Lecture Notes in Computer Sc

T0237817

Commenced Publication in 1973
Founding and Former Series Editors:
Gerhard Goos, Juris Hartmanis, and Jan van Leeuwen

George Danezis   Philippe Golle (Eds.)

Privacy Enhancing Technologies

6th International Workshop, PET 2006
Cambridge, UK, June 28-30, 2006
Revised Selected Papers

 Springer

Volume Editors

George Danezis
Katholieke Universiteit Leuven
Kasteelpark Arenberg 10
B-3001 Leuven-Heverlee, Belgium
E-mail: George.Danezis@esat.kuleuven.be

Philippe Golle
Palo Alto Research Center
3333 Coyote Hill Rd
Palo Alto, CA 94304, USA
E-mail: Philippe.Golle@parc.com

Library of Congress Control Number: 2006938345

CR Subject Classification (1998): E.3, C.2, D.4.6, K.6.5, K.4, H.3, H.4

LNCS Sublibrary: SL 4 – Security and Cryptology

ISSN   0302-9743
ISBN-10   3-540-68790-4 Springer Berlin Heidelberg New York
ISBN-13   978-3-540-68790-0 Springer Berlin Heidelberg New York

Springer is a part of Springer Science+Business Media

springer.com

© Springer-Verlag Berlin Heidelberg 2006
Printed in Germany

Typesetting: Camera-ready by author, data conversion by Scientific Publishing Services, Chennai, India
Printed on acid-free paper   SPIN: 11957454   06/3142   5 4 3 2 1 0

Foreword

The 6th Workshop on Privacy Enhancing Technologies, PET 2006, was held at Robinson College, Cambridge (UK), on June 28-3 2006. The workshop received 91 full paper submissions out of which 24 were selected for presentation. As a rule, papers were reviewed by 3 independent members of the Program Committee, and often also by external reviewers. A further two-week long online discussion took place amongst the PC to reach consensus on all submissions. The ultimate responsibility for the final selection of papers rests on the program chairs.

The ratio of acceptance puts PET in league with other premiere computer security venues, and guarantees a high quality scientific program. Yet PET also retains its character as a workshop, by providing a venue where promising new ideas can be presented and discussed by the privacy community. Identifying high quality, as well as high potential, submissions was a difficult balancing act. The program chairs would like to thank the Program Committee of PET 2006 for their invaluable work in helping select the best submissions:

- Alessandro Acquisti, Heinz School, Carnegie Mellon University, USA
- Mikhail Atallah, Purdue University, USA
- Michael Backes, Saarland University, Germany
- Alastair Beresford, University of Cambridge, UK
- Nikita Borisov, University of Illinois at Urbana-Champaign, USA
- Jan Camenisch, IBM Zurich Research Laboratory, Switzerland
- Kim Cameron, Microsoft, USA
- Fred Cate, Indiana University at Bloomington, USA
- Roger Dingledine, The Free Haven Project, USA
- Hannes Federrath, University of Regensburg, Germany
- Simone Fischer-Hübner, Karlstad University, Sweden
- Ian Goldberg, Zero Knowledge Systems, Canada
- Markus Jakobsson, Indiana University at Bloomington, USA
- Dennis Kügler, Federal Office for Information Security, Germany
- Brian Levine, University of Massachusetts at Amherst, USA
- David Molnar, University of California at Berkeley, USA
- Andreas Pfitzmann, Dresden University of Technology, Germany
- Mike Reiter, Carnegie Mellon University, USA
- Andrei Serjantov, The Free Haven Project, UK
- Paul Syverson, Naval Research Lab, USA
- Matthew Wright, University of Texas at Arlington, USA

Additional reviewers included Christer Andersson, Marina Blanton, Katrin Borcea-Pfitzmann, Sebastian Clauß, Richard Clayton, Hatim Daginawala, Markus Duermuth, Nick Feamster, Keith Frikken, Rachel Greenstadt, Thomas Heydt-Benjamin, Ari Juels, Lea Kissner, Stefan Köpsell, Klaus K. Kursawe, Pil Joong

Lee, Jiangtao Li, Katja Liesebach, Leonardo A. Martucci, Nick Mathewson, Steven J. Murdoch, Gregory Neuven, Amit Sahai, Antje Schneidewind, Dagmar Schufeld, Sid Stamm, Sandra Steinbrecher, Madhu Venkateshaiah, and Lasse Øverlier. Their help was very much appreciated.

We are especially grateful to our General Chair, Richard Clayton, from the University of Cambridge Computer Laboratory, for taking care of all local arrangements. Thomas Herlea, from the K.U. Leuven, was kind enough to help us with the online submission and reviewing system.

PET 2006 was collocated with two events. WEIS 2006, the Workshop on the Economics of Information Security, shared a session with PET on the economics of privacy and surveillance. We are very grateful to Ross Anderson, WEIS Chair, and Tyler Moore, WEIS General Chair, who took care of local arrangements, for their help in coordinating the two events. Secondly, WOTE 2006, the Workshop on Trustworthy Elections, coordinated by Peter Ryan, shared the last two days of the workshop. Participants of both workshops were free to circulate between all sessions, and social activities during the day were shared to maximize the synergy between the two communities.

PET 2006 was made possible, and more affordable, thanks to the continuing generous sponsorship of Microsoft. We are particularly indebted to Caspar Bowden and JC Cannon, who actively contributed to the success of the workshop by providing this sponsorship and support. Roger Dingledine was kind enough to manage and distribute the stipends to those participants who needed them.

The PET prize, sponsored by Microsoft and the Office of the Information and Privacy Commissioner of Ontario, was this year awarded through an independent prize committee headed by Alessandro Acquisti, to whom we are thankful. The 2006 prize was awarded to Daniel Solove for his paper entitled "A Taxonomy of Privacy". The award ceremony took place at Microsoft Research Cambridge, along with live demonstrations of privacy technology.

October 2006   George Danezis and Philippe Golle
                                                              Program Chairs
                                                                   PET 2006

Table of Contents

6th Workshop on Privacy Enhancing Technologies

Privacy for Public Transportation*

Thomas S. Heydt-Benjamin, Hee-Jin Chae, Benessa Defend, and Kevin Fu

University of Massachusetts, Amherst, MA 01003, USA
{tshb, chae, defend, kevinfu}@cs.umass.edu

Abstract. We propose an application of recent advances in e-cash, anonymous credentials, and proxy re-encryption to the problem of privacy in public transit systems with electronic ticketing. We discuss some of the interesting features of transit ticketing as a problem domain, and provide an architecture sufficient for the needs of a typical metropolitan transit system. Our system maintains the security required by the transit authority and the user while significantly increasing passenger privacy. Our hybrid approach to ticketing allows use of passive RFID transponders as well as higher powered computing devices such as smartphones or PDAs. We demonstrate security and privacy features offered by our hybrid system that are unavailable in a homogeneous passive transponder architecture, and which are advantageous for users of passive as well as active devices.

1 Introduction

Public transportation ticketing systems must be able to handle large volumes of passenger transactions while providing the minimum possible impedance to travel. Therefore, it is hardly surprising that some of the world's busiest public transportation systems are at the forefront of electronic payment technology. Unfortunately, current systems have been designed such that passengers sacrifice privacy in order to take advantage of the convenience of electronic payment. Moreover, because of the inherent broadcast nature of RF, as systems migrate from contact based technologies like mag-stripe to contactless technologies there is increased risk to privacy and security [1,2,3,4,5].

The traditional passive RFID transponder is a severely resource constrained computing device. Manufacturing cost is usually a primary design criterion, resulting in transponders with little memory and processing power. Even in more expensive passive transponders, current technology limits the amount of memory and the complexity of the microprocessor that can fit into common form-factors. Furthermore, since passive transponders are powered by electrical induction from the reader's antenna, an RFID tag must power up, receive, process, and transmit within the brief time that a user holds the tag within the reader's electric field. Consequently, many of the security protocols that we would use for communication between other kinds of computers are inappropriate for the RFID plat-

---

* This research was partially supported by NSF CNS-052072 and a Ford Foundation Diversity Fellowship.

G. Danezis and P. Golle (Eds.): PET 2006, LNCS 4258, pp. 1–19, 2006.

form [6]. However, despite their resource constraints, cards with cryptographic co-processors are capable of executing carefully crafted protocols [7,8,9,10,11].

As the abilities of contactless smart cards have increased, new cryptographic primitives suitable for these resource constrained devices have been developed. Not only do recent contributions to the field of e-cash and anonymous credentials require much less memory, but the communications required for the zero-knowledge proofs are also greatly reduced [12,13,14]. The key management problem for a transit system involving hundreds of readers and hundreds of thousands of tickets has traditionally been difficult. We apply recent advances in re-encryption and re-signatures to place the burden of key management on the more powerful computers in the system, requiring the tickets to store only the public portion of a single highly secure key pair whose private portion can be protected in offline storage [15,16].

1.1   Background

In 2004, passengers took approximately 9 billion trips through public transportation systems in the United States [17]. Existing systems maintain a database of all transactions, associating them with the identities of passengers whenever possible, such as when a credit card is used in conjunction with the transit card [18,19,20]. If communication between a ticket and a transit authority is not properly secured, arbitrary third party adversaries might then have inappropriate access to user data. Many of the currently deployed systems are proprietary [21], and thus closed to scientific scrutiny. Recent historical examples, such as the black-box cryptanalysis of TI's major RFID security mechanism [22], reinforce that eschewing peer review often leads to insecure systems. Even if the RF communication in a transit system is secure, the user's data may still be at risk. The Washington D.C. Metro operated for years without a clearly defined privacy policy [23,24,25]. Until recently, users of this system had no legal protection preventing the sale or sharing of their data with third parties. Privacy preserving protocols are needed to protect this large volume of sensitive data.

The utility of privacy to the individual consumer is clear, however the very consumer data that we wish to protect has long been considered valuable to the transit authority. We feel that at a certain point organizations such as transit authorities may wish to scale back on the amount of consumer data they collect. They may come to view such information as a greater liability than an asset since they stand to loose both money and reputation if the data leaks to adversarial parties. Additionally, growing public unease about ubiquitous surveillance may lead to legislation, commercial pressure, or societal pressure forcing companies to adopt stronger privacy technologies. Ultimately a new equilibrium may be achieved in which systems may be designed to permit gathering of useful business data while reassuring the consumer by providing scientific guarantees that such data will be appropriately anonymized.

Many large transit systems are still in the process of choosing and implementing new ticket technologies. The San Francisco Bay Area Rapid Transit (BART) system, for example, had over 91 million passengers in 2004 [26] and is currently in the process of considering how best to implement future RFID ticketing. BART has expressed willingness to listen to suggestions from the scientific community. We hope that our community will respond with protocols that give transit authorities the proper tools.

1.2   Our Contributions

Our research makes three primary contributions that address the challenges of privacy and security in public transportation:

1. We motivate the study of transit system payment as a problem domain with interesting properties and many open problems for research.
2. We propose a framework for reasoning about transit system payment security and privacy.
3. We present novel designs for systems offering RF electronic payment which we discuss in the context of our proposed framework.

Our design provides a payment system suitable for the needs of a typical transit system, in which the transit agency retains the ability to implement a variable rate fare structure. The movements of a user of our protocols cannot be tracked through the transit system by the transit authority nor by a third-party adversary. Our novel authentication protocol built around the re-encryption primitive [15] provides verification of reader authorization and also provides a secure channel in a manner well suited to the resource constraints of the various systems. Reader authorization in our design is efficient and secure, and does not require propagation of revocation information.

2   Related Work

Other researchers have proposed the use of actively powered devices for payment system or RFID anonymity [27,28,29]. By contrast we propose a hybrid system which takes advantage of the abilities of more powerful devices such as smartphones, while remaining compatible with more commonly deployed passively powered RFID transponders. Additionally, whereas much prior work exists relating to electronic payment, our focus is on a specific real-world problem domain, with consideration for such issues as the trade-offs between anonymity and certain mandatory and optional transit requirements.

The Advanced Fare Payment Systems Company [30] provides an overview of different types of cards that could be used for transit systems ticketing. They do not give details about card security and mention gathering user data as an advantage of implementing RFID, which contrasts with our goal of protecting user data.

There is much existing work on RFID security, including resistance to tracking and hotlisting attacks [31,4,32,33]. However, our paper is unique in considering them in the specific context of public transit. RFID privacy techniques such as Blocker Tags [34] and Faraday cages, which prevent communication with a transponder, are insufficient since they do not protect privacy when a ticket must be legitimately read.

Systems exist which address the security needs of RF transit ticketing, but do not significantly consider privacy of user data. Many publications consider unique card serial numbers as a requirement for fraud detection [35,36]. We propose the use of advanced anonymous credentials and e-cash systems, which can detect fraud while maintaining the anonymity of the honest user.

3   The Problem Domain of Transit System Payment

Transit systems have historically been at the forefront of experimenting with new payment technologies [18,21]. Yet increased security often comes at the expense of privacy. For instance, a transit card that records a passenger's travel history may reduce fraud at the expense of privacy. Below we discuss several challenges to providing freedom from ubiquitous surveillance while also maintaining or increasing security.

A cryptographic transit ticket is a resource constrained computing device. Such tickets are currently implemented on passive RFID transponders with severe limits on power, memory, and CPU, and in more advanced systems on higher powered embedded computing devices (HPDs), such as cell phones or PDAs. These resource constraints raise many compelling questions, as the systems requirements frequently force trade-offs with security or privacy features. However, it is also the case that considering a cryptosystem in the context of a very specific problem, rather than examining it in its general and abstract theory, may permit abbreviations of feature sets which lower the resource requirements of strong cryptosystems. For example, we may assume that the value stored on an e-cash based transit ticket will decrease monotonically. Not offering support for adding tokens to the ticket's wallet may allow savings of memory, transaction time, and CPU time. Transit tickets have limited communications bandwidth, but we will see below that this is an asset to security as well as a constraint.

A remarkable element of the problem domain lies in consideration of hybrid systems, which include both HPDs and passive transponders. HPDs can offer security and privacy benefits not only to the HPD user, but also to the passive transponder user. We examine one such case in section 6. In order for an HPD to enhance the security and privacy of a passive transponder user, however, the HPD and the passive transponder must be difficult to distinguish from one another. If a system permits heterogeneous HPDs based on different technologies from different hardware manufacturers, it may be challenging to ascertain this difficulty. We believe that there are many interesting problems related to this issue such as the problem of building an HPD which behaves as much like a passive transponder as possible, the problem of building a passive transponder with less predictable power and communications patterns, the problem of building readers with highly accurate antenna power analysis for attacking transponder indistinguishability, and other similar problems.

Cloning detection for temporally bounded tickets (such as weekly or monthly commuting passes) is another fundamental problem related to transit system payment. In general, smartcard manufacturers rely on tamper resistance for cloning prevention [37]. We consider this to be insufficient, as tamper resistance has been shown to be weak in many cases [38]. Cloning detection for anonymous credentials systems exists [39] (and we assume such detection in our design), however these detection schemes are most effective in systems that require credential holders to be online simultaneously. Such mechanisms are insufficient for the needs of transit systems, yet the nature of transit systems may allow other bounds (like the aforementioned communications constraints) on adversarial behavior which will serve to provide more appropriate cloning detection.

For simplicity, we have assumed a strongly connected transit system in which all readers have a reliable network connecting them to central transit authority computers. There are many things to be considered if support is to be offered for weakly-connected networks. For example, we believe that ticket revocation information and other such data could be propagated using disruption tolerant networking techniques, such as packet ferrying [40,41,42]. Bus readers with embedded wireless networked computers and even tickets themselves may ferry data as they move through the system.

In this paper we assume that the user of the HPD is able to back up their virtual tickets through some mechanism external to our protocols. Another interesting facet of the domain of transit system payment is the question of how the user of a traditional transponder can back up their ticket without compromising their privacy. Ideally, the transit authority could retain a secure copy of the ticket at the time of purchase, but it is critical that user authorization be required in order to decrypt this backup copy. One possibility that we have considered is that when a smart credit card is used to purchase a ticket, the credit card could provide a mechanism for encryption of the ticket data which could then safely be stored by the transit authority. An ideal such mechanism could optionally allow for anonymity revocation by an authorized entity such as a judicial system when such is desirable or required by law.

The forward secrecy available to a user, should an adversarial transit authority obtain physical possession of the user's ticket, will be highly dependent on the underlying e-cash and anonymous credentials systems. The choice of a specific cryptographic primitive will determine what information the authority can learn given full knowledge of the ticket's data and all past transactions.

These are just a few of the problems worthy of study in the domain of public transit payment. Some of these problems are not unique to transit payment, but consideration of a specific real-world application may lead to development of more general techniques.

4   Definitions and Notation

We apply the traditional meanings of security, anonymity and privacy. We consider a protocol to be secure if it is as difficult to violate the semantics of the protocol as it is to break the underlying cryptographic primitives, and we consider anonymity to mean indistinguishability within a group of transit users. Therefore the degree of anonymity provided to some user u with the transit system in a particular state, is the size of the set of users that are indistinguishable from u up to the strength of the underlying cryptographic primitives. We consider the degree of privacy offered by a transit system to be the degree of difficulty with which an adversary can link a user's identity (such as name or credit card number) with their actions within the transit system over time. For example, the purchase of a ticket with a credit card will be an identifying transaction since the user's name is presented to the system, but the overall system provides privacy to the extent that it is difficult to link this purchase with other events such as entrances and exits. Thus the system may know when and where a user purchases a ticket, but will not know to where the user travels, nor whether they transfer or otherwise re-enter the system.

4.1   Adversaries

Transit system user $= U$: U possesses the ticket TX and may read or modify any of the ticket data. We assume that U will do any thing she can that will maximize her expected economic utility. U is willing to break the rules of any protocol if it is to her advantage, and if it helps her U may have a non-standard transponder with any reasonable design parameters. We assume that U will help other users steal service from the transit authority as long as such action does not require significant resources from her.

The Transit Authority $= TA$: The TA is assumed to be controlled by entities hostile to anonymity who wish to identify and track all users of the transit system. If it can be in any way advantageous, TA will carry out extra (unauthorized) transactions using concealed readers both inside and outside of the transit system. We categorize any entity which knows TA's private key as being equivalent to TA.

We will not consider the various denial-of-service attacks that TA may perform upon U. It may be interesting in the future to consider mechanisms by which U can be protected from spurious charges or cancellation of valid tickets, but existing systems do not offer any such protection and this is not the focus of this paper.

The malicious 3rd party M: M is assumed to be able to read and or modify all data that is broadcast via RF. In order to provide a worst case analysis, we will assume that M has an RFID reader which can read/write to any tag over any arbitrary distance, and which can act as a perfect man-in-the-middle between a transponder and another reader. M is interested in doing anything that would maximize M's expected economic utility, and will also attempt to degrade the anonymity of users of the system.

4.2   Semantics Required from Credential and E-Cash Systems

Our protocols are designed to work with any anonymous credentials system that obeys the semantics outlined below. These semantics are similar to those described in [12] which provides a system compatible with our needs. We have found [13] to be quite suitable to the resource constraints of a passive RFID transponder, and we have begun working on a proof-of-concept implementation of our system based on this credentials system.

$FormNym(TX, TA)$: A session between the ticket TX and the credentials granting organization or their designee. TX and TA negotiate a pseudonym $N_{(TX,TA)}$ part of which is stored by each party, and additional cryptographic validating tags sufficient for TA to later verify $N_{(TX,TA)}$ without TA having any knowledge of TX's private information (such as a master private key).

$GrantCred(N, \lambda, TA)$: A session between TX and TA (or designee) in which TX identifies itself to TA by the previously negotiated pseudonym $N_{(TX,TA)}$, and specifies the range of parameters $\lambda \subseteq \Lambda$ for which the credential shall be valid. TA creates a credential $C_{(TX,\lambda,TA)}$ which shall be valid only for the specified $\lambda \subseteq \Lambda$, and grants it to TX. The credential thus formed can be demonstrated without revealing TX or N, but given TX or N the credential can be revoked.

$VerifyCred(N, \tau, F)$: A session between the TX and some verifier (the fare-gate F) in which TX proves possession of credential $C_{(TX,\lambda,TA)}$, and TX furthermore demonstrates that the credential is valid for the parameter $\tau \in \lambda$. This can be accomplished without F knowing any private information belonging to TX or TA, and F cannot determine anything about λ other than $\tau \in \lambda$.

$RevokeCred(N, TA)$: Given knowledge of N the TA may revoke all credentials grated to pseudonym N, and given TX the TA may revoke all credentials granted to TX regardless of pseudonym. We assume that N is revealed when cloning of multi-show credentials is detected (as in [39]), and when double-spending of single-show credentials is detected.

The e-cash semantics that we require are similar to those provided by [14,43]:

$CreateTokens(TA, TX, \nu)$: A session between the Transit Authority TA and the ticket TX in which the TA creates a number ν of valid tokens. These tokens are transmitted and stored on TX. The wallet thus generated must be small enough to fit on a contactless smart card.

$SpendTokens(TA, TX, \nu)$: A session between the TA and the TX in which the TX spends ν tokens. The TX transmits the tokens to the TA and then deletes those tokens. This transaction must be unlinkable with $CreateTokens$ unless double-spending has occurred.

5   A Semantic Framework for Transit System Payment

In this section we examine the basic properties of transit system payment and offer an analysis of the degree of identification inherent in each transaction. For simplicity we will consider only the case of a strongly connected transit system, in which every faregate has a network connection to a central TA database. Our

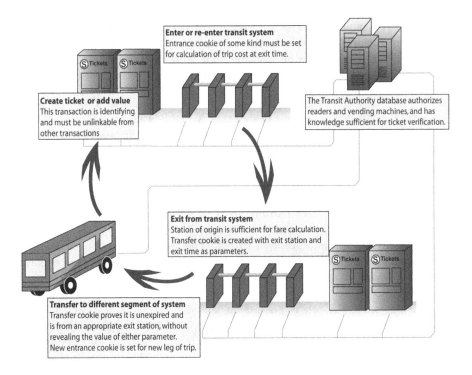

Fig. 1. The major pieces of a transit payment system

system is tolerant of intermittently connected faregates, however for brevity we will save further consideration of these features for future work. We will discuss the semantics of a transit system similar to that depicted in Figure 1 which is a variable-rate system with transfer between two components (bus and subway). Fixed-rate payment and additional transfer components can be trivially composed from these semantics.

$createTicket(TV, TX, U) \rightarrow TX$: A transaction between a ticket vendor (TV, designated by the TA through appropriate cryptographic keys), a ticket TX, and some form of payment external to the transit system. Such forms of payment may be anonymous, such as paper currency, or they may be identifying, such as credit cards. For simplicity we will assume the worst case: that all ticket creation transactions fully identify the user (indicated by U). A privacy-preserving transit system must therefore ensure that future transactions of TX cannot be linked to the ticket creation transaction.

$enter(F, TX) \rightarrow C_E(F)$: A transaction between a faregate F, and a ticket TX. In order to enter the system the ticket must demonstrate its validity to F. The final fare cannot be calculated until exit-time, therefore an entry cookie C_E of some sort must be generated so that TX may later demonstrate at which F it entered the system. TA and F require no information other than that sufficient to accomplish payment and proof of validity. In a privacy-preserving system no other information should be leaked.

$exit(F, TX, C_E) \rightarrow C_T(F, e)$: When the user leaves a section of the transit system, a transaction is required between the exit faregate F, and the ticket TX. The ticket must prove the validity of its entrance cookie C_E and pay the fare for the trip, and in return it is given a transfer C_T. This cookie is parameterized with the point of exit F (for determining to which segments the user may transfer) and a time epoch e (to permit transfer expiration). TA and F require only payment or proof of appropriate credential and C_E which should reveal only where the user entered. In order to prevent fraud, C_E should prevent double-spending.

$transfer(F, C_T) \rightarrow C_E(F)$: C_T is proven to F. The proof mechanism (which should be zero-knowledge) ensures that C_T's parameters fall within the range permissible for a valid transfer: i.e. the user is transferring from a permissible section of the transit system, and the transfer is not expired. The C_E generated by this transaction is done so by the same means as in the *enter* transaction. C_T should be double-spending proof. In an ideal privacy-preserving system, the only information that should be revealed is that the transfer has not yet been spent, that it is not yet expired, and that it comes from some exit faregate within a range of acceptable such faregates.

$addValue(TV, TX, U) \rightarrow TX'$: All value is taken off (is spent) of TX, the user provides additional value from an external payment source, and then the transaction proceeds as in initial ticket creation. This provides a new ticket TX', which is unlinkable with TX and with U.

$cancel(TA, TX, U)$: In this transaction, given full disclosure of TX the TA can cancel the entire ticket, spending all tokens and optionally paying the remaining balance of the card to some entity U. As previously mentioned, the user of the HPD is assumed to have the ability to back up any tickets stored on their HPD. Additionally, the TA may offer a mechanism for secure backup of traditional transponders. A user may reclaim the remaining balance of a lost card by performing a *cancel* on the backup of the ticket. *cancel* is also the transaction that the TA uses to destroy tickets which are identified by fraud detection.

6   A Design for Anonymous Transit System Payment

We consider two kinds of tickets: the passive RFID transponder and the embedded system such as the cell phone or PDA. We refer to the latter as a High Powered computing Device (HPD) in order to distinguish it from the passively powered transponder. We choose these two kinds of tickets because of their wide-deployment and non-trivial security and privacy properties. A HPD with an RF transmitter can follow the same protocols as the passive transponder. Thus, transit systems with existing RFID deployments can implement our hybrid design without requiring separate faregate hardware for each technology.

In addition to traditional HPD features, such as increased security through PIN or biometric user authentication [27], we assume an HPD can be backed up and restored by a user to some external storage (much like common PDA synchronization). We also assume that HPDs exist for which users can observe, debug, and modify the programming. Such devices are important because they provide the basis of assurance of detection of certain kinds of adversarial action on the part of the transit system. An open HPD platform allows interested users to monitor the transit system to observe that it follows its stated protocols and does not, for example, charge too little or too much for a particular transaction. HPD properties specific to transit systems include the ability to kill a transfer immediately after receipt if the user knows that they will not be transferring, and the ability to report a spurious balance in a transit system with protocols requiring the ticket's remaining balance to be disclosed. Note that this latter property increases not only the privacy of the HPD user, but that of the passive ticket as well.

For simplicity we assume that HPDs and passive transponders are indistinguishable to TA with respect to communications. We defer examination of this assumption to future work as there are many arguments both for it and against it under different circumstances.

In the remainder of this section, we will discuss the details of our design for transit system payment using e-cash and anonymous credentials and consider the security and privacy implications of each transaction.

6.1 Authentication and Session Key Creation

We propose Re-Encryption based Authentication (REA); a novel method for authentication of an authorized reader to a ticket. This method is secure and well matched to the computation and storage resources of the various computers involved in a transit system. The burden of key management is shouldered by the main transit authority computers, which is appropriate since they have the least resource constraints. In our system the TA must daily generate delegation keys which are only good for that day, and then distribute them to each authorized reader. Revocation of a reader is accomplished by simply failing to issue that reader a delegation key for a new day.

Possession of a non-expired delegation key permits F to re-encrypt messages from TX according to the protocol depicted in Figure 2. TX can accomplish authentication and negotiation of a session with only a single public key operation. In this system, TX only needs to store a single public key. This is appropriate to the transponder's storage constraints, and is superior to a system that would require TX to store revocation information.

In the challenge-response protocol, the authorized reader F, sends the current time t to TX. This step is necessary since some passive RFID transponders are not able to support real time clocks. This time is then concatenated together with a random number of length l_n (which is a security parameter) to form the session key S, which is then transmitted to F encrypted with TA's public key (it is reasonable to assume that K_{TA}^+ is built into TX at the factory). F demonstrates that it is authorized by using its delegation key to transform C into a form which it can then decrypt with its own private key. The fact that F is

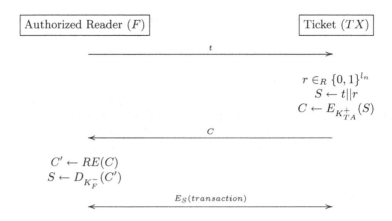

Fig. 2. Authentication of reader to ticket using re-encryption (RE) allows F to translate ciphertext encrypted with K_{TA}^+ to ciphertext which can be decrypted with K_F^-. Thus the private key of TA remains offline. This re-encryption can only happen if F possesses an appropriate non-expired delegation key. Proof of possession of this delegation key is the mechanism by which F demonstrates that it is authorized. This protocol provides a secure channel while matching the resource constraints of the different devices.

then able to reply to TX with a well-formed message encrypted with session-key S demonstrates that F is authorized (possesses a non-expired delegation key).

Once TX is satisfied that it is talking to an authorized reader it updates its logical clock to value t. If it ever receives a communication with a timestamp less than t, the communication will be assumed to be adversarial, and the protocol will be aborted. TX also uses t to refuse to divulge any information about cookies it holds which have expired.

Since t increases monotonically (which can be monitored by HPDs, and discrepancies will also be eventually caught by passive transponders) and r is chosen by TX, neither F nor TX can cheat at this protocol in such a way as to make a re-play attack possible. S can only be decrypted by a reader with an unexpired delegation key (up to the strength of the underlying public-key and re-signature cryptosystems). This suffices for the security (up to underlying primitives) of the challenge-response.

6.2 $createTicket(TV, TX, U) \rightarrow TX$

Once the session key S is negotiated as discussed above, a stored-value ticket can be created by calling $CreateTokens(TV, TX, \nu)$ resulting in a new wallet which is then stored on TX. The protocol for creation of a temporally bounded ticket is similar, except that in place of $CreateTokens$, $FormNym$ and $GrantCred$ must be executed with respect to some time interval λ which the user has chosen and purchased. We assume the existence of some function which maps from t to a particular credential expiration epoch $\tau \in \lambda$.

As with all of our other protocols, transactions such as $CreateTokens$, $FormNym$, and $GrantCred$ are protected by the session key S, thus preventing the various attacks of middleman adversary M. We omit the means by which payment is proven to TA since solutions to this problem are so well understood.

Privacy of ticket creation: We assume the worst case scenario in which a user purchases or adds value with a credit card, making this a fully-identifying transaction. In this case TV (and by extension TA) gains knowledge of a tuple (U, t, TV, ν), where ν is initial balance of TX. We will consider the privacy of the rest of the system in terms of how difficult it is to link future transactions with this initial transaction.

6.3 $enter(F, TX) \rightarrow C_E(F)$

Upon entrance to the transit system, TX must either prove that it possesses an unexpired credential using $VerifyCred(N, \tau, F)$, or if it is a stored-value card it must accept an entrance cookie C_E. In our system this cookie is a one-show credential parameterized by the identity of the station at which we enter the system L. The cookie is formed with a call to $FormNym$ and then $GrantCred$.

Privacy of $enter$: In the case of the temporally bounded ticket, the only information that is revealed by TX is the possession of a valid credential which is not expired for the present day. TA could attempt to learn TX's λ by running this transaction multiple times with increasing values of t, but since TX's logical clock increases monotonically this would have the effect of destroying the ticket, thus preventing this attack from being used for fingerprinting and tracking TX.

In the case of the stored-value ticket, no meaningful information is revealed during this transaction. It is worthy to note, however, that TX could be tricked into carrying an identifying cookie if an adversarial TA could provide a unique L with each transaction. In order to detect such adversarial behavior, HPDs should carry a table mapping from station id L to station name. The HPD software and user can easily detect invalid values of L. Since TA cannot distinguish between an HPD and a passive transponder, this is another example of how HPDs in a hybrid system offer benefits to users of lower cost passive tickets.

6.4 $exit(F, TX, C_E) \rightarrow C_T(F, e)$

In the case where TX is a temporally bounded ticket, exit from the system is exactly the same as entrance.

In the case where TX is a stored-value ticket, the entrance cookie C_E must now be revealed. TX deletes C_E from its memory as soon as its validity has been proven, and therefore avoids being tracked in the future based on any property of C_E. C_E gives TA knowledge of the location at which TX entered the system, so TA can now calculate the cost of the trip. This cost is transmitted to TX and is payed according to the $SpendTokens$ primitive. As a convenience to the user, TX transmits its remaining balance to the faregate so that it may be displayed to the user. After all of this occurs, a transfer cookie C_T is negotiated between TX and TA. The creation of C_T proceeds the same way as with C_E, except that C_T is parameterized by both an expiration time e as well as the exit station identity.

Privacy of *exit*: For simplicity of argument, we shall strengthen our adversary by assuming that TA can calculate with perfect knowledge the amount of time it would take for TX to move from its point of purchase to the exit faregate F.

If the system is to provide the convenience of displaying remaining balance at the faregate, the user of the passive transponder must necessarily lose a certain degree of anonymity. We will consider the size of TX's anonymity set. Since the station of entry is disclosed by our protocol, let set α be the set of all tickets which if they had travelled here from their station of entry would be arriving now (at time t). Let set β be the set of all tickets which have the same balance as TX and that were purchased within a time interval such that they could just now be arriving at the current faregate F. Let set γ be the set of all tickets which have the same balance as TX but that were not purchased within a time interval such that they could be just now arriving at the current faregate F. With respect to the information possessed by TA, TX's anonymity set is then $(\alpha \cap \beta) \cup \gamma$. Assuming that the fare structure is set up such that there is a reasonable distribution of possible balances, this anonymity set should be of acceptable size.

It is here that users of HPDs may offer greater privacy to users of traditional transponders. HPDs are capable of displaying remaining balance on their own screens, therefore the HPD user does not need to see the balance on the screen of the faregate. Consequently, HPDs could be programmed to either transmit a random "balance", or could even intentionally choose a "balance" with probability inversely proportional to that of the expected real system balance distribution. With many such HPDs in a system, and with no way of knowing which tickets are reporting false balances, the task of correlating exit balances with identified ticket purchases becomes quite challenging. Let set δ be the set of tickets falsely reporting the same balance as TX, then the new anonymity set of the traditional transponder is $(\alpha \cap \beta) \cup \gamma \cup \delta$. At the same time, this is advantageous to the user of the HPD who now enjoys greater anonymity since they can no longer be distinguished by their balance.

6.5 $transfer(F, C_T) \rightarrow C_F(F)$

For temporally bounded tickets, this transaction is the same as *enter*.

Stored-value tickets begin by proving that their transfer is unexpired, and is from an exit station in the set of stations which may transfer here. If these things are true, then a new type of transfer C_F is minted through the same means as C_E, except that C_F is distinguishable from an entry cookie. When the user exits at the final destination, TA can now compute a balance discounted according to the transit system's transfer rules. TX always deletes cookies from its memory as soon as they have been verified by TA.

Privacy of *transfer*: Some information about both the station at which C_T was minted, and the time epoch τ of genesis are revealed during the transfer verification. The size of the anonymity set will be the number of tickets issued during τ which are valid at the verifying station. Since TX will only agree to verify C_T once, an adversary cannot test different values of τ and F to reduce the size of TX's anonymity set. At this point in the system, it would be quite difficult indeed to trace TX back to its original purchase. Although the anonymity at each intermediate step is less than total, in a transit system with a reasonable passenger volume tracking a particular user quickly becomes infeasible.

6.6 $addValue(TV, TX, U) \rightarrow TX'$

In the case of a temporally bounded TX, the remaining time on the card (λ) can be determined by verifying the card's credential for increasing t until the expiration date is found. At this point, of course, the card has been destroyed, and must be re-initialized with a brand new Nym and Credential for a new, longer time period. This is accomplished as in $createTicket$.

The procedure for the stored-value TX is quite similar: The remaining tokens are spent via $SpendToken$, and a new wallet is created for this value plus whatever new value the user has purchased.

Privacy of $addValue$: In the worst case, the user will choose to refill their ticket using a credit card. In this case, of course, this is a fully identifying transaction. We will consider the case where the user pays for additional value through some anonymous means.

For the temporally bounded TX, the size of the anonymity set in this transaction will be the number of tickets in circulation with the same remaining λ. For most transit systems it seems likely that the more distinguishing λ values would be the longest such values (year-long passes and such). Fortunately it is unlikely that the owner of a ticket would desire to add time to a ticket which already has a great deal of time remaining.

There is an attack on the anonymity of the temporally bounded TX in which an adversarial TA reduces the size of TX's anonymity set by spuriously executing an addValue transaction in order to fingerprint TX's λ, and then creates a new Nym and Credential for TX. In our system, TX has a number of protections against this attack. First of all, such spurious transactions can clearly be detected and reported by HPDs. Secondly, the passive transponder can keep track of the most recent λ and refuse to accept a new λ that is not at least one day greater than the old. This latter defense would mean that an adversarial TA would have to give a free extra day for every fingerprint, and the fingerprint would become increasingly meaningless as the value of λ diverged further and further from the identifying purchase.

The only information that the TA gains from the stored-value TX is the remaining balance. It should be noted that this is a circumstance where the HPD cannot give a false balance, as the balance is checked by actually spending the remaining tokens. The anonymity set of TX during this transaction will be the number of TX in circulation with the same balance. Fortunately it is likely that users will add value to their tickets only when the ticket runs low. In this case the ticket will be likely to have a common balance.

6.7 $cancel(TA, TX, U)$

Given all of the information on TX, TA may cancel the ticket, and any clones it may have. In the case of a stored-value ticket, TA executes *spendToken* on all remaining tokens in TX's wallet, optionally reimbursing the user, if it is the user who is canceling the ticket (rather than the TA choosing to cancel due to detected fraud).

In the case of the temporally bounded ticket, TA optionally determines the remaining value by the same mechanism as in the *addValue* transaction, and then executes *RevokeCred* which will cancel TX and any clones thereof.

7 Alternative Approaches

If a transit authority chooses passive transponders which lack sufficient resources for the primary design outlined above, there are many alternatives to be considered which are much cheaper to implement, but do not provide the same strength of anonymity as our primary design.

Entry (C_E) and transfer (C_T) cookies can be realized with no processing required from the transponder above the cost of authenticating the reader. The TA can compute and transmit $C_E := M_{K_{TA}^-}(S)$, where S is the session-key containing a timestamp and a nonce. The TA can store the cookie along with the identity of the entry station. Note that the cookie can be signed by the reader using a re-signature key. For protection against tracking, the ticket will only disclose a cookie once, and thus can be tracked only by the TA and only for the duration of a single trip. This cookie design provides privacy, in that there is still no way to link a ticket to its fully identifying purchase, however it clearly does not meet the anonymity goals outlined in our payment semantics.

Another alternative design provides temporally bounded tickets through the same mechanisms as the stored value tickets. In this design, day passes are created with a large quantity of valueless e-cash tokens parameterized with an expiration date. The tokens are essentially used as single-show credentials. This system falls short of the true semantics of temporally bounded tickets in that the ticket may not be used an unbounded number of times during its period of validity. However, it may be cheaper to implement a system based on one primary underlying set of cryptographic protocols.

8 Future Work

Before a transit payment system is ready for deployment, its various components should individually and in aggregate be stated in formal notation with a clear security model and proofs of security within that model. We hope that future work will consider specific cryptosystems within the semantic framework that we have proposed here, and will provide appropriate proofs up to the assumptions supported by the chosen cryptographic schemes.

A problem clearly exists with maintaining an anonymous credential on a virtual card which the user has full ability to read and modify. In the naïve system there is little to prevent a dishonest user from selling many copies of a valid credential, and this would be quite difficult to detect given the anonymous nature of the credentials. Some work has been done on fraud detection in simultaneous use of the cloned credentials, which is quite suitable for other problem domains such as online game licensing [39]. In our problem domain, however, many kinds of fraud will go undetected with high probability. We are investigating novel mechanisms for cloning detection in anonymous credential systems, which we hope will offer a solution to this currently open problem.

9   Conclusion

We have (1) demonstrated that transit systems are an important problem domain for the study of security and privacy, (2) presented a framework for formal consideration of transit system ticketing, and (3) provided designs sufficient for implementation of a secure privacy preserving transit system. Our approach uses e-cash, anonymous credentials, and proxy re-encryption to increase passenger privacy without compromising the secure payment requirements of the transit authority. Yet many theoretical and practical challenges remain for further study in how to balance the privacy concerns of passengers with the security needs of transit authorities.

Acknowledgments

We are grateful to Anna Lysyanskaya for discussions about cloning detection for anonymous credentials systems, and to Ben Adida and Susan Hohenberger for discussion about the feasibility of re-encryption based authentication. For proofreading and presentation advice we thank Jeremy Barth, Ed Costello, Marc Liberatore, and Boris Margolin. For his implementation help we thank Russell Silva. Finally, we thank our anonymous reviewers for their suggestions and encouragement.

References

1. Juels, A., Molnar, D., Wagner, D.: Security and Privacy Issues in E-passports. In: Conference on Security and Privacy for Emerging Areas in Communication Networks – SecureComm, Athens, Greece, IEEE (2005)
2. Molnar, D., Wagner, D.: Privacy and Security in Library RFID: Issues, Practices, and Architectures. In Pfitzmann, B., Liu, P., eds.: Conference on Computer and Communications Security – ACM CCS, Washington DC, USA, ACM, ACM Press (2004) 210–219
3. Avoine, G., Oechslin, P.: RFID Traceability: A Multilayer Problem. In Patrick, A., Yung, M., eds.: Financial Cryptography – FC'05. Volume 3570 of Lecture Notes in Computer Science., Roseau, The Commonwealth Of Dominica, IFCA, Springer-Verlag (2005) 125–140

4. Dimitriou, T.: A Lightweight RFID Protocol to Protect Against Traceability and Cloning Attacks. In: Conference on Security and Privacy for Emerging Areas in Communication Networks – SecureComm, Athens, Greece, IEEE (2005)
5. Sarma, S., Weis, S., Engels, D.: Radio-Frequency Identification: Security Risks and Challenges. Cryptobytes, RSA Laboratories **6** (2003) 2–9
6. Vajda, I., Buttyán, L.: Lightweight Authentication Protocols for Low-Cost RFID Tags. In: Second Workshop on Security in Ubiquitous Computing – Ubicomp 2003, Seattle, WA, USA (2003)
7. Handschuh, H., Paillier, P.: Smart Card Crypto-Coprocessors for Public Key Cryptography. In Quisquitar, J.J., Schneier, B., eds.: Smart Card Research and Applications, SPLNCS. Volume 1820. (2000) 386–394
8. Trichina, E., Bucci, M., Seta, D.D., Luzzi, R.: Supplemental Cryptographic Hardware for Smart Cards. IEEE Micro **21** (2001) 26–35
9. Mohammed, E., Emarah, A., El-Shennawy, K.: Elliptic Curve Cryptosystems on Smart Cards. In: SEC '02: Proceedings of the IFIP TC11 17th International Conference on Information Security, Deventer, The Netherlands, The Netherlands, Kluwer, B.V. (2002) 311–322
10. Poupard, G., Stern, J.: On the Fly Signatures Based on Factoring. In: CCS '99: Proceedings of the 6th ACM conference on Computer and communications security, New York, NY, USA, ACM Press (1999) 37–45
11. Juels, A.: Minimalist Cryptography for Low-Cost RFID Tags. In Blundo, C., Cimato, S., eds.: International Conference on Security in Communication Networks – SCN 2004. Volume 3352 of Lecture Notes in Computer Science., Amalfi, Italia, Springer-Verlag (2004) 149–164
12. Camenisch, J., Lysyanskaya, A.: An Efficient System for Non-transferable Anonymous Credentials with Optional Anonymity Revocation. In: EUROCRYPT, Innsbruck(Typrol), Austria, IACR (2001)
13. Camenisch, J., Lysyanskaya, A.: Signature Schemes and Anonymous Credentials from Bilinear Maps. In: CRYPTO, Santa Barbara, CA, USA (2004)
14. Camenisch, J., Hohenberger, S., Lysyanskaya, A.: Compact E-Cash. In: EUROCRYPT, Aarhus, Denmark, IACR (2005) 302–321
15. Ateniese, G., Fu, K., Green, M., Hohenberger, S.: Improved Proxy Re-Encryption Schemes with Applications to Secure Distributed Storage. In: Proceedings of the 12th Annual Network and Distributed System Security Symposium (NDSS). (2005)
16. Ateniese, G., Hohenberger, S.: Proxy Re-Signatures: New Definitions, Algorithms, and Applications. In: Proceedings of the 12th ACM conference on Computer and communications security (CCS '05), Alexandria, VA, USA, ACM, ACM Press (2005) 310–319
17. Federal Transit Administration: Federal Transit Administration National Transit Database. WWW (2006) `http://www.ntdprogram.com`.
18. The Smart Card Alliance: Hong Kong Octopus Card. WWW (2006) `http://www.smarcardalliance.org/pdf/about_alliance/user_profiles/Hong_Kong_Octopus_Card.pdf`.
19. Winters, N.: Personal Privacy and Popular Ubiquitous Technology. In: Ubiconf, London, United Kingdom (2004)
20. Roschke, G.: Notes from an Information Law Student. WWW (2006) Last viewed February 24, 2006, `http://luminousvoid.net/archives/16/wmata-responds`.
21. Maxey, C., Benjamin, P.: Seamless Fare Collection: Using Smart Cards for Multiple-Mode Transit Trips. WWW (2006) `www.apta.com/research/info/briefings/documents/maxey.pdf`.

22. Bono, S., Green, M., Stubblefield, A., Juels, A., Rubin, A., Szydlo, M.: Security Analysis of a Cryptographically-Enabled RFID Device. In: USENIX Security Symposium, Baltimore, Maryland, USA, USENIX (2005) 1–16
23. The Smart Card Alliance: Smart Card Talk Standards. The Smart Card Alliance Newsletter (2006) Jan. issue.
24. Washington Metropolitan Area Transit Authority: WMATA Privacy Policy Proposal. WWW (2006) http://www.wmata.com/about/parp2.cfm.
25. Washington Metropolitan Area Transit Authority: WMATA Privacy Policy. WWW (2006) http://www.wmata.com/about/parp_docs/pi_9_2_0.pdf.
26. San Francisco Bay Area Rapid Transit District: Bay Area Rapid Transit (BART) Fiscal Year 2004 Annual Report. WWW (2006)
27. Chaum, D.: Security without Identification: Transaction Systems to Make Big Brother Obsolete. CACM **28** (1985)
28. Guerineau, P.: Active RFID Technology Applied to Security Improvement and Statistical Control in Public Transit. In: Automatic Fare Collection. New Horizons in Public Transport with Smart Cards, Brussels, Belgium, International Union of Public Transport (2002)
29. Juels, A., Syverson, P., Bailey, D.: High-Power Proxies for Enhancing RFID Privacy and Utility. In: Proceedings of Privacy Enhancing Technologies workshop (PET 2005). (2005)
30. McDaniel, T.L., Haendler, F.: Advanced RF Cards for Fare Collection. In: Commercial Applications and Dual-Use Technology Conference Proceedings, National Telesystems Conference (1993) 31–35
31. Ateniese, G., Camenisch, J., de Medeiros, B.: Untraceable RFID Tags via Insubvertible Encryption. In: Conference on Computer and Communications Security – CCS'05, Alexandria, Virginia, USA, ACM, ACM Press (2005)
32. Kang, J., Nyang, D.: RFID Authentication Protocol with Strong Resistance Against Traceability and Denial of Service Attacks. In Molva, R., Tsudik, G., Westhoff, D., eds.: European Workshop on Security and Privacy in Ad hoc and Sensor Networks – ESAS'05. Volume 3813 of Lecture Notes in Computer Science., Visegrad, Hungary, Springer-Verlag (2005) 164–175
33. Ranasinghe, D., Engels, D., Cole, P.: Low-Cost RFID Systems: Confronting Security and Privacy. In: Auto-ID Labs Research Workshop, Zurich, Switzerland (2004)
34. Juels, A., Rivest, R., Szydlo, M.: The Blocker Tag: Selective Blocking of RFID Tags for Consumer Privacy. In Atluri, V., ed.: 8th ACM Conference on Compuer and Communications Security. (2003) 103–111
35. Attoh-Okine, N., Shen, L.: Security Issues of Emerging Smart Cards Fare Collection Application in Mass Transit. In: Vehicle Navigation and Information Systems Conference. (1995) 523–526
36. Sim, L., Seow, E., Prakasam, S.: Implementing an Enhanced Integrated Fare System for Singapore. Public Transport International **53** (2004) 34–37
37. Neve, M., Peeters, E., Samyde, D., Quisquater, J.J.: Memories: A Survey of Their Secure Uses in Smart Cards. In: IEEE Security in Storage Workshop. (2003) 62–72
38. Anderson, R., Kuhn, M.: Tamper Resistance - A Cautionary Note. In: The Second USENIX Workshop on Electronic Commerce Proceedings. (1996) 1–11
39. Damgård, I., Dupont, K., Pedersen, M.Ø.: Unclonable Group Identification. Cryptology ePrint Archive, Report 2005/170 (2005) http://eprint.iacr.org/.
40. Burgess, J., Gallagher, B., Jensen, D., Levine, B.: Maxprop: Routing for vehicle-based disruption-tolerant networks. In: Proc. IEEE INFOCOM. (2006)

41. Zhao, W., Ammar, M., Zegura, E.: A Message Ferrying Approach for Data Delivery in Sparse Mobile Ad Hoc Networks. In: MobiHoc '04: Proceedings of the 5th ACM international symposium on Mobile ad hoc networking and computing, New York, NY, USA, ACM Press (2004) 187–198
42. Zhao, W., Ammar, M.H.: Message Ferrying: Proactive Routing in Highly-Partitioned Wireless Ad Hoc Networks. In: FTDCS '03: Proceedings of the The Ninth IEEE Workshop on Future Trends of Distributed Computing Systems (FT-DCS'03), Washington, DC, USA, IEEE Computer Society (2003) 308
43. Chaum, D., Fiat, A., Naor, M.: Untraceable Electronic Cash. In: CRYPTO '88: Proceedings on Advances in Cryptology, New York, NY, USA, Springer-Verlag New York, Inc. (1990) 319–327

Ignoring the Great Firewall of China

Richard Clayton, Steven J. Murdoch, and Robert N.M. Watson

University of Cambridge, Computer Laboratory, William Gates Building,
15 JJ Thomson Avenue, Cambridge CB3 0FD, United Kingdom
{richard.clayton, steven.murdoch, robert.watson}@cl.cam.ac.uk

Abstract. The so-called "Great Firewall of China" operates, in part, by inspecting TCP packets for keywords that are to be blocked. If the keyword is present, TCP reset packets (viz: with the RST flag set) are sent to both endpoints of the connection, which then close. However, because the original packets are passed through the firewall unscathed, if the endpoints completely ignore the firewall's resets, then the connection will proceed unhindered. Once one connection has been blocked, the firewall makes further easy-to-evade attempts to block further connections from the same machine. This latter behaviour can be leveraged into a denial-of-service attack on third-party machines.

1 Introduction

The People's Republic of China operates an Internet filtering system which is widely considered to be one of the most sophisticated in the world [9]. It works, in part, by inspecting web (HTTP) traffic to determine if specific keywords are present [8]. These keywords relate to matters such as groups that the Chinese Government has banned, political ideologies that they consider unacceptable and historical events that the regime does not wish to have discussed.

It is straightforward to determine that the keyword-based blocking is occurring within the routers that handle the connections between China and the rest of the world [14]. These routers use devices based upon intrusion detection system (IDS) technology to determine whether the content of packets matches the Chinese Government's filtering rules. If a connection from a client to a webserver is to be blocked then the router injects forged TCP resets (with the RST flag bit set) into the data streams so that the endpoints will abandon the connection. Once blocking has begun, it will remain in place for many minutes and further attempts by the same client to fetch material from same website will immediately be disallowed by the injection of further forged resets.

In Section 2 of this paper we discuss the methods available to countries that wish to prevent their citizens from accessing particular Internet content and the strengths and weaknesses that have been identified by previous investigators. In Section 3 we present the packet traces we obtained from each endpoint of some connections that were blocked by the Chinese firewall system. In Section 4 we propose a model for the operation of this firewall to explain the results we have obtained. Then in Section 5 we show that by ignoring the TCP resets being issued

G. Danezis and P. Golle (Eds.): PET 2006, LNCS 4258, pp. 20–35, 2006.

by the firewall we are able to successfully transfer material that was supposed to be blocked, and discuss why this may prove difficult for the firewall operators to address. In Section 6 we show how the blocking action of the firewall can be leveraged into a denial-of-service attack on third party machines. Finally, in Section 7, we consider how websites outside of China might make their material easier to access despite the blocking, and we discuss the merits and demerits of this method of evading censorship.

2   Content Blocking Systems

Three distinct methods of content blocking – packet dropping, DNS poisoning and content inspection – have been identified in previous papers by Dornseif [5], who studied the blocking of right-wing and Nazi material in Nordrhein-Westfalen and Clayton [3] who studied the hybrid blocking system deployed by BT in the United Kingdom to block access to paedophile websites.

2.1   Packet Dropping Schemes

In a packet dropping scheme, all traffic to specific IP addresses is discarded and the content hosted there becomes inaccessible. This scheme is low cost and easy to deploy – firewalls and routers offer the necessary features as standard.

Packet dropping schemes suffer from two main problems. Firstly, the list of IP addresses must be kept up-to-date, which could pose some difficulties if the content provider wishes to make it hard for an ISP to block their websites (for details of the complexity, see the extensive discussion in [4]). Secondly, the system can suffer from "overblocking" – all of the other websites that share the same IP address will also be blocked. Edelman [6] investigated the potential extent of overblocking and found that 69.8% of the websites for .com, .org and .net domains shared an IP address with 50 or more other websites. Although some of these domain names will have merely been "parked", and providing a generic webpage, the detailed figures show a continuum of differing numbers of websites per IP address, reflecting the prevailing commercial practice of hosting as many websites as possible on every physical machine.

2.2   DNS Poisoning Schemes

In a DNS poisoning scheme, it is arranged that when the Domain Name System (DNS) is consulted to translate a textual hostname into a numeric IP address, no answer is returned; or an incorrect answer is given that leads the user to a generic site that serves up a warning about accessing forbidden content.

These schemes do not suffer from overblocking in that no other websites will be affected when access to a specific host is forbidden. However, it can be difficult to make them work correctly if all that is to be blocked is a website, and email contact is still to be permitted. Dornseif demonstrated that all of the ISPs in his sample had made at least one mistake in implementing DNS poisoning.

2.3   Content Inspection Schemes

Most content inspection schemes work by arranging for all traffic to pass through a proxy which refuses to serve any results for forbidden material. These systems can be made extremely precise, potentially blocking single web pages or single images, and permitting everything else to pass through unhindered.

The reason that proxy-based systems are not universally employed is that a system that can cope with the traffic volumes of a major network – or an entire country – would be extremely expensive. In Pennsylvania USA, a state statute requiring the blocking of sites adjudged to contain child pornography was struck down as unconstitutional in September 2004 [13]. For cost reasons, the Pennsylvanian ISPs had been using a mixture of packet dropping and DNS poisoning. The resultant overblocking and "prior restraint" were significant factors in the court's decision.

Nevertheless, proxy-based systems have been deployed in countries such as Saudi Arabia [7], Burma [10] and on specific network providers such as Telenor in Norway [12]. The UK-based BT system studied by Clayton was a hybrid design, utilising a low-cost cache, because only the packets destined for relevant IP addresses would be passed to it. Unfortunately, this permits users to "reverse-engineer" the list of blocked sites. Since these sites provide illegal images of children, this runs counter to the public policy aim of the system.

An alternative method of performing content inspection uses components from an Intrusion Detection System (IDS). The IDS equipment inspects the traffic as it passes by and determines whether or not the content is acceptable. When the content is to be blocked it will arrange for packets to be discarded at a nearby firewall or, in the case of the Chinese system, it will issue TCP reset packets so as to cause the offending connection to be closed.

An IDS-based system is significantly more flexible than the other schemes, and it is much less simple to circumvent. Both Dornseif [5] and Clayton [4] have extensive discussions on how to circumvent the different types of content blocking they identify. However, the IDS approach ought to be able to detect the traffic no matter what evasion scheme is tried, provided that the traffic remains in the clear and is not encrypted or obfuscated in a manner that the IDS cannot convert to a canonical form before coming to a decision.

3   How the Chinese Firewall Blocks Connections

In our experiments we were accessing a website based in China (within the Chinese firewall) from several machines based in Cambridge, England (outside the Chinese firewall). The Chinese firewall system, as currently deployed, is known to work entirely symmetrically[1] – detecting content to be filtered as it passes in both directions – and by issuing all the commands from the Cambridge end we avoided any possibility of infringing Chinese law.

---

[1] This symmetry is necessarily present because it permits the firewall to block both requests that are deemed to be unacceptable and the return of unacceptable content.

3.1 Blocking with Resets

Initially we accessed a simple web page, which arrived in an entirely normal manner, just as would be expected. As can be seen from the packet dump below, after the initial TCP three-way handshake (SYN, SYN/ACK, ACK) the client (using port 53382 in this instance) issues an HTTP GET command to the server's http port (tcp/80) for the top level page (/), which is then transferred normally. We were using Netcat (nc) to issue the request, rather than a web browser, so that we might avoid extraneous detail. The packet traces were captured by ethereal, but we present them in a generic format.

```
cam(53382)   → china(http) [SYN]
china(http)  → cam(53382)  [SYN, ACK]
cam(53382)   → china(http) [ACK]
cam(53382)   → china(http) GET / HTTP/1.0<cr><lf><cr><lf>
china(http)  → cam(53382)  HTTP/1.1 200 OK (text/html)<cr><lf> etc...
china(http)  → cam(53382)  ... more of the web page
cam(53382)   → china(http) [ACK]
             ... and so on until the page was complete
```

We then issued a request which included a small fragment of text that we expected to cause the connection to be blocked, and this promptly occurred:

```
cam(54190)   → china(http) [SYN]
china(http)  → cam(54190)  [SYN, ACK] TTL=39
cam(54190)   → china(http) [ACK]
cam(54190)   → china(http) GET /?falun HTTP/1.0<cr><lf><cr><lf>
china(http)  → cam(54190)  [RST] TTL=47, seq=1, ack=1
china(http)  → cam(54190)  [RST] TTL=47, seq=1461, ack=1
china(http)  → cam(54190)  [RST] TTL=47, seq=4381, ack=1
china(http)  → cam(54190)  HTTP/1.1 200 OK (text/html)<cr><lf> etc...
cam(54190)   → china(http) [RST] TTL=64, seq=25, ack zeroed
china(http)  → cam(54190)  ... more of the web page
cam(54190)   → china(http) [RST] TTL=64, seq=25, ack zeroed
china(http)  → cam(54190)  [RST] TTL=47, seq=2921, ack=25
```

The first three reset packets had sequence values that corresponded to the sequence number at the start of the GET packet, that value plus 1460 and that value plus 4380 (3 × 1460).[2] We believe that the firewall sends three different values to try and ensure that the reset is accepted by the sender, even if the sender has already received ACKs for "full-size" (1460 byte) packets from the destination. Setting the sequence value of the reset packet "correctly" is necessary because many implementations of TCP/IP now apply strict checks that the value is within the expected "window". The vulnerabilities inherent in failing to check for a valid sequence value were first pointed out by Watson in 2004 [15].

---

[2] When we enabled TCP timestamps, and the packets contained 12 bytes of TCP options, we observed that these values changed to multiples of 1448.

The trace also shows part of the web page arriving from the Chinese machine after the connection had already been aborted (we examine why this occurred below). The Cambridge machine therefore sent its own TCP resets in response to these two (now) unexpected packets. Note that it zeroed the acknowledgement fields, rather than using a value relative to the randomly chosen initial value.

All of the reset packets arrived with a time-to-live (TTL) field value of 47, whereas the packets from the Chinese webserver always had a TTL value of 39, indicating that they were from a different source. If both sources set an initial value of 64, then this would indicate the resets were generated 8 hops away from the webserver, which `traceroute` indicates is the second router within the China Netcom Corporation network (AS9929) after the traffic is passed across from the Sprint network (AS1239).

We also examined this blocked connection from the point of view of the Chinese webserver:

```
cam(54190)   → china(http) [SYN] TTL=42
china(http)  → cam(54190)  [SYN, ACK]
cam(54190)   → china(http) [ACK] TTL=42
cam(54190)   → china(http) GET /?falun HTTP/1.0<cr><lf><cr><lf>
china(http)  → cam(54190)  HTTP/1.1 200 OK (text/html)<cr><lf> etc...
china(http)  → cam(54190)  ...more of the web page
cam(54190)   → china(http) [RST] TTL=61, seq=25, ack=1
cam(54190)   → china(http) [RST] TTL=61, seq=1485, ack=1
cam(54190)   → china(http) [RST] TTL=61, seq=4405, ack=1
cam(54190)   → china(http) [RST] TTL=61, seq=25, ack=1
cam(54190)   → china(http) [RST] TTL=61, seq=25, ack=2921
cam(54190)   → china(http) [RST] TTL=42, seq=25, ack zeroed
cam(54190)   → china(http) [RST] TTL=42, seq=25, ack zeroed
```

As can be seen, when the "bad" packet was detected, the firewall also sent resets to the Chinese machine, but these resets arrived after the GET packet (and after the response had commenced). The last two resets (with zeroed ack values), were the ones that were sent by the Cambridge machine.

The other resets (generated because `falun` was present) arrived at the Chinese webserver with a TTL value of 61, which is consistent with them being generated 3 hops away with an initial count of 64. This differs from the 8-hop offset we observed from Cambridge. However, it is possible that there is more than one device that is generating resets – or the initial count may have been adjusted to be different from 64. We do not currently have any definitive explanation for the lack of symmetry that this observation represents.

The first three blocking resets were also set to a range (+25, +1485, +4405) of sequence numbers in an attempt to ensure that at least one was accepted, and in fact the +25 packet will have reset the connection.[3] The fourth and

---

[3] If the resets had arrived *before* the GET packet, then the resets would *not* have been accepted. The server is running FreeBSD and in this stage of a connection its TCP stack will, to provide protection against denial-of-service attacks, only accept a reset where the sequence number exactly matches the last acknowledgement sent. Before the GET arrives that value is +1, and hence all of the resets would be ineffective.

fifth resets received can be seen, by examining their acknowledgement values, to be responses to the two packets that the server managed to send before the connection was reset.

3.2 Immediate Reset of Connections

The firewall is not just inspecting content but has other blocking rules as well. Having made a "bad" connection we found that, for a short period, all web traffic between the same two hosts was blocked, before any determination could possibly have been made as to the content. This can also be seen in the previous example – but it applies to new connections as well. For example, immediately after the example documented above we saw this:

```
cam(54191)  → china(http) [SYN]
china(http) → cam(54191)  [SYN, ACK] TTL=41
cam(54191)  → china(http) [ACK]
china(http) → cam(54191)  [RST] TTL=49, seq=1
```

Here the reset packet came from the firewall (which sent a reset to the web-server as well). If the client manages to send out its GET packet before the reset arrives from the firewall then multiple resets arrive from the firewall (even if the GET is entirely innocuous). These are then followed by resets from the webserver – which usually receives the resets promptly and so it will have torn down the connection before the GET arrives.

It should be noted that the firewall does not attempt to reset the connection at the SYN stage but waits for the SYN/ACK. Although the client could immediately be sent valid reset packets when the SYN is seen, it is only when the SYN/ACK packet is observed that a reset can be constructed with valid values for the server to act upon.

In our experiments, we found that the length of time for which a pair of end-points would be prevented from communicating was somewhat variable. Sometimes the blocking would only last for a few minutes, yet at another time the block would be present for most of an hour. The average value was around 20 minutes, but because we saw significant clustering of times around specific values we suspect that different firewall system components may be setting different time delays; and hence a better understanding of which component was to handle our traffic would enable us to predict the blocking period fairly accurately.

3.3 Application to Other Chinese Networks

We obtained a list of Chinese Autonomous Systems (ASs)[4] and from that generated a list of all Chinese subnets that were present in the global routing table. We then used a modified `tcptraceroute` to determine which ASs were handling traffic as it crossed from international networks into China, and from this learnt the identities of the major Chinese border networks. These turned out to be: AS4134, AS4837, AS7497, AS9800, AS9808, AS9929, AS17622, AS24301

---

[4] `http://bgpview.6test.edu.cn/bgp-view/cur_ana/ipv4cn/china_asnlist.shtml`

and AS24489. We then selected an example web server within each of these ASs and found that similar RST behaviour occurred on all of these networks except AS24489 (Trans-Eurasia Information Network). From this we conclude that our results are extremely typical of the "Great Firewall of China", as it exists in late May 2006, but are not necessarily universally applicable.

4   Design of the Chinese Firewall

Based on the results of our experiments, and descriptions of the type of devices and technologies known to be employed in China – such as Cisco's "Secure Intrusion Detection System" [2] – we propose the following model for the operation of a router that is a part of the Chinese firewall. This model fits our observations well, but it remains speculative because the Chinese network providers do not publish any specifications of their systems.

When a packet arrives at the router it is immediately placed into an appropriate queue for onward transmission. The packets are also passed to an out-of-band IDS device within which their content is inspected. If the packet is considered to be "bad" by the IDS device (because of a keyword match) then three TCP reset packets – with the three different sequence numbers – are generated for each endpoint and given to the router to be transmitted to their destinations.

We do not expect that the IDS, being a logically separate device, will have the capability to remove "bad" packets from the router transmission queue (especially since they might have already been transmitted before a decision is made). Hence it is limited to emitting resets to cause connections to close.

If there is some congestion within the router, and the IDS device is keeping up, then the reset packet will be sent ahead of the "bad" packet; and this is what we mainly observed in our experiments, although sometimes it would lag behind. The values chosen for the reset packets strongly suggest that the designers were concerned that if there is some congestion within the IDS device, compared with the router, then several "bad" packets may have already been transmitted and so the reset packets will reach the destination after these have arrived.

Once the IDS system has detected behaviour it wishes to block, it might add a simple discard rule to the main router, rather than issuing resets. We strongly suspect that this does not scale well within major, high-speed, routers, but that scaling the blocking within the IDS systems is cheaper and easier.

We have already observed, from the time periods for which connections were blocked, that there seemed to be several devices providing the firewall functionality. We ran a further experiment which sent 256 packets containing the offending string through the firewall. Although these packets came from a single machine, we set their source addresses to 256 consecutive IP address values, viz: the Chinese firewall would believe that 256 different, albeit related, machines were sending content that was to be blocked. We observed that the reset packets that were returned to us would sometimes arrive "out of order".

The modern Internet generally arranges for packets to be processed in FIFO (first-in, first-out) queues, so the simplest explanation for the lack of ordering was that different packets had been passed to different IDS systems, whose own FIFO queues were not equally loaded at the moment they issued the resets. Unfortunately, we found that the experiment engendered so much packet loss (not all of the resets were returned for all of the connections) that it was not possible to form a view as to how far out of order packets could come – and hence establish a lower bound on the number of parallel IDS devices. We intend to return to this experiment at a later time.

4.1   Firewall "State"

There is no evidence that the out-of-band IDS devices communicate with each other so as to create a shared notion of the "state" of connections that pass through the firewall. Experiments demonstrate that triggering a firewall in one border network did not affect the traffic passing through another.

Even where "state" might be expected to be preserved – within the IDS devices – there is no stateful TCP inspection: splitting the ?falun query across packets is sufficient to avoid detection. Furthermore, the devices are unaware of whether an open connection exists, so that for many of our tests we did not perform the three-way handshake to open a connection but just sent the packet containing the HTTP GET request. In fact, apart from the ongoing blocking of traffic after the initial detection occurs, there is no evidence for the IDS devices doing anything other than acting upon one packet at a time.

5   Deliberately Ignoring Resets

The firewall relies entirely upon the endpoints implementing the TCP protocol [11] in a standards-compliant manner and aborting the connection when a reset packet is received. The firewall could sometimes be slightly caught out, as we noted above, when the resets beat the GET packet to the destination and so they were ignored by the careful validation that was applied. Nevertheless, the connection was successfully torn down as soon as the next packet transited the firewall, and hence this didn't make much overall difference.

But now consider what happens if the endpoints do *not* conform to the standards and the TCP resets are entirely ignored. We might expect the firewall to have no impact on HTTP transfers, despite them triggering the IDS system.

We therefore conducted a further experiment with both of the endpoints ignoring TCP resets. We could have achieved this in a number of different ways, but we chose to set appropriate rules within packet filtering firewalls. Within Linux we installed iptables and gave the command:

```
iptables -A INPUT -p tcp --tcp-flags RST RST -j DROP
```

which specifies that incoming TCP packets with the RST flag set are to be discarded. If we had been using FreeBSD's ipfw the command would have been:

```
ipfw add 1000 drop tcp from any to me tcpflags rst in
```

Once we were discarding TCP resets we found that we could indeed transfer a web page without any blocking occurring. Examining the traffic at the
Cambridge end of the connection we saw the results:

```
cam(55817)   → china(http) [SYN]
china(http)  → cam(55817)  [SYN, ACK] TTL=41
cam(55817)   → china(http) [ACK]
cam(55817)   → china(http) GET /?falun HTTP/1.0<cr><lf><cr><lf>
china(http)  → cam(55817)  [RST] TTL=49, seq=1
china(http)  → cam(55817)  [RST] TTL=49, seq=1
china(http)  → cam(55817)  [RST] TTL=49, seq=1
china(http)  → cam(55817)  HTTP/1.1 200 OK (text/html)<cr><lf> etc
china(http)  → cam(55817)  ...more of the web page
cam(55817)   → china(http) [ACK] seq=25, ack=2921
china(http)  → cam(55817)  ...more of the web page
china(http)  → cam(55817)  [RST] TTL=49, seq=1461
china(http)  → cam(55817)  [RST] TTL=49, seq=2921
china(http)  → cam(55817)  [RST] TTL=49, seq=4381
cam(55817)   → china(http) [ACK] seq=25, ack=4381
china(http)  → cam(55817)  [RST] TTL=49, seq=2921
china(http)  → cam(55817)  ...more of the web page
china(http)  → cam(55817)  ...more of the web page
cam(55817)   → china(http) [ACK] seq=25, ack=7301
china(http)  → cam(55817)  [RST] TTL=49, seq=5841
china(http)  → cam(55817)  [RST] TTL=49, seq=7301
china(http)  → cam(55817)  [RST] TTL=49, seq=4381
china(http)  → cam(55817)  ...more of the web page
china(http)  → cam(55817)  [RST] TTL=49, seq=8761
            ...and so on until the page was complete
```

viz: the web page was transferred in a normal manner except for the TCP reset
packets generated by the firewall. Since these were all ignored (there were 28
resets sent in total), they had no effect on the client's TCP/IP stack – which
continued to accept the incoming web page, issuing ACKs as appropriate. A
similar pattern of RSTs mixed in amongst the real traffic could also be seen at
the Chinese end.

Hence, by simply ignoring the packets sent by the "Great Firewall", we made
it entirely ineffective! This will doubtless disappoint its implementers.

5.1   Blocking with Confusion

As well as blocking further connections by issuing TCP resets once the connection was established, we observed that parts of the firewall occasionally used an
additional strategy. On some pairs of endpoints (apparently at random), we saw
a forged SYN/ACK packet arrive from the firewall. This contained an apparently
random (and hence invalid) sequence number.

If the SYN/ACK packet generated at the firewall arrives at the client before
the real SYN/ACK then the connection fails. The sequence of events is that the

client records the random sequence number from the specious SYN/ACK and returns what the server considers to be an incorrect ACK value. This triggers a reset packet and the client closes. In practice, there are a number of other packets in a typical trace when the client is prompt in sending its GET, causing both the firewall and the server to respond with further resets:

```
cam(38104)    → china(http) [SYN]
china(http) → cam(38104)    [SYN, ACK] TTL=105
cam(38104)    → china(http) [ACK]
cam(38104)    → china(http) GET / HTTP/1.0<cr><lf><cr><lf>
china(http) → cam(38104)    [RST] TTL=45, seq=1
china(http) → cam(38104)    [RST] TTL=45, seq=1
china(http) → cam(38104)    [SYN, ACK] TTL=37
cam(38104)    → china(http) [RST] TTL=64, seq=1
china(http) → cam(38104)    [RST] TTL=49, seq=1
china(http) → cam(38104)    [RST] TTL=45, seq=3770952438
china(http) → cam(38104)    [RST] TTL=45, seq=1
china(http) → cam(38104)    [RST] TTL=45, seq=1
china(http) → cam(38104)    [RST] TTL=37, seq=1
china(http) → cam(38104)    [RST] TTL=37, seq=1
```

Dealing with this new firewall strategy is more difficult than dealing with the forged reset packets. The problem is that even if the client ignores the (entirely valid) reset from the server, it continues to have an incorrect understanding of the server's sequence number, and it cannot "synchronise" with the server to complete the three-way handshake and connect.

Of course if, as occasionally happens, the specious SYN/ACK from the firewall arrives *after* the SYN/ACK from the webserver, it will be ignored by the client and will not cause any confusion. The firewall still attempts to tear down the connection with forged reset packets but, just as before, ignoring these resets means that a blocked web page can still be viewed.

Deciding which of two incoming SYN/ACK packets is genuine is clearly essential. In the examples we saw they were easy to distinguish, the firewall version had a distinctive TTL value, no DF flag, and no TCP options were set. They are therefore, at present, just as easy to filter as resets and the Chinese firewall is once again ineffective. Moreover, this strategy is only used once an attempt has been made to block a previous connection, and hence the expected TTL value for the server could be remembered by the client, whereas the firewall will not know what value to place into its forged packet.

However, with increasing sophistication in the firewall, it might manage to forge SYN/ACK packets with no detectable differences. The client could simply take the view that the firewall packet was the one arriving first. However, if the firewall countered this by sometimes delaying its SYN/ACK packet (allowing a naïve system to get access, but defeating a more sophisticated system!) then a complex "game" could result with ever more abstruse strategies. It should be noted that webpage fetching often involves multiple connections and so the firewall operators might feel that they had "won" the game by blocking a proportion of accesses, rather than all of them.

An effective client strategy (with the prerequisite that both client and server are discarding resets) is to arrange to treat all incoming SYN/ACK packets (the firewall might in future send more than one) as valid. The client should then record their sequence values and ACK all of them. The client then continues to consider all values to be potentially correct (holding appropriate state within the TCP stack) until it receives an ACK from the server that confirms which value is actually correct. This is somewhat complex to achieve and beyond the capabilities of simple packet-filtering systems such as `iptables` or `ipfw`.

A further round of this new "game" would be for the firewall to forge an ACK for all of the client's packets. It should be possible for the client to see through this subterfuge by discarding values for which a genuine looking RST is received from the server, so the firewall would need to forge these – and once again the strategies can become arbitrarily complex. The endpoints do have an advantage in that they can eventually conclude whether packets are being generated by other, stateful, endpoint or by a stateless firewall. However, should the firewall start to keep "state" then this major architectural change (albeit almost certainly at significant cost) would open up many other strategies, and the advantage would swing decisively to the firewall.

Unfortunately, it must be noted that firewall generated SYN/ACK packets cannot be securely dealt with by a change to the TCP/IP stack at the server end of the connection. The server is in a position to work out that the client is continually responding with the "wrong" ACK value and retrospectively alter its own state to correspond with the value from the forged SYN/ACK packet. However, doing this would permit access by systems that forged the source IP addresses so as to pretend to be another machine [1].

Making secure connections in the presence of adversaries that can "sniff" packets and add forged packets of their own has of course been well studied in the context of cryptographic key exchange protocols. The open question is to what extent fairly simple modifications to existing TCP/IP stacks will continue to be sufficient to overcome the strategies available to the Chinese firewall operators, given the architectural limitations of their current design.

6   Denial-of-Service Attacks

As we have already noted, a single TCP packet containing a request such as `?falun` is sufficient to trigger blocking between the destination address and source address for periods of up to an hour. If the source of the packet is forged, this permits a (somewhat limited) denial-of-service attack which will prevent a particular pair of endpoints from communicating. However, depending upon their motives, this might be sufficient for some attackers. For example, it might be possible to identify the machines used by regional government offices and prevent them accessing "Windows Update"; or prevent a particular ministry accessing specific UN websites; or prevent access by Chinese embassies abroad to particular Chinese websites "back home".

Our calculations suggest that the denial-of-service could be reasonably effective even if operated by a lone individual on a dial-up connection. Such an individual could generate approximately 100 triggering packets per second, and hence – assuming that blocking was in place for the average period of 20 minutes – some 120 000 pairs of end-points could be permanently prevented from communicating.

Of course, current denial-of-service attacks are seldom instantiated by single dial-up machines, but by large numbers of machines on much faster connections. Hence the 120 000 value can be multiplied up to taste. However, it may well be that the IDS components of the firewall do not have the ability to record substantial numbers of blocked connections – so the actual impact is likely to be limited by this type of resource consideration. It should also be noted that while the IDS is handling an attempted denial-of-service attack it will have fewer resources to devote to recording information about other connections – thereby temporarily reducing its effectiveness.

6.1   Limitations on the Denial-of-Service Attack

Further experiments showed that the firewall's blocking was somewhat more complex than we have explained so far; and hence a denial-of-service attack would not necessarily be quite as effective as it initially seemed.

Firstly, the blocking is only applied to further connections with similar port numbers. The algorithm being used by the firewall only blocks the 128 TCP port numbers whose most significant 7 bits of value match the connection that triggered the blocking. For a system such as Windows that uses ephemeral port numbers sequentially this would mean that an average of 64 further connections would be blocked (therefore occasionally, if a port number such as 4095 was used in a triggering connection, there would be no further blocking). Conversely on a system such as OpenBSD which uses ephemeral port numbers pseudo-randomly, then the chance of another connection being blocked is only about 1 in 500.

We do not have a definitive explanation as to why the firewall behaves this way. It would seem much simpler are more effective to just block every connection to the same endpoints, without worrying about the port number.[5] It is possible that the aim is to avoid penalising other users of Network Address Translation (NAT) devices, when just one user has been blocked, or it may that the port number helps determine which particular IDS machine is given the packet. However, it may just be that the behaviour is meant to appear mysterious – and hence more menacing.

From the point of view of a denial-of-service attacker, the consequence is that all possible port number ranges must be blocked, unless there are special circumstances which allow the attacker to guess which ephemeral port numbers will be used in the near future. This increases, by a factor of about 500, the number of packets that must be sent to ensure one machine is blocked.

Secondly, not all IP addresses had their traffic inspected. Every hour we sent a rapid burst of requests containing "?falun", one packet from each of a block

---

[5] HTTP traffic was blocked not only on tcp/http port 80, but also on other port numbers. However, only a single server port was ever blocked – no adjacent ports were affected – nor was tcp/https (port 443) blocked when port 80 was.

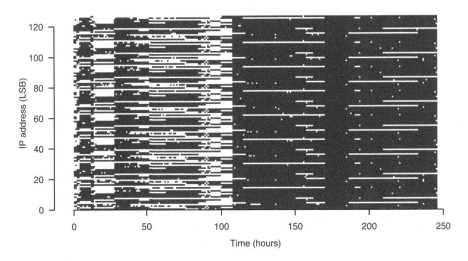

Fig. 1. Blocking of "bad" strings by the Chinese firewall. We tested from 256 adjacent IP addresses once an hour for 10 days in early February 2006. Results for the first 128 are shown; the pattern was very similar for the others. The dark blobs indicate that the access was blocked, and white that there was no blocking. When the result was indeterminate (no response at all) the colour is a mid-gray. An obvious change in firewall configuration (to block more IP addresses) is visible after 110 hours.

of 256 consecutive IP addresses. Initially, about two-thirds of each set of packets were blocked, with the address selection varying over time. However, after a few days, almost all packets caused blocking behaviour. We were unable to reverse-engineer the algorithm that determined which IP addresses had their packets scanned, although distinctive patterns (see Figure 1) within the IP address selections strongly suggest that quite a simple mechanism has been deployed. The most likely explanation is a lack of resources – two-thirds of the traffic may be all that the content scanning system can handle. Clearly, if a proportion of machines are being excused packet inspection at a particular time, then at that time, it will not be possible to mount a denial-of-service attack on them.

Finally, we observe that these experiments, as is the case with all the experiments we made, were performed using a small number of endpoints both outside and within China. Although we saw reasonably consistent results, with a system as complex as the "Great Firewall of China" it is entirely possible that we failed to observe significant aspects of its behaviour. Hence, although we believe that a denial-of-service attack may succeed in many circumstances, we cannot say that an attack on an arbitrary pair of endpoints would succeed.

7   Strategic Considerations

In order for traffic to pass unhindered through the Chinese firewall machines it is necessary for *both* endpoints to ignore resets. Machines in the "rest of the world" that wish to be accessed from China should have no difficulty in arranging for a reconfiguration. However, the individual at the Chinese end of the connection may not wish to install special software. Their difficulty is that the firewall may not only be blocking connections but also logging what it has done. This might lead to an investigation, and the specially installed software would be discovered and an unenlightened view might be taken of the motives for installing it.

The packet inspection capabilities of the Chinese firewall can also be evaded by the use of encryption. If the authorities detected encrypted traffic, perhaps by statistical analysis of the content, then the same problem of specially installed software would arise when the endpoint was visited. However, since encryption systems typically discard session keys, it might not be possible to demonstrate that the traffic had been, say, pornography rather than political speech. In the case where the firewall is breached by discarding resets, the content will be available to the firewall in the clear, so that the authorities could consult their logs and treat the two types of access differently. As a result, some might view discarding reset packets as having an advantage over the use of encryption.

The Chinese authorities might be forced to take a more tolerant view of the use of reset discarding software by their citizens if this was to become universally deployed, and the resets were discarded for completely unrelated reasons.

Other work on "software firewalls" has shown that TCP resets are routinely discarded with few side effects (see Section 4.7 of [4]). Their main purpose is to provide a rapid way of reporting that incoming traffic is unwelcome. However, if the remote machine is well-behaved then very little more traffic will arrive if the packets are simply ignored, rather than responded to with a reset.

Nevertheless, some people may not wish to discard every TCP reset, and an alternative strategy is possible.[6] At present, inspection of the TTL values provides a simple method of distinguishing the resets generated by the firewall from any resets sent by the other end of the connection. In particular, we note that Watson's reset attack [15], whereby third parties forge resets to close down connections, is usually resisted by careful validation of the sequence numbers of reset packets. Validating the TTL value in the reset packet to ensure that it is similar to the TTL value seen for the rest of the connection would improve the chances of spotting forged resets generally. One of the present authors has developed a 20-line patch for FreeBSD [16] that discards resets whose TTL radically differs from other incoming packets on the connection. Experience so far has been very positive. It is unlikely that other operating systems or "personal firewalls" would find it onerous to provide the same facility.

Of course, the Chinese firewall can be adapted to make the proposed method of circumvention harder to achieve – in particular, it could trivially ensure that the TTL value was correct on reset packets sent in the same direction as triggering packets, although getting it correct for resets sent in the other direction would be difficult because Internet routing is often asymmetric and so the firewall cannot expect to see both directions of traffic.

---

[6] In future the Chinese firewall might block connections with FIN packets rather than resets. Ignoring all FIN packets would upset normal operations; this alternative strategy would then be the more appropriate.

However, it will continue to be complex to arrange to remove packets from router queues (or even delay them until a decision on their content has been made). Unless packets can be prevented from reaching their destination, our basic method – of ignoring everything the firewall says – will continue to work.

A completely different firewall strategy would be to refuse to route any further packets to sites that have triggered the blocking behaviour. However, we have already noted that this may scale very badly, because it must be done "in-line" with the fast path through the routers – and of course, full-scale blocking would increase the effectiveness of the denial-of-service attacks we discussed above.

8   Conclusions

We have demonstrated that the "Great Firewall of China" relies on inspecting packets for specific content. When filtering rules are triggered, forged reset packets are sent to each endpoint of the TCP connection. However, the genuine packets traverse the firewall unchanged, and hence by ignoring the resets, traffic can be exchanged unhindered. Further connections to the same destination are also blocked (although only if closely related port numbers are used), but ignoring resets will continue to permit unhindered access.

This result will be of considerable significance to the Chinese authorities, who will presumably wish to strengthen their systems to fix the holes in their firewall, although as we have noted, this may not be especially easy to achieve.

However, the result may be of less significance to Chinese residents who wish to access content unhindered, because their activity can still be logged and investigated. Only if the ignoring of reset packets becomes commonplace will residents be able to claim that their firewall evasion was inadvertent. This is not entirely far-fetched because validating TCP resets to see if they have been forged is a reasonable precaution for TCP/IP stack vendors to take.

We have also shown that a side-effect of the blocking is the potential for a denial-of-service attack, albeit one that can only be used to attack particular pairs of endpoints. It is perhaps unsurprising that a blocking mechanism can be used to block things – but without adding significant amounts of "state" to the firewall we do not see an easy way to prevent attacks.

The results we have demonstrated are also relevant to other countries, institutions and enterprises that use similar reset mechanisms to protect their interests. They should carefully note that the blocking entirely relies upon the acquiescence of those who are being blocked. Smaller countries than China may run a greater risk of denial-of-service, because they are likely to have fewer endpoints within their borders, so the firewall may not run out of resources to store details of blocked connections before the effect becomes significant.

Acknowledgments

We wish to acknowledge the assistance of a Chinese national we will not name (and who was entirely unaware of the nature of our experiment, and whose web pages contain no illicit material) in providing an extremely convincing practical demonstration of a theoretical idea. Richard Clayton is currently working on the spamHINTS project, funded by Intel Research.

References

1. Bellovin, S.: Defending Against Sequence Number Attacks. RFC1948, IETF, May 1996.
2. Carter, E.: Secure Intrusion Detection Systems. Cisco Press (2001)
3. Clayton, R.: Failures in a Hybrid Content Blocking System. Fifth Privacy Enhancing Technologies Workshop, PET 2005, Dubrovnik, Croatia, 30 May–1 June 2005.
4. Clayton, R.: Anonymity and Traceability in Cyberspace. Tech Report UCAM-CL-TR-653, Computer Laboratory, University of Cambridge (2005)
5. Dornseif, M.: Government mandated blocking of foreign Web content. In von Knop, J., Haverkamp, W. and Jessen, E. (ed): Security, E-Learning, E-Services: Proceedings of the 17. DFN-Arbeitstagung über Kommunikationsnetze, Düsseldorf 2003, Lecture Notes in Informatics, pp. 617–648.
6. Edelman, B.: Web Sites Sharing IP Addresses: Prevalence and Significance. Berkman Center for Internet and Society (February 2003)
   http://cyber.law.harvard.edu/people/edelman/ip-sharing/
7. King Abdulaziz City for Science and Technology: Local content filtering Procedure. Internet Services Unit, KACST (2004). http://www.isu.net.sa/saudi-internet/contenet-filtring/filtring-mechanism.htm
8. The OpenNet Initiative: Probing Chinese search engine filtering. Bulletin 005, (August 2004) http://www.opennetinitiative.net/bulletins/005/
9. The OpenNet Initiative: Internet Filtering in China in 2004–2005: A Country Study (June 2004) http://www.opennetinitiative.net/studies/china/ONI_China_Country_Study.pdf
10. The OpenNet Initiative: Internet Filtering in Burma in 2005: A Country Study (October 2004)
    http://www.opennetinitiative.net/burma/ONI_Burma_Country_Study.pdf
11. Postel, J. (ed.): Transmission Control Protocol: DARPA Internet Program Protocol Specification. RFC 793, IETF (1981)
12. Telenor Norge: Telenor and KRIPOS introduce Internet child pornography filter. Telenor Press Release, 21 September 2004.
    http://presse.telenor.no/PR/200409/961319_5.html
13. US District Court for the Eastern District of Pennsylvania: CDT, ACLU, Plantagenet Inc. v Pappert, 337 F.Supp.2d 606, 10 September 2004.
14. Villeneuve, N.: Censorship Is In the Router. (3 June 2005)
    http://ice.citizenlab.org/?p=113
15. Watson, P.: Slipping in the Window: TCP Reset Attacks. CanSecWest/core04 (2004)
16. Watson, R.: 20060607-tcp-ttl.diff. June 2006,
    http://www.cl.cam.ac.uk/~rnw24/patches/

Imagined Communities:
Awareness, Information Sharing, and Privacy on the Facebook

Alessandro Acquisti[1] and Ralph Gross[2]

[1] H. John Heinz III School of Public Policy and Management
[2] Data Privacy Laboratory, School of Computer Science
Carnegie Mellon University, Pittsburgh, PA 15213

Abstract. Online social networks such as Friendster, MySpace, or the Facebook have experienced exponential growth in membership in recent years. These networks offer attractive means for interaction and communication, but also raise privacy and security concerns. In this study we survey a representative sample of the members of the Facebook (a social network for colleges and high schools) at a US academic institution, and compare the survey data to information retrieved from the network itself. We look for underlying demographic or behavioral differences between the communities of the network's members and non-members; we analyze the impact of privacy concerns on members' behavior; we compare members' stated attitudes with actual behavior; and we document the changes in behavior subsequent to privacy-related information exposure. We find that an individual's privacy concerns are only a weak predictor of his membership to the network. Also privacy concerned individuals join the network and reveal great amounts of personal information. Some manage their privacy concerns by trusting their ability to control the information they provide and the external access to it. However, we also find evidence of members' misconceptions about the online community's actual size and composition, and about the visibility of members' profiles.

1 Introduction

"Students living in the scholarship halls [of Kansas University] were written up in early February for pictures on facebook.com that indicated a party violating the scholarship halls alcohol policy" [1]. "'Stan Smith' (not his real name) is a sophomore at Norwich University. He is majoring in criminal justice even though he admits to shoplifting on his MySpace page" [2]. "Corporations are investing in text-recognition software from vendors such as SAP and IBM to monitor blogs by employees and job candidates" [3]. Although online social networks are offering novel opportunities for interaction among their users, they seem to attract non-users' attention particularly because of the privacy concerns they raise. Such concerns may be well placed; however, online social networks are no longer niche phenomena: millions of people around the world, young and old, knowingly and willingly use Friendster, MySpace, Match.com, LinkedIn,

G. Danezis and P. Golle (Eds.): PET 2006, LNCS 4258, pp. 36–58, 2006.

and hundred other sites to communicate, find friends, dates, and jobs - and in doing so, they wittingly reveal highly personal information to friends as well as strangers.

Nobody is literally forced to join an online social network, and most networks we know about *encourage*, but do not *force* users to reveal - for instance - their dates of birth, their cell phone numbers, or where they currently live. And yet, one cannot help but marvel at the nature, amount, and detail of the personal information some users provide, and ponder how informed this information sharing is. Changing cultural trends, familiarity and confidence in digital technologies, lack of exposure or memory of egregious misuses of personal data by others may all play a role in this unprecedented phenomenon of information revelation. Yet, online social networks' security and access controls are weak by design - to leverage their value as network goods and enhance their growth by making registration, access, and sharing of information uncomplicated. At the same time, the costs of mining and storing data continue to decline. Combined, the two features imply that information provided even on ostensibly private social networks is, effectively, public data, that could exist for as long as anybody has an incentive to maintain it. Many entities - from marketers to employers to national and foreign security agencies - may have those incentives.

In this paper we combine survey analysis and data mining to study one such network, catered to college and high school communities: the Facebook (FB). We survey a representative sample of FB members at a US campus. We study their privacy concerns, their usage of FB, their attitudes towards it as well as their awareness of the nature of its community and the visibility of their own profiles. In particular, we look for underlying demographic or behavioral differences between the communities of the network's members and non-members; we analyze the impact of privacy concerns on members' behavior; we compare members' stated attitudes with actual behavior; and we document the change in behavior subsequent information exposure: who uses the Facebook? Why? Are there significant differences between users and non-users? Why do people reveal more or less personal information? How well do they know the workings of the network?

Our study is based on a survey instrument, but is complemented by analysis of data mined from the network before and after the survey was administered. We show that there are significant demographic differences between FB member and non-members; that although FB members express, in general, significant concern about their privacy, they are not particularly concerned for their privacy *on* FB; that a minority yet significant share of the FB population at the Campus we surveyed is unaware of the actual exposure and visibility of the information they publish on FB; and we document that priming about FB's information practices can alter some of its members' behavior.

The rest of the paper is organized as follows. In Section 2 we discuss the evolution of online social networks and FB in particular. In Section 3 we highlight the methods of our analysis. In Section 4 we present our results. In Section 5 we compare survey results to network data.

2   Online Social Networks

At the most basic level, an online social network is an Internet community where individuals interact, often through profiles that (re)present their public persona (and their networks of connections) to others. Although the concept of computer-based communities dates back to the early days of computer networks, only after the advent of the commercial Internet did such communities meet public success. Following the SixDegrees.com experience in 1997, hundreds of social networks spurred online (see [4] for an extended discussion), sometimes growing very rapidly, thereby attracting the attention of both media and academia. In particular, [5], [6], and [7] have taken ethnographic and sociological approaches to the study of online self-representation; [8] have focused on the value of online social networks as recommender systems; [4] have discussed information sharing and privacy on online social networks, using FB as a case study; [9] have demonstrated how information revealed in social networks can be exploited for "social" phishing; [10] has studied identity-sharing behavior in online social networks.

2.1   The Facebook

The Facebook is a social network catered to college and high school communities. Among online social networks, FB stands out for three reasons: its success among the college crowd; the amount and the quality of personal information users make available on it; and the fact that, unlike other networks for young users, that information is personally identified. Accordingly, FB is of interest to researchers in two respects: 1) as a mass social phenomenon in itself ; 2) as an unique window of observation on the privacy attitudes and the patterns of information revelation among young individuals.

FB has spread to thousands of college campuses (and now also high schools) across the United States, attracting more than 9 million (and counting) users. FB's market penetration is impressive: it can draw more than 80% of the undergraduate population in many colleges. The amount, quality, and value of the information provided is impressive too: not only are FB profiles most often personally and uniquely identified, but by default they show contact information (including personal addresses and cell phone numbers) and additional data rarely available on other networks.

FB requires a college's email account for a participant to be admitted to the online social network of that college. As discussed in [4], this increases the expectations of validity of the personal information therein provided, as well as the perception of the online space as a closed, trusted, and trustworthy community (college-oriented social networking sites are, ostensibly, based "on a shared real space" [11]). However, there are reasons to believe that FB networks more closely resemble *imagined* [12] communities (see also [4]): in most online social networks, security, access controls, and privacy are weak *by design*; the easier it is for people to join and to find points of contact with other users (by providing vast amounts of personal information, and by perusing equally vast amounts of data provided by others), the higher the utility of the network to the users themselves, and the higher its commercial value for the network's owners and managers. FB, unlike other online networks, offers its members very granular and powerful control on the privacy (in terms of searchability and visibility) of their personal information. Yet its privacy default settings are very permeable: at the time of writing, by default participants' profiles are *searchable* by anybody else on the FB network, and actually *readable* by any member at the same college and geographical location. In addition, external access to a college FB community (e.g., by non-students/faculty/staff/alumni, or by non-college-affiliated individuals) is so easy [4], that the network is effectively an open community, and its data effectively public.

3   Methods

Our study aims at casting a light on the patterns and motivations of information revelation of college students on FB. It is based on a survey instrument administered to a sample of students at a North American college Institution, complemented by analysis of data mined from the FB network community of that Institution.

3.1   Recruiting Methods

Participants to the survey were recruited in three ways: through a list of subjects interested in participating in experimental studies maintained at the Institution where the study took place (and containing around 4,000 subscribed subjects); through an electronic billboard dedicated to experiments and studies, with an unknown (to us) number of campus community subscribers; and through fliers posted around campus. The above two lists are populated in majority by undergraduate students. The emails and the fliers sought participants to a survey on "online networks," and offered a compensation of $6, plus the possibility to win a $100 prize in a lottery among all participants.

Around 7,000 profiles were mined from the FB network of the same Institution. In order to automate access to the Facebook we used Perl scripts [13], specifically the Perl LWP library [14], which is designed for downloading and parsing HTML pages. The data was mined before and after the survey was administered.

3.2   Survey Design

The survey questionnaire contained around forty questions: an initial set of screening questions; a consent section; a set of calibration questions (to ascertain the respondents' privacy attitudes without priming them on the subject of our study: privacy questions were interspersed with questions on topics such as economic policy, the threat of terrorism, same-sex marriage, and so on); and, next, FB-related questions. Specifically, we asked respondents to answer questions about their usage, their knowledge, and their attitudes towards FB. Finally, the survey contained a set of demographics questions.

Only respondents currently affiliated with the Institution were allowed to take the survey (students, staff, and faculty). Respondents received somewhat different questions depending on whether they were current FB members, previous members, or never members. The survey is available on request from the authors.

3.3 Statistical Analysis

We analyzed survey results using STATA 8.0 on Windows and other *ad hoc* scripts. The study was performed on dichotomous, categorical (especially 7-point Likert scales), and continuous variables. We performed a number of different tests - including Pearson product-moment correlations to study relations between continuous variables, χ^2 and t tests to study categorical variables and means, Wilcoxon signed-rank test and Wilcoxon/Mann-Whitey test for non-normal distributions, as well as logit, probit, and linear multivariate regressions.

4 Results

A total of 506 respondents accessed the survey. One-hundred-eleven (21.9%) were not currently affiliated with the college Institution where we conducted our study, or did not have a email address within that Institution's domain. They were not allowed to take the rest of the survey. A separate set of 32 (8.2%) participants had taken part in a previous pilot survey and were also not allowed to take the survey. Of the remaining respondents, 318 subjects actually completed the initial calibration questions. Out of this set, 278 (87.4%) had heard about FB, 40 had not. In this group, 225 (70.8%) had a profile on FB, 85 (26.7%) never had one, and 8 (2.5%) had an account but deactivated it. Within those three groups, respectively 209, 81, and 7 participants completed the whole survey. We focus our analysis on that set - from which we further removed 3 observations from the non-members group, since we had reasons to believe that the responses had been created by the same individual. This left us with a total of 294 respondents.

4.1 Participants

In absolute terms, we had exactly the same number of male participants taking the survey as female participants, 147. We classified participants depending on whether they were current members of the FB campus network (we will refer to them as "members"), never members, or no longer members (we will often refer to the last two groups collectively as "non-members").

A slight majority of FB members in our sample (52.63%) are male. Our sample slightly over-represents females when compared to the target FB population, whose data we mined from the network (male represent 63.04% of the Institution's FB network, but it is important to note that the gender distribution at the Institution is itself similarly skewed). However, we know from the information mined from the network that 79.6% of all the Institution's undergraduate males are on the FB (91.92% of our sample of male undergrads are FB members) and 75.5% of all the Institution's undergraduate females are on the FB

(94.94% of our sample of female undergrads are FB members). In other words (and expectably), our total sample of respondents slightly over-represents FB members.

The gender distribution of our sample is reversed among respondents who were never or are no longer members of FB: 56.46% are female. This gender difference between current members and current non-members is not statistically significant (Pearson $\chi^2(1) = 2.0025$, $Pr = 0.157$). However, when we test usage by contrasting actual FB users and non-members plus members who claim to " I never login/use" their profile, the gender difference becomes more radical (54.19% of *users* are male, but only 40.66% of *non users* are) and significant (Pearson $\chi^2(1) = 4.5995$ $Pr = 0.032$). See Figure 1 for the gender distribution in the three FB member groups.

User	What is your gender		Total
	Male	Female	
Current FB Member	110	99	209
	52.63	47.37	100.00
	74.83	67.35	71.09
Former FB Member	3	4	7
	42.86	57.14	100.00
	2.04	2.72	2.38
Never FB Member	34	44	78
	43.59	56.41	100.00
	23.13	29.93	26.53
Total	147	147	294
	50.00	50.00	100.00
	100.00	100.00	100.00

Fig. 1. Gender distribution of the survey participants for the three FB member groups

There is no significant difference among the distributions of undergraduate versus graduate students in our sample and in the overall FB population.

Overall, sixty-four percent of our respondents (64.29%) are undergraduate students; 25.17% are graduate students; 1.36% are faculty; and 9.18% are staff. We did not consider alumni in our study. This distribution slightly oversamples undergraduate students when compared to the actual Institution's population (total student population in 2005/06: 10,017. Undergraduate students: 54.8%). This was expected, considering the available recruiting tools and the comparatively higher propensity of undergraduate students to take paid surveys and experiments. However, when checking for current FB membership in our sample, we find that undergraduates dominate the picture (84.21%), followed by graduate students (14.35%) and staff (1.44%). These numbers are comparable to the distribution of the target population discused in [4] when correcting for alumni (91.21% were undergraduate students on the Facebook network).

Again, the distribution of non-members is reversed: graduate students dominate (51.76%), followed by staff (28.24%). The distributions of user types

| | | Are you... | | | |
User	Undergrad	Graduate	Faculty	Staff	Total
Current FB Member	176	30	0	3	209
	84.21	14.35	0.00	1.44	100.00
	93.12	40.54	0.00	11.11	71.09
Former FB Member	2	4	0	1	7
	28.57	57.14	0.00	14.29	100.00
	1.06	5.41	0.00	3.70	2.38
Never FB Member	11	40	4	23	78
	14.10	51.28	5.13	29.49	100.00
	5.82	54.05	100.00	85.19	26.53
Total	189	74	4	27	294
	64.29	25.17	1.36	9.18	100.00
	100.00	100.00	100.00	100.00	100.00

Fig. 2. Distribution of survey participant status for FB members, non-members and people who never had a FB account

(undergraduates, graduates, staff, or faculty) by FB membership status are significantly diverse (Pearson $\chi^2(3) = 135.3337 \ Pr = 0.000$). See Figure 2 for a breakdown of the academic status of survey participants across the three FB groups.

Unsurprisingly, age is a strong predictor of membership (see Figure 3). Non-members tend to be older (a mean of 30 years versus a mean of 21) but their age is also more broadly distributed (sd 8.840476 vs. sd 2.08514). The difference in the mean age by membership is strongly significant ($t = $ -14.6175, $Pr<t = 0.0000$).

| | | group_age | | | |
usercomb	17-24	25-34	35-44	45+	Total
Current member	204	4	1	0	209
	97.61	1.91	0.48	0.00	100.00
	88.31	9.30	9.09	0.00	71.09
Current non member	27	39	10	9	85
	31.76	45.88	11.76	10.59	100.00
	11.69	90.70	90.91	100.00	28.91
Total	231	43	11	9	294
	78.57	14.63	3.74	3.06	100.00
	100.00	100.00	100.00	100.00	100.00

Fig. 3. Distribution of age for FB members and non-members

4.2   Privacy Attitudes

Age and student status are correlated with FB membership - but what else is? Well, of course, having heard of the network is a precondition for membership. Thirty-four participants had never heard of the FB - nearly half of the staff that took our survey, a little less than 23% of the graduate students, and a negligible portion of the undergraduate students (1.59%).

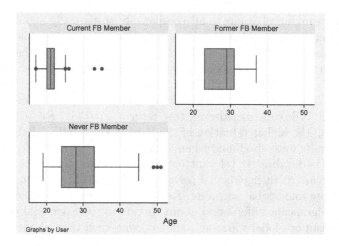

Fig. 4. Box-plots of age distribution for different membership status

However, together with age and student status (with the two obviously being highly correlated), another relevant distinction between members and non-members may arise from privacy attitudes and privacy concerns.

Before we asked questions about FB, our survey ascertained the privacy attitudes of participants with a battery of questions modelled after the Alan Westin's studies [15], with a number of modifications. In particular, in order not to prime the subjects, questions about privacy attitudes were interspersed with questions about attitudes towards economic policy and the state of the economy, social issues such as same-sex marriage, or security questions related to the fear of terrorism. In addition, while all instruments asked the respondent to rank agreement, concern, worries, or importance on a 7-point Likert scale, the questions ranged from general ones (e.g., "How *important* do you consider the following issues in the public debate?"), to more and more specific (e.g., "How do you *personally* value the *importance* of the following issues for your own life on a day-to-day basis?"), and personal ones (e.g., "Specifically, how *worried* would you be if" [a certain scenario took place]).

"Privacy policy" was on average considered a highly *important* issue in the *public debate* by our respondents (mean on the 7-point Likert scale: 5.411, where 1 is "Not important at all" and 7 is "very important"; *sd*: 1.393795). In fact, it was regarded a more important issue in the public debate than the threat of terrorism ($t = 2.4534$, $Pr>t = 0.0074$; the statistical significance of the perceived superiority was confirmed by a Wilcoxon signed-rank test: $z = 2.184$ $Pr>|z|=0.0290$) and same sex marriage ($t = 10.5089$, $Pr>t = 0.0000$; Wilcoxon signed-rank test: $z = 9.103$ $Pr>|z|= 0.0000$); but less important than education policy (mean: 5.93; *sd*: 1.16) or economic policy (mean: 5.79; *sd*: 1.21). The slightly larger mean valuation of the importance of privacy policy over environmental policy was not significant. (These results are comparable to those found in previous studies, such as [16].)

The same ranking of values (and comparably statistically significant differences) was found when asking for "How do you personally value the *importance* of the following issues for your *own life* on a *day-to-day basis?*" The mean value for the importance of privacy policy was 5.09. For all categories, subjects assigned slightly (but statistically significantly) more importance to the issue in the *public debate* than in *their own life* on a day-to-day basis (in the privacy policy case, a Wilcoxon signed-rank test returns $z = 3.62 \ Pr > |z| = 0.0003$ when checking the higher valuation of the issue in the public debate).

Similar results were also found when asking for the respondents' *concern* with a number of issues directly relevant to them: the state of the economy where they live, threats to their personal privacy, the threat of terrorism, the risks of climate change and global warming. Respondents were more concerned (with statistically significant differences) about threats to their personal privacy than about terrorism or global warming, but less concerned than about the state of the economy.

Finally, we asked how *worried* respondents would be if a number of specific events took place in their lives. The highest level of concern was registered for "A stranger knew where you live and the location and schedule of the classes you take" (mean of 5.78, with 45.58% of respondents choosing the 7th point in the Likert scale, "very worried," and more than 81% selecting Likert points above 4). This was followed by "Five years from now, complete strangers would be able to find out easily your sexual orientation, the name of your current partner, and your current political views" (mean of 5.55, with 36.39% - the relative majority - choosing the 7th point in the Likert scale, and more than 78% with points above 4), followed, in order, by the 'global warming' scenario ("The United States rejected all new initiatives to control climate change and reduce global warming"), the security scenario ("It was very easy for foreign nationals to cross the borders undetected"), the 'contacts' scenario ("A friend of a friend that you do not even know knew your name, your email, your home phone number, and your instant messaging nickname"), and the 'same-sex' scenario ("Two people of the same sex were allowed to marry in your State").

Privacy Attitudes and Membership Status. Privacy concerns are not equally distributed across FB members and non-members populations: a two-sided t test that the mean Likert value for the "importance" of privacy policy is *higher* for non-members (5.67 in the non-members group, 5.30 in the members group) is significant ($t = -2.0431$, $Pr<t = 0.0210$). Similar statistically significant differences arise when checking for the level of *concern* for privacy threats and for *worries* associated with the privacy scenarios described above. The test becomes slightly less significant when checking for member/non-member differences in the assigned importance of privacy policy on a day-to-day basis.

Importantly, in general no comparable statistically significant differences between the groups can be found in other categories. For example, worries about the global warming scenario gain a mean Likert valuation of 5.36 in the members sample and 5.4 in the non-members sample. (A statistically significant difference can be found however for the general threat of terrorism and for the personal worry over marriage between two people of same sex: higher values in the non-members group may be explained by their higher mean age.)

We also used two-sample Wilcoxon rank-sum (Mann-Whitney) tests to study the distributions of the sensitivities to the various scenarios. We found additional evidence that the sensitivity towards privacy is stronger among non-members than members. In the "A stranger knew where you live and the location and schedule of the classes you take" scenario, concerns are higher in the non-member population - the Mann-Whitney test that the two distributions are the same returns $z = -3.086$ $Pr > |z| = 0.0020$. Similar results are found for the "Five years from now, complete strangers would be able to find out easily your sexual orientation, the name of your current partner, and your current political views" scenario ($z = -2.502$ $Pr > |z| = 0.0124$), and the "A friend of a friend that you do not even know knew your name, your email, your home phone number, and your instant messaging nickname" scenario. Importantly, no such differences were found to be significant for the same sex marriage scenario, the illegal aliens scenario, and the US rejecting initiatives to control climate change scenario.

Overall, the distributions of reported intensity of privacy concerns tend to be more skewed towards higher values, and less normally-distributed for non-members. For the most invasive scenarios, however, *both* members and non-members' distributions are not normal, with the distribution for non-members more skewed towards the higher values on the right (see Figure 5). These results do not change after accounting for people who do not know about FB - the t tests simply become more significant.

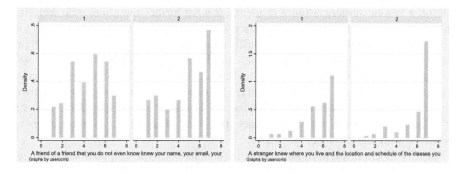

Fig. 5. Distribution of privacy attitudes for FB members (columns marked "1") and non-members (columns marked "2"; this set includes both people that never had a profile and those who had a profile but deactivated it) for an exemplary scenario

Disentangling Age, Student Status, and Privacy Concerns. An obvious hypothesis about FB membership is that individual privacy concerns will be inversely correlated with the probability of joining FB. However, while non FB members seem to have higher average privacy concerns than members (over the scenarios we tested), we cannot directly conclude that the higher one's general

usercomb	Threats to your personal privacy						
	1	2	3	4	5	6	7
Current member	6	15	20	28	46	52	42
	2.87	7.18	9.57	13.40	22.01	24.88	20.10
	100.00	71.43	80.00	68.29	71.88	76.47	60.87
Current non member	0	6	5	13	18	16	27
	0.00	7.06	5.88	15.29	21.18	18.82	31.76
	0.00	28.57	20.00	31.71	28.13	23.53	39.13
Total	6	21	25	41	64	68	69
	2.04	7.14	8.50	13.95	21.77	23.13	23.47
	100.00	100.00	100.00	100.00	100.00	100.00	100.00

Fig. 6. Distribution of levels of concern for threats to personal privacy for FB members and non-members

privacy concerns, the less likely he will be a FB member. Figure 6, for instance, shows the distribution of levels of concern for privacy threats for both FB members and non-members. A measure of correlation provided by Pearson $\chi^2(6)$ is not significant ($\chi^2(6)=8.0467$, $Pr = 0.235$). (Pearson χ^2 is significant when studying the "stranger knows where you live scenario:" $\chi^2(6) = 16.5665$, $Pr = 0.011$; likelihood-ratio $\chi^2(6) = 17.4785$, $Pr = 0.008$.)

In addition, privacy concerns may also be correlated with gender,[3] and status (undergraduate, graduate, faculty, staff).[4] This makes it difficult to understand the actual impact of privacy attitudes and concerns and various other personal characteristics on FB membership.

For instance, when we focus on the undergraduate respondents in our sample, we find that even the undergraduates who expressed the highest level of concern for threats to their personal privacy are still in vast majority joining the Facebook: 89.74% of them. We also find that the mean level of concern is not statistically different between undergraduates who are members and those who are not. (Among undergraduate students, 2 were former members who were no longer members at the time of the survey; their expressed level of concern for threats was 5 and 7; one user was still a member but claimed to never login - his concern level is 6). On the other hand, among respondents who are *not* undergraduates, the mean concern level of non-members (controlling for those who have heard about the FB) is 5.41; the mean for members is 4.81. A two-side Student t test shows that the difference is mildly significant: $Ha : diff < t = -1.5346$ and $Pr < t = 0.0646$). In fact, the ratio of members to non-members decreases with the intensity of concern.

In order to disentangle these complex relations between age, respondent type, and privacy concerns - that we hypothesize are all factors affecting FB membership - we employed multivariate regression analysis.

In a first approach, we used k-means multivariate clustering techniques [17] to cluster respondents according to their privacy attitudes: we used all the

---

[3] For instance, female respondents in general report statistically significantly higher average concerns for privacy over the various scenarios and instruments we discussed above.

[4] We did not find a significant correlation between age and a number of indicators of privacy concerns in our sample; however, our sample cannot be considered representative of the population of age over 25.

```
Logit estimates                            Number of obs   =         260
                                           LR chi2( 9)     =      130.27
                                           Prob > chi2     =      0.0000
Log likelihood =    -63.57221              Pseudo R2       =      0.5061
```

user_logit	Coef.	Std. Err.	z	P>|z|	[95% Conf. Interval]	
age	-.5632942	.1385778	-4.06	0.000	-.8349017	-.2916866
undergrad	.9950484	.5923704	1.68	0.093	-.1659763	2.156073
Iprivacy~2	4.906447	2.119911	2.31	0.021	.7514989	9.061395
Iprivacy~3	.2758868	.5935938	0.46	0.642	-.8875356	1.439309
Iprivacy~4	1.043322	.8747547	1.19	0.233	-.6711654	2.75781
Iprivacy~5	1.598968	1.113793	1.44	0.151	-.5840251	3.781961
Iprivacy~6	.6435271	.6934733	0.93	0.353	-.7156556	2.00271
Iprivacy~7	1.451756	1.173762	1.24	0.216	-.8487741	3.752287
gender	.1879386	.4760592	0.39	0.693	-.7451203	1.120997
_cons	12.81519	3.278655	3.91	0.000	6.389147	19.24124

Fig. 7. Results of logit regression on FB membership using demographical characteristics and k-means clustered privacy attitudes (unstandardized effect coefficients)

```
Logit estimates                            Number of obs   =         260
                                           LR chi2( 4)     =      121.80
                                           Prob > chi2     =      0.0000
Log likelihood =    -67.804697             Pseudo R2       =      0.4732
```

user_logit	Coef.	Std. Err.	z	P>|z|	[95% Conf. Interval]	
age	-.4953475	.1236441	-4.01	0.000	-.7376856	-.2530095
undergrad	1.025618	.5752887	1.78	0.075	-.1019268	2.153164
privacy_at~n	-.5152155	.2212539	-2.33	0.020	-.9488651	-.0815658
gender	.1798292	.4576217	0.39	0.694	-.7170929	1.076751
_cons	14.69864	3.322535	4.42	0.000	8.186591	21.21069

Fig. 8. Results of logit regression on FB membership using demographical characteristics and mean privacy attitudes (unstandardized effect coefficients)

7-Likert scale responses relevant to privacy (from importance assigned to privacy policy, to worries about specific scenarios) and created a new categorical variable called _Iprivacy_. We employed that variable in logistical regressions (logit and probit) over the dependent variable user_logit, a dichotomous variable representing membership to the FB network (user_logit=1; or lack thereof, user_logit=0). We also used age (age), a dummy variable representing gender (male if gender=1), and a dummy variable representing student status (undergraduate if undergrad=1) as independent variables. We restricted the analysis to respondents who had heard about FB. The results of the regression are reported in Figure 7. The model has a good fit, explaining more than half of the variance between members and non-members of FB. As expected, age and undergraduate status are significant while gender is not. The signs of the regression are as expected: being an undergraduate increases the probability of being a member, and age decreases it. Interestingly, at least one of the categorical clusters for privacy attitudes (represented by the variables _Iprivacy_~2,3,4,5,6,7, measured against the base cluster _Iprivacy_~1 - the one with the highest level of concerns) is significant, with a large positive impact on the probability of being a member.

In a second approach, we took the means of all the 7-Likert scale responses relevant to privacy and constructed a new categorical variable ($privacy\_at{\sim}n$), that we used in the second regression reported in Figure 8.

The results are comparable to those from the previous regression. Both regressions show that even when controlling for age, status, and gender, one's privacy concerns have *some* impact on the decision to join the network, and the student status has some impact independent from age.[5] However, and importantly, this impact really only exists for the non undergraduate population: when restricting the analysis to the undergraduate population, neither the privacy cluster nor the privacy mean variables are significant. They are, however, significant ($Pr > z$: 0.024) when focusing on the non undergraduate population. In other words: privacy concerns may drive older and senior college members away from FB. Even high privacy concerns, however, are *not* driving undergraduate students away from it. Non-members have higher generic privacy concerns than FB members. These results suggest that FB membership among undergraduates is *not* just a matter of their not being concerned, in general, about their privacy - other reasons must be explored.

4.3   Reported Facebook Usage

In order to understand what motivates even privacy concerned individual to share personal information on the Facebook, we need to study what the network itself is used for. Asking participants this question directly is likely to generate responses biased by self-selection and fear of stigma. Sure enough, by far, FB members deny FB is useful to them for dating or self-promotion. Instead, members claim that the FB is very useful to them for learning about and finding classmates (4.93 mean on a 7-point Likert scale) and for making it more convenient for people to get in touch with them (4.92), but deny any usefulness for other activities. Other possible applications of FB - such as dating, finding people who share one's interests, getting more people to become one's friends, showing information about oneself/advertising oneself - are ranked very low. In fact, for those applications, the relative majority of participants chooses the minimal Likert point to describe their usefulness (coded as "not at all" useful). Still, while their mean Likert value remains low, male participants find FB slightly more useful for dating than female.

And yet, when asking participants to rate *how often*, on average, their *peers* use FB for the same activities, the results change dramatically: learning about classmates and the convenience factor of staying in contact are still ranked very highly, but now "Showing information about themselves/advertising themselves," "Making them more popular," or "Finding dates" suddenly become very popular. See how the distributions almost invert in Figure 9.

Information Provided. What information do FB members provide, and of what quality? Many members are quite selective in the type of information they

---

[5] As noted above, in our sample age alone is not significantly correlated with privacy concerns.

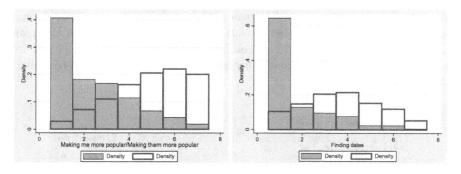

Fig. 9. Do as I preach, not as I do - How useful is FB for you (grey boxes) vs. how often do you believe other members use FB for (transparent boxes)?

What personal information do you provide on the FaceBook and how accurate is that information?			
	I don't provide this information	I provide this information and it is complete and accurate	I provide this information but it is intentionally not complete or not accurate
Birthday	12% (29)	84% (195)	3% (8)
Cell phone number	59% (138)	39% (90)	2% (4)
Home phone number	89% (207)	10% (24)	0% (1)
Personal address	73% (169)	24% (55)	3% (8)
Schedule of classes	54% (126)	42% (97)	4% (9)
AIM	24% (56)	75% (173)	1% (3)
Political views	42% (97)	53% (122)	6% (13)
Sexual orientation	38% (88)	59% (138)	3% (6)
Partner's name	71% (164)	28% (65)	1% (3)

Fig. 10. Information provided by FB members

provide - for instance, most publish their birthdays but hide their cell phone numbers. However, interestingly, our survey participants' answers imply that if a certain type of information is provided at all, it is likely to be of good quality: complete and accurate (see Figure 10).[6]

When controlling for participants who have abandoned the Facebook, we find out that as users they were less likely than continuing members to provide information such as their birthday (85.71% do not provide this information, while 86.12% of current members claim they *do* provide it - Pearson $\chi^2(2) = 33.9440$ $Pr = 0.000$), AIM (Pearson $\chi^2(2) = 14.2265$ $Pr = 0.001$), cellphone number, home phone number, personal address, political orientation, sexual orientation, and partner's name (the differences between non-members and members across the last six categories however are not statistical significant).

Female members are not more or less likely than male members to provide accurate and complete information about their birthday, schedule of classes, partner's name, AIM, or political views. However, they are much *less* likely to

---

[6] Also such survey answers that elicit personal admissions about the quality of the data provided on FB may be, in turn, biased. However, since survey participants were not asked to disclose the actual information whose quality they were asked to evaluate, we have no reason to believe that their incentives to offer inaccurate answers were significant.

provide their sexual orientation (Pearson $\chi^2(2) = 11.3201$ $Pr = 0.003$), personal address (Pearson $\chi^2(2) = 10.5484$ $Pr = 0.005$), and cell phone number (Pearson $\chi^2(2) = 10.9174$ $Pr = 0.004$). This confirms the results reported in [4], where less than 29% of females were found providing cell phone information, compared to 50% of male.

On average, how often do you login to FaceBook?

	Response Percent	Response Total
More than once a day	21.6%	50
Once a day	25.4%	59
More than once a week, but in general less than once a day	22.4%	52
Once a week	8.6%	20
Less than once a week	6%	14
More than once a month, but in general less than once a week	6%	14
Once a month	6%	14
I still have a profile, but I never login/use it.	3.9%	9

On average, how often do you update your profile on FaceBook?

	Response Percent	Response Total
More than once a week	2.6%	6
Once a week	6%	14
More than once a month, but in general less than once a week	17.2%	40
Once a month	50.4%	117
Never	23.7%	55

Fig. 11. Frequency of login and profile update

Self-selection Bias? Often, survey participants are less privacy conscious than non participants. For obvious reasons, this self-selection bias is particularly problematic for survey studies that focus on privacy. Are our respondents a biased sample of the Institution's FB population - biased in the sense that they provide more information than the average FB members?

We did not find strong evidence of that. Since we mined the network before the survey was administered, we were able to compare information revelation by survey participants and non survey participants. It is true that, on average, our survey takers provide slightly more information than the average FB member. However, the differences in general do not pass a Fisher's exact test for significance, except for personal address and classes (where non participants provide statistically significant less information) and political views (in which the difference is barely significant).

Attitudes vs. Behavior. We detected little or no relation between participants' reported privacy attitudes and their likelihood of providing certain information, even when controlling, separately, for male and female members. For instance, when comparing the propensity to provide birthday and the Likert values reported in the answers to the privacy threat question described at the beginning of Section 4.2, no statistically significant difference emerged: Pearson $\chi^2(12) = 5.2712$ $Pr = 0.948$. Comparable results were found when testing sexual orientation (Pearson $\chi^2(12) = 10.7678$ $Pr = 0.549$), partner's name (Pearson

$\chi^2(12) = 15.1178$ $Pr = 0.235$), cell phone number (Pearson $\chi^2(12) = 19.0821$ $Pr = 0.087$), or personal address.

We obtained the same results when using the cluster variable that summarizes each respondent's privacy attitudes (see Section 4.2), both when using standard Pearson's χ^2 as well as when using Student's t test (the latter was used when comparing the mean privacy concern across respondents who provided or did not provide accurate information about various data types).

Combined with the results discussed in 4.2, the above evidence may suggest that privacy attitudes have some effect on determining who joins the network, but after one has joined, there is very little marginal difference in information revelation across groups - which may be the result of perceived peer pressure or herding behavior.

If anything, we found new confirmations of a privacy attitude/behavior dichotomy [18]. Almost 16% of respondents who expressed the highest concern (7 on the Likert scale) for the scenario in which a stranger knew their schedule of classes and where they lived, provide nevertheless both pieces of information (in fact, almost 22% provide at least their address, and almost 40% provide their schedule of classes).

Similarly, around 16% of respondents who expressed the highest concern for the scenario in which someone 5 years from now could know their current sexual orientation, partner's name, and political orientation, provide nevertheless all three types of information - although we can observe a *descending* share of members that provide that information as their reported concerns *increase*. Still, more than 48% of those with the highest concern for that scenario reveal at least their current sexual orientation; 21% provide at least their partner's name (although we did not control for the share of respondents who are currently in relationships); and almost 47% provide at least their political orientation.

4.4   Awareness of Facebook Rules and Profile Visibility

How knowledgeable is the average FB member about the network's features and their implications in terms of profile visibility?

By default, everyone on the Facebook appears in searches of everyone else, and every profile at a certain Institution can be read by every member of FB at that Institution. However, the FB provides an extensive privacy policy and offers very granular control to users to choose what information to reveal to whom. As mentioned above, relative to a FB member, other users can either be friends, friends of friends, non-friend users at the same institution, non-friend users at a different institution, and non-friend users at the same geographical location as the user but at a different university (for example, Harvard vs. MIT). Users can select their profile visibility (who can read their profiles) as well as their profile searchability (who can find a snapshot of their profiles through the search features) by type of users. More granular control is given on contact information, such as phone numbers.

And yet, among current members, 30% claim not to know whether FB grants any way to manage who can search for and find their profile, or think that they

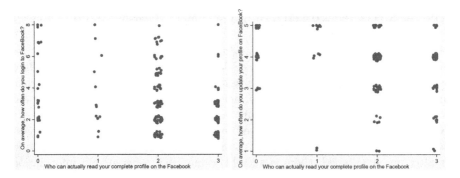

Fig. 12. Self-awareness of ability to control who can see one's profile, by frequency of login (left) and frequency of update (right). On the x-axis, the value 0 means "Do not know" if there is any way to control; 1 means "No control"; 2 means "Some control" and 3 means "Complete control." On the y-axis, higher values mean *less* frequent login or update.

are given no such control. Eighteen percent do not know whether FB grants any way to manage who can actually read their profile, or think that they are given no such control. These numbers are not significantly altered by removing the 13 members who claim never to login to their account. In fact, even frequency of login does not explain the lack of information for some members. On the other hand, members who claim to login more than once a day are also more likely to believe that they have "complete" control on whom can search their profile.

Awareness of one's ability to control who can see one's profile is not affected by the frequency of login, but *is* affected by the frequency of update (a Pearson $\chi^2(12) = 28.9182\ Pr = 0.004$ shows that the distribution is significant): see Figure 12. Note the difference between the two graphs and, specifically, the distribution by frequency of update for respondents who answered "Do not know" or "No control" (graph on the right).

Twenty-two percent of our sample do not know what the FB privacy settings are or do not remember if they have ever changed them. Around 25% do not know what the location settings are.

To summarize, the majority of FB members claim to know about ways to control visibility and searchability of their profiles, but a significant minority of members are unaware of those tools and options.

Self-reported Visibility. More specifically, we asked FB members to discuss how visible and searchable their own profiles were. We focused on those participants who had claimed never to have changed their privacy settings (that by default make their profile searchable by everybody on FB and visible to anybody at the same Institution), or who did not know what those settings were.

Almost every such respondent realizes that anybody at their Institution can search their profile. However, 24% incorrectly do not believe that anybody on FB can in fact search their profile. Misunderstandings about visibility can also go in the opposite direction: for instance, 16% of current members believe, incorrectly, that *anybody* on FB can read their profile.

In fact, when asked to guess how many people could search for their profile on FB (respondents could answer by selecting the following possible answers from a drop-box: a few hundred, a few thousands, tens of thousands, hundreds of thousands, millions), the *relative* majority of members who did not alter their default settings answered, correctly, "Millions." However, *more than half* actually underestimated the number to tens of thousands or less.

In short, the majority of FB members seem to be aware of the true visibility of their profile - but a *significant minority* is vastly underestimating the reach and openness of their own profile. Does this matter at all? In other words, would these respondents be bothered if they realized that their profile is more visible than what they believe?

The answer is complex. First, when asked whether the current visibility and searchability of the profile is adequate for the user, or whether he or she would like to restrict it or expand it, the vast majority of members (77% in the case of searchability; 68% in the case of visibility) claim to be satisfied with what they have - most of them do not want more or less visibility or searchability for their profiles (although 13% want less searchability and 20% want less visibility) than what they (correctly or incorrectly) believe to have. Secondly, as we discuss further below in Section 4.5, FB members remain wary of whom can access their profiles, but claim to manage their privacy fears by controlling the information they reveal.

4.5   Attitudes Towards the Facebook

So far we have glanced at indirect evidence of a number of different reasons for the dichotomy between FB members' stated privacy concerns (high) and actual information hiding strategies (mixed, but often low also for members with high stated concerns). Those reasons include peer pressure and unawareness of the true visibility of their profiles.

Another possible reason is the level of trust FB members assign to the network itself. On average, FB members trust the system quite a bit (and in general trust its members *more* than members of comparable services, like Friendster or MySpace - see Figure 13).

This happens notwithstanding the fact that almost 77% of respondents claimed not to have read FB's privacy policy (the real number is probably higher); and that many of them mistakenly believe that FB does not collect information about them from other sources regardless of their use of the site (67%), that FB does not combine information about them collected from other sources (70%), or that FB does not share personal information with third parties (56%). (We note that having read, or claiming to have read, the privacy policy, does *not* make respondents more knowledgeable about FB's activities.)

While respondent are mildly concerned about who can access their personal information and how it can be used, they are not, in general, concerned about the information itself, mostly because they control that information and, with less

How much do you trust	Do not trust at all						Trust completely	N/A	Response Average
The FaceBook (the Company)	5% (10)	8% (17)	17% (38)	24% (53)	25% (56)	14% (32)	4% (8)	3% (7)	4.20
Your own friends on FaceBook	1% (3)	1% (3)	3% (6)	7% (15)	26% (57)	38% (84)	22% (49)	2% (4)	5.62
CMU Facebook users	3% (7)	6% (13)	14% (32)	26% (58)	32% (70)	15% (33)	3% (7)	0% (1)	4.35
Friends of your friends on FaceBook	6% (13)	8% (17)	15% (33)	27% (60)	24% (54)	14% (31)	4% (9)	2% (4)	4.17
On average, FaceBook users not connected to you	13% (28)	17% (38)	23% (51)	27% (60)	12% (27)	5% (10)	1% (3)	2% (4)	3.29
If you use or know about MySpace, MySpace users not connected to you	15% (33)	9% (19)	6% (14)	12% (26)	4% (9)	1% (2)	1% (3)	52% (115)	2.78
If you use or know about Friendster, Friendster users not connected to you	16% (35)	8% (17)	8% (17)	12% (27)	5% (12)	2% (4)	0% (1)	49% (108)	2.82

Fig. 13. How FB members assign trust

emphasis, because believe to have some control on its access. Respondents are fully aware that a social network is based on information sharing: the strongest motivator they have in providing more information are reported, in fact, as "having fun" and "revealing enough information so that necessary/useful to me and other people to benefit from FaceBook."

However, psychological motivations can also explain why information revelation seems disconnected from the privacy concerns. When asked to express whether they considered the current public concern for privacy on social network sites such as the FaceBook or MySpace to be appropriate (using a 7-point Likert scale, from "Not appropriate at all" to "Very much appropriate"), the response average was rather high (4.55). In fact, the majority of respondents agree (from mildly to very much) with the idea that the information *other* FB members reveal may create privacy risks to *those* members (that is, the other members; average response on a 7-point Likert scale: 4.92) - even though they tend to be less concerned about their *own* privacy on FB (average response on a 7-point Likert scale: 3.60; Student's t test shows that this is significantly less than the concern for other members: $t = -10.1863$, P $<t = 0.0000$; also a Wilcoxon matched pair test provides a similar result: $z = -8.738$, $Pr <|z| = 0.0000$).

In fact, 33% of our respondents believe that it is either impossible or quite difficult for individuals not affiliated with an university to access FB network of that university. "Facebook is for the students" says a student interviewed in [19]. But considering the number of attacks described in [4] or any recent media report on the usage of FB by police, employers, and parents, it seems in fact that for a significant fraction of users the FB is only an *imagined* community.

5   Survey and Network Data

In order to justify conclusions informed by a survey, the validity of the answers provided by the subjects has to be addressed. For this study we were in the *unique* position to be able to *directly* compare the answers provided by the participants with visible FB profiles to the information they actually provide in the profile (downloaded and archived immediately before the survey was administered). This section compares the survey responses with profile data and examines survey impacts in the form of changes to FB profiles of survey participants.

5.1 Comparison Between Reported Answers and Actual Data

In order to gauge the accuracy of the survey responses, we compared the answers given to a question about revealing certain types of information (specifically, birthday, cell phone, home phone, current address, schedule of classes, AIM screenname, political views, sexual orientation and the name of their partner) with the data from the actual (visible) profiles. We found that 77.84% of the answers were exactly accurate: if participants said that they revealed a certain type of information, that information was in fact present; if they wrote it was not present, in fact it was not. A little more than 8% revealed more than they said they do (i.e. they claim the information is not present when in fact it is). A little more than 11% revealed less then they claimed they do. In fact, 1.86% claimed that they provide false information on their profile (information is there that they claim is intentionally false or incomplete), and 0.71% have missing false information (they claimed the information they provide is false or incomplete, when in fact there was no information).

We could not locate the FB profiles for 13 self-reported members that participated in the survey. For the participants with CMU email address, 2 of them did mention in the survey that they had restricted visibility, searchability, or access to certain contact information, and 3 wrote that not all CMU users could see their profile.

5.2 Survey Impacts

For this analysis, we eliminated the survey responses for users whose profile we could not locate on the network, ending up with 196 profiles out of the 209 self-proclaimed FB members participants. We downloaded information from the network immediately before and after administering the survey, both for users who responded to it and those who did not, and then compared the profiles.

First, we found a statistically significant difference in the byte size of the resulting files. The mean byte size decreased in both the experiment and the control group, but the experiment group changed significantly more than the control group (paired t test $Pr < t = 0.0060$). See Figure 14 for histograms of the file size changes for both groups. However, no significant changes were found when evaluating *individual* data fields: 5 survey participants reduced the information they provided compared to 4 profiles in the control group that similarly removed specific information.

After further investigation, we found that what happened was the following: the 9 profiles with the highest byte change (all >10kb) were in fact the ones that completely changed the visibility of their profile. They represent slightly more than 5% of our sample of current FB members (whose profile before the survey was visible). Out of this group 6 were female and 3 male. In the control group

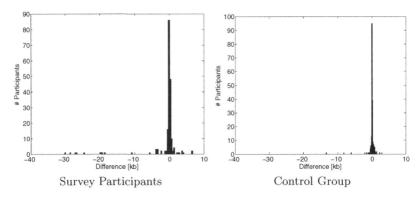

Fig. 14. Changes in profile sizes for survey participants and a control group. The sizes for the survey participants changed significantly more.

only 2 profiles changed visibility. This difference is statistically significant (χ^2 $Pr<0.05$).

While the difference is significant and somewhat surprising, the magnitude in terms of number of members that changed their behavior is relatively small. One should note that this change happened even without us providing the survey participants with a real threat scenario. In addition, although privacy concerned individuals are on FB, only a fraction of them may have such high concerns to be induced to abandon the network just by questions about its privacy implications. In fact, we found that this group of "switchers" have higher means in terms of average privacy attitudes, and their distributions of privacy attitudes are skewed towards the right (that is, towards higher concerns) - than non "switchers," although such differences are not statistically significant.

6   Discussion and Future Work

Online social networks offer exciting new opportunities for interaction and communication, but also raise new privacy concerns. Among them, the Facebook stands out for its vast membership, its unique and personally identifiable data, and the window it offers on the information revelation behavior of millions of young adults.

In our study we have combined survey instruments with data mined from a FB community at a North American college Institution. We looked for demographic or behavioral differences between the communities of the network's members and non-members, and searching for motivations driving the behavior of its members. Our analysis is going to be complemented by other experiments, but we can summarize here a number of initial results.

Age and student status obviously are the most significant factors in determining FB membership. However, we observe that privacy attitudes also play a role, but only for the non undergraduate population. In fact, most of highly privacy concerned undergraduates still join the network. While a relative majority of FB members in our sample are aware of the visibility of their profiles, a significant minority is not. The 'aware' group seems to rely on their own ability to control the information they disseminate as the preferred means of managing and addressing their own privacy concerns. However, we documented significant dichotomies between specific privacy concerns and actual information revelation behavior. In addition, misunderstanding or ignorance of the Facebook (the Company)'s treatment of personal data are also very common.

It is interesting to note that a pilot study we ran in September 2005 provided similar results, but also small, yet significant differences in terms of members' awareness of their profile visibility and their ability to control it: respondents a few months ago appeared less aware of privacy risks and of means of managing their own profiles. This evidence may suggest that the widespread public attention on privacy risks of online social networks is affecting, albeit marginally, some of their users.

Acknowledgements

This research was supported by CMU Berkman Faculty Development Fund and CMU CyLab. We would like to thank Lorrie Cranor, Charis Kaskiris, Julia Gideon, Jens Grossklags, and Bradley Malin for their insights and suggestions in the development of the survey protocol, and three anonymous referees for their useful comments.

References

1. Parker, R.: Alcohol policy violated. Kansan.com **February 28** (2006)
2. Youngwood, S.: Networking by the 'book'. The Times Argus **February 26** (2006)
3. Kharif, O.: Big brother is reading your blog. BusinessWeek online **February 28** (2006)
4. Gross, R., Acquisti, A.: Privacy and information revelation in online social networks. In: Proceedings of the ACM CCS Workshop on Privacy in the Electronic Society (WPES '05). (2005)
5. d. boyd: Reflections on friendster, trust and intimacy. In: Intimate (Ubiquitous) Computing Workshop - Ubicomp 2003, October 12-15, Seattle, Washington, USA. (2003)
6. d. boyd: Friendster and publicly articulated social networking. In: Conference on Human Factors and Computing Systems (CHI 2004), April 24-29, Vienna, Austria. (2004)
7. Donath, J., d. boyd: Public displays of connection. BT Technology Journal **22** (2004) 71–82
8. Liu, H., Maes, P.: Interestmap: Harvesting social network profiles for recommendations. In: Beyond Personalization - IUI 2005, January 9, San Diego, California, USA. (2005)
9. Jagatic, T., Johnson, N., Jakobsson, M., Menczer, F.: Social phishing. Communications of the ACM **Forthcoming** (2006)

10. Stutzman, F.: An evaluation of identity-sharing behavior in social network communities. In: Proceedings of the 2006 iDMAa and IMS Code Conference, Oxford, Ohio. (2006)
11. Sege, I.: Where everybody knows your name. Boston.com **April 27** (2005)
12. Anderson, B.: Imagined Communities: Reflections on the Origin and Spread of Nationalism. Revised edn. Verso, London and New York (1991)
13. Wall, L., Christiansen, T., Orwant, J.: Programming Perl. 3rd edn. O'Reilly (2000)
14. Burke, S.: Perl & LWP. O'Reilly (2002)
15. Westin, A.F.: Harris-equifax consumer privacy survey (1991). Technical report, Equifax, Inc., Atlanta, GA (1991)
16. Acquisti, A., Grossklags, J.: Privacy and rationality in decision making. IEEE Security & Privacy **January-February** (2005) 24–30
17. Berry, M., Linoff, G.: Data Mining Techniques for Marketing, Sales and Customer Support. Wiley, New York (1997)
18. Acquisti, A.: Privacy in electronic commerce and the economics of immediate gratification. In: Proceedings of the ACM Conference on Electronic Commerce (EC '04). (2004) 21–29
19. Kornblum, J., Marklein, M.B.: What you say online could haunt you. USA Today **March 8** (2006)

Enhancing Consumer Privacy in the Liberty Alliance Identity Federation and Web Services Frameworks

Mansour Alsaleh and Carlisle Adams

School of Information Technology and Engineering (SITE),
University of Ottawa
{malsaleh, cadams}@site.uottawa.ca

Abstract. Internet usage has been growing significantly, and the issue of online privacy has become a correspondingly greater concern. Several recent surveys show that users' concern about the privacy of their personal information reduces their use of electronic businesses and Internet services; furthermore, many users choose to provide false data in order to protect their real identities. Identity federation aims to assemble an identity virtually from a user's personal information stored across several distinct identity management systems. Liberty Alliance is one of the most recognized projects in developing an open standard for federated network identity. While one of the key objectives of the Liberty Alliance is to enable consumers to protect the privacy and security of their network identity information, this paper identifies and analyzes possible privacy breaches within the Liberty identity Federation Framework and Liberty identity Web Services Framework. Proposals for improvement in both these frameworks are discussed.

1 Introduction

Privacy is of particular concern to Internet users. Collecting personal information without users' awareness, sharing personal information between businesses without users' consent, using personal information for purposes other than stated, and the inability to access, change, or delete personal information, are among the main privacy concerns for many users. In 2003, industry watchdog Gartner Group predicted that by 2006, the first barrier to electronic business and commerce will be user concerns over information privacy [9]. A March 2000 Business-Week/Harris Poll shows that 86% of users want a Web site to obtain opt-in consent before collecting user name, address, phone number, or financial information. The same poll shows that 88% of users support opt-in as the standard before a Web site shares personal information with others [6]. A Pew Internet & American Life Project survey in 2000 found that 54% of Internet users believe that Web site tracking of users is harmful and invasive to user privacy; 24% of users reported giving false information to a Web site and 20% gave alternative or secondary e-mail addresses to Web sites [8].

Users maintain many separate accounts on different Internet businesses and services. Web sites almost always keep a profile for each visitor; this profile will contain more Personally Identifiable Information (PII) when the user registers his/her

G. Danezis and P. Golle (Eds.): PET 2006, LNCS 4258 , pp. 59–77, 2006.

information (otherwise, the Web site may identify the user by other means such as a browser cookie, or an IP address). Users usually need distinct authentication credentials (e.g. user name and a password) to access their profiles. Managing user profiles is a costly process for both users and service providers. Identity federation enables users to link, assemble and control an identity virtually from separate accounts where a user can control sharing of his/her identity attributes between service providers. Identity federation defines mechanisms for enterprises to share identity information between domains. These mechanisms include single sign-on (SSO), authorization, identity mapping and account linking, and directory services. The SSO mechanism reduces redundant logons whereby a user can login once with a member of a federate group and gain access to resources of multiple members among the group without signing-on again. In addition to fewer redundant logons, identity federation has the advantages of reducing the administrative costs of user profiles for service providers and keeping more accurate and up-to-date information about users [22].

One of the early identity federation frameworks is Microsoft's Passport. It deploys a centralized framework where there is just one identity provider (Microsoft). Any time a user logs into a Passport-participating site, the site is immediately able to access the information in the user's Passport account. Users' privacy concerns (users have no privacy with respect to the identity provider which is Microsoft) and the concept of a single trusted third party led to limited adoption of this architecture [12]. Microsoft carried out a significant upgrade to Passport and changed the service name to Windows Live ID. The new service overcomes the limitation of not supporting multiple identity management by utilizing a new Microsoft model, InfoCard, which is an identity selector that enables users to manage and exchange their digital identities [5]. InfoCard supports more than one identity provider (not just Microsoft) and the identity provider can be the user machine itself. One major drawback of InfoCard is that users lose their digital identities when using a different machine (unless the user uses an external security token such as a smartcard).

Set up at the instigation of Sun Microsystems in 2001, the Liberty Alliance is a consortium of technology vendors and consumer-facing enterprises formed to develop an open standard for federated network identity. The Liberty Alliance project is based on the concept of enabling users to connect multiple sets of personal information which exist across several e-commerce providers into a single easy-to-manage federated identity. This allows for the convenience of an SSO mechanism as well as easier administration of personal information across multiple service providers [15, 26]. Liberty Alliance is one of the most prominent federated identity standard proposals.

Although one of the key objectives of Liberty Alliance is to enable consumers to protect the privacy and security of their network identity information, the multidiscipline specifications Liberty covers make it vulnerable to a variety of privacy breaches. In this paper, we identify and analyze possible privacy breaches within the Liberty Identity Federation Framework and the Liberty Identity Web Services Framework. The main focus will be on identifying privacy concerns that are not discussed at all, or in much depth in Liberty specifications or Liberty privacy and security documentations. We believe that enhancing consumer privacy in these frameworks will increase consumer trust in using Liberty-enabled providers' services and thus will lead to greater adoption of Liberty standards. Our goal is that this paper helps to complement the current Liberty security and privacy documents by addressing possible privacy breaches and proposals for improvement.

The remainder of the paper is structured as follows. In the next section, we discuss related work. This is followed by a brief introduction to the Liberty Alliance project in 3.1. In particular, in section 3.2, we illustrate the concept of identity federation and SSO through a simple user case scenario. In section 4, we discuss some of the privacy requirements in identity federation systems and we highlight best privacy practices. In section 5.1, we give a detailed user case scenario that integrates the usage of both the Liberty Identity Federation Framework (ID-FF) and the Liberty Identity Web Services Framework (ID-WSF). In Section 5.2 we then identify and analyze possible privacy breaches within the different transactions of the given scenario and discuss proposals for improvement. We propose three new services that can merge with the current Liberty ID-FF and ID-WSF frameworks in section 5.3. We conclude by summarizing our recommendations to enhance consumer privacy within the Liberty frameworks.

2 Related Work

In addition to specification documents, Liberty Alliance has published several non-normative documents pertaining to security and privacy in their multi-level specifications. In [24], the author addressed some privacy laws, privacy and security fair information practices, and implementation guidance for organizations using the Liberty Alliance specifications. In particular, [7, 14] provided an overview of the security and privacy issues in ID-WSF technology and briefly explained potential security and privacy ramifications of the technology used in ID-WSF. The authors in [16] investigated the topic of identity theft in Liberty Alliance Project and showed how a cross-organizational and a vendor-neutral method of approaching the problem can work where piecemeal approaches will not. Varney and Sheckler [25] gave guidelines to assist businesses deploying Liberty-enabled solutions by identifying and addressing certain privacy and security issues that arise in business-to-consumer applications. The authors in [1] provided a high-level example of how to manage privacy preferences within Liberty Alliance's ID-WSF framework.

Recently, some academic publications have discussed the security and privacy in the Liberty Alliance project. Pfitzmann [19] evaluated the privacy of the Liberty Alliance phase 1 specifications that concern the browser single sign-on protocol. Later, an update for this paper evaluated the privacy on the same part of the Liberty project but for phase 2 of the specifications. The majority of the privacy concerns in this paper are about the user giving clear consents for transactions that happen between the different providers. A non-technical overview in [17] showed some scenarios by which federated identity management can actually help address certain aspects of the identity theft problem. The paper pointed out that federated identity management connects together previously isolated collections of identity information, which might be perceived as contributing to the identity theft problem because it exacerbates the ramifications of any successful attack. The concern is that if one of the user identity provider accounts is compromised, then all the related service provider federated accounts will be compromised as well.

The paper then suggested new mechanisms against identity theft in these scenarios, mainly in the authentication part. The authors in [4] proposed a flexible and privacy-preserving approach that allowed a user to establish a unique identifier and then proceed to establish other complex identity attributes in a federation. A solution to the problem of identity theft based on cryptographic techniques was presented.

Ahn and Lam [2] investigated the privacy issues in federated identity management focusing on the Liberty Alliance project. The authors discussed the privacy requirements using business scenarios. They proposed a privacy preferences expression language that uses the user preferences language PREP as a basis. The paper did not give any user interface proposal that could be used to store his/her preferences in the suggested customized PREP language. Easy-to-use and clear user interface that give the user full control in specifying privacy preferences for his/her personal information seems to be a significant challenge. The authors in [3] identified information assurance requirements in federated identity management. The paper briefly discussed privacy concerns in federated identity management with the Liberty Alliance project. A security model for authentication and access control for federated systems is described in [23]. The model supports single sign-on for users, a high level of autonomy for database custodians, and low maintenance overhead. The paper is concerned with securing read-only access to sensitive data as it is transmitted and delivered as part of federated database projects. A short survey of privacy issues within current browser-based attribute-exchange protocols is given in [21]; moreover, this paper presented design decisions that are mandatory to fulfill the privacy requirements. Pfitzmann and Waidner [20] gave an overview of the security and privacy properties desirable for the zero-footprint and browser-stateless constraints. The paper proposed a new protocol for browser-based attribute-exchange with better privacy and scalability. The privacy policies for attributes exchange are discussed in detail. In [11], the author first discussed the shortcomings of the existing Attribute Release Policies (ARP). XACML was then recommended as a suitable base language for ARPs. The proposed architecture suggested the integration of XACML ARPs into SAML-based identity providers and it specified the policy evaluation workflows. Gross [10] went through a security analysis of the SAML single sign-on browser profile, revealing several security flaws in the Liberty Alliance specification of this profile. Countermeasures and solutions to these attacks are proposed.

In this paper, we look at the Liberty ID-FF and ID-WSF and identify potential privacy breaches that were not discussed at all, or in much depth in the above work.

3   Overview of Liberty Alliance Project

In section 3.1 we give a brief introduction to the Liberty Alliance project. In section 3.2, we provide a simple user case scenario that illustrates the concept of identity federation and SSO.

3.1   Liberty Alliance Project

The Liberty Alliance project objective is to create open, technical specifications that enable SSO mechanism through federated network identification using emerging network access devices, and to support a permission-based attribute sharing framework to enable users' control over the use and disclosure of their personal information. The Liberty Alliance project has obtained support from over 150 well known businesses and organizations in the last few years and they were involved in the development of the specifications. The Liberty architecture consists of a multi-level specification set that has three major components. First is the Liberty ID-FF which defines a framework for federating identities and a mechanism for SSO using a federated identity. ID-FF allows a user with multiple accounts at different Liberty-enabled (LE) sites to link these accounts for future SSO. The second component is the Liberty ID-WSF which defines a framework for Web services that allows providers to share users' identities in a permission-based mode. ID-WSF offers features like Permission Based Attribute Sharing, Identity Service Discovery (to discover identity and attribute providers), and Interaction Service (a mechanism to obtain permissions from a user). The third is the Liberty Identity Service Interface Specifications (ID-SIS) that defines service interfaces for each identity-based Web service so that providers can exchange different parts of identity interoperably. These might include services such as registration, contact book, calendar, geo-location, or alerts [13-15, 26]. The privacy analysis in this paper is for the Liberty ID-FF version 1.2 and ID-WSF version 2.0. The Security Assertion Markup Language (SAML) version 2.0, an OASIS Standard, includes many new features derived from the Liberty ID-FF v1.2 specification that were contributed to the OASIS Security Services TC. Some new key features are the following: the use of pseudonyms, attribute profiles for attribute exchange, single logout, common domain cookie for identity provider discovery, and metadata for expressing SAML configuration. The new added features in SAML V2.0 enable SSO and Identity federation mechanisms. Therefore, SAML V2.0 can supersede the Liberty ID-FF V1.2 [18].

3.2 Liberty Use Case Scenario

Identity federation and SSO are the two main features offered by the Liberty Alliance project (ID-FF in particular). To best describe these features, we will go through the following use case scenario. In this scenario, a sales employee (SE) in a hardware company (compABC) goes to a business exhibition in a different province to promote compABC's new product. SE needs to book a hotel room, so she checks her favorite hotels-search Web site (hotserABC) to find a good hotel deal that is close from the exhibition location. hotserABC identifies SE after she logs in using her credentials (e.g., user name and a password). All that is required is to choose the hotel and specify the booking date where hotserABC will locate her profile and book the room. Moreover, SE gives her consent to hotserABC to introduce her to some members of the affinity group (e.g., car rental Web site). hotserABC is an LE Web site and it is SE's identity provider (IdP) in this scenario. At a later time, she clicks on a car rental company (carrntABC) that is a member of the affinity group (or the circle of trust, CoT). carrntABC, which is SE's service provider (SP), will recognize that the visitor is an LE user and that hotserABC is the visitor's IdP. SE may have a local account with carrntABC and in this case, she will typically login to carrntABC. carrntABC will offer to federate her local identity with her IdP, hotserABC, where she gives her consent to federate.

Identity federation between the two Web sites will enable the use of an SSO mechanism. If SE logs in to hotserABC and then visits carrntABC (while the Web session is still valid with hotserABC), she will not need to login to carrntABC. In fact, carrntABC will get authentication assertions from her IdP (either through browser redirect or a back-channel) that SE has been already authenticated with the IdP. When SE logs out from hotserABC, the authentication status (logout notice) is sent by hotserABC to carrntABC and all other SPs within the CoT where SE identity federation occurs with her IdP (and which were visited within the same Web session). Furthermore, Identity federation will enable the IdP and SP to exchange SE's personal in formation attributes upon her permission. For example, carrntABC will get SE's geographical information and perhaps her credit card number from hotserABC in order to conduct the car rental transaction. Identity federation does not imply that IdP will expose user identity by sharing user's identifiable attributes with the SP. The user IdP always shares a unique pseudonym with the SP to identify the user. This unique pseudonym is valid just between these two providers and means nothing to any other provider in the CoT. Therefore, if the user wants to conceal her identity from the SP, her IdP can provide authentication status (and maybe authorization information as well) to the SP by using this unique pseudonym that will refer to the user and preserve her anonymity. In this case, the SP still gets some non-identifiable attributes about the user (e.g., time zone information for better customization). SE can eliminate linkage between her accounts at an identity provider and a service provider, such that the identity provider no longer provides user identity to the service provider, and the service provider no longer accepts user identity from the identity provider. This process is called defederation. Within the same CoT, the user can have multiple identities linked to one or more identity providers. The user can choose which IdP to federate with when she visits a SP. A more detailed scenario will be provided in section 5.1 that will show the ID-WSF key features and will reveal more underlying layers.

4   Privacy Requirements in Identity Federation

Identity federation architectures have many components that need to satisfy user privacy concerns. The Liberty Alliance project takes into consideration different fair information practices; in particular, the Organization for Economic Co-operation and Development (OECD) and the Online Privacy Alliance (OPA) guidelines. Using these guidelines, Liberty offers the following set of fair information practices [24]:

♦ **Notice:** Consumer-facing LE Providers should provide to the user clear notice of who is collecting the information, what information they collect, how they collect it, how they provide choice, access, security, quality, relevance and timeliness to users, whether they disclose the information collected to other entities, and whether other entities are collecting information through them.

♦ **Choice:** Consumer-facing LE Providers should offer users choices, to the extent appropriate given the circumstances, regarding what PII is collected and how the PII is used beyond the use for which the information was provided. In addition, consumer facing LE Providers should allow users to review, verify, or update consents previously given or denied.

♦ **User Access to PII:** Consumer-facing LE Providers that maintain PII should offer, consistent with and as required by relevant law, a user reasonable access to view the non-proprietary PII that it collects from the user or maintains about him.

♦ **Complaint Resolution:** LE Providers should offer a complaint resolution mechanism for users who believe their PII has been mishandled.

♦ **Relevance:** LE Providers should use PII for the purpose for which it was collected, or the purposes about which the user has consented.

♦ **Quality:** Consumer-facing LE Providers that collect and maintain PII should permit users a reasonable opportunity to provide corrections to the PII that is stored by such entities.

♦ **Timeliness:** LE Providers should retain PII only so long as is necessary or requested and consistent with a retention policy accepted by the user.

♦ **Security:** LE Providers should take reasonable steps to protect and provide an adequate level of security for PII.

5 Privacy Analysis of Liberty ID-FF and ID-WSF

In this section we present a detailed use case scenario, and identify possible privacy breaches within the different transactions of the scenario and discuss proposals for improvement.

5.1 Use Case Scenario Using Liberty ID-FF and ID-WSF

In this section, we will use a more detailed scenario than the one given in Section 3.2 to show typical message flow between the different parties. The scenario will integrate the usage of both the Liberty ID-FF and ID-WSF. In this scenario, a user (usrABC) deals with an online payment Web site, payABC, that keeps some of the user attributes (e.g., name, address, credit card information, and so on). Several e-commerce Web sites have business relationships with payABC and they are within the same CoT. usrABC wants a cell phone, so she subscribes first with a wireless service provider and then she can buy a cell phone. Therefore she will visit a phone service provider (phnABC) to sign a wireless service contract. Next, usrABC will visit an online electronics store (eleABC) to buy a cell phone that is compatible with phnABC service. The typical sequence diagram for the identity federation process between the identity provider and the service providers is depicted in Figure 1.

In this scenario, it is assumed that identity federation has occurred between phnABC and payABC, and between eleABC and payABC. Thus, there are business relationships between these Web sites and they are in the same CoT. In step 1, the user visits the phnABC Web site where she is redirected to the payABC Web site since she has not been authenticated (step 2.a and 2.b). payABC will authenticate the user by asking her to provide her credentials in case she has not yet been authenticated. Then, payABC as usrABC's IdP redirects her back to the SP1 Web site (phnABC) with an artifact that points to the corresponding authentication assertion phABC will use the artifact and send a back-channel Get SAML Assertion message to the IdP in step 4.a. The IdP (payABC) replies with the corresponding SAML authentication assertion in step 4.b that indicates that the user is authenticated.

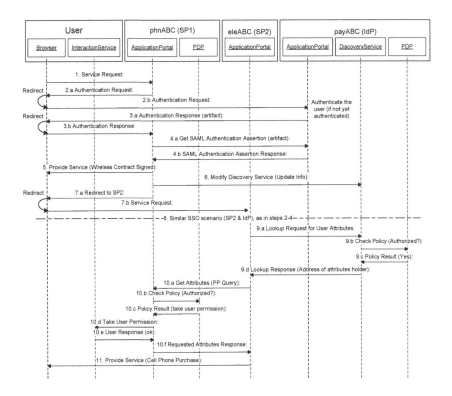

Fig. 1. User case scenario typical sequence flow using the Liberty ID-FF and ID-WSF

Next, the user will be informed of the SSO confirmation and in step 5, chooses her wireless plan. The SP1 (phnABC) needs some basic information about the user (e.g., name, address, or credit card information) in order to complete the wireless contract. In this case, phnABC either: (a) asks the user for her personal information which is then provided (e.g., by completing a form); (b) has an old profile of the user (local account) and asks the user for any needed updates; or (c) checks with the discovery service (which is hosted by the IdP in this example) and receives the needed information from the corresponding Attribute Provider (which is the IdP). The way of obtaining user's information is both a design choice and user choice. SP1 maintains the user's attributes (e.g., wireless service type, SIM card compatibility) and is able to act as an Attribute Provider. By being requested by usrABC or by asking permission from the user (either immediately via a Web form if the user is still connected to the Web site, or via the Interaction Service), SP1 registers its resource offering to the Discovery Service (DS).

This process is performed by sending an ID-WSF Discovery Service Modify message as in step 6.

Now, since the user needs a cell phone to use the wireless service, phnABC offers the user links to online electronic stores to order the needed device. These stores are expected to have business relationships with phnABC, and most likely they are within the same CoT. The user picks eleABC and she is directed to their Web site in step 7. Note that the user has the choice to visit different electronic stores and it is not necessary to be redirected from phnABC. In step 8, the user is authenticated by her IdP (payABC) using the SSO mechanism in a similar way as steps 2 to 4. After authentication confirmation, the user gets service from SP2. eleABC needs to know more about the user wireless service to offer her the sales promotions on the compatible devices (which are cell phones). SP2 does not maintain user attributes. Therefore, at the request of the user, SP2 tries to retrieve the user's attributes from other Web sites. This process is achieved by sending the ID-WSF Query message (lookup request) to DS in step 9.a. Note that SP2 uses ResourceOffering of DS, which it received from IdP with the ID-FF AuthnResponse (i.e., ResourceOffering of DS is embedded in the ID-FF AuthnResponse that was exchanged earlier). In step 9.b, the IdP acts as a Policy Enforcement Point (PEP) and sends a request to the Policy Decision Point (PDP) to find out whether SP2 is authorized to get information about the attribute provider possessing the user attributes (e.g. WSDL for the desired service). The access policy set by the user in the IdP PDP allows this in step 9.c. In this scenario, the IdP is both a PEP and a PDP. It is possible that the PDP service is hosted by another service or identity provider within the same CoT. In step 9.d, the DS responds to SP2 with an ID-WSF Discovery Service QueryResponse in which ResourceOfferings (by SP1) that match with specified ResourceID and ServiceType are embedded. SP2 receives SP1's ResourceOffering, and sends an ID-SIS Personal Profile Query message to SP1 in step 10.a (Get Attributes), to receive the necessary attributes of the user. This message is defined in the ID-WSF Data Service Template specification. SP1 checks its local policy by sending an authorization request to the hosted PDP service as in step 10.b (SP1 is both a PEP and a PDP). Since the user never gave permission for SP2, there is no permit or deny policy result. Therefore, SP1 requires the user permission first, if she is available online. SP1 sends a request for user permission in step 10.d to the Interaction Service (IS). IS is often a user agent that enables providers to interact with the owner of a resource to obtain his/her consent for particular resource exposure. After the user gives consent in step 10.e, SP1 responds to SP2 with an ID-SIS Personal Profile QueryResponse message in which the user's attributes (e.g., SIM type) are embedded (step 10.f). The user will then be able to see the sales promotions on compatible cell phones and purchase the one she likes. Likewise, SP2 can obtain needed user information (e.g., name, address, or credit card information) by requesting the user IdP or contacting the user SP1.

In general, service providers can register some of the user's attributes with the user DS upon his/her permission/request. For instance, browsing or shopping preferences may be kept at the SP. In the Liberty Alliance project, steps 2, 3, 4, and 8 are defined by the Liberty ID-FF specification; steps 6, 9, 10.b, 10.c, 10.d, and 10.e are defined by the Liberty ID-WSF specification; and steps 10.a and 10.f are defined by the Liberty ID-SIS specification. However, the PDP services are outside the scope of Liberty.

5.2 Possible Privacy Breaches: Identification, Analysis, and Proposals

We now identify and analyze possible privacy breaches and concerns within the Liberty ID-FF and ID-WSF frameworks throughout the scenario presented in 5.1. Moreover, we propose several improvements to the frameworks to enhance consumer privacy. Most of the privacy issues discussed here are not identified within Liberty specification documents or non-normative security and privacy documents (e.g. [14, 24]). In addition, we will clarify any privacy concerns that are not clearly explained. In this privacy analysis, most of the identified possible privacy breaches are not necessarily because of direct privacy flaws in the Liberty specifications. In fact, the various design options in resolving the non-determinism of the Liberty specifications are what could cause the majority of these privacy breaches. Moreover, some of these breaches are indirect results of privacy weaknesses in Internet protocols and browsers, upon which the Liberty specifications are built. It is also important to note that the proposed solutions to the identified privacy breaches are not intended to be complete, fully-specified solutions. Rather, many of these proposals are actually recommendations or improvements to enhance consumer privacy in a general sense. More strict, privacy-aware, and comprehensive Liberty specifications (taking these proposals into consideration) will help to diminish these privacy concerns; ultimately, this will enhance consumer privacy in federated frameworks.

In the CoT, the user usually trusts some providers more than others. Identity providers are usually the most trusted parties. In fact, the user chooses the IdP because she trusts it more than other providers. The same case applies to the user attribute provider. IdPs themselves trust some SPs more than others and so they deal with them differently according to the SPs' security and privacy policies and practices. Moreover, providers interact with the Liberty services differently according to the trustworthiness of the provider hosting the service. We will assume this in the discussion below. For each subsection, we will list the possible privacy breaches together with the proposed solutions.

5.2.1 Identity Federation

♦ *Privacy Concern.* The idea of IdP introducing the user to members of the affinity group seems a simple direct concept, but this introduction could lead to a privacy contravention. It is not sufficient that IdP gets a general user consent to introduce the user. Some SPs' privacy polices may not match with the user privacy preferences. In this case, giving only one general consent may lead to a privacy breach.

Proposed Solution. The IdP needs to get a user consent for every single introduction with a member in the CoT. Moreover, the user needs to have the choice of knowing the privacy practices of every member that s/he will be introduced to and whether it matches the user's privacy preferences or not. This seems to be a lot of work for the user (since one of the Liberty objectives is to enable simplified and fast user sign-on through federated network identification). However, aside from the fact that this introduction only happens once, there are several ways to facilitate the verification of providers' privacy polices by the user. As we propose in 5.3.1, if the user can specify the privacy preferences in advance and there is an automated mechanism to compare SP privacy policy with the user privacy preferences, then this can act in place of the user and give warnings in case of discrepancies. If it is difficult to go through this process before the introduction step, then this can be done when the user visits the SP and before federation. Adding a new member to the affinity group at a later time requires obtaining another consent from the user for introduction. In this case, the IdP will either interact with the user via the Interaction Service, or wait for the user login in order to get the introduction permission for the new member. The IdP should enable a mechanism for the user to opt-out from the introduction consent for each member independently.

♦ *Privacy Concern.* Nonrepudiable clear user consent for Identity federation between IdP and SP is another important requirement. Giving this consent to the SP side may cause some privacy impacts. This is because any SP is always trusted less than other providers and it is not easy to prove that the user has given consent for the identity federation between SP and IdP.

Proposed Solution. It is always preferable that the user gives this consent to the IdP side [19]. Therefore, there should be a mechanism to enable the SP to interact with the user IdP through a back-channel and request a user consent. Then the IdP will contact the user via the user agent interaction service as defined in ID-WSF. In this case, the IdP will probably authenticate the user first and then get a nonrepudiable user consent.

♦ *Privacy Concern.* Some design options in the Liberty specification enable SPs (especially the ones to whom a user agrees to be introduced) to know some basic information about the user even before federating the identity with the user IdP. Examples of this information are user IdPs list, user preferred IdP (or the most recently established IdP session which is the last one in the list), and other introduction details. Moreover, SPs could exchange such information with each other.

Proposed Solution. Introduction information should remain private (by both the user and his IdP) regardless of what introduction technique is used, either via the Identity Provider Introduction Profile (i.e. Common Domain Cookie) or when the user agent is a LE client or proxy (LECP). When the user gives his consent to be introduced to a SP, the SP should not know any information about this introduction until the user visits the SP website and he wants to federate. For example, if the user has more than one IdP, then the SP should not know the user's preferred IdP unless the user wants to federate his identity with the SP. The SP (where the user federated his identity) should protect the privacy of this information (user IdPs list and user preferred IdP). Furthermore, other SPs should not even know that the user has given consent to be introduced to a specific SP.

5.2.2 Single Sign-On

♦ *Privacy Concern.* Federation domain cookie: one of the design choices in ID-FF is to use a federation common domain cookie. This cookie can be used to find out whether the user has been authenticated recently by the IdP. Note that the most recently established identity provider session is the last one in the list. This cookie is accessible by any federated SP in the CoT (when the user visits the SP Web site). This represents a privacy breach since other members in the CoT do not need to always know the user's authentication status (the most recent IdP that authenticated the user). For example, in our scenario, if the user has a local account with SP2 and wants to access the SP2 Web site using only her local credentials, then it is not necessary for SP2 to know her authentication status with her IdP.

Proposed Solution. This cookie should not be used to reveal user authentication status (the most recent IdP that authenticated the user). Moreover, this cookie should not divulge the user's preferred IdP or any other information (other than a list of user IdPs). If we remove the restriction that the most recently established IdP session should be the last one in the common domain cookie IdPs list (so the list becomes random), then the visited SP would not be able to discover the last IdP the user logged into. SP should always be able to contact the user IdP through a back-channel and request user authentication status if necessary.

♦ *Privacy Concern.* Browser redirect for SSO: The ID-FF specification has the option for browser-redirect messages to carry some information. This information may contain users' personal information (either identifiable or not). Since redirect message length is limited and it is not usually encrypted, this is a privacy breach (in case of eavesdropping attacks).

Proposed Solution. There should be a strict rule to not include any valuable information in the redirect itself. For example, in step 3.a, the artifact that comes with the authentication response redirect should not contain any user PII. The artifact should be always an arbitrary number that is known only to the IdP. Any PII that the IdP needs to send to the SP should be through a back-channel between them using encrypted SAML assertions.

♦ *Privacy Concern.* Redirection between SPs: When the user is redirected from SP1 to SP2, SP2 will know that the user came from SP1. This is a potential user privacy breach as an indirect result of privacy weakness in Internet protocols and browsers. Let us assume that SP1 and SP2 have different access policies to the user attributes stored in her IdP, so SP1 may get a user attribute that SP2 is not authorized to get and vice versa. SP1 gets a non-identifiable attribute att1 from the user IdP according to the user privacy policy and SP2 gets a non-identifiable attribute att2 from the user IdP according to the corresponding user privacy policy. SP1 is not authorized to get att2 and SP2 is not authorized to get att1 where none of them is intended to know any PII about the user. The IdP uses a unique user pseudonym to deal with each SP, so SP1 and SP2 have no way to link the user. However if SP2 knows that the user was redirected from SP1, then SP2 knows it is the same user and they can exchange att1 and att2 illegally. Moreover, knowing att1 and att2 could lead to deducing identifiable attributes and may reveal user identity. In addition, SP2 may show customized ads for the user knowing that she just visited phnABC.

Proposed Solution. This situation requires more attention from the user IdP. For example, the IdP may decide not to expose att2 to SP2 when it notices successive authentication requests (SP1 followed by SP2). An audit trail mechanism at either a trusted third party or the IdP could help in discovering such cooperation so that the appropriate actions are taken.

♦ *Privacy Concern.* Authentication information: federated SPs have the right to re-authenticate the user (via his IdP) whenever they want. Moreover, they can query the user IdP for the authentication method and other related detail (e.g., password length). This information helps SPs to evaluate the authentication mechanism. The

SP may ask for stronger authentication or ask the user to re-authenticate before carrying out some transactions at the SP. However, this information can be a threat to the user privacy and security in the case of a malicious SP. The authentication method information and authentication repetition can help the attacker to figure out user access credentials.

Proposed Solution. To limit these consequences, the user should have control over which SPs can get this information, either through direct consent or through her privacy preferences. Furthermore, the user IdP may warn the user after a specific number of re-authentications within the same session, or apply strict security mechanisms for further re-authentications.

5.2.3 Discovery Service

♦ *Privacy Concern.* If the user policy within DS PDP allows the SP to get the address of the user attribute resource holder, the SP may locally store the address information. When the user changes the DS PDP at a later time, the same SP may no longer be allowed to get the address of the resource holder. However, the SP still has the resource address stored locally.

Proposed Solution. The SP must not store the resource address after getting the needed resources. The existence of a mandatory trusted third party that can monitor SP privacy policies and monitor privacy practices can help in diminishing this privacy breach. Another option is that the DS should give the SP the resource address in an artifact with a timestamp (signed by the DS). So that the resource holder (Attribute Provider) will accept the SP attribute request only if the artifact is not expired.

♦ *Privacy Concern.* Using the current ID-WSF specification, the SP can request resource-holder address for more than one user attribute within the same request message as in step 9.a; however the SP may use only one Usage Directive SOAP header to specify only one usage purpose and other usage information (e.g., retention time). This may lead to a privacy breach since the declared purpose may apply only to some requested attributes.

Proposed Solution. There must be a separate Usage Directive SOAP header for each attribute resource-holder address where the attribute requester must send a request that contains the purpose for the request, the retention period, and other necessary usage information. The response should contain elements for any privacy obligations that are to be imposed upon the requester. Alternatively, if the SP will request more than one address in one lookup request message with one Usage Directive header, then there should be a standard way to express more than one purpose and other usage information within the single usage field of the lookup request.

♦ *Privacy Concern.* Privacy expression language: Lack of standard privacy expressions could lead to inconsistent interpretation of data privacy directives.

Proposed Solution. A standard fine-grained, machine-readable, and dynamic privacy expression language (e.g., XACML) will enable providers to understand the syntax and semantics of privacy elements. The standard language will be used by both the PDP at the discovery service and the PDP at the attribute provider.

5.2.4 Interaction Service

♦ *Privacy Concern.* The user SP (or may be the user Attribute Provider or IdP) can fabricate user consent. Moreover, an unencrypted channel between the user and one of her providers may enable the attacker to illegitimately post a user consent. In the ID-WSF IS specification, the `<InteractionRequest>` can include a "`signed`" attribute which indicates that recipient (e.g., IS) should attempt to obtain a signed `<InteractionStatement>` from the user, so the SP can ask the user to sign his consent. However, it is not clear how the user can control the integrity of either the request or the response. The user has no direct way to force the SP to sign a request for consent. Moreover, the user can not sign the response if the SP did not ask for the signature. This enables user non-repudiation (user can not deny his consent) but not SP non-repudiation.

Proposed Solution. There must be a mechanism in the specification to enable users to control the integrity of consent request messages. Furthermore, it is usually hard for users to manage digital signature mechanisms. Hence, it is more appropriate that IS signs user consents on behalf of the user. This however requires that the user logs in to the IS first (e.g., userID and password) before giving his consent. In this case, the IS must be trusted by the user.

♦ *Privacy Concern.* ISs hosted by other providers may have privacy impacts.

Proposed Solution. If the IS is not hosted by the user agent itself then the provider hosting the user IS should be very trusted by the user. The fact that the interaction service is responsible for gathering user consents makes it a very sensitive service. User IdP is one trusted provider that could host user IS.

♦ *Privacy Concern.* With the current ID-WSF specification, SP is able to deny its query to the user, as well as user consent (or user deny) returned. There is no suggested way that enables the user or a trusted third party to verify this exchange.

Proposed Solution. SP queries to the user should be recorded by the interaction service. SPs should digitally sign each query to the user; moreover, SPs should sign a confirmation of receipt for the user consent (or denial) together with the request itself (with timestamp). This provides an audit trail mechanism in case of any dispute.

5.2.5 User Attribute Access Control

♦ *Privacy Concern.* SP cooperation: if the user deals with two SPs, and each of them knows some identifiable attributes of a user, then there is a risk of attribute exchange between them.

Proposed Solution. An audit trail mechanism can help in exposing such leakages. The fact that the user can check her personal information usage will enable her to discover any unauthorized attribute sharing. The existence of a trusted third party for the audit trail will give more confidence to the user. In addition, the existence of a seal service (as in section 5.3.2) will enable the user to carefully select her SPs.

♦ *Privacy Concern.* Attribute deduction: if an SP collects more than one non-identifiable attribute about the same user for different needs on different sessions, this SP may be able to deduce an identifiable user attribute that leads to user identity. Furthermore, if more than one SP collects non-identifiable attributes about the user and they are able to infer that it is the same user, then they may work together to deduce an identifiable user attribute.

Proposed Solution. A privacy seal trusted third party that can certify and monitor SP privacy policies, monitor privacy practices, and monitor cooperation, can help to diminish this privacy concern. More privacy precautions are also needed by attribute providers.

♦ ***Privacy Concern.*** ID-WSF architecture enables an SP to request more than one user attribute from the attribute provider within the same request message as in step 10.a (the provided user scenario in section 5.1); however the attribute requester may use only one Usage Directive SOAP header to specify the usage purpose and other usage information. This may violate user privacy since the declared purpose and other directives may apply only to some requested attributes. Moreover, the attribute provider response could have only one field for attribute obligations and other usage directives.

Proposed Solution. There must be a separate Usage Directive SOAP header for each attribute, and the attribute requester must send a request that contains the purpose for each attribute and any other necessary data privacy directives (preferably using a standard usage directive language). The response should contain elements for any privacy obligations that are to be imposed upon the requester. (See Discovery Service privacy concern above.)

♦ ***Privacy Concern.*** If the attribute provider relies on the discovery service to be the PEP, then this could lead to a privacy violation. The SP can reuse or share the information about the attribute provider holding the user's attributes, so the same SP or other providers may access the user's attributes illegitimately.

Proposed Solution. Both the discovery service and the attribute provider should act as a PEP. At the attribute provider, the PEP must always be designed as a back-line guard by the entity hosting or exposing the resource (as in step 10). On the other hand, the discovery service PEP acts as a first-line guard for user information access (as in step 9).

♦ ***Privacy Concern.*** If there is a conflict between the attribute provider local access control policy and the user privacy policy at the attribute provider PDP, then unexpected decision results may occur.

Proposed Solution. Each attribute provider should predefine a conflict strategy to deal with this case. For example, a deny-overrides combining algorithm (see XACML) can be used to deny the attribute request if either policy denies it.

5.3   Proposal for New Services in ID-FF and ID-WSF

In this section, we propose three new services that can merge with the current Liberty ID-FF and ID-WSF frameworks. These services enhance user privacy when using Liberty-enabled sites and services.

5.3.1   User Privacy Preferences Service

One of the main objectives of identity federation is to enable simplified and fast user sign-on while browsing to different service providers. Thus, when the user visits an SP Web site, he will be automatically signed on and some of his information may be transferred from his IdP to the visited SP (upon a previous user permission) for better customization and service. Nevertheless, as we noted in the previous section, to enhance user privacy, we need to make the user aware of the excessive transactions occuring and to request his permission in many cases. Consequently, the user may be overwhelmed by many access permission requests and so identity federation will no longer be a fast, easy-to-use mechanism.

We propose a user privacy preferences service that can be part of the ID-WSF specification. The new service will enable the user to enter his default privacy preferences. A user can have several preferences categorized by a generic classification of SPs according to different levels of privacy practices. The best place to host this service appears to be the user IdP. A Liberty-enabled user agent can host this service too; however, the user may then not be able to use his privacy preferences in case of using a different machine. Using this service, some access permission requests (e.g., step 10.d) can be directed first to the user privacy preferences service to find out whether the user's default preferences allow the requested access.

This new service will raise some new privacy concerns. For instance, SPs should not know the user's privacy preferences unless required. A detailed specification is needed for this service; however, the service does not have to be mandatory but can be a design option when deploying the Liberty ID-WSF specification. It is also possible to integrate the proposed service with some existing techniques such as, for example, browser-based privacy preferences languages (e.g., APPEL in P3P).

5.3.2 Privacy Seal Service

It is always difficult to ensure that a user attribute requester will adhere to its stated privacy policy and its declared purposes and other attribute usage directives. If no technical mechanism exists, the user will need to rely on his trust of the attribute requester. Here, we propose a Liberty privacy seal service by a trusted third party that can certify and monitor identity and service providers' privacy policies, monitor privacy practices, and resolve any user disputes. The user will need this service in many cases. At the time of federation introduction, this service will assure the user that an SP privacy policy accurately states what personal information the SP gathers and how it is handled. Moreover, this service can be consulted by an attribute provider PDP before revealing any information. Typically, a trusted third party is the best place to host the service. The service can be part of the ID-WSF specification. It can help tremendously in increasing user trust in using Liberty-enabled services. It is important to note, however, that Web privacy seal organizations do not always revoke a seal certification from a business even after privacy violations have occurred. This indicates the need for strict rules (e.g., an automatic revocation mechanism) when deploying a Liberty seal service.

5.3.3 Audit Trail Service

Using the existing Liberty architecture, a user may have many privacy concerns about the different providers exchanging his personal information without his permission. In addition, many other transactions need to be recorded (for example, transactions in steps 6, 9, and 10). The user needs to know if any privacy violation has been committed by any SP so he can take the appropriate action for future transactions and so that he can update his privacy preferences accordingly. An audit trail service as part of the

Liberty architecture can achieve this task. The user (and probably his IdP) can access this service to review the transaction record. The provider hosting this service may need to notify the user in case of potentially dangerous violations. This provider may be the same one who hosts the Liberty privacy seal service.

6 Conclusion

This paper has looked at the Liberty Identity Federation and the Liberty Identity Web Services frameworks from the perspective of user privacy. In particular, we presented a detailed user experience scenario that integrates both these frameworks, and identified and analyzed possible privacy breaches within the different transactions of the scenario. In each case, we discussed proposals for improvements that would enhance privacy. Furthermore, three new services were proposed (a user privacy preferences service, a privacy seal service, and an audit trail service) that can merge with the current Liberty ID-FF and ID-WSF frameworks.

Some directions for future work in this area include finding additional privacy breaches, analyzing SAML V2.0 and the Liberty Identity Service Interface Specifications (ID-SIS) framework (privacy analysis), and specifying the three new proposed services in greater detail. We expect to report on some of this work in a future paper.

Acknowledgments

We thank Liam Peyton and Paul Madsen for helpful discussions. This research was supported in part by the Natural Sciences and Engineering Research Council of Canada (NSERC) and the Ontario Research Network for Electronic Commerce (ORNEC).

References

1. Aarts, R., Björksten, M., Deadman, S., Duserick, B., Karhuluoma, N., et al., *"Liberty architecture framework for supporting Privacy Preference Expression Languages (PPELs)"*. Nov 2003, Version 1.0, Liberty Alliance Project. Available from: http://www.projectliberty.org/about/whitepapers.php.
2. Ahn, G.-J. and Lam, J. "Managing privacy preferences for federated identity management". In *Proceedings of the 2005 workshop on Digital identity management*, Fairfax, VA, USA, November 2005. ACM Press.
3. Ahn, G.-J., Shin, D., and Hong, S.-P. "Information Assurance in Federated Identity Management: Experimentations and Issues". In *Proceedings of the 5th International Conference on Web Information Systems Engineering: Web Information Systems – WISE 2004*, Brisbane, Australia, November 2004. LNCS, Volume 3306, Jan 2004, Pages 78 - 89.
4. Bhargav-Spantzel, A., Squicciarini, A. C., and Bertino, E. "Establishing and protecting digital identity in federation systems". In *Proceedings of the 2005 workshop on Digital identity management*, Fairfax, VA, USA, November 2005. ACM Press.
5. Brown, K. "Security Briefs: Step-by-Step Guide to InfoCard". April 2006. MSDN Magazine, Microsoft. Available from: http://msdn.microsoft.com/msdnmag/issues/06/05/SecurityBriefs/default.aspx [Accessed: April 25, 2006].
6. BusinessWeek online. "Business Week/Harris Poll: A Growing Threat". March, 2000. Available from: http://businessweek.com/2000/00_12/b3673010.htm [Accessed: January 16, 2006].

7. Ellison, G. and Madsen, P., *"Liberty ID-WSF Security Mechanisms"*, version 2.0-03, Liberty Alliance Project. Available from: http://www.projectliberty.org/resources/specifications.php.

8. Fox, S. "Trust and Privacy Online: Why Americans Want to Rewrite the Rules". August 2000. Pew Internet & American Life Project. Available from http://: www.pewinternet.org/pdfs/PIP_Trust_Privacy_Report.pdf [Accessed: February 17, 2006].

9. Gartner Group. 2003. Industry watchdog Gartner Group. Available from: http://www.gartner.com [Accessed: October 21, 2005].

10. Groß, T. "Security analysis of the SAML Single Sign-on Browser/Artifact profile". In *Proceedings of the 19th Annual Computer Security Applications Conference.*, Dec 2003. IEEE.

11. Hommel, W. "Using XACML for Privacy Control in SAML-Based Identity Federations". In *Proceedings of the TC-11International Conference, CMS 2005*, Salzburg, Austria, September 2005. Lecture Notes in Computer Science, Volume 3677, Sep 2005, Pages 160 - 169.

12. Johnston, S. J. "Pondering Passport: Do You Trust Microsoft With Your Data?" September, 2001. PCWorld.com. Available from: http://pcworld.about.com/news/Sep242001id63244.htm [Accessed: January 10, 2006].

13. Kellomäki, S. and Lockhart, R., *"Liberty ID-SIS Personal Profile Service Specification"*. 2003, Version 1.1, Liberty Alliance Project. Available from: http://www.projectliberty.org/resources/specifications.php.

14. Landau, S., *"Liberty ID-WSF Security & Privacy Overview"*. 2003, Version 1.0, Liberty Alliance Project. Available from: http://www.projectliberty.org/resources/specifications.php.

15. Liberty Alliance Project. Available from: http://www.projectliberty.org/ [Accessed: October 2005].

16. Liberty Alliance Project. "Liberty Alliance Whitepaper: Identity Theft Primer". December 2005. Available from: http://www.projectliberty.org/resources/id_Theft_Primer_Final.pdf [Accessed: January 2006].

17. Madsen, P. and Takahashi, Y. K. K. "Federated identity management for protecting users from ID theft". In *Proceedings of the 2005 workshop on Digital identity management*, Fairfax, VA, USA, November 2005. ACM Press.

18. OASIS Security Services (SAML) TC. "Security Assertion Markup Language (SAML)". OASIS Standards. Available from: http://www.oasis-open.org/committees/tc_home.php?wg_abbrev=security [Accessed: December 2005].

19. Pfitzmann, B. "Privacy in Enterprise Identity Federation - Policies for Liberty Single Signon -". In *Proceedings of the 3rd Workshop on Privacy Enhancing Technologies (PET)*, Dresden, Germany, March 2003. Lecture Notes in Computer Science, Volume 2760, Dec 2003, Pages 189 - 204.

20. Pfitzmann, B. and Waidner, M. "Federated Identity-Management Protocols — Where User Authentication Protocols May Go". In *Proceedings of the 11th Cambridge Workshop on Security Protocols*, Cambridge, UK, April 2003. Lecture Notes in Computer Science, Volume 3364, Pages 153 - 174.

21. Pfitzmann, B. and Waidner, M. "Privacy in browser-based attribute exchange". In *Proceedings of the 2002 ACM workshop on Privacy in the Electronic Society*, Washington, DC, USA, November 2002. ACM Press.

22. SourceID. "Digital Identity Basics". Available from: http://www.sourceid.org/content/primer [Accessed: December 2005].

23. Taylor, K. and Murty, J. "Implementing role based access control for federated information systems on the web". In *Proceedings of the Australasian information security workshop conference on ACSW frontiers 2003 - Volume 21*, Adelaide, Australia, 2003. ACM Press.

24. Varney, C. and Hartson, H., *"Privacy and Security Best Practices"*. November 2003, Version 2.0, Liberty Alliance Project. Available from: http://www.projectliberty.org/resources/specifications.php.
25. Varney, C. and Sheckler, V., *"Deployment Guidelines for Policy Decision Makers"*. September 2005, Version 2.9, Liberty Alliance Project. Available from: http://www.projectliberty. org/about/whitepapers.php.
26. Wason, T., *"Liberty ID-FF Architecture Overview"*. 2004, Version: 1.2-errata-v1.0, Liberty Alliance Project. Available from: http:// www.projectliberty.org/resources/ specifications.php.

Traceable and Automatic Compliance of Privacy Policies in Federated Digital Identity Management

Anna Squicciarini, Abhilasha Bhargav-Spantzel,
Alexei Czeskis, and Elisa Bertino

Computer Science Department, Purdue University
{squiccia,bhargav,aczeskis,bertino}@cs.purdue.edu

Abstract. Digital identity is defined as the digital representation of the information known about a specific individual or organization. An emerging approach for protecting identities of individuals while at the same time enhancing user convenience is to focus on inter-organization management of identity information. This is referred to as *federated identity management*. In this paper we develop an approach to support privacy controlled sharing of identity attributes and harmonization of privacy policies in federated environments. Policy harmonizations mechanisms make it possible to determine whether or not the transfer of identity attributes from one entity to another violate the privacy policies stated by the former. We also provide mechanisms for tracing the release of user's identity attributes within the federation. Such approach entails a form of accountability since an entity non-compliant with the users original privacy preferences can be identified. Finally, a comprehensive security analysis details security properties is also offered.

1 Introduction

Digital identity is defined as the digital representation of the information known about a specific individual or organization. As such, it encompasses not only login names (often referred to as *nyms*), but many additional pieces of information, referred to as *identity attributes* or *identifiers*, about users. Managing identity attributes raises a number of challenges. On one hand, these attributes often need to be shared among several parties in order to speed up and facilitate user authentication and access control, and thus enhancing usability of digital identities. On the other hand, identity attributes need to be protected because they may convey sensitive information that individuals may not be willing to share unless specific conditions are satisfied. An emerging approach for protecting identities of individuals while at the same time enhancing user convenience is to focus on inter-organization management of identity information. This is referred to as *federated identity management*. Specifically, the goal of a federated approach to digital identity management is to provide users with protected environments enabling identity attribute sharing. As such, federations provide

G. Danezis and P. Golle (Eds.): PET 2006, LNCS 4258, pp. 78–98, 2006.

a controlled method by which federated service providers (SP's) can provide more integrated and complete services to a qualified group of individuals within certain sets of business transactions. To date several on-going initiatives are developing standard protocols and platforms for the federated management of digital identities (see Table 5 in Appendix C for a summary of these initiatives).

Although federating identities greatly simplifies the task of collecting and distributing user attributes in the federation, no satisfying mechanisms are currently provided to protect users privacy and for privacy policy matching in collaborative environments. As SP's in a federation correspond to independent entities, they may adopt privacy practices that are not homogeneous. Uncontrolled identity information sharing may result in privacy breaches and threats like identity theft or phishing, and in the lack of compliance with respect to the privacy policies advertised by the various SP's.

A suitable solution to the problem of privacy in a federated environment should satisfy two important requirements. The first requirement is to provide mechanisms for facilitating privacy policies matching and harmonization among federated SP's. Such mechanisms would make it possible to determine whether or not the transfer of identity attributes from one SP to another would violate the privacy policies stated by the former. Notice that allowing a SP to transfer identity information to another SP is important in order to maximize user convenience and extend the notion of single-sign on to encompass a large variety of identity attributes. The second requirement is to provide mechanisms making it possible for users to trace their identity information across the federation, and verify whether it has been managed according to their privacy preferences. Privacy conscious users may in fact have their own preferences concerning the use of their identity attributes.

In this paper, we address these requirements by developing an approach that supports the privacy controlled sharing of identity attributes and the harmonization of privacy policies based on the notion of *subsumption*. Subsumption is used on policies defined over equal or similar class of data in order to determine if they are in conflict or if one implies the other. To facilitate policy harmonization in a federation, we assume some predefined policy templates to be available for policy specification. The SP's may either exploit the templates or may specify customized policies describing their own practices.

We base our approach on a rich privacy vocabulary rather than on the vocabulary provided by P3P[1]. We employ EPAL[2] vocabulary hierarchies to address the limited expressive power of the original P3P vocabulary. Moreover, we make use of an ontology to establish a common vocabulary for attributes, credentials, and data produced and exchanged across the federation. The use of an ontology makes it possible for the interacting parties to automatically detect semantic relationships among different attributes and reason about policy subsumption. To help users in verifying whether their privacy preferences have been enforced as required, we provide mechanisms for tracing the release of user's identity attributes. Our policy tracing is a method determining if such information has been transmitted from one SP to another along a path without violating the user's privacy preferences. We assume a tamper proof logging system to be in place. As a result, our protocol is also effective in the presence of malicious parties. In addition, if the policy tracing algorithm is executed a sufficient number of times, the user can check the enforcement of his/her privacy requirements over the whole federation

We cast our discussion in the context of the FAMTN (*Federated Attribute Management and Trust Negotiation*) system [3]. FAMTN is characterized by two types of entities: FAMTN SP's (FSP's for brevity) and users. A FSP is an entity providing a service to a user, if the user satisfies the policy requirements of the service. In addition, FSP's also manage and collect identity related information of federated users. As such a user will register at his/her own local FSP and then he/she will submit other identity attributes and credentials while interacting with FSP's to gain access to specific services or data. As no centralized identity provider exists, such information is not be stored at a unique server but is distributed among the various respective FSP's the user has visited. At the end of each interaction, the user obtains a receipt, referred to as *trust ticket*, that keeps track of relevant information concerning the interaction, like the purpose, the involved FSP and a time stamp. FSP's, besides interacting with users to provide them with services, also interact among each other in order to support the federated management of digital identities. FSP's, and more in general SP's in an IdM (Identity Management) system, exchange user attributes and credentials to automatically authorize users to access services and resources and so to avoid requiring multiple submissions of these attributes and credentials from users. It is important to notice that even though our approaches are cast in the context of FAMTN, they can be easily applied to other federated systems.

To the best of our knowledge, no previous approaches exist that provide privacy policy harmonization and tracing in federated environments for digital identity management. In the paper we also present a scenario motivating the development of the outlined techniques and we discuss how these techniques can be applied to specific domains characterized by a broad disclosure of sensitive information across federated domains.

The remainder of the paper is organized as follows. In the next section we introduce the motivating scenario that will be used throughout the paper. In Section 3 we provide preliminary concepts and definitions concerning ontologies and privacy policies. In Section 4 we illustrate the different mechanisms to policy specification and describe our algorithms for policy subsumption and tracing. In particular, Section 4.3 we illustrate the policy tracing algorithm and in Section 4.4 we present a detailed security analysis. In Sections 5 we discuss related work. Finally, we conclude the paper in Section 6 with pointers to future work.

2 Motivating Scenario

Health industry payers and providers maintain large volumes of confidential health information along with other sensitive personal and financial data and conduct many transactions electronically. In this arena an individual's digital identity includes his/her medical history, which is made up of (often disjoint) medical records from different health institutions. Privacy of medical records and medical-related identity information requires particular attention. To analyze the specific requirements and challenges of this environment we consider the example of an on-line federation of hospitals and organizations collaborating with each other, named *Trusted_Health*. We assume each federated organization being composed by service providers collecting users' information and interacting with users and other service providers through negotiations. In particular, we refer to the scenario of a user Alice who is a student of Purdue University.

We start from Alice getting an X-Ray performed at a city clinic called Lafayette-Health, part of the *Trusted_Health* federation. The resulting X-Ray report is stored with the privacy preferences of Alice at Lafayette-Health itself. Lafayette-Health collects medical records of its patients according to some privacy policies publicly available. Alice's report (along with her privacy preferences) is subsequently sent to her insurance company MedInsure, for filing her claim. *Trusted_Health* federation promotes privacy practices harmonization within the various institution by providing templates for possible policies describing different approach to data practices. Both Lafayette-Health and Medinsure specify policies using such templates. As such upon transmission of data between the two entities, MedInsure can easily verify whether its applied privacy policy is subsumed by the Lafayette-Health one. At a later date, Purdue Health Clinic requests the X-Ray information from Lafayette-Health for a routine check up and update of her health information. Purdue Health Clinic has all health related information of Alice. After three weeks Alice visits another university, State-U, and finds an X-Ray as a study sample in one of their biology classes. Even though the Alice's personal identifying information, such as name, SSN, and Purdue Identification Number, have been suppressed from the record provided with the X-Ray, such record still provides medical data, such as abnormalities seen in the x-rays, and supporting general data, such as gender, age, race, height, weight. Alice finds that this information perfectly fits her.

Therefore, how can Alice make sure that her privacy policy with respect to the X-Ray was not violated as this information was shared among the different institutions? Can Alice know which entity has managed her own data and according to which privacy practices?

3   Preliminary Notions

Our approach relies on the two important notions of ontology and privacy policies. In what follows we provide background information about these notions that is relevant for the subsequent discussion in the paper.

3.1   Ontologies

To properly apply and enforce privacy policies in a federation, interacting entities need to share a common vocabulary to facilitate communication and sharing of information. In particular, the meaning of a given attribute is to be understood in an unambiguous manner, so that other possibly related attributes are also automatically protected. In fact, same information can be often expressed through different attributes and be a generalization or a specialization of other attributes. With respect to our example of Section 2, the X-Ray report is the main data related to Alice in *Trusted_Health*. This information may be referred to as *medical document* in the Insurance company MedInsure and *Bone Sample* in the biology department. Here the *medical document* may not have all the details of the original X-Ray report and might differ from the features of attribute used in the *Bone Sample*.

To model semantic relationships, we borrow ideas from work on ontologies [4,5,6]. In our work, we consider an ontology as a set of *concepts* together with relationships among these concepts. Specifically, the ontology assigns semantics to attributes, credentials and other identity related data, by defining two main classes. The first is the general class of identity related attributes, that are independent from any specific domain. Attributes like name, address and job position, fall in this class. The second class represents identity information that is specific to a given federated domain. In our scenario, this class includes information dealing with health state of an individual, his/her medical record information, blood type, diagnosis and so forth. For simplicity, we assume that the two class of information are disjoint, that is, there are no attributes which fall in both classes.

Each *concept* in the ontology is associated with a name, a set of keywords, a set of general purpose attributes names and a set of domain dependent attribute names. The formal definition is given below.

Definition 1. [Concept] *A concept, denoted by C_i, is a tuple $\langle Name_i, KeywordSet_i, D\_Id\_Attr_i, Dom\_Attr_i \rangle$, where $Name_i$ is the concept name, $KeywordSet_i$ is a set of keywords associated with C_i, $D\_Id\_Attributes_i$ is a set of credential type and/or attribute names and Dom_Attr_i is the set of domain related attribute names. $KeywordSet_i$ describes the set of all possible keywords used to describe concept C_i. Each element in $KeywordSet_i$ is a synonymous of $Name_i$. Each attribute or credential type in $D\_Id\_Attr_i$ implements concept.* □

$\langle Xray, \{\}, xray, \{xray, \ medicaldocument, \ bonesample\} \rangle$ is an example of concept.

For any two distinct concepts C and C', where $C = \langle Name_i, KeywordSet_i, D\_Id\_Attr_i, Dom\_Attr_i \rangle$ and $C' = \langle Name_i, KeywordSet'_i, D\_Id\_Attr'_i, Dom\_Attr'_i \rangle$, the following conditions hold: $KeywordSet \cap KeywordSet' = emptyset$ and $D\_Id\_Attr_i \cap D\_Id\_Attr'_i = emptyset$. As such, any keyword belongs to exactly one concept. Similarly, we assume each attribute to be associated with exactly one concept.

An ontology is a partially ordered set of concepts $\{C_1, \ldots, C_n\}$. The order relationship, denoted by $\prec$, represents a generalization relationship between concepts. $C_i \prec C_k$ if concept C_k is a generalization of concept C_i. This means that information conveyed by concept C_k can be used to infer information conveyed

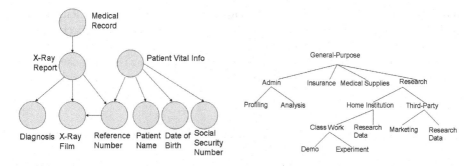

Fig. 1. Example of a Concept-Graph of an X-Ray Medical Report

Fig. 2. Example of a purpose hierarchy for generic medical data

by concept C_i. For instance, the concept *Patient Vital Info* is a more general concept than *Patient Name* (denoted as *Patient Vital Info* $\prec$ *Patient Name*), since the Patient Vital Info imply the knowledge of his/her name. As an example, in Figure 1 we report graphical representation of concepts Medical Report, X-Ray, Diagnosis etc. In Figure, the parent node is a generalization of the child.

We assume the existence of an ontology which is shared and agreed upon by the various FSP's in a FAMTN system. Note that such an ontology is in most cases obtained through an integration process taking into account ontologies possibly existing at the various FSP's. A large number of integration techniques and methodologies have been developed for semantic ontologies [7]. For example matching techniques have been developed to determine semantic mappings between concepts of different related ontologies [5], that can be used in our context. Also, we assume the ontology to be stored for reference in a repository available to all the federated users. In what follows, we refer to the ontology shared in the federation as *federated ontology* in order to distinguish it from ontologies that are local to the various FSP's.

3.2 Privacy Policies

Privacy policies state who the *recipients* will be for the user *data*, the *purpose* for which this data will be used, and how long the data will be *retained*. Data in a privacy policy can be represented at different levels of granularity. They can refer to aggregate data, or they can refer to more specific piece of information, such as, last name or social security number. In our work, we adopt the terminology of the P3P standard [1]. The data element refers to smallest granularity data. Examples of data elements are social security number and last name. In our context, data elements actually correspond to ontological concepts. The current vocabulary adopted by the P3P standard is, however, not adequate for automatically and efficiently matching policies. We need to operate on a more articulated dictionary, using which we can compare and relate different values assigned to a same element of the policy. In particular, it is important to extend and define semantics relationships among elements in the *purpose* element and in the *recipient* elements. To achieve this goal, we consider the hierarchy developed for APPEL [8], a very well known language supporting the specification of privacy preferences by users. The referred data schema for the purpose is illustrated in Figure 2. In Appendix A we report details about the P3P syntax and the APPEL language.

4   Matching Privacy Policies in a Federation

FSP's can exchange user attributes and credentials to automatically authorize users without asking them to submit the same information multiple times. Further, in a medical environment, FSP's may need to access medical records to perform internal activities, such as evaluation of the health state of a patient or definition of patient eligibility to a given exam. We also notice here that sharing patient records may provide important benefits to the patient themselves, in that a physician may have available all information concerning a given patient and therefore perform a more informed diagnosis.

To enable secure information sharing across FSP's, we must assert that the privacy policies of all the FSP's that receive information pertaining to a given individual comply with the privacy preferences of this individual. In a system, like FAMTN, a compliance check can be executed between two FSP's when one FSP (referred to as FSP1) requests one or more user attributes from another FSP (referred to as FSP2). Instead of matching policies against the user preferences, FSP2 can more easily verify whether or not its policies subsume FSP1's. Subsumption reasoning is used on policies defined over equal or similar class of data in order to determine if they conflict.[1] To enhance flexibility and facilitate the task of policy specification of federated providers, we consider two different ways of specifying privacy policies: using *policy templates* or specifying *customized policies*. We assume a profile of policy templates to be pre-defined and available for privacy policy specification. We also assume privacy policy templates to be defined by the federated entities as preliminary agreement of the possible practices of the entities. We will further elaborate on this aspect in our future work.

A FSP may choose to use one of the available templates or can specify its own, customized privacy policies. Similarly, users can specify privacy requirements according to available specific pre-defined templates or they can specify their own requirements. The same FSP can specify policies using templates for some data and specify a customized privacy policy for other. Whether or not the enforced policies are instances of a template, a conservative approach is taken whereby if a request has even the slightest possibility of violating a privacy preference or policy due to some ambiguity, the request will be denied. Essentially, there are only two cases for each interaction: success or failure. A value like *Incompatible* or similar is never returned; instead only *Not Found* is returned. This generic

---

[1] Note that information about the availability of user attributes at FSP2 site is known because of the usage of trust tickets, as illustrated in Section 1.

reply is returned to avoid leak of information from FSP2 to FSP1 based on FSP1 reply (e.g., FSP2 learns that FSP1 has some data if an *Incompatible* reply is given).

4.1 Policy Templates

As introduced, FSP's can simplify the task of policy specification by using policy templates. Each template has a predefined set of values and is standardized across the federation. Each FSP can choose a template $T_i{}^2$ from the set $\{T_1, \ldots, T_n\}$ of available templates. The templates in such set are totally ordered based on the strictness approach that will be followed for data disclosure. Specifically, templates are in descending order, then T_i defines practices that are stricter than those defined by policy template T_k, if $k > i$. In other words, T_k subsumes T_i. To simplify the process of policy specification, templates can be used to specify privacy practices for whole records, attributes or user credentials. In order for information to be released between two FSP's, the associated policies must be compatible. Here, by compatible policies we mean that if data is being released from FSP2 to FSP1, then privacy policy enforced by FSP1's policy should be equal or stricter than the policy applied by FSP2.

As suggested by [9], an example of set of policy templates ordered according the strictness is: { *Strict, Cautious, Moderate, Flexible, Casual* }. Adopting the notation adopted by [9] for the P3P syntax, we provide examples of such policy templates in Tables 1, 2, 3.

Table 1. Sample Strict Policy

Element	Value
Purpose	current
Access	all
Recipient	ours
Retention	stated-purpose, legal-requirement

Table 2. Sample Moderate Policy

Element	Value
Purpose	current, pseudo-analysis, contact
Access	all
Recipient	ours, same
Retention	stated-purpose, legal-requirement

The understanding of the policy illustrated in Table 1 is that data may be used only for the current activity and cannot be shared with others. Element *Recipient* is set to *ours*, meaning that the owner has full access to data and (as by *retention* element) data is kept only as long as the purpose requires or as mandated by law.

The policy template shown in Table 2 is a possible moderate policy and is to be interpreted as follows. The data it refers to may be used for this activity and can be shared with others having the same business practices. Statistical

---

[2] In what follows we refer to T_x as identifiers uniquely identifying the templates, while x denotes the position in the ordering.

records may be kept only with non-identifying information. The understanding of the *Access* element is that owner can be contacted with suggestions concerning treatments or drugs. As in the example of Table 1, owner has full access to data. Data is kept only as long as purpose requires or as mandated by law.

Table 3. Sample Casual Policy

Element	Value
Purpose	current, contact, other-purpose
Access	none
Recipient	ours, other-recipient, unrelated
Retention	indefinitely

Table 4. Policy supporting the privacy requirements described in Example 1

Element	Value
Purpose	current, pseudo-analysis
Access	all
Recipient	ours
Retention	stated-purpose, legal-requirement

In Table 3 a template for a casual policy is reported. The translation on such policy in natural language is as follows. Data may be used for virtually any activity, as stated by the *Purpose* element. Information may be shared with any unrelated entity irrespective of their policies. Owners can be contacted with suggestions concerning treatment or pharmaceutical. Owners may not be able to access or correct data. Finally, as reported by the *Retention* element, data may be kept indefinitely.

If both parties use pre-defined policy templates, policy comparison is straightforward: pre-defined policy templates are totally sorted based on the requirements that need to be met in order to release data. Policy subsumption reasoning is defined by Algorithm 1, encoding the protocol that performs local matching from the perspective of the *FSP1*, which is servicing a request for an attribute A from another service provider *FSP2*. Note that both parties are using policy templates totally sorted in descending order, thus T_k subsumes T_i if $k > i$. Assume that templates $\{T_k, T_i\}$ represent $\{Pol1, Pol2\}$ respectfully, then $isMoreStrict(Pol1, Pol2)$ at line 13 can be performed by checking if $k \leq i$.

It is important to note that the definition of policy templates is to be agreed upon by the federation members. When all entities in a federation use the policy template approach, it is simple to perform policy matching. However, policy templates inherently lack flexibility, and limit the range of preferences and intentions that users and FSP's can express, as illustrated by the following example.

Example 1. *Consider our motivating scenario. Alice might want to use a* Strict *policy as in Table 1, but might also want her data to be shared for statistical/research purposes as long as it cannot be linked to her. She is not able to use a* Cautious *or* Modest *policy because they are not strict enough. Therefore, she*

Algorithm 1. FSP1 services FSP2's request

Require: *Request*
 1: $Attr \Leftarrow Request.Attribute$
 2: $userID \Leftarrow Request.userID$
 3: $Policy \Leftarrow Request.getPolicyOf(Attr)$
 4: $myPolicy \Leftarrow this.userID.getPolicyOf(Attr)$
 5: **if** $Attr \notin this.userID.AttrList$ **then**
 6:     $this.log.Add(Request, notFound, time)$
 7:     **return** $notFound$
 8: **end if**
 9: **if** $isMoreStrict(Policy, myPolicy)$ **then**
10:     $this.log.Add(Request, tooStrict, time)$
11:     **return** $notFound$
12: **end if**
13: $this.log.Add(Request, released, time)$
14: **return** $this.userID.getAttribute(Attr)$

*is not able to completely express her preferences because the privacy preferences
are preset for each policy.*

4.2   Customized Privacy Policies

Customized privacy policies are designed by FSP which can arbitrarily create a
rules that describe how data will be managed. These policies give FSP's a flexible and expressive method for defining their privacy preferences and practices.
However, customized policies are more difficult to specify, match and, typically,
to enforce. Moreover, this flexibility increases the difficulty of policy matching.
It is fair to assume that federation members may refer to similar terms with
different names. For example, FSP1 and FSP2 may refer to the same group of
people as *faculty* or *staff*. In order to determine the relationship between two
different terms while performing local matching we make use of the federated
ontology introduced in Section 3. It would indeed be misleading and error-prone
to enforce a controlled vocabulary across a federation of disjoint entities without
the help of the ontology.

The algorithm for performing local matching between customized FSP policies
is identical to Algorithm 1. However, determining the relative policy strictness
is a more articulated process. This is reflected by modifications to the *isMore-
Strict()* function in order to use the ontology as in Algorithm 2.

An example of a possible customized policy is reported in Table 4, which
solves the problem presented by Example 1. The policy states that data may be
used only for this activity and cannot be shared with others. Statistical records
may be kept only with non-identifying information. Data is kept only as long as
purpose requires or according to the length mandated by law.

An explanation of Algorithm 2 follows. To evaluate the relationship between
two given policies, *Pol1* and *Pol2*, associated respectively with the requester

---

Algorithm 2. isMoreStrict(Pol1, Pol2)

Require: $Pol1, Pol2$ are objects
 1: //For all data elements of Pol1
 2: **for all** $E1 \mid E1 \in Pol1.dataElements$ **do**
 3:     //Get corresponding element from Pol2
 4:     $E2 \Leftarrow getElement(Pol2, E1.name)$;
 5:     **if** $E2 == NULL$ **then**
 6:         **return** NO
 7:     **end if**

 8:     //For all purposes of Pol1.E1
 9:     **for all** $P1 \mid P1 \in Pol1.getPurps(E1.name)$ **do**
10:         $P2 \Leftarrow getPurp(Pol2, E2.name, P1.name)$;
11:         **if** $P2 == NULL \parallel P1 \subseteq P2$ **then**
12:             **return** NO
13:         **end if**
14:     **end for**

15:     //For all retentions of Pol1.E1
16:     **for all** $Ret1 \mid Ret1 \in Pol1.getRets(E1.name)$ **do**
17:         $Ret2 \Leftarrow getRets(Pol2, E2.name, Ret1.name)$;
18:         **if** $P2 == NULL \parallel Ret1 \subseteq Ret2$ **then**
19:             **return** NO
20:         **end if**
21:     **end for**

22:     //For all recipients Pol1.E1
23:     **for all** $Rec1 \mid Rec1 \in Pol1.getRecs(E1.name)$ **do**
24:         $Rec2 \Leftarrow getRets(Pol2, E2.name, Rec1.name)$;
25:         **if** $Rec2 == NULL \parallel Rec1 \subseteq Rec2$ **then**
26:             **return** NO
27:         **end if**
28:     **end for**
29: **end for**
30: **return** YES

---

and the data holder, it is sufficient to analyze the purposes, recipients, and retentions for all data being requested from $Pol1$. Therefore, at line 2, every data element that is being requested by holder of $Pol1$ is evaluated, to determine whether the requester's intended use of the data element is subsumed by those in $Pol2$. Note that (at line 4) we exploit the federated ontology to determine an equal data element or if an equal one does not exist the closest generalization in $Pol2$. Next the algorithm proceeds by examining each purpose in $Pol1$ pertaining to this data element, checking if it is a subset of the purposes pertaining to the same data element from $Pol2$. The same comparisons are then performed for the retention and recipient conditions of the policies. As shown, comparison of purposes, recipients, and retentions are based on the semantic

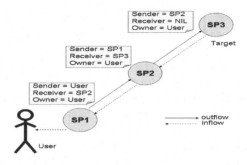

Fig. 3. Example of Policy Tracing execution

hierarchical nature of our vocabulary mentioned in Section 3 (proposed by [2]). Finally, if the purposes, retentions, and recipients of the requesting policy are all subsets of the servicing policy, a positive result is returned. Otherwise the result is negative.

4.3   Policy Tracing Algorithm

Policy tracing is a method for verifying if data have been transmitted from FSP_1 to FSP_k in a path that did not violate the user's privacy preferences. A trace can be initiated by a user who wishes to verify whether his/her privacy preferences have been properly applied as the data was passed to a target FSP (FSP_k in this case). Our solution for tracing is accomplished by a *Policy Tracing* algorithm, illustrated in Algorithm 3. Algorithm *Policy Tracing* is defined in terms of a series of message handlers which provide the necessary functionalities. Intuitively, the algorithm provides a tour of local match verifications, and policy compliance at each step starting from the sink peer FSP_k. The compliance depends on the transcript of the matching assumed to be stored in a tamper proof device at each FSP. Messages for the traces are propagated from the sink FSP to the user. Depending on the direction of the message, represented as an arrow in Figure 3, we define a prover FSP which is at the head of the arrow and a verifier which is at the tail. At each step, compliance is checked by the verifier, which retrieves the prover's logs. The GM_TRACEFAIL method ensures that if a point of failure is found the failure message returns to the target FSP. In case no point of failure is found, the trace message is propagated until it reaches the user. Behavior to signal success or failure could be implemented as a return to the calling algorithm.

To ease the presentation, we provide a detailed example illustrating the main steps of the algorithm (please refer to Figure 3). Alice finds her data at the FSP called SP3. As an initial step Alice checks if her privacy preferences matches the policies of SP3 using the local matching algorithm provided in Section 4.

The algorithm starts with the GM_START module which will spawns off a trace thread. The *inflow* thread goes from SP3 through SP2 and SP1 until it reaches Alice. For each thread instance the GM_TRACE function is called. SP3 first retrieves the sender of the data (which is also the head of the arrow representing the flow) from the log associated with this data. We assume that each such log contains the *sender, receiver* and the *owner* of the data. In the example, SP2 is the sender of the data contained at SP3 and Alice is the owner Now SP3 verifies that the transcript generated at the time of matching at SP2 is correct and does satisfy the privacy policy constraints. If this is true then GM_TRACE is called recursively until the message reaches the user. Otherwise, a GM_TRACEFAIL module is initiated by the verifier which recursively sends a failure message hop by hop to the target. GM_TRACEFAIL will reach the target because the entities in the GM_TRACEFAIL path have been verified to be honest.

Note that if executed multiple times from various sink FSP's a user can control the data related to him shared within the federation and match his/her privacy preferences with respect to all FSP's policies.

4.4   Security Analysis

The policy tracing algorithm is resistant to several types of attacks. Specifically, we address the cases of semi-honest, single malicious, and colluding malicious parties. By semi-honest, we mean parties that will follow the tracing protocol, but try to learn as much information as they can during the interaction. Malicious parties, in our case, correspond to parties that have not performed the local matching correctly and have released user data to parties whose rules for use of data violate the data owner's privacy requirements. Malicious parties may not follow the trace-back protocol and will attempt to circumvent being caught. Colluding malicious parties are multiple parties who can freely exchange user data meanwhile possibly violating the data owner's privacy requirements. One colluding party will never reveal information indicating policy violation by any other colluding party.

The following cases highlight the security features of our tracing algorithm:

Case 1. *All semi-honest parties.*

If all the parties are semi-honest, the initial local matching of the sink and user will always be compliant and the policy matching will be executed successfully.

This is because of the strict subsumption property of the local matching performed at each step when the data is released between any FSP's.

Case 2. *A single malicious party.*

A single malicious party in a trace is identified efficiently by a single execution of the tracing algorithm. The tracing begins at the information sink, that is, the FSP at which user found his/her data. We assume that the sink party is semi-honest (as such, it will follow the protocol)[3]. Let us assume FSP_{k-j}, $j < k$, be the malicious party and FSP_k be the sink FSP. As

---

[3] At this stage further release of the users data from the sink is not investigated. We trust the sink until proof of the contrary is found.

Algorithm 3. Policy Tracing Message Handlers

Require: TargetFSP T, DataObject D {sender, receiver, owner }
 1: **GM_START:**
 2: PostMessage(GM_START, inflow)
 3: **if** (T.containsData(D)) **then**
 4:   PassMessage(GM_TRACE (T,D,inflow), D.sender)
 5: **else**
 6:   PostMessage(GM_FAILURE)
 7: **end if**
 8: **GM_TRACE(Target T, DataObject D, flowtype f):**
 9: **if** (f == inflow *and* I am D.owner) **then**
10:   PostMessage(GM_SUCCESS)
11: **else**
12:   **if** (f==inflow) **then**
13:     sender = D.sender
14:     **if** (localMatchVerify(sender, my ID, data) == TRUE) **then**
15:       PassMessage(GM_TRACE(T,D,f),sender)
16:     **else**
17:       PassMessage(GM_TRACEFAIL(T,D,my ID, outflow)
18:     **end if**
19:   **end if**
20:   **if** (f==outflow) **then**
21:     receiver = D.receiver
22:     **if** (localMatch(my ID, receiver, data) == TRUE) **then**
23:       PassMessage(GM_TRACE(T,D,f),receiver)
24:     **else**
25:       PassMessage(GM_TRACEFAIL(T,D,my ID, inflow)
26:     **end if**
27:   **end if**
28: **end if**

29: **GM_TRACEFAIL(Target T, DataObject D, FailurePoint P, flowtype f):**

30: **if** (f == inflow *and* I am D.owner) or (f == outflow *and* I am T) **then**
31:   signal FALSE
32:   PostMessage(GM_FAILURE || at point P)
33: **else**
34:   **if** (f==inflow) **then**
35:     sender = D.sender
36:     PassMessage(GM_TRACEFAIL(T,D,P,f)
37:   **end if**
38:   **if** (f==outflow) **then**
39:     receiver = D.receiver
40:     PassMessage(GM_TRACEFAIL(T,D,P,f)
41:   **end if**
42: **end if**

the trace continues a recursive procedure is called such that FSP_k checks FSP_{k-1}, FSP_{k-1} checks FSP_{k-2}, and so on. This procedure continues until $FSP_{k-(j-1)}$ is reached. Note that the trace has been executed by honest parties till this point. More precisely, each party's transcript is checked by an honest party before it is delegated the task of checking its parent. Then as $FSP_{k-(j-1)}$ checks FSP_{k-j}'s transcript and finds an error, it will send a GM_TRACEFAIL message towards the sink such that the resulting error is notified at the sink.

Case 3. *Non-consecutive malicious parties.*

Once the first malicious party is found, as described above, there could still be other parties along the data path who are also dishonest. Again, assume FSP_{k-j}, $1 \leq j < k$, be the malicious party and FSP_k be the sink FSP. After FSP_{k-j} is identified as malicious (as in above example), FSP_{k-j-1} which is the FSP from whom FSP_{k-j}, received data is assigned as the next sink. In this case FSP_{k-j-1} is assumed to be trusted to not have released the data incorrectly. If FSP_{k-j-1}, is found non compliant with the users original policy then the only possibility is that other parties in the rest of the path are malicious. Hence, the tracing mechanism is called repeatedly in order to catch multiple malicious parties along the original trace of the data. In case FSP_{k-j-1} is compliant then there the release of data till this point has been executed correctly and no further trace is needed.

Case 4. *Consecutive or colluding malicious parties.*

The presence of colluding parties can be detected if the sink's policy is not subsumed by the user's policy, and after the trace no GM_TRACEFAIL message is propagated to the user. In this case we require the transcript verification run at each node by a trusted third party (TTP) in a brute force manner. This TTP can also be the sink or the user itself. TTP follows the same trace protocol with the only difference that it does the verifications. Once an error is found, the GM_TRACEFAIL message is propagated exactly the same as the original protocol.

5   Related Work

Our work is originally motivated from the existing initiatives related to federated digital identity management whose goal is to provide a controlled and protected environment for managing identities of federated users. In this section we first explore the most relevant federated digital identity management initiatives and then overview work related to privacy policy specification and enforcement.

In the corporate world there are several emerging standards for identity federation like Liberty Alliance [10] (LA) and WS-Federation. Because the projects are very similar we describe the former in more detail. LA is based on SAML and provides open standards for SSO with decentralized authentication. SSO allows a user to sign-on once at a Liberty-enabled site in order to be seamlessly signed-on when navigating to another site without the need to authenticate again. This group of Liberty-enabled sites is a part of what is called a *circle of trust*, which is a federation of SP's and identity providers having business relationships based on the Liberty architecture. The identity provider is a Liberty-enabled entity that creates, maintains and manages identity information of users and gives this information to the SP's. As compared to LA which has the identity provider as the only identity provisioning entity, our approach can protect sharing even when the provisioning is being done from the service providers that the user has visited. Such an approach provides privacy, flexibility and usability to the identity system. This is especially useful in the context of health data where the leakage of such information can have serious consequences.

Shibboleth [11] is an initiative by universities that are members of Internet2. The goal of such initiative is to develop and deploy new middleware technologies that can facilitate inter-institutional collaboration and access to digital contents. It uses the concept of federation of user attributes. When a user at an institution tries to use a resource at another, Shibboleth sends attributes about the user to the remote destination, rather than making the user log into that destination, thus enabling a seamless access. The receiver can check whether the attributes satisfy its own policies. Our approach differs with respect to Shibboleth in that we do not rely on a central identity provider providing all user attributes. User attributes in our framework are distributed within the different federation members, each of which can effectively be an identity provider. We also provide a mechanism for local and global matching which have not been well defined in federated identity management systems.

Regarding privacy, lots of researchers are actively working on privacy policy specification. The Platform for Privacy Preferences Project (P3P) is an attempt to provide a standardized, XML based policy specification language that can be used to specify an organizations privacy practices in a way that can be parsed and used by policy-checking agents on the users behalf [12].

Many user software agents are currently available for use (e.g. Privacy Bird2, Privacy Companion3, Internet Explorer 6.04), which handle policy checking and invoke the required actions that need to occur when a websites policy is found to conflict with the user's preferences. These actions range from blocking a particular webpage from being displayed, to placing a warning icon in the users browser status bar.

E-P3P[13] is a privacy policy language for expressing an enterprise-wide privacy policy. Its goals are different than P3P, in that it is geared towards internal policy enforcement and business practices, rather than expression of a policy to a user agent. As such, it supports enterprise-defined user roles, purposes, and arbitrary conditions and obligations that must be fulfilled. E-P3P expresses a privacy policy in abstract user role and data categories. The association of these with actual data and users or user groups in a system is outside the scope of E-P3P. E-P3P assumes an enterprise-wide policy, where users can opt-in or opt-out.

Finally, a work more closely related to ours is represented by IBMs Enterprise Privacy Authorization Language (EPAL) [2]. EPAL's authors propose an approach to achieve machine enforceable policies [14]. Like P3P, EPAL is an XML-based privacy policy specification language, specifically designed for organizations to specify internal privacy policies. EPAL policies can be used internally and amongst the organization and its business partners to ensure compliance different purposes and scopes, but to evaluate each languages expressiveness for specifying natural language privacy policies. In our work, we do not propose a new language. Rather, we focus on the deployment of protocols to facilitate privacy policy harmonization within federated entities. Further, differently from EPAL, we propose an approach to check users' privacy preferences compliance based on policy traceability.

6   Conclusion

In this paper we address the problem of privacy in a federated environment. In particular, we attempt to satisfy two important requirements. The first requirement is to provide mechanisms for facilitating privacy policies matching and harmonization among federated SP's. The second requirement is to provide mechanisms making it possible for users to trace their identity information across the federation, and verify whether it has been managed according to their privacy preferences.

To achieve such goals we have developed an approach that supports the privacy controlled sharing of identity attributes and the harmonization of privacy policies based on the notion of subsumption. This approach relies on the P3P language and federated ontology. Two well defined ways of specifying privacy policies have been proposed, that is, by use of pre-defined policy templates or by defining customized policies. We have also devised two main protocols to provide harmonization of the privacy policies at the local and global levels respectively. Our approach entails a form of accountability since an entity non-compliant with the users original privacy preferences can be identified. A comprehensive security analysis details security properties offered by our approach.

An interesting challenge that must be addressed to achieve effective privacy protection is maintaining data management consistency, as privacy practices and preferences might change over time. In the current work we do not take into account update of such policies after the data has been released. We will address such an issue in our future work.

In addition, we plan to extend this work along several other directions. The first concerns the conservative approach we took while determining the subsumption criteria for the local matching to avoid inference. We will further explore other inference problems to allow flexible subsumption criteria. Second, in our current work we assume privacy policy templates to be defined by the federated entities as preliminary agreement of the possible practices of the entities. We plan to define reasonable templates and their extension for customized policies. Third we are developing more articulated conflict resolution techniques in the tracing algorithm, taking into account the exact mismatch that occurred due to which the policies were non-compliant. We believe this will provide a mechanism to extend the search of multiple malicious and colluding parties such that all non-compliant entities are held accountable.

Acknowledgement

The work reported in this paper has been sponsored by NSF under the ITR Project 0428554 "The Design and Use of Digital Identities". Intel has provided the fellowship to fund Alexei Czeskis.

References

1. http://www.w3.org/TR/P3P/:   (The Platform for Privacy Preferences 1.0 (P3P1.1) specification)
2. http://www.zurich.ibm.com/security/enterprise privacy/epal/: (EPAL 1.0 Specification)
3. Spantzel, A.B., Squicciarini, A.C., Bertino, E.: Integrating federated digital identity management and trust negotiation. In: Review for the IEEE Security and Privacy Magazine. (2005)
4. Gruber, T.R.: A translation approach to portable ontology specifications. Knowledge Acquisition 5(2) (1993) 199–220
5. Doan, A., Madhavan, J., Domingos, P., Halevy, A.: Ontology Matching: A Machine Learning Approach (2003)
6. Uschold, M., Gruninger, M.: Ontologies: Principles, Methods, and Applications. Knowledge Engineering Review 11(2) (1996) 93–155
7. Maedche, A., Motik, B., NunoSilva, Volz, R.: MAFRA – a MApping FRAmework for distributed ontologies. Lecture Notes in Computer Science 2473 (2002) 235–241
8. http://www.w3.org/TR/P3P preferences/: (P3P Preference Exchange Language 1.0 (APPEL1.0))
9. Alliance, L.: Liberty architecture framework for supporting privacy preference expression languages (ppel's) (2003)
10. http://www.projectliberty.org: (Liberty Alliance Project)
11. http://shibboleth.internet2.edu: (Shibboleth, Internet2)
12. Cranor, L.F.: P3P: Making privacy policies more useful. Volume 1. (2003) 50–55
13. Paul Ashley, Satoshi Hada, G.K., Schunter, M.: E-P3P Privacy Policies and Privacy Authorization. In: Proceedings of the Workshop on Privacy in the Electronic Society (WPES). (2001)
14. Stufflebeam, W.H., Antón, A.I., He, Q., Jain, N.: Specifying privacy policies with P3P and EPAL: lessons learned. In: Proceedings of the Workshop on Privacy in the Electronic Society (WPES). (2004) 35
15. http://www.switch.ch/aai/documents.html: (Switchaai Federation)
16. http://www.incommonfederation.org/: (InCommon Federation)
17. http://www.csc.fi/suomi/funet/middleware/:
    (HAKA Federation Finland Federation)

18. Overhage, S., Thomas, P.: Ws-specification: Specifying web services using uddi improvements. In: Revised Papers from the NODe 2002 Web and Database-Related Workshops on Web, Web-Services, and Database Systems, London, UK, Springer-Verlag (2003) 100–119

A   P3P Policy Language

A P3P privacy policy is specified by one policy element that includes the following major elements: *entity, access, extension,* and *statement.* The *entity* element identifies the legal entity making the representation of privacy practices contained in the policy. The access element indicates whether the site allows users to access the various kind of information collected about them. The *extension* is an optional element describing a website's self defined extension to the P3P specification. One or more *statement* elements are defined in a policy. A statement is the core of the policy as it defines the data and the data categories collected by the site, as well as the purposes, recipients and retention of that data. Each statement contain the following:

- *data* denotes a data element. In P3P each DATA element has a set of categories associated with it. Some categories are implicitly specified by the base P3P data schema whereas some others are defined by the policy itself;
- *purp* denotes purposes for data processing; *purpose* element assumes on or more pre-defined value in {*current, admin, tailoring, pseudoanalysis*}.
- *retention* denotes the type of retention and assumes values in {*no-retention, stated-purpose, legal-requirement, business-practice, indefinitely*} according to the P3P standard taxonomy;
- *recipient* is the legal entity, or domain, beyond the service provider and its agents where data may be distributed; *recipient* can assume one value in {*ours, legal, delivery, unrelated, ...*};

Example 1. Consider the following P3P policy:

```
<STATEMENT>
  <PURPOSE>
   <individual-decision required=
    "opt-out"/> </PURPOSE>
  <RECIPIENT><ours/></RECIPIENT>
  <RETENTION><stated-purpose/>
  </RETENTION>
  <DATA-GROUP>
    <DATA ref="#user.name.given"/>
    <DATA ref="#dynamic.cookies">
      <CATEGORIES><preference/>
       <uniqueid/>
      </CATEGORIES>
```

```
    </DATA>
   </DATA-GROUP>
  </STATEMENT>
```

Since P3P has not been specifically conceived for negotiations within federation, its syntax include data elements that are not of interest to trust negotiations, such as *click-stream*. In the following, we always limit our analysis to elements having a corresponding concept in our reference ontology. Such data elements can then be used to evaluate privacy concepts.

B   APPEL Preference Language

With respect to APPEL(ACCENT Project Policy Environment/Language) the privacy preferences are expressed in as a list of RULEs [8]. These rules are matched against a policy in the order in which they appear. A rule consists of two parts:

- Rule behavior (Rule head): Specifies the action to be taken if the rule fires. The behavior can be request, implying that the policy conforms to preferences specified in the rule body. It can be block, implying that the policy does not respect user's preferences.
- Rule body: Provides the pattern that is matched against a policy. The format of a pattern follows the XML structure used in specifying privacy policies described earlier.

An APPEL rule is satisfied by matching its constituent expressions and recursively their subexpressions. Every APPEL expression has a connective attribute that defines the logical operators between its subexpressions. An example of an APPEL policy is as follows:

```
<appel:RULESET>
 <appel:RULE behavior="block">
   <POLICY>
     <STATEMENT>
      <PURPOSE appel:connective="or">
      <contact/>
      <telemarketing/>
      </PURPOSE>
     </STATEMENT>
   </POLICY>
 </appel:RULE>

<appel:RULE behavior="request"/>
  <appel:OTHERWISE/>
  </appel:RULE>
</appel:RULESET>
```

C   Federation Examples

Table 5. Federation Examples

SWITCHaai Federation [15] The SWITCHaai Federation is a group of organizations like universities, hospitals and libraries, that have agreed to cooperate regarding inter-organizational authentication and authorization. They operate a Shibboleth-based authentication and authorization infrastructure (AAI).
InCommon [16] By using Shibboleth authentication and authorization technology, InCommon intends to make sharing of protected resources easier, enabling collaboration between InCommon participants which protects privacy. Access decisions to protected resources are based on user attributes contributed by the user's home institution. InCommon became operational on 5 April 2005.
HAKA Federation [17] The HAKA Federation in Finland entered its production phase in late 2004. The Federation was set up in 2003, currently including 2 (of 20) universities and 1 (of 29) polytechnics as Identity Providers, and 4 service providers, including the National Library Portal (Nelli). In Finland, the libraries in higher education traditionally co-operate widely in licensing electronic journals. It is based on Shibboleth.
Microsoft, IBM, WS* [18] In April 2002, Microsoft and IBM published a joint whitepaper outlining a roadmap for developing a set of Web service security specifications. Their first jointly-developed specification, WS-Security, offers a mechanism for attaching security tokens to messages, including tokens related to identity.
Liberty Alliance [10] The Liberty Alliance is a consortium of approximately 170 companies that develops specifications for federated identity management. It works on creating a single comprehensive federated identity specification. In March 2003, it released a new blueprint that described three separate specifications that can be used together or independently: First is the Identity Federation Framework (ID-FF) allows single sign-on and account linking between partners with established trust relationships. Second is Identity Web Services Framework (ID-WSF), allows groups of trusted partners to link to other groups, and gives users control over how their information is shared. Finally Identity Services Interface Specifications (ID-SIS) will build a set of interoperable services on top of the ID-WSF.

Privacy Injector — Automated Privacy Enforcement Through Aspects

Chris Vanden Berghe[1,2] and Matthias Schunter[1]

[1] IBM Research, Zurich Research Laboratory
Säumerstrasse 4, CH-8803 Rüschlikon, Switzerland
{vbc, mts}@zurich.ibm.com
[2] Katholieke Universiteit Leuven
Celestijnenlaan 200A, B-3001 Leuven, Belgium
chrisvdb@cs.kuleuven.be

Abstract. Protection of personal data is essential for customer acceptance. Even though existing privacy policies can describe how data shall be handled, privacy enforcement remains a challenge. Especially for existing applications, it is unclear how one can effectively ensure correct data handling without completely redesigning the applications. In this paper we introduce Privacy Injector, which allows us to add privacy enforcement to existing applications.

Conceptually Privacy Injector consists of two complementary parts, namely, a privacy metadata tracking and a privacy policy enforcement part. We show how Privacy Injector protects the complete life cycle of personal data by providing us with a practical implementation of the "sticky policy paradigm." Throughout the collection, transformation, disclosure and deletion of personal data, Privacy Injector will automatically assign, preserve and update privacy metadata as well as enforce the privacy policy. As our approach is policy-agnostic, we can enforce any policy language that describes which actions may be performed on which data.

1 Introduction

An increasing number of enterprises make privacy promises to meet customer demand or to implement privacy regulations. As a consequence, enterprises aim at protecting data against accidental misuse, including unwarranted disclosure and over-retention. Recent approaches towards formalizing privacy regulations have addressed the issue of how permitted data usage can be formalized [3,10,14,16]. However, in practice two major challenges remain. The first challenge is to assess the actual privacy status of an enterprise, i.e., what data is stored and what data has been collected under what policy. The second challenge is how to enforce the given privacy promise consistently throughout existing and new applications.

A first step in addressing these challenges has been the "sticky policy paradigm" as proposed in Karjoth et al. [16]. This paradigm requires that a privacy promise made to a data subject stick to the data to later identify how this data can be used. For cross-enterprise transfer, policy refinement can be used to enforce sticky policies [3]. However, for enterprise-internal use, there is no clear concept how policies can be reliably

G. Danezis and P. Golle (Eds.): PET 2006, LNCS 4258, pp. 99–117, 2006.

associated with data and how policies can be managed. This holds in particular for existing enterprise applications in which privacy enforcement was not included as a non-functional design requirement.

In this paper we introduce Privacy Injector, which leverages the Aspect-Oriented Software Development (AOSD) [9] paradigm to modularize and encapsulate privacy enforcement. This allows us to add privacy enforcement functionality late in the software development cycle or even in the maintenance phase of applications. Privacy Injector consists of a *privacy metadata tracking* part and a *privacy policy enforcement* part. The former is a practical implementation of the aforementioned sticky policy paradigm, whereas the latter is responsible for the actual enforcement of the sticky policies.

The privacy metadata tracking part consists of three components. The first component, *privacy metadata assignment*, is responsible for assigning the appropriate privacy metadata to data that enters the system. This is achieved by instrumenting the input vectors of the execution platform, i.e., all functions responsible for collecting external data. The second component, *metadata-preserving data operations*, is responsible for preserving and updating this privacy metadata when operations are performed on this data. This is achieved by instrumenting all data operations to update the privacy metadata to reflect changes resulting from the operations. The third component, *metadata persistence*, is responsible for preserving, restoring, updating and removing privacy metadata when data is made persistent, retrieved, modified or removed, respectively. This is accomplished by leveraging the event systems exposed by persistence services.

The privacy policy enforcement part ensures that the appropriate tests and actions specified by the privacy policy are performed upon usage and disclosure of the data. The different ways in which data can be disclosed are called output vectors, which are again instrumented and retrofitted with the policy-enforcing functionality. For example, when an application calls the API for sending e-mail, this function is intercepted and the required conditions and obligations, as described by the privacy metadata attached to the function's parameters, are checked and the necessary actions performed.

We rely on the Aspect-Oriented Software Development paradigm for implementing the instrumentation, i.e., for making the connection between Privacy Injector and the target application. Our method is platform-independent, although we focus on Java to illustrate our concepts for this paper. Privacy Injector does not require the source code of the target applications; however it makes some assumptions about the target applications that will be discussed later in this paper.

The goal of this work is to show that Privacy Injector provides a useful methodology for implementing the sticky policy paradigm and enforcing privacy in applications in which privacy enforcement was not included as a design goal. In this paper we focus on preventing *unwarranted disclosure of personal data*; other possible and potentially valuable use-cases, e.g., preventing over-retention of personal data, are only touched upon briefly.

1.1 Outline

In Section 2 we discuss related work on privacy policies, privacy enforcement, flow control, and aspect-oriented software development. In Section 3 we discuss the life cycle of personal data. In Section 4 we introduce Privacy Injector conceptually, whereas

Section 5 is devoted the implementation details of our prototype. In Section 6 describes the benefits and limitations of our approach, and Section 7 concludes the paper.

2   Related Work

2.1   Privacy Policies and Policy Attachment

We distinguish privacy policies and privacy notices. Formalized privacy policies were described in [3,10,14,16]. Privacy policy languages formalize which users can perform which operations on given data types for which purpose [5]. In addition, privacy policies can specify conditions (such as usage only during day-time; see [21]) or obligations (such as limited retention; see [4,7,13,27]). Similarly to the approach described in this paper, privacy policies aim at enterprise-internal use.

Privacy notices, on the other hand, formalize the privacy promises of an enterprise to end-users. The World Wide Web Consortium has standardized the Platform for Privacy Preferences (P3P) that allows enterprises to declare which data is collected and how it will be used [22]. The adoption rate of P3P, however, remains relatively low [8].

When comparing the two approaches, languages for enterprise-internal privacy practices and technical privacy policy enforcement offer finer-grained distinction of users, purposes, etc.

An open challenge is how to implement sound policy management for privacy policies and how policies can be enforced, namely, how policies can be attached to data and how they can be enforced automatically. Karjoth et al. [16] propose the "sticky policy paradigm" that defines that a privacy promise made to the data subject should stick to the data to later identify how this data may be used. As addressed in [2,3], sticky policy transfer between enterprises can be implemented using policy comparison. Policy attachment and enforcement for legacy applications remain an open challenge.

2.2   Privacy Policy Enforcement

Privacy policy enforcement has several aspects, depending on the life cycle of the personal data that is collected and used (see Section 3). For data protection during collection, consistent use of privacy notices is essential. Privacy notices can be formalized using P3P [22], whereas their consistent use can be verified using the Watchfire tool [30]. Enforcement of privacy policies depends heavily on the systems that store and handle personal data. IBM has published technologies for declaring and enforcing privacy policies for Java Beans [12].

For policy enforcement inside databases, the concept of Hippocratic databases has been described in [1]. The core idea is to use SQL rewriting to include policy evaluation into the (modified) databased query that is actually being processed. This enables the database to automatically return the subset of records where usage is authorized. For newly built applications in which policy authorization can be delegated to an authorization engine, various authorization engines have been designed, including the one described in [21]. These engines enable an application to query whether a certain use of data is allowed.

2.3   Flow Control

Language-based information flow security was surveyed by Sabelfeld and Myers in [28]. The main focus of current research is to statically determine potential flows and whether a program complies with a desired flow-control policy. Flow-control approaches that perform static checking need to perform a worst-case analysis to catch all potential violations. To resolve this problem, Myers [19,20] proposes a Java extension called JFlow that annotates Java code using flow-control constructs. This enables a pre-compiler that performs a static verification and then generates Java code that performs additional run-time checks.

The advantage of Privacy Injector over the existing approaches lies mainly in its practical applicability. For example, it does not require to have the application's source code available. Nor does it require a modified runtime or special language constructs; a simple configuration file specifying the policy suffices in most cases. Finally, no flow-control policy must be known at compile time, in contrast to the existing approaches where this forms a major obstacle in their acceptance because the privacy policy actually consented to is only determined at run-time.

Three design choices contribute to this improved practical applicability: the use of the AOSD paradigm, some assumptions made about the applications (discussed further) and a different adversary model. Rather than aiming at also identifying and preventing hidden information flow, we focus on an adversary model in which a non-malicious developer accidentally uses or discloses data in a manner violating the privacy policy.

2.4   Aspect-Oriented Software Development

Aspect-Oriented Software Development (AOSD) [9] is a software engineering paradigm that enables the *Separation of Concerns* [23], i.e., the breaking down of applications into components that minimize the overlap in functionality. In particular, AOSD focuses on the modularization and encapsulation of cross-cutting concerns.

Cross-cutting concerns are areas of interest that cannot easily be separated and encapsulated through existing software development paradigms such as object-oriented or procedural programming. Logging is the archetypical example, as it touches every logged component, and existing software development paradigms force program code responsible for the logging functionality to be scattered throughout these components.

AOSD refers to software development as a whole, including design, testing, etc., whereas Aspect-Oriented Programming (AOP) [18] refers specifically to the programming part. Several distinct AOP implementations exist, each providing language constructs to express both the cross-cutting concerns (the advice) as well as the points in the application at which the advice should be integrated (the join points), and tools for performing the actual integration (weaving). In this work we will use AspectJ [17,25], which is the most popular and widely supported AOP implementation for Java.

AspectJ provides a fine-grained qualification of the join points, called pointcuts, enabling instrumentation of methods, constructors, field access, etc., of which the selection is based on a combination of name, return type, parameters, etc. The actual weaving step of AspectJ is performed at the byte-code level, and thus no access to the target application's source code is required to provide it with additional functionality.

Although the principle of separation of concerns originally served mainly as a guideline for structuring application functionality, it has more recently been applied to separate the non-functional from the functional application requirements. One important non-functional application requirement that has proved difficult to separate or modularize with standard software development tools and methodologies is security. One reason for that is the cross-cutting nature of security. In [31] De Win et al. investigate the usefulness of AOP for secure software development.

3 The Life Cycle of Personal Data

Protecting personal data throughout its entire life cycle is essential to implement a given privacy notice. We now define a life cycle model of personal data as well as the corresponding privacy metadata that is required to track the life cycle and usage of personal data. Figure 1 shows the UML sequence diagram representation [6] of the life cycle of some personal data given out by data subject DS to enterprise A, which stores it in storage A and discloses it in turn to enterprise B. The arrows represent the direction of the data flow resulting from an action, the parameters represent the context required for enforcing the privacy of a particular action. The quotes represent changes to the parameters, e.g., *consent* is the consent given by the data subject to enterprise A, whereas *consent'* refers to the consent given to enterprise B (i.e., a subset of the original consent) and *consent"* refers to the additional consent requested by enterprise B. The boxed area shows the domain in which Privacy Injector is active, i.e., the enterprise-internal usage of personal data. Privacy enforcement for cross-enterprise transfer can however also benefit from it. In Section 4 we show how the life cycle phases are protected by Privacy Injector.

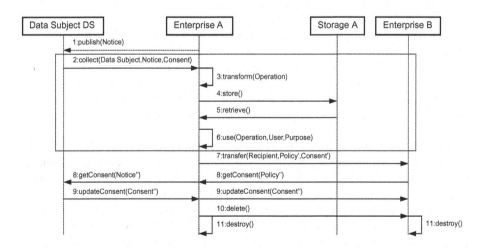

Fig. 1. Life cycle and flow of personal data

Publication (1): Before actual collection of personal data, the enterprise publishes a privacy notice describing the intended use of the the data subject's personal data. This is typically done by displaying a notice on a website or as part of a web form. This flow is independent of the actual data flows and is therefore represented by a dotted line.

Collection (2): Data subject DS consents with the privacy notice and sends personal information to the enterprise. During this data-collection flow, the collecting enterprise associates the personal data with the privacy metadata required to enforce its privacy notice to the data subject. The privacy metadata includes the following:

> *Data Subject*: The person whose personal data has been collected
> *Privacy policy*: The privacy policy that governs the data's usage
> *Consent*: Opt-in and opt-out choices as collected from the data subject

The identifier for the data subject is needed if the privacy notice promises notification under certain circumstances. The privacy policy formalizes the intended use of the data and governs the data's usage. The privacy policy is a refinement of the privacy notice that has been consented to by the data subject. For example, whereas a notice may say "we share your data with our partners for processing orders", the privacy policy should list the actual partners. It is complemented by the consent, which defines opt-in and opt-out choices that refine the usages defined in the privacy policy.

Transformation (3): Most data is subjected to several transformation operations throughout its lifetime. These transformation operations typically normalize, merge and extract data to make it suitable for its environment and purpose. Although these operations are very common, they constitute a challenge that has not been addressed by earlier approaches. In particular, ensuring that the associated privacy metadata remains consistent with the transformed data is non-trivial.

Storage and Retrieval (4 & 5): One common type of data operation is storage and retrieval using a database or other persistent storage. The privacy metadata associated with the personal data should "survive" such storage and retrieval operations. For this, the privacy metadata is stored and retrieved together with the data it belongs to. Persistent storage media, e.g., relational databases, are typically not metadata-aware, and this functionality will thus have to be provisioned by another system component.

Usage (6): When data is accessed by a certain user of the enterprise to perform a certain operation for a given purpose, this usage must be authorized. The context (operation, user and purpose) must be compared with the conditions described in the privacy policy that is configured by the consent associated with the data. The usage can then either be authorized and the obligations carried out, or else usage can be denied and potential mis-use logged for auditing purposes. The actual context information required to make the authorization decision is privacy-policy-dependent. In some cases the privacy policy applies to the entire enterprise and thus no user information is required. In other cases, additional context information, for example, about the country in which the operation takes place, might be required.

Cross-enterprise transfer (7-11): Transfer of personal data is a special type of usage in which there is a protocol between two enterprises. The sending enterprise first verifies whether the personal data may be transferred to the recipient. If the privacy policy and consent allow such a transfer, the data is transferred together with the original privacy policy and consent or else with a refined privacy policy and consent that adhere to the original privacy policy and consent (see [3,2,15] for a policy management framework for disclosures). For proper disclosure management, additional privacy metadata is needed:

Sources: Organizations where data has been obtained
(Recipient,Policy',Consent'): Recipients plus governing policies and consents

If an enterprise wants to use data for a purpose that has not been consented to during collection, it can recursively request consent from the party from whom the data was obtained (8 & 9). If a collecting enterprise has promised complete deletion, then it can trigger recursive deletion of the data by requesting deletion to all data recipients and then deleting its own data after obtaining appropriate acknowledgements (10 & 11).

4   Privacy Injector

In this section we introduce Privacy Injector, which leverages the AOSD paradigm to modularize and encapsulate privacy enforcement. This allows us to add privacy enforcement functionality late in the software development cycle or even to existing applications. Privacy Injector builds upon the idea behind context-sensitive string evaluation (CSSE) [24], which defines a metadata tracking and validation system used for preventing injection attacks. This paper shows how we can leverage and extend this idea to create a practical privacy enforcement. Privacy Injector consists of two complementary parts: a *privacy metadata tracking* part and a *privacy policy enforcement* part. The former is a practical implementation of the aforementioned sticky policy paradigm, whereas the latter is responsible for the actual enforcement of the sticky policies.

4.1   Privacy Metadata Tracking

Three components make up the privacy metadata tracking part: the *Privacy metadata assignment* component is responsible for assigning the appropriate privacy metadata to data that enters the system. The *metadata-preserving data operations* component is responsible for preserving and updating this privacy metadata when operations are performed on it. And the *metadata persistence* component is responsible for preserving, restoring, updating or removing privacy metadata when data is made persistent, retrieved, modified or removed, respectively.

Note that these components are mostly application- and enterprise-independent, and thus only need to be developed once per execution platform (e.g., Java, .NET) and can be used on a wide variety of applications and enterprises. Application- or enterprise-specific customizations are possible through configuration settings. In the remainder of this section, we describe the privacy policy-tracking components in more detail.

Privacy Metadata Assignment. The initial step in a policy-tracking system is the assignment of privacy metadata to personal data. In Privacy Injector, this is the responsibility of the privacy metadata assignment component and performed upon entry of personal data into the system through one of the input vectors. Typical input vectors include parameters from web requests, direct input, web services requests, e-mail, etc.

The assignment of the privacy metadata is achieved through instrumentation of the API functions exposed by the execution platform responsible for the input vectors. For example, by instrumenting the API functions for retrieving the contents of cookies contained in web requests, we ensure that all data returned by these functions will have the appropriate privacy metadata assigned to it. Input received from persistent storage is treated separately by the metadata persistence component.

The privacy metadata assignment component operates fully automatically; therefore it relies on a configuration file that specifies for each input vector the conditions under which certain privacy metadata is to be assigned to data of this input vector. A simple policy could specify that no user-provided web request parameters with the name "credit card" are to be made persistent. A more complex policy could add that the restriction is only applicable under certain conditions, e.g., if the request originates from a particular country. The relevant conditions depend on the input vector. A conservative default can be specified in case some input does not match the specified conditions.

As implementing privacy metadata assignment using traditional software development methodologies requires code scattered throughout the applications, it can be seen as a cross-cutting concern that is suited for modularization through AOSD. AOSD allows us to modularize this functionality into advice and pointcuts: the former contains the actual program code responsible for the policy assignment, whereas the latter describe how the input vectors are to be intercepted and instrumented with the advice.

The location and representation of the privacy metadata are implementation choices. Conceptually, the policy travels together with the personal data. In practical implementations, however, the privacy metadata can be either stored in a system-wide policy repository or truly be part of the data. The representation of the privacy metadata is also an implementation issue, and, depending on the needs, it is possible to assign arbitrary privacy metadata containing any combination of data (e.g., consent data, data subject) and privacy policy in either declarative or programmatic form.

Metadata-Preserving Data Operations. During its life cycle, data undergoes a chain of operations that normalize and transform it into the desired form. A privacy metadata tracking system has to ensure that the privacy metadata assigned is not lost but correctly updated when such operations are performed on the data. In Privacy Injector, this is the responsibility of the metadata-preserving data operations component.

To achieve this, all data-manipulation operations are intercepted and instrumented to update the privacy metadata to reflect changes resulting from the operations on the data, i.e., to make them "metadata-preserving." For example, when two strings are concatenated, the privacy metadata of the resulting string will have to reflect to which policy its different fragments adhere. Note that we intercept data operations at the level of the primitive data types of the execution platform.

For this paper, we assume that personal data is stored in strings, and concentrate on the string-level representation of data and corresponding string-manipulation functions. This is not an inherent limitation, and our method can equally be applied to other data types and their corresponding data-manipulation functions. In the case of strings, we assign privacy metadata per string fragment, as opposed to per string as a whole. This allows fine-grained specification of which fragments adhere to which policy and hence execution of the checks defined by the policy on only the relevant fragments.

Different transformation operations will yield different effects on the privacy metadata. Some operations, for example, changing the case of textual data, will have no influence on the privacy status of the data and such operations do not affect the privacy metadata. Other operations, for example anonymization [29], yield data that is no longer personal and thus privacy metadata needs to be removed or updated to reflect this. Yet other operations will result in a more complex interaction with the privacy metadata. An example of a very interesting and common operation is the merging of data.

There are two complementary approaches for handling the metadata of merged personal data. The first is fine-grained policy association, in which different policies are associated with the individual parts that constitute the data. The second approach is policy algebras, in which the appropriate merged metadata is calculated. When no accurate policy algebra is known for the operation, a conservative approach is to have the merged data governed by the policies of all input data. In the exceptional case of contradictory policies the most conservative action has to be selected or human intervention has to be requested.

Metadata Persistence. A particularly important data operation is persistence, most commonly in relational databases. Privacy Injector specifies a metadata persistence component responsible for preserving, restoring, updating or removing privacy metadata when data is stored, retrieved, modified or removed, respectively. One possibility to implement this component to use a technique similar to the other components, namely, the interception and instrumentation of the appropriate persistence functions. Another related technique is SQL rewriting as used in Hippocratic databases [1]. However, implementing either of these techniques is a daunting task as it would require parsing and syntactical analysis of each SQL query to ensure correct privacy metadata persistence.

As an alternative, we propose a new technique that leverages the event system exposed by persistence services. The goal of such services is to abstract data persistence away from the applications. Applications therefore no longer perform SQL queries directly, but rely on the persistence service to store, retrieve and update their objects. The developers only describe the mapping of a particular object to database tables, and it is the responsibility of the persistence service to perform the actual mapping between the objects and the database. The best known persistence service is Hibernate [26].

The proposed metadata persistence component builds upon the fine-grained event systems exposed by persistence services. Upon storing an object in the database, the metadata persistence component will receive an event and examine the privacy metadata of the object. When indeed privacy metadata is attached to this object, it will also be made persistent. Similarly, when an object is restored, updated or removed, a corresponding event will be sent to the metadata persistence component, which will respectively restore, update or remove the persisted privacy metadata.

This rather unconventional use of the event system exposed by persistence services allows us to turn the difficult problem of policy persistence into a more manageable one as no parsing or syntactical analysis of SQL queries is required. On the other hand, this comes at the expense of a reduced applicability of our method. We believe, however, that the current trend towards the use of persistence services for enterprise applications will continue as such persistence services themselves are rapidly becoming more mature and the resulting applications prove more flexible and easier to maintain.

4.2 Privacy Policy Enforcement

The privacy policy enforcement part ensures that the appropriate tests and actions specified by the privacy policy are performed upon usage and disclosure of the data. The different ways in which data can be disclosed are called output vectors, which are again intercepted and instrumented with the policy-enforcing functionality. For example, when an application calls the API for sending e-mail, this function is intercepted and the required conditions and obligations, as described by the privacy metadata attached to the function's parameters, are checked and the necessary actions performed.

Privacy Injector is policy-agnostic and only responsible for ensuring that the specified policy is notified of all relevant uses of the personal data and provided with the correct contextual information. The policy itself is executable, and can either be programmatically defined or interpret a declarative privacy policy configured during the privacy policy assignment.

As such, the conditions and actions supported are only limited by the expressiveness of the programming or privacy policy language used. Conditions are typically specified in function of the context of the usage or disclosure (e.g., usage/disclosure type, time of day, recipient, ...) and the attached privacy metadata (e.g., data subject, consent, type of data, ...). Practically, actions are mostly limited by their effect on the target application. Typical actions include logging the request, blocking the request (e.g., by throwing an exception), notifying the data subject, delaying the request while asking for additional consent, etc. Yet another possible action is changing or removing the personal information being disclosed, e.g., obscuring all but 4 digits of a credit-card number. This can however impact the application in unforeseen ways, and should thus be done with utmost caution.

5 Prototype Implementation

In this section we introduce a prototype implementation of Privacy Injector and focus on the technical aspects of implementing the concepts introduced in Section 4. Implementing a complex system such as Privacy Injector involves making several important and less important design decisions. Although we describe many of the particular design decisions we made in the prototype, the goal of this section is not to convince the reader that these are the best ones possible. The goal is rather to demonstrate the practical feasibility of Privacy Injector, to learn and find limitations, and finally to provide a feeling of how a production system might look.

5.1   Architecture

Our prototype targets Java applications and is implemented in AspectJ; it consists of a combination of Java classes and aspects that together form a general-purpose and highly flexible privacy enforcement framework. In its current state, the prototype does not include support for metadata persistence.

All interception points (input vectors, string operations, and output vectors) target API calls of the applications to the underlying Java platform, and the prototype can thus be seen as a layer between these two. An advantage of this choice, compared with instrumenting the platform itself, is that this API layer is standard over all platform implementations. This make our prototype compatible with all Java implementations.

The datatype targeted is strings for the reasons discussed in Section 4.1. Privacy metadata (PM) are objects that contain the privacy context as well as the privacy policy. Strings and PM objects are linked together by means of a central repository.

The focus is on extensibility rather than completeness. For example, only a few input and output vectors are implemented, but implementations for more can easily be plugged in. The prototype does, however, contain its own minimalist policy language that allows full declarative configuration of the prototype for many common tasks.

We distinguish between four components, which will be detailed further below: configuration, PM assignment, PM preservation, and policy enforcement. These components map largely to the conceptual components of Section 4.

5.2   Configuration

The prototype supports configuration through an XML-based configuration file, which enables most common and many less common tasks be achieved without programming. At the same time, it also supports flexible programmatic configuration through user-provided interceptors for input and output vectors, or specialized PM factories, i.e., classes that generate PM objects.

Figure 2 depicts the set of Java classes that form the configuration component and the three steps that make up the configuration phase: reading of the configuration file, initialization of the specified PM factories, and registration of the PM factories with the relevant input vectors.

The first step entails reading and parsing the XML-based configuration file. This configuration file specifies the PM factories and their initialization context, as well as the conditions under which data received from certain input vectors is assigned PM from these factories. An example configuration file looks as follows:

```
<PIConfiguration>
  <PM id="onlyLocalEmail" factory="pi.pmfactory.Generic">
    <!-- initialization context -->
  </PM>
  <PMAssignment>
    <inputvector>pi.inputVector.Http</inputvector>
    <conditions>
      <regexp target="http.requestedUrl">some regexp</regexp>
      <test>com.company.pi.RequestorTest</test>
      <regexp target="http.requestedParam">another regexp</regexp>
    </conditions>
    <PM ref="onlyLocalEmail"/>
  </PMAssignment>
</PIConfiguration>
```

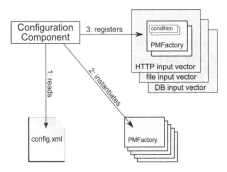

Fig. 2. Configuration phase of the prototype

The second step is to initialize the specified PM factories described in the <PM> elements of the configuration file. A PM factory is a Java class that follows the factory design pattern [11] to create specialized PM objects. In this excerpt one PM factory of type "pi.pmfactory.Generic" and with id "onlyLocalEmail" is specified. The PM element also contains an optional initialization context (not shown here), which will be discussed as part of the PM assignment phase.

The third and final step is to configure the actual PM assignment by linking the different PM factories with the relevant input vectors. This link is described in the <PMAssignment> elements of the configuration file and contains a reference to the relevant input vector, the conditions under which PM should be assigned, and a reference to the PM factory responsible for creating the PM objects. Two types of conditions are supported: regular expressions on the context exposed by the input vector (e.g., the requestedURL in case of the HTTP input vector) and arbitrary user-provided programmatic tests. These conditions are then initialized (e.g., regular expressions are pre-compiled for efficiency) and together with the PM factory registered at the interceptor for the input vector specified.

After these three steps, Privacy Injector is fully configured, and assignment of PM can commence.

5.3   PM Assignment

The PM-assignment component is responsible for assigning the specified PM objects to data received by the target application through one of its input vectors. As this requires the ability to intercept input-vector API calls made by the target application, the PM-assignment component consists of AspectJ aspects rather than plain Java classes. The core part is an abstract aspect that is subclassed by concrete aspects, which are organized per input vector and responsible for the actual interception and PM assignment. The framework can easily be extended further by plugging in a new aspect targetting the desired input vector. Figure 3 shows the four steps involved: interception of the input, validation of the conditions, creation of the PM, and assignment of the PM to the data.

The interception step is driven by the pointcuts and advice (cf. Section 2.4) declared in the aspects. The pointcuts specify join points for all the relevant methods pertaining to the input vector. For the HTTP input vector, on which

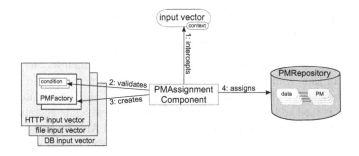

Fig. 3. Privacy metadata assignment phase of the prototype

is the prototype focuses, this means all methods for extracting data from an HTTP request object. For example, `javax.servlet.Servlet.getParameter()` or `javax.servlet.http.Cookie.getValue()`. The advice used is so-called *after advice*, which is executed after the call to the API function returns, and is capable of inspecting the returned value before it is passed on to the calling application.

Each input vector has a (possibly empty) set of PM factories that were registered with it during the configuration phase. In the second step the conditions associated with these PM factories are validated. These conditions are typically tests on the context exposed by the aspect, i.e., on the set of parameters relevant to that particular input vector. For the HTTP input vector, such a condition could be related to the resource requested or to the authentication status of the requester. Only if all conditions of a PM factory hold, is the third step performed on that PM Factory. Otherwise, control will be returned to the application without assigning PM.

In the third step, the actual PM object is created by calling the creation method of the PM factory. A PM factory is a factory that creates objects that subclass the PM class. The configuration file can specify an arbitrary user-provided factory or the generic one as in our example. The latter provides less flexibility, but requires only configuration and no programming from the user's part. The configuration excerpt shows the PM factory initialization context used to configure the generic factory:

```
<PM id="onlyLocalEmail" factory="pi.pmfactory.Generic">
  <context>
    <param name="inputVector"/>
    <param name="http.requester" as="dataSubject"/>
    <param name="http.requestTime" as="timestamp"/>
    <text as="comment">some comment</text>
  </context>
  <policies>
    <!-- description of policies -->
  </policies>
</PM>
```

This initialization context is passed on to the PM factory during its initialization in the configuration phase. The syntax of the initialization context is PM-factory-specific; shown here is the syntax for the generic PM factory. The initialization context contains two parts: the context, which describes the metadata that should be maintained, and the policies, which describes the policy (cf. Section 5.5). In our example, the generic PM factory is configured to maintain four pieces of metadata in the PM objects it generates:

the input vector, the requester, the time of the request, and a comment. The `as` specifies the name under which the metadata is accessible.

In the final step, the PM generated is packaged into a PM container and stored in the central PM repository. A PM container is a data structure that allows one to associate multiple PM objects with possibly overlapping string fragments. It also provides an API for convenient and efficient lookup and manipulation of the associated PM. This PM container is then added to the central PM repository, which is essentially a weak hash table enabling efficient lookup through an specialized API. By using a *weak* hash table [1] the PM of data that is no longer in use will be removed automatically.

After this step all input data that fulfilled the specified conditions will have the appropriate PM associated with it.

5.4   PM Preservation

The goal of this phase is to preserve and update the PM assigned in the assignment phase. Efficiency is a major concern of this phase as almost every string operation is affected, even if none of the operands contain PM. And, as in a typical application only a small fraction of the strings has PM attached, special care should be taken to make operations on these strings particularly low-overhead. Figure 4 shows the four steps of the PM preservation phase: interception of the data operations, retrieval of the PM, updating of the PM, and storage of the PM.

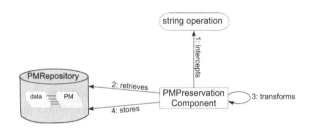

Fig. 4. Metadata-preservation phase of the prototype

In the interception step, all relevant string operations are intercepted. Java has two types of string-like data, String and StringBuffer, with the difference between the two being that the former is immutable whereas the latter is not. This means that the relevant operations are operations that have at least one stringbuffer operand or that return a string and have at least one string operand. The PM preservation component provides pointcuts for all calls to these functions.

In the second step, the PM of all operands is retrieved from the PM repository. The repository has an API for doing this, requiring only one efficient hash table lookup per operand. If no PM is found, control is returned to the application.

The third step requires by far the largest development effort as it needs the ability to reflect the semantics of all relevant string operations on the PM correctly. For our

---

[1] A special type of hash table whose elements do not count as referents for the garbage collector.

prototype, we initially focused on the most common operations. Many of the operations fall into the class of operations that return string(buffers) that merely have a copy of the original PM of their operands attached or no PM at all. In the former case, the original PM is cloned, in the latter control is returned to the application. Other operations require more complex manipulation of the PM, e.g., a merge of the PM of two operands or a selection of a fragment of the PM. For this we leverage the API provided by the PMContainer class, which facilitates common operations such as retrieval of the PM of string fragments and merging of PM containers.

The final step is storing the updated PM in the PM repository.

5.5   Policy Enforcement

In this last phase, the actual enforcement of the privacy policy is performed. The framework is responsible for notifying and providing the context to the PM objects attached to data passed to an output vector. The actual validation of the conditions and execution of the appropriate actions are the responsibility of the PM objects.

Recall that PM objects are created by PM factories that can be either user-provided or of the generic type. Factories can contain a hard-coded programmatic policy or a declarative one, described in a factory-specific manner in the <PM> part of the configuration file. By plugging in a policy language interpreter, the framework can be extended to support arbitrary policy languages. The following XML shows an example of the configuration of the generic PM factory:

```
<PM id="onlyLocalEmail" factory="pi.pmfactory.Generic">
  <context>
    <!-- stored privacy context, discussed in PM Assignment -->
  </context>
  <policies>
    <policy>
      <outputvector>email</outputvector>
      <conditions>
        <regexp target="email.recipient">^.+@mycompany.com$</regexp>
      </conditions>
      <actions>
        <log file="/path/to/log/file"/>
      </actions>
    </policy>
    <default>
      <actions>
        <custom method="pi.Actions.pageOperator"/>
        <exception class="pi.IllegalDisclosureException">
          disclosure not in accordance with privacy policy
        </exception>
      </actions>
    </default>
  </policies>
</PM>
```

The <policy> element pertains to the email output vector, and describes which actions have to be performed under which conditions. The conditions are specified using a syntax identical to that of the PM assignment conditions and can refer to both context exposed by the output vector and metadata stored in the PM object. In the example, the condition specifies a limitation on the domain of the email recipients. If all conditions hold, the specified action, in this case log, is performed. If for none of the specified policies, both output vector and conditions match, the optional default policy actions are performed. In the example, a custom method is executed and an exception is thrown.

Figure 5 shows the three steps of the policy-enforcement phase: interception of the output vectors, retrieval of the PM, and execution of the specified policy.

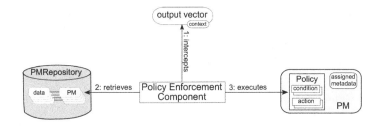

Fig. 5. Policy-enforcement phase of the prototype

Our primary focus is prevention of unwarranted disclosure of personal data. The first step of the policy-enforcement step will then also be to intercept all calls to output vectors, as this is where disclosure takes place. The output vector in our example is the Java mail API. We defined aspects grouped per output vector that provide pointcuts for all calls to methods used for sending data through the output vector. The advice is so-called *around advice* that allows us to alter the program flow, for example by throwing exceptions or altering the data passed to the output vector.

The next step is to verify whether the data being sent has PM attached to it. This is done in the same way as in the PM preservation phase by checking the PM repository. If the data has no PM attached to it, control is returned to the program and the disclosure is allowed to take place unchanged.

In the final step the policy specified by the PM is executed. For this, a pre-defined method is invoked which receives the context surrounding the call to the output vector, e.g., which output vector, the parameters, etc. Using the provided context together with the metadata stored in the PM object, the appropriate actions are performed. The generic PM factory supports logging, exception throwing, and executing arbitrary commands.

6   Discussion

6.1   Assumptions and Limitations

In this section we discuss limitations and assumptions related to Privacy Injector.

The most important assumption made by Privacy Injector is the use of a persistence service by the target application. This is because, as mentioned in Section 4, the meta-data persistence component relies on the event system of the persistence service for correctly preserving metadata when data is stored and retrieved. The impact of the assumption is eased by the momentum persistence services currently enjoy.

We also assume that for privacy enforcement we are mainly interested in textual data and hence that, at finest granularity, privacy-related data is contained in variables of the string type. This can be considered a pragmatic consideration that will suffice for many real-world applications. Related to this is the assumption that applications do not access strings in a low-level manner, but through the string API functions. This holds in almost all cases for high-level languages such as Java, but might not hold for C.

Privacy Injector is inherently platform-independent, but assumes a provision for intercepting library functions, either at the platform layer (instrumentation of the library functions) or at the application layer (instrumentation of the library function calls).

Finally, Privacy Injector is particularly suited for preventing unwarranted disclosure of personal data, as the focus on the limited and well-defined set of input and output vectors provided by the platform allows the creation of a reusable framework. For usecases with other requirements, it currently remains an open question whether the desired functionality can also be made generally applicable.

6.2 Correctness

When implementing a privacy-enforcement system, it is reasonable to expect a certain level of guarantee that the system enforces the policy as specified. As Privacy Injector is a complex system that interacts with all components of a system, a formal correctness proof is beyond the state of the art. When assessing the possibility to create a complete and correct Privacy Injector implementation, one has to keep two properties in mind.

The first is that the Privacy Injector framework is largely reusable and requires implementation only once. This has the advantage that it can be done by experts that submit it to rigorous testing, resulting in high-quality code.

The second is that Privacy Injector can implement a fail-safe mode, by requiring that metadata be assigned to all data and failing when this assertion does not hold. When no real privacy metadata is attached to the data, a placeholder indicating that the metadata framework functioned correctly is attached. Related to this, a policy should always specify a safe default action when none of the conditions specified hold (as in the example provided in Section 5).

7   Conclusions and Future Work

In this paper we introduced Privacy Injector, which leverages the Aspect-Oriented Software Development paradigm to create a fully modularized privacy-enforcement system. Privacy Injector can be seen as a practical implementation of the sticky policy paradigm and conceptually consists of two complementary parts, namely a privacy metadata tracking and a privacy policy enforcement part.

We showed how these two parts together protect the entire life cycle of personal data. Throughout the collection, transformation, disclosure and deletion of personal data, Privacy Injector will automatically assign, preserve and update privacy metadata as well as enforce the privacy policy specified. Through the use of aspects, Privacy Injector can be used to add privacy enforcement to existing applications as well as a framework for building privacy-aware applications.

We also described a prototype implementation of Privacy Injector, aimed at demonstrating the practical feasibility of the concepts introduced in the paper. For this prototype we focused on Java and relied on the AspectJ flavor of the Aspect-Oriented

Software Development paradigm. We focused on disclosure control to prevent unwarranted disclosure of personal data.

Currently, we are further extending our prototype to include support for metadata persistence through the use of the fine-grained event system provided by Hibernate. This will allow us to test our prototype in a real-world environment. As future work, we will add a provision for storing accounting information in the privacy metadata, providing us with the ability to keep a detailed history of all operations performed on any piece of personal information.

References

1. Rakesh Agrawal, Jerry Kiernan, Ramakrishnan Srikant, and Yirong Xu. Hippocratic databases. In *Proceedings of the 28th Int'l Conf. on Very Large Databases (VLDB), Hong Kong*, 2002.
2. Michael Backes, Walid Bagga, Günter Karjoth, and Matthias Schunter. Efficient comparison of enterprise privacy policies. *19th ACM Symposium on Applied Computing, Special Track Security, Nicosia, Cyprus*, 2004.
3. Michael Backes, Birgit Pfitzmann, and Matthias Schunter. A toolkit for managing enterprise privacy policies. *8th European Symposium on Research in Computer Security (ESORICS 2003), Lecture Notes in Computer Science*, 2808:162–180, 2003.
4. Claudio Bettini, Sushil Jajodia, X. Sean Wang, and Duminda Wijesekerat. Obligation monitoring in policy management. In *Proceedings of the 3rd IEEE International Workshop on Policies for Distributed Systems and Networks (POLICY)*, pages 2–12, 2002.
5. Piero A. Bonatti, Ernesto Damiani, Sabrina De Capitani di Vimercati, and Pierangela Samarati. A component-based architecture for secure data publication. In *Proceedings of the 17th Annual Computer Security Applications Conference*, pages 309–318, 2001.
6. Grady Booch, Jim Rumbaugh, and Ivar Jacobson. *The Unified Modeling Language User Guide*. Addison-Wesley, 1998.
7. N. Damianou, N. Dulay, E. Lupo, and M. Sloman. The ponder policy specification language. *Policies for Distributed Systems and Networks (Policy 2001), Lecture Notes in Computer Science 1995*, pages 18–39, 2001.
8. S. Egelman, L. Cranor, and A. Chowdhury. An analysis of p3p-enabled web sites among top-20 search results. In *Proceedings of the Eighth International Conference on Electronic Commerce*, 2006.
9. Robert Filman, Tzilla Elrad, Siobhán Clarke, and Mehmet Akşit. *Aspect-Oriented Software Development*. Addison-Wesley, 2004.
10. Simone Fischer-Hübner. *IT-security and privacy: Design and use of privacy-enhancing security mechanisms*, volume 1958 of *Lecture Notes in Computer Science*. Springer, 2002.
11. E. Gamma, R. Helm, R. Johnson, and J. Vlissides. *Design Patterns: Elements of Reusable Object-Oriented Software*. Addison-Wesley, 1995.
12. IBM. Declarative privacy monitoring. Web page at http://alphaworks.ibm.com/tech/dpm.
13. Sushil Jajodia, Michiharu Kudo, and V. S. Subrahmanian. Provisional authorization. In *Proceedings of the E-commerce Security and Privacy*, pages 133–159. Kluwer Academic Publishers, 2001.
14. Günter Karjoth and Matthias Schunter. A privacy policy model for enterprises. In *Proceedings of the 15th IEEE Computer Security Foundations Workshop (CSFW)*, pages 271–281, 2002.

15. Günter Karjoth, Matthias Schunter, and Els Van Herreweghen. Enterprise privacy practices vs. privacy promises - how to promise what you can keep. *4th IEEE International Workshop on Policies for Distributed Systems and Networks (Policy '03), Lake Como, Italy*, pages 135–146, 2003.

16. Günter Karjoth, Matthias Schunter, and Michael Waidner. The platform for enterprise privacy practices – privacy-enabled management of customer data. In *Proceedings of the Privacy Enhancing Technologies Conference*, volume 2482 of *Lecture Notes in Computer Science*, pages 69–84. Springer, 2002.

17. Gregor Kiczales, Erik Hilsdale, Jim Hugunin, Mik Kersten, Jeffrey Palm, and William G. Griswold. An overview of AspectJ. *Lecture Notes in Computer Science*, 2072:327–355, 2001.

18. Gregor Kiczales, John Lamping, Anurag Menhdhekar, Chris Maeda, Cristina Lopes, Jean-Marc Loingtier, and John Irwin. Aspect-oriented programming. In Mehmet Akşit and Satoshi Matsuoka, editors, *Proceedings of the European Conference on Object-Oriented Programming*, volume 1241, pages 220–242. Springer-Verlag, Berlin, Heidelberg, and New York, 1997.

19. A. Myers and B. Liskov. Protecting privacy using the decentralized label model. *ACM Transactions on Software Engineering and Methodology*, pages 410–442, 2000.

20. Andrew C. Myers. JFlow: Practical mostly-static information flow control. In *Proceedings of the Symposium on Principles of Programming Languages*, pages 228–241, 1999.

21. Oasis. eXtensible Access Control Markup Language (XACML). Web page at http://www.oasis-open.org/committees/tc_home.php?wg_abbrev=xacml.

22. Platform for Privacy Preferences (P3P). W3C Recommendation, April 2002. http://www.w3.org/TR/2002/REC-P3P-20020416/.

23. David L. Parnas. On the criteria to be used in decomposing systems into modules, 1972.

24. Tadeusz Pietraszek and Chris Vanden Berghe. Defending against injection attacks through context-sensitive string evaluation. In *Proceedings of the 8th International Symposium on Recent Advances in Intrusion Detection (RAID2005)*, pages 124–145, 2005.

25. AspectJ Project. The AspectJ home page. Web page at http://eclipse.org/aspectj/.

26. Hibernate Project. Hibernate. Web page at http://hibernate.org/.

27. Carlos Ribeiro, Andre Zuquete, Paulo Ferreira, and Paulo Guedes. SPL: An access control language for security policies with complex constraints. In *Proceedings of the Network and Distributed System Security Symposium (NDSS)*, 2001.

28. A. Sabelfeld and A. Myers. Language-based information-flow security, 2003.

29. Latanya Sweene. k-anonymity: A model for protecting privacy. *International Journal of Uncertainty, Fuzziness and Knowledge-Based Systems*, 10(5):557–570, 2002.

30. Watchfire. Watchfire. Web page at http://watchfire.com/.

31. Bart De Win, Frank Piessens, Wouter Joosen, and Tine Verhanneman. On the importance of the separation-of-concerns principle in secure software engineering. In *Proceedings of the ACSA Workshop on the Application of Engineering Principles to System Security Design*, pages 1–10, 2003.

A Systemic Approach to Automate
Privacy Policy Enforcement in Enterprises

Marco Casassa Mont[1] and Robert Thyne[2]

[1] Hewlett-Packard Laboratories, Trusted Systems Lab,
Bristol, United Kingdom
marco.casassa-mont@hp.com
[2] Hewlett-Packard, Software Business Organisation,
Toronto, Canada
robert.thyne@hp.com

Abstract. It is common practice for enterprises and other organisations to ask people to disclose their personal data in order to grant them access to services and engage in transactions. This practice is not going to disappear, at least in the foreseeable future. Most enterprises need personal information to run their businesses and provide the required services, many of whom have turned to identity management solutions to do this in an efficient and automated way. Privacy laws dictate how enterprises should handle personal data in a privacy compliant way: this requires dealing with privacy rights, permissions and obligations. It involves operational and compliance aspects. Currently much is done by means of manual processes, which make them difficult and expensive to comply with. A key requirement for enterprises is being able to leverage their investments in identity management solutions. This paper focuses on how to automate the enforcement of privacy within enterprises in a systemic way, in particular privacy-aware access to personal data and enforcement of privacy obligations: this is still open to innovation. We introduce our work in these areas: core concepts are described along with our policy enforcement models and related technologies. Two prototypes have been built as a proof of concept and integrated with state-of-the-art (commercial) identity management solutions to demonstrate the feasibility of our work. We provide technical details, discuss open issues and our next steps.

Keywords: privacy, policy enforcement, privacy-aware access control, obligation management, identity management.

1 Introduction

Privacy management is important for enterprises and organisations that handle identities and personal data of customers, employees and business partners: it has implications on their compliance with regulations, their reputation, their brand and customers' satisfaction [19,20].

Privacy laws [1,2] and privacy guidelines, such as OECD [3], dictate that enterprises should clearly state the purposes for which they are collecting personal data and should take into account the consent given by data subjects (users) to use their data

G. Danezis and P. Golle (Eds.): PET 2006, LNCS 4258 , pp. 118–134, 2006.

for these purposes. In addition, personal data should be deleted once its retention is not required anymore. Openness and transparency over how data is processed, manipulated and disclosed to third parties are also key requirements. Data subjects should be notified of changes affecting the management of their personal data and they should retain a degree of control over it. Compliance to all these aspects must be monitored and any violations promptly reported and addressed. Furthermore large enterprises that are geographically distributed across different nations might need to comply with different privacy laws. Privacy policies can be used to represent privacy laws and guidelines: they describe data subjects' rights on their personal data, permissions given to enterprises and obligations that enterprises need to fulfil when handling personal data.

On one hand, enterprises have been investing in identity management solutions to automate the management of personal and identity information. This includes solutions to store personal and confidential data and use it for access control and authorization purposes. On top of this single-sign-on mechanisms and federated identity management solutions have been developed to simplify and enable multi-party interactions. Provisioning and user account management solutions have also been developed to simplify users' self-registration process and provision users' information to various enterprises' systems and data repositories. On the other hand, in terms of privacy management, much is still done by means of manual processes, which make them difficult and expensive to comply. Simplification of the involved processes and better control are key enterprise requirements: this leads towards the need to introduce automation also for privacy management.

Most of the technical work currently done in this space focuses on auditing and reporting solutions to analyse logged events and check them against privacy policies. This addresses compliance aspects of privacy management. However, operational aspects of privacy must also be addressed. In particular, the enforcement of privacy policies is very important to guarantee that personal data is accessed, used, disclosed and managed according to these policies. Often privacy policies are hardcoded into enterprise applications and services or managed with very vertical, ad-hoc solutions, in specific contexts. This approach is not adaptive to changes and does not scale. The enforcement of privacy rights, permissions and obligations on confidential and personal data requires the mapping of these concepts into rules, constraints and access control, the meaning of which must be unambiguous so that it can be deployed and enforced by software solutions. This still requires following best practices and good behaviours. However, automating aspects of the enforcement of privacy policies can really help enterprises to improve their practice and simplify the overall management. This paper describes our systemic approach to automate the enforcement of privacy policies (inclusive of obligations). Our technology can be integrated with enterprise middleware solutions, in particular identity management solutions.

2 Addressed Problem

This paper focuses on the problem of how to automate the enforcement of privacy policies within enterprises by keeping into account privacy laws, enterprise guidelines and data subjects' privacy preferences. As anticipated, privacy policies dictate privacy rights, permissions and obligations. Addressing the problem of automating their enforcement requires dealing with: (1) *privacy-aware access to personal data*; (2) *enforcement of privacy obligations*.

Our goal is to address this by developing a privacy enforcement framework and a systemic approach that can be leveraged by current enterprise identity management solutions.

3 Important Issues and Requirements

In the remaining part of this paper, for simplicity, we will use in an interchangeable way the terms: "data subjects", "people" and "users". We consider scenarios where users are asked by enterprises (e.g. a service provider) or other organisations to disclose their personal information in order to access services, engage in transactions or access information.

We want to enable *users* to specify their privacy preferences and dictate obligations on how their data should be managed, give explicit consent and specify limitations about the usage of their data. We want to provide them with degrees of control on their personal data. We also want to enable *enterprises* to: keep into account users' privacy preferences and enforce them; explicitly author privacy policies and obligations, deploy and enforce them during accesses, manipulations and transmission of personal data. Enterprises need tools to achieve this but at the same time ideally they would like to leverage their investments in identity management solutions.

The (technological) enforcement of privacy permissions and rights (on stored personal data) requires extended access control and authorization mechanisms that check these privacy permissions against data requestors' credentials, check the consistency of data requestors' intent against stated purposes and take into account the consent given by data subjects [19]. This applies, for example, to enterprise services or applications that need to access and manipulate personal data for various reasons. Traditional access control systems are necessary but not sufficient to enforce privacy policies on personal data. They are mainly based on "access control lists" and enforcement mechanisms that keep into account only the identities of data requestors, their rights and permissions and the types of actions that are allowed/disallowed on the involved resources. These systems do not keep into account additional aspects relevant to privacy enforcement: the *stated purposes* for collecting data and data subjects' consent - i.e. properties usually associated to collected data - the *intent of data requestors* and any additional enterprise or customized data subjects' *constraints*. To address the above issues and move towards privacy-aware access control systems to protect personal data, it is important to satisfy the following core requirements: (1) *Explicit modeling of personal data stored by enterprises*; (2) *Explicit definition, authoring and lifecycle management of privacy policies*; (3) *Explicit deployment and enforcement of privacy policies*; (4) *Integration with traditional access control and identity management systems*; (5) *Simplicity of usage of all the involved system*; (6) *Support for auditing*. A more comprehensive analysis of these aspects can be found in [19].

Even more complex is the case of dealing with the enforcement of privacy obligations [20,21]. Privacy obligations dictate criteria for a privacy-aware information lifecycle management. They might require the deletion or transformation of confidential data after a predefined (potentially very long) period of time, periodic notifications and requests for authorization to data subjects, fulfilment of opt-in/opt-out choices made by data owners, ongoing compliance with laws' obligations and internal guidelines. Privacy obligations can have ongoing aspects that need to be monitored and satisfied over a long period of time. All these tasks are challenging for enterprises because of the need for specific IT infrastructures and processes able to manipulate confidential data as dictated by privacy obligations. It is important that privacy obligation management solutions address the following core requirements: (1) *Explicit modeling and representation of privacy obligations*; (2) *Association of obligations to data*; (3) *Being able to timely enforce privacy obligations*; (4) *Mapping obligations into enforceable actions*; (5) *Compliance of refined obligations to high-level policies*; (6) *Tracking the evolutions of obligation policies*; (7) *Dealing with long-term obligation aspects*; (8) *Accountability management*; (9) *Monitoring obligations*; (10) *User involvement*. A comprehensive analysis and discussion of these aspects can be found in [20,21].

4 Our Work

This section describes our work to automate the enforcement of privacy policies and privacy obligations on personal data stored by enterprises. Our approach consists of researching and building solutions that can be leveraged by current enterprise identity management solutions. In particular, our approach focuses on the following (typical) enterprise identity management processes (already supported by current identity management solutions), which occur when a new user wants to access services or applications that might require financial or business transactions:

1. The user (data subject) is asked to access a self-registration web site and provide their personal information and other requested data. Some privacy preferences might also be asked to the user and stored. The user later on will be allowed to change their information and preferences;
2. Provisioning and user account management solutions are used to manipulate user's information and store (parts of) it within relevant enterprise data storages. The same provisioning solutions will take care of creating user accounts across enterprise' relevant systems and set proper access control on these resources. These provisioning tools will track any changes to the stored information and ensure that information is kept aligned and consistent;
3. As an effect of the previous provisioning step, authorization and access control systems have been provisioned (by means of access control constraints, new user accounts, etc.) and will be able to and grant (or deny) access to services.

The above steps usually focus only on the automation of identity management aspects. Privacy aspects are either not included or their enforcement is not automated. In addition, personal data is stored in enterprise data repositories subject only to security aspects. As summarised in Figure 1, our work wants to:

1. Enable users to explicitly define their privacy preferences and customise them during their self-registration phase;

2. Use users' privacy preferences, during the provisioning phase, to:
    a. Configure extended access control systems to provide privacy-aware access to personal data: this includes ensuring that these systems can keep track of stated purposes, data subjects' consent and other privacy constraints;
    b. Turn parts of these privacy preferences (such as deletion date of data, notification choices, etc.) into explicit privacy obligations to be enforced by enterprises.
3. Allow enterprises to author, deploy and enforce "enterprise-side" privacy policies and privacy obligations derived from privacy laws and internal guidelines.

Section 4.1 describes our work on privacy-aware access control. We introduce our privacy-aware access control model. We illustrate a prototype that we have built by leveraging and extending HP Select Access [14] (a state-of-the-art access control solution) to deal with privacy policy enforcement on personal data.

Section 4.2 describes our work on privacy obligation management within enterprises. It provides details of our obligation management model along with our prototype of an obligation management system. We also describe how we have successfully integrated it with HP Select Identity [23], a state-of-the-art provisioning and user account management solution.

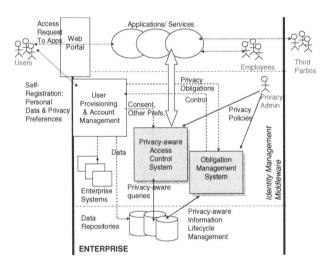

Fig. 1. Automation of Privacy Enforcement within Identity Management Solutions

4.1 Privacy Policy Enforcement

Our approach to enforce privacy policies on stored personal data is based on a privacy-aware access control model. This model extends traditional access control models (based on users/groups, users' credentials and rights, access control lists and related policies) by explicitly dealing with the *stated purposes* for which data is collected, checking - at the access request time - the *intent* of requestors against these purposes, dealing with data subjects' *consent* and enforcing additional access conditions and constraints defined by data subjects and/or enterprise administrators [1,2,3] – see Figure 2. The main aspects of this model are:

a) **A mechanism for the explicit modelling of personal data that are subject to privacy policies:** this mechanism provides a description of data including the type of the data repository (database, LDAP directory, etc.), its location, the schema of these data, types of attributes, etc.;

b) **An integrated mechanism for authoring privacy policies along with traditional access control policies:** it is a Policy Authoring Point (PAP) to allow privacy administrators to describe and author privacy policy constraints and conditions (including how to check consent and data purpose against requestors' intent and how to deal with data filtering and transformation, etc.) along with more traditional access control policies based on security criteria (e.g. who can access which resource, given their rights and permissions);

c) **An integrated authorization framework for deploying both access control and privacy-based policies and making related access decisions:** it is an integrated Policy Decision Point (PDP);

d) **A run-time mechanism –referred to as the "Data Enforcer" - for intercepting attempts to access personal data and enforcing decisions based on privacy policies and contextual information**, e.g., intent of requestors, their roles and identities, etc. It is a Policy Enforcement Point (PEP). This mechanism is in charge (among other things) of dealing with the transformation of queries to access personal data (e.g. SQL queries) and filtering part of the requested data, if their access is not authorised for privacy reasons.

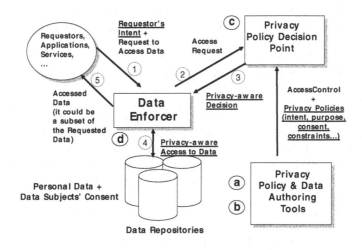

Fig. 2. Model of our Privacy-aware Access Control System

The Data Enforcer component plays a key role to enforce privacy policies on personal data. At "run-time", attempts to access personal data are intercepted and managed in the following way - Figure 2:

1. A request from a data requestor to access personal data is intercepted by the data enforcer. Available information about the requestor (credentials, identity, etc.) is collected, along with their *intent* (that can be explicitly passed as a parameter or could be predefined in the application/service making the request);
2. The data enforcer interacts with the privacy policy decision point by passing information about the request (including the intent) and the requestor;
3. The privacy policy decision point makes a decision, based on available privacy policies and the context (request, requestor's information, etc.). This decision is sent back to the data enforcer. It can be any of the following types:
   - *Deny*: access to data is denied;
   - *Deny + conditions*: access to data is denied. Some conditions are sent back to the requestors. The satisfaction of these conditions (for example passing the intent or authenticating) could change the outcome of the decision;
   - *Allow*: access to data is granted;
   - *Allow + conditions:* access to (part of the) data is allowed, under the satisfaction of the attached conditions. Among other things, these conditions might require data filtering, transformations and manipulations.
4. The data enforcer enforces this decision. In particular, if the decision is "*Allow + conditions*" the data enforcer might have to manipulate the query (query pre-processing) and/or transform the requested personal data (result post-processing), before returning the result to the data requestor;
5. Data (or alternatively no data) is returned to the data requestor, based on the enforced decision.

Figure 3 shows a simple example based on this model where an attempt to access personal data is made by an enterprise employee. In this example, the employee's declared *intent* (i.e. *marketing*) is consistent with the declared *purposes* of data (*marketing, research*). However the employee is trying to access – via a SQL query - more data than she is allowed to. The SQL query is intercepted by the enforcement point (data enforcer) and transformed on-the-fly (before being submitted to the database) in a way to include constraints based on data subjects' consent and the filtering of data. The transformed query is then submitted to the database. In this example privacy is achieved by pre-processing and transforming the query before actually interacting with the database.

We implemented our privacy enforcement model by leveraging and extending HP Select Access. HP Select Access [14] is a leading-edge access control product. It provides policy authoring, policy decision and policy enforcement capabilities via the following components:

- **Policy Builder:** it is a graphical tool to author access control policies (PAP) on resources managed by the system;
- **Validator:** it is a Policy Decision Point (PDP). It makes access control decisions based on the access control policies (authored with the Policy Builder) and contextual information, such as the identity of a requestor;
- **Web Enforcer plug-in:** it is a Policy Enforcement Point (PEP) for web resources.

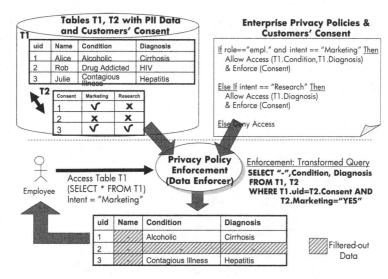

Fig. 3. Example of Privacy Policy Enforcement

The current commercial version of HP Select Access does not handle data as managed resources: it only deals with traditional access control policies on web resources. Additional functionalities have been added to HP Select Access (HP SA) in our proto-type, to explicitly deal with privacy-aware access control on personal data, as shown in Figure 4:

The specific extensions are:

- The HP SA Policy Builder has been extended to represent "data resources" (data-bases, LDAP directories, virtual-directories, their schemas, etc.) in addition to traditional IT resources (such as web resources);

- The HP SA Policy Builder has been extended to *graphically* author privacy poli-cies on "data resources" in addition to traditional access control policies: a set of additional plug-ins has been implemented to allow checking (at the enforcement time) the requestor's intent against the stated data storage purposes, take into ac-count data subjects' consent and data retention policies and describe how the ac-cessed personal data must be filtered, obfuscated or manipulated, etc. By using this tool administrators can manage the lifecycle of both privacy and security policies, in an integrated environment – based on the same principles and GUI. This simpli-fies the overall policy management process and differentiates our approach from re-lated work (see section 5);

- The HP SA Validator has been extended to make privacy-aware decisions. Plug-ins, correspondent to the ones used in the Policy Builder, have been implemented. This enhanced-version of the Validator can now also make "*Allow + conditions*" decisions as described in our model;

- A Data Enforcer has been built and added to the framework: this is a new feature which has been added to HP Select Access. It is in charge of enforcing privacy decisions made by the Validator, as previously described in our model. We

envisage that a family of data enforcers sharing a common logic but differentiated by add-ons dealing with different types of data resources (e.g. databases,
LDAP directories, virtual directories, etc.) need to be built, because of the different semantic of different data repositories. As a proof of concept, we implemented a data enforcer as a JDBC proxy for RDBMS databases.

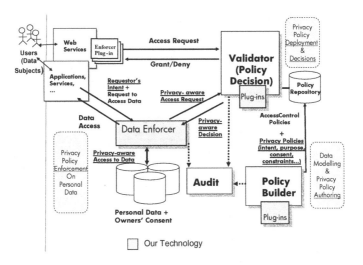

Fig. 4. Extended HP Select Access to deal with Privacy Policy Enforcement

The above functionalities address and satisfy the core requirements described in
section 3 for privacy enforcement on personal data. Policy authoring and enforcement
processes are audited by the HP Select Access's Audit Server, for accountability and
compliance management.

Figure 5 provides additional details about the data enforcer that we developed to
intercept SQL queries for RDBMS databases and enforce privacy policies on the
requested data.

This data enforcer is based on a JDBC Proxy (JDBC driver). Applications and services do not need to be modified apart from having to use this JDBC driver. Standard
JDBC APIs are used. The data enforcer intercepts applications' SQL queries and
processes them.

The *intent* (reason for accessing data) of a data requestor (e.g. application) could be
implicit in its role: this ensures the most transparent interaction between applications
and our data enforcer. In case the *intent* information has to be explicitly passed by the
application to the data enforcer, we support two mechanisms to achieve this: (1) the
intent information is added by the application at the end of its SQL query – before
submitting it; (2) the *intent* information is passed as a property object by the application, via the JDBC API getConnection method.

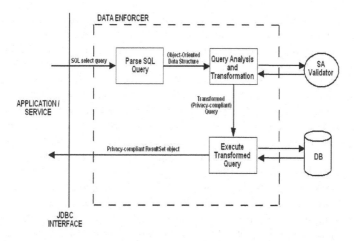

Fig. 5. Internal architecture of the Data Enforcer

The "**Parse SQL Query**" component intercepts incoming SQL queries (SELECT, UPDATE, CREATE, etc.), parses them and generates an explicit tree-based (object-oriented) representation of these queries. This representation clearly identifies, given an arbitrary SQL query, what the involved *data resources* are (e.g. DB tables, fields, etc.), *intent* information, SQL conditions on data, etc. The "**Query Analysis and Transformation**" component - for each involved data resource - checks with the Validator if any privacy policy applies. In doing this it will pass relevant contextual information (requestor's identity, *intent*, etc.) to the Validator. If privacy policies apply, related decisions are recorded. They might include the filtering of some of the data associated to specific fields, the fact that consent has to be enforced, etc. The transformation of the SQL query happens on-the-fly: for example, if specific fields need to be filtered out (because a privacy policy says so), these fields are replaced in the query representation with default values (as described in the policies). If data subjects' consent has to be enforced, additional JOIN conditions are added into the query representation to check for data subjects' consent information. See Figure 3 for an example. The outcome of this module is a transformed SQL query that keeps into account all the stated privacy constraints and is still compatible with the original stated SQL query. This query is sent from the "**Execute Transformed Query**" to the RDBMS system and executed by the real SQL engine. The result of this privacy-compliant query is sent back to the application/service.

4.2 Privacy Obligation Management

Our work in this area focuses on the explicit management and enforcement of privacy obligations on personal data stored by enterprises. In our model, privacy obligations are "first class" entities, i.e. they are explicit entities that are modeled and managed to provide a privacy-aware lifecycle management of personal data: this includes data deletion, data transformation, dealing with notifications, etc. A related obligation management framework is introduced to manage these privacy obligations. In our vision their management and enforcement must be independent from the management and enforcement of privacy-aware access control policies [20,21]. For example, deletion of personal data has to happen independently from the fact that this data has ever been accessed. This differentiates our approach from related work (see section 5).

A privacy obligation is an "object" that includes (at least) the following aspects: *Obligation Identifier*; *Targeted Personal Data*; *Triggering Events* (e.g. time-based events); *Actions* (e.g. data deletion, sending notifications). Different categories of privacy obligations need to be managed and enforced by enterprises: *transactional obligations*; *data retention and handling obligations*; *other types of event-driven obligations*. A complementary classification of our managed privacy obligations is based on their activation timeframe and period of validity: *short-term obligations*; *long-term obligations*; *ongoing obligations*.

In our obligation management framework (a) data subjects can explicitly define their privacy preferences on their personal data at the disclosure time (e.g. during a self-registration process) or at any subsequent time; (b) privacy preferences are automatically turned into privacy obligations based on supported privacy obligation templates; (c) enterprise privacy administrators can associate other privacy obligations, for example dictated by laws or internal guidelines.

Our obligation management framework handles these obligations by providing the following core functionalities: (1) *scheduling the enforcement of privacy obligations*; (2) *enforcement of privacy obligations*; (3) *Monitoring the fulfilment of privacy obligations*.

These functionalities can be accessed by enterprise privacy administrators and potentially also by data subjects, for example to monitor their personal data and check for privacy compliance. Figure 6 shows the high-level architecture of our obligation management system.

A comprehensive description of this obligation management system can be found in [20,21]. A working prototype has been implemented in the context of the EU PRIME project [22], as a proof of concept, providing the core functionalities: scheduling, enforcement and monitoring of privacy obligations. At the moment the managed obligations are restricted to handling time-based and access based events. The supported actions include deletion of data and notifications. Short-term, long-term and ongoing obligations are supported. Our work addresses the core issues and requirements described in section 3.

This obligation management can be considered as an additional component of current enterprises' identity management solutions. In particular it can be integrated with the self-registration, customization and account management capabilities of identity provisioning systems to allow users and administrators to describe and handle privacy preferences and turn them into privacy obligations for the enterprise. In this context our system allows for the explicit representation and management of privacy obligations, along with the coordination of their overall enforcement and monitoring.

To demonstrate how this can be achieved for real, we integrated our Obligation Management System (OMS) with HP Select Identity, as shown in Figure 7. HP Select Identity [23] is a state-of-the-art solution to manage digital identities within and between large enterprises. It automates the process of provisioning, managing and terminating user accounts and access privileges by keeping all this information consistent and synchronised across provisioned platforms, applications and services (within and between enterprise boundaries). Interactions with these third party systems (i.e. data repositories, legacy applications, services, etc.) are achieved via *Connectors*. These third parties can provide feedback to HP Select Identity (via agent-based mechanisms) about changes to their local copies of provisioned data, by calling its Web Service API.

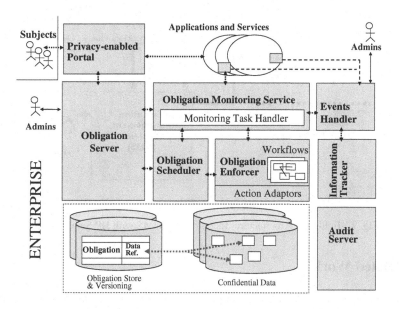

Fig. 6. High-level Architecture of our Obligation Management System

As shown in Figure 7, in our integrated prototype we use (1) HP Select Identity self-registration capabilities to allow users to specify their privacy constraints and preferences along with required personal data. Personal data is provisioned by HP Select Identity to various enterprise systems and data repositories (2). Please notice that at this stage external systems – *such as our privacy-aware access control system* – can be configured with privacy preferences and related constraints. Specifically, privacy preferences are also processed by our OMS connector (2), turned into privacy obligations (based on predefined templates) and pushed to the OMS system (3). Privacy obligations are then scheduled, enforced and monitored by our OMS system (4). We leverage the workflow and user/identity management capabilities of HP Select Identity to enforce aspects of privacy obligations (5). Our system retains control of the supervision of obligations and their monitoring (6). HP Select Identity enforces obligations constraints, such as deletion of identities, data transformation, etc. At the moment the deletion of personal data (as the effect of enforcing obligations) is achieved by triggering HP Select Identity workflows, whilst the obligation management system handles the notifications to users.

HP Select Identity audits the overall lifecycle of managed personal data. The Audit Server within the OMS system can be used to specifically audit how privacy obligations are authored, managed and enforced.

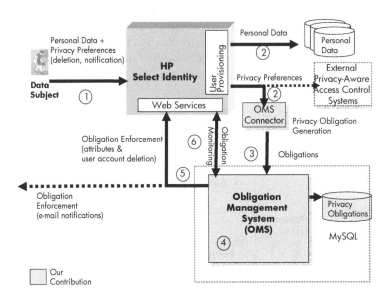

Fig. 7. High-level Architecture: Integration of OMS with HP Select Identity

5 Related Work

A common approach adopted by enterprises to enforce privacy-aware access control policies on personal data consists of hardcoding them within applications and services or building ad hoc solutions. This approach is suitable for very simple and static environments: it shows all its limitations and maintenance costs in case of complex and dynamic organizations that need to adapt to changes. As described in the requirements section, to explicitly address the automation problem, a model of the relevant personal data is required. Privacy policies need to be authored, deployed, enforced and audited. This requires the definition of a comprehensive privacy-aware access control model and systems that implement it. Relevant work in this direction, for privacy management and enforcement in enterprises is described in [4,5,6,7]. An Enterprise Privacy Architecture (EPA/E-P3P) is introduced and described in [7]. This approach is further refined and described in the Enterprise Privacy Authorization Language (EPAL) specification [8]. However these papers mainly provide general guidelines and do not describe an overall deployable solution within current identity management solutions.

The content of Figure 1 is compatible with [4,5,6,7]. Our work differentiates from this because: (1) we do not focus our effort in defining a new privacy-oriented access control language (such as EPAL). Instead, we ensure that privacy aspects (e.g. dealing with data purposes, consent, etc.) can be managed by current identity management systems, by leveraging and extending their capabilities; (2) our approach to obligation management is not subordinated to access control, as instead recommended by [4,5,6,7]; (3) we described how our privacy management capabilities can actually be integrated with state-of-the art identity management solutions.

Important related work on actual privacy enforcement on personal data has been done on Hippocratic databases [9] and similarly on Oracle databases (Private Virtual database/Privacy Manager component). The drawback of this approach is that it mainly focuses at the database level, specifically on RDBMS data repository architectures and related data schemas. The enforcement of privacy policies need to span across a broad variety of data repositories and legacy systems to include LDAP directories, meta/virtual directories, file systems and legacy systems. It might need to incorporate higher-level views and perspectives than just the database-level perspective.

In terms of commercially available solutions, IBM Tivoli Privacy Manager [10, 11] provides mechanisms for defining fine-grained privacy policies and associating them to data. On one hand this solution provides the required privacy enforcement functionalities. On the other hand this approach dictates strong constraints on how applications need to be developed and how personal data has to be stored and administered: it might require some duplications of administrative and enforcement frameworks (e.g. it requires the parallel usage of Tivoli Access Manager) and it is vertically-based on other IBM products and solutions. Other products, such as HP Select Federation [12] and ePok [13], focus on single-sign-on and related privacy aspects: they enforce privacy rules on personal data in federated environment when these data are disclosed by an organization (or an identity provider) to other parties.

Our work on privacy-aware access control specifically addresses the problem of enforcing privacy policies on personal data stored in a broad variety of data repositories within enterprises. This is a major differentiator compared to related work. Personal data can be accessed by different types of requestors, including people, applications and services. It includes related aspects of modeling the managed data and authoring privacy policies. Our work aims at not being invasive for applications and services: privacy policies are managed in an explicit way, in conjunction with traditional access control policies and not hardcoded in applications and services. We avoid duplication of efforts by providing a single, integrated framework for authoring, administering and enforcing both traditional access control and privacy policies. This has been demonstrated in the way we leveraged and extended HP Select Access [14] to enforce privacy policies on personal data – along with security policies.

In terms of managing and enforcing privacy obligations, relevant work is described in [4,5,6,7,8], in particular the EPAL specification. As previously described, their approach to handling privacy obligations is driven from an authorization and access control perspective. However, privacy obligations typically cannot be managed solely from an authorization-based perspective. Similar observations apply to XACML.

Our approach addresses this issue. In our work obligation policies are first-class entities with their explicit and independent management. Our architecture has high-level commonalities with the architecture described in [4,5,6,7] but in our work we further refine the concept of obligations and their enforcement. We split the enforcement mechanisms in two parts by including a scheduling mechanism and an enforcement mechanism allowing for workflow automation and human intervention.

Approaches to deal with (privacy) obligations have already been implemented in products, in particular for data retention [15] and in a variety of document management systems. Nevertheless, these approaches are very specific, focused on particular domains and handle simple obligation policies on files and documents, not really on personal data. Our work aims at pushing the barrier even further to create an obligation management framework that can be leveraged in multiple contexts, for different purposes and that can be actually integrated with state-of-the-art identity management solutions. The feasibility of our work in the real world has been demonstrated by integrating it with HP Select Identity [23] – in a context of user provisioning and user account management.

A lot of work has been done in representing privacy policies, including obligations such as [16,17]. Paper [24] provides a formal definition and classification of obligations, in a data protection context. Relevant work on mechanisms to associate policies to data is described in [4,5,6,7,18]. We can leverage aspects of this work to provide a stronger association of obligation policies to confidential data.

6 Discussion and Next Steps

Our prototypes are proof of concepts. However they show the feasibility of our work to address the enforcement of privacy policies and obligations in a systemic way, integrated with state-of-the-art identity management solutions. We are refining and extending them for their potential productisation. It is important to highlight the fact that our models and technologies are general purpose: they can be leveraged, integrated and deployed in other identity management contexts, beyond HP identity management solutions.

We believe that, by leveraging and extending current identity management solutions, we reduce the barrier that enterprises might have in adopting our privacy management solutions - if compared to other approaches where new, additional privacy solutions need to be used. We are currently exploring opportunities for technological trials with HP customers to further investigate this point.

Another important aspect characterising our work is the way we manage privacy policies. As anticipated, our management of privacy-aware access control policies is integrated with the management of traditional (security-based) access control policies. This simplifies administrators' tasks that only need to use one tool and a related GUI. We also automate the creation of privacy obligations, based on predefined templates - at least in the context of user provisioning and account management. However additional work needs to be performed in terms of implementing a more comprehensive lifecycle management of privacy obligations. "User studies" can help to show how data subjects and administrators deal with the overall system. We are collaborating with Karlstad University on this topic.

At the moment the enforcement of privacy policies in HP Select Access mainly consists in enforcing data subjects' consent, constraints on data purposes and data expirations via data filtering. Current performance tests and analysis (done on databases of sizes from 100K to 500K records) are promising. No noticeable loss of performance (i.e. the time spent between sending a query to a RDBMS and retrieving the last returned record) has been registered so far, on common SQL queries. More tests and experiments are in progress on different varieties of SQL queries. We are also planning to: (1) explore the implications of post-processing queries (post-processing of query results) to extend the current set of managed privacy constraints; (2) explore the enforcement of privacy policies on LDAP repositories and virtual directories.

In terms of privacy obligation enforcement, we are currently refining the integration of our obligation management system with HP Select Identity, specifically to leverage as much as possible the provisioning and workflow capabilities of HP Select Identity to enforce obligations' actions. Additional work and research in the space of privacy obligations is going to be done in PRIME [22]: in particular we plan to research on how to make the obligation management system scalable to cope with large amounts of personal data. A promising research topic to explore is the management of parametric obligations that apply to a large subset of personal data subject to similar privacy preferences.

7 Conclusions

Privacy management is becoming more and more important for enterprises to ensure their compliance to regulation, their governance objectives and address customers' preferences and rights. This paper focuses on how to automate the enforcement of privacy policies and privacy obligations on personal data, stored and accessed by enterprises. We discussed a privacy-aware access control model to enforce privacy policies on personal data - including handling the purpose of data, checking data requestors' intent against data purposes and enforcement of data subjects' consent. We also analysed aspects and concepts related to privacy obligations, considered in our model as "first-class" entities (i.e. not subordinated to access control) and introduced our obligation management framework to schedule, enforce and monitor them.

Working prototypes have been implemented and integrated with state-of-the art identity mangement solutions: specifically we described our work to add privacy policy enforcement to HP Select Access and the integration of obligation management and enforcement capabilities with HP Select Identity, within the context of user provisioning. These technologies are ready for commercial exploitation. Research and development work continues to refine our technolgies and implement adiditional functionalities, in particular in the context of the PRIME project.

References

1. C. Laurant: Privacy International: Privacy and Human Rights 2003: an International Survey of Privacy Laws and Developments, Electronic Privacy Information Center (EPIC), Privacy International. http://www.privacyinternational.org/survey/phr2003/ 2003
2. Online Privacy Alliance: Guidelines for Online Privacy Policies, http://www.privacyalliance.org/, Online Privacy Alliance, 2004
3. OECD: OECD Guidelines on the Protection of Privacy and Transborder Flows of Personal Data, http://www1.oecd.org/publications/e-book/9302011E.PDF, 1980
4. G. Karjoth, M. Schunter: A Privacy Policy Model for Enterprises, IBM Research, Zurich. 15th IEEE Computer Foundations Workshop, 2002
5. G. Karjoth, M. Schunter, M. Waidner: Platform for Enterprise Privacy Practices: Privacy-enabled Management of Customer Data, 2nd Workshop on Privacy Enhancing Technologies, Lecture Notes in Computer Science, Springer Verlang, 2002
6. M. Schunter, P. Ashley: The Platform for Enterprise Privacy Practices, IBM Zurich Research Laboratory, 2002

7. G. Karjoth, M. Schunter, M. Waidner: Privacy-enabled Services for Enterprises, IBM Zurich Research Laboratory, TrustBus 2002, 2002

8. IBM: The Enterprise Privacy Authorization Language (EPAL), EPAL 1.1 specification, http://www.zurich.ibm.com/security/enterprise-privacy/epal/, IBM, 2004

9. R. Agrawal, J. Kiernan, R. Srikant, Y. Xu: Hippocratic Databases, http://www.almaden.ibm.com/cs/people/srikant/papers/vldb02.pdf, IBM Almaden Research Center, 2002

10. IBM Tivoli Privacy Manager: Privacy manager main web page, http://www-306.ibm.com/software/tivoli/products/privacy-mgr-e-bus/, 2005

11. IBM Tivoli Privacy Manager: online technical documentation, http://publib.boulder.ibm.com/tividd/td/PrivacyManagerfore-business1.1.html, 2005

12. HP: HP Select Federation - Product and Solution Overview, http://www.managementsoftware.hp.com/products/slctfed/, 2005

13. ePok: identity management solution - Trusted Data Exchange Server, http://www.epokinc.com/, 2005

14. HP: HP OpenView SelectAccess - Overview and Features, http://www.openview.hp.com/products/select, 2005

15. IBM: IBM Tivoli Storage Manager for Data Retention, 2004

16. C. Bettini, S. Jajodia, X. Sean Wang, D. Wijesekera: Obligation Monitoring in Policy Management, 2002

17. N. Damianou, N. Dulay, E. Lupu, M. Sloman: The Ponder Policy Specification Language, 2001

18. M. Casassa Mont, S. Pearson, P. Bramhall: Towards Accountable Management of Privacy and Identity Information, ESORICS 2003, 2003

19. M. Casassa Mont, R. Thyne, P. Bramhall: Privacy Enforcement with HP Select Access for Regulatory Compliance, HPL-2005-10, 2005

20. M, Casassa Mont: Dealing with Privacy Obligations: Important Aspects and Technical Approaches, TrustBus 2004, 2004

21. M. Casassa Mont: Dealing with Privacy Obligations in Enterprises, ISSE 2004, 2004

22. PRIME: Privacy and Identity Management for Europe, European RTD Integrated Project under the FP6/IST Programme, http://www.prime-project.eu/, 2006

23. HP: HP OpenView Select Identity – Overview and Features, http://www.openview.hp.com/products/slctid/index.html, 2005

24. M. Hilty, D. Basin, A. Pretschner: On Obligations, Information Security, ETH Zurich, Switzerland, 10th ESORICS, 2005

One Big File Is Not Enough: A Critical Evaluation of the Dominant Free-Space Sanitization Technique

Simson L. Garfinkel[1] and David J. Malan[2]

[1] Center for Research on Computation and Society, Harvard University
simsong@acm.org
[2] Division of Engineering and Applied Sciences, Harvard University
malan@post.harvard.edu

Abstract. Many of today's privacy-preserving tools create a big file that fills up a hard drive or USB storage device in an effort to overwrite all of the "deleted files" that the media contain. But while this technique is widespread, it is largely unvalidated.

We evaluate the effectiveness of the "big file technique" using sector-by-sector disk imaging on file systems running under Windows, Mac OS, Linux, and FreeBSD. We find the big file is effective in overwriting file data on FAT32, NTFS, and HFS, but not on Ext2fs, Ext3fs, or Reiserfs. In one case, a total of 248 individual files consisting of 1.75MB of disk space could be recovered in their entirety. Also, file metadata such as filenames are rarely overwritten. We present a theoretical analysis of the file sanitization problem and evaluate the effectiveness of a commercial implementation that implements an improved strategy.

1 Introduction

It is widely known that the Unix `unlink()` and Windows `DeleteFile()` system calls do not actually overwrite the disk sectors associated with files that are "deleted." These calls merely remove the directory entries for the files from their containing directory. The file sectors are added to the list of available sectors and are overwritten only when they are allocated to other files. As a result, the contents of these "deleted" files can frequently be recovered from *free space* or *slack space* using forensic tools like EnCase [18] or The Sleuth Kit [6].[1]

While the ability to recover accidentally deleted files is useful, many users need to erase files so that recovery is not possible. For example, an individual selling a

---

[1] In this paper, we use the term *free space* to describe disk sectors or clusters of disk sectors that are on the file system's "free list" and can be allocated to newly-created files. The term *slack space* refers to sectors that, while not currently allocated to files, are not on the free list. On FAT file systems, a cluster might consist of eight sectors but only the first sector might be used by a file. Because FAT allocates storage by clusters, not sectors, there is no way for the remaining seven sectors in the cluster to be allocated to a second file; these sectors are part of the slack space.

G. Danezis and P. Golle (Eds.): PET 2006, LNCS 4258, pp. 135–151, 2006.

laptop might need to remove confidential documents before relinquishing control of the device. Alas, the tools for deleting files provided with most computers do not satisfy this need.

One solution is to change operating systems so that files are actually overwritten when they are unlinked. A second is to provide special-purpose tools for that purpose. A third is to provide users with tools that sanitize the free space on their computers, so that already-unlinked files are actually eradicated. For this last solution, a common technique is to open a file for writing and to write one or more patterns to this file until the media is full. Figure 1 presents pseudocode for this technique.

```
procedure bigfile:
  char buf[65536]
  f = open("/volume/bigfile", "w")
  repeat until error writing file:
    write(f, buf)
  close(f)
  if (bigfile+smallfile requested) run smallfile procedure
  unlink("/volume/bigfile")
```

Fig. 1. Pseudocode for the "big file technique," which involves creating one big file that will (hopefully) overwrite all sectors currently on a volume's free list that possibly contain data from long-since "deleted" (*i.e.*, merely unlinked) files. Since some file systems limit the maximum size of a file to $2^{32} - 1$ bytes, in practice it is necessary to create multiple big files until no new files can be created, then to delete them all.

```
procedure smallfile:
  char buf[512]
  i = 0
  repeat until error opening file:
    f = open("/volume/smallfile" + i, "w")
    repeat until error writing file:
      write(f, buf)
    close(f)
    i = i + 1
```

Fig. 2. Pseudocode for the "small file technique," which involves creating numerous small files that will (hopefully) overwrite regions of the file system that are too small or fragmented to be allocated to the big file in Figure 1. This pseudocode should be run following the `close(f)` function in Figure 1 and before the `unlink()` function.

Despite the popularity of this "big file" technique, there are reasons to suspect that it leaves unscathed some sectors corresponding to deleted information. First, while the big file might expand to occupy all data sectors on the file system, in most cases it cannot overwrite file names or other metadata associated with the unlinked files. Second, the big file cannot occupy "slack space" since these sectors, by definition, are not on the free list. Third, file systems that use a log or journal to achieve high reliability might not allow the big file to overwrite the journal; overwriting the journal with user data would defeat the journal's purpose of providing disaster recovery.

Our analysis finds that the big file technique is highly effective, but not perfect, for erasing user data on the MSDOS, FAT, and HFS file systems. The technique fails to erase many file names and other kinds of metadata. And when applied to Linux's Ext2fs, Ext3fs, Reiserfs, and XFS file systems, the technique fails—sometimes spectacularly. We found a modified technique, which we call "Big+Small" and present in pseudocode in Figure 2, is dramatically more effective.

2   Vendor-Supplied Tools

Tools exist for Windows and Mac OS alike that claim the ability to overwrite disk sectors associated with files that have been previously deleted.

2.1   Windows' CIPHER.EXE

Included with Windows XP and Windows Server 2003 (and available as a download for Windows 2000) is CIPHER.EXE, a command-line tool for NTFS that includes an "ability to overwrite data that you have deleted so that it cannot be recovered and accessed" [8,9]. The program's /w option "[r]emoves data from available unused disk space on the entire volume." [23]

We executed CIPHER.EXE /W on a 364MB ATA hard disk while tracing all of the tool's file system activity with Filemon for Windows 7.02 [22]. During our trace, CIPHER.EXE appeared to:

1. Create and open a file for writing (called \EFSTMPWP\fil2.tmp);
2. Write 512KB at a time to the opened file in non-cached mode until the disk was nearly full;
3. Overwrite portions of \$LogFile, \$BitMap, and \$Mft in non-cached mode;
4. Write 512KB at a time again to the opened file in non-cached mode until one such write failed with an error indicating insufficient space;
5. Write only 512B at a time to the opened file in non-cached mode until one such write failed with an error indicating insufficient space;
6. Create and open an additional file for writing (called \EFSTMPWP\0.E);
7. Write 8B at a time to the new file in cached and non-cached modes until one such non-cached write failed with an error indicating insufficient space;
8. Repeat steps 6 to 7 (calling the files \EFSTMPWP\1.E, \EFSTMPWP\2.E, ...) until one such non-cached write and one such creation failed with errors indicating insufficient space;
9. Overwrite additional portions of \$LogFile in non-cached mode;
10. Close and delete all opened files and their containing directory;

11. Repeat steps 1 to 10 twice (calling the largest files \EFSTMPWP\fil3.tmp and \EFSTMPWP\fil4.tmp).

All the while, CIPHER.EXE's output indicated only that the tool was "Writing 0x00," "Writing 0xFF," and "Writing Random Numbers."[2]

2.2 The Apple Disk Utility

Included with Mac OS 10.4 is a version of Apple Disk Utility [3] that offers the ability to "Erase Free Space" in any of three ways: "Zero Out Deleted Files," "7-Pass Erase of Deleted Files," or "35-Pass Erase of Deleted Files."[3] The tool advises that "These options erase files deleted to prevent their recovery. All files that you have not deleted are left unchanged." We were not able to trace the operation of this tool.

2.3 Third-Party Tools

Several third parties offer tools that claim the ability to wipe unallocated space thoroughly (see Section 5). We tested two such tools: SDelete 1.4 [21], which implements an algorithm that is similar to CIPHER.EXE's, and Eraser 5.3 [16].

3 Experimental

We designed an experiment to evaluate the effectiveness of the big file technique for sanitizing information in free and slack space using file systems created on a "512MB"[4] Cruzer Mini USB drive manufactured by the SanDisk Corporation and on a virtual disk drive of precisely the same size that was mounted as a Unix "device." We used this procedure for each experimental run:

1. Every *user addressable* sector of the device or virtual drive was cleared with the Unix dd command by copying /dev/zero to the raw device.[5]

---

[2] The technique of writing a character, its complement, and a random number is specified by the US Department of Defense Clearing and Sanitization Matrix which is present in numerous DoD publications, including DOD 5220.22-M [12].

[3] The number 35 is a reference to Gutmann's Usenix paper, "Secure Deletion of Data from Magnetic and Solid-State Memory" [19], which describes a procedure that might recover data from magnetic media after that data had been overwritten and a set of patterns which could be written to the media to make this sort of recovery more difficult. Although Gutmann has repeatedly said that there is no possible reason to use the entire 35-pass technique described in the paper, many tools nevertheless implement it.

[4] Despite the fact that the Cruzer USB drive is labeled as having "512MB" of storage, a footnote on the package revealed that the manufacturer used the letters "MB" to mean "million bytes." Most operating systems, in contrast, use the phrase "MB" to mean $1024 \times 1024 = 1,048,576$ bytes. Thus, the Cruzer Mini USB drive that we used actually had 488MB of storage.

[5] This experiment specifically did not attempt to read previous contents of a block after it had been overwritten. For the purposes of this experiment, we assumed that once a data block was overwritten, its previous contents were gone.

2. The drive was formatted with the file system under study.
3. The drive was filled with one big file entirely filled with blocks of the letter "S". This file was then deleted.
4. We ran a program that we both designed and wrote called stamp that created a predetermined set of directories and files on the drive. Some of the directory and file names contained the letter "a" and are herein referred to as *A directories* and *A files*, while others contained the letter "b" and are herein referred to as *B directories* and *B files*.
5. The drive was unmounted and moved to an imaging workstation, where it was imaged using aimage [15]. The resulting image is herein referred to as the *stamped* image.
6. The drive was returned to the operating system under study, mounted, and the *B files* and *B directories* were deleted.
7. The drive was unmounted and re-imaged. The resulting image is herein referred to as the *deleted* image.
8. The drive was returned to the operating system under study, mounted, and the free-space sanitizer was run.
9. The drive was unmounted and re-imaged; the resulting image was subsequently examined for artifacts of sanitization.

It was necessary to configure Windows to treat the removable USB device as a fixed drive so that we could format the device with NTFS.[6]

To facilitate analysis, each directory and file created in the file system was given a unique name consisting of a 12-digit number and the letter "a" or "b". Files were created in a variety of file sizes from 129 to 1,798,300 bytes. A total of 80 *A files* and 80 *B files* files were placed in the root directory. In addition, a total of 10 subdirectories were created—5 *A directories* and 5 *B directories*. The *A directories* were given 80 *A files* and 80 *B files* each, while the *B directories* were given 160 *B files*. (No *A files* were placed in the *B directories* because the *B directories* themselves were scheduled for deletion.) The contents of the files were likewise written with a recognizable pattern consisting of 512-byte records that contained the file's number and byte offset. The final record of the file included a flag indicating that it was the final record. Table 1 lists the directories and files that were written to the media as part of this "stamping" procedure.

A specially written program called report analyzed the disk images for traces of the *B* directory names, file names, and file contents. File names were also

---

[6] Although some drivers might suppress multiple writes to a disk and only write the final version of each block, this optimization would not affect our protocol as we unmounted and physically removed the Cruzer USB device prior to each imaging session. Also, while many flash storage devices employ "leveling" to ensure that individual flash cells are not overly rewritten, such leveling necessarily happens beneath the level of the block device abstraction, and not within the file system implementation. If leveling happened in the file system, then every file system would need to be specially modified in order to operate with flash devices. This is clearly not the case. To the file system, the USB device really does look like just another block-addressable device.

Table 1. The directories and files written to each file system as part of the "stamping" procedure. The total number of 512-byte sectors is based on a calculation of file sizes made by the **stamp** program, rather than an analysis of the actual space required on the disk by the files.

	# entries in root	# in A directories	# in B directories	total entries in partition	# 512-byte disk sectors
A dirs	5	n/a	n/a	5	n/a
B dirs	5	n/a	n/a	5	n/a
A files	80	80 (each) 400 (total)	0 0	480	138,426
B files	80	80 (each) 400 (total)	160 (each) 800 (total)	1,280	369,136
S-filled Sectors	n/a	n/a	n/a	n/a	$\approx 450,000^{a}$

^{a} The actual number of "S" sectors depends on the file system overhead.

scavenged from the disk images using **fls**, part of The Sleuth Kit [6], and the Unix **strings** command. While we were frequently able to recover all of the *B file names* and *B directory names* from our disk partitions, we were never able to recover all of the *B file contents*. This represents a minor failing of our experimental technique, but does not invalidate our primary conclusion because our technique can only err in failing to find information that is present on the disk, rather than mistaking non-information for information.

We also scanned for sectors that were filled with the letter "S". These sectors literally contained data from a previous file (the first file created) that was not allocated to any of the stamped files and could not be allocated to the sanitizing big file. That is, these sectors were part of the slack space.

3.1   Windows XP with Service Pack 2

Windows XP with Service Pack 2 supports two native file systems: FAT32 and NTFS. In each case the disk was zeroed on a Unix computer and then formatted on the Windows system using Windows' **FORMAT.EXE**.

There are two ways to delete files on Windows: they can be programmatically deleted using the **DeleteFile()** system call; or they can be deleted through the graphical user interface by dragging them to the "Recycle Bin" and then chosing to "Empty Recycle Bin," which causes each file in the Recycle Bin directory to be deleted with the system call. In our tests we deleted each file with the **DeleteFile()** system call.

We present the results for each file system in Table 2. Each column indicates the amount of metadata or data for the *B directories and files* that could be recovered using our image analysis technique. The "Data Sectors" column indicates the number of sectors from *B files* that could be recovered. (A total of 405,865 *B* sectors were written.) Since each individual block of each file was numbered, it was possible to note when a complete file could be recovered; that information is presented in the "# Complete Files" column. We classified each complete file as to whether it was "Small" (between 1 and 9 disk sectors, inclusive), "Medium" (between 10 and 99 disk sectors, inclusive), or "Large" (100 or more disk sectors). We also present the total number of complete files. Finally, the "S" sectors column indicates the number of recovered sectors that were filled with the letter "S"—this is the amount of recoverable information from the first big file that now resides in the slack space.

For each file system, the row labeled "Stamped" serves as a control for the recovery program; it shows the amount of B metadata and data that could be recovered by our recovery utility after the data was written to the file system but before any attempt had been made at deletion or sanitization. The row labeled "Deleted" shows the amount of metadata and program data that could be recovered after the files had been deleted with the Windows `DeleteFile()` system call. Finally, the row labeled `CIPHER.EXE /W` shows what could be recovered after Microsoft's sanitization utility was run. Similar results are reported for SDelete, Eraser, and our own big file implementation.

Image analysis shows that on FAT file systems `CIPHER.EXE` was very but not completely effective at overwriting deleted information on both FAT and NTFS volumes. On FAT the program was very effective at overwriting sectors that belonged to unallocated clusters, but the program was unable to overwrite slack space at the end of partially allocated clusters: a total of 1,734 sectors were left behind (the same number of sectors left behind by the Big+Little technique.) On NTFS both `CIPHER.EXE` and Big+Little were effective at overwriting all of the data in slack space.

A serious failing with both `CIPHER.EXE` and the Big+Little techniques is that both left behind large number of metadata in the form of the names of deleted files and directories. Of all the tools we tested, only Eraser made a serious attempt to overwrite this information, and Eraser still left approximately did not do a complete job.

3.2 Mac OS 10.4

Mac OS 10.4 includes native support for three file systems: Apple's Hierarchical File System (HFS), a modified version of HFS that supports journaling, and Microsoft's FAT file system (which Apple calls the "MSDOS" file system). We evaluated each; testing the FAT file system under Mac OS allowed us to see how a file system's sanitization properties are impacted by different implementations.

As with Windows, there are two ways to delete files on the Macintosh: programmatically with the `unlink()` system call and through the graphical user interface by dragging files to the Trash Can. Apple, however, has created two ways to empty the Trash Can: an "Empty Trash..." command and a "Secure Empty Trash" command (which uses Apple's user-level `srm` Secure Remove command). In this section we evaluate performance of Apple's file system with `unlink()`; we evaluate `srm` in Section 4.3.

We hypothesized that the Erase Free Space command on Apple's MSDOS and HFS file systems would have results similar to running `CIPHER.EXE` under

Table 2. Results of separately using the big file technique, Microsoft's CIPHER.EXE program, Eraser, and SDelete to sanitize the free space using Microsoft Windows with Service Pack 2 FAT and NTFS file systems. The first two columns indicate the number of deleted directory and file names recovered. The third column is the number sectors recovered from previously-deleted files. The next four columns indicate the number of complete files that could be recovered. Last is the number of unsanitizied slack sectors that recovered. Smaller numbers are better.

	# B Metadata		# B Data	# Complete B Files				"S"
	Dirnames	Filenames	Sectors	Small	Medium	Large	Total	Sectors
FAT								
Stamped	5	1280	368,992	320	304	624	1,248	491,006
Deleted	5	480	368,992	320	304	624	1,248	491,006
Bigfile	4	480	75	0	2	0	2	1,763
Big+Little	4	480	0	0	0	0	0	1,734
CIPHER.EXE /W	5	480	0	0	0	0	0	1,734
NTFS								
Stamped	5	1280	369,056	305	304	624	1,233	478,240
Deleted	5	1280	369,045	305	304	624	1,233	478,240
Bigfile	5	1280	75	1	0	0	1	9
Big+Little	5	1273	75	1	0	0	1	0
CIPHER.EXE /W	5	1273	65	0	0	0	0	0
Eraser	5	294	0	0	0	0	0	0
SDelete	5	1262	60	0	0	0	0	0

Windows with the FAT file system, while HFS with journaling would be similar to our results with Windows's NTFS file system.

As Table 3 shows, the big file technique was once again highly successful at erasing the free space on the partition formatted with the FAT file system. The big file was also very effective at sanitizing the HFS file system, although a total of 24 B sectors, including one complete medium-sized file, were left unsanitized. The technique was less effective with the journaled version of HFS: 71 sectors including 4 complete files were left behind. Presumably the few unsanitized sectors correspond to those that were in the journal. We were surprised that the unlink() call on the non-journaled version of HFS eradicated file names as well. We confirmed the absence of deleted file and directory names by searching for them with EnCase 5. Some, but not all, of the file names remain on the journaled file system. We suspect that the names that are left behind are in the journal.

3.3   Linux 2.6.12

We tested an Ubuntu Linux distribution with a 2.6.12 kernel using our technique. Ubuntu comes with many file systems; we tested vfat (FAT32), Ext2fs, Ext3fs, Reiserfs 3.6, and XFS file systems. Results appear in Table 4.

Table 3. Test results of Mac OS 10.4.4 with Apple's MSDOS, HFS, and Journaled HFS file systems. The "Bigfile" row shows the results of sanitizing the "Deleted" file system with our own program that creates a single big file, while "Erase Free Space" shows the results of sanitizing with the Mac OS 10.4.4 Disk Utility. While the big file technique does a good job overwriting the sectors associated with deleted files, Apple's Disk Utility does better.

	# B Metadata		# B Data	# Complete B Files				"S"
	Dirnames	Filenames	Sectors	Small	Medium	Large	Total	Sectors
Mac OS 10.4.6 "MSDOS" (FAT)								
Stamped	5	1280	369,048	320	304	624	1,248	484,512
Deleted	5	1280	369,048	320	304	624	1,248	484,512
Bigfile	5	1279	6	0	0	0	0	0
Big+Little	5	1279	0	0	0	0	0	0
Erase Free Space	5	1278	0	0	0	0	0	0
Mac OS 10.4.4 HFS								
Stamped	5	739	369,048	320	304	624	1,248	468,736
Deleted	5	0	369,048	320	304	624	1,248	468,736
Bigfile	5	0	24	0	1	0	1	0
Big+Little	5	0	0	0	0	0	0	0
Erase Free Space	5	0	0	0	0	0	0	0
Mac OS 10.4.6 HFS, Journaled								
Stamped	5	739	369,050	320	304	624	1,248	454,784
Deleted	5	739	369,050	320	304	624	1,248	454,784
Bigfile	5	739	71	0	4	0	4	0
Big+little	5	739	2	0	0	0	0	0
Erase Free Space	5	739	2	0	0	0	0	0

Because there is no overwriting program provided with Linux, the big file technique was implemented with a specially-written program that created a single big file filled with repetitions of the letter "E". Strikingly, the big file left a large number of B sectors—and in many cases complete files—when applied to Ext2fs, Ext3fs, Reiserfs, and XFS file systems. With Ext3, roughly 1% of the user data was left unsanitized by the technique, with 85 small and 91 medium-sized files being recoverable in their entirety.

We also tested the improved "big file + little file" technique with the Linux file systems.In all cases the improved technique did significantly better, but only on the "vfat" file system did the technique erase all of the data; XFS was the only file system on which metadata was affected at all.

3.4   FreeBSD 6.0

We tested FreeBSD 6.0 with the Unix File System version 2 (UFS2) and FreeBSD's support for FAT32. The big file left hundreds of complete files on

Table 4. Results of applying our tests to the Ubuntu Linux distribution with the 2.6.12 kernel shows that the big file technique generally fails on Linux-specific file systems. Tested file systems include Linux "vfat" (FAT with long file names), Ext2, Ext3, Reiserfs, and XFS. The rows labeled "Bigfile" show the metadata and sectors left unwritten after execution of the bigfile routine, while the "Big + Little" show the amount remaining following the application of both techniques. In general, the combination of the two techniques is more effective than the big file technique alone, but it is not perfect.

	# B Metadata		# B Data	# Complete B Files				"S"
	Dirnames	Filenames	Sectors	Small	Medium	Large	Total	Sectors
Linux vfat								
Stamped	5	1280	369,048	320	304	624	1,248	489,982
Deleted	5	1280	369,048	320	304	624	1,248	489,982
Bigfile	5	1278	0	0	0	0	0	1,734
Big + Little	5	1278	0	0	0	0	0	1,734
Linux Ext2fs								
Stamped	5	1280	369,048	320	304	624	1,248	455,970
Deleted	5	1280	369,048	320	304	624	1,248	455,970
Bigfile	5	1278	6	0	0	0	0	0
Big + Little	5	1278	0	0	0	0	0	0
Linux Ext3								
Stamped	5	1280	369,048	320	304	624	1,248	439,308
Deleted	5	1280	369,048	320	304	624	1,248	439,308
Bigfile	5	1280	3,567	85	91	0	176	224
Big + Little	5	1280	24	0	0	0	0	0
Linux Reiserfs 3.6								
Stamped	5	1281	370,451	64	304	624	992	421,661
Deleted	5	1281	370,358	64	304	624	992	421,669
Bigfile	5	1281	1,460	0	0	0	0	96
Big + Little	5	1281	1,460	0	0	0	0	96
XFS								
Stamped	5	1282	370,635	320	304	624	1,248	470,451
Deleted	5	1283	370,125	320	304	624	1,248	470,451
Bigfile	5	801	1,004	0	0	0	0	44
Big + Little	5	801	957	0	0	0	0	44

the FreeBSD UFS2 file system—nearly 2MB of data on a 488MB device. The technique also left a relatively large number of complete B *files*—both small and medium-sized files. These small files might be stored directly in the UFS inodes and thus occupy space not available to a big file. We do not have an explanation as to why so many medium-sized files were recovered.

4 Beyond One Big File

Although the big file technique does a good job sanitizing file content from free space, on every system we tested it fails to properly sanitize metadata. Here we evaluate the problem of free space sanitization from a theoretical prospective, discuss approaches for removing hidden information from computer systems, and evaluate the effectiveness of Apple's Secure Empty Trash file sanitizer.

Table 5. Results of testing FreeBSD 6.0 with FreeBSD's native MSDOS and UFS2 implementations shows that the big file technique largely works on the FAT file system but leaves some data behind on UFS2 file systems

	# B Metadata Dirnames	Filenames	# B Data Sectors	# Complete B Files Small	Medium	Large	Total	"S" Sectors
FreeBSD "MSDOS" (FAT)								
Stamped	5	1280	369,048	320	304	624	1,248	484,680
Deleted	5	1280	369,048	320	304	624	1,248	484,680
Bigfile	5	1278	16	0	0	0	0	56
Big + Little	5	1278	0	0	0	0	0	0
FreeBSD UFS2								
Stamped	5	1280	369,048	320	304	624	1,248	454,724
Deleted	5	1280	369,048	320	304	624	1,248	454,724
Bigfile	5	1280	3,504	152	96	0	248	256
Big + Little	5	1278	2,865	106	74	0	180	152

4.1 Sanitization Patterns

Garfinkel describes two design patterns or properties that can help address the problem of hidden data in computer systems:

1. **Explicit User Audit** [14, p. 325]: All user-generated information in the computer should be accessible through the computer's standard user interface, without the need to use special-purpose forensic tools.
2. **Complete Delete** [14, p. 328]: When the user attempts to delete information, the information should be overwritten so that it cannot be recovered.

These patterns apply equally well to hidden data in file systems and other data-holding structures. For example, there have been many cases in which "deleted" data has been recovered from Adobe Acrobat and Microsoft Word files [26, 29, 25]. These cases are a result of the Acrobat and Word file formats not implementing Explicit User Audit and the failure of Microsoft Word to implement Complete Delete.

As Section 3 shows, today's operating systems do not implement either of these patterns and this failing is not remedied by running existing free space and slack space sanitization tools.

4.2   Approaches for Removing Hidden Information

Let s_n be disk sector n and f be an arbitrary file. The set S_f is then the set of sectors $s_0 \ldots s_n$ that are used to hold f's data and metadata. If I is the information in file f, then the process of creating S_f could be described by:

$$S_f \leftarrow s_0 \ldots s_n \leftarrow I$$

Let S_R be the set of disk sectors that correspond to resident files and their metadata. Using this notation, the act of creating the new file f adds that files sectors to the list of resident sectors. That is,

$$S_R \leftarrow S_R \cup S_f.$$

Let S_D be the set of sectors that correspond to deleted files. In today's operating systems, deleting a file does not overwrite the information that the files contain; deleting a file simply moves that file's sectors from S_R to S_D:

$$S_R \leftarrow (S_R - S_f)$$
$$S_D \leftarrow S_D \cup S_f$$

The Explicit User Audit property can be satisfied simply by assuring that are no sectors in the file system that are both hidden and contain data. That is, we need to ensure that $S_D = \emptyset$. There are four ways to achieve this result:

1. Allow no deletion. If nothing can be deleted, then the problem of hidden dirty sectors will never arise. This approach ensures that $S_D = \emptyset$ by forbidding any modifications to S_D.
2. Have the operating system explicitly clear sectors on the target operating system before returning them to the free list. In this way is hidden data never created. (Bauer and Priyantha describe such an implementation for the Linux operating system [4].) This approach clears the sectors in S_f.
3. Create a second volume large enough to hold all resident files. Explicitly clear all sectors on the second volume,[7] then create a new file system on it.[8] Recursively copy all of the files from the root directory on the target volume to the root directory of the second volume.[9] Discard the target volume and treat the second volume as the target volume. Symbolically, this approach copies S_R to another volume and then destroys S_D. This approach is similar to a stop-and-copy garbage collection algorithm [34] and results in the only data on the new target volume being data that could be explicitly reached from the root directory of the original target volume.
4. Starting at the root directory of the target volume, recursively enumerate or otherwise mark every sector number that is used for file data or metadata. The sectors that remain will be the union of those sectors on the free list

---

[7] *e.g.*, `dd if=/dev/zero of=volume.iso`

[8] *e.g.*, `mdconfig -a -t vnode -f volume.iso -u 0; newfs /dev/md0`

[9] *e.g.*, `cp -pR /volume1 /volume2`

and those sectors that cannot be allocated but which do not currently hold user data. These sectors are then cleared. Symbolically, this approach clears the sectors in S_D. This approach is similar to a mark-and-sweep garbage collection algorithms [34]. Every sector that does not contain data is cleared.

These techniques have analogs when discussing data left in document files.

For example, the several cases in which confidential or classified information has leaked in Adobe Acrobat files is almost certainly a result of the way that Microsoft Word interacts with Adobe Acrobat's PDF Writer when "highlighted" words are printed. Microsoft Word allows text to be highlighted by selecting the words and then choosing the "highlight" tool from the Word formatting menu. Normally words are highlighted with the color yellow, which causes the words to stand out as if someone had colored them with a yellow "highlighter" pen. However, Word allows the color of the highlighting tool to be set by the user.

If the highlighter is set to use the color black, it can be used to redact information visually from a Microsoft Word document—that is, the information that is highlighted with black can not be seen on the computer's screen, nor will it be visible if the document is printed. An examination of the printer codes generated by Microsoft Word reveals why: Word highlights by first drawing a rectangular box in the specified highlighting color, after which it draws on top of the box. When the color black is used to highlight black text, the result is black text printed on a black background, resulting in text that cannot be discerned. However, the text is nevertheless present and can be revealed through a variety of means.

One approach for removing hidden data from a Microsoft Word document is to select and copy all of the text, then to paste the text into a new document. This technique, which was recently endorsed by the US National Security Agency [1], is similar to approach #3 above. Unfortunately, the technique does not work for included images or OLE objects, which must be handled separately. Current versions of Microsoft Office also have a "Remove Hidden Data" option in their file menu, although the mechanism of action is not documented.

4.3   Specific File Eradication Tools

An alternative to using the big file technique to sanitize disk sectors after files are deleted is to use a tool that is specifically designed to securely delete confidential information. Such tools typically use the file system `rename()` primitive to overwrite the file name and use a combination of `open()`, `write()` and `seek()` calls to repeatedly overwrite file contents. As previously noted, these techniques may not be effective on file systems that use journals or log files.

We evaluated three such tools: SDelete's file deletion capability, Eraser's file deletion capability, and the "Secure Empty Trash" command built into Mac OS 10.4.4. We found that SDelete did a perfect job removing the B sectors containing data but that it left approximately one-sixth of the metadata associated with the B filenames. Eraser left approximately 5% of the data sectors, including 78 complete files. Mac OS "Secure Empty Trash" command also did a perfect job deleting data, but it did not delete all of the directory and file names: many could be recovered. Details appear in Table 6.

All of these commands suffer from usability problems. While free, both SDelete and Eraser are third-party programs that must be specially downloaded and run: we believe that most Windows users do not know that these commands exist. Meanwhile, the implementation of Secure Empty Trash is incomplete. Although the command appears on the Finder's File menu, it does not appear on the Trash Can's context-sensitive menu (made visible by control-clicking on the trash can). Chosing "Secure Empty Trash" locks the trash can so that it cannot be used until the operation is finished. Secure Empty Trash is very slow—performing it on the file system in Table 6 took over an hour, compared with seconds simply empty the trash. (This is a result of Apple's decision to overwrite each sector with seven passes of random data.) Finally, if the user inadvertently empties the trash, there is no way to go back and securely empty the trash.

Table 6. Mac OS 10.4.4 Journaled HFS with Secure Empty Trash

	# B Metadata		# B Data	# Complete B Files			
	Dirnames	Filenames	Sectors	Small	Medium	Large	Total
Windows XP FAT32							
Stamped	5	1280	368,992	320	304	624	1,248
deleted with SDelete	3	480	0	0	0	0	0
deleted with Eraser	0	0	0	0	0	0	0
Windows XP NTFS							
Stamped	5	1280	369,056	305	304	624	1,233
deleted with SDelete	5	1262	60	0	0	0	0
deleted with Eraser	5	294	0	0	0	0	0
Mac OS 10.4.4 Journaled HFS							
Stamped	5	739	369,050	320	304	624	1,248
Dragged to Trash	5	739	369,050	320	304	624	1,248
Secure Empty Trash	1	43	0	0	0	0	0

5   Related Work

Although ours is the first work to vet the big file technique itself, there are several works analyzing sanitization tools.

A study by Guidance Software, authors of EnCase, found specific problems with Microsoft's `CIPHER.EXE`: "All unallocated space was filled with random values (which greatly affected file compression in the evidence file); however, the cipher tool affected only the unallocated clusters and a very small portion of the MFT; 10–15 records were overwritten in the MFT, and the majority of the records marked for deletion went untouched) [sic]. The utility does not affect other items of evidentiary interest on the typical NTFS partition, such as: file slack, registry files, the pagefile and file shortcuts." [30]

Geiger found defects in six counter-forensic tools [17]: Webroot Software's Window Washer 5.5 [31], NeoImagic Computing's Windows & Internet Cleaner Professional 3.60 [24], CyberScrub's CyberScrub Professional 3.5 [11], White-Canyon's SecureClean 4 [32], Robin Hood Software's Evidence Eliminator 5.0 [27], and Acronis's Acronis Privacy Expert 7.0 [2].

Burke and Craiger found similar defects [5] with Robin Hood Software's Evidence Eliminator 5.0, IDM Computer Solutions's UltraSentry 2.0 [20], CyberScrub's CyberScrub Privacy Suite 4.0, EAST Technologies' East-Tec Eraser 2005 [13], and Sami Tolvanen's Eraser 5.3 [16].

Chow *et. al.*, studied the lifetime of such sensitive data as password and encryption keys in the slack space of Unix-based computer systems using whole-system simulation. They discovered that such information, if not explicitly deleted, has a potentially indefinite lifespan [7].

One deficiency in our technique was that our stamped file systems did not contain fragmented files, because all of the files were written to the disk in a single operation. As noted by Rowe, creating realistic "fake" file systems is a non-trivial problem [28].

Finally, throughout this paper we have assumed that overwriting a sector on a hard drive with a single pass of zeros is sufficient to place the data previously in that sector beyond the possibility of recovery with conventional tools. Although Gutmann's 1996 paper discussed the possibility of recovering overwritten data using sophisticated laboratory equipment [19], the paper clearly states that the techniques only work on drives that use now-obsolete recording techniques. In a postscript added to the version of the paper that is available on the web, Gutmann states that two overwrites of random data is more than sufficient to render data irrecoverable on modern disk drives. While many researchers have claimed that a well-funded adversaries can recover overwritten data, after more than 10 years of searching we have been unable to verify or even corroborate any such claim. Crescenzo *et al.* also discuss techniques for overwriting secrets such as cryptographic key material. [10] In our opinion, such extraordinary measures do not seem to be warranted for the vast majority of computer users.

6   Conclusion

Clearly, there are two simple ways to erase the contents of any file system. The first is to physically destroy the storage device. The second is to erase every sector of the device using a command such as `dd`.

The technique of using one big file to sanitize the free space of an active file system has been widely implemented in many privacy-protecting and anti-forensic tools. We have found that the technique is effective at removing the contents of deleted files on FAT and NTFS file systems but that it rarely erases file names. The technique is less successful on many Linux file systems, leaving as much as 1.5% of user data unsanitized.

We found that the big file technique can be significantly improved by creating numerous small files a sector at a time after the big file is created but before it is deleted, but that even this improvement leaves a significant amount of residual information on many file systems.

The primary problem with the big file technique is that it sanitizes deleted files as a side effect of another file system operation—the operation of creating a big file. Results are inconsistent because the behavior of this side effect is not specified. "A program that has not been specified cannot be incorrect; it can only be surprising." [33]

Privacy protection should be a primary goal of modern operating systems. As such, they should give the user easy-to-use tools for deleting information. Apple's "Secure Empty Trash" is an example of such a tool, but its unnecessarily poor performance is a usability barrier to its use. A better approach would be to build this behavior directly into the `unlink()` and `DeleteFile()` system calls so that all deleted files are properly overwritten.

The test programs developed for this paper, along with the disk images that we created, can be downloaded from `http://www.simson.net/bigfile/`.

Acknowledgments

Simson L. Garfinkel is supported by a postdoctoral fellowship from the Center for Research on Computation and Society at the Division of Engineering and Applied Sciences at Harvard University. David J. Malan is funded in part by NSF Trusted Computing grant CCR-0310877. We thank Microsoft for the copy of MSDN that was used for the preparation of this paper.

We thank Michael D. Smith of Harvard University for his support of this work and his review of this paper. We also thank Walter Bender, Scott Bradner, Jesse Burns, Richard M. Conlan, Matthew Geiger, Peter Gutmann, Beth Rosenberg, and the anonymous reviewers for their helpful comments on this paper.

References

1. Redacting with confidence: How to safely publish sanitized reports converted from word to pdf. Technical Report I333-015R-2005, Architectures and Applications Division of the Systems and Network Attack Center (SNAC), Information Assurance Directorate, National Security Agency, 2005.
2. Acronis, Inc. `http://www.acronis.com/`.
3. Apple Computer, Inc. Apple Disk Utility, 2006.
4. Steven Bauer and Nissanka B. Priyantha. Secure data deletion for Linux file systems. In *Proc. 10th Usenix Security Symposium*, pages 153–164, San Antonio, Texas, 2001. Usenix.
5. Paul K. Burke and Philip Craiger. Digital Trace Evidence from Secure Deletion Programs. In *Proceedings of the Second Annual IFIP WG 11.9 International Conference on Digital Forensics*, Orlando, Florida, January 2006.
6. Brian Carrier. The Sleuth Kit & Autopsy: Forensics tools for Linux and other Unixes, 2005.
7. Jim Chow, Ben Pfaff, Tal Garfinkel, Kevin Christopher, and Mendel Rosenblum. Understanding data lifetime via whole system simulation. In *Proc. of the 13th Usenix Security Symposium*. Usenix, August 9–13 2004.

8. Microsoft Corporation. How To Use Cipher.exe to Overwrite Deleted Data in Windows, July 2004.
9. Microsoft Corporation. Windows 2000 Security Tool: New Cipher.exe Tool. http://www.microsoft.com/downloads/release.asp?releaseid=30925, March 2004.
10. Giovanni Di Crescenzo, Niels Fergurson, Russell Impagliazzo, and Markus Jakobsson. How to forget a secret. In *16th International Symposium on Theoretical Aspects of Computer Science (STACS '99)*, pages 500–509. Springer Verlag, 1999.
11. CyberScrub LLC. http://www.cyberscrub.com/.
12. Cleaning and sanitization matrix, January 1995. Chapter 8.
13. EAST Technologies. http://www.east-tec.com/.
14. Simson L. Garfinkel. *Design Principles and Patterns for Computer Systems that are Simultaneously Secure and Usable*. PhD thesis, MIT, Cambridge, MA, April 26 2005.
15. Simson L. Garfinkel, David J. Malan, Karl-Alexander Dubec, Christopher C. Stevens, and Cecile Pham. Disk imaging with the advanced forensic format, library and tools. In *Research Advances in Digital Forensics (Second Annual IFIP WG 11.9 International Conference on Digital Forensics)*. Springer, January 2006. (To appear in Fall 2006).
16. Garrett Trant. Eraser. http://www.heidi.ie/eraser/.
17. Matthew Geiger. Evaluating Commercial Counter-Forensic Tools. In *Proceedings of the 5th Annual Digital Forensic Research Workshop*, New Orleans, Louisiana, August 2005.
18. Guidance Software, Inc. EnCase Forensic.
19. Peter Gutmann. Secure deletion of data from magnetic and solid-state memory. In *Sixth USENIX Security Symposium Proceedings*, San Jose, California, July 22-25 1996. Usenix. Online paper has been updated since presentation in 1996.
20. IDM Computer Solutions, Inc. http://www.ultrasentry.com/.
21. Mark Russinovich. SDelete, 2003.
22. Mark Russinovich and Bryce Cogswell. Filemon for Windows.
23. Microsoft. Cipher.exe security tool for the encrypting file system. January 31 2006.
24. NeoImagic Computing, Inc. http://www.neoimagic.com/.
25. Dawn S. Onley. Pdf user slip-up gives dod lesson in protecting classified information. *Government Computer News*, 24, April 16 2005.
26. Kevin Poulsen. Justice e-censorship gaffe sparks controversy. *SecurityFocus*, October 23 2003.
27. Robin Hood Software Ltd. http://www.evidence-eliminator.com/.
28. Neil C. Rowe. Automatic detection of fake file systems. In *International Conference on Intelligence Analysis Methods and Tools*, May 2005.
29. Stephen Shankland and Scott Ard. Document shows SCO prepped lawsuit against BofA. *News.Com*, March 4 2004.
30. Kimberly Stone and Richard Keightley. Can Computer Investigations Survive Windows XP? Technical report, Guidance Software, Pasadena, California, December 2001.
31. Webroot Software, Inc. http://www.webroot.com/.
32. WhiteCanyon, Inc. http://www.whitecanyon.com/.
33. W. D. Young, W. E. Boebeit, and R. Y. Kain. Proving a computer system secure. *The Scientific Honeyweller*, 6(2):18–27, July 1985. Reprinted in Computer and Network Security, M. D. Abrams and H. J. Podell, eds., IEEE Computer Security Press, 1986.
34. Benjamin Zorn. Comparing mark-and sweep and stop-and-copy garbage collection. In *LFP '90: Proceedings of the 1990 ACM conference on LISP and functional programming*, pages 87–98, New York, NY, USA, 1990. ACM Press.

Protecting Privacy with the MPEG-21 IPMP Framework

Nicholas Paul Sheppard and Reihaneh Safavi-Naini

School of Information Technology and Computer Science
The University of Wollongong, NSW, 2522, Australia
{nps, rei}@uow.edu.au

Abstract. A number of authors have observed a duality between privacy protection and copyright protection, and, in particular, observed how digital rights management technology may be used as the basis of a privacy protection system. In this paper, we describe our experiences in implementing a privacy protection system based on the *Intellectual Property Management and Protection* ("IPMP") components of the MPEG-21 Multimedia Framework. Our approach allows individuals to express their privacy preferences in a way enabling automatic enforcement by data users' computers. This required the design of an extension to the MPEG Rights Expression Language to cater for privacy applications, and the development of software that allowed individuals' information and privacy preferences to be securely collected, stored and interpreted.

1   Introduction

The increasing use of electronic records in commerce, government, health and other fields has led to public fears about the potential mis-uses of private data. Once personal information has been submitted to an organisation, the subject of that information no longer controls what becomes of it, and organisations or rogue parties within organisations have the potential to mis-use the information through negligence or dishonesty.

While some organisations publish privacy protection policies, there is no technological guarantee that the policy espoused by the organisation will actually be followed by the people who have access to personal information. Furthermore, the privacy policies offered by organisations may not always meet the requirements or desires of the individuals who are the subjects of personal information held by those organisations.

Digital rights management ("DRM") provides protection for information by making access to information depend on satisfying the conditions imposed by a *licence* written in a machine-enforceable *rights expression language*. DRM technology is widely used in copyright protection applications, but can also be applied to privacy protection [14] by developing licences that represent individuals' preferences for use of their personal information. The digital rights management approach to privacy is detailed in Section 2.

G. Danezis and P. Golle (Eds.): PET 2006, LNCS 4258, pp. 152–171, 2006.
© Springer-Verlag Berlin Heidelberg 2006

The MPEG-21 Multimedia Framework [9] is a framework for creating, distributing, navigating, using and controlling multimedia content, currently under development by the Motion Picture Experts Group ("MPEG"). Of particular interest to this paper, MPEG-21 proposes to incorporate an *Intellectual Property Management and Protection* framework within which content providers can control the use and distribution of multimedia content. In this paper, we consider that "multimedia content" might include personal information such as contact details and financial records. We will give an outline of the relevent components of the MPEG-21 Framework in Section 3.

The MPEG Rights Expression Language supplies a vocabulary of elements useful in copyright protection applications, but lacks elements that are useful in privacy protection applications. In Section 4, we outline how we developed a "privacy extension schema" (in the sense of XML Schema) for MPEG REL, based on a study of vocabularies developed for the Platform for Privacy Preferences [22] and Enterprise Privacy Authorization Language [19]. Our extension allows individuals to express how they allow their data to be used in terms of actions and conditions that can be interpreted by an automated computer terminal.

In Section 5, we describe the extension of an existing MPEG-21-based digital rights management system to a privacy protection scenario. Our implementation allows a service provider to collect individuals' data in the form of XML documents, while the use and distribution of these documents is restricted according to conditions supplied by the data's owner.

Our system demonstrates the fundamentals of the DRM approach to privacy, but leaves substantial opportunity for further work in a number of areas including the composition of licences, management of protected information and provision for exceptional circumstances. We will conclude the paper with a discussion of outstanding issues in Section 6.

2   Digital Rights Management and Privacy Protection

Zittrain [24] observed a duality between protection of private data, and protection of copyrighted material: in both cases, we have a provider who wishes to make some information available to a third party in return for some financial reward or service, but does not wish to make the information publicly available. Technical approaches to protecting copyright, therefore, might be expected to yield insights into technical approaches to protecting privacy.

Kenny and Korba [14] later examined applying digital rights management technology in the context of the European Union's Data Protection Directive. Unlike models of privacy protection in which the privacy policy is developed by the database operator, the digital rights management model permits the data subject to choose the policy to be applied to his or her data.

Figure 1 shows the architecture of a typical digital rights management system. Data is created by a *provider*, and transmitted in a protected (for example, encrypted) form to a *user* via some distribution channel. In order to access the protected data, the user must obtain a *licence* from the licence issuer. A licence is a document containing the terms of use of the data and the cryptographic information required to access the protected content.

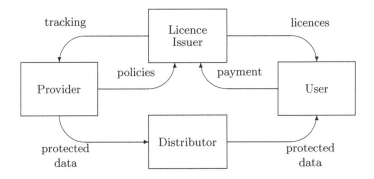

Fig. 1. A typical digital rights management system

Protected data may only be accessed using special terminals certified to behave in accordance with the terms specified in the licence, and not to reveal the unprotected content or decryption keys to the human user of the terminal. By controlling the licences that are made available to users via the licence issuer, the provider can control whether or not content is copied between users, how many times content is used, and so on.

In a privacy protection context, the provider is a *data subject* whose privacy is at stake should an item of data be mis-used in some way. A *data user* may require access to the data for some purpose, such as completing a transaction requested by the data subject. In order to gain access to the data, the data user must obtain a licence from the licence issuer. Licences issued by the licence issuer are controlled in some way by the data subject, either directly or by having the issuer act according a policy supplied by the data subject. The data user can then access the data according to the terms of the licence.

Several DRM-like approaches to privacy protection have been reported in the literature, often for specific applications such as location privacy. We are not aware of any attempt, however, to develop a privacy protection system in the digital rights management model as complete as those currently available for copyright protection.

Cha and Joung's *On-Line Personal Data Licensing* ("OPDL") system [3] allows data subjects to issue licences using a *personal data licensor*. The personal data licensor is much like the licence issuer in a digital rights management system. OPDL licences are based on the policy language defined by the Platform for Privacy Preferences ("P3P") [22]. P3P, however, was not designed for this purpose and does not provide for automated enforcement of the policies expressed in its policy language. In OPDL, licences are simply stored and made available to any audit of the privacy practices of the data collector.

Hong and Landay's *Confab* architecture [8] for ubiquitous computing allows items of data to be associated with a "privacy tag" (licence). The privacy tag specifies the conditions under which the data may be retained, and provides an e-mail address to which notifications of disclosure can be sent. The tag does not specify how the data may be used or shared, however.

The most similar system to the one described in this paper is the *Personal DRM* ("PDRM") system of Gunter, et al. [7]. PDRM is a location privacy system in which individuals may make their current location available in order to receive some service, such as alerting them to the proximity of their friends. Individuals' privacy is protected by associating their location data with a licence written in the Extensible Rights Markup Language ("XrML") [4], which is the predecessor of the language used by MPEG-21 and in this paper.

PDRM's XrML, however, makes extensive use of P3P policy files to describe users' privacy preferences and Gunter, et al. do not describe any method by which these preferences can be enforced. For the system described in the present paper, we developed a rights expression language within the model used by both XrML and MPEG-21 that can be enforced using the standard algorithm for interpreting these languages.

3   MPEG-21

Unlike the well-known MPEG-1, -2 and -4 standards, MPEG-21 does not define the way in which individual multimedia presentations are encoded, but defines ways in which atomic multimedia objects can be used, combined, navigated and referenced. It consists of numerous parts, some of which have been ratified by the International Standards Organisation as the ISO/IEC 21000 series of standards, while others remain under development. In this section, we will give an overview of the components of MPEG-21 required to understand this paper.

3.1   Digital Items

The core notion in MPEG-21 is the notion of a *digital item* [10], which represents a collection of multimedia objects related in some way. Digital items are described using the XML-based *digital item declaration language* ("DIDL"), which organises content and meta-data into a hierarchical structure. For the purposes of this paper, the most important elements are:

Resources. Atomic multimedia objects such as images, sounds and videos.
Components. Resources together with their descriptors.
Descriptors. Meta-data, such as identifiers, MPEG-7 descriptors, etc.

Figure 2 shows a simple digital item declaration, similar to the digital items used in our system. It consists of a single item containing a single component. The resource is an XML document contained by the *MyXML* tags (the body of the document has been omitted for brevity), and is identified by the URN `urn:smartinternet:doc1`.

```
<didl:DIDL>
  <didl:Item>
    <didl:Component>
      <didl:Descriptor>
        <didl:Statement>
          <dii:Identifier>urn:smartinternet:doc:1</dii:Identifier>
        </didl:Statement>
      </didl:Descriptor>
      <didl:Resource>
        <myxml:MyXML>...</myxml:MyXML>
      </didl:Resource>
    </didl:Component>
  </didl:Item>
</didl:DIDL>
```

Fig. 2. A simple digital item declaration

3.2   Intellectual Property Management and Protection

Intellectual property management and protection ("IPMP") is MPEG's term for digital rights management [11]. MPEG-21 does not fix a particular digital rights management system, but assumes that IPMP functionality is provided by vendor-specific *IPMP tools* that can be downloaded and made accessible to the terminal as necessary. IPMP tools may implement basic functions such as decryption and watermarking, or may implement complete digital rights management systems in their own right.

We say a resource is *governed* if it is protected by one or more IPMP tools. Each governed resource is associated with a plaintext identifier and an *IPMP information descriptor* that associates the resource with a licence and describes the IPMP tools required to access the resource. If the conditions of the licence are satisfied, the terminal must obtain and instantiate the IPMP tools in order to access the resource.

A large part of the work done on our original digital rights management system involved the design and implementation of IPMP tools. The security architecture used by our tools is described in Appendix B, but the technical detail of their implementation is beyond the scope of the present paper.

3.3   Rights Expression Language

Though MPEG-21 does not define a full digital rights management system, it does define a rights expression language known as "MPEG REL" [12]. MPEG REL is closely based on the Extensible Rights Markup Language ("XrML") [4].

An MPEG REL licence is structured as a collection of *grants* issued by some licence issuer. Each grant awards some *right* over some specified *resource* to a specified *principal*, that is, user of a resource. Each grant may be subject to a *condition*, such that the right contained in the grant cannot be exercised unless the condition is satisfied.

In order to perform some action on a resource, a user (principal) must possess a licence containing a grant that awards the right to perform that action on that resource, and satisfy the associated condition. This must be checked by the terminal prior to exercising the right.

MPEG REL is defined as a collection of three XML schemata, called the *core schema* (denoted by the XML namespace prefix r in this paper), the *standard extension schema* (prefix sx) and the *multimedia extension schema* (prefix mx). These schemata define the fundamental elements of the language, some widely-useful conditions, and elements useful in copyright protection applications, respectively. We will later discuss the development of a *privacy extension schema* for use in privacy protection applications. We will denote elements of the privacy extension schema by the namespace prefix px.

Figure 3 shows an example of an MPEG REL grant allowing a principal (r:keyHolder) identified by his or her public key to print a resource (mx:diReference) identified by a digital item identifier urn:smartinternet:doc1. The principal is only permitted to print the resource once (sx:ExerciseLimit).

```
<r:grant>
  <r:keyHolder>
    <r:info>
      <dsig:KeyValue>
        <dsig:RSAKeyValue>...</dsig:RSAKeyValue>
      </dsig:KeyValue>
  </r:keyHolder>
  <mx:print/>
  <mx:diReference>
    <mx:identifier>urn:smartinternet:doc1</mx:identifier>
  </mx:diReference>
  <sx:ExerciseLimit>
    <sx:count>1</sx:count>
  </sx:ExerciseLimit>
<r:grant>
```

Fig. 3. An MPEG REL grant

XrML and MPEG REL are provided with a vocabulary useful in copyright protection applications. In the following section, we will discuss extending MPEG REL with a vocabulary suitable for privacy protection applications.

4   Expressing Privacy Preferences in MPEG REL

As described in Section 2, previous authors have attempted to enlist the P3P policy language for expressing the privacy preferences of data subjects. The intention of P3P, however, is to inform data subjects of the global privacy practices of Internet service providers. Here, we require data subjects to specify their preferences regarding the handling of a particular item of data. P3P seems poorly suited to the latter task since it provides no way of identifying a specific item of data or a specific data user. Furthermore, P3P does not provide for automated enforcement of privacy policies and we are not aware of any algorithms for determining whether or not a given action is permissible, given a P3P policy.

Recognising the shortcomings of P3P as an enforcement tool, researchers at IBM proposed the Enterprise Privacy Authorization Language ("EPAL") [19]. EPAL is intended to express an organisation's privacy policy in such a way as to make it enforceable by an access control system. EPAL's structure is very similar to that of MPEG REL and other access control languages such as the Extensible Access Control Markup Language ("XACML") [17]: policies in all of these languages consist of a series of rules expressing the right of some actor to perform some action on some object, subject to certain conditions and obligations. EPAL has an additional element called *purpose* that makes permission conditional on the action being performed for some particular purpose.

EPAL and XACML, however, require each organisation to define its own vocabulary of actors, actions, etc. for use in their access control policies. In our application, it seems highly impractical to require data subjects to use a different vocabulary for every service provider with which he or she interacts.

MPEG REL is specifically designed for the digital rights management model, provides a vocabulary that is constant across all service providers, and specifies an algorithm for determining whether or not a given action is permissible. However, the existing MPEG REL vocabulary was designed with only copyright protection applications in mind and it lacks elements to describe principals, rights and conditions that may be useful in privacy protection applications. For example, privacy protection systems often restrict the use of data to a particular transaction, but MPEG REL does not define any conditions that support this.

For the purposes of the prototype system described in Section 5, we designed a preliminary privacy extension schema by examining existing vocabularies for P3P (including drafts of P3P Version 1.1) and EPAL [18]. The detailed syntax of the extension was worked out by attempting to write licences for a variety of simple scenarios, and making corrections as necessary until the licences we wanted could be written reasonably conveniently. The resulting schema was applied to the customer service application considered in this paper.

The detailed development of a comprehensive privacy extension schema is left as the topic for another paper. In this section, we will simply summarise the major observations we made while developing our schema. A summary of the schema we derived is given in Appendix A.

Purposes. Perhaps the most conspicuous difference between MPEG REL and languages developed in privacy protection is the latter's use of "purposes". Different languages make somewhat different uses of the term – P3P Version 1.1 even goes so far as to use the term twice: once as "purpose" then again as "primary purpose". Purposes are widely used in human-readable privacy policies, but to be enforceable by machine they need to be interpreted as some combination of a particular principal exercising a particular right under certain conditions.

P3P's notion of a "purpose" generally corresponds to a combination of a right and one or more conditions in MPEG REL. For example, P3P's `contact` and `telemarketing` purposes can be interpreted as the right to contact someone, under the condition that it not be by telephone or be by telephone, respectively.

The use of "purpose" in EPAL at first recalls a condition in MPEG REL, and of course it would be possible to simply create an MPEG REL condition called `Purpose` that made a grant available only if the right was exercised for some specified purpose. This is, in fact, how purposes are treated in the Privacy Policy Profile of XACML Version 2.0. In our schema, we chose to create a different condition for every purpose that we interpreted in this way – this makes the vocabulary of purposes shared by all uses of the language.

However, a number of the purposes identified in [18] may be better implemented as roles in the sense of a role-based access control system. For example, it is much more straightforward to check that a principal is acting in the role of a police officer than it is to check directly that he or she is carrying out law enforcement. MPEG REL supports role-based principals using the `PropertyPossessor` principal (e.g. a principal who possesses the property of being a police officer). We will give more detail about how these elements are used in Section 5.

Obligations. EPAL and XACML distinguish "conditions" and "obligations" that represent conditions that must be true before access is permitted, and actions that must be carried out after access is permitted. MPEG REL conflates obligations with conditions – we can think of obligations as being post-conditions and EPAL/XACML-style conditions as being pre-conditions. It is straightforward to express widely-used obligations involving notification and data retention, for example, using `TrackReport` and `ValidityInterval` conditions in MPEG REL.

Recipients. P3P and [18] consider "recipients" who have data disclosed to them by someone with direct access to the database, but who do not have direct access to the database themselves. In the model used by P3P and EPAL, it makes sense to make the discloser to be the principal of an access control rule and make the identity of the recipient a condition. In the digital rights management model, however, it makes more sense to identify the recipient as the principal of a grant that is given directly to that recipient. The "discloser" can give the data to the recipient in its protected form without needing to access the data him- or herself.

5   Enforcing Privacy Preferences with SITDRM

In order to explore the digital rights management approach to privacy protection, we applied our existing implementation of MPEG-21's IPMP Components – known as "SITDRM" – to a privacy protection scenario.

SITDRM was designed to allow businesses to license multimedia works from their web site, using the MPEG-21 IPMP framework to ensure that buyers complied with the terms of the licence they had purchased. In the project described by this paper, we took the IPMP technology that underpins SITDRM and

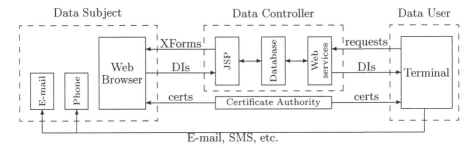

Fig. 4. SITDRM Enterprise Architecture

applied it to the protection of customer records submitted via a company's web site. We call the new system "SITDRM Enterprise".

Figure 4 shows an overview of the SITDRM Enterprise system. We assume that some service provider (the data controller) requires information to be collected from its customers (data subjects), and that all of this information is stored in some central database. The service provider's employees (data users) then require access to the information in order to carry out their jobs and provide service to the customers.

Customers submit their information via a form on the service provider's web site. In our example, the document contained the customer's postal address, e-mail address and telephone number formatted as an XML document using the Extensible Customer Information Language ("xCIL") [16]. In principle, the service provider can set up the web site to collect any information formatted as an XML document. At the same time, customers may design an MPEG REL licence that describes how this information may be used.

Upon submitting the form, the customer's web browser converts the resulting XML document into the governed resource of an MPEG-21 digital item, and issues the licence designed by the customer. The governed item and issued licence are then transmitted to the data controller for storage.

Employees who require access to a customer's data may download the governed item from the data controller. Upon attempting to perform some action on the item, the employee's terminal asks the data controller for a licence that authorises this action. If an appropriate licence is found, the action is permitted to continue. Otherwise, the action is rejected.

In general, governed items and licences can also be passed on to third parties (such as related companies) via e-mail or the like. If the customer has granted a licence that permits the third party to access his or her data, the third party can access this data as for employees of the original service provider. Our initial scenario considers data distributed within one company only, however.

5.1   Security Architecture

SITDRM Enterprise uses the same techniques used to preserve the integrity of the digital rights management as were used in the original copyright protection application. Our fundamental requirement is that every terminal be tamper-resistant and be supplied with a public/private key pair of which the private key is known only to the terminal – in particular, it is not known to the human user of the terminal. We further assume that a public key infrastructure exists that allows all public keys to be verified.

Every governed resource is encrypted using a unique *resource key*. Any licence that grants permission to use this resource must contain the resource key encrypted either by the public key of the terminal on which the resource is to be used, or by a key that can be obtained from a second licence without which the first licence would be invalid. In this way, a resource can only be decrypted by a tamper-resistant terminal in possession of a valid set of licences. The integrity of licences is ensured by having them signed by their issuer.

For clarity of the main body of this paper, we have omitted the details of cryptographic operations in the remainder of this section. A complete description of SITDRM's security architecture is given in Appendix B.

5.2 Licences

Two kinds of licences are used in SITDRM Enterprise: *membership certificates* permit individual data users to act as members of roles using the `PossessProperty` right, while *resource licences* permit members of roles to perform actions using the `PropertyPossessor` principal.

In order for a particular data user to carry out an action on a document, he or she must obtain both a resource licence that permits some role to carry out that action, and a membership certificate that makes him or her a member of that role. Examples of a membership certificate and a resource licence are given in Figures 5 and 6, respectively.

```
<r:grant>
  <r:keyHolder>
    <r:info>
      <dsig:KeyValue>
        <dsig:RSAKeyValue>...</dsig:RSAKeyValue>
      </dsig:KeyValue>
  </r:keyHolder>
  <sx:possessProperty/>
  <sx:propertyUri definition="urn:smartinternet:customer-service"/>
</r:grant>
```

Fig. 5. A membership certificate for the `urn:smartinternet:customer-service` role

Membership certificates can be obtained from a *role issuer* operated by the service provider. The role issuer is simply a licence issuer in the sense described in Section 2. We assume that the role issuer is operated by some reputable administrator who is trusted to issue membership certificates only to individuals who have reason to act in those roles. In a real company, we might expect the

```
<r:grant>
  <r:propertyPossessor>
    <sx:propertyUri definition="urn:smartinternet:customer-service"/>
  </r:propertyPossessor>
  <mx:play/>
  <mx:diReference>
    <mx:identifier>urn:smartinternet:customers:123</mx:identifier>
  </mx:diReference>
</r:grant>
```

Fig. 6. A licence that allows members of the `urn:smartinternet:customer-service` role to view the document `urn:smartinternet:customers:123`

role issuer to be under the control of human resources staff who assign roles to employees according to the terms of their employment.

Resource licences are issued by data subjects. The details of generating and issuing appropriate licences will be discussed in Section 5.3.

5.3 Submitting Governed Documents

A service provider who wishes to collect information from his or her customers may design a form for doing so using XForms [23]. XForms' ability to manipulate arbitrary XML documents without programming makes it very appealing to web designers who need to present documents written in machine-oriented languages such as xCIL and MPEG REL in way that is accessible to human users.

Every XForms form is associated with an XML document called the *instance document*. Every control on the form is identified with a node of the instance document using an XPath expression [21], and the user's input to a control determines the content of the associated XML node. Initial values for controls can be supplied by the data controller by supplying an initial instance document containing those values. When the user chooses to submit the form, the instance document is uploaded to the server.

The present application uses two kinds of instance documents: data and licences. We require that the former kind be encrypted before it is uploaded to the server, and that the latter kind be signed before it is uploaded. For this purpose, we added a new attribute to the **submission** element of XForms – called *transform* – that indicates what kind of post-processing should be applied to the instance document prior to uploading it. We use transformations called *govern* and *issue* that cause the instance document to be converted into an MPEG-21 governed digital item and issued as licence, respectively.

A simple form for editing a document and a licence is shown in Figure 7. Each **model** element in the head of the HTML page describes one instance document, and every control on the form is associated with a model using the **model** attribute. In the example, model **d** represents the document and model **l** represents the licence. The submit button and other details have been omitted or abbreviated for brevity.

```
<h:head>
  <f:model id="d">
    <f:instance src="/templates/document.xml"/>
    <f:submission action="/submission/document" transform="govern"/>
  </f:model>
  <f:model id="l">
    <f:instance src="/templates/licence.xml"/>
    <f:submission action="/submission/licence" transform="issue"/>
  </f:model>
</h:head>

<h:body>
    <f:input model="d" ref="/ci:xCIL/.../ci:ContactNumber">
      <f:label>Phone Number</f:label>
    </f:input>
    <f:input model="l"
             ref="/r:license/.../px:ContactMethodUri/@definition">
      <f:label>Voice or SMS</f:label>
    </f:input>
</h:body>
```

Fig. 7. A form for editing a document and a licence

The form in Figure 7 initialises the instance documents from templates on the server called `document.xml` and `licence.xml`. In our example application, the document template is a skeleton xCIL document whose fields will be filled in by the form controls.

The licence template, however, is a near-complete licence similar to the one shown in Figure 8. This template supplies technical information such as the identifier for the role that will be using the information, while allowing the data subject to change the permissible contact method using the form. Data subjects may view the complete technical details of the licence using a toolbar option.

In principle it is possible to design a form that allows the data subject to make any change to the licence he or she wishes. Such a form, however, would likely be very intimidating to users and we expect that most users would only be

```
<r:grant>
  <r:propertyPossessor>
    <sx:propertyUri definition="urn:smartinternet:customer-service"/>
  </r:propertyPossessor>
  <px:contact/>
  <px:contactMethods>
    <px:contactMethodUri definition="changeme"/>
  </px:contactMethods>
</r:grant>
```

Fig. 8. A licence template for Figure 7

interested in modifying a few simple conditions like the one shown in Figure 8. We will discuss this issue further in Section 6.

5.4   Accessing Governed Documents

Anyone with access to the data controller is permitted to download any of the documents and licences stored there. Documents and licences so obtained may be further distributed using other channels, for example, by e-mailing them to other companies or saving them to physical media. However, a governed document can only be accessed on a DRM-compliant terminal and only if that terminal is provided with licences that permit access to that document.

In our implementation, a DRM-compliant terminal is represented by an application called "IPDoc" that allows users to download governed documents from the server and perform actions on them if there are licences permitting them to do so. Some screenshots from IPDoc are shown in Figure 9.

(a)   (b)

Fig. 9. IPDoc: (a) the main window and log-in dialogue and (b) a document window

IPDoc's main window lists the identifiers of all of the documents in the database. Before any documents can be used, the user must log-in with a name and password, and specify the task that he or she intends to perform – in this case, either "renewals" or "marketing". Of course the latter selection is open to abuse since the computer cannot check what the user actually intends, but it serves to at least prevent honest users from using or disclosing data by mistake.

When the user selects a document from the main window, IPDoc downloads the document from the database and opens a new window with menu options for performing various actions on the document. If the user chooses to perform an action on a document, IPDoc first searches for any licence that permits that action. If it finds one, and that licence requires the user to be a member of a particular role in order to be used, it then searches for a membership certificate that permits the current user to act in that role. If it finds one, the action is permitted. Otherwise the action is rejected and an error message is displayed.

6   Lessons Learnt and Future Work

Composing Licences. To be enforceable, licences must be expressed in terms of the internal structure and procedures of the service provider. Data subjects, however, are unlikely to find this representation very convenient or meaningful when attempting to express their privacy preferences.

Our XForms-based approach allows licences to be represented in a more convenient way by using careful web design, but is limited to making direct associations between form controls and MPEG REL licence elements. Nor does it assure a data subject that the licence being produced accurately represents their privacy preferences unless they have a detailed understanding of MPEG REL and the time to examine the licence.

Improving the way that licences are presented to users and giving data subjects greater assurance that licences match their preferences is the subject of further research. Possible approaches include auditing of web sites by consumer agencies, protocols for negotiating privacy policies [5,13,20] and the introduction of a formal human-readable representation of privacy preferences that can be mapped to computer-readable licences by machine.

Selecting Documents. Our implementation allows data users to select documents based on the identifier associated with the document. This may be acceptable if the identifiers used are meaningful, or if documents can be chosen automatically by a computer system that knows which document ought to be processed next (for example, by maintaining a queue of jobs to be done). However, we can imagine situations in which more useful information would be required in order for a user to decide which document is the one that he or she is looking for – for example, if a user were looking for documents concerning a particular topic.

DIDL allows meta-data to be associated with a resource by placing it in a `Descriptor` element contained within the component that contains the resource. This descriptor need not be encrypted even if the resource is governed, and can be used by a data user to identify resources that he or she might be interested in. Obviously, however, meta-data may itself constitute private information.

Possible solutions include the use of a trusted search engine [15] and encrypted keyword search [1]. These topics are beyond the scope of this paper.

Exceptions. Our system allows data to be used in any situation that can be foreseen by the data subject at the time the data is created. However, it is easy to imagine unforeseen exceptional circumstances – such as a medical emergency – in which it may be desirable to over-ride the restrictions imposed by a licence.

Even if a data subject could foresee all of the exceptional circumstances in which data might need to be accessible, it seems likely that encoding all of them into a licence would be cumbersome and inefficient. Furthermore, there may be cases (notably in law enforcement) where the data subject may not have any incentive to encode exceptions.

These exceptions can be considered loosely analogous to the fair dealing or fair use exceptions of copyright law, which allow content users to make some copies of copyrighted content without the explicit permission of the copyright owner. Dealing with these exceptions is very difficult [6], though some authors have proposed methods using a trusted escrow agent who is able to over-ride a DRM system if a case for an exception can be made [2]. The development of analogous systems for privacy is left as future work.

7   Conclusion

SITDRM Enterprise shows how a DRM framework originally developed for copyright protection can be applied to privacy protection. It shows how data subjects' preferences for the use of their data can be encoded in such a way as to enable a computer system to – so far as is possible using current technology – ensure that those preferences are adhered to by data users.

Compared to models in which private data is governed by a central policy set by the organisation's privacy officer, the digital rights management model permits data subjects to control the policy to which their data is subject and ensures that this policy is applied in any organisation to which the data might travel. The need to compose, manage and interpret large numbers of licences, however, makes the system somewhat more complex than one in which all data is subject to a central policy. In particular, the average user may require technological assistance to be able to produce useful and accurate licences conveniently.

In designing SITDRM Enterprise, it quickly became apparent that the architecture we had designed might work just as well for protecting internal documents generated by company employees as it does for protecting external documents submitted by data subjects. One might wonder if it is possible to develop a "grand unified rights management system" that could be deployed in any application where there are rights to be protected. Our work with SITDRM may suggest that this is possible, but it remains to be be seen whether or not a unified rights management system could be as practical and effective as one designed for a specific purpose.

Acknowledgements

This work was partly funded by the Co-operative Research Centre for Smart Internet Technology, Australia. We would particularly like to thank members of the User-Centred Design Group within the Smart Internet CRC for stimulating discussion in this area.

References

1. D. Boneh, G. Di Crescenzo, R. Ostrovsky, and G. Persiano. Public key encryption with keyword search. In *EUROCRYPT*, pages 506–522, 2004.
2. D. L. Burk and J. E. Cohen. Fair use infrastructure for copyright management systems. *Harvard Journal of Law and Technology*, 15:41–83, 2001.
3. S.-C. Cha and Y.-J. Joung. From P3P to data licenses. In *Workshop on Privacy Enhancing Technologies*, pages 205–221, 2003.
4. ContentGuard. Extensible Rights Markup Language. http://www.xrml.org, 2004.
5. K. El-Khatib. A privacy negotiation protocol for web services. In *Workshop on Collaboration Agents: Autonomous Agents for Collaborative Environments*, 2003.
6. J. S. Erickson and D. K. Mulligan. The technical and legal dangers of code-based fair use enforcement. *Proceedings of the IEEE*, 92:985–996, 2004.

7. C. A. Gunter, M. J. May, and S. G. Stubblebine. A formal privacy system and its application to location based services. In *Workshop on Privacy Enhancing Technologies*, pages 256–282, 2004.
8. J. I. Hong and J. A. Landay. An architecture for privacy-sensitive ubiquitous computing. In *International Conference On Mobile Systems, Applications And Services*, pages 177–189, 2004.
9. International Standards Organisation. Information technology – multimedia framework (MPEG-21) – part 1: Vision, technologies and strategy. ISO/IEC 21000-1:2001.
10. International Standards Organisation. Information technology – multimedia framework (MPEG-21) – part 2: Digital item declaration. ISO/IEC 21000-2:2003.
11. International Standards Organisation. Information technology – multimedia framework (MPEG-21) – part 4: Intellectual property management and protection components. ISO/IEC 21000-4:2006.
12. International Standards Organisation. Information technology – multimedia framework (MPEG-21) – part 5: Rights expression language. ISO/IEC 21000-5:2004.
13. K. Irwin and T. Yu. Determining user privacy preferences by asking the right questions: An automated approach. In *ACM Workshop on Privacy in the Electronic Society*, pages 47–50, 2005.
14. S. Kenny and L. Korba. Applying digital rights management systems to privacy rights. *Computers & Security*, 21:648–664, 2002.
15. E. Mykletun and G. Tsudik. Incorporating a secure coprocessor in the database-as-a-service model. In *International Workshop on Innovative Architecture for Future Generation High Performance Processors and Systems*, pages 38–44, 2005.
16. Organization for the Advancement of Structured Information Standards. OASIS Customer Information Quality TC. http://www.oasis-open.org/committees/ciq/, 2004.
17. Organization for the Advancement of Structured Information Standards. OASIS eXtensible Access Control Markup Language TC. http://www.oasis-open.org/committees/xacml/, 2004.
18. C. Powers, S. Adler, and B. Wishart. EPAL translation of the Freedom of Information and Protection of Privacy Act. White paper, Ontario Information and Privacy Commissioner, 11 March 2004. http://www.ipc.on.ca/docs/EPAL%20FI1.pdf.
19. M. Schunter and C. Powers. The Enterprise Privacy Authorization Language (EPAL 1.1). http://www.zurich.ibm.com/security/enterprise-privacy/epal, 2003.
20. A. Tumer, A. Dogac, and I. H. Toroslu. A semantic based privacy framework for web services. In *Proceedings of WWW '03 Workshop on E-Services and the Semantic Web*, 2003.
21. W3 Consortium. XML Path Language (XPath). http://www.w3.org/TR/xpath, 1999.
22. W3 Consortium. Platform for Privacy Preferences (P3P) project. http://www.w3.org/P3P, 2004.
23. W3 Consortium. XForms. http://www.w3.org/MarkUp/Forms, 2005.
24. J. Zittrain. What the publisher can teach the patient: Property and privacy in an era of trusted privication. *Stanford Law Review*, 52, 2000.

A A Privacy Extension Schema for MPEG REL

The multimedia extension of MPEG REL provides methods of identifying an item of content that seem sufficient for privacy protection applications, and so there does not appear to be any need to introduce new kinds of resource in our privacy extension.

The MPEG REL core schema provides methods of identifying roles and individuals that seem sufficient for privacy protection applications. However, it seems useful to allow the destination of a transfer right (such as Embed) to be a database or other object that is an MPEG REL resource in its own right. Since the syntax of the Destination condition requires the destination to specified as a principal, we must introduce a new principal – which we call ResourcePrincipal – that makes a resource into a principal. (Of course, we could also modify the syntax of the Destination condition in the multimedia extension schema.)

Table 1 lists the new rights that we identified for inclusion in our privacy extension schema, and Table 2 lists the conditions. For the most part, these are derived by decomposing the "purposes" and "primary purposes" of P3P into a combination of an action and the conditions under which that action may take place. Of course, a number of the actions and conditions so derived are already present in the standard extension and multimedia extension schemata, and we have not duplicated such elements in our privacy extension schema.

Table 1. Rights in our privacy extension schema

Right	Description
Contact	Use the resource to establish a communications channel
Export	Export the resource to an ungoverned application or database
Query	Submit the resource as a query to a service
Tailor	Use the resource for a transient adaptation of a second resource

Note that the Export right is present in XrML, but not in MPEG REL. This right seemed to us to be necessary for allowing data to be exported to a specific application or database that performed some function that lay outside the domain of a terminal of the kind postulated by MPEG-21. The historical purpose of P3P, for example, contemplates data being exported to some historical archive. It is unlikely, however, that such an archive would be maintained by a terminal like IPDoc.

Table 2. Conditions in our our privacy extension schema

Condition	Description
ContactMethod	Only if the specified means of contact is used
Dealing	Only in the context of a particular session or goal
Pseudonym	Only if the data is anonymised or pseudonymised

A number of "primary purposes" used in P3P Version 1.1 suggest the use of a Content condition that restricts the kind of material present on a communications channel to news, entertainment, marketing, etc. We are not aware of any computer system that can vet the contents of a channel in this way and so have chosen not to include such a condition in our privacy extension schema. Restrictions of this sort can be achieved to some degree using the `Dealing` condition, however, as demonstrated in our example scenario described in Section 5.

B Security Architecture

In order to preserve the integrity of the digital rights management system, governed content must only be usable under the terms imposed by a licence supplied by the licence issuer. To this end, we require that

- content may only be accessed by use of a secure terminal trusted to comply with the terms of any licence associated with the content; and
- terminals must be able to verify the authenticity and integrity of any licences purporting to grant privileges over content.

B.1 Key Infrastructure

We assume that every trusted terminal T has a private key $\bar{K}_T$ and corresponding public key K_T, and that the authenticity of the public key K_T can be verified by licence issuers using some public key infrastructure. The private key $\bar{K}_T$ is known only to the terminal; in particular, it is not known to the human user of the terminal. In our implementation, we use the well-known RSA algorithm for all public key cryptographic operations.

We similarly assume that every human user u (both data subjects and data users) of the system has a private key $\bar{K}_u$ and public key K_u. This key pair is used both for identifying the beneficiary of a licence using the MPEG REL `KeyHolder` principal, and for signing licences issued by data subjects. We also assume that every human user has a secret symmetric *master key* k_u that will be used for encrypting his or her data according to an algorithm described below.

Finally, each role R is associated with a key pair $\bar{K}_R$ and K_R that is used for encrypting keys to be delivered to that role. We assume that the public key for all of the roles in the system can be obtained from the certificate authority.

B.2 Resource Encryption

Every document x to be submitted to the data controller must be encrypted with a unique resource key k_x. In order to generate a unique resource key, we require every document x to be associated with a unique digital item identifier i_x. A unique resource key is then generated according to the formula

$$k_x = \text{HMAC-SHA1}(k_u, i_r)$$

where k_u is the master key of the user who created the document. We use the AES algorithm for all symmetric encryption.

In SITDRM Enterprise, uniqueness of resource identifiers is ensured by assuming that every data controller is associated with a unique URI stem. Every time the data submission form is downloaded from the web server, the data controller uses a counter to generate a new suffix to its URI stem. In our example, the data controller was assigned the stem `urn:au:com:smartinternet` and documents are numbered `urn:au:com:smartinternet:customer:1`, `urn:au:com:smartinternet:customer:2`, etc. in the order in which they are submitted.

B.3   Licences

In SITDRM, every grant of a licence that permits some action to be performed must contain the key required to perform that action. For security, the key must be encrypted in such a way as to render it inaccessible to any party except one that is entitled to perform the action.

Every resource licence is required to contain the resource key for the resource to which it refers, encrypted by the public key of the role to which that licence is awarded. In order to access the resource key, the private key of the role must be obtained from a membership certificate for that role.

Since data users are not assumed to be trusted, it is not sufficient to encrypt the private key of a role using the public key of the data user for whom a membership certificate is intended – this would allow a dishonest data user to obtain the resource key for a resource. Instead, we require that membership certificates only be usable on a particular terminal, that is, that a data user may only act as a member of the role when he or she is using a particular terminal (presumably one that is owned and operated by the data user's employer).

The private key of a role is encrypted using the public key of the terminal on which the membership certificate is to be used, and inserted into the membership certificate. In this way, the terminal can decrypt the role's private key from the membership certificate and use this in turn to decrypt the resource key in a resource licence. The terminal is trusted not to reveal the role's private key, the resource key or the decrypted resource to its human user.

Membership certificates are signed by the role issuer. We assume that a trusted version of the role issuer's public key can be obtained from the certificate authority. Any terminal can then verify the integrity of a membership certificate by verifying the signature of the role issuer on that certificate.

Unfortunately, the same approach does not suffice for resource licences. Since all of the humans who use the system have the ability to issue resource licences, it is possible for a dishonest user to issue a licence for a document created by any data subject. This can be done by copying the encrypted resource key and encrypted resource into an arbitrary licence, and signing this licence using the dishonest user's private key. The forged licence will be accepted as valid by the terminal for which the original licence was intended.

There is a fairly simple fix for this problem, though we have not yet implemented it in SITDRM Enterprise. The strategy is to insert a secret into both the encrypted resource and the signed licence, such that the terminal is able to recover the secret from both (using its private key) and check that they match.

An attacker is then unable to generate a valid signature for a licence on this resource since he or she is unable to insert the secret.

Let n_x be a random nonce chosen by the data subject every time he or she encrypts a document x. The nonce is appended to the document prior to encryption. That is, the encrypted document is $\hat{x} = e(k_x, x \parallel n_x)$ where $e(k, m)$ denotes symmetric encryption of message m with key k and $\parallel$ denotes concatenation.

Let E be a public key encryption algorithm and S be a signature algorithm, using parameters analogous to e above. The data subject u can compute a signed licence $\hat{L}$ as follows:

1. Compute $\hat{k}_x^* = E(\bar{K}_u, n_x \parallel k_x)$, that is, the nonce and content key encrypted using the private key of the data subject.
2. Compute $\hat{k}_x = E(K_T, \hat{k}_x^*)$, that is, the nonce and content key further encrypted using the public key of the terminal.
3. Compute $\sigma = S(\bar{K}_u, L \parallel \hat{k}_x \parallel K_u)$, that is, the data subject's signature on the original licence L and encrypted nonce and content key.
4. Compute the signed licence $\hat{L} = L \parallel \hat{k}_x \parallel K_u \parallel \sigma$.

A terminal can then verify the signature on such a licence as follows:

1. Check that σ is a valid signature for $L \parallel \hat{k}_x \parallel K_u$. If not, stop.
2. Decrypt $\hat{k}_x$ using $\bar{K}_T$ to obtain $\hat{k}_x^*$.
3. Decrypt $\hat{k}_x^*$ using K_u to obtain n_x and k_x.
4. Decrypt $\hat{x}$ to obtain n_x and x. If the n_x obtained from $\hat{x}$ is not the same as that obtained from $\hat{L}$, stop.

It is straightforward to check that the algorithm is both correct and secure, assuming that the encryption algorithm E and signature algorithm S are secure.

Personal Rights Management - Taming Camera-Phones for Individual Privacy Enforcement

Mina Deng[1,*], Lothar Fritsch[2,**], and Klaus Kursawe[1,***]

[1] Katholieke Universiteit Leuven, ESAT/COSIC, Kasteelpark Arenberg 10,
B-3001 Leuven-Heverlee, Belgium
[2] Chair of M-Commerce and Multilateral Security, Johann Wolfgang
Goethe-University, 60054 Frankfurt am Main, Germany
{Mina.Deng, Klaus.Kursawe}@esat.kuleuven.ac.be,
Lothar.Fritsch@m-lehrstuhl.de

Abstract. With ubiquitous use of digital camera devices, especially in mobile phones, privacy is no longer threatened by governments and companies only. The new technology creates a new threat by ordinary people, who could take and distribute pictures of an individual with no risk and little cost in any situation in public or private spaces. Fast distribution via web based photo albums, online communities and web pages expose an individual's private life to the public. Social and legal measures are increasingly taken to deal with this problem, but they are hard to enforce in practice. In this paper, we proposed a model for privacy infrastructures aiming for the distribution channel such that as soon as the picture is publicly available, the exposed individual has a chance to find it and take proper action in the first place. The implementation issues of the proposed protocol are discussed. Digital rights management techniques are applied in our proposed infrastructure, and data identification techniques such as digital watermarking and robust perceptual hashing are proposed to enhance the distributed content identification.

Keywords: privacy protection, model for privacy infrastructures, mobile camera phones, data identification techniques.

1 Introduction

Over the last years, privacy protection has become a major issue, and both the European Union and the US are investing significantly into research on this area.

* Mina Deng's work was partially supported by the Concerted Research Action (GOA) Ambiorics 2005/11 of the Flemish Government, the Research Foundation - Flanders (FWO-Vlaanderen), and the research institute IBBT of the Flemish Government.
** Lothar Fritsch's work was partially supported by the IST PRIME and IST FIDIS projects, he state of Hessen and T-Mobile, but expresses his opinion only.
*** Klaus Kursawe is now working for Philips Research Eindhoven.

G. Danezis and P. Golle (Eds.): PET 2006, LNCS 4258, pp. 172–189, 2006.
© Springer-Verlag Berlin Heidelberg 2006

However, almost all of the current work assumes an asymmetric model; the privacy violator is a corporate or governmental institution (or at least an employee thereof), while the victim is a normal citizen. Correspondingly, the main research areas cover issues such as identity management, policy enforcement, and anonymous communication. In the last years, however, a new privacy threat has emerged that cannot be addressed by such means. Due to improvements as well as the growing distribution of various handhold devices, an increasing number of people are equipped with miniature cameras (in their mobile phones) and voice recorders (in their music players).

1.1 Problem Statement

Until the 1990s, public distribution of images could only happen in the press, either in print or in electronic broadcast media. To challenge the unauthorized distribution of an individual's image, a media company could be identified and contacted. Furthermore, the media company usually would know who the photographer was.

With the advent of the Internet as a public communication platform, fast and global distribution of images in public with Web pages became common means. Scanned photos then were available from an unknown number of private Web pages. The availability of digital cameras reduced the cost and shortened the time it took to put images online. However, due to the physical dimension pointing a digital camera at a person can still be noticed in many situations.

In recent years, camera-phones were introduced. The build-in camera lens on a mobile phone can hardly be recognized, which brings the possibility that anyone who holds a camera-phone in an individual's surroundings could be taking a photo of the individual without being noticed. The individual won't be able to see a camera while being photographed or filmed, and won't know whether his images are put on the Web or not.

With massive numbers of camera-phones out in the public, photos can be taken at any place. News stories about offenders being caught while shooting photos under women's dresses in public are available from the United States, Japan, Great Britain, Malaysia or even Saudi Arabia. Web sites like Voyeur-web.com have been around longer than digital camera phones exist to even commercially distribute the content. While this intrusive and offensive use of cameras is regarded illegal in many places in the world, other uses seem to create benefits for society - other news stories tell of offenders being identified thanks to camera-phone photos taken by bystanders of a crime. Considering the favorable uses of camera-phones in public, a solution that does detect, but not prevent from taking photos in public places may seem appropriate.

It has already shown to be a significant problem. At some beaches and in various companies, camera-phones are completely banned, and a number of countries have significantly increased the penalty for illegally taken pictures. Unfortunately, these countermeasures are by far not sufficient, as a growing number of Web sites boasting such pictures demonstrates. As it is impossible and unwanted to enforce a broad ban on camera-phones, and technical measures such as a simulated shutter noise when a picture is taken appear to be insufficient, we propose a novel way to complement such measures.

This paper deals with the challenge of protecting one's private data, such as image, and privacy issues attached to it. With respect to new mobile technologies and distribution channels, we sketch a privacy threat posed by millions of privately owned cameras in mobile phones.

Instead of preventing the picture from being taken, or call attention on the photographer when he takes the picture, we attack the distribution channel: if an inappropriate picture of an individual is taken and published, the victim has a fair chance of being the first one to actually find this picture, which enables her to request the pictures removal or invoke legal actions before significant privacy violation is done. The authors are aware that in extreme cases, it will be impossible to remove a picture from the Internet by legal means. However, we expect that most of the privacy violations we address are done in a context where the publisher could be convinced to remove the offending material without a legal escalation. To achieve this, we propose that each picture receives an identity, which is contained in the picture and broadcasted to the victim that is photographed. Although this approach may be insufficient against a highly dedicated attacker, it can help to prevent privacy violations from becoming a mass phenomenon, without inhibiting the use of camera-phones, motivating users to manipulate their devices, or significantly increasing the costs of the devices.

This paper is organized as follows. The legal situation is first reviewed and traditional law as well as recent efforts to tackle the issue with new laws or technological solutions is reviewed. Then the privacy threat is defined, where the attacker and attack scenarios are discussed. We introduce a basic protocol on an abstract level, and define the attack model. At a general architecture level, we propose an evolution approach from Digital Rights Management to Personal Rights Management. We propose the protocol based on content identification techniques such as digital watermarking or perceptual image hashing and broadcast channels to enable individuals to take notice when being photographed. Afterwards, we analyze the hardware infrastructure to implement our protocol, and investigate possible attacks on the hardware. Following this, we describe the software implementation of the protocol, both on the side of the camera device and on Internet search engines. Finally, we discuss various modifications of the basic scheme, and draw conclusions towards the feasibility of the technology on mobile phones with particular respect to already existing digital rights management (DRM) technologies.

1.2   Examples of Legal Context

Because of the fast growth of Internet new technologies as well as the incompatible policies between the different countries, in this context, privacy issues are complex. From a technical perspective, due to Directive 95/46/EC of the European Parliament and the Council of 24 October 1995 [3], describes the protection of individuals regarding the processing and free movement of their personal data.

The right to privacy in the *EU* is defined as a human right under Article 8 of the 1950 European Convention of Human Rights and Fundamental Freedoms (ECHR). The implicit principles and constructs of The Directive define the enforcement and the representation of data protection. The terms privacy and data protection are often used interchangeably, though they are not necessarily equivalent. The Directive applies to all sectors of public life, with some exceptions. It specifies the data protection rights afforded to "data subjects", plus the requirements and responsibilities obligated for "data controllers" and by association "data processors" [10].

Several countries enacted laws against unauthorized taking of photos with individuals. More countries are debating legislation that is intended to ban cameraphones or their use. Some examples are given below.

In *Germany*, a copyright law ("Kunsturhebergesetz") protects one's own image against unauthorized publication since Bismarks's times. Photos can legally be taken without authorization, but their distribution without authorization, even to small audiences, is illegal. Exceptions are photos taken in public places at events where (press) photography usually happens. Also, individuals of "public interest" (e.g. politicians, actors, celebrities) can be photographed and published with limited restriction (see [11]).

In *Australia*, under the Commonwealth Crimes Act 1914 - Part VIIB, Section 85ZE it is an offence for "a person to knowingly or recklessly use a telecommunications service supplied by a carrier in such a way as would be regarded by reasonable persons being, in all the circumstances, offensive". In addition, following the widespread introduction of the internet, state laws were changed to address this issue. For example the Crimes Act in Victoria was amended in 1995 to include the offence of 'Stalking'. This includes telephoning and sending electronic messages with the intention of causing physical or mental harm.

While many countries do have legislation about camera based privacy invasions and the distribution of photos without consent of the photographed individuals, the question of the enforcement remains.

1.3 Current Solutions

The problem of secret photography has been recognized by most of the involved parties, including the manufacturers, politics and private citizens. Some actions have been taken, though with limited effect.

One solution is to fortify the privacy right on personal pictures and increased the punishment for the publication of such by *tougher laws*. However, this right may be hard to enforce. The photographed individual may never find out about the publication neither could do anything about it. Even though an offender was caught on the scene, the phone could already digitally transmit the photo away. Even with laws enacted, the only choice of an individual would be to arrest the offender instead of waiting for the police to show up. This is not a setting that helps all members of a society with their privacy rights.

The second approach is to *ban the use of camera-phones* in places, such as public swimming pools, gyms and Saunas, where illegal photographing is subjected. Though banning camera-phones could be the first choice in some places, this approach is only suitable for controlled areas with a high risk of secret photographing, such as companies or confidential institutes to counter espionage. The approach has also lead to the situation that even some mobile phone producers banned their own devices from their premises, e.g. Samsung and Motorola.

A more common sense solution is to add a sufficient loud *shutter-noise* such that whenever a picture is taken, it can be noticed by the environment. However, the feature is often poorly implemented. For example, if a mobile phone is switched into silent mode, the shutter noise is also turned off. Besides, given the noise pollution created by mobile phones anyhow, adding shutter noise can add to the annoyance of the technology. More, it violates the privacy of the photographer, as people around immediately learns about who being present with a camera. The approach is mostly ineffective, because the noise can be hard to heard due to general background noise or the environment, e.g. in a Discotheque, and it usually does not help the victim.

Given the difficulty to prevent pictures from being taken without dramatically infringing the rights of harmless photographers, our approach targets the distribution channel rather than the creation of the picture, i.e. pictures can be taken without restrictions. However, the individual is made aware that some picture has been taken. As soon as the picture appear on the Internet, she has a realistic chance to locate it at an early point in time, when it is still possible to inhibit the distribution by legal means. As an added value, outside of protecting the victim's privacy, this technology can also be used to distribute pictures to interested parties.

Another solution is to *enforce safe zones by broadcast*. Several businesses have developed a so-called safe haven technology which is intended to create zones where a broadcast unit tells cameraphones that photographing is forbidden there [33]. It enables digital cameras within a variety of electronic devices to be disabled including camera phones, camera PDA's, digital cameras and multipurpose MP3 players. HP is developing a privacy technology that can jam still and video cameras and blur faces of people who don't want to have their picture taken [31]. While this approach empowers property owners to define non-photographing zones, it also restricts a user's freedom of taking pictures with consent in the area. Another problem is that here is a need to implement the receiver technology into all manufacturers' handsets for an effect. Furthermore, to protect individual rights, one needs a portable unit. This only could guarantee personal rights independent from one's property protection policy.

1.4   The Privacy Tradeoff

In order to protect the privacy rights of the parties involved in our setting, it is necessary to make a tradeoff between the interests of the individual being photographed and the photographer. As the balance between the right to privacy and the right to photograph, we will now state the minimum rights of each party that should be preserved.

Ideally, the individual should have the right to give consent to every picture she plays a major role in; this is the actual right granted by law in the European Union. This right is hard to enforce technologically, however, as it includes judgment on when a picture is a picture of a person, or just a picture of a marketplace that happens to have people on it. As a minimum, the individual has the right to know she has been photographed, and to have a chance to get an early warning if the picture is being published, which allows her to take appropriate steps in needed.

As long as the photographer does not infringe any personal rights, he should have the right to take pictures without any major obstacles. In this, the protocol should preferably be passive, and not prevent him from taking pictures unless under well defined and measurable circumstances. Furthermore, the photographer has the right to stay anonymous, as long as he does not infringe anybody else's rights. Finally, the photographer has the right to modify his device; for example, the camera in a PDA should not stop working if the operating system is modified or replaced.

2 An Infrastructure for Personal Rights Management

2.1 Attack Model

Possible attacks from both the technical and privacy aspects will be discussed. From a technical point of view, even with a technically perfect scheme, an attacker could easily circumvent the entire system by using a traditional camera with strong zoom optics or a traditional mini-camera. The problem is not only in the professional voyeurs, but also in the wide deployment of photographic devices and the ease of secret photographing. We assume the attacker can do simple modifications to the device and the picture, and that the corresponding instructions will eventually be published on the Internet. For instance, there are Internet sources to offer modified operating systems for mobile phones to turn off the noise generated while taking a picture. On the other hand, there are many possible attacks for content identification techniques proposed in the literature. However, there is always a balance between the risks for the service provider if the watermarking or hashing scheme is circumvent, and the benefit for the attacker to attempt to break the scheme compare to the amount of effort spent.

From the privacy and legal point of view, it is an unavoidable issue that we want to protect the rights of the harmless photographers: unless we treat every owner of a mobile phone like a criminal, there will possible for a sufficiently motivate attacker to escape from the scheme. Apart from making the technology stronger and therefore less attractive to the attackers, our protocol also has their merit if combined with legal measures. By attacking the scheme, it demonstrates a photographer has a "criminal intend". Therefore, it is easier to distinguish a normally harmless person that just couldn't resist taking a picture in a particular situation from a semiprofessional voyeur with manipulated equipment.

2.2   Basic Protocol

Players. There are three major players in our setting: the photographer, the individual, and the search engine. The *photographer (Bob)* is the person who takes the pictures. Bob uses a camera-phone, which is a mobile phone with a build in camera. From a privacy point of view, Bob has the rights not to be inhibited while taking the pictures and has his identity preserved as long as he does not infringe the rights of anybody. Bob also has the right to perform some "standard" changes to his camera-phone, such as updating the operating system.

The *individual (Alice)* is the person that is photographed by the photographer. The interest of Alice is to have a control over the pictures taken of her. It means that in case she is the focus point of the picture, this picture should (ideally) not been taking without her consent. In our protocol, we grant her a lesser right: If a picture taken from her is published, she gets a fair chance to find out early. Alice uses a receiver, which registers the identities of pictures taken in her vicinity. The receiver could be her own mobile phone or a specialized piece of hardware. It can also be integrated in the infrastructure provided by external parties, for instance, the owner of a discotheque or even the GSM operators.

Finally, the *search engine* searches the Internet for picture identities and makes them publicly available. They are similar as any Internet search engines, with slightly modified rules.

The Protocol. A possible scenario of our scheme will be discussed in this section. The goal is to let an individual "Alice" detect unauthorized publication of personal images taken by others "Bob". We name the complete setting a Personal Rights Management (PRM) system.

In the first step, Bob secretly takes private photos of unaware Alice with malicious intent, as shown in Fig. 1. Luckily, the camera on Bob's mobile phone applies PRM to the photo when it is taken. The photo can be identified and marked by using several data protection techniques, such as digital watermarking, robust perceptual hashing, or Digital Rights Management technology. In case digital watermarking techniques are used, Bob's camera embeds the image content identification in the picture. In case robust perceptual hashing techniques are used, Bob's camera sends the image hash values optionally together with a thumbnail of the picture itself. All the possible techniques used for content identification will be discussed in the software implementation section.

On the other hand, the identity of the photo is broadcast with a short-range radio. Alice's receiver picks up the picture identification information and stores it for later use, as shown in Fig. 1.

An alternative approach is that Alice broadcasts pseudorandom (and changing, e.g. through means of a hash-chain) identifiers that are picked up by Bob's phone; instead of broadcasting a picture identifier, Bob's camera embeds the identifier of every individual present at that time into the picture. This saves complexity on Alice's side, and may help if the communication between the devices is slightly unreliable; however, it does require every individual that wants to trace their pictures to permanently broadcast some (though changing) identifer, which may have other undesired consequences.

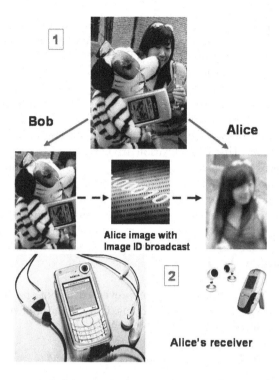

Fig. 1. The first two steps of the protocol, communication between Alice and Bob. Bob secretly takes private photos of unaware Alice with malicious intent. Alice's image together with identification information are sent to the receiver of Alice.

Fig. 2. The last two steps of the protocol, Bob publishes the unauthorized photo from Alice to an online community which is very unfavorable to Alice. Alice can detect the unauthorized publishing of the photo using the PRM search engine.

In the next step, Bob publishes the unauthorized photo from Alice to an online community which is very unfavorable to Alice. Alice would take action on this if she knew the photo was published. Luckily, Alice can detect the unauthorized publishing of the photo using the PRM search engine (see Fig. 2). When Bob puts the picture from Alice on the Internet, the specialized search engines find it and index it by the extracted watermark or the perceptual image hash values. Alice uploads the collected photo marks or identification numbers to a specialized search engine. Then the search engine checks photos published on the web by photo identifications. Upon notification from the search engine, Alice checks whether the photos found have her image on them and takes appropriate actions to protect her privacy. Note that while it is hardly possible to remove data from the Internet if the publisher is determined to keep it public, we assume that in most real cases the publisher can be identified due to the publishing medium, and convinced to remove the offending material either of the publisher's own accord or by legal means; the possibility for malicious publishers to get away publishing pictures seems unavoidable unless we want to restrict the privacy of photographers.

In summary, the photo taking is not prevented. From the beginning to the end, Alice and Bob both remain anonymous. Only upon publishing of an image, the image will be detected and reported to Alice.

2.3   Architecture Evolution from DRM to PRM

At an system architecture level, there is a potential of adapting Digital Rights Management (DRM) systems for the purpose of Personal Rights Management (PRM) according to the legal requirements. DRM technology, developed for protecting intellectual property rights, appears to have features that would allow the development of a system-based approach to data protection compliance, i.e. Personal Rights Management.

DRM architectures support description, trading, protection, monitoring and tracking of the use of digital content. These technologies may be contained within operating systems, program software, or in the hardware of a device.

PRM manages personal data from the data subject, the originator and the owner of the personal data. The Directive [3] defines the authorities and boundaries of the relationships between each of the participants. The driving purpose behind DRM, thus the content distribution management, relates easily to data protection constructs constraining the exchange of personal data [18].

For the purpose of expressing privacy in a PRM system, the Open Digital Rights Language (ODRL) [1] and extensible rights mark-up language (XrML) [2] can be applied, which are similar as the rights expression languages used in a DRM system.

Korba et al.[18] propose an adaptation of DRM functionality to provide PRM for individuals by assigning names to the functional parts in the DRM setting from the privacy enhancing techniques vocabulary. Thus it brings some form of taxonomy or meta-design for PRM.

3   Hardware Implementation

3.1   Basic Proposal

The hardware and software implementations of the proposed protocol will be discussed in the following sections. We assume that no mobile phone manufacturer will be willing to add a completely new communication technology into the devices to enable a protocol such as the one presented above. Therefore, we restrict ourselves to the current hardware available in the market. Three possible communication standards, Infrared, Bluetooth, and GSM network, can be used to establish the link between camera-phone from Bob and the receiver from Alice.

Infrared. One feature of infrared communication is that it is directed, i.e., the signal can be sent in a way that only the devices in the view of the camera can receive it. The penalty paid is that the bandwidth of infrared communication is fairly low, and the transmitting distance might be too small. It can cause a problem on the receiving side: if the receiver is not directed to the camera, it may not get any signal at all. It is fairly easy to block the communication by simply gluing an object onto the infrared port. This problem can be solved by building the receiver into the enabling function of camera lens. This way, blocking the communication would disable the ability to take pictures. The second problem could be to block the communication by jamming the signal with a strong infrared light. Though the problem is harder to deal with, it is possible to design a camera that can not take pictures if exposed to a strong infrared signal. However, another problem arises when the jamming signal may be directed and allow for a denial of service attack, i.e., preventing all camera phones to take pictures at all.

Bluetooth. Bluetooth communication is the complement of Infrared. The communication is very difficult to jam, and the bandwidth is sufficient even for interactive protocols. The disadvantage is that a Bluetooth signal is undirected and all devices that are not in the visual scope of the camera get the signal as well. Another disadvantage is that currently enabling Bluetooth on a phone may pose a security risk. Recent studies [7] show that many Bluetooth phones are open to attacks that may reveal the entire phone memory, including the address book, the calendar etc. Thus, unless the security of this technique can be improved, to protect the privacy of Alice's pictures she may have to risk a privacy-invasion on her phone book.

GSM-Network. It is by the nature of mobile phones to communicate on the GSM network. However, the GSM protocol is ill-suited for device-to device communication. Adding this capacity would require major changes in the GSM standard, which is unlikely to happen for the purpose of protecting people form illegal pictures. It would be possible to use the base-station as an intermediate in a way that the photographer's device sends a signal to the base-station, which in turn sends a cell broadcast to all devices in the area. This creates new problems.

One on hand, many devices that don't have anything to do with the picture will be noticed altogether. On the other hand, phones at the same location may be locked into another cell or use a different provider.

All of the Above. A combination of those techniques can be proposed, for instance, an infrared flash could be used to command the device to listen to a Bluetooth signal or a GSM cellular broadcast. If implemented properly, this could combine the advantages of all technologies. As the infrared signal only has to carry a binary signal, the low bandwidth and limited range are not problematic anymore. As receivers neither see the flash nor listen to the radio signals, they can be configured not to pick up the pictures out of their interests, though it can't be excluded that they do.

3.2   Attacks on the Hardware

A few examples are given here on how an attacker can disable the proposed functionality by manipulating their devices. For some mobile phones, the shutter noise can be manipulated to be turned off when the entire phone is put in silent mode. For our protocol, it is possible to block the transmission by deactivating Bluetooth or by using it to communicate with another device while the picture is taken. Some users directly modify their mobile phone hardware to detach the infrared light or the Bluetooth antenna. For some mobile phones, there are some firmware to manipulate the corresponding functionality available on the Internet, and it is easy to perform by a normal audience. However, mobile phone manufacturers have recently started to think about other functionalities that a user may not manipulate, e.g., Superdistribution and Micropayment from Nokia. It is foreseeable that this problem will be solved in the near future, e.g. by using a core-operating system which cannot be changed by the owner and building the real operating system on top of this core, or by TCPA/TCG-like technologies.

4   Software Implementation

4.1   Digital Image Watermarking

Digital watermarking is a technique for embedding information in digital content without perceptually altering its appearance [12]. In our system, one intuitive way could be to append a visible watermark on the host image. The visible watermark can be any information that identifies the photographer and/or the time stamping analogous to analog cameras. However, the obvious drawback is that an attacker can easily remove the watermark by an image editing software despite of destroying the watermarked region of the image.

Various imperceptible robust image watermarking applications are studied [17,14]. In the system we proposed, the key point is to identify the secretly photographed image rather than to authenticate the image integrity. This is because Alice is more interested to identify whether the image is from her or not. The owners' and/or user's information can be embedded directly into the images to protect copyright. And a rather high level of robustness against malicious attacks is required.

For watermarking system, it should be computationally infeasible to extract the watermark information even if the algorithm of the watermarking principle is known. Therefore, secret or public keys should be used to provide the security of watermarking.

The design of a watermarking algorithm always involved a tradeoff between robustness, imperceptibility and capacity [21]. In our proposed scheme, the optimal balance among these three attributes should be found if properly designed. The capacity of the watermark doesn't have to be large, thus extra robustness could be gained. In order to get optimal robustness, watermark should be embedded just below the perceptual level, and the knowledge of human vision systems (HVS) are applied to the imperceptible watermarking schemes [30]. A few benchmarking of watermarking to provide a fair evaluation of watermarking parameters are introduced, such as Stirmark [29], Optimark [35], and Checkmark [28], etc.

From a practical point of view, with an expected 70 million camera-phones sold by 2006, a 40-bit image identifier should be sufficient even for high usage of the cameras. Although there are no firm numbers, to embed a 40-bit watermark into a picture with 640*480 pixels is quite realistic. For example, the Stirmark [29] can perform the test with 100 bit watermarks on 512*512, 24-bit colored pictures.

When facing a general audience, in order to prevent that everyone has the ability to extract the watermark information from the picture, public key watermarking scheme is used. The photographer embeds the watermark by the public key of the search engine, and the search engine can extract the watermark by using its private key.

4.2   Search Engines

The final player of our protocol is a search engine that allows the individual to locate the pictures on the Internet. The search engines could work just like any ordinary ones, except for the ability to extract the identification information from the pictures and use it as an index. It requires that the watermark extraction or other algorithms to be computationally feasible. Commercial web spiders are already available for copyright protection. As reported in [32], Digimarc, a company which holds most of the core patents on digital watermarking, introduced a tool called MarcSpider [22], purported to crawl the web to search images, test them for watermarks and report on infringers. Due to the fact that crawling the web quickly became an intractable task, as well as that only a small number of copyrighted images installed on the web, MarcSpider didn't work out as a huge success.

Some counter technologies have been developed to hide the pictures from the spider, for example by splitting it into many small pictures or by embedding it using JavaScript. This is another point where a sufficiently motivated attacker can circumvent the scheme, which is hard to deal with unless the privacy of the photographer is inhibited.

There could be a privacy problem introduced by the search engine, such as profiling of all watermarks Alice submits in order to create an album of Alice's life. To avoid linking of ID and image requests, we assume that the search engine is to be used with some anonymous connection.

5   Modifications

5.1   Perceptual Robust Image Hashing

The watermark-based approach is expected to be sensitive to malicious modifications of the media, thus brings the robustness issue dependent on applications. When the watermark is embedded into the host data, the data content is altered and image manipulations may be localized in most schemes [34].

Robust perceptual hashing, which can be used in multimedia applications both for data identification and robust data authentication, is meant to complement digital watermarking. The main advantage for perceptual hashing schemes is that the data is neither altered nor degraded. If a malicious attack on a watermarking scheme succeeded, the watermark would be destroyed. However, the perceptual hash value will remain the same as long as the perceptual features of the data are unchanged. This is also the reason why perceptual hashing is used instead of cryptographic hashing, which is very sensitive to a single input bit. Perceptual hash functions can be particularly useful to identify illegal copies, since the illegal content are usually lossy copies of the original.

The main requirement of our scheme is the image identification. An occasional collision between two picture-identities does not cause a significant trouble, although it merely poses a minor annoyance to a user. Therefore, the picture identity does not need to be excessively long. With a k-bit identifier, we need $1.2 * 2^k$ pictures for the to get 0.5 probability of a collision. Therefore, it is proper to apply perceptual hashing schemes to our application.

Four requirements for image hash functions are defined in [24]. A generic image hashing can be achieved into two steps: feature extraction and secure compression of the feature vector. It is shown that the robust feature vector detection is the key point for robust image hashing. Various feature extraction methods are developed based on different concepts, such as by using wavelet [24,27,26], DCT [13], matrix invariance [19], different descriptors [25]. [23] propose a frame to achieve feature extraction in three steps: quantization, bit assignment, and error correcting code. Many algorithms are proposed for the second step that secure compress the feature vector, including those based on cryptographic hash functions procedure [34], error correcting codes [24,27], and secure compression for authentication applications [16]. Various image hashing methods are analyzed and the experiment results are compared in [34,8].

Having generality and robustness as the two attributes, a feature detection algorithm can be considered robust if it identifies the same feature locations independent of different attacks, such as Stirmark attacks, compression, image processing or geometric distortions. Hamming distances between the hash values of perceptually similar images and between different images can be examined to evaluate the algorithm.

5.2   Broadcasting a Sample Picture

In addition to the image identifier, a strongly compressed sample version of the picture could be broadcasted as well. This would inform the individual whether there is a need to take immediate action or not, e.g . when a specially compromising picture has been taken or a credit card has been photographed. However, this costs a significant bandwidth, and significantly infringes the privacy of the photographer. Due to the content of the image taken by the photographer is broadcasted, the photographer could be identified, and therefore, the privacy of the photographer could be violated. Besides, the intellectual property of the photographer, i.e. his work of art in arranging and taking the photo, could be infringed by broadcasting it to the world.

5.3   Hybrid DRM Solutions

Several DRM techniques can be integrated into our scheme. In a generic DRM mechanism, digital watermarking and perceptual hashing are used for content protection and/or identification, while encryption and digital signature are used for content confidentiality and integrity [20]. New watermarking based techniques can be used to identify, trace and control the use of digital copy and enhance the content protection thus strongly improve DRM [21,32]. In the application of mobile DRM, watermarking has been suggested as an key technology for *media identification* [36,15], especially since user's identity is known in mobile networks. It is expected that the market will thrive by delivering multimedia content through Multimedia Messaging Service (MMS). The content should be wrapped in DRM packages prior to distribution. The proposed DRM technology for the Open Mobile Alliance (OMA) specifies three different methods that vary in complexity requirements, and that offer different levels of security for the distributed content [6]. *Privacy tracing* with the defense of intellectual property rights and *copy protection* where a copy-bit is un-removal from the host content [21] which require different level of requirement of watermarking robustness.

Encryption and watermarking are to be combined as two defensive lines to enhance DRM. For image content, selective encryption [5] is introduced to encrypt a portion of the compressed data. In our proposed scheme, to protect the photographer's privacy, the watermarking embedded information can be further encrypted by the user's ID as a secrete key, so that only the authenticated party can extract the information [4]. A watermark can be used to serve as a proof of ownership but is vulnerable to attacks such as average and collusion attacks [37]. In addition to ensuring that a watermark cannot be removed, the DRM system has to ensure that a fake watermark cannot be inserted. [21] analyze several DRM scenarios related to image distribution, and propose a fair and efficient benchmarking of open-source web based evaluation system. Benchmarking parameters and requirements are scenario dependent.

While we discuss the image content protection or identification from a technical perspective, it is important to note that any technique that allows a user to assert their ownership of any digital object must also be placed in the context of intellectual property right law [30].

6   Conclusions

Camera-phones have been used in much more malicious ways than just to invade privacy, and control over one's image is hard to enforce today. Several reports have been published of cases where credit card information has been obtained by secret photographing of the card. The problem is analyzed from both the privacy and technical aspects in this paper, and possible solutions are proposed. There is a tradeoff between the privacy rights of the individual to have control over images and the privacy rights of the photographer. It is of limited effort for initiatives to enact laws to ban the unauthorized photos when lacking of a technological support for the enforcement and prosecution. On the other hand, users and consumers reject technology that presses restrictions on them. While we are aware that our solution- due to the conflicting interests we need to satisfy- leaves a number of issues unresolved, we believe that a great advantage for individual privacy can be achieved by the proposed personal rights management.

We propose a detection system that combines cryptographic and data protection technologies together with legal regulations in order to control the distribution of private photos online. The scheme can empower individuals to detect and act upon violations without putting strong restrictions on cameras and photographers. Content identification mechanisms such as digital watermarking and robust perceptual hashing are integrated to enhance a PRM system. Techniques to apply in our scheme are discussed and possible attacks together with hard- and software solutions are analyzed.

To evaluate the usability of our proposed scheme, it is not difficult for one to imagine that it will require a significant amount of time and energy if Alice has to check hundreds of pictures per day from search engines. However, as a normal individual the chance that Alice gets a high amount of images taken is fairly low. This scheme can be interesting for celebrities though, who are able to afford hiring people to do the checking work in order to make sure that their personal rights are not violated.

Given the potential commercial value of the privacy market, an investment in Personal Rights Management appears to be worthwhile both in terms of what has to be done to achieve compliance with current legislative requirements and to meet privacy policies towards building a stronger trust relationship with clients.

7   Future Work

The general concept of Personal Rights Management is designed to keep protection as well as to track the sharing process of personal data. Based on the PRM concept to control personal images as we proposed in this paper, further research can be focused on working out the protocol prototype implementations and security. TCPA/TCG- like trusted computing platforms or DRM systems could be integrated to the prototype to achieve an generic PRM architectures.

We discussed the time problem if Alice has to check hundreds of pictures per day. We propose to ease the problem by adding location data and biometric (facial etc.) recognition algorithms to search engines to reduce complexity for Alice. Future research could work out on how to implement this feature.

New applications of PRM could be expended into other aspects of peer to peer privacy violations. While private images taking are the most eminent area of privacy issues caused by peers, other threats are emerging. There is a vast increase of video camera-phones on the market, which brings a similar privacy threat as the privacy image scenario. There are many mp3 players equipped with recording functions. Though the tendency yet to put electronically recorded conversations or videos online on a large scale is not as high yet, the mere presence of such a high number of uncontrolled recording devices may pose a significant problem in the future. A recent story of a high school teacher Jay Bennish in the US shows an example for a problem caused by privately owned recording equipment. The teacher's speech was investigated, because of a student's recording in class and complained to the principal [9]. Another emerging problem is the ever increasing number of Weblogs, combined with search engines to efficiently find personal information therein. Furthermore, PRM scenarios could be applied to protect personal geographical location data as well.

Acknowledgements

The authors would like to thank Claudia Diaz for her constructive comments on our work and the valuable comments from the anonymous reviewers.

References

1. *Open Digital Rights Language (ODRL).* http://www.odrl.net.
2. *XrML is being contributed to the standards body OASIS Rights Language Technical Committee as its foundation technology.* http://www.xrml.org.
3. Directive 95/46/ec of the european parliament and the council of 24 october 1995. *Official Journal L 281, 23/11/1995,* page 0031 0050, 1995.
4. A. Adelsbach, S. Katzenbeisser, and H. Veith. Watermarking schemes provably secure against copy and ambiguity attacks. In *Digital Rights Management Workshop,* pages 111–119, 2003.
5. L. Agi and L. Cong. An empirical study of secure mpeg video transmissions. In *In Proc. of the Internet society symposium on network and distributed system security,* San Diego, CA, February 1996.
6. Open Mobile Alliance. *OMA digital rights management version 1.0.* OMA. http://www.openmobilealliance.org/documents.html.
7. John Blau. *Cracks appear in Bluetooth security.* NetworkWorld.com, Feb. 2004. http://www.networkworld.com/news/2004/0211cracksappear.html.

8. P. Cardin. *Robust signal representation for image identification and hashing.* Student Literature survey, 2005.

9. CNN. *Teacher's Bush remarks investigated - Some students protest teacher being put on leave,* March 2006.   http://www.cnn.com/2006/EDUCATION/03/03/teacher.bush.ap/?section=cnn_topstories.

10. L. Deitz. Privacy and security ecs privacy directive: protecting personal data and ensuring its free movement. *Computers and Security Journal,* pages 25–46.

11. Alexander Dix. Das Recht am eigenen Bild – Anachronismus im Zeitalter des Internet ? In *Mediale (Selbst-)Darstellung und Datenschutz, Konferenz des LfD NRW,* 2000.

12. R. J. Anderson F.A.P. Petitcolas and M. G. Kuhn. Information hiding-a survey. volume 87, pages 1062–1078, 1999.

13. Jiri Fridrich and Miroslav Goljan. Robust hash functions for digital watermarkin, March. 2000.

14. F. Hartung and M. Kutter. Multimedia watermarking techniques. In *special issue on protecting of multimedia contents,* volume 87, pages 1079–1107. Proceedings of the IEEE, July 1999.

15. F. Hartung and F. Ramme. Digital rights management and watermarking for multimedia content for m-commerce. In *IEEE communications magazine,* volume 38, pages 78–84, Nov. 2000.

16. M. Johnson and K. Ramchandran. Dither-based secure image hashing using distributed coding. In *ICIP (2),* pages 751–754, 2003.

17. S. Katzenbeisser and F.A.P. Petitcolas. *Information hiding techniques for steganography and digital watermarking.* Artech House, INC., 2000.

18. L. Korba and S. Kenny. Towards meeting the privacy challenge: Adapting drm. In *Security and Privacy in Digital Rights Management, ACM CCS-9 Workshop (DRM 2002),* pages 118–136, November 2002.

19. S. Kozat, M. Kivanç Mihçak, and R. Venkatesan. robust perceptual hashing via matrix invariance. In *Proc. Of IEEE international conference on image processing ICIP,* Singapore, Sept. 2004. Springer-Verlag.

20. W. Ku and C. Chi. Survey on the technological aspects of digital rights management. In *ISC,* pages 391–403, 2004.

21. Benoit M. Macq, Jana Dittmann, and Edward J. Delp. Benchmarking of image watermarking algorithms for digital rights management. *Proceedings of the IEEE,* 92(6):971–984, 2004.

22. MarcSpider. *Digimarc image tracking service.* DigiMarc corporation, 2001. http://www.digimarc.com/products/imagebridge/MarcSpider/default.asp.

23. Elizabeth P. McCarthy, Felix Balado, Guenole C. M. Silverstre, and Neil J. Hurley. A framework for soft hashing and its application to robust image hashing. In IS&T/SPIE, editor, *In Proc. of SPIE, Security, Steganography, and Watermarking of Multimedia Contents VII,* volume 5681, pages 5681–06, San Jose, CA, USA, January 2005.

24. M. Kivanç Mihçak and R. Venkatesan. New iterative geometric methods for robust perceptual image hashing. In *ACM CCS-8 Workshop on Security and Privacy in Digital Rights Management,* pages 13–21, London, UK, 2002. Springer-Verlag.

25. Krystian Mikolajczyk and Cordelia Schmid. A performance evaluation of local descriptors. Submitted to PAMI, 2004.

26. V. Monga and B. L. Evans. Robust perceptual image hashing using feature points. In *Proc. IEEE Int. Conf. on Image Processing,* Singapore, Oct. 2004. Singapore.

27. V. Monga, D. Vats, and B. L. Evans. Image authentication under geometric attacks via structure matching. In *Proc. IEEE Int. Conf. on Multimedia & Expo*, London, UK, July 2005. Amsterdam, The Netherlands.

28. S. Pereira, S. Voloshynovskiy, M. Madueno, S. Marchand-Maillet, and T. Pun. Second generation benchmarking and application oriented evaluation. In *IHW '01: Proceedings of the 4th International Workshop on Information Hiding*, pages 340–353. Springer-Verlag, 2001.

29. F.A. Petitcolas, M. Steinebach, F. Raynal, J. Dittmann, C. Fontaine, and N. Fates. Public automated web-based evaluation service for watermarking schemes: Stirmark benchmark. In *SPIE International Symposium on Electronic Imaging 2001*, volume 4314 of *Proceedings of the SPIE*, pages 575–584. SPIE, 2001. Security and Watermarking of Multimedia Contents III.

30. C. I. Podilchuk R. B. Wolfgang and E. J. Delp. Perceptual watermarks for digital images and video. In *special issues on identification and protection of multimedia information*, pages 40–51. IEEE, 1998.

31. Emily Raymond. *HP Developing Picture Jamming Technology to Block Unwanted Photographs*. http://www.digitalcamerainfo.com/d/News.htm.

32. B. Rosenblatt. Steganography revisited: watermarking comes in from the cold. 3(5), June 2003.

33. Sensaura. *UK companies team to solve worldwide camera phone privacy abuse. British Safe Haven technology enables digital cameras to be disabled in a localized environment.* Sensaura press release, Sept. 2003. http://www.sensaura.com/news/pr.php?article=2003_09_11.inc.

34. C. J. Skrepth and A. Uhl. Robust hash functions for visual data: An experimental comparison. In *Iberian Conference on Pattern Recognition and Image Analysis*, pages 986–993, 2003.

35. V. Solachidis, A. Tefas, N. Nikolaidis, S. Tsekeridou, A. Nikolaidis, and I.Pitas. A benchmarking protocol for watermarking methods. In *Int. Conf. on Image Processing (ICIP'01)*, volume 21, pages 1023–1026. IEEE, October 2001.

36. M. Trimeche and F. Chebil. Digital rights management for visual content in mobile applications. In *First International Symposium on Control, Communications and Signal Processing*. IEEE, March 2004.

37. M. Wu, W. Trappe, Z. Wang, and K. J. R. Liu. Collision resistant fingerprinting for multimedia. In *Signal Processing magazine*, volume 21, pages 15–27. IEEE, March 2004.

Improving Sender Anonymity in a Structured Overlay with Imprecise Routing*

Giuseppe Ciaccio

DISI, Università di Genova
via Dodecaneso 35, 16146 Genova, Italy
`ciaccio@disi.unige.it`

Abstract. In the framework of peer to peer distributed systems, the problem of anonymity in structured overlay networks remains a quite elusive one. It is especially unclear how to evaluate and improve *sender* anonymity, that is, untraceability of the peers who issue messages to other participants in the overlay. In a structured overlay organized as a chordal ring, we have found that a technique originally developed for *recipient* anonymity also improves sender anonymity. The technique is based on the use of imprecise entries in the routing tables of each participating peer. Simulations show that the sender anonymity, as measured in terms of average size of anonymity set, decreases slightly if the peers use imprecise routing; yet, the anonymity takes a better distribution, with good anonymity levels becoming more likely at the expenses of very high and very low levels. A better quality of anonymity service is thus provided to participants.

1 Introduction and Motivation

Overlay networks are receiving a lot of attention by the research community, as flexible and scalable low-level infrastructures for distributed applications of many kinds: network storage [18,13,39], naming [12], content publication [16,11,3,37,46, 40],multicast/anycast [36,6,31], and communication security [33,47]. They have also been proposed as general networking infrastructures [17,44,20,19], because of their potential ability to decouple network addresses from physical placements of cooperating hosts, an important feature for privacy and mobility.

The vast population of existing or proposed overlay systems can be broadly divided into two families, namely, unstructured overlays and structured overlays.

Structured overlays [35,14,30,23,38,29,48] are receiving far more attention lately, because of performance guarantees they can in principle provide thanks to their regular topologies. Regular topologies allow routing algorithms to provably converge, and a careful choice of entries in routing tables can reduce the number of routing hops to even a constant quantity, independent of the overlay size [22,27]. The most known example of a structured overlay is the chordal ring [45] (Figure 1): N peers are arranged in a circle, and each can route messages

---

* This research is supported by the Italian FIRB project *Webminds*.

G. Danezis and P. Golle (Eds.): PET 2006, LNCS 4258, pp. 190–207, 2006.
© Springer-Verlag Berlin Heidelberg 2006

via its own *successor* in the ring as well as a small $(O(\log(N)))$ number of other peers, called *fingers*, whose "distances" increase according to a geometric progression. With this organization, a message can be delivered in $O(\log(N))$ hops according to a so called "greedy" routing (Figure 2 and Section 3.1).

On the other hand, unstructured overlays like Freenet [11] and GNUnet [2] first leveraged techniques to enhance identity privacy or *anonymity* of participant entities.

Both families of overlays share a common goal, namely, to implement a layer of virtual addressing and message routing on top of the Internet addressing and packet routing infrastructure. Each host participating to the overlay is said to be *responsible* for (or *owner* of) a range of overlay virtual addresses. Messages can be issued by any participant, and are targeted to overlay addresses rather than Internet addresses; the routing algorithm of the overlay implements the correspondence between the target address (an overlay address) and the destination host (an Internet address).

In this respect we easily identify at least two anonymization possibilities. Mostly researched upon is *sender* anonymity, namely, the untraceability of the Internet address of a host which issued a given message. Indirection based on source rewriting, usual cryptographic machinery, or, even better, mix chains [7,4], can help hide the identity of a message sender, that is, improve sender anonymity. But there is another face of the coin, namely, *recipient* anonymity, which in this context means hiding the correspondence between any given overlay address A (the target of a message) and the Internet address of the peer who is responsible for A (the actual receiver of the message).

In a distributed system for content publication, the actions of producing and making use of a content are implemented by letting each participant send suitable messages (respectively "write" and "read") to other entities in the network which happen to store the information. In such a kind of systems, sender anonymity is thus a key ingredient for protecting the privacy of those people who are either producing or making use of any contents. On the other side, recipient anonymity is a key ingredient for censorship resistance, in that it makes it difficult for a censor to locate and then attack the physical place where the target piece of information is stored. In a distributed storage system (but also in the real world), censorship resistance without user privacy makes no sense: readers of unlawful information, when identified, can be prosecuted. Thus, sender anonymity and recipient anonymity may not live separated from each other, and any potential trade-off between these two features must be considered with the greatest care.

The overall goal of our investigation is to understand and improve both the user privacy and the censorship-resistance properties of structured overlay networks. In a previous work of ours [10] we have proposed a technique, that we have called *imprecise routing*, aimed at enhancing the censorship resistance of a chordal ring. The technique, based on the use of deliberately inaccurate entries in the routing tables of all peers, has been shown to be effective in hiding, to some extent, the correspondence between overlay addresses and Internet addresses, without compromising the nice routing properties of this family of overlay networks. In other words we were able to enforce recipient anonymity in the overlay, thus providing a necessary condition for censorship resistance, without sacrificing too much the routing efficiency. In this paper we report about the subsequent step, namely, a study of the interplay between recipient anonymity (related to the censorship resistance) and sender anonymity (related to privacy of users) when the technique of imprecise routing is in place. We have carried out simulations which shows that imprecise routing is beneficial to sender anonymity as well: with imprecise routing, the amount of sender anonymity takes a better distribution, with good anonymity levels becoming more likely at the expenses of very high and very low levels. A more uniform and effective quality of anonymity service is thus provided to participants.

The paper is structured as follows: after defining the adversarial model and the anonymity metrics (Section 2), we recall the ideas behind imprecise routing (Section 3). Then, we report the results of our simulation study on sender anonymity with imprecise routing (Section 4). After a brief survey on the few existing works in the field (Section 5), the paper closes with a summary of conclusions and open issues, in which we also mention NEBLO, a working implementation of the concepts accounted in this paper.

2   Preliminary Assumptions

We believe that the entire work presented here could be adapted to any structured overlay. Nevertheless, for practical purposes we had to choose a reference model of overlay network. We focused on the most successful such model, namely, the aforementioned chordal ring.

The overlay supports the abstraction of a generic *address space*, consisting of the set of 2^k binary words of k bits ordered as a circle modulo 2^k. This space is mapped onto the ring of peers in consecutive chunks or *address intervals*; thus, each peer *owns* a well defined address interval. For the purpose of our work, it is uninteresting to give meaning to the data possibly "stored" at each overlay address. In other words we choose an application-neutral standpoint, and therefore prefer the terms "overlay network" and "address space" to the more popular "distributed hash table" and "key space".

Our discussion assumes an adversarial model that, following Diaz et al. [15], we term "internal, local, and passive"; that is, the adversary controls and can orchestrate a number of peers in the system, each of which complies to the overlay protocol and does not generate malicious traffic, but can maliciously gather information from its internal routing tables as well as any messages it happens to forward.

In order to enforce some sender anonymity, our system relies on pure indirection with no mixes nor cover traffic; in such a case, the adversary has no convenience in injecting extra traffic in the system. Violations of the routing algorithm can be excluded from our adversarial model, because in a structured overlay the routing choices are constrained by the overlay graph, and thus any violation could be easily detected. Global adversaries, either external (capable of observing possibly any message across the entire overlay) or internal (capable of controlling possibly any peer in the network) appear to be unrealistic in a large peer to peer system. So, we conclude that our model of an "internal, local, and passive" adversary is reasonable in a stable overlay. However, when a peer first joins the overlay, or whenever it tries to rebuild its own routing table, an "active" adversary is given chance to take over by playing a suitable protocol; this shall be briefly discussed in Section 6.

We also assume that the overlay protocol does not explicitly disclose the identity of any participant.

Various metrics for sender anonymity have been proposed so far [8,2,5,15,41]. In this paper we conform to other existing studies on structured overlays [26,32, 42] by adopting the size of the anonymity set [8] as a metrics. The anonymity set is the set of those participants who are considered as being possible senders for a given message. The adversary will make its best to narrow down the anonymity set, usually by making use of routing information concerning the intercepted message. If a message is not intercepted by the adversary, the anonymity set is conventionally the whole set of those participants not colluding with the adversary.

Some of the proposed anonymity metrics are based on the entropy within the anonymity set and thus might be more accurate in some cases. We now show why these metrics are unneeded in our scenario. The first adversarial peer P_A who happens to intercept a given message M has the shortest distance from the sender of M. P_A directly knows the peer P_l which it has received M from, whereas the possible predecessors of P_l in the routing path followed by M are unknown. Based on the knowledge of the (greedy) routing algorithm of the chordal ring (Section 3.1), the best P_A can do is to compute how many well-formed routes cross with one another at P_l, and hence the size of the smallest set of possible originators of M (which P_l indeed belongs to), with no chance of discriminating any better within that set (whose members are unknown to P_A, with the only exception of P_l). Later interceptions of M by other adversarial peers are of no help: they occur at greater distance from the sender, and the routing rules does not depend upon the sender, so a later interception cannot gather more information than an earlier one.

3   Imprecise Routing

3.1   Generalized Chordal Rings

Let us consider a set of peers logically organized into an overlay shaped as a ring. Each peer has a link to its own *successor* in the ring; "to have a link" means to store $\langle IPaddress, listeningport \rangle$ of the linked peer in the own routing table. If peer P owns the address interval from A_l to A_u in the address space, and peer Q is the successor of P, then all addresses owned by Q are greater than A_u (modulo 2^k). For better resiliency, each peer has a *successor list*, rather that just one immediate successor. This allows a peer to talk directly to its successor's successor to seal the ring in case the successor has gone (the extension to the case of multiple adjacent faulty peers is straightforward).

In order to keep the routing path below an acceptable size, each peer also knows additional peers called the *fingers*. We present here a generalized version of the concept originally introduced by Stoica et al. [45]. [1] A finger is a link (an entry in the own routing table), pointing to a distant peer in the overlay. The distance is measured between (one of the bounds of) the local address interval and (the corresponding bound of) the address interval owned by the remote peer. Each peer maintains its own list of fingers, the elements of which are ordered by increasing distance. Finger distances obey a mathematical requirement that we call the *distance rule*. The distance rule is often geometric on base 2. Given a bottom value C, called *cutoff*, the first finger has the largest possible distance $\leq C$ from local peer, the second finger has the largest possible distance $\leq 2C$, the third finger has distance $\leq 4C$, and so on, up to spanning half of the address space. The finger at distance $C \cdot 2^m$ is said to have *magnitude* m; we will also call it the "finger m" for brevity. Clearly, each peer can have at most $O(\log(N))$ fingers. A ring of peers, enhanced by fingers, becomes what we call a chordal ring. Figure 1 illustrates this concept.

The routing algorithm takes advantage of fingers in a so-called "greedy" way (Figure 2). When a peer P gets an incoming message whose destination address is A, it acts as follows:

1. P checks out if A is locally owned; if so, the message has arrived and no routing is needed;
2. otherwise, P computes the residual distance D yet to be travelled by the message, as the difference between A and (one of the bounds of) the locally owned address interval;
3. P chooses the finger of largest magnitude whose distance does not exceed D, and forwards the message to it. If no such finger is found, P forwards to successor.

In a chordal ring with complete finger tables conforming to a geometric distance rule, a total travel distance of D is covered in $O(\log_2(D/C))$ hops.

The most efficient way to build and maintain a finger table takes advantage from the recursive nature of the geometric distance rule. To find the finger 0, P sends a suitable request along its successor chain, until the most distant peer still within cutoff distance C is found. To find a finger of magnitude $m > 0$, P asks its own current finger $m - 1$ to be contacted by its finger $m - 1$. [2] Such an *incremental procedure* minimizes the number of contacted peers, so it should be preferred when anonymity is of concern, because it can minimize the information leak towards potential adversaries.

---

[1] Similar concepts are found in every scalable overlay.

[2] In case the address interval of P spans the entire cutoff distance, the finger of magnitude 0 could not be found. In this case P starts by directly searching its finger of magnitude n along successor chain within distance $C \cdot (n + 1)$, where n is such that $C \cdot (n + 1)$ is larger than the size of P's address interval.

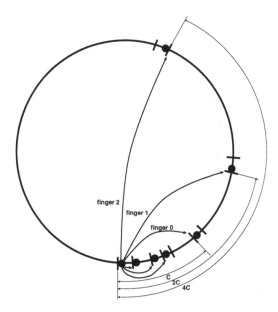

Fig. 1. An instance of a chordal ring. Each peer is responsible for a contiguous interval of overlay addresses. Each peer has links to some successors, and other links called "fingers" pointing to peers at distances C, 2*C, 4*C, etc., where C is a parameter of the system. With N participants, each peer "knows" $O(log(N))$ other peers, and can easily infer their overlay addresses thanks to the above geometric progression.

3.2   Improving Recipient Anonymity with Imprecise Routing

Recipient anonymity is broken when the adversary knows which peer (identified by IP address) is responsible for which overlay address. Clearly, the above (traditional, after Chord [45]) definition of fingers poses two serious threats on recipient anonymity, namely:

1. If peer P has peer Q as its own finger of magnitude m, then P knows that Q's address interval is more or less at distance $C \cdot 2^m$ from itself. Thus, Q's address interval is indirectly disclosed to P. In general, in a ring counting N peers, each participant has $O(\log(N))$ fingers and thus can deduce the address intervals of as many other peers. A malicious coalition counting $O(N/\log(N))$ peers can thus build a *map of the overlay*, namely, a map where all participants (identified by their IP addresses) are related to the overlay addresses they are responsible for.
2. When searching finger 0, peer P exposes its own address interval to the whole successor chain up to the finger. This can help an adversarial coalition to harvest useful information for building the aforementioned map of the overlay.

The two anonymity flaws above are impossible to fix, because they are implied by the traditional definition of fingers. To improve recipient anonymity

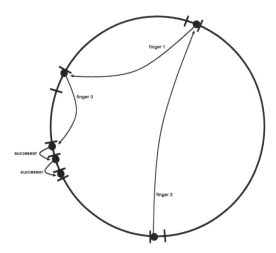

Fig. 2. "Greedy" routing in a chordal ring. With N participants and complete routing tables, $O(\log(N))$ hops are sufficient.

we must shift to a slightly different definition.Our goal is to obfuscate part of the topological information conveyed by traditional fingers, and to protect peers against excessive exposure when they search their fingers of magnitude 0. The solution envisaged in our previous work [10], is that a routing table should only be allowed to contain a small and fixed amount of exact addressing information, whereas most of the information in the table should be deliberately made *imprecise* by construction. Such construction, whose details are reported in [10], ensures that the distance of any finger of generic magnitude m is never fully known; the optimal distance of $C \cdot 2^m$ is affected by a random and unknown error in $[0, C \cdot 2^{m-1}[$, so that the actual distance is an unknown random value in $[C \cdot 2^{m-1}, C \cdot 2^m[$. [3] (Figure 3).

Such an amount of finger imprecision is a good device for recipient anonymity. The higher a finger's magnitude, the lesser the information the finger conveys about the remote peer it points to. As a result, only large adversarial coalitions can harvest sufficiently exact information from finger tables. In [10] we have also shown that routing convergence in a logarithmic number of hops is preserved even with imprecise routing.

4   Imprecise Routing and Sender Anonymity

Imprecise routing is aimed at recipient anonymity, yet its use would be impractical, if sender anonymity was compromised by this. But we come to the main contribution of this paper: not only imprecise routing does not compromise sender

---

[3] The distribution of distance corresponds to the convolution of $m+2$ uniform random variables over $[0, C/4[$.

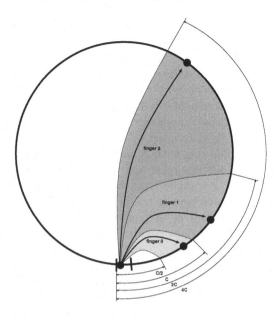

Fig. 3. A chordal ring (successors omitted) in which the fingers are affected by an unknown random error. The average error increases proportionally with the distance of the peer. This way, no peer can infer much about the overlay addresses of other peers, and this improves recipient anonymity. Yet, $O(log(N))$ hops are still sufficient to route messages towards an arbitrary destination.

anonymity, it is even beneficial in improving the quality of sender anonymity provided to participants.

To validate such a claim we have built a simulator for a chordal ring over an address space made of 32-bit addresses. By acting upon a handful of parameters, we could simulate rings with imprecise fingers as well as traditional rings with exact fingers.

In the systems with imprecise fingers, all fingers are built according to the incremental procedure outlined in Section 3.1. The cutoff distance C is a critical parameter because it affects the average number of successors in between each peer and its corresponding finger 0. If C was too small, the inaccuracy affecting the routing tables would be small as well, with lesser guarantees of recipient anonymity. Therefore, C should depend on the number N of participants in the overlay. For a ring with N participants, our simulator initializes the parameter C as follows: the initial value is set to cover 20 bits of overlay address, then this value is doubled again and again until it exceeds the quantity $10 * 2^{32}/N$, namely, ten times the average size of each peer's address interval. This ensures that C is chosen in such a way that the distance between each peer and its corresponding finger 0 covers 10 consecutive peers on average. In a real-world system, hovever, C should be a fixed parameter known to all peers. In order to allow C to be constant in a real system with an unpredictable and unknown number of participants, each peer might just evaluate the size of its own address interval and, based on this, decide the minimum magnitude of the first finger to be inserted in the routing table. Setting a minimum magnitude $M > 0$ is tantamount to applying a scale factor 2^M to the cutoff distance C, without forcing other partecipants to do the same (which would be impossible).

By contrast, in the systems with exact routing tables, fingers are computed explicitly rather than incrementally, in order to avoid that higher magnitude fingers could be affected by cumulated inaccuracy arising from fingers of lower magnitude. The cutoff distance is set to 1 as with traditional chordal rings.

After creating a sample ring with N uniformly distributed peers, the simulator fills up each peer's successor list and finger table; fingers can be imprecise or exact, depending on a compile-time flag. The simulator then generates all the routing paths from each peer to the peer owning the overlay address 0 (any destination address is equivalent to 0 modulo rotational transformation of the chordal ring). At this point, the simulator generates a number of sample adversarial configurations over the ring; the fraction f of adversaries over the entire population is specified at runtime, and the simulator obtains each adversarial configuration by marking each peer as adversary with probability f. For each adversarial configuration, the simulator computes statistics of the anonymity sets of all "honest" peers, by processing the set of all routing paths as follows:

1. For each "honest" peer P, scan the routing path from P to address 0 until the first adversarial peer is found. Let us call $last(P)$ the result of the scan. If the path does not meet adversaries, $last(P)$ is assigned the pair $\langle -1, -1 \rangle$; otherwise $last(P)$ is assigned the pair $\langle C, m \rangle$, where C is the first adversarial peer found along the path, and m is the magnitude of the finger which was the last hop in the path up to C, or -1 if such last hop was a successor link. The reason why we take the magnitude of last hop into account shall become clear at the next step.

2. For each adversarial peer C, count all "honest" peers P such that $last(P) = \langle C, m \rangle$ with given m. Let us call $a(C, m)$ such count. $a(C, m)$ is the size of the anonymity set that the colluder C can associate to a generic lookup for address 0 that it could intercept. The reason why this anonymity set depends on m is that C can indeed discriminate among possible originators of a lookup by looking at which incoming link the lookup has came from; intuitively, a lookup coming from the immediate predecessor may have a lot of possible originators, whereas a lookup coming from a link corresponding to the finger of greatest magnitude may only have one originator (namely, the opposite peer on the ring).

3. For each "honest" peer P, if $last(P) = \langle C, m \rangle = \langle -1, -1 \rangle$ then the anonymity set size from P's point of view is equal to the total number of "honest" peers in the ring, namely, $f \cdot N$; otherwise, the anonymity set size is equal to $a(C, m)$. The case of unintercepted lookup is thus taken into account when estimating the average sender anonymity from the sender viewpoint. [4]

---

[4] Actually, the simulator does not require three distinct scans of the entire set of peers in order to accomplish the above three steps.

The results have been obtained by running the simulator over 500 sample rings of given size, each with 100 sample adversarial configurations with given percentage of attackers.

Let us first discuss the average sender anonymity as a function of the distance between sender and recipient (this distance is normalized to the size of the complete address space):

- The overall result is that, with imprecise fingers, the average sender anonymity as a function of distance from destination is often lower but always more uniform, compared to traditional fingers. This is displayed by Figure 4, where chordal rings with both kinds of fingers are compared with one another with varying percentage of attackers. By averaging along the whole range of distances, we see that a system with 10000 peers and 30% attackers yields a sender anonymity of 689 when using traditional fingers and 272 with imprecise fingers, a 61% loss. With 50% attackers the loss is 41% but the level of anonymity is however too small (anonymity decreases from 71 to 42). On the other hand, with 10% attackers the loss is just 27% (from 4620 to 3379). Systems with 1000 peers show a lesser impact of imprecise fingers on sender anonymity (maximum loss is 33%, at 30% attackers). To summarize, with imprecise fingers the average sender anonymity becomes less dependent on the target of queries, while the resulting loss of anonymity is not substantial unless the system is large and highly compromised by the adversary. The fundamental reason for this behaviour, is that the routing paths with imprecise fingers become longer (mainly because of the cutoff distance), and more uniform (because of the randomization). Longer paths yield lower sender anonymity, because messages are more likely to get intercepted. However, as we shall see at the end of this Section, randomization leads to a more effective anonymity distibution.
- Another important insight is that, on average, the sender anonymity is in both cases fairly large when the percentage of attackers is not overwhelming. It becomes very poor when this percentage raises 50%, but a system with so many attackers should be considered as highly compromised indeed.

However, the average sender anonymity alone is not informative enough. The variability around the average value must also be considered. We have observed that the variance is always strong, regardless of the fingers being imprecise or not. Figure 5 shows the frequency distribution of sender anonymity in chordal rings with 1000 peers and three different percentages of attackers, averaged along the whole range of distances from destination. The choice between imprecise or traditional fingers leads to deeply different distributions of sender anonymity: with imprecise fingers all distributions span a large interval of pretty good anonymity levels, as opposed to traditional fingers which only span too small or very large anonymity levels. In other words, imprecise fingers increase the probability of getting a fairly good sender anonymity. The same conclusion can be drawn for

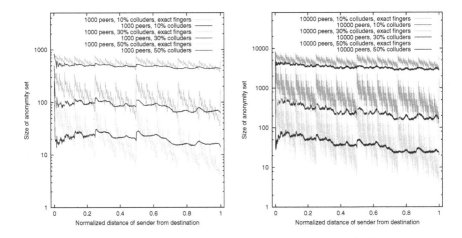

Fig. 4. Average sender anonymity in simulated chordal rings with 1000 and 10000 peers and three different percentages of attackers. Systems with imprecise fingers are compared to systems with exact fingers. The order of captions reflects the order of the curves from top to bottom. Imprecise fingers yield a lower but more regular sender anonymity compared to exact fingers.

systems with 10000 peers (Figure 6). It is the author's opinion that such a better distribution compensates for the lower average level of sender anonymity.

Finally, our overlay with imprecise routing differs from a traditional chordal ring because of two distinct features, namely, the imprecise fingers, and a cutoff distance far greater than 1. In order to understand how these two additional features contribute to sender anonymity we need to separate them from each other. To this end, we have considered a "hybrid" chordal ring in which the imprecision has been eliminated from our fingers. Recall that a generic imprecise finger of magnitude m points to a distance randomly distributed within $[C \cdot 2^{m-1}, C \cdot 2^m[$. The random distribution is obtained as sum of several uniform distributions, so the expectation is always at the middle of the interval. If we remove the imprecision from our overlay, yet we want to preserve the average length of routing paths, each imprecise finger must be replaced by an exact finger whose distance falls at the middle of the interval, namely, $0.75 \cdot C \cdot 2^m$. This is tantamount to running a chordal ring with exact fingers and cutoff distance scaled down by a factor of 0.75.

By running the simulator on such "hybrid" chordal ring, we obtain a distribution of sender anonymity (Figure 7) very similar to a traditional Chord (which has cutoff distance 1); the differences only affect the regions of very low and very high anonymity degrees, with no significant changes in between. We thus conclude that the improvement in the distribution of sender anonymity, observed in the chordal rings with imprecise routing, is effectively due to finger imprecision rather than the large cutoff distance.

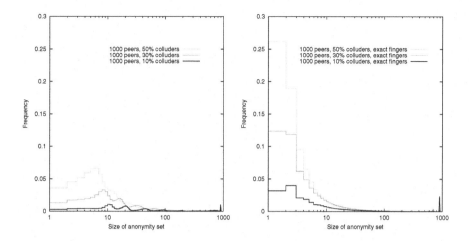

Fig. 5. Average frequency distribution of sender anonymity in simulated chordal rings with 1000 peers and both imprecise and traditional fingers, with three different percentages of attackers. The spikes at right correspond to the cases when messages are not intercepted, yielding the largest possible anonymity set. All curves are heavily affected by the x scale being logarithmic; this must be taken into account when comparing curves from different scenarios.

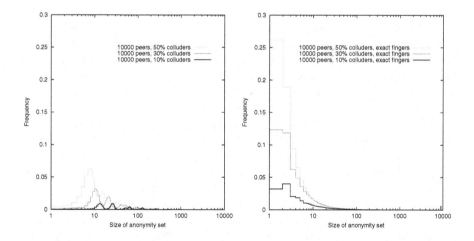

Fig. 6. Average frequency distribution of sender anonymity in simulated chordal rings with 10000 peers and both imprecise and traditional fingers, with three different percentages of attackers. The spikes at right, corresponding to the cases when messages are not intercepted, are too small to be visible. All curves are heavily affected by the x scale being logarithmic; this must be taken into account when comparing curves from different scenarios.

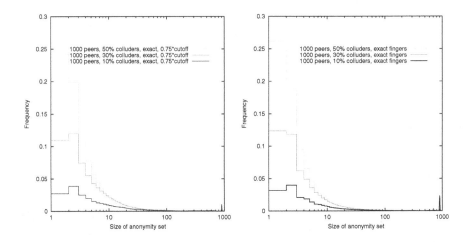

Fig. 7. Average frequency distribution of sender anonymity in simulated chordal rings with 1000 peers and three different percentages of attackers. Left: "hybrid" system with exact fingers and cutoff distance scaled down by a factor of 0.75. Right: traditional Chord system with exact fingers. The differences only affect the regions of very low and very high anonymity.

5   Related Work

There are very few attempts to improve anonymity in structured overlays. Achord [25] is an enhancement of Chord [45] with anonymity features. Aiming at enforcing sender anonymity, Achord implements recursive-style [45] routing (because of the indirection) and forces each response to travel back to sender along the same route previously tracked by the corresponding request (so that the sender address need not be disclosed to the receiver; this trick is also cited by Borisov and Waddle [5]).

Other studies [26,5,32] focus on measuring sender anonymity in plain Chord. According to O'Donnell and Vaikuntanathan [32], Chord provides a good amount of sender anonymity in terms of size of anonymity set. This is in apparent contradiction with Kannan and Bansal [26]. Apparently, the difference between these two works is that the former considers the anonymity from the attacker point of view, whereas the latter chooses the point of view of the generic "honest" sender. In addition, the latter work shows an analytical mistake, since the event that a lookup is not intercepted by any adversary is overlooked in the anonymity evaluation. Such an event is not so unlikely, and its impact on the average anonymity set size makes a difference. As we have seen in Section 4, in order to estimate the sender anonymity of our system, we follow the approach suggested by Borisov and Waddle [5] by choosing simulation rather than analytical tools. We too choose the sender viewpoint when estimating sender anonymity, but do not forget about the weight of unintercepted messages, so our results look better that the ones in [26].

Agyaat [43] provides a compromise between anonymity and efficiency by means of a two-level hybrid organization in which the Chord structured overlay works together with the Gnutella unstructured system. Gnutella-like "clouds" are connected with one another by means of a Chord ring. It is an interesting and very effective approach that deserves a deeper anonymity analysis.

Imprecise routing information is at the core of unstructured overlays. With Freenet, for example, a message directed to key A is routed towards a node P if P has previously been able to route back responses from keys "similar" to A [11]. Thus, a routing table entry that points to P does not say anything about the keys actually stored at P, nor does it say much about the placement of P in the overlay topology. GNUnet [2] and MUTE [37] follow a similar approach, with some more randomness. Also SkipNet [24] and Skip Graphs [1], both inspired to the Skip List data structure [34], and Symphony [29], make use of somehow randomized routing entries, although not for anonymity purposes.

The technique of choosing fingers so that they point to sub-optimal distances is also cited by Gummadi et al. [21], as a means of improving routing resilience and neighbour selection while retaining logarithmic-sized routing paths. We have exploited this well known degree of flexibility offered by chordal rings, in order to improve anonymity rather than resilience or neighbour proximity.

6   Conclusions and Open Issues

The most important result reported in this paper concerns sender anonymity. Previous work has shown that the use of some randomization on long-range connections in structured overlay networks provides better recipient anonymity without sacrificing the nice properties of structured overlays (provable routing convergence and, to some extent, performance). However, we were also concerned with the impact on sender anonymity: the proposed solution would have been impractical, was recipient anonymity obtained at the expenses of sender anonymity. Luckily, the simulations reported in this paper show that the *average* sender anonymity decreases but not so dramatically, and this decrease is compensated by a *better distribution* of the sender anonymity levels: good levels become more likely at the expenses of very low and very high levels.

As an aside, this paper also presents a deep evaluation of sender anonymity of traditional generalized chordal rings.

Our result can be summarized by saying that anonymous routing can be accomplished even in a chordal ring, and can be done in $O(\log(N))$ hops where N is the number of peers in the overlay. If we liked slogans, we would say that anonymity can be asymptotically efficient. The cutoff distance of the chordal ring is one of the parameters that directly affects the path lengths; future investigations are thus in order, concerning the role of cutoff distance in the trade-offs between anonymity, efficiency, and availability.

The choice of the chordal ring as a reference overlay for our study was not just driven by popularity reasons. In their interesting paper [21], Gummadi et al. have shown that chordal rings provide good resilience to peer failures, a remarkable advantage for real peer-to-peer systems. Although it would be in principle interesting to evaluate the anonymity properties of constant-degree overlays such as Viceroy [28], there is the suspect (a certainty for Viceroy [21]) that constant-degree networks of small degree might have poor resilience against peer failures.

An unexplored security issue is about the algorithm by which a new peer joins the overlay. In order to preserve anonymity, it is crucial that colluding peers be given no control on which position in the overlay they are going to occupy. The obvious, and widely adopted, rule based on the pair $\langle IPaddress, port \rangle$ of the newcomer appears weak as long as the adversary is able to use an IP domain of choice. We are also working at this critical security issue.

A main security concern is about the incremental procedure outlined in Section 3.1, that each peer should follow when building its own finger table. Let us suppose the generic peer P wants to locate its own finger 0. It issues a request which travels along the successor chain until a valid candidate is met. But, if the request meets an adversarial peer, from then on the whole incremental procedure can be diverged towards the adversarial coalition. The finger 0 would be an adversary, and the same would occur with all fingers of greater magnitude, and thus the sender anonymity of P would be entirely compromised. No variant of such a procedure can prevent this kind of opportunistic attack from occurring: any kind of search for fingers may possibly end up in a colluder, and from there on the search can be fully managed within the adversarial coalition. We thus conclude that full sender anonymity is impossible to achieve as long as routing tables are built by running the routing protocol itself, no matter the overlay being structured or not. Yet, one could wonder about algorithms for finger location that decrease the strike probability of this opportunistic attack.

We have managed to embody the mechanism of imprecise routing tables into NEBLO [9], a chordal ring overlay with anonymity features. NEBLO is still in beta development stage, yet it has already been released to the community, under the GNU General Public Licence.

References

1. J. Aspnes and G. Shah. Skip Graphs. In *Proc. of the 14th Annual ACM-SIAM Symp. on Discrete Algorithms (SODA '03)*, January 2003.
2. K. Bennett and C. Grothoff. GAP: Practical Anonymous Networking. In *Proc. of Workshop on Privacy Enhancing Technologies (PET 2003)*, Dresden, Germany, March 2003.
3. K. Bennett, C. Grothoff, T. Horozov, and I. Patrascu. Efficient Sharing of Encrypted Data. In *Proc. of ACISP 2002*, pages 107–120. Springer-Verlag, July 2002.
4. O. Berthold, H. Federrath, and S. Köpsell. Web MIXes: A System for Anonymous and Unobservable Internet Access. In H. Federrath, editor, *Proc. of Designing Privacy Enhancing Technologies: Workshop on Design Issues in Anonymity and Unobservability (PET)*, pages 115–129. Springer-Verlag, LNCS 2009, July 2000.
5. Nikita Borisov and Jason Waddle. Anonymity in Structured Peer-to-Peer Networks. gnunet.org/papers/borisov_waddle.pdf, December 2003.

6. M. Castro, P. Druschel, A. M. Kermarrec, and A. Rowstron. Scribe: A Large-scale and Decentralized Application-level Multicast Infrastructure. *IEEE Journal on Selected Areas in Communications, special issue on Network Support for Multicast Communications*, 20(8), October 2002.

7. D. Chaum. Untraceable electronic mail, return addresses, and digital pseudonyms. *Communications of the ACM*, 4(2), February 1981.

8. D. Chaum. The Dining Cryptographers Problem: Unconditional Sender and Recipient Untraceability. *Journal of Cryptology*, 1(1):65–75, 1988.

9. G. Ciaccio. The NEBLO homepage, http://www.disi.unige.it/project/neblo/.

10. G. Ciaccio. Recipient Anonymity in a Structured Overlay. In *Proc. of the International Conference on Internet and Web Applications and Services (ICIW'06)*, Guadeloupe, French Caribbean, February 2006. IEEE.

11. I. Clarke, O. Sandberg, B. Wiley, and T. W. Hong. Freenet: A Distributed Anonymous Information Storage and Retrieval System. In *Proc. of Designing Privacy Enhancing Technologies: Workshop on Design Issues in Anonymity and Unobservability (PET)*, pages 46–66, July 2000.

12. R. Cox, A. Muthitacharoen, and R. Morris. Serving DNS using a Peer-to-Peer Lookup Service. In *Proc. of the 1st International Peer To Peer Systems Workshop (IPTPS02)*, March 2002.

13. F. Dabek, M. F. Kaashoek, D. Karger, R. Morris, and I. Stoica. Wide-area Cooperative Storage with CFS. In *Proc. of 18th ACM Symp. on Operating Systems Principles*, October 2001.

14. F. Dabek, J. Li, E. Sit, J. Robertson, M. F. Kaashoek, and R. Morris. Designing a DHT for low latency and high throughput. In *Proc. of the 1st USENIX Symposium on Networked Systems Design and Implementation (NSDI '04)*, San Francisco, CA, March 2004.

15. Claudia Díaz, Stefaan Seys, Joris Claessens, and Bart Preneel. Towards measuring anonymity. In Roger Dingledine and Paul Syverson, editors, *Proc. of Privacy Enhancing Technologies Workshop (PET 2002)*. Springer-Verlag, LNCS 2482, April 2002.

16. R. Dingledine, M. J. Freedman, and D. Molnar. The Free Haven Project: Distributed Anonymous Storage Service. In H. Federrath, editor, *Proc. of Designing Privacy Enhancing Technologies: Workshop on Design Issues in Anonymity and Unobservability (PET)*. Springer-Verlag, LNCS 2009, July 2000.

17. J. Eriksson, M. Faloutsos, and S. Krishnamurthy. PeerNet: Pushing Peer-to-Peer Down the Stack. In *Proc. of the 2nd International Workshop on Peer-to-Peer Systems (IPTPS03)*, Berkeley, CA, 2003.

18. J. Kubiatowicz et al. Oceanstore: An Architecture for Global-scale Persistent Storage. In *Proc. of ACM ASPLOS*, November 2000.

19. Michael J. Freedman and Robert Morris. Tarzan: A peer-to-peer anonymizing network layer. In *Proc. of the 9th ACM Conference on Computer and Communications Security (CCS 2002)*, Washington, DC, November 2002.

20. I. Goldberg. *A Pseudonymous Communications Infrastructure for the Internet*. PhD thesis, UC Berkeley, December 2000.

21. K. Gummadi, R. Gummadi, S. Gribble, S. Ratnasamy, S. Shenker, and I. Stoica. The Impact of DHT Routing Geometry on Resilience and Proximity. In *Proc. of ACM SIGCOMM*, August 2003.

22. A. Gupta, B. Liskov, and R. Rodrigues. One Hop Lookups for Peer-to-peer Overlays. In *Proc. of the 9th Workshop on Hot Topics in Operating Systems (HotOS-IX)*, Lihue, Hawaii, May 2003.

23. I. Gupta, K. Birman, P. Linga, A. Demers, and R. van Renesse. Kelips: Building an Efficient and Stable P2P DHT Through Increased Memory and Background Overhead. In *Proc. of the 2nd International Workshop on Peer-to-Peer Systems (IPTPS03)*, Berkeley, CA, 2003.

24. N. Harvey, M. B. Jones, S. Saroiu, M. Theimer, and A. Wolman. Skipnet: A Scalable Overlay Network with Practical Locality Properties. In *Proc. of the 4th USENIX Symposium on Internet Technologies and Systems (USITS '03)*, March 2003.

25. S. Hazel and B. Wiley. Achord: A Variant of the Chord Lookup Service for Use in Censorship Resistant Peer-to-Peer Publishing Systems. In *Proc. of the 1st International Peer To Peer Systems Workshop (IPTPS02)*, March 2002.

26. J. Kannan and M. Bansal. Anonymity in Chord. www.cs.berkeley.edu/ kjk/chord-anon.ps, December 2002.

27. B. Leong and J. Li. Achieving One-Hop DHT Lookup and Strong Stabilization by Passing Tokens. In *Proc. of the 12th International Conference on Networks (ICON)*, November 2004.

28. D. Malkhi, M. Naor, and D. Ratajczak. Viceroy: A Scalable and Dynamic Emulation of the Butterfly. In *Proc. of ACM PODC*, August 2002.

29. G. S. Manku, M. Bawa, and P. Raghavan. Symphony: Distributed Hashing in a Small World. In *Proc. of the fourth USENIX Symposium on Internet Technologies and Systems (USITS'03*, Seattle, WA, March 2003.

30. P. Maymounkov and D. Mazières. Kademlia: A Peer-to-peer Information System Based on the XOR Metric. In *Proc. of the 1st International Peer To Peer Systems Workshop (IPTPS02)*, March 2002.

31. A. Mislove, G. Oberoi, A. Post, C. Reis, P. Druschel, and D. S. Wallach. AP3: Cooperative, Decentralized Anonymous Communication. In *Proc. of 11th ACM SIGOPS European Workshop*, Leuven, Belgium, September 2004.

32. C. O'Donnell and V. Vaikuntanathan. Information Leak in the Chord Lookup Protocol. In *Proc. of the 4th IEEE Int.l Conf. on Peer-to-Peer Computing (P2P2004)*, Zurich, Switzerland, August 2004.

33. P. Perlegos. DoS Defense in Structured Peer-to-Peer Networks. Technical Report UCB-CSD-04-1309, U.C. Berkeley, March 2004.

34. W. Pugh. Skip Lists: a Probabilistic Alternative to Balanced Trees. *Comm. of ACM*, 33(6):668–676, 1990.

35. S. Ratnasamy, P. Francis, M. Handley, R. Karp, and S. Shenker. A Scalable Content-Addressable Network. In *Proc. of ACM SIGCOMM*, August 2001.

36. S. Ratnasamy, M. Handley, R. Karp, and S. Shenker. Application-level Multicast Using Content-addressable Networks. In *Proc. of 3rd Int.l Workshop on Networked Group Communication*, November 2001.

37. J. Rohrer. MUTE: Simple, Anonymous File Sharing. http://mute-net.sourceforge.net/.

38. A. Rowstron and P. Druschel. Pastry: Scalable, Distributed Object Location and Routing for Large-scale Peer-to-peer Systems. In *Proc. of Int.l Conf. on Distributed System Platforms*, November 2001.

39. A. Rowstron and P. Druschel. Storage Management and Caching in PAST, a Large-scale, Persistent Peer-to-peer Storage Utility. In *Proc. of 18th ACM Symp. on Operating Systems Principles*, October 2001.

40. A. Serjantov. Anonymizing Censorship Resistant Systems. In *Proc. of the 1st International Peer To Peer Systems Workshop (IPTPS02)*, March 2002.

41. Andrei Serjantov and George Danezis. Towards an information theoretic metric for anonymity. In Roger Dingledine and Paul Syverson, editors, *Proc. of Privacy Enhancing Technologies Workshop (PET 2002)*. Springer-Verlag, LNCS 2482, April 2002.

42. Rob Sherwood, Bobby Bhattacharjee, and Aravind Srinivasan. P5: A protocol for scalable anonymous communication. In *Proc. of the 2002 IEEE Symposium on Security and Privacy*, May 2002.

43. A. Singh and L. Liu. Agyaat: Providing Mutually Anonymous Services over Structured P2P Networks. Technical Report GIT-CERCS-04-12, Georgia Inst. of Tech. CERCS, 2004.

44. I. Stoica, D. Adkins, S. Zhuang, S. Shenker, and S. Surana. Internet Indirection Infrastructure. In *Proc. of ACM SIGCOMM*, August 2002.

45. I. Stoica, R. Morris, D. Karger, M. F. Kaashoek, and H. Balakrishnan. Chord: a Scalable Peer-to-peer Lookup Service for Internet Applications. In *Proc. of ACM SIGCOMM*, August 2001.

46. M. Waldman, A. Rubin, and L. Cranor. Publius: A Robust, Tamper-evident, Censorship-resistant and Source-anonymous Web Publishing System. In *Proc. of the 9th USENIX Security Symposium*, pages 59–72, August 2000.

47. J. Wang, L. Lu, and A. Chien. Tolerating Denial-of-Service Attacks Using Overlay Networks - Impact of Topology. In *Proc. of ACM Workshop on Survivable and Self-Regenerative Systems*, October 2003.

48. B. Y. Zhao, J. D. Kubiatowicz, and A. D. Joseph. Tapestry: An Infrastructure for Fault-resilient Wide-area Location and Routing. Technical Report UCB-CSD-01-1141, U.C. Berkeley, April 2001.

Selectively Traceable Anonymity

Luis von Ahn[1], Andrew Bortz[2], Nicholas J. Hopper[3], and Kevin O'Neill[4]

[1] Carnegie Mellon University, Pittsburgh, PA USA
[2] Stanford University, Palo Alto, CA USA
[3] University of Minnesota, Minneapolis, MN USA
[4] Cornell University, Ithaca, NY USA

Abstract. Anonymous communication can, by its very nature, facilitate socially unacceptable behavior; such abuse of anonymity is a serious impediment to its widespread deployment. This paper studies two notions related to the prevention of abuse. The first is *selective traceability*, the property that a message's sender can be traced with the help of an explicitly stated set of parties. The second is *noncoercibility*, the property that no party can convince an adversary (using technical means) that he was not the sender of a message. We show that, in principal, almost any anonymity scheme can be made selectively traceable, and that a particular anonymity scheme can be modified to be noncoercible.

1 Introduction

Anonymous communication has several important potential applications, including anonymous email for "whistle-blowing," anonymous web browsing to access useful but possibly embarrassing or incriminating information (e.g., "how to deal with a drug addiction"), and mechanisms to ensure individual privacy in electronic transactions. At the same time, there are obvious ways in which anonymity protocols could be used for antisocial or criminal purposes such as slander, threats, and transfer of illegal content. In some cases, especially when the anonymity guarantees are strong, the negative consequences of allowing users to communicate anonymously can outweigh the benefits. This is a potential stumbling block for the widespread adoption of anonymizing systems.[1]

Systems for anonymous communication have generally tried to provide the strongest possible guarantees while providing some reasonable level of efficiency and ease-of-use, but, surprisingly, have usually not addressed "revoking" the anonymity of a message in a formal manner.[2] In this paper we argue that it would be useful to have anonymity protocols that *explicitly* allow the tracing of

---

[1] We note that there are naturally other stumbling blocks to the widespread adoption of current anonymity systems, such as ease-of-use, ease-of-installation, and public awareness.

[2] One exception is the mechanisms in various anonymous cash and election protocols that allow revoking the anonymity of a user who double-spends or double-votes.

G. Danezis and P. Golle (Eds.): PET 2006, LNCS 4258, pp. 208–222, 2006.

a message's sender whenever a set of fair and sensible conditions is met.[3] To this effect, we define *selectively traceable anonymous communication*, which allows tracing a message when a *tracing policy* is satisfied, such as a fixed fraction of the participants voting to trace the message.

Another reason for examining tracing in anonymity protocols is that some existing anonymity protocols already allow a slightly different form of tracing by allowing participants to *prove* that they did not send some particular message. If a protocol has this property, we call it *coercible*, because participants can be coerced into proving that they did not send a particular message. Coercibility is related to tracing in that a coercible protocol allows gradual and uncoordinated tracing: every participant except the sender can show that they did not send the message. If the anonymity set of a message is small, this can be easier than tracing through other means. The notion of uncoercible anonymity is similar to the notions of coercibility in election protocols [18], *deniability* in encryption [7], and *adaptive security* in multiparty computation [8].

We present two definitions of traceable anonymity. In one, which we refer to as *weak traceable anonymity*, a message should be traced whenever the tracing policy is satisfied; in the other, *strong traceable anonymity*, nothing about the sender of a message should be learned unless the tracing policy is satisfied. To clarify the distinction between these definitions, we mention that a weak traceable protocol can be coercible: the message can be traced when the tracing policy is satisfied, but something about the identity of the sender can be revealed even if the tracing policy is not satisfied if any participants prove that they did not send the message. A strong traceable protocol does not allow such coercion.

In this paper, we present definitions and several technical results relating to selectively traceable anonymous communication. Our technical results include:

A generic transformation that adds selective traceability. We show that a large class of systems for anonymous communication can, in principle, be transformed into systems with selectively traceable anonymity, using a construction that first appears in [20]: append an anonymous "group signature" to every message sent on an anonymous channel and *require the receivers to drop all messages that are not signed*. We note that this transformation suffers from an incentive problem: receivers have no incentive to drop unsigned messages, and thus senders have no incentive to sign messsages. We show that, in principle, almost any anonymity scheme can be transformed to avoid this problem without sacrificing anonymity.

Two efficient transformations from specific DC-Net-like protocols. We show efficient transformations from two specific DC-Net-based protocols: [1,15]. The transformations do not affect the efficiency of the underlying non-traceable protocols and yield security against malicious adversaries.

---

[3] We note that in some situations, such extreme remedies may not be required. It is an interesting question to determine what conditions allow weaker solutions to counter abuse.

Coercibility results. We discuss the notion of coercibility in anonymous communication, and show how the DC-Net-based protocols in [1,15] allow coercion. We show a simple modification to the [1] protocol that gives noncoercibility. We also show that our generic transformations do not alter the coercibility (or noncoercibility) of the underlying protocols. These results show that, in principle, strong traceable anonymity can be acheived.

2 Threshold Cryptography and Group Signatures

We use two main building blocks for the technical results that follow: threshold El Gamal decryption and group signatures. The first technique generalizes El Gamal encryption so that private keys are distributed among a number of principals; the second provides a way for a principal to sign a message anonymously in such a way that the signer's anonymity can be revoked by the group manager.

Distributed El Gamal Decryption [21]. We will use a public-key encryption system to encrypt information that identifies the sender of a message. To do so in a way that respects a particular tracing policy, however, we want decryption to occur only when all the voters in some tracing set T agree to take part. In other words, we require a cryptosystem with the following features:

1. There is an "aggregate" public key y that can be used to encrypt messages, as with regular public-key cryptosystems.
2. Each voter v_i has a secret private key x_i that can be used to "partially" decrypt a ciphertext C, and decryption is computationally hard unless all the voters in some tracing set T take part in the decryption.

Group Signatures. Group signature schemes [12] provide a way for members of a group to sign messages anonymously. That is, they allow a member of a group to digitally sign a document in such a way that it may be verified that the document was signed by a group member, but not which particular group member signed it unless a designated group manager "opens" the signature.

Definition 1 (From [3]). *A group signature scheme is a digital signature scheme comprised of the following five procedures:*

- SETUP *outputs the initial group public key GPK (including all system parameters) and the secret key for the group manager.*
- JOIN *allows a new user to join the group. The user's output is a membership certificate and a membership secret.*
- SIGN(m), *given GPK, a membership certificate and secret, and a message m, outputs a group signature on m.*
- VERIFY *establishes the validity of an alleged group signature σ on message m with respect to GPK.*
- OPEN *given a message m with valid group signature σ, the key GPK and the group manager's secret key, determines the identity of the signer.*

Group signature schemes must satisfy a variety of properties. Signatures produced using SIGN must be accepted using VERIFY, for example, and the actual signer of a message should remain anonymous until the signature is opened by the group manager. For more details, see [3].

Many group signature schemes (e.g., [3,20]) implement OPEN as an instance of El Gamal decryption. In these schemes the group manager can be distributed so that each instance of OPEN operates according to a threshold scheme.

3   Selective Traceability

Tracing, like anonymity, may be abused. Accordingly, we want to avoid any requirements that tracing information be logged or enforaced by any single, central authority, since in many cases the primary reason for having an anonymity protocol is to provide protection against central authorities. To describe a general framework for traceable schemes, it will therefore be important to specify *who* is able to trace. The setting we consider is as follows: there is a finite set G of *users* who may be able to send or receive messages anonymously, and there is a finite set V of *voters* who are authorized to trace a message. There is also a set $\mathcal{V} \subseteq 2^V$, the *tracing policy*, such that an act of tracing only occurs when all the members of a *tracing set* $T \in \mathcal{V}$ agree to it. (We assume that $\mathcal{V}$ is *monotone*, so that if $T \in \mathcal{V}$ and $T \subseteq T'$, then $T' \in \mathcal{V}$. It therefore suffices to consider only the minimal sets in $\mathcal{V}$.) We call $(G, V, \mathcal{V})$ a *tracing scheme*. Some examples of tracing policies include:

1. The trivial tracing policy, in which explicit tracing by voters is not allowed, can be represented with $\mathcal{V} = \emptyset$. (For many protocols, a sufficiently large subset of the users of a system can cooperate to trace messages; but this is an implicit process, rather than one enforced by the protocol.)
2. Given V and an integer $1 \le t \le |V|$, let $\mathcal{V}(t) = \{R \subseteq V \mid |R| = t\}$. $\mathcal{V}(t)$ is a *threshold tracing policy*, with parameter t. Tracing occurs only when at least t members of V agree that tracing should occur.
3. Let V be the set of n members of a legislative body (e.g., the US Senate's 100 members or the UK House of Commons' 646 members); then $\mathcal{V}(\lfloor n/2 \rfloor + 1)$ is the policy that says a legislative act is required to trace a message.

We note that there is a close relationship between the tracing scheme $\mathcal{V}$ of a selectively traceable anonymity protocol and the "trust model" of any anonymity protocol. In particular, when a static set of nodes must be trusted not to reveal the sender of all messages, it is clear that the tracing policy must include this subset as an element. On the other hand, a tracing policy explicitly specifies sets of voters (not necessarily participants) who may trace a message regardless of its origin or destination; a participant must therefore trust these sets of voters. In the case of a tracing policy, however, these sets are always static, and always have the power to trace a message; in many existing anonymity protocols, the set of nodes that can trace any particular message varies by message. Thus "trust models" are mostly a side-effect of the protocols employed by some anonymous communication schemes, whereas tracing policies are conscious decisions to allow tracing the anonymity of a message.

3.1 Generic Transformations

In this section we present a method to convert a generic anonymous communication protocol to a new protocol that permits selective tracing. We assume that there is an independent set V of voters and a threshold tracing policy $\mathcal{V} \subseteq 2^V$. (We remark that any monotone tracing policy may be implemented using our method, though in the worst case the length of the shares may be exponential in the size of the voting set. Here we focus only on the threshold case.) We do not assume anything about the voters except that they can be trusted with a secret share of the El Gamal private key that will be used for decryption. The voters may be principals in the original anonymous communication scheme, but this isn't a necessary requirement. For this work, we make the simplifying assumption that a group manager enforces some binding between a user's identity in the JOIN protocol and that user's physical identity.

Let $\mathcal{M}$ be the set of possible *anonymous messages*, which are generated by one party to be processed for anonymous delivery to another party, and let $\mathcal{PM}$ be the set of *protocol messages*, which are exchanged by parties during the execution of the protocol. Our generic transformation applies to protocols that include a finite number of parties $\{P_1, \ldots, P_n\}$ and include the primitive operations SEND, PROCESS, and RECOVER, which we now describe. (These operations use a set of public parameters selected by an initial setup stage, and each player P_i may use his secret parameters S_i in any stage):

- SEND: a procedure executed by P_i that takes as input an anonymous message $m \in \mathcal{M}$ and a recipient P_j, and outputs a list c of pairs $(c_{i,j}, P_j)$ where $c_{i,j}$ is a protocol message to be sent to P_j.
- PROCESS: a procedure executed by P_j that takes as input a list of pairs $(c_{i,j}, P_i)$, where the $c_{i,j}$ are protocol messages received from P_i, and outputs a new list c' of pairs $(c'_{j,k}, P'_k)$ where $c'_{j,k}$ is a protocol message to be sent to P'_k. (We remark that there may be several rounds of PROCESS operations during a single execution of the protocol.)
- RECOVER: a procedure executed by P_j that takes as input a list c (or multiple vectors) of pairs $(c_{i,j}, P_i)$, where the $c_{i,j}$ are protocol messages received from P_i, and outputs a list of pairs (m_k, P'_k) where each m_k is an anonymous message to send to P'_k.

All well-known anonymity protocols in the security literature implement variants of these protocols. With mixes and onion-routing protocols, for example, a PROCESS step takes a batch of protocol messages and shuffles and forwards them along to other parties, possibly after performing some operation on the messages such as encryption and/or decryption.

Transformation 1: The first transformation we consider (already mentioned in [20]) affects the SEND and RECOVER steps of a given protocol. In the new protocol the sender P_i must sign the message $m \in \mathcal{M}$ to get a group signature σ, and the resulting message $m' = (m, \sigma)$ is the one that must be processed by the SEND operation. For any party P_j executing a RECOVER operation to recover a message m, P_j must ensure that m has been signed using a group signature and must discard the message if it has not been signed.

If a receiver P_k presents an anonymous message to the voting group V for tracing, a tracing set $T \in \mathcal{V}$ may open the signature to reveal the sender.

A significant problem with Transformation 1 is that nothing stops the party P_j executing RECOVER from reading a recovered unsigned message, or sending it on to its intended recipient — regardless of whether P_j is simply curious or is attempting to subvert the tracing scheme. As soon as unsigned messages are read instead of dropped, senders have no incentive to sign messages that they may later be blamed for, and the system degrades into a non-traceable protocol. Of course one could appoint a trusted "auditor" to check that all messages are signed before delivery but this would both have the effect of severely degrading the anonymity of the system (the auditor sees ALL messages delivered!) and would create a single point of failure for the anonymity protocol; we seek a solution that violates anonymity for traceability *only* to the extent that it enforces the tracing policy.

Transformation 2: In most anonymity protocols, the PROCESS step involves protocol messages from which the original anonymous message m cannot be efficiently recovered by the party executing the step. The message may be encrypted, for example, or split into shares using some secret-sharing scheme. (One exception to this is the Crowds framework [23], where messages may be sent in plaintext. Protocol participants essentially flip a coin to decide whether to execute a PROCESS or a RECOVER operation, and they can see the anonymous messages at every step.) The transformation we outline below may be applied whenever it is impossible or computationally infeasible to recover m from the PROCESS step.

Our solution to the game-theoretic problem of Transformation 1 is to require that an agent P_j executing a PROCESS step must check that the protocol messages $c_{1,j}, \ldots, c_{n,j}$ are all generated from underlying anonymous messages that have been signed using the group signature scheme. To do this without revealing anything about the underlying message, we use noninteractive zero-knowledge (NIZK) proofs [5]; briefly, these are objects that prove the truth of a statement without revealing anything about the proof. Essentially, we define *valid* protocol messages to be those that are the output of SEND on a signed-message, or PROCESS on a set of valid messages; then modify the SEND procedure to output of NIZK of validity, and modify the PROCESS procedure to verify the validity of all inputs and output a NIZK of the validity of its outputs. Full details appear in [2].

Efficiency. We stress that the point of this general scheme is not to suggest a protocol that should be used in practice, but to show that *in principle*, any anonymity scheme can provide selective traceability. Indeed, the most efficient general constructions of NIZKs [17] have length roughly $6000T$ bits, where T

is the number of bit operations required to verify that $x \in L$ given witness w. Since in the previous transformation, this involves (at minimum) verifying a group signature or checking a NIZK, and the most efficient such signatures require roughly $T = 10^6$ bit operations per verification, the generic transformation cannot be considered practical.

3.2   More Efficient Transformations

In this section, we will demonstrate simple modifications to allow selective tracing of two DC-Net-based protocols: k-AMT [1] and a protocol due to Golle and Juels [15] which we refer to as GJ. Both protocols make slight alterations to the basic DC-Net protocol [10] to implement a shared channel; these modified protocols are then run in several parallel copies, and cryptographic mechanisms are employed to prove that each participant broadcasts on at most one channel, ensuring fair access to the medium. Our approach considers the messages sent on each channel orthogonally and allows determining who has broadcast on a single channel, so for ease of exposition we will describe the protocols here only in terms of a single shared channel.

k-**AMT.** The k-AMT protocol implements a shared channel as a secure multiparty sum computation, using Pedersen commitments[4] to ensure correctness. Here we assume that player P_i wants to send message X_i. The basic protocol has four phases:

1. **Commitment Phase**
   - P_i splits $X_i \in \mathbb{Z}_q$ into n random shares $s_{i,1}, ..., s_{i,n}$, and chooses $r_{i,j} \leftarrow \mathbb{Z}_q$
   - P_i computes and broadcasts commitments $\{C_{i,j} = C_{r_{i,j}}(s_{i,j}) : 1 \leq j \leq n\}$.
2. **Sharing Phase**
   - For each $j \neq i$, $P_i \longrightarrow P_j \ : \ (r_{i,j}, s_{i,j})$.
   - P_j checks that $C_{r_{i,j}}(s_{i,j}) = C_{i,j}$
3. **Broadcast Phase**
   - P_i computes and broadcasts $R_i = \sum_j r_{j,i} \bmod q$ and $S_i = \sum_j s_{j,i} \bmod q$.
   - All players check that $C_{R_i}(S_i) = \prod_j C_{j,i} \bmod p$
4. **Result.** Each player computes $X = \sum_i S_i \bmod q$ and $R = \sum_i R_i \bmod q$; if $C_R(X) = \prod_{i,j} C_{i,j} \bmod p$, the player outputs the anonymous message X.

As was previously mentioned, k-AMT actually runs several parallel copies of this protocol and includes procedures for proving that a party has transmitted on at most one parallel channel or "slot." Here we will describe how to augment the basic protocol so that it is selectively traceable. It should be clear that these modifications are orthogonal to those additional procedures.

The new protocol exploits the relationship between El Gamal encryption and Pedersen commitments to allow the voters to "decrypt" the commitments generated in Phase 1 (when the tracing policy is satisfied). Here we describe the necessary modifications.

---

[4] If p, q are primes such that $p = 2q + 1$, and $g, h \in \mathbb{Z}_p^*$ both have order q, a Pedersen commitment to the value $x \in \mathbb{Z}_q$ is generated by randomly choosing $r \in \mathbb{Z}_q$ and computing $C_r(x) = g^x h^r$.

1. **Initialization:** As a group, choose securely an El Gamal key pair (G, x, y) where $y = G^x$, such that the private key x is shared by threshold secret sharing according to the desired tracing policy, as in Section 2.

2. **Commitment Phase:** In addition to the $\{C_{i,j} : j \in [M]\}$ commitments broadcast by party P_i, we will have P_i broadcast a certificate that can be proven correct for a given set of commitments, but can only be opened by the owner of the private key of the El Gamal encryption scheme above. Assuming that a round of k-AMT is correctly computed, we are guaranteed that $S_i = \prod_j C_{i,j} = g^{X_i} h^{R_i}$, where $R_i = \sum_j r_{i,j}$. Let $a_i = G^{R_i}$ and $b_i = g^{-X_i} y^{R_i}$. Together, a_i and b_i form an El Gamal encryption of g^{-X_i} with the public key y.

   Finally, we compute σ_i to be an efficient noninteractive proof of knowledge that the discrete log of a_i with respect to base G is the same as the discrete log of $S_i b_i$ with respect to base hy. The certificate broadcast in addition to the commitments is just (a_i, b_i, σ_i).

Now, to trace a message: identify the slot that it was transmitted on, obtain a number of parties as required by the tracing policy, and securely compute the decryption M of each party's certificate for that slot. For all participants who sent nothing on the channel we have $X_i = 0$, and thus $M = g^{-X_i} = 1$. All other participants transmitted something on the channel, and in particular if only one participant i sent a message we have $X = X_i$, and thus $M \cdot g^X = 1$.

To compute σ_i, we want to show that $\log_G a_i = \log_{hy} S_i b_i$. In general, to prove that $\log_g y = \log_h z$ when $\log_g h$ is unknown and hard to compute, it suffices to prove knowledge of $\log_{g/h}(y/z)$. (If there exists a such that $y = g^a$ and $z = h^a$, then because $g^a z = h^a y$ we have $\log_{g/h}(y/z) = a$. If $y = g^a$ and $z = h^b$, with $a \neq b$, then knowledge of $\log_{g/h}(y/z)$ can easily be used to compute $\log_g h$.) Therefore, σ_i is a noninteractive proof of knowledge of $\log_{G/hy}(a_i/S_i b_i)$, and can be computed efficiently using standard techniques.[5] Note that this modification doesn't affect the asymptotic efficiency of the underlying protocol.

We prove in [2] that under the Decisional Diffie-Hellman assumption, the protocol remains secure against computationally bounded adversaries that have not corrupted a tracing set.

The GJ DC-Net Protocol. The GJ DC-Net protocol takes advantage of bilinear maps to perform many Diffie-Hellman key exchanges noninteractively, thus achieving a single-round (noninteractive) DC-net protocol. The protocol works over groups $\mathbb{G}_1, \mathbb{G}_2$ of prime order q, and with an admissible bilinear map $\hat{e} : \mathbb{G}_1 \times \mathbb{G}_1 \to \mathbb{G}_2$. (A map is bilinear if $\hat{e}(aP, bP) = \hat{e}(P, P)^{ab}$.) We denote the group operation in $\mathbb{G}_1$ using additive notation, and the group operation in $\mathbb{G}_2$ using multiplicative notation, as is common when dealing with admissible

---

[5] In the random oracle model, a proof of knowledge of $\alpha = \log_\gamma \beta$ has the form $(\zeta = \gamma^\rho, \lambda = \alpha H(\zeta) + \rho)$, where $\rho \in_R \mathbb{Z}_q$ and $H : \mathbb{Z}_p^* \to \mathbb{Z}_q$ is a random oracle; the proof is accepted if $\gamma^\lambda = \beta^{H(\zeta)} \zeta$; interactive versions of this protocol first appear in [11].

bilinear maps. ($\mathbb{G}_1$ is typically an elliptic curve group.) We let $P \in \mathbb{G}_1$ be a public parameter and assume all parties know a map $H : \{0,1\}^* \to \mathbb{G}_1$, which we will model as a random oracle. As previously mentioned, the GJ protocol is actually comprised of several parallel executions of a simple shared channel along with some auxiliary information that proves a player has transmitted on at most one channel; for simplicity, and because our modifications are orthogonal, we describe only the single channel and omit the auxiliary information. For a description of the full protocol, see [15].

1. **Setup Phase:** Every player P_i picks private key $x_i \in \mathbb{Z}_q$ and publishes $y_i = x_i P$ as his public key.
2. **Pad Construction:** Let s be some unique identifier of a particular execution of the shared channel. (For example, a running count appended to the list of users). All players compute the element $Q_s \in \mathbb{G}_1$ as $Q_s = H(s)$. Then each pair of players (noninteractively) computes a shared Diffie-Hellman key

$$k_{i,j}(s) = \hat{e}(y_j, x_i Q_s) = \hat{e}(P, Q_s)^{x_i x_j} = \hat{e}(y_i, x_j Q_s) = k_{j,i}(s) \ .$$

   Each player i computes his "pad" $p_i(s) = \prod_j k_{i,j}(s)^{\delta_{i,j}}$, where $\delta_{i,j} = -1$ if $i < j$ and 1 otherwise.
3. **Transmission:** In session s, we let the intended message of P_i be the element $m_i(s) \in \mathbb{G}_2$, where $m_i(s)$ is the identity element $1 \in \mathbb{G}_2$ if P_i has no message to send. To transmit, each player P_i publishes value $W_i(s) = m_i(s)p_i(s)$.
4. **Message Extraction:** The final message is extracted by computing

$$m(s) = \prod_i W_i(s) = \prod_i m_i(s) \prod_j k_{i,j}(s)^{\delta_{i,j}} = \prod_i m_i(s) \ ,$$

   since $k_{i,j}(s)^{\delta_{i,j}} = k_{j,i}(s)^{-\delta_{j,i}}$. Thus if exactly one $m_i(s) \neq 1$, then we have $m(s) = m_i(s)$.

To support selective tracing, the only modification to the previous procedures is in the setup phase: after generating key pair (x_i, y_i) and publishing y_i, player P_i will share his private key x_i among the voters in a similar fashion to that described in section 2. Then to trace the message $m(s)$, the voters will compute the pads $p_i(s)$ for each i using their shares. If the published value $W_i(s) = m(s)p_i(s)$, then P_i is the sender. We formally describe the new procedures in [2]. We note that in the full GJ protocol [15] shares of the private keys x_i are distributed amongst the *players* to allow any two-thirds of them to reconstruct the pads of players who do not participate in any given session. So, even though this is done for different reasons, the GJ protocol silently implements a threshold tracing scheme, with $V = \{P_1, \ldots, P_n\}$ and $\mathcal{V} = \mathcal{V}(\frac{2n}{3})$.

4   Coercibility in Anonymous Protocols

Informally, we say that an anonymity protocol is *coercible* if every player who did not send a message can produce a proof that this is the case. More formally, consider a "proof protocol" $\mathbb{P}$ between a player P_i and a verifier V, where the difference in the probabilities that V "accepts the proof" when P_i sent the message and P_i did not send the message is at least some value ρ_P. We call a protocol ρ-coercible if, over all $\mathbb{P}$, $\rho = \max(\rho_P)$. In other words, ρ measures the confidence of the best proof procedure. If a protocol is 1-coercible, only the legitimate sender of a message cannot exculpate himself (but everybody else can); if a protocol is 0-coercible the verifier should not believe any proofs. If ϵ is negligible, we say that a protocol that is $(1 - \epsilon)$-coercible is *strongly coercible*, and that a protocol that is at most ϵ-coercible is *noncoercible*. If a protocol is ρ-coercible for some constant ρ, we say that it is *plausibly noncoercible*.

In this section we assume that all the players in the protocol Π are plausible senders of any message m. Assuming that all the players belong to the same "anonymity set" (i.e., the set of players who could have sent a particular message) lets us ignore "proofs of innocence" that can arise simply because two players belong to different anonymity sets.

Formally, for an anonymous communications protocol Π we define coercibility as follows:

- A *proof procedure* $\mathbb{P}$ is a pair $(\mathcal{P}, \mathcal{V})$ of programs such that $\mathcal{V}$ outputs either acc (for *accept*) or rej (for *reject*). (Intuitively, $\mathcal{P}$ can be thought of as a program that is run by some player P_i.)
- After the public parameters of Π are chosen, $\mathcal{V}$ is allowed to choose a message m as a function of the parameters. This is the message that, if sent during an execution of the protocol, $\mathcal{V}$ will ask players in Π to prove they have not sent.
- Let $view_X(P_j : m)$ denote the *view* of party X in the anonymity protocol Π when P_j sends message m and m is delivered. The view includes X's inputs (including random tape) and any protocol messages sent and received during the execution of Π.
- Let A denote any adversary who cannot compromise the anonymity guarantee of Π. For any player X, denote by $view_A(X : m)$ the views of all parties corrupted by A as well as all protocol messages from Π that A observes. Essentially, A will serve as $\mathcal{V}$'s agent in Π: we allow the verifier access to A's view of Π to help in deciding whether to accept $\mathcal{P}$'s proof that P_i didn't send m. Denote by $\mathbb{P}_i(X : m)$ the output of $\mathcal{V}$ (on input m and $view_A(X : m)$) when interacting with $\mathcal{P}$ (on input m and $view_{P_i}(X : m)$).
- We say that Π is ρ-*coercible* if there is a proof procedure $\mathbb{P}$, an adversary A, and players P_i and P_j such that

$$|\Pr[\mathbb{P}_i(P_j : m) = \mathsf{acc}\,] - \Pr[\mathbb{P}_i(P_i : m) = \mathsf{acc}\,]| \geq \rho \,,$$

regardless of P_i's actions in the second case.

Notice that this definition is weak in the sense that the verifier is allowed to choose the message. In other words, the protocol is coercible if there *exists* a message and adversary such that some player can prove that she did not send the message. (This makes noncoercibility a stronger definition, because it rules out any convincing proofs of innocence.) As we will demonstrate, the coercibility of several protocols from the literature is much stronger — and therefore more problematic — because it allows any player to prove she is not the sender of any message she did not send.

Coercibility for group signature schemes can be defined analogously. We remark that noncoercibility of group signatures satisfying the security definitions of [4] is implied by the "full anonymity" condition.

Recently, Danezis and Clulow [13] have introduced the notion of *compulsion-resistant* anonymity protocols. In their setting, an adversary may *compel* certain noncooperative nodes to reveal their secrets (via, for example decrypting ciphertexts or revealing logs or secret keys) in an attempt to trace a message back to its sender. Noncoercibility and compulsion-resistance are related in that both concern the ability of an adversary to trace a message after it has been sent. Our notion is different from compulsion-resistance in several ways. First, a coercive adversary is given a complete transcript of a protocol execution, whereas the perhaps more realistic (but weaker) "compulsive" adversary has only an anonymous reply block. Second, our constructions consider mainly DC-Net based protocols whereas [13] is concerned mainly with mix-based protocols. Finally, the goals of noncoercibility and compulsion-resistance differ somewhat: a noncoercible protocol aims to make compulsory revelation of secrets useless because no such revelation will convincingly exonerate a nonsender, whereas a compulsion-resistant protocol aims to make such compulsory tracing prohibitively expensive.

4.1   Coercibility in Various Anonymity Protocols

In the simplest formulation of Chaum's mix-net protocol [9], each party sends a message to the mix, who decrypts and shuffles the messages before forwarding them to the recipients. This protocol is clearly coercible against a global passive adversary: if P_i sent ciphertext c_i to the mix, and c_i does not decrypt to m, he can open c_i to plaintext $p_i \neq m$ to the verifier. The true sender, on the other hand, cannot. It is similarly clear that, in the worst case, any forwarding-based scheme which relies on static public or shared keys allows similar acts of exculpation to a global passive adversary: by decrypting all received ciphertexts and opening all sent ciphertexts, P_i can prove that he was not the originator of any message he did not send. Clearly some players will be reluctant to sacrifice their anonymity entirely in order to give such proofs. It is conceivable, however, that the consequences of non-exculpation could be serious enough that such a privacy loss would be acceptable to P_i. In this work we leave open the interesting question whether such forwarding-based protocols remain coercible in settings that employ forward-security or against different adversarial models.

In Section 3.2 we focused on selective tracing in protocols based on DC-Nets, in part because of the reliance of those protocols on cryptographic techniques that are amenable to tracing. For similar reasons, both of those protocols are coercible. Here we show how participants in those protocols are able to prove easily that they did not send particular messages that were sent by other participants during an execution of the protocol.

In a GJ DC-Net, player P_i can prove that he didn't send a message during session s by publishing the quantity $z_i(s) = x_i Q_s$. (Note that $z_i(s)$ doesn't reveal anything about P_i's private key x_i.) From $z_i(s)$, P_i's pad $p_i(s)$ can be publicly computed as $p_i(s) = \prod_j k_{i,j}(s)^{\delta_{i,j}} = \prod_j \hat{e}(y_j, z_i(s))^{\delta_{i,j}}$. $W_i(s)$ — the value publically declared by P_i — will be the same as $p_i(s)$ if and only if P_i did not send the message.

In k-AMT, player P_i broadcasts commitments $C_{i,j} = C_{r_{i,j}}(s_{i,j})$ of the random shares $s_{i,1}, ..., s_{i,n}$ broadcast to the other players when P_i sends message X_i. If P_i wants to prove that she did not send a message, i.e., that $X_i = 0$, she needs only to open the commitments $C_{i,j}$ by announcing the shares $s_{i,j}$ and the random values $r_{i,j}$. (Opening a commitment $C_{i,j}$ to some value $s'_{i,j} \neq s_{i,j}$ is as computationally hard as computing $\log_g(h)$, where g and h are the generators used in the commitment scheme.) Other users can easily check that $\sum_j s_{i,j} = 0$, thus proving that P_i did not send the message in question.

We note, however, that k-AMT can be modified to be noncoercible. The key idea is that when $\log_g h$ *is* known, a player can open a commitment to any value (Pedersen commitments are thus *equivocable*), and in particular can show that his commitments sum to zero, even if they do not. We can thus modify the k-AMT protocol to start each round by choosing a new h so that $\log_g h$ is uniformly chosen and can be recovered exactly when $2n/3$ players reveal their secret information; each round continues as before, and at the end of each round $\log_g h$ is revealed. We note that Pedersen [22] gives an appropriate protocol for choosing h with these properties. We also note that this modification to k-AMT is incompatible with the tracing modification of Section 3.2. Thus, while applying the generic transformation to this modification of k-AMT can result in a strong selectively traceable protocol, no *efficient* construction is known.

4.2   Coercibility Preservation

Here we show that the general transformations in Section 3 preserve (up to a negligible additive factor) the coercibility of the underlying (non-traceable) anonymous communications protocol, given that the selected group signature scheme is noncoercible. That is, we will show that any proof system that has an acceptance gap of ρ in the transformed protocol can be converted into a proof system with acceptance gap at least $\rho - \mu$ for the underlying anonymous protocol if the group signature scheme is at most μ-coercible. This implies that using a noncoercible anonymous protocol will result in a noncoercible selectively traceable protocol.

Group Signature transformation. Let Π denote an anonymous communication protocol and let Π^* denote the protocol that results from applying Transformation 1 to Π. Suppose that Π^* is ρ-coercible and that the group signature scheme $\mathcal{GS}$ used in the transformation is at most μ-coercible. Then there must be a proof procedure $\mathbb{P}^* = (\mathcal{P}^*, \mathcal{V}^*)$ for Π^* with acceptance gap ρ, for some adversary A^* and a pair of players P_i and P_j. We construct a proof procedure $\mathbb{P}$ for Π, which "simulates" the group signature part of Π^* so that it can run $\mathbb{P}^*$:

- On input the public parameters from Π, $\mathcal{V}$ plays the role of the group manager in $\mathcal{GS}$ to pick a group public key GPK. $\mathcal{V}$ appends GPK to the parameters (producing a set of public parameters consistent with Π^*) and runs $\mathcal{V}^*$ to choose a message m^*. $\mathcal{V}$ computes a signing key for P_j and computes $\sigma^* = \mathtt{SIGN}_j(m^*)$. $\mathcal{V}$ also chooses the message $m = (m^*, \sigma^*)$.
- $\mathcal{V}$ and $\mathcal{P}$ jointly execute the JOIN protocol from $\mathcal{GS}$ to produce P_i's signing key. This is so that when $\mathcal{P}$ runs $\mathcal{P}^*$ he can supply a transcript of the JOIN protocol. (Note however, that if P_i sends m in Π, this view will be slightly different than if P_i sent m^* in Π^*, because m is signed by P_j. We prove, essentially, that the noncoercibility of $\mathcal{GS}$ means that this doesn't matter for the acceptance probabilities.)
- $\mathcal{V}$ appends GPK and σ^* to his input $view_A$ to form a view $view_A^*$ consistent with Π^*. Similarly, $\mathcal{P}$ appends GPK and his signing key and σ^* to $view_i$ to form a view $view_i^*$ consistent with Π^*.
- $\mathcal{V}$ executes $\mathcal{V}^*(m^*, view_A^*)$, and $\mathcal{P}$ executes $\mathcal{P}^*(m^*, view_i^*)$.
- $\mathcal{P}$ proves in zero-knowledge that his actions are consistent with the extra inputs computed with $\mathcal{V}$. If this proof fails, or $\mathcal{P}$ aborts the protocol, $\mathcal{V}$ outputs $\mathtt{rej}$. Otherwise $\mathcal{V}$ outputs the decision of $\mathcal{V}^*$. This prevents $\mathcal{P}$ from cheating (using different inputs) to increase the acceptance probability.

Let us compute the acceptance gap of $\mathbb{P}$. To do so, we will imagine an experiment in which Π^* delivers m^* with a group signature from either P_i or P_j. Denote the event that P_i's signing key is used by S_i, and the event that P_j's key is used by S_j. Then we have that:

$$\begin{aligned}
\rho &\le |\Pr[\mathbb{P}_i^*(P_i:m)=\mathtt{acc} \mid S_i] - \Pr[\mathbb{P}_i^*(P_j:m)=\mathtt{acc} \mid S_j]| \\
&\le |\Pr[\mathbb{P}_i^*(P_i:m)=\mathtt{acc} \mid S_i] - \Pr[\mathbb{P}_i^*(P_i:m)=\mathtt{acc} \mid S_j]| \\
&\quad + |\Pr[\mathbb{P}_i^*(P_i:m)=\mathtt{acc} \mid S_j] - \Pr[\mathbb{P}_i^*(P_j:m)=\mathtt{acc} \mid S_j]| \\
&= |\Pr[\mathbb{P}_i^*(P_i:m)=\mathtt{acc} \mid S_i] - \Pr[\mathbb{P}_i^*(P_i:m)=\mathtt{acc} \mid S_j]| \\
&\quad + |\Pr[\mathbb{P}_i(P_i:m)=\mathtt{acc}] - \Pr[\mathbb{P}_i(P_j:m)=\mathtt{acc}]| \\
&\le \mu + |\Pr[\mathbb{P}_i(P_i:m)=\mathtt{acc}] - \Pr[\mathbb{P}_i(P_j:m)=\mathtt{acc}]|
\end{aligned}$$

where the second line follows by the triangle inequality, the third follows from the definition of the proof procedure $\mathbb{P}$ — it is running $\mathbb{P}^*$ exactly in the (imaginary) case that S_j happens — and the last follows because $\mathcal{GS}$ is at most μ-coercible.[6] Thus we have that

$$|\Pr[\mathbb{P}_i(P_i:m)=\mathtt{acc}] - \Pr[\mathbb{P}_i(P_j:m)=\mathtt{acc}]| \ge \rho - \mu .$$

---

[6] Suppose that $|\Pr[\mathbb{P}_i^*(P_i:m)=\mathtt{acc} \mid S_i] - \Pr[\mathbb{P}_i^*(P_i:m)=\mathtt{acc} \mid S_j]| > \mu$. Then $\mathbb{P}$ gives a way for P_i to prove that he did not generate the group signature σ^* with acceptance gap greater than μ: $\mathcal{V}$ and $\mathcal{P}$ run Π^* together, with $\mathcal{V}$ playing the roles of other parties, and $\mathcal{P}$ sends m^* using the group signature σ^*. Then they run $\mathbb{P}$ on their views of this execution; the acceptance gap will be preserved.

NIZK transformation. Let Π denote an anonymous communication protocol that results from applying Transformation 1, and let Π^* denote the result of applying Transformation 2 to Π, that is, adding the NIZK proofs to the protocol. We also show that if Π^* is ρ-coercible then Π is at least $\rho - \epsilon$ coercible, for a negligible function ϵ. Informally, this is because NIZK proofs are *simulatable*: a party who can choose the common reference string used for the proof can, without a witness, produce simulated proofs that are indistinguishable from accepting proofs. Because both $\mathcal{P}$ and $\mathcal{V}$ may need to generate proofs on strings that the other has not seen, they will use a *secure two-party computation protocol* [26] to generate the CRS and any simulated proofs so that neither learns anything about the CRS except the proofs they need to emulate Π^*. The formal proof appears in [2].

5   Conclusion

In this paper we have discussed selective tracing and coercibility as two issues that designers of anonymity protocols should bear in mind. We have described a framework for describing tracing policies that we believe to be general enough to capture most situations where fair and sensible tracing policies are desired. We have shown that, in principle, strong selectively traceable anonymity schemes for any tracing policy can be implemented by modifying a recent protocol of [1].

Extending this work to protocols based on mixes is one possible direction for future work. Our proposed "Transformation 2" (in Section 3) is extremely inefficient in both space and time — more efficient transformations that apply to specific protocols (or at least to mix-style protocols) are highly desirable.

We are not advocating anonymity tracing as a necessary feature of anonymity protocols, but rather suggesting that any tracing — whether implicit (e.g., coercible protocols) or explicit — should be examined carefully so that system designers can make more specific anonymity guarantees. While it is rarely a good idea to have tracing possible by the action of a single trusted authority, it may be easier to deploy an anonymity protocol in some contexts if it includes some tracing functionality. To that end, we want to develop systems that provide flexible tracing policies that are less likely to be abused. Finally, the issue of traceable anonymity presents interesting technical problems that may help to further the goals of anonymity research. We hope that this will be the case.

Acknowledgments. The authors thank Roger Dingledine, Joe Halpern, Yongdae Kim, Nick Matthewson, David Molnar, Hovav Shacham, Gun Sïrer, the attendees of the Stanford Security Lunch and the Minnesota Security and Cryptography Seminar, and several anonymous referees for helpful discussions and comments. This work was supported by the US National Science Foundation under grants CCR-0122581, CCR-0058982, and CNS-0546162, and the US Army Research Office and the CyLab Center at Carnegie Mellon University.

References

1. L. von Ahn, A. Bortz, and N. J. Hopper. k-anonymous message transmission. In *10th Conference on Computer and Communications Security*, pp. 122–130, 2003.
2. L. von Ahn, A. Bortz, N. J. Hopper, and K. O'Neill. Selectively Traceable Anonymity. Minnesota Digital Technology Center Research Report 2006/14, June 2006. URL: http://dtc.umn.edu/publications/reports/2006_14.pdf.
3. G. Ateniese, J. Camenisch, M. Joye and G. Tsudik. A Practical and Provably Secure Coalition-Resistant Group Signature Scheme. *CRYPTO 2000*, pp. 255–270.
4. M. Bellare, D. Micciancio and B. Warinschi. Foundations of Group Signatures. In *Eurocrypt 2003*, (LNCS 2656), pp. 614–629.
5. M. Blum, A. De Santis, S. Micali, and G. Persiano. Noninteractive Zero-Knowledge Proof Systems. *SIAM Journal on Computation*, 20(6): 1084–1118, 1991.
6. D. Boneh. The Decision Diffie-Hellman Problem. *Proc. 3rd ANTS*, pp 48–63, 1998.
7. R. Canetti, C. Dwork, M. Naor, and R. Ostrovsky. Deniable Encryption. In *CRYPTO 97*, pp. 90–104.
8. R. Canetti, U. Feige, O. Goldreich, and M. Naor. Adaptively Secure Multiparty Computation. *MIT LCS Technical Reports* TR96-682, 1996.
9. D. Chaum. Untraceable electronic mail, return addresses, and digital pseudonyms. In *Communications of the ACM* 4(2), February 1981.
10. D. Chaum. The dining cryptographers problem: Unconditional sender and recipient untraceability. *Journal of Cryptology*, 1(1):65–75, 1988.
11. D. Chaum, J. Evertse, J. van de Graaf and R. Peralta. Demonstrating Possession of a Discrete Logarithm Without Revealing It. In *CRYPTO'86*, pp. 200–212.
12. D. Chaum and E. van Heyst. Group Signatures. In *EUROCRYPT '91*, pp. 257–265.
13. G. Danezis and J. Clulow. Compulsion Resistant Anonymous Communications. In *7th Information Hiding Workshop*, June 2005.
14. Y. Dodis, A. Kiayias, A. Nicolosi and V. Shoup. Anonymous Identification in Ad-Hoc Groups. In *EUROCRYPT '04*.
15. P. Golle and A. Juels. Dining Cryptographers Revisited. In *EUROCRYPT '04*.
16. T.C. Greene. Net anonymity service back-doored. *The Register*, 21 August, 2003.
17. J. Groth, R. Ostrovsky and A. Sahai. Perfect Non-Interactive Zero Knowledge for NP. *Electronic Colloquium on Computational Complexity* report TR05-097, 2005.
18. A. Juels and. M. Jakobsson. Coercion-Resistant Electronic Elections. *Cryptology ePrint Archive Report 2002/165*, 2002.
19. J. Katz and M. Yung. Threshold Cryptosystems Based on Factoring. In *Asiacrypt 2002*, pp. 192–205.
20. A. Kiayias, Y. Tsiounis and M. Yung. Traceable Signatures. In: *Advances in Cryptology – Eurocrypt 2004*, 2004.
21. T.P. Pedersen. A threshold cryptosystem without a trusted party. In *Eurocrypt '91*, pp.522–526.
22. T.P. Pedersen. Efficient and information theoretic secure verifiable secret sharing. In *CRYPTO '91*.
23. M. Reiter and A. Rubin. Crowds: Anonymity for web transactions. *ACM Transactions on Information and System Security*, 1(1):66–92, 1998.
24. A. Shamir. How to share a secret. *Communications of the ACM*, 22:612–613, 1979.
25. V. Shoup. Practical Threshold Signatures. In *Eurocrypt 2000*.
26. A. C. Yao. How to Generate and Exchange Secrets. In *Proc. 27th IEEE FOCS*, pp. 162–167, 1986.

Valet Services:
Improving Hidden Servers
with a Personal Touch

Lasse Øverlier[1,2] and Paul Syverson[3]

[1] Norwegian Defence Research Establishment, P.B. 25, 2027 Kjeller, Norway
lasse.overlier@ffi.no
http://www.ffi.no/
[2] Gjøvik University College, P.B. 191, 2802 Gjøvik, Norway
lasse@hig.no
http://www.hig.no/
[3] Center for High Assurance Computer Systems
Naval Research Laboratory Code 5540, Washington, DC 20375
syverson@itd.nrl.navy.mil
http://chacs.nrl.navy.mil/

Abstract. Location hidden services have received increasing attention as a means to resist censorship and protect the identity of service operators. Research and vulnerability analysis to date has mainly focused on how to locate the hidden service. But while the hiding techniques have improved, almost no progress has been made in increasing the resistance against DoS attacks directly or indirectly on hidden services. In this paper we suggest improvements that should be easy to adopt within the existing hidden service design, improvements that will both reduce vulnerability to DoS attacks and add QoS as a service option. In addition we show how to hide not just the location but the existence of the hidden service from everyone but the users knowing its service address. Not even the public directory servers will know how a private hidden service can be contacted, or know it exists.

1 Introduction

Hidden Servers are a means to offering attack-resistant services. A server that is accessible but hidden can resist a variety of threats simply because it cannot be found. These threats include physical and logical threats to the service itself. But they also include threats to the people offering the service and attempts to prevent general access to the service provided.

Since 2004, hidden services have been offered that use Tor to underly services offered from hidden locations. These were introduced [11] as resistant to distributed DoS since they were designed to require a DDoS attack on the entire Tor network in order to attack a hidden server.

Recent events have placed Tor prominently in the international media as a tool to allow people to access Internet sites even if they are behind filtering firewalls

G. Danezis and P. Golle (Eds.): PET 2006, LNCS 4258, pp. 223–244, 2006.
© Springer-Verlag Berlin Heidelberg 2006

or if the large commercial search engines are cooperating with local authorities to provide only censored offerings. However, at least as important as obtaining information is the ability for people in these environments to disseminate information. Besides resisting DDoS and physical threats, hidden servers have also been recommended for preserving the anonymity of the service offerer and to resist censorship. Specifically, Undergroundmedia.org has published a guide to "Torcasting" (anonymity-preserving and censorship-resistant podcasting). And both the Electronic Frontier Foundation and Reporters Without Borders have issued guides that describe using hidden services via Tor to protect the safety of dissidents as well as to resist censorship. Even in more open societies bloggers have lost their jobs because employers were unhappy about the blog sites.

Hidden services thus have a clear value and appeal. But, their resistance to some adversaries is limited. In [17], we demonstrated location attacks on hidden servers deployed behind Tor that locate a hidden server quickly and easily, often within minutes. The suggested countermeasures to those attacks have been implemented. But other threats remain. Hidden servers are accessed via a publicly listed small set of relatively long-lived *Introduction Points*. Anyone with access to a hidden service can easily discover the Introduction Points. This can lead to a DoS race that the hidden server is likely to lose, since setting up Introduction Points and disseminating associated information is somewhat resource intensive. To address this limitation in the current hidden service design we propose the introduction of *Valet nodes*. There can be far more Valet nodes than Introduction Points associated with a hidden server. Relatedly, it is much easier to generate and disseminate Valet node information than Introduction Point information.

In Sect. 2 we present previous work on hidden services and availability together with a brief look into how Tor's hidden services work. In Sect. 3 we give a description of the Valet node design. In Sect. 4 we discuss the security of the design. In Sect. 5 we present our conclusions.

2   Previous Work on Availability and Hidden Services

Location hidden services build upon anonymous communication, which was first described by David Chaum [7] in 1981. Most of the early work in this area focused on high-latency communications, like email. Low-latency anonymous communication, such as currently dominates Internet traffic, got new focus in the late 1990's with the the introduction of onion routing [14]. In 1995, shortly before onion routing was initially deployed, the first low-latency commercial proxy for web traffic, the Anonymizer [2], became available. Proxy services like Anonymizer and Proxify [19] work by mixing traffic from multiple clients through a single point so that any accessed servers are only able to trace back clients to the anonymizing proxy, and not to the actual users. This requires complete trust in the proxy provider and will unfortunately be easy to abuse since we now have a single point of failure, a single point of compromise, and *a single point of attack*.

Distributed low-latency anonymous communication systems include the original onion routing [14], the Freedom Network [6] (deployed in 1999), and the current version of onion routing, Tor [11]. These are more resistant to the above mentioned vulnerabilities because they proxy communication through multiple hops; at each hop the communication changes its appearance by adding or removing a layer of encryption (depending on whether it is traveling from the circuit originator to responder or vice versa). They all use public-key cryptography to distribute session keys to the nodes along a route, thus establishing a circuit. Each session key is shared between the circuit initiator (client) and the one node that was given that key in establishing the circuit. Data that passes along the circuit uses these session keys. Both Freedom and Tor have a default circuit length of three nodes. For more details consult the above cited work. Another low-latency distributed system is JAP/Web MIXes [4]. It is based on mix cascades (all traffic shares the same fixed path) and thus, unlike the above systems, its security is not based on hiding the points at which traffic enters and leaves the network. It is thus not directly usable for hidden services as they are described below.

The property of hiding the location of a service in order to sustain availability was introduced in Ross Anderson's Eternity Service [1]. Focusing on availability and longevity of data, the Eternity service stores files at multiple locations, encrypted and prepaid for, during a certain period of time. Freenet[8] was the first system to use a peer-to-peer network with the goal of censorship resistance, enabling a service to have (some) availability even when only one of the nodes is available. Splitting the stored files up into minor pieces and storing them on multiple nodes of the network also added robustness. However it has numerous security vulnerabilities, e.g., clients must trust the first nodes they connect to for all network discovery and hence anonymity protection. Both Freenet and GNUnet[3] communication builds upon mix-net[7] technology for sending messages to other nodes, and must trust the availability of the underlying network. Publius [15] was designed to guarantee persistence of stored files, like Eternity and unlike Freenet. Tangler [27] additionally makes newly published files dependent on previous ones, called *entanglement*, thereby distributing incentives for storing other nodes' files as well. Free Haven [10] uses a network of nodes with a reputation system involving contracts between nodes to store data for others. But Free Haven does not define the underlying anonymous communication channel, and this is where many of the availability issues are located.

Tor is not a publishing service and does not store information like the above mentioned censorship-resistant systems, but Tor facilitates something called *hidden services*. The hidden service design supports the anonymous access of common services, e.g. a web service, enabling users of the network to connect to these services without knowing the server's location (IP address). Tor builds this functionality upon the assumption that if a node cannot be located, it cannot be (easily) stopped or in other means shut down. The hidden service design relies on a rendezvous server, which mates anonymous circuits from two principals so that each relies only on himself to build a secure circuit. The first published design for a rendezvous service was for anonymous ISDN telephony [18] rather than Internet communication. As such it had very different assumptions and requirements from the rendezvous servers we describe, some of which we have already noted above. A rendezvous server for IRC chat was mentioned in [14]; however, the first detailed design for a rendezvous server for Internet communication was by Goldberg [13]. It differs in many ways from rendezvous servers as used by Tor's hidden services, and we will not discuss Goldberg's design further here.

2.1 Location-Hidden Services in Tor

In the current implementation of Tor, a connection to a hidden service involves five important nodes in addition to the nodes used for basic anonymous communication over Tor.

- HS, the Hidden Server offering some kind of (hidden) service to the users of the Tor network, e.g. web pages, mail accounts, login service, etc.
- C, the client connecting to the Hidden Server.
- DS, a Directory Server containing information about the Tor network nodes and used as the point of contact for information on where to contact hidden services.
- RP, the Rendezvous Point is the only node in the data tunnel that is known to both sides.
- IPo, the Introduction Point where the Hidden Server is listening for connections to the hidden service.

A normal setup of communication between a client and a hidden service is done as shown in Fig. 1. All the displayed connections are anonymized, i.e., they are routed through several anonymizing nodes on their path towards the other end. Every arrow and connection in the figure represents an anonymous channel consisting of at least two or more intermediate nodes. (Hereafter, we use 'node' to refer exclusively to nodes of the underlying anonymization network, sometimes also called 'server nodes'. Although we are considering the Tor network specifically, the setup would apply as well if some other anonymizing network were used to underly the hidden service protocol. Unlike the other principals above, C and HS may be anonymization nodes or they may be merely clients external to the anonymization network.)

First the Hidden Server connects (1) to a node in the Tor network and asks if it is OK for the node to act as an Introduction Point for his service. If the node accepts, we keep the circuit open and continue; otherwise HS tries another node until successful. These connections are kept open forever, i.e., until one of the nodes restarts or decides to pull it down.[1] Next, the Hidden Server contacts (2) the Directory Server and asks it to publish the contact information of its hidden service. The hidden service is now ready to receive connection requests from clients.

In order to communicate with the service the Client obtains a special URL, a *.onion* address, that it can understand and that has been posted to a public site

---

[1] In Tor any node in a circuit can initiate a circuit teardown.

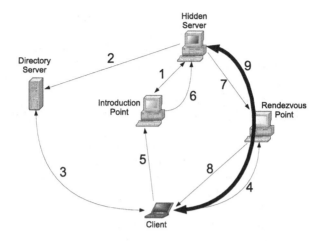

Fig. 1. Normal use of hidden services and rendezvous servers

or otherwise given to the Client out-of-band. The Client then connects (3) to DS and uses the *.onion* address to ask for the contact information of the identified service and retrieves it if it exists (including the addresses of Introduction Points). There can be multiple Introduction Points per service. The Client then selects a node in the network to act as a Rendezvous Point, connects (4) to it and asks it to listen for connections from a hidden service on C's behalf. The Client repeats this until a Rendezvous Point has accepted, and then contacts (5) the Introduction Point and asks it to forward the information about the selected RP.[2] The Introduction Point forwards (6) this message to the Hidden Server, which determines whether to connect to the Rendezvous Point or not. If OK, the Hidden Server connects (7) to RP and asks to be connected to the waiting rendezvous circuit, and RP then forwards (8) this connection request to the Client.

Now RP can start passing data between the two connections and the result is an anonymous data tunnel (9) from C to HS through RP.

2.2 Threats to Hidden Services

Until now most papers on anonymizing networks have focused on the threats of locating users and services in the network, and addressed different threat scenarios like intersection attacks [22,29] and traffic analysis [21,24].

A large adversary will be able to correlate network traffic going into and out from a distributed anonymizing network. For hidden services inside such a network this will also be true if large (or critical[3]) portions of the network can be observed at any given time. Using techniques from Serjantov and Sewell [24]

---

[2] Optionally, this could also include authentication information for the service to determine from whom to accept connections.

[3] E.g. smaller bounded parts of the network including the communicating nodes.

even a smaller adversary can match timing to and from nodes in the network. If a suspected communication channel is to be verified, e.g. "A is talking to B", this will quite easily be confirmed by simple statistical methods. Murdoch and Danezis [16] controlled a service accessed by clients through the Tor network and thereby were able to trace the route of traffic through the Tor network (but not all the way to the client). This attack involved probing the entire network. It was achieved on an earlier and much smaller Tor network than now exists.

In [17], we demonstrated on a live anonymizing network how effective intersection attacks can be in locating hidden servers and clients. The paper also describes other vulnerabilities in the hidden services design that makes it simple for an attacker to locate the Hidden Server.

All these attacks address how to *locate* either the user or the hidden service. But there are other threats that are important, like preventing Denial-of-Service attacks. This is of major concern when we are trying to achieve availability for the service, because even if the adversary cannot locate the server, the next best thing will be to shut down the possible access methods (or channels) for contacting it.

In [25] Stavrou and Keromytis describes how to use an indirection-based overlay network (ION) for DDoS protection by using packet replication and packet path diversity combined with redirection-based authentication. This is currently not applicable to the current implementation of the Tor hidden service protocol as Tor is based on TCP communication and the described ION requires a stateless protocol.

In the current Tor design, hidden services publish their contact information on a directory server describing to any user how she can connect to them. This information contains, amongst other things, a signed public key and a list of Introduction Points to contact in order to get a connection to the hidden service (cf. Sect. 2.1). This list can be abused by an attacker targeting all the Introduction Points with a DoS attack and thereby disabling the hidden service.

In addition, if a node is chosen to be an Introduction Point for a hidden service, it will be able to easily discover this through the general availability of the contact information retrieved from the directory services. This availability makes it possible for an adversary to shut down a service by attacking its Introduction Points, and also makes it possible to stop some selected services, e.g. by threatening all Introduction Points to avoid being associated with a particular service descriptor.

The directory server will also be able to see all hidden services that are published and can enumerate them, identify when they first became available, identify all their Introduction Points, and contact all the services (that do not require additional authorization).

If the directory servers are compromised, or if all of them are subject to a DoS attack, this could effectively shut down the entire network. For more information on this consult [11]. We do not address this possibility here.

3   Valet Service

Valet service adds another layer of protection to the hidden service design. By re-enabling some parts of the reply-onion technology from the original onion routing design [14], we will hide the Introduction Points from the users, and we will also extend the functionality of the hidden service.

3.1   Overview

We introduce a method of accessing the Introduction Points without knowing their location. This is quite similar to the situation of hiding the hidden service in the first place, but now we want to hide more nodes (all Introduction Points), and we want to make only a few of the contact points visible to any user or node in the network at a specific time.

To accomplish this we introduce *Valet Service nodes*, or simply *Valet nodes*. These nodes are the new contact points for the Client, they can be different for different clients or groups of clients and will enable the service to maintain a limited number of Introduction Points, but multiple contact points. So neither the public nor the real users know about the identity of several of these nodes at a time. We also avoid having the Valet nodes knowing which services they are assisting, and we make sure that the Valet nodes do not know more than one Introduction Point per connection request. The information about these Valet Service nodes are found in Contact Information tickets which will be discussed later.

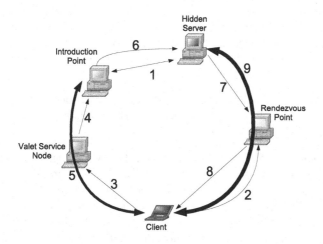

Fig. 2. Use of Valet Service

In Fig. 2 we illustrate that the Hidden Server tunnels (1) out to at least one Introduction Point, and creates a listener for contact requests. The Client tunnels (2) out to a Rendezvous Point as in the original setup, and constructs the rendezvous information (including, e.g., authentication information) that it will send to the Hidden Server.

Using information about the Valet Service nodes in the Contact Information ticket, the Client tunnels (3) out to the Valet node. The Valet node receives a Valet token encrypted with its public key, and containing information about the Introduction Point. The Valet node then extends (4) the circuit to the Introduction Point so that the Client now can communicate directly (5) and securely with the Introduction Point without knowing who this is, just that it is communicating with a node authorized by the Hidden Server.   ˙

The Client then uses information from the Contact Information ticket to authenticate the connection through the Introduction Point (IPo) and delivers to it the client's message to be forwarded (6) to the Hidden Server.

Based on the received information, the hidden service now determines whether to contact (7) the Rendezvous Point and complete the anonymous tunnel (8&9) setup with the Client, or to drop the request.

There are several challenges in this extension of the protocol, e.g., lost and expired tickets and the selection of contact information, but we will address these after a more detailed description of how Valet services work.

3.2   Description

We divide the connection phase of contacting the hidden service into five parts:

1. The Hidden Server's setup of the Introduction Points and the construction and distribution of the Contact Information tickets.
2. The Client setting up a Rendezvous Point and contacting the Valet node.
3. The Valet node extending the circuit to the Introduction Point.
4. The Client authenticating and sending contact and authentication information to the Introduction Point, which forwards this to the Hidden Server.
5. The Hidden Server contacting the Rendezvous Point and finalizing the connection with the Client.

We will address the construction and distribution of the Contact Information tickets at the end so the reader will learn how the information is used and hence better understand why it contains what it does.

Client Contacting Valet Service Node. Following Fig. 2, we assume that the Hidden Server has set up (1) a set of Introduction Points to be used by the clients and distributed information about how to connect to them. (See discussion of "Distributing tickets" below in this section.)

Contact Information tickets are shown in Table 1. Each contains a signed list of Valet nodes that are allowed to contact the Introduction Points and optional authentication information.

Before the contact to the Valet node can be completed the Client must first have selected a Rendezvous Point and connected to it (2) through an anonymizing tunnel. The Client will instruct RP to listen for authenticated connections and pass this RP contact information along to the Hidden Server.

Now the Client selects one of the Valet nodes listed in the Contact Information ticket and constructs a tunnel (3) to it, similar to the tunnel it created to the Introduction Point in the original version.

Table 1. Contact Information ticket

$ValetServiceNode_1$	One Valet node to forward the Client's information to an Introduction Point
$TimestampVS_1$	Expiry time of this Valet Token
$ValetToken_1$	Identifier for this Valet's connection to one or more Introduction Points, encrypted with the Valet node's public key
$PublicServiceKeyIPo_1$	Provides the client with the public service key of IPo_1
$ValetServiceNode_{2\&3...}$	Other Valet node(s)
$TicketID$	Ticket identifier for client to show to IPo and HS
$TimeStampCI$	Validity period for information in Contact Information ticket
$AuthorizeCtoHS$	Optional authorization information for ticket (or for C) to connect to HS

Valet Node Contacting Introduction Point. At this point the Client needs to extend the circuit to the Introduction Point. The extra functionality of adding the Valet node requires that we must have a method of assuring that we are talking to the Introduction Point without knowing its location or public key. This can be solved by having the Introduction Point associate a special *service key* with each associated hidden service contact point. This IPo service key pair and a corresponding key identifier, is generated by the Hidden Server, and the private part of the key pair together with the key identifier is transferred to the Introduction Point upon setup of the listener. In other words, when acting as an Introduction Point, the node will use the given private key for authenticating in an extension of the tunnel to it, and not its usual private node key. In addition the Introduction Point is told which Valet nodes are allowed to use this key when connecting. The public part of the service key is sent to the client through the Contact Information ticket shown in Table 1. The Introduction Point is not given the public service key thus making it harder to find out the hidden service with which it is associated.

The Client must send information to the Valet Service node that the Client itself is unable to read. The Client finds this information in the Contact Information ticket as the *Valet Token*, see Table 2, and it is encrypted (by the Hidden Service) using the public key of the Valet Service node. The token contains the identity of the Introduction Point, a time stamp, and a *Valet Identifier*. The Valet Identifier is used for identifying to the Introduction Point what service key to use and for confirming which Valet Service node is allowed to extend to it using this key. The Valet Identifier is signed with the private service key (IPo verifies the signature by producing the signature itself) and encrypted with the public node key of the Introduction Point.

But the Client also needs to give information to the Introduction Point upon extension of a tunnel similar to the way a usual tunnel extension is done. The message, an *Extend Tunnel Message*, contains normal circuit extension parameters, including a DH start g^x, added replay protection and identification of the

Table 2. Content of Valet Token including the Valet Identifier

IPo_1	Identity of Introduction Point
$TimeStampIPo_1$	Valet Token's validity period
$\{ValetIdentifierIPo_1\}_{sign,enc}$	Identifies the connection at Introduction Point IPo_1
$\rightarrow privateIPo_1ServiceKeyID$	The key for IPo_1 to use for extension of the circuit
$\rightarrow ValetServiceNodeID_1$	Identifies the Valet node allowed to extend to IPo_1
$\rightarrow TimeStampIPo_1$	Valet Identifier's validity period

Valet node. The Extend Tunnel Message is encrypted with the public part of the service key to ensure that only the Introduction Point can receive the message.

So the Client creates an *Extend Tunnel Message* and submits (3) this together with the *Valet Token* to the Valet node asking it to extend the tunnel (circuit) to the Introduction Point inside the Valet Token. The Valet node extracts the identity of the Introduction Point from the Valet Token and extends (4) the circuit to this node by forwarding the Extend Tunnel Message. The Introduction Point checks the message for the correct Valet node, correct key ID and signatures, and replies to the Client to complete the DH exchange using g^y and a verification of correct key, as in current design. The Client now has a secure communication channel (5) to the Introduction Point without knowing its real identity. And the Introduction Point knows which of the hidden service descriptors the channel is associated with, and as before it knows nothing about the Client's identity.

Client Contacting Hidden Service. Now the Client has to send the Rendezvous Point's contact information to the Hidden Service via the Introduction Point. The Client sends (5) the *TicketID* found in the Contact Information ticket to the Introduction Point to identify the use of the ticket, and it also attaches a time stamp and the information going to the Hidden Service (encrypted with the Hidden Service's public key). The Introduction Point checks the *TicketID* and *TimeStampIPo* and then forwards (6) the Hidden Server message (see Table 3) containing contact information of the Rendezvous Point together with the first part of a DH-key exchange and optional authentication information. If we wanted to identify the Valet node used for contacting the hidden service, we could do this in the authentication field. The message is protected from interception by the Valet node via the DH-key the Client exchanged with IPo.

Hidden Server Contacting Rendezvous Point. After authorizing the connection from the Client, the Hidden Server connects (7) to the Rendezvous Point to finalize the connection of the anonymous tunnel.

The Rendezvous Point authenticates the request based on the *RendezvousPoint* information the Hidden Server received from the Client (Table 3), and then forwards (8) the finalization of the Client to Hidden Server DH key exchange with the (optional) new Contact Information ticket to the Client. Then the Rendezvous Point connects the two tunnels forming (9) the authenticated, secure and anonymous channel between the Client and the Hidden Server.

Table 3. Message from Client to Introduction Point

$TicketID$	Information for IPo to verify ticket access before forwarding message to HS
$TimeStampIPo$	to verify validity period
The following is encrypted with HS's public key	
$RendezvousPoint$	Contact and authentication information for HS to contact the RP
g^x	First part of Client's ephemeral DH-exchange with Hidden Server
$TimeStampHS$	period of validity of this request
$TicketID$	Information to identify the ticket to HS
$AuthorizeCtoHS$	(optional) authentication information for ticket or for C towards HS

Constructing Contact Information Tickets. Uptime history and bandwidth availability are the most important factors when the hidden service is constructing contact information tickets for its clients. [4] The hidden service first has to select a set of nodes with high uptime to use as Introduction Points and as Valet nodes. For each of the Introduction Points the hidden service constructs a service-access public-key pair and submits one part, the "private"[5] key to the Introduction Point, and the other "public" key is to be put into the Contact Information ticket as shown in Table. 1. The key pair is given an identifier, $privateIPo_1ServiceKeyID$, to help identify the use of the correct key upon connection requests. In addition the hidden service constructs $TicketID$s allowing different clients (i.e. different tickets) to connect to the same Introduction Point. These $TicketID$s are sent to the Introduction Point together with the private key and the key identifier upon setup of the Introduction Point's listener.

So, after selecting a Valet node, the hidden service is now ready to construct the Contact Information ticket. First it packs the service key ID together with a validity period and the identity of the Valet node into the *Valet Identifier*. The private *service* key is then used to sign the Valet Identifier before it is encrypted with the public *node* key of the Introduction Point (cf. Table 2).

The Valet Identifier is then put into the *Valet Token* together with a time stamp and the identity (the public node key) of the Introduction Point. The Valet Token is encrypted with the public key of the Valet node and put into the Contact Information ticket together with its public node key and the public service key of the associated Introduction Point.

The Contact Information ticket is now built up of identifiers of Valet nodes, a Valet node validity period, and the corresponding Valet Token with the associated public service key of the Introduction Point. There can be as many Valet nodes listed in a ticket as the hidden service finds appropriate. The ticket will also contain a $TicketID$, a validity period for the ticket, and optional au-

---

[4] In Tor there currently exists no certification of this information as this would require active measurements of a nodes' capacity and availability during operation.

[5] The key is generated by HS not IPo, but used as a private key by HS (signing) and IPo (decrypting).

thentication information to be used when the Client connects to the Hidden Server.

Distributing Tickets. For distribution of the tickets we must look at two different scenarios; authorized users only or also allowing anonymous users. The different vulnerabilities of these will be discussed in Sect. 4. In either scenario, although especially applicable to anonymous users, another distinction is whether traditional directory servers are used or distributed hash tables (DHTs). We first present distribution via directory servers since this is closer to the current usage over the Tor network.

By using the protocol described here the hidden service will be able to keep track of users and build a "reputation" for a user or a group of users. This is of course something an authenticated user might be subjected to by a service anyway, but we will use this to create QoS for both types of users, authenticated and anonymous.

Each time a user is connecting to a hidden service he either sends publicly known information (contained in a ticket publicly available at a Directory Server), or some authentication based on information he shares with the hidden service. Now the hidden service is able to set up different QoS based on what category the client is in. E.g. an authorized client can have access to a larger number of Valet nodes, Introduction Points, or even just use higher bandwidth nodes in IPo and RP connections than an anonymous user will get. We can also imagine that a hidden service will use more trusted or higher bandwidth nodes in some of its tunnels based on this information. Anonymous users may also be given different QoS based on previous experience, e.g. an anonymous user connecting for the thousandth time could get better (or worse?) QoS than a first time user. This would imply either a pseudonymous user profile or a bearer instrument for tracking reputation.

In the existing hidden service design one major problem is that everyone can find all the Introduction Points to any service for which they know the *.onion* address. Another threat to security is that the Directory Server is able to identify and count all services and their startup times, and in addition locate all their contact information since the listings are not encrypted (but signed). We suggest in this paper a simple countermeasure addressing these issues.

First we must look at the two different scenarios:

1. The service is to be publicly available if a client knows the *.onion* address.
2. The service is open to authorized clients with valid tickets already received, e.g. through an off-line distribution channel, and will not use the Directory Servers.

The latter scenario is managed by the functionality of the network. As noted, ticket control is then maintained through the connections, but to counter the first scenario we propose the following simple scheme.

The Client has somehow (e.g. by a link on a web page, phone call, letter, etc.) received the *q.onion* address of the service to contact, where q is derived from the public key of the service, e.g. $q = hash(PK + value)$. We use this address to create the service descriptor index, e.g. $hash(q +' 1')$, to use at the Directory Server. The downloaded value, Q, is the Content Information ticket encrypted with a symmetric encryption scheme using a key derived from the public key, e.g., $hash(q +' 2')$. So both the descriptor index and the descriptor content are hidden from the Directory Server. Now a client must be in possession of the public key (or the $q.onion$) address of the hidden service in order to find and decrypt its Contact Information ticket. After receiving Q, the Client extracts the content, finds the public key, checks whether the signature matches, and does a confirmation to see if this key really is the one corresponding to the $q.onion$ address. If so, she has confirmed receiving correct contact information for this service.

Since there is no way of deriving $hash(q +' 2')$ from $hash(q +' 1')$ without having q, the Directory Server cannot find the contact information of unknown *.onion* addresses.

So what about private entries? If we want to permit groups of users to connect with different QoS, the hidden service gives them different cookies, grouping them so they e.g., can use $hash(q +' 1' + cookie)$ for lookup, and $hash(q +' 2' + cookie)$ for decrypting. Now we are also making it impossible for the Directory Server to count how many services it has listed. In addition, the cookies can be based on the client's authentication data, enabling only that specific client to download and decrypt the associated Contact Information ticket.

The scheme should also be expanded by using a date/time value inside the hash calculation to include a time period, e.g., current date, so a listing can exist anonymously without revealing when the service started to exist. Combining this with a time stamp could have the Directory Server store the entry for a longer (or shorter) period of time than default. And of course for authenticated users we only need to give the Client several Contact Information tickets with varying lifetimes. Typically any client should always have a long-term ticket and one or more short-term tickets.

In order to verify an update of information inside the directory service during the entry's life time, we propose a simple reverse hash chain scheme where the initial contact to the Directory Server is followed by an iterated hash value, $v_n = hash^n(v)$, known only to the hidden service itself. For each update of this index (e.g. of $hash(q +' 1' + date)$) the new encrypted ticket is accompanied by the value, v_{k-1}, enabling the directory server/DHT to verify the update using $v_k = hash(v_{k-1})$.

To adapt to the current and future improvements in hash collision techniques it is probably wise to increase the number of bits used in the .onion address from today's 80-bit (16 * base32(5-bit) characters) address to e.g. 256-bit (using 44 * base64[6](6-bit) characters, including an eight-bit version and extension value as the first byte of the address). An evaluation of hash algorithms will not be discussed here.

Distributed Hash Tables. The list of Tor servers is sensitive in at least two ways. First, it is the means by which clients bootstrap into anonymity: we cannot as-

---

[6] Use "special" base64 e.g., '/'→'-', '+'→'_'

sume that clients can anonymously obtain an initial list of Tor nodes. Second, the list of nodes is sensitive. If different sets of nodes are given to different users, then it is possible to separate the source of traffic according to the nodes carrying it.

Neither of these is as much of an issue for hidden services. The IP addresses of clients acquiring information on available hidden services may be assumed to already be anonymized. Since there is neither a need for, nor a preexisting expectation of, an authoritative list of hidden services, partitioning is less of an issue as well. In any case, there is nothing to prevent someone from listing at directory servers two or more distinct sets of information for the same hidden service and selectively announcing one or the other set to distinct individuals.

For this reason, authoritative directory servers for hidden services as a core part of the Tor network are not necessary. Indeed, the primary motivation for their use initially has been one of convenience: they are an available and already used infrastructure for Tor users that distributes one kind of server information (Tor nodes). So, it was easy to add another kind (hidden servers). Obviously it would be better not to overload these servers in either functionality or workload.

One could set up another set of directory servers specifically for hidden services, but given the above considerations, hidden services would seem to be an advantageous application for distributed hash tables (DHTs), such as CAN [20], Chord [26], Pastry [23], or Tapestry [30].

DHTs are decentralized systems that can be used to support many applications including file storage and retrieval. They are known for their efficient tradeoffs of decentralization, scalability, robustness and routing efficiency. Their application in anonymous communication is not as straightforward as is sometimes supposed, and require careful design to avoid security pitfalls [5,9]. Presenting a careful design is beyond the scope of this paper. However, we note that the basic design of *.onion* addresses based on hashing of keys are naturally amenable to DHTs.

4   Security

4.1   Availability

The greatest threat to availability in the original hidden service design is the collection of all Introduction Points in the information stored on the Directory Server. This makes it easy to either *directly* attack the Introduction Points, or *indirectly* attack them, e.g. by threatening the Directory Server or the Introduction Point operator not to list a specific service.

By using tickets and Valet nodes we have enabled the possibility of a hidden service to exist entirely on its own without anyone being able to identify it unless he can either guess or by some other method get ahold of the public key (or the *.onion* address) of the service. If a group of people can distribute the *.onion* address in private, no one should be able to find the service used, or know of its very existence.

We have addressed two types of hidden service users – *the authorized user* and *the anonymous user*. The hidden service might want to offer different QoS to the different users, in addition to the persistent and general need to provide availability. The anonymous user might allow himself to be recognized as a previous user of the service without revealing his identity, much like the use of *cookies* in HTTP[12]. For example, such an anonymous user might over time be considered trustworthy (enough) to be given higher availability and bandwidth than plain anonymous users. So we can have QoS also for anonymous connections. Availability and QoS for an authorized user can be very flexible, based on what the Hidden Servers require.

In addition, in our design it is impossible for the Directory Servers to count and identify the services as they can in the currently deployed hidden service system. Further, they will now only be able to extract the total number of "client groups"—not likely to be useful information. More important is the removal of the Directory Server's ability to confirm the existence of a service. Now a service will be able to announce its Contact Information on a Directory Server and remain private/unannounced.

But most important, the Introduction Points are hidden from the users, from the Directory Servers, and from the public. We have thus enhanced the availability of the Introduction Points. If the Contact Information tickets are publicly accessible, we must assume that a Valet node or an Introduction Point with reasonable effort will be able to determine which hidden service is using that Introduction Point. But only knowing one or two Introduction Points still leaves the others available for use.

Finding the Introduction Points. is still possible for an adversary. If we select a small number of Valet nodes this will move us closer to the original hidden service design, as the Valet nodes now are the vulnerable points of a potential DoS attack. If the number of Valet nodes is huge, we make it easier for an adversary to collect all the Introduction Points through owning a Valet node in all "groups" associated with each Introduction Point. So we have to find a trade-off, and we expect to be better off in the lower count case.

Using n as the number of nodes in the network, c as the number of compromised nodes, i as the number of Introduction Points, and v as the number of Valet nodes per Introduction Point, we can get an expression for the probability of revealing all the Introduction Points to the adversary. The probability P_s for a specific combination of c compromised nodes in $i+1$ groups is given by Eq. 1.

$$P_s(x_j \text{ in Valet group } j) = \frac{\binom{G_0}{x_0}\binom{G_1}{x_1}\cdots\binom{G_i}{x_i}}{\binom{n}{c}} = \frac{\binom{n-i\cdot v}{c-x_1-\ldots-x_i}\binom{v}{x_1}\cdots\binom{v}{x_i}}{\binom{n}{c}} \quad (1)$$

Here 0 is the index for being outside all the Valet node groups, i.e., $G_0 = n - i \cdot v$, $x_0 = c - x_1 - x_2 - \ldots - x_i$. and all other G_j are given to be v. The number of compromised nodes c must be larger or equal to the number of Introduction Points i, otherwise the probability will be zero.

$$P(n, c, v, i) = \sum_{x_1, x_2 \ldots, x_i} \frac{\binom{n - i \cdot v}{c - \sum_1^i x_j}\binom{v}{x_1} \cdots \binom{v}{x_i}}{\binom{n}{c}} \tag{2}$$

The probability of the adversary having concurrent presence in all groups is given by Eq. 2 where $c \geq i$ and we sum over the values: $x_1 = 1, \ldots, min(v, c - i + 1)$; $x_2 = 1, \ldots, min(v, c - i - x_1 + 2)$; $x_3 = 1, \ldots, min(v, c - i - x_1 - x_2 + 3)$; up to $x_i = 1, \ldots, min(v, c - \sum_{j=1}^{i-1} x_j)$, where the upper limit of the x-values is v as indicated.

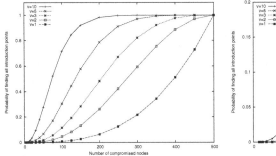 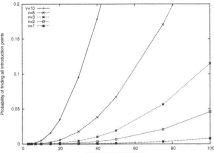

Fig. 3. Probability of finding all $i=3$ Introduction Points each using v Valet nodes in a $n=500$ network

Fig. 4. Lower left corner of Fig. 3

Figure 3 and 4 shows how the use of Valet nodes hides the Introduction Points in the current system using three IPos. The probability is plotted against the number of compromised nodes, c, in a system with $n = 500$ nodes in total. Even when using ten Valet nodes per IPo the adversary must control 25 nodes in order to have a 10% chance of locating all three Introduction Points. Using only three Valet nodes per IPo the adversary must control almost 100 nodes to achieve the same probability.

As described in Sect. 2.2, the probability of locating all Introduction Points for a hidden service is 1 in the current implementation, independent of how many network nodes the adversary controls. Figure 5 shows the probability of an adversary, controlling c nodes of the network, to be able to locate all the i Introduction Points when using Valet nodes. The more Valet nodes added per IPo, the higher the probability of locating all (presence in all groups), and if we add more IPos keeping the number of Valet nodes constant, the probability goes down. We observe that the number of Valet nodes is a more significant factor than the number of Introduction Points. E.g. the strongest protection occurs in the case of using only a single Valet node per IPo, but this will, as previously mentioned, affect the service's availability. Using only one Valet node gives an insider adversary the same number of nodes to attack. We also observe that when using nine Introduction Points and only one Valet node per IPo, the adversary

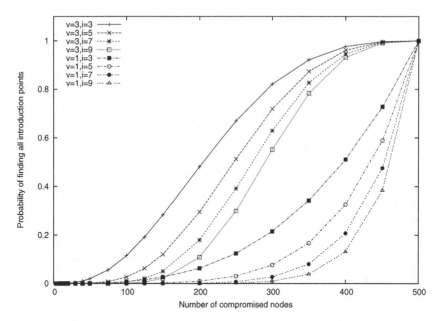

Fig. 5. Probability of finding all i Introduction Points, each using v Valet nodes in a network of $n=500$ nodes

will have to control around 400 nodes in order to have the same 10% probability of locating them all.

Even if the service is now involving more nodes in the network, unavailability will only happen if all Introduction Points are down or if the combination of either all the IPos or their associated Valet nodes are down at the same time. Given that the Introduction Points now are hidden from the public, we find that the removal of targeted DoS attacks is more significant than the introduction of more nodes. In Fig. 6 we compare the relative distributions of a network of 100 and 1000 nodes and observe only tiny variations in the probability distribution caused by the changing relative sizes of i and v compared to c and n.

Based on this we estimate that good protection of the service should consist of at least three Introduction Points combined with at least two Valet nodes per Introduction Point, and should be combined with the possibility of differentiated QoS as described in Sect. 4.2.

4.2   Quality of Service

As described in Sect. 3.2 we can now differentiate QoS for the users. But there are potential problems with the described methods.

If a user wants to stay anonymous and untraceable, he must start with a public ticket every time (the paranoid variant), or trust the service to supply semi-public tickets for every connection, which e.g. the user can check by connecting multiple

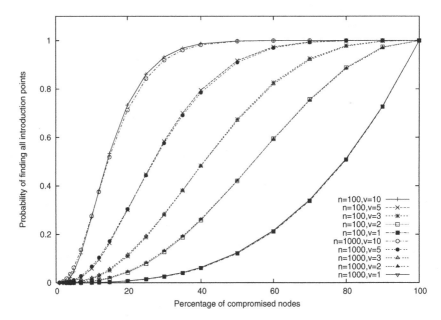

Fig. 6. Comparing $n=1000$ to an upscaled $n=100$ for a service using three Introduction Points with varying number of Valet nodes

times using the public ticket(s). As these are open public services connected to by anonymous clients, this is a simple verification.

When it comes to authorized users, a service may access the Rendezvous Point through different nodes giving a specific ("deserved") bandwidth to the user. This might reduce the set of nodes the service is selecting from during set up of the tunnel.

4.3   MitM Attack

The Valet Service node will not be an additional danger for performing a man-in-the-middle attack because the Client is able to authenticate the Introduction Point by the use of its service key pair. And, as in the current version of the hidden service protocol, the Introduction Point will not be able to perform a MitM attack due to the authentication of the hidden service.

4.4   DoS Attacks

A client connecting multiple times to a Valet node and sending messages requesting decryption of the Valet Token and extension of circuits may cause a problem for the Valet node. But a Valet node should only need to unpack a Token once, and then may cache it for later reuse within its lifetime. The other actions are normal extension, involving the Client, and simple forwarding of information, so this should not be easy to abuse. By not accepting extension requests twice for the same tunnel, the attacker may be forced to set up a new tunnel through another node before every attempt.

Sending multiple connection requests to the Introduction Point could be a potential problem. But if all Introduction Points tear down their connection circuits upon finishing a connection, the Client will be forced to perform too many operations compared with the effect created on the Introduction Point. If it becomes necessary, an Introduction Point can simply ignore service requests from specific Valet nodes.

If the chosen Valet node is down, a Client simply chooses another Valet node in the ticket. If they are all down or unavailable, this will affect every client using the same ticket. But the Valet nodes should be as many and constructed in such a way that it is possible for a user to either use a long term ticket previously received, or use an anonymous ticket for a first connection. There should be enough variety in the construction of the tickets to make it prohibitively difficult for an adversary to take down all Valet nodes of a service even if she did know them all.

This should apply to the Introduction Points as well, so we must make certain that Valet nodes only know the same Introduction Point for the same service to minimize this threat factor.

A large threat to the public tickets scheme is uploading of false tickets to the Directory Servers (or into the DHT). For known services it is easy to counter by signing, but for encrypted tickets this is an issue. We proposed a reverse hash chain scheme (Sect. 3.2) to counter this since the false updates will be invalid. But the scheme will raise issues in synchronization of directory servers and DHTs, which we will not address here.

4.5   Ticket Problems

If a client lost its ticket or the ticket expires, it must either use a long term ticket, or download a new contact information ticket from the network. If authentication is required, or if the client has a privileged QoS, this can now be resubmitted and the next ticket received should get the client back on the same level of QoS. Another way of restoring QoS even to anonymous users is to store this information in separate cookies alongside the tickets.

So, what if the public key of the hidden service has become exposed to someone who should not have it? Will we have any possibility to hide the hidden service again once we are "found"? Not with today's design. But if we require authentication and there is suspicion of someone knowing the .onion address and thereby having the Contact Information (e.g. by lots of valid connection requests with false authentication information), the protocol could be extended to distribute new public key information with the new Contact Information upon the next authenticated request.

4.6   Colluding Connection Nodes

If one of the service's Valet nodes happens to be colluding with the Client, it will be able to collect information about at least one Introduction Point to this service. This takes us to the same scenario as in the current version of the hidden service design, except that now we also have several other Introduction Points that will continue to route users to the service, thus maintaining availability. Adversary Alice must now own a node in every set of Valet Service nodes used for the Introduction Points, something which should be highly unlikely if the grouping of nodes are constructed with this in mind.

Alice will not be able to find out if she owns an Introduction Point unless she also owns the corresponding Valet node or the Client. As a Valet node she will know if she also controls the Introduction Point, but she will not be able to confirm which service this is until she gets the corresponding ticket. As a Client there is the possibility of matching the DH-exchange and thereby determine if she controls the Introduction Point. But even if Alice should happen to find one of her nodes as an Introduction Point, this would still not reveal any additional information over the currently deployed system, where a node can trivially know the service for which it is chosen to be an Introduction Point.

5   Conclusion

Hidden services are now widely deployed and of increasing interest for individuals, corporations, governments, and organizations. We have here presented an extension of the current hidden service design that improves availability and resistance to DoS through the introduction of Valet nodes, which hide service Introduction Points. The new design also facilitates the use of "completely hidden services": only clients that know a hidden service's *.onion* address or its public key will be able to connect to it or even verify it's existence. The new protocol also allows differentiation of the quality of service given to clients, regardless of whether they are anonymous or authenticated.

References

1. Ross J. Anderson. The eternity service. In *Proceedings of Pragocrypt '96*, 1996.
2. The Anonymizer. http://www.anonymizer.com/.
3. Krista Bennett and Christian Grothoff. GAP – practical anonymous networking. In Roger Dingledine, editor, *Proceedings of Privacy Enhancing Technologies workshop (PET 2003)*. Springer-Verlag, LNCS 2760, March 2003.
4. Oliver Berthold, Hannes Federrath, and Stefan Köpsell. Web MIXes: A system for anonymous and unobservable Internet access. In H. Federrath, editor, *Proceedings of Designing Privacy Enhancing Technologies: Workshop on Design Issues in Anonymity and Unobservability*, pages 115–129. Springer-Verlag, LNCS 2009, July 2000.
5. Nikita Borisov. *Anonymous Routing in Structured Peer-to-Peer Overlays*. PhD thesis, UC Berkeley, Spring 2005.
6. Philippe Boucher, Adam Shostack, and Ian Goldberg. Freedom systems 2.0 architecture. White paper, Zero Knowledge Systems, Inc., December 2000.
7. David Chaum. Untraceable electronic mail, return addresses, and digital pseudonyms. *Communications of the ACM*, 4(2), February 1981.

8. Ian Clarke, Oskar Sandberg, Brandon Wiley, and Theodore W. Hong. Freenet: A distributed anonymous information storage and retrieval system. In *Proceedings of Designing Privacy Enhancing Technologies: Workshop on Design Issues in Anonymity and Unobservability*, pages 46–66, July 2000.

9. George Danezis, Chris Lesniewski-Laas, M. Frans Kaashoek, and Ross Anderson. Sybil-resistant dht routing. In *Computer Security – ESORICS 2005*, September 2005.

10. Roger Dingledine, Michael J. Freedman, and David Molnar. The Free Haven Project: Distributed anonymous storage service. In H. Federrath, editor, *Proceedings of Designing Privacy Enhancing Technologies: Workshop on Design Issues in Anonymity and Unobservability*. Springer-Verlag, LNCS 2009, July 2000.

11. Roger Dingledine, Nick Mathewson, and Paul Syverson. Tor: The second-generation onion router. In *Proceedings of the 13th USENIX Security Symposium*, August 2004.

12. R. Fielding, J. Gettys, J. Mogul, H. Frystyk, L. Masinter, P. Leach, and T. Berners-Lee. Hypertext transfer protocol – http/1.1. IETF RFC 2616, June 1999.

13. Ian Goldberg. *A Pseudonymous Communications Infrastructure for the Internet*. PhD thesis, UC Berkeley, December 2000.

14. David M. Goldschlag, Michael G. Reed, and Paul F. Syverson. Hiding Routing Information. In R. Anderson, editor, *Proceedings of Information Hiding: First International Workshop*, pages 137–150. Springer-Verlag, LNCS 1174, May 1996.

15. Aviel D. Rubin Marc Waldman and Lorrie Faith Cranor. Publius: A robust, tamper-evident, censorship-resistant, web publishing system. In *Proceedings of the 9th USENIX Security Symposium*, pages 59–72, August 2000.

16. Steven J. Murdoch and George Danezis. Low-cost traffic analysis of Tor. In *Proceedings of the 2005 IEEE Symposium on Security and Privacy*. IEEE CS, May 2005.

17. Lasse Øverlier and Paul Syverson. Locating hidden servers. In *Proceedings of the 2006 IEEE Symposium on Security and Privacy*. IEEE CS, May 2006.

18. Andreas Pfitzmann, Birgit Pfitzmann, and Michael Waidner. ISDN-mixes: Untraceable communication with very small bandwidth overhead. In *Proceedings of the GI/ITG Conference on Communication in Distributed Systems*, pages 451–463, February 1991.

19. Proxify.com. http://www.proxify.com/.

20. Sylvia Ratnasamy, Paul Francis, Mark Handley, Richard Karp, and Scott Schenker. A scalable content-addressable network. In *SIGCOMM '01: Proceedings of the 2001 conference on Applications, technologies, architectures, and protocols for computer communications*, pages 161–172, New York, NY, USA, 2001. ACM Press.

21. Jean-François Raymond. Traffic Analysis: Protocols, Attacks, Design Issues, and Open Problems. In H. Federrath, editor, *Proceedings of Designing Privacy Enhancing Technologies: Workshop on Design Issues in Anonymity and Unobservability*, pages 10–29. Springer-Verlag, LNCS 2009, July 2000.

22. Michael Reiter and Aviel Rubin. Crowds: Anonymity for web transactions. *ACM Transactions on Information and System Security*, 1(1), June 1998.

23. Antony Rowstron and Peter Druschel. Pastry: Scalable, distributed object location and routing for large-scale peer-to-peer systems. In *IFIP/ACM International Conference on Distributed Systems Platforms (Middleware)*, pages 329–350, November 2001.

24. Andrei Serjantov and Peter Sewell. Passive attack analysis for connection-based anonymity systems. In *Computer Security – ESORICS 2003*, October 2003.

25. Angelos Stavrou and Angelos D. Keromytis. Countering DoS attacks with stateless multipath overlays. In *CCS '05: Proceedings of the 12th ACM conference on Computer and communications security*, pages 249–259, New York, NY, USA, 2005. ACM Press.

26. Ion Stoica, Robert Morris, David Karger, M. Frans Kaashoek, and Hari Balakrishnan. Chord: A scalable peer-to-peer lookup service for internet applications. In *SIGCOMM '01: Proceedings of the 2001 conference on Applications, technologies, architectures, and protocols for computer communications*, pages 149–160, New York, NY, USA, 2001. ACM Press.

27. Marc Waldman and David Mazières. Tangler: a censorship-resistant publishing system based on document entanglements. In *Proceedings of the 8th ACM Conference on Computer and Communications Security (CCS 2001)*, pages 126–135, November 2001.

28. Matthew Wright, Micah Adler, Brian Neil Levine, and Clay Shields. An analysis of the degradation of anonymous protocols. In *Proceedings of the Network and Distributed Security Symposium - NDSS '02*. IEEE, February 2002.

29. Matthew K. Wright, Micah Adler, Brian Neil Levine, and Clay Shields. The predecessor attack: An analysis of a threat to anonymous communications systems. *ACM Trans. Inf. Syst. Secur.*, 7(4):489–522, 2004. A preliminary version of this paper appeared in [28].

30. Ben Y. Zhao, Ling Huang, Jeremy Stribling, Sean C. Rhea, Anthony D. Joseph, and John Kubiatowicz. Tapestry: A resilient global-scale overlay for service deployment. *IEEE Journal on Selected Areas in Communications*, 22(1):41–53, 2004.

Blending Different Latency Traffic
with Alpha-mixing

Roger Dingledine[1], Andrei Serjantov[2], and Paul Syverson[3]

[1] The Free Haven Project
arma@freehaven.net
[2] The Free Haven Project
aas23@freehaven.net
[3] Naval Research Laboratory
syverson@itd.nrl.navy.mil

Abstract. Currently fielded anonymous communication systems either introduce too much delay and thus have few users and little security, or have many users but too little delay to provide protection against large attackers. By combining the user bases into the same network, and ensuring that all traffic is mixed together, we hope to lower delay and improve anonymity for both sets of users.

Alpha-mixing is an approach that can be added to traditional batching strategies to let senders specify for each message whether they prefer security or speed. Here we describe how to add alpha-mixing to various mix designs, and show that mix networks with this feature can provide increased anonymity for all senders in the network. Along the way we encounter subtle issues to do with the attacker's knowledge of the security parameters of the users.

1 Introduction

Anonymous communication systems today don't provide much protection against a large attacker. Tor [11] and JAP [3] have hundreds of thousands of concurrent users, but their low latency and low overhead mean they do not defend against an adversary who observes most of the network. At the other end of the spectrum, Mixminion's design [5] theoretically provides strong security against a global attacker by adding high variance in latency, but this latency has crippled adoption — which in turn decreases the security that the network can provide, discouraging even the users who need high security [2,10].

Here we design a hybrid mix batching strategy that combines users with different anonymity and performance goals into the same network.

In our scheme each sender communicates an α – a security parameter – to each mix along the route of her message. The time the message spends inside each mix (and hence the anonymity it accumulates) then depends on the size of this security parameter. The message's α value at each mix decrements based on certain events, and when it reaches zero it is reintegrated back into the mix network. Our scheme can be combined with any of the standard mix types such

G. Danezis and P. Golle (Eds.): PET 2006, LNCS 4258, pp. 245–257, 2006.
© Springer-Verlag Berlin Heidelberg 2006

as timed mixes, pool mixes, etc. [14] to give each sender more control over the anonymity/performance tradeoff of her message.

Users that desire better anonymity then have the opportunity to obtain it by increasing α for their messages. More importantly, there is a network effect: when the attacker knows little about the security parameters chosen by individual users, all senders will benefit because of the mere *possibility* that they chose a higher α.

In this paper we start by outlining some simple alpha-mix designs and analysing the anonymity properties they can provide to users with different security preferences. Next we look at the strategies users should follow when picking the security parameter for each mix in the message's path. In Section 5, we look at the incentives users have for choosing a high security parameter themselves rather than expecting others to take the latency penalty (and thus provide more anonymity to everyone). Lastly we consider more sophisticated alpha-mixing strategies which should provide better properties but are hard to analyse.

2   Deterministic-Alpha Mix

While *threshold mixes* fire only when a sufficient number of messages have arrived, *timed mixes* simply fire at regular intervals. Timed mixes may be appropriate for traffic for which timeliness matters, since with threshold mixes the time until the next firing is unpredictable without assumptions about the rate of incoming messages. On the other hand, threshold mixes can provide minimum anonymity properties.

"Deterministic" here refers to the algorithm by which messages change α after each mix firing. Later we will consider algorithms that will change alpha probabilistically, for example based on the number of messages with certain alpha values in the mix. In this section, all messages simply drop one alpha level after each mix firing.

Timed deterministic-alpha mix: The mix fires every t seconds. All messages for which $\alpha = 0$ are sent out.[1] All remaining messages have their α decremented by one. New messages that arrive before the next firing are buffered based on their initial α and are placed at the according α level.

Threshold deterministic-alpha mix: This is the same as the timed version, except that the mix fires when at least a threshold n of messages with $\alpha = 0$ are in the mix. Note that since the number of messages with $\alpha = 1$ may be above the firing threshold, some batches may include more than n messages. (When many messages with $\alpha > 0$ are waiting in a mix before a threshold number of $\alpha = 0$ accumulate, this is analogous to the situation where many mixes in a

---

[1] We do not describe the reordering of messages or changing of their appearance in this paper. We assume that messages emerging from a mix have an appearance that cannot be correlated with their appearance upon entering the mix and that the order of all $\alpha = 0$ messages is randomly permuted before they are sent.

free-route threshold-mix net are waiting and nearly full while messages are being accumulated at relatively empty mixes.)

As we will see, one of the virtues of alpha mixing is that the timed/threshold distinction for mixes can blur, and it becomes more a distinction for firing strategies of individual messages than of mixes. For our initial analysis we will assume a steady-state network with constant rate of incoming messages, which means against a passive adversary the anonymity properties are equivalent.

It is also possible to have a threshold-or-timed alpha mix in which all messages are decremented in the alpha stack if either t seconds have passed or n messages have arrived. Similarly, one can have a threshold-and-timed alpha mix to reduce the effective rate of flooding attacks [14]. Even more complex variants of these designs are discussed in Section 6.

2.1 Deterministic-Alpha Mix: Anonymity Against a Local Passive Adversary

Here we describe the anonymity for a threshold alpha mix during steady-state (i.e., messages arrive with various alphas at a regular rate, and the mix fires at regular intervals).

We assume the adversary does not know the specific alpha of any message entering the mix, e.g., that this is provided to the mix encrypted together with the message. However, we do allow that the adversary might know the strategy by which alpha was chosen; we examine this issue further in Section 2.2. What should that strategy be? It would seem that choosing higher alphas would correspond to greater anonymity for messages. We now make this more precise.

Claim. Given any set of other messages in a threshold deterministic-alpha mix, a message has greater anonymity if it is assigned an alpha from a broader range (chosen uniformly) than from a narrower range.

Proof. Suppose messages occur with some distribution of alphas in a mix with firing threshold n. A sender will assign to message M an initial α_M for a particular mix in a given position in the message's path. Suppose the adversary knows the strategy chosen by the sender. Assume the choice of strategies are between choosing α_M from either a range of 0 to j or a range of 0 to $k > j$. The anonymity set size increases by $n(k - j)$ if the broader range is chosen. (In information-theoretic terms, the entropy has increased by $\log(n(k - j))$.) If the adversary does not know the strategy, then we cannot put a precise number on his uncertainty. However, the less predictable the range is to the adversary, the greater the uncertainty is, even if we cannot say how much. She can either guess too small a range and risk not seeing the output message at all, or guess too large and include many additional batches in the anonymity set for the message. (These points carry over mutatis mutandis when we reason probabilistically rather than just possibilistically.)

If the adversary does know the strategy (although still not the actual α) for each incoming message, then the anonymity of M is less affected by the strategy that other messages use for choosing α in a steady-state network. However, if the strategies are not known, then choosing α from a broader range increases the anonymity for other messages in the mix as well, although it is difficult to say by how much. If the distribution of strategies across all messages in the mix at any time is known to the adversary, however, then it is clear that increasing the range from which α is chosen for any unknown one of those messages increases the uncertainty about the future batch in which any of the messages still in the mix will emerge. Thus,

Claim. Assume a set of messages in a steady-state deterministic-alpha mix. Assume the α_M for any message M is chosen uniformly at random from the range given by $0 \leq \alpha_M \leq k_M$. Then anonymity increases for every message M in the mix if any $k_{M'}$ increases.

The key is not that a high α necessarily provides better security, but rather that when the variance of our α is high, its value within the range is hard for the attacker to predict.

In summary, for threshold mixes or steady-state timed mixes, choosing α from a broader range improves the anonymity for that message whether the adversary knows one's strategy or not. Further, if the adversary knows nothing about the strategies of choosing alphas or knows simply the distribution of strategies, then increasing the α-range for any message improves anonymity for all messages.

2.2 Attacker Knowledge

In the previous section we noted that the anonymity properties provided by alpha mixes depend on what the attacker knows about the security parameters of the users. Specifically, while choosing from a wider range of alphas improves anonymity, an attacker can reduce anonymity if he has information about which alphas are chosen. We illustrate this on a simple example.

Consider sender anonymity in the setting of just one mix, illustrated on two rounds only (equivalently, suppose maximum alpha is 1):

Round 1: $I_1 = i_{1,1} \ldots i_{m,1}$ entered the mix, messages $o_{1,1} \ldots o_{x,1}$ came out.
Round 2: $I_2 = i_{1,2} \ldots i_{n,2}$ entered, messages $o_{1,2} \ldots o_{y,2}$ came out.

Let $\alpha(x)$ be the set of possible alphas of message x as known by the attacker. Note that if the attacker knows nothing, then $\forall x,\ \alpha(x) = \{0,1\}$.

Our target message is $o_{1,2}$. The sender anonymity set (in messages) is:

$$\{x | x \in I_1 \wedge 1 \in \alpha(x)\} \cup \{y | y \in I_2 \wedge 0 \in \alpha(y)\}$$

Hence (almost) any knowledge of alphas by the attacker degrades anonymity. Note that complete knowledge of alphas by the attacker *may* leave the message with no anonymity; however, this is extremely unlikely (or amounts to a rather expensive variant of the trickle attack).

Indeed, when analysing alpha mixes we need not constrain ourselves to reasoning about anonymity sets. We now compute the anonymity probability distribution, but first we need a little more formalization of the assumptions. Essentially, where we allowed the attacker possibilistic knowledge about the alphas of the messages, we now allow him (better) probabilistic knowledge.

Notation: call α_M the alpha in message M. Hence the attacker knows the probability distributions $P(\alpha_M = a)$ for every message M with a ranging from 0 to a_{max}.

Now, the anonymity probability distribution:

$$\text{Normalise}(\{p|M \in I_1 \wedge p = P(\alpha_M = 0)\} \cup \{p|M \in I_2 \wedge p = P(\alpha_M = 1)\})$$

and the anonymity is the entropy of this distribution. Clearly, the more the attacker knows about alpha, the lower the anonymity.

2.3   Correlating Message Content with Requested Security

Now let us study an interesting example which has long been known intuitively... Suppose the attacker knows that sender S only sends with a high security parameter (let's say alpha of 5). He now sees a message from sender S at round 0, and a message detailing Enron's finances emerges at round 5. Suppose further that all other messages have an alpha of 0. Our above definitions give the target message the anonymity set of all the senders of round 5 union S. Nevertheless, we conjecture the attacker will tend to suspect that S sent the message. How can we reconcile the intuition of the attacker with our formalism above and how can we design the system to avoid such a judgement?

The attacker is likely to be correct — what we ignore here is the fact that the choice of the security parameter is likely *conditional* on the importance of the message and the attacker has used this fact to form his judgement. In order to avoid this, we must (paradoxically!) ignore this fact completely and pick alphas from a distribution which is independent of the receiver and the message's content. Of course, we cannot defeat this attack entirely because the sender's distribution will still be conditional on her utility function: messages from users with higher security needs will in fact still behave differently.

There are still external factors to consider. We'd like to go a step further and make the sender's software enforce that she doesn't vary alpha based on each message's receiver or content. This approach would best convince the attacker that the sender *could not* have changed it. Also, if a given user is the only sender with extremely high alpha values, then intersection attacks over time (watching the high-value messages and what senders were active before each) will reveal her [4,13]. But we will ignore these black-box network attacks since they are not the focus of this paper.

Below we will see that some strategies for choosing the alpha values are more effective than others at preventing the attacker from learning the security preferences of senders.

3   Allocating $\sum \alpha$ Against a Distributed Adversary

In the previous section we discussed the fact that an adversary who can learn about the sender's alphas can weaken her anonymity. For example, sending only high value messages and picking high security parameters for them can actually decrease anonymity.

In this section we examine an attack that a compromised mix can perform to deduce the sender's alphas, and we deal with the problem of allocating the overall message's security parameter $\Sigma\alpha$ over the mixes in the message's path. There are two problems to solve. Firstly, if a bad mix observes one of the alphas, it should get as little information as possible about the other alphas of this message.[2] Secondly, it should be hard for the bad mixes to link any alpha parameter to a particular sender, i.e. figure out how much any sender is concerned about security.

One possible solution for picking a sequence of $\alpha^{(i)}$ (where the "(i)" represents the ith mix in the route) is simply to pick from a uniform distribution over the partitions of $\Sigma\alpha$ into ℓ buckets where the buckets themselves are indistinguishable. The number of such partitions are given by

$$\sum_{k=1}^{\ell} Q(\Sigma\alpha, k)$$

where Q denotes the number of ways of partitioning $\Sigma\alpha$ into exactly k distinct parts. Generating values from such a distribution is possible, for instance, using the algorithm described in [7]. This seems to deal with the first problem (the analysis to show this is beyond the scope of this paper). For the second part, it depends what the sender wants to protect: does she care about having an estimate of the security parameter associated with just herself, with herself and the recipient, or just the recipient? Note that if the first and the last mixes are bad and can observe a "higher security" message passing through each of them, they can conjecture that it is one of a relatively small set of sensitive messages. There are a variety of properties to explore in this area; we merely observe that by reordering the value that we obtain from the uniform distribution over partitions, we can make sure that the minimum values in that partition are sent to the first and the last mix. For example, if $\Sigma\alpha = 5$, then the distribution is uniform over: $\{5, 0, 0, 0\}, \{4, 1, 0, 0\}, \{3, 2, 0, 0\}, \{3, 1, 1, 0\}, \{2, 1, 1, 1\}$. Supposing we draw the partition $\{3, 1, 1, 0\}$, we reorder it into $\{0, 3, 1, 1\}$ and hence obtain a sequence of alphas to insert into the message.

If we wish to guarantee that neither the first nor the last mix can locally know anything about the sensitivity level of a message, we can simply stipulate for message M that $\alpha_M^{(0)} = \alpha_M^{(n)} = 0$ (for a path length of $n + 1$). Similarly we could stipulate that $\alpha_M^{(1)} = \alpha_M^{(n-1)} \leq 1$, etc. The tradeoff is that with each such move we are reducing what an adversary observing just the endpoints can learn about sensitivity of messages, but a more concentrated set of nodes in the center learn more about the sensitivity of messages. Against an adversary who controls the central node(s) combined with, e.g., a global passive observer, our protection is diminished. We can gain advantage against both types of adversaries by

---

[2] Note the similarity between picking an alpha and message splitting [15] — in both cases they are distributions over partitions.

increasing path length, with the usual concomitant risk to robustness of delivery that comes with increased path length.

4   Dummies

Our focus so far has been on steady-state networks with passive adversaries. However, we want to provide uncertainty even in edge cases where there is a momentarily lull in traffic [8,9,14]. An active attacker can arrange an edge case via blending attacks, but a passive attacker can also simply wait for an edge case to occur. For timed mixes there will be occasions when only a single message enters and leaves the mix in a given round. Alpha mixes have a clear advantage here since there is no guarantee that the message that exited the mix is the same message that entered. The attack is never exact (guaranteed to recognize a target message as it exits the mix) unless the adversary can bound the range of α with certainty for all messages he observes.

We provide a very lightweight dummy policy that guarantees that no exact attack is possible against an alpha mix, even for active attackers: simply initialize the mix with a single dummy message set at an arbitrary alpha. Before firing, always check the mix for the presence of a dummy somewhere in the alpha-stack. If none is present, add one.

But what do we mean by "arbitrary alpha"? Obviously it must occur within some finite range. It could be uniformly chosen between 0 and the maximum expected α. If a message is ever received with a higher α, then the maximum should be raised to this level. Such a strategy will prevent any exact attack, but it will still allow most practical attacks that dummies are intended to counter (active or passive) because most traffic will not have high alpha. Thus, a single message entering and a single message exiting a timed mix in a single firing interval are much more likely to be the same message than a dummy.

A strategy that should maximize uncertainty at least in the edge cases would be to insert dummies according to the expected distribution of α_M for messages M entering the mix. The expected distribution can be determined by observation. Mixes joining the network can be initialized with a default expected distribution averaged from one or more mixes already in the network. If the network is uninitialized, individual mixes can be initialized with a uniform strategy (as above), or better a geometric one, e.g., add a dummy at level α with probability $2^{-(\alpha+1)}$. Dummy policy can then be periodically shifted to reflect the distribution of alphas for actual traffic through the mix. More research remains here to make this dummy approach resistant to an adversary who sends lots of messages with non-standard alphas into a particular mix to influence its view of a typical value for alpha.

If active attacks are suspected, the amount of dummy traffic added to the alpha stack can be increased according to the expected duration of and strength of the blocking (assuming timed deterministic-alpha mixes, for which there is no point in flooding) and the anonymity one intends to maintain for messages so attacked.

The easiest way to disguise dummies from others in the network is to route them in a circuit leading back to the mix that generates them [6]. The length of the path should be randomly chosen as suggested in [14]. Obviously the alphas chosen for the dummy message at other mixes in the path should be distributed to minimize recognition of the message as a dummy; hence some dummies should follow an alpha pattern as if they had entered the network at that mix and others should appear to be in mid path as they emerge from the mix (cf. Section 3).

5   Strategic Choice of Alpha

As observed in Section 2.1, the anonymity of any message can be improved by greater uncertainty about the alpha level of *other* messages. Since Alice benefits from the fact that other people might choose non-zero α for their messages, she has an incentive to take advantage of this by choosing a lower α to get better performance but still have good security. This can be viewed as a commons: everybody will hope that somebody else takes the latency hit.

There are two ways to resolve this risk. First, note that not all users have the same sensitivity level: some users favor performance and others favor anonymity. Three factors are most important in characterizing the utility function for our users: their need for anonymity, their willingness to accept delay, and their guess at (expectation of) the current alpha levels in the network. In [2] it was shown that there can be optimal levels of free riding: more-sensitive users have incentive to provide "free" communications service for less-sensitive users by running network nodes because this will still provide additional value in the form of better anonymity protection for the more-sensitive users. This can provide adequate incentive even if there are many others running nodes. Similarly, while the existence of higher α traffic may reduce Alice's incentive to set higher α levels for her own traffic, it does not eliminate that incentive.

Second, when Alice chooses her alphas' range based on her sensitivity and timeliness constraints for her own messages, she gets increased autonomy and control over her own security and utility. Indeed, if an adversary can make reasonable guesses about a choice of alpha range for a message, then much higher or much lower alphas for other messages in a mix might actually decrease the anonymity set for a target message. For example, consider a mix containing a target message with low alpha and an ancillary message that is either from about the same alpha range or from a much larger alpha range than the target message. If the adversary learns that the second message has a larger range, then his uncertainty about the target message decreases.

Even more significantly, however, security is hard to get right when it doesn't depend on the strategic behavior of others. Users of the system are not likely to have such fine-tuned knowledge of the system, the behavior of others, and their own needs. Thus if we can prescribe recommendations for choice of alpha, for example based on analysis and observed patterns within the network, we can expect most people to heed them. (On the other hand, they may not — we can also expect hyperbolic discounting of risk, disregard of risk for expedience, etc. [1].)

Alpha mixing itself is likely to affect the applications that can be securely used and how, so recommendations are likely to evolve. Initial recommendations can be guided by existing anonymity networks. Traffic that must arrive in realtime obviously must have $\sum \alpha = 0$. For more sensitive traffic, we might initially try to follow networks such as Mixminion and Mixmaster. But how can we do that? These use a dynamic batching strategy in which messages are chosen for the current batch randomly by the mix from a collective pool, while alpha mixing is based on individual choices made by the sender. We now turn to various generalizations on the basic deterministic-alpha mix design, including ways to combine these features.

6 Beta Alpha: Variations on Alpha Mixing

In the previous sections, we investigated and analysed some basic alpha mixing designs and the incentive questions and attacks that arise from them. In this section we introduce and briefly discuss some more complex designs that are harder to analyse fully but may provide better protection against stronger attacks.

6.1 Preventing End-to-End Timing Attacks on Alpha Mixnets

The prior work that is probably most similar to alpha mixing is stop-and-go mixing [12]. In stop-and-go mixing, the sender gives to each mix in the path a time interval. If the message arrives within the interval, it is sent at the end of the interval, otherwise it is discarded. This approach is similar to the timed deterministic-alpha mix described above, but an important difference is that a stop-and-go mixnet must be entirely synchronized to prevent losing messages. Alpha mixes offer predictable delivery times, but will still mix and deliver messages even if some nodes in the path are not adequately synchronized. On the other hand, this flexibility is also a flaw: an adversary that is global-passive except for being able to delay messages from a single sender could batch up a victim's messages and send them through an alpha mixnet all at once. Unless all the messages have $\sum \alpha = 0$ the adversary will gain limited information from this attack, but he can still learn more than from a stop-and-go mixnet.

We could include timestamps along with the α that each mix receives, and require that the message be dropped if it arrives more than some delta from the timestamp. This would make timed alpha mixes essentially equivalent to stop-and-go mixes, which might prove useful against timing correlations by such an adversary. For example, Alice might send one hundred messages to Bob that are sensitive so each has $\sum \alpha^{(i)}$ chosen uniformly at random from a range of 0 to 10. An adversary that can block all messages from Alice during this period and send them into the network will see approximately ten messages delivered to Bob immediately followed by approximately ten messages in each of the next nine time intervals. However, we need not resort to assuming a synchronized network. Instead of including any timestamps, Alice could choose $\sum \alpha^{(i)}$ from some private distribution on a private range (not necessarily including 0). This would (1) prevent such an attack if the adversary cannot predict her distribution, (2) still have as much predictability on delivery time as stop-and-go mixes, and (3) unlike stop-and-go, still allow eventual delivery of all messages (unless they're dropped by the attacker). We are not primarily focused in this paper on end-to-end timing attacks, and we will say no more about them.

6.2   Variations on Deterministic-Alpha Mixing

In the basic threshold deterministic-alpha mix, if there are *threshold* $= n$ messages in each of alpha levels 0 through ℓ, all of the messages in levels 0 through ℓ will be sent at once; however, messages from the different levels will not be mixed together. The mix will send all messages with $\alpha = 0$, lower the stack, send the next batch of messages that now have $\alpha = 0$, etc. An adversary may not know exactly where level i ends and level $i + 1$ begins because there may be more than n messages in a given level, but if more than n messages emerge he can know that the last messages to emerge were considered more sensitive by their senders than the first, in a stepped linear order of sensitivity. And by sending in messages of his own at known alpha levels above 0 the adversary can learn the exact levels of the messages that emerge between his messages. Then, by flooding first $\alpha = \ell$, then $\alpha = \ell - 1$, ..., then $\alpha = 0$, the adversary can guarantee a flush of the mix all the way up to $\alpha = \ell$ while also learning the alpha level of most of the messages.

The simplest solution is simply to mix all messages that emerge at once. This will prevent an adversary from watching the order in which messages exit during a flush and thus learning about their sensitivity. The stronger attack we worry about is the blending attack: an adversary emptying the mix of all messages up to the highest reasonably expected level, trickling in a message, then flooding with $\alpha = 0$ messages repeatedly to learn the sensitivity of that message and its next destination. Batching all outgoing messages together, combined with the dummy schemes presented in Section 4, would substantially reduce the risk from blending.

We could also use a threshold-and-timed mix, which would prevent the adversary from triggering an alpha-stack dump because only messages of one alpha level will emerge in each time interval. It is unclear what the local advantage is of this vs. the above multilevel-batching threshold mix. In addition, having threshold-and-timed batching would preclude the predictability advantages of timed mixes while the multilevel-batching approach could potentially offer faster performance. The primary risk of not having timing limitations on mix firing is the end-to-end effects that the adversary could induce by flooding, which would not be countered by our dummy scheme. However, that assumes a powerful adversary that can flood and watch the entire network. The nice thing about alpha mixing is that we can still have both good realtime properties and threshold protections together.

There are various ways to have realtime and threshold properties together in one mix design. We note two of them next.

6.3 Dynamic-Alpha Mixing

In this design, alphas are assigned to messages as they have been all along, except instead of deterministically decreasing by one after each mix firing, there is a probabilistic function f that dictates how they decrement:

$$\alpha_{M,i+1} = f(\alpha_{M,i}, Pool(\alpha_{M,i})) \text{ where}$$
$$Pool(\alpha_{M,i}) = |\{M' : 1 \le \alpha_{M',i-1} \le \alpha_{M,i-1}\}|$$

We believe that f would typically be monotonically nonincreasing. The sender gives f_M to a mix along with α_M. We would expect that there be some small number of easy-to-compute fs that can be chosen. The idea is that alphas decrease but only as a function of the current alpha level of the message and how many messages are in the pool below it. We have also limited the input of f to messages that arrived with a non-zero alpha, although this is not necessary. This effectively puts each message in a dynamic pool, which could also be timed.

6.4 Tau Mixing

We have been describing alpha all along as a level which determines a batch of messages that a given message will be sent with, after (or possibly also together with) the messages in the alpha levels that are below it in the stack. This lends itself naturally to the batching concept familiar in the mix literature. Intuitively, threshold batching implies unpredictable delays since we don't know how long it will take for a threshold number of messages to accumulate at $\alpha = 0$. Timed mixing on the other hand will allow a predictable delay by providing an upper bound on latency. But because timed mixing also provides a *lower* bound on latency, threshold batching can be faster because it can allow messages to be processed as quickly as they arrive, provided the batch size does not get in the way.

   This is the idea behind tau mixing: a message M arrives at a mix with an associated threshold τ_M of how many other messages must be sent by the mix between the arrival and sending of M. Multiple messages that have the same tau can be sent together after mixing, e.g., three messages that arrive with $\tau = 2$ are sent together. Messages that are to be sent as quickly as possible are assigned $\tau_M = 0$. This can provide realtime properties limited only by the processing speed of the network components. For example, if a message with $\tau = 0$ arrives at a mix containing messages with current $\tau = 1$, $\tau = 2$, and $\tau = 3$, the latter three should be mixed and sent together after sending the former. (We assume messages with initial $\tau = 0$ should always be sent as quickly as they arrive without the delay associated with mixing.) Messages that are more sensitive should be assigned a $\sum \tau_M^{(i)}$ from a private distribution on a range that increases with sensitivity. Many of the same features of alpha mixing apply, including the dummy strategy discussion, the techniques for allocating $\sum \tau$ across the mixes in the path, and so on.

If taus are purely threshold values, then an adversary that is powerful enough to perform a sustained flush of the entire network will be able to conduct end-to-end timing correlations on more sensitive messages (assuming we stick to a purely internally routed dummy scheme). To address this attack, both a threshold and a random minimum delay at each mix can be given as security parameter. This will prevent effective flushing unless the adversary can also perform sustained blocking of all inputs to the mixnet, and even then the attack will be substantially slowed.

7   Conclusion

In this paper we have presented a mixing technique that works together with traditional batching strategies to allow senders with varying anonymity and performance goals to share the same network and have their traffic mixed. Aside from simply letting high-sensitivity users choose to get higher anonymity for their messages, the key property it provides is a network effect: when *some* users ask for higher anonymity, *all* users can benefit.

While we proved anonymity properties for the simplest versions of alpha mixing, we have only begun to explore the possibilities and analysis of this design. Future work includes:

Multiple messages and stream-based communication: This paper has assumed the *single-message model*, where each sender produces individual uncorrelated messages. We did describe countermeasures to end-to-end timing correlations in Section 6; however, we have not carefully examined the implications of stream-based communication. Much of the reason for the success of Tor and JAP is not just the low overhead, but rather their support for bidirectional streams. But the *stream model* introduces many end-to-end anonymity attacks that seem hard to resolve simply with better batching strategies.

A full analysis of the alpha mix design: In this paper we have added to mixes an additional user-defined security parameter and explored some scenarios of attacker's knowledge about it. However, the more complex dynamic-alpha mixes and tau mixes are yet to be analysed; this seems difficult as we need to make some assumptions both about how users choose their security parameters and what the attacker knows about them.

User behavior: However much we postulate about how users behave, there is no substitute for actually getting user profiles and learning how to create incentives for secure behavior. We expect that unless we protect our users, they will try to condition their security parameter on the threat level of the message; as we have seen above this reduces rather than increases anonymity.

References

1. Alessandro Acquisti. Privacy in electronic commerce and the economics of immediate gratification. In *ACM Conference on Electronic Commerce*, pages 21–29, 2004.
2. Alessandro Acquisti, Roger Dingledine, and Paul Syverson. On the economics of anonymity. In Rebecca N. Wright, editor, *Financial Cryptography*. Springer-Verlag, LNCS 2742, Jan 2003.
3. Oliver Berthold, Hannes Federrath, and Stefan Köpsell. Web MIXes: A system for anonymous and unobservable Internet access. In H. Federrath, editor, *Designing Privacy Enhancing Technologies: Workshop on Design Issue in Anonymity and Unobservability*, pages 115–129. Springer-Verlag, LNCS 2009, 2000.
4. George Danezis. Statistical disclosure attacks: Traffic confirmation in open environments. In Gritzalis, Vimercati, Samarati, and Katsikas, editors, *Proceedings of Security and Privacy in the Age of Uncertainty, (SEC2003)*, pages 421–426, Athens, May 2003. IFIP TC11, Kluwer.
5. George Danezis, Roger Dingledine, and Nick Mathewson. Mixminion: Design of a type III anonymous remailer protocol. In *2003 IEEE Symposium on Security and Privacy*, pages 2–15. IEEE CS, May 2003.
6. George Danezis and Len Sassaman. Heartbeat traffic to counter (n-1) attacks. In *Proceedings of the Workshop on Privacy in the Electronic Society (WPES 2003)*, Washington, DC, USA, October 2003.
7. Luc Devroye. *Non-Uniform Random Variate Generation*. Springer-Verlag, 1986. Available from: ⟨http://cgm.cs.mcgill.ca/~luc/rnbookindex.html⟩.
8. Claudia Díaz, Len Sassaman, and Evelyne Dewitte. Comparison between two practical mix designs. In *Proceedings of ESORICS 2004*, LNCS, France, September 2004.
9. Claudia Díaz and Andrei Serjantov. Generalising mixes. In Roger Dingledine, editor, *Proceedings of the Privacy Enhancing Technologies workshop (PET 2003)*. Springer-Verlag, LNCS 2760, March 2003.
10. Roger Dingledine and Nick Mathewson. Anonymity loves company: Usability and the network effect. In *Proceedings of Workshop on Economics and Information Security (WEIS06)*, June 2006.
11. Roger Dingledine, Nick Mathewson, and Paul Syverson. Tor: The Second-Generation Onion Router. In *Proceedings of the 13th USENIX Security Symposium*, Aug 2004.
12. Dogan Kesdogan, Jan Egner, and Roland Büschkes. Stop-and-go MIXes: Providing probabilistic anonymity in an open system. In David Aucsmith, editor, *Proceedings of Information Hiding Workshop (IH 1998)*. Springer-Verlag, LNCS 1525, 1998.
13. Nick Mathewson and Roger Dingledine. Practical traffic analysis: Extending and resisting statistical disclosure. In *Proceedings of Privacy Enhancing Technologies workshop (PET 2004)*, volume 3424 of *LNCS*, May 2004.
14. Andrei Serjantov, Roger Dingledine, and Paul Syverson. From a trickle to a flood: Active attacks on several mix types. In F. Petitcolas, editor, *Proceedings of Information Hiding Workshop (IH 2002)*. Springer-Verlag, LNCS 2578, October 2002.
15. Andrei Serjantov and Steven J. Murdoch. Message splitting against the partial adversary. In George Danezis and David Martin, editors, *Proceedings of Privacy Enhancing Technologies workshop (PET 2005)*. Springer-Verlag, May 2005.

Private Resource Pairing

Joseph A. Calandrino* and Alfred C. Weaver

University of Virginia
Charlottesville, Virginia
{jac4dt, acw}@cs.virginia.edu

Abstract. Protection of information confidentiality can result in obstruction of legitimate access to necessary resources. This paper explores the problem of pairing resource requestors and providers such that neither must sacrifice privacy. While solutions to similar problems exist, these solutions are inadequate or inefficient in the context of private resource pairing. This work explores private resource-pairing solutions under two models of participant behavior: honest-but-curious behavior and potentially malicious behavior. Without compromising security, the foundation of these solutions demonstrates significant performance benefits over a popular solution to the similar private matching problem.

1 Introduction

In privacy-critical scenarios, the need to protect information confidentiality can impede valid resource requests. Resource providers may refuse to even confirm possession of a resource to requestors that have not demonstrated a need to access the resource. Such a scenario would force requestors to first reveal their queries accompanied by justifications. As a request query alone may contain or imply confidential data, requestors need some assurance that a provider can satisfy a request before revelation of the request. If both entities refuse to compromise privacy, a reasonable request could go unfulfilled. Private resource pairing links resource providers and legitimate requestors while preserving privacy.

Several recent papers have explored the similar private matching problem, in which operators of two separate databases wish to establish common entries without revealing non-matching elements [2,8,11,12]. By treating request queries as single-entry databases and forcing providers to maintain databases of resource metadata, existing solutions to the private matching problem can, with minor modification, solve the private resource-pairing problem for honest-but-curious

---

* This research was partially performed under an appointment to the Department of Homeland Security (DHS) Scholarship and Fellowship Program, administered by the Oak Ridge Institute for Science and Education (ORISE) through an interagency agreement between the U.S. Department of Energy (DOE) and DHS. ORISE is managed by Oak Ridge Associated Universities (ORAU) under DOE contract number DE-AC05-06OR23100. All opinions expressed in this paper are the author's and do not necessarily reflect the policies and views of DHS, DOE, or ORAU/ORISE.

G. Danezis and P. Golle (Eds.): PET 2006, LNCS 4258, pp. 258–276, 2006.

participants. This paper presents schemes with two primary advantages over such a solution:

- Efficiency: The unique constraints of private resource pairing allow the use of pre-computation and other techniques that significantly decrease the computational costs of searches over a popular private matching solution.
- Security: While a private matching solution exists that prevents participant dishonesty [12], its technique is incompatible with private resource pairing. This paper proposes several methods for thwarting dishonest behavior.

1.1 Motivating Scenarios

Under a number of circumstances, a solution to the private resource-pairing problem would allow organizations to come closer to the ideal of precisely pairing entities with needed resources. Two such scenarios arise in the medical and national intelligence domains.

Medical Scenario. Suppose that an incapacitated tourist with no identification arrives at a hospital in the United States. The safety of any treatment for the patient's condition is highly dependent upon her medical history. In addition, the patient's condition, while serious, will not dramatically deteriorate during the time a doctor would require to review the patient's record. Further, assume that some biometric or combination of biometrics could allow unique, perfectly reproducible identification of any human. Prior to administering treatment, the hospital may wish to use the patient's biometric to make an emergency request for relevant records from all health centers in the country or a particular region.

In the United States, no centralized repository exists for medical records, and security and medical data ownership issues presently preclude the use of such a repository [18]. Therefore, a searching party would need to approach numerous medical centers and inquire as to whether those centers possess records related to the patient. Given a reasonable alternative, most people would prefer not to disclose their hospital visits to unnecessary parties. To comply with federal medical privacy standards, health centers are also unlikely to disclose lists of their patients [14]. In this scenario, a system for privately pairing record requestors and possessors would be desirable to protect patient privacy. Such a system must enforce requestor need to know and prevent provider forgery of record possession.

National Intelligence Scenario. Presume that a security analyst determines that a particular landmark may be at risk. Numerous agencies may possess data related to the landmark or threat. To protect information confidentiality, agencies may have strict policies against revealing even metadata pertaining to resources they possess. For example, an agency may have records of related threats but wish to appear unaware of the threats by restricting access to both the records and data regarding the records. Similarly, the analyst may be reluctant to reveal the metadata that interests her. In this scenario, necessary privacy hampers necessary availability. A private pairing method would be desirable to link the analyst with resources essential to assess and respond to the threat.

1.2   Paper Overview

The remainder of this paper is organized as follows. Section 2 presents existing work related to private resource pairing. Section 3 sets forth security goals. Section 4 provides a system for privately pairing resource requestors and providers given that entities are honest but curious. Section 5 suggests extensions to the system to prevent malicious behavior. Section 6 evaluates the theoretical cost, applied performance, and security of the honest but curious protocol as compared to a private matching solution. Finally, section 7 presents a summary and recommendations for future work.

Throughout this paper, assume that all sets are totally ordered, are transmitted in order, and are initially ordered by element insertion time.

2   Related Work

2.1   Private Matching

In 2003, Agrawal, Evfimievski, and Srikant presented the notion of minimal information sharing across private databases [2]. Their paper establishes protocols to allow two entities maintaining separate databases to determine query results across both databases without revealing information beyond the result or requiring a trusted third party. Agrawal et al. address the intersection query problem, also known as the private matching problem, and several other query types. Assuming Alice wishes to learn the intersection between her and Bob's databases, the Agrawal, Evfimievski, and Srikant private matching solution (AgES) is:

1. Alice and Bob agree on a commutative encryption function, f, and select appropriate secret keys, $e_A, e_B \in keyF$. Note that, for commutative encryption, $f_{e_A}(f_{e_B}(x)) = f_{e_B}(f_{e_A}(x))$ given $x \in domF$ and $e_A, e_B \in keyF$.
2. Alice and Bob, using a common one-way collision resistant hash function [11] from $domD$ (the domain of potential database entries) to $domF$, hash all entries in their databases: $A_h = \{h(a) | a \in A\}$ and $B_h = \{h(b) | b \in B\}$.
3. Alice and Bob encrypt the elements in A_h and B_h, producing $A_{e_A} = \{f_{e_A}(a_h) | a_h \in A_h\}$ and $B_{e_B} = \{f_{e_B}(b_h) | b_h \in B_h\}$ then reorder A_{e_h} and B_{e_h} lexicographically. Alice maintains the dataset $\{(a, f_{e_A}(h(a))) | a \in A\}$.
4. Alice and Bob exchange A_{e_A} and B_{e_B}.
5. Alice computes $B_{e_B, e_A} = \{f_{e_A}(b_{e_B}) | b_{e_B} \in B_{e_B}\} = \{f_{e_A}(f_{e_B}(b_h)) | b_h \in B_h\}$. Bob computes $A_{e_A, e_B} = \{f_{e_B}(a_{e_A}) | a_{e_A} \in A_{e_A}\} \; (= \{f_{e_A}(f_{e_B}(a_h)) | a_h \in A_h\})$ and uses the result to create the set $\{(f_{e_A}(a_h), f_{e_A}(f_{e_B}(a_h))) | a_h \in A_h\}$.
6. Bob returns $\{(f_{e_A}(a_h), f_{e_A}(f_{e_B}(a_h))) | a_h \in A_h\}$ to Alice.

7. Alice joins $\{(a, f_{e_A}(h(a)))|a \in A\}$ and $\{(f_{e_A}(a_h), f_{e_A}(f_{e_B}(a_h)))|a_h \in A_h\}$ on $f_{e_A}(h(a))$ to get $\{(a, f_{e_A}(f_{e_B}(h(a))))|a \in A\}$.

8. Alice extracts all $a \in A$ such that the corresponding $f_{e_A}(f_{e_B}(a))$ matches some value in B_{e_B, e_A}. These values comprise the intersection of A and B.

Agrawal et al. demonstrate the computation and communication benefits of their protocol over a solution using circuit-based protocols.

AgES assumes semi-honest, or honest-but-curious, behavior of protocol participants. This means that entities adhere to the protocol but may analyze data to derive additional information [2,9]. For example, neither Alice nor Bob will falsely claim element possession, but Alice may perform cryptanalysis on B_{e_B}. Entities may demonstrate semi-honesty at minimum to protect their reputations, but a lack of protection measures is often inadequate. Entities may even prefer protocols in which they cannot lie to prevent false accusations of impropriety.

Li, Tygar, and Hellerstein explore private matching solutions under semi-honest and malicious models [12]. A malicious model assumes that entities may lie or deviate arbitrarily from the protocol. To prevent bogus possession claims, Li et al. propose data ownership certificates (DOCs). DOCs are not directly applicable to private resource pairing, however. A requestor may not possess a desired resource, so the requestor may not have its metadata's DOCs. Both entities must have DOCs to verify each other's[1]. While this property is desirable for private matching, an alternate solution is necessary for private resource pairing.

Li et al. present a hash-based alternative to AgES, but this alternative fails to ensure privacy without DOCs. Assume Alice and Bob agree on a hash function and trade hashed items. From that point on, Alice can guess and check for any item she desires, regardless of whether she possesses that item, in Bob's set.

Freedman, Nissim, and Pinkas as well as Kissner and Song have proposed private matching protocols based on homomorphic encryption [8,11]. Future research may wish to explore private resource pairing using homomorphic encryption. Note that the notion of malicious behavior in [8] and [11] differs from that of [12] and this paper, which consider *ownership* of data. For example, assume that businesses have databases of customers indexed by unique consumer identifiers. If the space of identifiers is small, a business may falsely claim all consumers as customers. Ownership mechanisms can expose or prevent dishonesty.

2.2   Additional Work

Private information retrieval (PIR) allows parties to retrieve database entries without disclosing which entries they desire [7]. Unfortunately, PIR offers no

---

[1] For the certified hash and certified AgES protocols in [12], Bob provides Alice with $\sigma = \{b||B\}_{sk}$ for each value b he possesses, where B is a unique id for Bob. Alice must possess pk to verify σ (the verification method is VERIFY($pk, b||B, \sigma$)). If everyone knew pk, the only unknown is b. If b's domain is small and Bob is honest, Alice could mount a brute force attack, running VERIFY for all possible values of b for the σ value until VERIFY returns true. When VERIFY returns true, Alice can be confident that she found the entry in Bob's database corresponding to the σ value. Repeating this process for all of Bob's σ values yields all values in Bob's database.

assurance that parties need the data they retrieve. Nonetheless, an efficient PIR implementation would be useful to this paper's solutions (see sections 4 and 5).

Waters, Balfanz, Durfee, and Smetters present a method to allow searches on encrypted audit logs [21]. The scheme could protect provider privacy and enforce need to know for resource requestors. Requestors would need to reveal potentially confidential search strings to a third party, however.

Song, Wagner, and Perrig present a means of searching on encrypted data [20]. Their work allows the use of encrypted queries to search encrypted data on untrusted servers. Unfortunately, to make an encrypted query, the entity that encrypted the data (or a third party) must learn the query. For private pairing, providers would learn requestors' searches.

Zero-knowledge proofs allow a prover to demonstrate possession of a piece of information to a verifier without revealing the information. For example, a prover could demonstrate possession of Alice's unique identity-confirming key without revealing the key itself [17]. Unfortunately, a verifier must know the precise information for which a prover will seek to demonstrate possession, even if the information itself can remain private. For example, a verifier must know that the prover is demonstrating possession of Alice's key. Thus, such proofs would require one party to publicly reveal its requests or possessions.

3   Security Criteria

Li et al. [12] offer three goals for assessing the security of private matching solutions under semi-honest and malicious scenarios. This paper adopts two of the goals (the third is not applicable): (1) the protocol leaks no information beyond input size and (2) participants cannot lie regarding element possession. If parties cannot lie regarding possession, AgES leaks no information even in a malicious scenario [12]. Any protocol trivially prevents lying in a semi-honest scenario. Note that Li et al. do not address lying via omission. Allowance of nondisclosure may be desirable, so this paper presents a compromise: individuals can check that their resources are available (see section 5.2). With several exceptions (see section 4.2), [12] and this paper allow collusion.

Devious parties may mount other attacks, such as denial-of-service attacks against protocol participants. While more efficient solutions may be more resistant to some attacks, this paper does not explicitly consider these threats.

4   Semi-honest Case Solution

This paper first presents a protocol for private resource pairing under a semi-honest behavior model. Section 5 presents extensions to the semi-honest protocol to allow enforcement of need to know and proof of resource possession.

4.1   Basic Scheme

A one-time setup process is necessary for participants in this private resource pairing protocol. Resource requestors and providers, which may be overlapping sets, agree on a common commutative encryption scheme and hash function. Providers choose random encryption keys and hash then encrypt metadata pertaining to their resources. Finally, providers publish the encryptions to potential requestors directly or to host servers. By maintaining constant keys and publishing encryptions a single time, providers can efficiently handle searches later.

When a requestor wishes to search for and acquire resources tagged with a given piece of metadata, it chooses a random encryption/decryption key pair and hashes then encrypts the metadata. The requestor gives the ciphertext to the provider, who encrypts the ciphertext again using its key and returns the result. The requestor decrypts the ciphertext and matches the result to provider-published records. If the requestor finds a match, it approaches the provider and requests resources related to the metadata. By decrypting a single item of metadata rather than re-encrypting every published piece of metadata, requestors decrease their computation. A more rigorous explanation follows shortly.

4.2 Assumptions

This protocol makes several assumptions. First, a requestor's identity alone must imply nothing confidential to providers or servers. Second, providers must publish encrypted metadata all at once (i.e., provider metadata must not change frequently), or others must be unable to draw undesirable conclusions from metadata publication order, modification, or removal. If providers use host servers, requestors must download all data from a given server. Otherwise, a server could infer whether and on what encrypted value a search is satisfied even if the underlying metadata is unknown. Private information retrieval may be unreasonable: even a search over sorted data will require $\log n$ values. Also, servers must be unable to collude to determine which servers a requestor checks. If servers colluded, they could identify the provider that satisfied a request or infer that a request went unsatisfied. Finally, this paper assumes that metadata is not fuzzy.

4.3 Detailed Process

This paper's protocol for private resource pairing under the semi-honest model (henceforth shPRP) requires separate setup and search processes.

Setup. The setup process for a resource provider, P, with resource metadata $M_P \subseteq M$, where M is the set of all possible metadata, is:

1. P, all other providers, and all potential requestors agree on a commutative encryption function, f, and a common one-way collision resistant hash function, h, that maps from $dom M$ to $dom F$.
2. P selects a random encryption key, e_P, such that $e_P \in key F$.
3. P computes hashes of its resource metadata: $P_h = \{h(m_P)|m_P \in M_P\}$.
4. P encrypts the elements in P_h, producing $P_{e_P} = \{f_{e_P}(p_h)|p_h \in P_h\}$.

5. P reorders P_{e_P} lexicographically if others could infer private information from M_P's order.
6. P publishes P_{e_P} to potential requestors, host servers, or both.

If an escrow service is desirable, P may provide e_P, the related decryption key, or both to the service. If P publishes metadata to host servers, P must choose a signature scheme and accompany each published item with a signature.

Search and Acquisition. The following process allows a resource requestor, R, to obtain access to P's resources with metadata m:

1. R generates a random encryption key, $e_R \in keyF$, and the corresponding decryption key, d_R.
   - R must generate a new random key pair each time it enters the search process. If R reuses a key, providers could determine whether R previously sought the same value, even if they cannot identity the value.
   - If R is also a provider, R must not use its provider key. Otherwise, R's published data would reveal whether R already possesses resources with the metadata it seeks.
2. R computes the hash of m: $m_h = h(m)$.
3. R encrypts m_h: $m_{e_R} = f_{e_R}(m_h)$.
4. R presents m_{e_R} to P.
5. P encrypts m_{e_R}: $m_{e_R,e_P} = f_{e_P}(m_{e_R}) = f_{e_P}(f_{e_R}(m_h)) = f_{e_R}(f_{e_P}(m_h))$.
6. P returns m_{e_R,e_P} to R.
7. R decrypts m_{e_R,e_P}: $m_{e_P} = f_{d_R}(m_{e_R,e_P}) = f_{e_P}(m_h)$.
8. If P hosts its data on a server, R downloads P_{e_P}, the accompanying signatures, and any items necessary to verify P's signatures (public key, etc.).
9. R searches P_{e_P} for a match to m_{e_P}.
   - If R finds a match and P_{e_P} is from a server, R may verify the corresponding signature.
   - If R finds no match and P_{e_P} is from a server, R may verify signatures to ensure that the server did not remove data.
10. If R finds a match, R asks P for resources with metadata m.

5   Malicious Case Extensions

As section 6.3 argues, shPRP does not leak information even under a malicious model. Therefore, malicious case extensions must protect against two forms of potential participant dishonesty without leaking information. First, dishonest requestors could request either metadata searches for or direct access to resources for which they have no valid need. Providers can eliminate this issue by forcing requestors to prove their need to search for metadata and access resources. Second, dishonest providers could falsely claim possession of resources to coax requestors to reveal secret search metadata. By forcing providers to prove possession of resources related to metadata, the protocol can prevent this issue. This section considers a number of possible scenarios and, for completeness, offers solutions under each scenario. Under several scenarios, the solution uses a trusted external party, which future work may be able to eliminate.

Note that the modified protocol retains all assumptions of section 4.2.

5.1   Proving Need to Know

To prevent superfluous searches and resource accesses, resource providers must have the ability to verify the legitimacy of requests. To demonstrate the need to perform a search or to access a given resource, requestors present tickets to potential providers in steps four and ten of the shPRP search and acquisition process (see section 4.3). In step four, the ticket only verifies the right to search for the encrypted metadata, m_{e_R}; it does not reveal the metadata. In step ten, the ticket contains plaintext metadata, since the provider cannot confirm that m_{e_R} represents m. Note that, to generate tickets containing m_{e_R} and m, the ticket supplier must receive both items and verify that m_{e_R} represents m.

The process by which a requestor, R, may acquire tickets from a supplier, S, is as follows (the order of steps two and three is arbitrary):

1. R presents m and m_{e_R} to S.
2. S verifies that m_{e_R} represents m:
   (a) S generates a random encryption key, $e_S \in keyF$ for the common requestor/provider commutative encryption function.
   (b) Using the common hash function, S computes the hash of m: $m_h = h(m)$.
   (c) S encrypts m_h: $m_{e_S} = f_{e_S}(m_h)$.
   (d) S presents m_{e_S} to R.
   (e) R encrypts m_{e_S}: $m_{e_S,e_R} = f_{e_R}(m_{e_S}) = f_{e_R}(f_{e_S}(m_h)) = f_{e_S}(f_{e_R}(m_h))$.
   (f) R returns m_{e_S,e_R} to S.
   (g) S encrypts m_{e_R}: $m_{e_R,e_S} = f_{e_S}(m_{e_R})$ $(= f_{e_S}(f_{e_R}(m_h))$ if m_{e_R} is valid).
   (h) S checks that m_{e_S,e_R} matches m_{e_R,e_S}.
3. S verifies R's right to search for and acquire resources with metadata m (implementation specific verification process).
4. S returns tickets for m and m_{e_R}.

Tickets can be universal or restricted to a subset of potential providers if circumstances warrant only a limited search. A network of trust must connect ticket suppliers so providers can confirm the validity of any ticket. Various models exist for establishing trust, such as direct and distributed trust models [13]. This choice is implementation-specific; the use of any model is acceptable.

Two ticket supplier models exist: internal and external. Both models assume that ticket suppliers cannot initiate searches and will not collude with malicious requestors to allow illicit access to data or resources.

An internal supplier model assumes that potential requestors are part of larger organizations and that they may reveal searches to ticket-granting parties in their organizations. The ticket-granting party verifies that present conditions warrant a search. In the medical scenario, a set of trained hospital administrators could be on-call for search verification. When a doctor explains the situation, the verifier can determine, based on established standards, whether the situation warrants a search. If the verifier concludes that it does, she can provide the doctor with appropriately constrained tickets. This solution presumes the existence of robust audit mechanisms and severe penalties to deter and detect collusion.

In the event that no impartial party exists inside a requestor's organization, requestors and providers could form agreements, contractual or otherwise, with trusted external parties to verify the need to search. In this case, requestors must also trust the verification party with their search metadata. External verification is appropriate and perhaps necessary for cases such as business agreements in which parties agree to limited, circumstance-dependent resource sharing. Members of either business may possess bias in interpretation of the agreement, creating the possible need for an impartial arbitrator.

5.2   Proving Resource Possession

As with proving need to know, this section presents two models for proving resource possession. In one model, metadata implies an obvious owner of all associated resources. For example, a patient with a unique biometric could have legal control over medical records tied to her biometric [14], making her the effective owner of the records. Under the second model, metadata either does not imply an owner or implies numerous owners. For example, "explosives" may be applicable to many intelligence resources, but the word does not imply an owner of those resources. A solution under the second model is also applicable to the first, since entities can ignore implied ownership. A solution for the first scenario is preferable when possible, however, as it allows owners to better control their resources. In both cases, solutions rely on identity-based signatures.

Identity-Based Signatures. Identity-based cryptosystems and signature schemes, first proposed by Shamir, allow the use of one's identity as its public key [19]. For example, Alice may sign her messages using a private key associated with her unique identity ("alice@petworkshop.org"). To verify her signature, Bob can simply pass the message, the signature, a master public key, public parameters, and "alice@petworkshop.org" to a verification method. Bob does not need to acquire Alice's public key to verify her signatures. Alice needs to obtain her private key from a private key generator, however, unless she possesses the system's master secret, which allows the generation of private keys for all identities. Shamir presented the first identity-based signature (IBS) scheme in [19].

Key Privacy, IBC Privacy, and IBS Privacy. Bellare, Boldyreva, Desai, and Pointcheval [3] first formalized the property of key privacy in public-key cryptosystems. Given this property, an adversary that possesses a piece of ciphertext cannot gain a non-negligible advantage in determining which public key out of a given set produced the ciphertext. For example, RSA lacks key privacy because an adversary can gain an advantage based on the public modulus [3].

Calandrino and Weaver [6] extend the notion of key privacy to multiple identity-based cryptosystem instantiations. If a cryptosystem possesses IBC privacy, an adversary can gain no more than a negligible advantage in determining which instantiation produced a given piece of ciphertext. Instantiations may share common parameters if such a choice does not undermine security [6].

When metadata implies an owner, the possession scheme's security relies on IBS systems with a novel property called IBS privacy. Suppose that multiple instantiations of an IBS scheme exist. Instantiations may share some parameters but have unique master secrets, meaning that each instantiation produces a unique mapping between identities and private keys. Assume that an adversary chooses an identity, and an arbitrary instantiation produces the identity's signature of a nonce. The adversary receives the signature but not the nonce. If, for some parameters, no adversary can reliably determine the instantiation that produced the signature, the scheme provides IBS privacy under those parameters. Appendix A offers a more formal description.

Metadata Implies an Owner. Assume that metadata implies an owner of associated resources. To allow proof of resource possession, some setup is mandatory. Owners must agree on an IBS scheme and parameters necessary for IBS privacy. Each owner generates a unique instantiation of the scheme with the common parameters. Owners publish parameters needed to verify their signatures. Either requestors and providers or public repositories must maintain lists of owners' public parameters. If a repository maintains the data, private information retrieval or total repository downloads must be reasonable so repository operators cannot infer which owner's resources a requestor seeks. Given a large number of non-colluding servers, PIR may be feasible: requestors will seek a small amount of data at a predetermined index, the owner's identity.

To prove possession, additional steps are needed between steps four and five of the shPRP setup process (see section 4.3). For each metadata item $m_P \in M_P$:

1. P determines the owner, O, that m_P implies.
2. P presents m_P and the corresponding value $p_{e_P} \in P_{e_P}$ to O.
3. O verifies that p_{e_P} represents m_P:
   (a) O generates a random encryption key, $e_O \in keyF$ for the common requestor/provider commutative encryption function.
   (b) Using the common function, O computes the hash of m_P: $m_h = h(m_P)$.
   (c) O encrypts m_h: $m_{e_O} = f_{e_O}(m_h)$.
   (d) O presents m_{e_O} to P.
   (e) P encrypts m_{e_O}: $m_{e_O,e_P} = f_{e_P}(m_{e_O}) = f_{e_P}(f_{e_O}(m_h)) = f_{e_O}(f_{e_P}(m_h))$.
   (f) P returns m_{e_O,e_P} to O.
   (g) O encrypts p_{e_P}: $p_{e_P,e_O} = f_{e_O}(p_{e_P})$ $(= f_{e_O}(f_{e_P}(m_h))$ if p_{e_P} is valid).
   (h) O checks that p_{e_P,e_O} matches m_{e_O,e_P}.
4. O verifies that P possesses resources related to metadata m_P (implementation specific verification process).
5. O signs p_{e_P} using its IBS scheme instantiation and the private key associated with P's identity.
6. O returns the signature of p_{e_P} to P.
7. P downloads the public parameters for O's IBS scheme instantiation.
8. P verifies the signature of p_{e_P} using P's identity as the public key.

The order of steps three and four is arbitrary.

Signing with the private key associated with the provider's identity prevents two providers from using the same encryption keys and sharing signed values. Because values in P_{e_P} are polynomial-time indistinguishable from random values and owners use IBS private signature schemes, an adversary will have at most a negligible advantage in determining the owner behind any given signature.

Following acquisition of signatures, P can reorder them lexicographically and publish them. If P reordered by the original encryptions, adversaries could estimate the pre-signed data ranges and attempt to infer the signing instantiations.

If owners can privately retrieve server data, they can verify at any time that servers host their data to detect malicious data removal.

Because only an owner possesses its master secret, only it can produce its private keys and generate its signatures. Owners can delegate signing responsibilities to a trusted party and can provide master secrets to an escrow system. If one resource owner's master secret is compromised, only that owner's data is compromised. Generating a new master secret and replacing associated published signatures would be straightforward, but this procedure could be problematic if others could infer confidential information from updates. If an owner updates its parameters at nearly the same time a provider updates its published data, an adversary can infer that the provider's published metadata relates to the owner's resources. This paper leaves resolution of update issues to future work.

With two exceptions, the search process is the same for requestors as under shPRP. First, a requestor must obtain the owner's public parameters. Second, using the provider's identity as a public key, requestors must attempt to verify published values as the signature of m_{e_P} in step nine of the shPRP search process. If a value verifies, the provider possesses a desired resource.

In the medical scenario, patients could serve as owners of their medical records for the purpose of proving resource possession. When a patient receives medical care, she could provide her unique identifier to the medical center and authorize a delegated service to sign the encrypted hash of her identifier. If a hospital needs to retrieve the patient's records, it could use her identifier to retrieve the public parameters of her signature scheme instantiation and verify published signatures. Because medical centers would retain possession of records, such a system deliberately sidesteps disagreements over medical data ownership [18].

Metadata Does Not Imply an Owner. Assume that metadata does not imply a single owner of associated resources. Thus, no single party has a legitimate right to confirm or deny possession of resources associated with metadata. For requestors to accept possession claims, a trusted third party, centralized or distributed, seems necessary to validate provider possession based on established rules. Requestors can later verify possession without the third party, preventing the third party from collecting request data. The third party acts as a universal resource owner and maintains an identity-based signature system.

In this case, the publication process is the same as when metadata implies an owner, except the owner is always the trusted third party. The search and acquisition process is also the same, but requestors can store the single owner's parameters instead of retrieving parameters during each search. This scheme suffers from an issue common to identity-based cryptography: the key revocation problem. If any private key is compromised, the universal owner has two options:

- Publish a potentially huge exception list. In this case, the third party must maintain backup system(s) for the exceptions. Requestors would need to either store exception lists or have the ability to privately check the list.
- Change the master secret. This impractical option would entail reproducing all signatures. Gradual migration to a new master secret may be more reasonable. For example, if the key for "provider" is compromised, the party could immediately migrate all 'p' keys and gradually migrate other keys.

Fortunately, because the third party need not reveal or store private keys, private keys are nearly as difficult to compromise as the master secret.

6   Evaluation of shPRP

The AgES protocol offers the closest match to shPRP, making it the most logical comparison for theoretical cost, actual performance, and security. In a private resource-pairing scenario, AgES treats requestors as operators of one-entry databases containing the desired metadata. To fairly compare the protocols, several assumptions are necessary:

- Providers and requestors have settled on commutative encryption and hash functions prior to entering the protocol.
- Even if shPRP uses host servers, it does not create signatures. Signature costs would be dependent on implementation decisions.
- Once complete, AgES performs step ten of the shPRP search process.
- Providers publish lexicographically ordered encryptions.

shPRP has an inherent advantage over AgES because shPRP is a custom private resource-pairing solution. For example, the requirements of private matching prevent AgES's use of pre-computation. Nevertheless, as a leading private matching solution, AgES provides the most appropriate comparison.

6.1   Theoretical Costs

Assume that C_{g_e}, C_{g_d}, C_e, and C_d are the costs of generating public keys, generating private keys, encrypting, and decrypting for the chosen encryption scheme. C_h is the cost of hash computation with the chosen hash function. m and c are the metadata and metadata ciphertext lengths. A provider has p metadata items.

Under AgES, no setup procedure is necessary. For the search and acquisition process, the total computational cost is $2C_{g_e} + (C_h + 2C_e)(p+1) + p\log p + p$, while the communication cost is $(p+2)c + m$. Note that, with AgES, requestors and providers generate new private keys each time they enter the search and acquisition process. The setup process for shPRP has a total computational cost of $C_{g_e} + (C_h + C_e)p + p\log p$, while the communication cost is pc. The

Table 1. Computational cost comparison. See section 6.1 for variable definitions.

Setup		
	AgES	shPRP
Provider	-	$C_{g_e} + (C_h + C_e)p + p\log p$
Requestor	-	-
Total	-	$C_{g_e} + (C_h + C_e)p + p\log p$
Search and Acquisition		
	AgES	shPRP
Provider	$C_{g_e} + C_h p + C_e(p+1) + p\log p$	C_e
Requestor	$C_{g_e} + C_h + C_e(p+1) + p$	$C_{g_e} + C_{g_d} + C_h + C_e + C_d + \log p$
Total	$2C_{g_e} + (C_h + 2C_e)(p+1) + p\log p + p$	$C_{g_e} + C_{g_d} + C_h + 2C_e + C_d + \log p$

Table 2. Communication cost comparison. See section 6.1 for variable definitions.

	AgES	shPRP	
		w/ Host Server	w/o Host Server
Setup	-	pc	pc
Search and Acquisition	$(p+2)c + m$	$(p+2)c + m$	$2c + m$

computational cost for the search and acquisition process is $C_{g_e} + C_{g_d} + C_h + 2C_e + C_d + \log p$. If requestors download metadata from a server, the communication cost is $(p+2)c + m$. Otherwise, the communication cost is $2c + m$. Table 1 and Table 2 summarize these results in greater detail.

After the initial setup, shPRP significantly lightens the computational costs for requestors and providers while producing equivalent or better communication costs. Provider computational cost during the search and acquisition process is critical, as a reduction in cost allows providers to handle more requests per given time. The importance of reducing this cost underscores the value of performing pre-computation during the setup process. These theoretical results also suggest an improvement to the AgES private matching protocol. If, in the protocol of section 2.1, Alice has a smaller dataset than Bob and $C_e \approx C_d$, she should not encrypt Bob's set in step five. She should instead decrypt her $f_{e_A}(f_{e_B}(h(a)))$ values between steps seven and eight and match those against Bob's set.

6.2   Actual Performance

A series of tests compared the performance of AgES to shPRP. Java-based implementations of shPRP and portions of the AgES protocol allowed direct comparisons. SHA-1 and Pohlig-Hellman [15] with a common modulus served as the hash function and commutative encryption scheme respectively. The sorting algorithm was a modified mergesort with guaranteed $n\log n$ performance [10]. For the tests, providers maintained 10,000 metadata items. To achieve a fair comparison, the AgES implementation contained a straightforward optimization: requestors encrypt provider-published data line-by-line (instead of all at

Table 3. Comparison of actual computational costs. See section 6.2 for details.

		AgES	shPRP	Speedup
Setup	Provider	-	50,514 ms	-
	Requestor	-	-	-
	Total	-	50,514 ms	-
Search and Acquisition	Provider	50,530 ms	16 ms	3158
	Requestor	40,059 ms	116 ms	345
	Total	90,589 ms	132 ms	686

once), checking each result against the re-encryption of the desired metadata. When a match exists, the optimization reduces requestor encryptions by 50% on average. Tests ran on a 3.2 GHz Pentium 4 with 512 MB of RAM. Table 3 shows the results, and Appendix B offers additional details of the evaluation process.

These results demonstrate a strong performance benefit for shPRP. After the setup process, requestor computation time decreases by 99.7%, and provider computation time almost entirely disappears. Also note that shPRP scales better than AgES (see Table 1).

The results also demonstrate shPRP's practicality. Providers in shPRP always perform a single encryption during the search process, so a provider's expected computational cost is a constant, reasonable 16 ms for any amount of published metadata. The quantity of metadata has a marginal impact on requestor computational costs, as requestors search an ordered list of the encryptions. This cost grows logarithmically with the number of published values and averages only 116 ms for 10,000 metadata items, so shPRP is also computationally viable for requestors. A requestor's work is parallelizable, making shPRP even more practical. Search communication costs are negligible if a requestor stores all provider-published data. With host servers, however, communications costs can become a constraining factor for large quantities of published encryptions.

6.3   Security

Because shPRP is a modification of AgES, its security may rest on AgES's security as shown in [2] and [12] provided that, under the assumptions of section 4.2, the changes do not compromise security. The modifications are:

- Providers publicly reveal encrypted metadata.
- Providers may use an encryption key indefinitely.
- Providers may publish to host servers.
- Requestors decrypt re-encrypted data instead of re-encrypting provider data.

Appendix C argues that, under the given assumptions, none of these modifications adversely impacts security. This argument does not rely on semi-honest participant behavior, meaning that, like AgES [12], shPRP does not leak information even under a malicious behavioral model.

7   Summary and Conclusion

A chief concern of many privacy-critical organizations is protection of information against illegitimate access. This emphasis can result in restrictive systems that successfully thwart objectionable parties yet also deter privacy-constrained requestors with valid claims. Private resource pairing attempts to connect such resource requestors and providers without violating privacy. While existing work addresses similar issues, no known prior work directly addresses this issue in a satisfactory manner. Research on private resource pairing uncovered several interesting topics warranting further research, including weaknesses in the present system and extensions that would make the present system more useful.

Several weaknesses exist in the present private pairing model. During the search process, requestors receive indefinite search capabilities for a given piece of metadata. A provider's encrypted metadata is constant as long as its key remains constant. During that period, a provider may publish additional metadata that a requestor has no right to search. The present private resource-pairing scheme would also allow curious parties to make numerous undesirable inferences if a provider modifies its metadata set or an owner updates its key. In addition, the malicious case extensions rely on a trusted third party in several cases. Means of reducing or removing these weaknesses are desirable.

Additional research could also add functionality. For example, some entities may partition resources by classification levels and limit searches by requestor clearance level. If providers use multiple keys and verification tickets include clearance data, this paper's solutions are sufficient, but more elegant solutions may exist. Also, organizations may have valid reasons for revealing only a subset of metadata or resources related to metadata. A means of ensuring that providers reveal appropriate data would be helpful, particularly if owners do not exist or cannot monitor metadata. Finally, future projects may wish to examine cases where a requestor's identity is confidential, host servers may collude, or metadata is fuzzy ([16] may offer insight for working with fuzzy metadata).

This paper presents a practical semi-honest solution that, under the unique constraints of private resource pairing, offers a 686-time computational speedup over the similar AgES protocol without compromising security. In addition, this work suggests means of preventing malicious participant behavior. The shPRP protocol and its extensions for preventing malicious behavior provide a concrete basis for future work in private resource pairing.

Acknowledgments

We thank David Evans for helpful advice and assistance in finding related work as well as his helpful comments on this paper. We thank Alexandre Evfimievski for his clarification of the performance of the AgES protocol. We also thank Brent Waters for his useful advice during the early stages of this research.

References

1. M. Abdalla, M. Bellare, D. Catalano, E. Kiltz, T. Kohno, T. Lange, J. Malone-Lee, G. Neven, P. Paillier, H. Shi. Searchable encryption 2: Consistency properties, relation to anonymous IBE, and extensions (Full version). Cryptology ePrint Archive, Report 2005/254, 2005. http://eprint.iacr.org/2005/254/.

2. R. Agrawal, A. Evfimievski, R. Srikant. Information sharing across private databases. In Proceedings of the 2003 ACM SIGMOD International Conference on Management of Data, pages 86-97. ACM Press, 2003.

3. M. Bellare, A. Boldyreva, A. Desai, D. Pointcheval. Key-privacy in public-key encryption. In Proc. of Advances in Cryptology ASIACRYPT 01. Springer-Verlag, 2001. LNCS 2248.

4. D. Boneh, G. Di Crescenzo, R. Ostrovsky, G. Persiano. Public key encryption with keyword search. In Proc. of EUROCRYPT 2004, pages 506-522. Springer-Verlag, 2004. LNCS 3027.

5. D. Boneh, M. Franklin. Identity-based encryption from the Weil pairing. In Proc. of CRYPTO 2001, pages 213-229. Springer-Verlag, 2001. LNCS 2248.

6. J. A. Calandrino, A. C. Weaver. Identity-based cryptosystem privacy. University of Virginia Technical Report CS-2006-15. 2006.

7. B. Chor, O. Goldreich, E. Kushilevitz, M. Sudan. Private information retrieval. In Journal of the ACM, Vol. 45, No. 6, pages 965-982. ACM Press, 1998.

8. M. J. Freedman, K. Nissim, B. Pinkas. Efficient private matching and set intersection. In Proc. of EUROCRYPT 2004, pages 1-19. Springer-Verlag, 2004. LNCS 3027.

9. O. Goldreich. Secure multi-party computation. Manuscript, version 1.4. 2002. Available at http://www.wisdom.weizmann.ac.il/ oded/pp.html

10. Java 2 Platform Standard Edition 5.0 API Specification. 2004. Available at http://java.sun.com/j2se/1.5.0/docs/api/

11. L. Kissner, D. Song. Privacy-preserving set operations. In Proc. of CRYPTO 2005, pages 241 - 257. Springer-Verlag, 2005. LNCS 3621

12. Y. Li, J. D. Tygar, J. M. Hellerstein. Private matching. In Computer Security in the 21st Century, pages 25-50. Springer, 2005.

13. Liberty Alliance Project. Liberty Trust Models Guidelines. Version 1.0. 2003. Available at http://www.projectliberty.org/specs/liberty-trust-models-guidelines-v1.0.pdf

14. Office for Civil Rights, U.S. Department of Health and Human Services. Health Insurance Portability and Accountability Act (HIPAA). Available at http://www.hhs.gov/ocr/hipaa/

15. S. C. Pohlig, M. E. Hellman. An improved algorithm for computing logarithms over GF(p) and its cryptographic significance. In IEEE Transactions on Information Theory, IT-24, pages 106-110. 1978.

16. A. Sahai, B. Waters. Fuzzy identity based encryption. In Proc. of EUROCRYPT 2005, pages 457-473. Springer-Verlag, 2005. LNCS 3494.

17. B. Schneier. Applied Cryptography: Protocols, Algorithms, and Source Code in C. John Wiley & Sons, 1994.

18. R. Schoenberg, C. Safran. Internet based repository of medical records that retains patient confidentiality. In British Medical Journal, Volume 321, pages 1199-1203. 11 November 2000.

19. A. Shamir. Identity-based cryptosystems and signature schemes. In Proc. of CRYPTO 84, pages 47-53. Springer-Verlag, 1985. LNCS 196.

20. D. X. Song, D. Wagner, A. Perrig. Practical techniques for searches on encrypted data. In Proc. of 2000 IEEE Symposium on Security and Privacy. 2000.
21. B. R. Waters, D. Balfanz, G. Durfee, D. K. Smetters. Building an encrypted and searchable audit log. In Proc. of 11th Annual Network and Distributed System Security Symposium. 2004.

Appendix A: IBS Privacy

Define an identity-based signature scheme as a set of four algorithms: $IBS = (Setup, KeyExtract, Sign, Verify)$. $Setup$ accepts a security parameter, k, and any given common parameters, $commonParams$, and generates a set of public parameters, $params$; a random master secret, s; and the corresponding master public key, pk. $KeyExtract$ accepts a master secret, public parameters, and an identity, id, for which the private key, v_{id}, is to be extracted. $Sign$ accepts a user's secret key, public parameters, and a message, m, and it outputs the signature, sig. $Verify$ accepts a master public key, public parameters, an identity, a message, and a signature. It outputs true or false. If an identity-based signature scheme, IBS, possesses IBS privacy, an adversary, A, is unable to gain more than a negligible advantage at guessing the value b in the following experiment $(\text{Exp}_{IBS,A}^{ibs-priv-b}(k))$:

1. The challenger computes $(params_0, s_0, pk_0) = Setup(commonParams, k)$ and $(params_1, s_1, pk_1) = Setup(commonParams, k)$ and presents $params_0$, pk_0, $params_1$, and pk_1 to A.
2. A may use an oracle to derive secret keys for any identities under either instantiation. Eventually, A must choose a valid identity, id. A must not have queried for the secret keys corresponding to id. A returns id to the challenger and may save any state information.
3. The challenger randomly selects a bit $b \in \{0,1\}$ and a random nonce, n, within the message space, computes $sig = Sign(v_{id,b}, params_b, n)$, and returns sig to A.
4. A may use the oracle again to derive private keys but may not derive private keys associated with id. Eventually, A must submit a guess, b', for b based on all known information, including saved state data.

A's advantage is defined as:

$$\text{Adv}_{IBS,A}^{ibs-priv}(k) = \Pr[\text{Exp}_{IBS,A}^{ibs-priv-1}(k) = 1] - \Pr[\text{Exp}_{IBS,A}^{ibs-priv-0}(k) = 1]$$

A's advantage is negligible if $\text{Adv}_{IBS,A}^{ibs-priv}(k)$ is a negligible function over k.

Shamir's original identity-based signature scheme lacks IBS privacy. Each instantiation must use a different, publicly available modulus [19]. Thus, the same technique for distinguishing between public keys in RSA systems is applicable to this identity-based signature scheme.

Appendix B: Evaluation Process

Only shPRP providers have a setup process. Therefore, the setup duration for requestors and AgES providers is trivially zero. Fourteen trials, with the two highest and two lowest results excluded, established the average setup duration of shPRP providers. An equivalent procedure assessed shPRP provider performance during the search and acquisition process. In AgES, providers are active at two points during the search process: to supply encrypted metadata and to encrypt requestor metadata. These tasks precisely correspond to the shPRP provider setup and search processes. Thus, the AgES provider average is the sum of the shPRP averages for each task. AgES and shPRP requestors underwent two rounds of testing. In the first round, requestors performed fourteen searches for existing metadata. In the second round, requestors searched for fourteen nonexistent metadata items. The overall average was the mean of all results, excluding the two highest and two lowest results from each round. Results do not include time waiting on providers or downloading data.

Appendix C: Security of shPRP

Recall that the modifications of AgES for shPRP are:

- Providers publicly reveal encrypted metadata.
- Providers may use an encryption key indefinitely.
- Providers may publish to host servers.
- Requestors decrypt re-encrypted data instead of re-encrypting provider data.

This section argues that, given the assumptions of section 4.2, none of these changes result in shPRP leaking more information than AgES, which does not leak information in the semi-honest or malicious case.

Through public revelation of metadata, a provider, P, allows any curious entity (requestors, other providers, host servers, etc.) to acquire and analyze the provider's encrypted metadata hashes. This set of encrypted hashes is equivalent to the set that P, with metadata M_P, would provide to a curious party, C, with metadata set $M_C = \emptyset$, under the AgES protocol. Agrawal et al. demonstrate that C can learn only $|M_P|$ and $M_C \cap M_P = \emptyset$ from this data [2].

Similarly, shPRP's use of constant provider keys makes cryptanalysis no less difficult. C could store and perform cryptanalysis on the equivalent set of encrypted hashes it receives from P under the AgES protocol. In both cases, security against cryptanalysis is dependent on choice of commutative encryption function, hash function, and key length. The use of constant provider encryption keys does mean that the encryption of a piece of metadata will remain constant, however. Because encryptions remain constant and providers publicly disclose encrypted data, curious parties may observe and draw inferences from the publication time of data if providers do not publish data all at once. Also, a curious party could trivially observe modification or removal of encryptions.

To avoid issues with publication, modification, and removal, section 4.2 states that either providers must publish all data in unison or inferences must reveal no confidential data. Future work may establish a more satisfactory solution.

Provider signatures and the assumptions of section 4.2 prevent host servers from imperceptibly modifying data or drawing undesirable inferences. Beyond attacks that this paper explicitly does not consider (see section 3), host servers introduce no additional known weaknesses.

Finally, a requestor's choice to decrypt data rather than re-encrypt it has no impact on security. Nothing prevents entities from decrypting legitimately acquired data from the AgES protocol.

Honest-Verifier Private Disjointness Testing Without Random Oracles

Susan Hohenberger* and Stephen A. Weis**

Massachusetts Institute of Technology, Cambridge, MA, USA
{srhohen,sweis}@mit.edu

Abstract. We present an efficient construction of a *private disjointness testing* protocol that is secure against malicious provers and honest-but-curious (semi-honest) verifiers, without the use of random oracles. In a completely semi-honest setting, this construction implements a *private intersection cardinality* protocol. We formally define both private intersection cardinality and private disjointness testing protocols. We prove that our construction is secure under the *subgroup decision* and *subgroup computation* assumptions. A major advantage of our construction is that it does not require bilinear groups, random oracles, or non-interactive zero knowledge proofs. Applications of private intersection cardinality and disjointness testing protocols include privacy-preserving data mining and anonymous login systems.

Keywords: private disjointness testing, private intersection cardinality, subgroup decision assumption, private data mining, anonymous login.

1 Introduction

Suppose two parties, Alice and Bob, each have a private database of values, respectively denoted A and B, where the set cardinalities $|A|$ and $|B|$ are publicly known. Alice wishes to learn whether their two sets are disjoint, that is, whether $A \cap B = \emptyset$, or how large the intersection is, that is, $|A \cap B|$. In doing so, Alice cannot reveal information about her set A to Bob, who in turn does not want to reveal information about his set B, other than the bit $A \cap B \stackrel{?}{=} \emptyset$ or, perhaps, the size of the intersection $|A \cap B|$. These are respectively the *private disjointness testing* (PDT) and *private intersection cardinality* (PIC) problems.

For example, Alice may be a law enforcement agent ensuring that no suspects under investigation purchased tickets on a flight operated by Bob. Alice cannot simply reveal her list of suspects to Bob without compromising her investigation. Nor can Bob disclose any passenger names without explicit subpoenas. Yet, both parties have an interest in alerting Alice whether any suspects are on Bob's flight.

As another example, suppose Bob wants to anonymously login to Alice's system. Bob needs to prove that one of his identities in a (possibly singleton) set B

---

* Susan's work was supported by an NDSEG Fellowship.
** Stephen's work was supported by NSF Grant CCR-0326277.

intersects the set A of Alice's valid users. Alice should be convinced that Bob is a legitimate user, without learning which specific user he is. Thus, both parties wish to determine whether $|A \cap B| \neq 0$.

These types of private set operations may be implemented by several existing techniques. They may be viewed as a general two-party secure computation problem, solvable by classic secure multiparty computation techniques [12, 22]. Zero-knowledge sets [16] support private operations like disjointness testing, set union, and set intersection.

Unfortunately, these techniques have remained unused in practice due to their high computation, communication, and implementation costs. Oblivious polynomial evaluation protocols, such as those due to Naor and Pinkas [17], may also be applied to private set operations. However, using generalized oblivious polynomial evaluation for private set operations is inefficient in comparison to specialized protocols.

This paper builds on specialized private set operation protocols recently developed by Freedman, Nissim, and Pinkas (FNP) [11], and Kiayias and Mitrofanova (KM) [14], and offers a new construction that is more efficient in a malicious-prover setting. When both parties are honest-but-curious (semi-honest), the Hohenberger and Weis (HW) construction presented in this work is a *private intersection cardinality* protocol, where a verifier party (who is played by Alice in the above examples) learns $|A \cap B|$. The efficiency in this setting is equivalent to both FNP and KM, but is based on a different complexity assumption.

Note that in the context of "honest-verifier", we are using the term "honest" interchangeably with "semi-honest". This means the verifier *honestly* abides by the protocol, but may be *curious* and examine any received values to try to learn more about B. The notion of semi-honest or honest-but-curious was introduced in [12].

The HW construction improves on existing results in settings where the prover is malicious and the verifier is honest-but-curious. In this malicious-prover setting, the HW construction implements a *private disjointness testing* protocol. A malicious, polynomial-time bounded prover able to send arbitrary messages cannot convince a verifier that their sets intersect, unless they actually do. In the anonymous login example, Bob will not be able to login unless he possesses a legitimate identity string.

The HW honest-but-curious (semi-honest) private intersection cardinality protocol presented in this paper *as is* becomes a private disjointness testing protocol in the malicious-prover setting. By contrast, previous works require additional computations, such as adding zero-knowledge proofs [14] or homomorphic encryptions [11], to be made secure in a malicious-prover setting. Moreover, both FNP and KM require random oracles to be made secure in the presence of a malicious prover, whereas the HW construction does not.

1.1   The FNP Protocol Paradigm

The FNP protocol [11] is quite intuitive and simple, and is the design paradigm used in both the KM and HW protocols. An FNP invocation where Bob has

---

THE FNP PROTOCOL:

1. $\mathcal{V}$ chooses a random constant or irreducible polynomial $G(x)$.
2. $\mathcal{V}$ computes $f(x) = G(x) \cdot (\prod_{a_i \in A}(x - a_i)) = \sum \alpha_i x^i$.
3. If any $\alpha_i = 0$, restart the protocol.
4. $\mathcal{V}$ encrypts the coefficients of $f(x)$ with a homomorphic encryption scheme and sends the encryptions $c_i = E(\alpha_i)$ to $\mathcal{P}$.
5. Using the homomorphic properties of E, $\mathcal{P}$ obliviously evaluates $f(x)$ at some value b, obtaining $E(f(b))$.
6. $\mathcal{P}$ randomizes his evaluation as $c = E(Rf(b))$ and sends it to $\mathcal{V}$.
7. $\mathcal{V}$ decrypts c. If $D(c) = 0$, $\mathcal{V}$ knows $\mathcal{P}$'s value intersects with A.

Fig. 1. An overview of the Freedman, Nissim, and Pinkas (FNP) protocol

a singleton set is informally outlined in Figure 1. To provide further technical details, suppose (G, E, D) is a semantically-secure homomorphic encryption scheme. Let $\mathcal{V}$ have set $A = \{a_1, \ldots, a_n\}$ and $\mathcal{P}$ have set $B = \{b_1, \ldots, b_m\}$.

As shown in Figure 1, the verifier (also known as Alice) first selects a random constant or irreducible polynomial $G(x)$ (i.e. $G(x)$ will have no roots). The verifier than computes $f(x) = G(x) \cdot (\prod_{a_i \in A}(x - a_i)) = \sum \alpha_i x^i$. Note that the roots of f are exactly the values in the set A. The verifier then encrypts the α coefficients of f under a public key pk that she chooses, and sends them to the prover. That is, $\mathcal{V}$ encrypts each coefficient as $c_i = E_{pk}(\alpha_i)$ with a homomorphic cryptosystem, e.g., [18, 19].

Recall that homomorphic cryptosystems like Paillier's allow a party given $E_{pk}(x)$ and $E_{pk}(y)$ to obliviously compute $E_{pk}(x) \cdot E_{pk}(y) = E_{pk}(x + y)$, or to compute $E_{pk}(x)^z = E_{pk}(x \cdot z)$, where z is some constant. Note that given the encryptions c_i, these homomorphic operations are sufficient to obliviously evaluate the polynomial f. For example, the encryptions $c_0 = E_{pk}(4)$ and $c_1 = E_{pk}(3)$ commit the polynomial $f(x) = 3x + 4$. A second party may evaluate this at a particular value $x = 2$, by computing $c_1^2 \cdot c_0 = E_{pk}(3 \cdot 2) \cdot E_{pk}(4) = E_{pk}(6 + 4) = E_{pk}(10) = E_{pk}(f(2))$.

Thus, given coefficients encrypted as c_i values, the prover (Bob) may obliviously evaluate $f(b_i)$ for each element $b_i \in B$. Note that if $b_i \in A$, then $f(b_i) = 0$. The prover will now randomize all his obliviously evaluated $f(b_i)$ values by homomorphically multiplying them by a random nonzero value. That is, he computes $E_{pk}(f(b_i))^r = E_{pk}(r \cdot f(b_i))$ where r is a random nonzero value. Thus, if $f(b_i) = 0$, then the encryption of $E_{pk}(r \cdot f(b_i)) = E_{pk}(0)$. Otherwise, $E_{pk}(r \cdot f(b_i))$ is some random value. This hides any information about elements in the prover's set that are *not* in the verifier's set. The prover now sends these encrypted oblivious evaluations $E(r_i \cdot f(b_i))$ to the verifier. The verifier then decrypts and tests whether any of the resulting plaintexts are zero. If $b_i \in A$, then $f(b_i) = 0$, so if any decrypted values are zero, then the verifier believes there is an intersection with the prover's set. Note that the original FNP protocol reveals the elements in the intersection of the two sets, by having the prover return the ciphertext $E_{pk}(r \cdot f(b_i) + b_i)$ instead. Thus if $f(b_i) = 0$, the verifier obtains the elements of the intersection – not just the cardinality!

We focus on applications where the prover explicitly does not want to reveal anything about his set, except the size or existence of the intersection. For instance, the anonymous login application cannot have the verifier learn the actual intersection values. This paper will only focus on the private intersection cardinality protocol version of FNP, although finding actual intersection values will be discussed further in Section 7.

In the KM protocol [14], the same techniques as FNP are applied, except that it uses a new primitive called *superposed encryption* based on Pedersen commitments [20]. Superposed encryption is closely related to a homomorphic ElGamal variant first used in voting schemes by Cramer, Gennaro, and Schoenmakers [9]. In the KM protocol the prover returns to the verifier a single ciphertext $E_{pk}(r \cdot |A \cap B|)$, where r is a random value. Thus, this is specifically a PDT protocol rather than a PIC protocol. The verifier accepts if the ciphertext decrypts to zero and rejects otherwise.

Both the FNP and KM constructions, based on Paillier's homomorphic encryption [18, 19] and Pedersen's commitment scheme [20], suffer from a crucial flaw: *malicious adversaries may simply encrypt or commit to zero values*. For instance, in the FNP case, someone can simply encrypt 0 with the public key and convince the verifier that an intersection exists when it does not. This is a critical failure which both FNP and KM immediately recognize and address. To cope with malicious provers, FNP proposes a fix that relies on the random oracle model (ROM), despite its inherent problems [2, 7].

Fixing KM against malicious adversaries requires random oracles as well as universally-composable (UC) commitments [6] (which require a common reference string). While relatively efficient, the best known UC commitment schemes are interactive and would increase communication complexity by a quadratic factor [5, 8, 10].

The weakness of FNP and KM in the face of malicious provers begs the question: Can we implement an efficient private disjointness testing protocol without the use of random oracles or costly sub-protocols? This paper answers this question in the affirmative.

1.2   Overview of the HW Construction

This section provides intuition for understanding the Hohenberger and Weis (HW) construction in the context of prior work. Essentially, the main difference is that in both the FNP and KM protocols, a prover convinces a verifier to accept by returning an encryption of zero. If the prover was honest, then if the verifier receives an encryption of a zero value, it implies some element in $\mathcal{P}$'s set is also in $\mathcal{V}$'s set. However, if the prover is malicious, then he can easily encrypt a zero value from scratch and send it to the verifier. To prevent this, both FNP and KM must add costly computations to check that the prover follows a specified protocol.

To cope with malicious provers, the HW construction essentially substitutes a cryptographic primitive dubbed "testable and homomorphic commitments"

Table 1. Three private set protocols compared in different security settings. ROM stands for "Random Oracle Model", NIZK for "Non-Interactive Zero Knowledge", and UC for "Universally Composable".

Security Setting	FNP	KM	HW
Semi-Honest	Cardinality	Disjointness	**Cardinality**
Malicious Prover (Requirements)	Cardinality (ROM)	Disjointness (NIZK Proofs) (ROM)	**Disjointness** (**None**)
Malicious Verifier (Requirements)	Cardinality (Multiple Invocations)	Disjointness (UC-Commitments) (ROM)	See Section 7

in the place of Paillier's homomorphic encryption. Instead of encryptions of zero, elements belonging to the intersection of the two sets will be encoded to have a specific order in a multiplicative group. In other words, a prover convinces a verifier that an intersection exists by returning elements of a specific order.

The necessary complexity-theoretic assumptions are that it is hard to for a prover to decide whether group elements belong to a particular subgroup of unknown order, and that it is hard to compute elements in the subgroup. Under this *subgroup computation assumption*, computing an element of this order is hard for a prover, unless he correctly follows the protocol (and there *is* a nonempty intersection). Thus, in the malicious-prover setting, the HW construction is sound by default, whereas FNP and KM must augment their protocols with costly computations in the random oracle model.

In the HW construction presented in Section 4, the verifier begins, as in FNP, by selecting a random polynomial $f(\cdot)$ whose roots correspond to set A. The verifier computes a *testable and homomorphic commitment* (THC) of each coefficient, which is essentially a BGN encryption [3] set in group $\mathbb{G}$, which has order $n = pq$ where p and q are large primes.

For each element $b_i \in B$, the prover uses THCs to compute a value that will be a random element in $\mathbb{G}$ if $b_i \notin A$ or will be a random element of order p if $b_i \in A$. The verifier, with knowledge of p and q, can test the order of each element returned by the prover. In this way, the verifier learns the cardinality of the intersection, just as in FNP.

The main benefit, however, is that a malicious prover cannot, under the subgroup computation problem, compute an element of order p from scratch. As proven in the full version of this paper, the HW construction remains sound in the malicious-prover setting without any augmentation. As in the FNP PDT protocol, the verifier can *potentially* learn the cardinality of the intersection, but is not *guaranteed* to do so when talking with a malicious prover. That is, if the prover happens to be honest, the verifier will learn the cardinality – but there is no way to know whether a prover is honest. Table 1 compares the behavior of FNP, KM, and the HW construction in different security settings.

1.3 Related Work

Kissner and Song [15] offer FNP-inspired schemes for solving several closely related privacy-preserving set operations like set disjointness, cardinality, and set union. They offer improved efficiency compared to FNP in the multiparty, honest-but-curious setting. Again, when translated to the malicious adversary model, their constructions require relatively costly zero-knowledge proof of knowledge sub-protocols. In all fairness, Kissner and Song address a richer set of problems than simple disjointness testing like set union, set intersection, and multiplicity testing. They also work in a multiparty model, so it is not surprising that their solutions require more computation.

Constructions from both Pedersen's commitment scheme [20] and Paillier's homomorphic cryptosystem [18, 19] are both closely related to the "testable and homomorphic commitment" primitive in Section 4.2.

The Subgroup Decision Assumption (SDA) and the Subgroup Computation Assumption (SCA) described in Section 2.1 are crucial to proving security of the construction presented herein. Yamamura and Saito apply the SDA to the private information retrieval problem [21]. The composite residuosity assumptions made by Paillier are also closely related.

A similar *bilinear* subgroup complexity assumption is made by Boneh, Goh, and Nissim for their 2DNF ciphertext evaluation scheme [3]. Groth, Ostrovsky, and Sahai also make the same complexity assumption to implement noninteractive zero knowledge proofs [13].

2 Preliminaries

Notation. Let $\mathbb{Z}$ be the integers. Let $\text{negl}(\cdot)$ be a *negligible* function such that for all polynomials $p(\cdot)$ and all sufficiently large $k \in \mathbb{Z}$, we have $\text{negl}(k) < 1/p(k)$. We denote that two distributions C and D are perfectly indistinguishable using $C \approx D$ and computationally indistinguishable using $C \stackrel{c}{\approx} D$ notation. A $\mathcal{M}_{ppt}$ subscript will indicate that a interactive Turing machine $\mathcal{M}$ runs in probabilistic polynomial time. The value $ord(x)$ is the order of x. The transcript $\text{View}^{\mathcal{M}}[\mathcal{M}(x)\mathcal{N}(y)]$ will represent the view of algorithm $\mathcal{M}$ after interacting with algorithm $\mathcal{N}$ on inputs x and y, respectively. $\mathcal{M}$'s view includes its input, its randomness, and the public transcript of the protocol. We denote a distribution of views over random inputs as $\{\text{View}^{\mathcal{M}}[\mathcal{M}(x)\mathcal{N}(y)]\}$.

2.1 Complexity Assumptions

The complexity assumptions applied in the HW construction exist in various forms throughout the literature. The formalization here is closest to that of Yamamura and Saito [21]. Recently, Boneh, Goh, and Nissim introduced a stronger version of these assumptions for *bilinear* groups [3].

Definition 1 (Subgroup Decision Assumption (SDA) [3, 21]). *Let $S(1^k)$ be an algorithm that produces $(\mathbb{G},\ p,\ q)$ where $\mathbb{G}$ is a group of composite order*

$n = pq$, and $p < q$ are k-bit primes. Then, we say that the subgroup decision problem is hard in $\mathbb{G}$ if for all probabilistic polynomial time adversaries $\mathcal{A}$,

$$\Pr\left[(\mathbb{G}, p, q) \leftarrow S(1^k); \; n = pq; \; x_0 \leftarrow \mathbb{G}; \; x_1 \leftarrow x_0^q; \; b \leftarrow \{0, 1\};\right.$$
$$\left. b' \leftarrow \mathcal{A}(\mathbb{G}, n, x_b) : b = b'\right] \leq \frac{1}{2} + \text{negl}(k).$$

Basically, the SDA means that given the description of a group $\mathbb{G}$, in the form of a generator g, and its order $n = pq$, a probabilistic polynomial-time adversary cannot distinguish random elements of order p in $\mathbb{G}$ from random elements in $\mathbb{G}$. Clearly, if factoring is easy, then the SDA fails to hold. Similarly, someone able to compute discrete logarithms given $(\mathbb{G}, n, x)$ can decide this problem by computing $gcd(\log_g x, n)$, for some generator g. It is not clear how the SDA relates to the Decisional Diffie-Hellman (DDH) assumption.

Additionally, the security of the HW scheme requires the following computational assumption:

Definition 2 (Subgroup Computation Assumption (SCA)). *Let $S(1^k)$ be an algorithm that produces $(\mathbb{G}, p, q)$ where $\mathbb{G}$ is a group of composite order $n = pq$, and $p < q$ are k-bit primes. Then, we say that the subgroup computation problem is hard in $\mathbb{G}$ if for all probabilistic polynomial time adversaries $\mathcal{A}$,*

$$\Pr\left[(\mathbb{G}, p, q) \leftarrow S(1^k); \; n = pq; \; x \leftarrow \mathcal{A}(\mathbb{G}, n) : ord(x) = p\right] \leq \text{negl}(k).$$

An example group where these assumptions may be applied is a subgroup $\mathbb{G}$ of order $n = pq$, consisting of the quadratic residues of $\mathbb{Z}_{p'}$, where $p' = 2pq + 1$ and p', p, q are all primes. Of course, the HW construction can also operate over the bilinear groups where Boneh et al. [3] assume the subgroup decision problem is hard. It is not clear that the SDA assumption implies SCA, or vice versa, although a relation between the two seems plausible. Further exploration of both assumptions could be valuable in other schemes as well.

3   Problem Definitions

This section formally defines private intersection cardinality (PIC) and private disjointness testing (PDT) protocols. Let 1^k be a security parameter in unary. Let Q be the domain of values for this protocol such that $|Q| \in \Theta(2^k)$. Let the universe U be the set of all poly(k)-sized subsets of Q. For sets $A \in U$ and $B \in U$, define the *disjointness predicate* $D(A, B) = (A \cap B = \emptyset)$, that is, $D(A, B)$ will have value 1 if and only if A and B are disjoint.

Let verifier $\mathcal{V}$ and prover $\mathcal{P}$ be two probabilistic polynomial time interactive Turing machines. Each party takes as input a (possibly different) element of U and the interaction of $\mathcal{P}$ and $\mathcal{V}$ yields a result to $\mathcal{V}$ *only*.

3.1   Private Disjointness Testing Definition

Definition 3 (Honest-Verifier Private Disjointness Testing). *Two probabilistic polynomial time interactive Turing machines $(\mathcal{P}, \mathcal{V})$ define an Honest-Verifier Private Disjointness Testing protocol if the following conditions hold:*

1. **Completeness:** *For honest parties, the protocol works and the verifier learns the disjointness predicate; that is,*

$$\forall A \in U, \ \forall B \in U, \ \Pr\left[\mathcal{P}(B)\mathcal{V}(A) = D(A, B)\right] \geq (1 - \text{negl}(k))$$

where the probability is taken over the randomness of $\mathcal{P}$ and $\mathcal{V}$.

2. **Soundness:** *For a random set $A \in U$, the probability that the prover will convince the verifier to accept is negligible; that is,*

$$\forall \mathcal{P}^*_{ppt}, \ \Pr_{A \in U}\left[\mathcal{P}^*\mathcal{V}(A) \neq 0\right] \leq \text{negl}(k)$$

where probability is taken over the choice of $A \in U$ and the randomness of $\mathcal{P}^*$ and $\mathcal{V}$.

3. **Malicious-Prover Zero Knowledge (MPZK):** *A malicious prover learns nothing about the verifier's set; that is,*

$$\exists \mathcal{S}_{ppt}, \ \forall \mathcal{P}^*_{ppt}, \ \forall A \in U, \ \left\{ \textit{View}^{\mathcal{P}^*}\left[\mathcal{P}^*\mathcal{V}(A)\right] \right\} \overset{c}{\approx} \left\{ \textit{View}^{\mathcal{P}^*}\left[\mathcal{P}^*\mathcal{S}(1^{|A|})\right] \right\}$$

4. **Honest-Verifier Perfect Zero Knowledge (HVPZK):** *An honest-but-curious verifier learns nothing about the prover's set beyond the size of the intersection; that is,*

$$\exists \mathcal{S}_{ppt}, \ \forall A \in U, \ \forall B \in U, \ \left\{ \textit{View}^{\mathcal{V}}\left[\mathcal{P}(B)\mathcal{V}(A)\right] \right\} \approx \left\{ \mathcal{S}(A, 1^{|B|}, 1^{|A \cap B|}) \right\}$$

Note that an honest-but-curious verifier is allowed to *potentially* learn $|A \cap B|$, but he is not *guaranteed* to learn that value. One might define a stronger definition where rather than being provided $1^{|A \cap B|}$, the simulator would only be provided $D(A, B)$.

3.2   Private Intersection Cardinality Definition

Definition 4 (Honest-Verifier Private Intersection Cardinality). *An Honest-Verifier Private Intersection Cardinality protocol has the same setup as in Definition 3, except for the following differences:*

1. **Completeness:** *For honest parties, the protocol works and the verifier learns the cardinality predicate; that is,*

$$\forall A \in U, \ \forall B \in U, \ \Pr\left[\mathcal{P}(B)\mathcal{V}(A) = |A \cap B|\right] \geq (1 - \text{negl}(k))$$

where probability is taken over the randomness of $\mathcal{P}$ and $\mathcal{V}$.

2. **Cardinality Soundness:** *A malicious prover can not convince an honest verifier that the cardinality is larger than it really is; that is,*

$$\forall \mathcal{P}^*_{ppt}, \ \forall B \in U, \ \Pr_{A \in U}\left[\mathcal{P}^*(B)\mathcal{V}(A) > |A \cap B|\right] \leq \text{negl}(k)$$

where probability is taken over the choice of $A \in U$ and the randomness of $\mathcal{P}$ and $\mathcal{V}$.

3.3   Informal Explanation of the Definitions

Completeness means that a correct execution between two honest parties will return the correct value to $\mathcal{V}$ with negligible chance for error. In a PDT protocol, the correct value is the disjointness predicate $D(A, B)$ and in a PIC protocol it is the intersection cardinality $|A \cap B|$.

PDT soundness implies that on a random input set $A \in U$, $\mathcal{V}$ has a negligible chance of obtaining a non-zero result when interacting with any malicious probabilistic polynomial-time prover $\mathcal{P}^*$. That is, unless $\mathcal{P}^*$ actually knows a value in $\mathcal{V}$'s set, or is extremely lucky, then $\mathcal{V}$ will not be fooled into thinking otherwise. Neither the FNP nor KM protocols are sound by this definition. In those schemes, a verifier will believe that there is an intersection if it receives the value zero encrypted under a public-key. A malicious prover could trivially violate the soundness property by encrypting zero itself.

PIC soundness is similar to the PDT soundness definition, except that for any set B, and random set A, the protocol has a negligible chance of returning a value greater than $|A \cap B|$ to a verifier $\mathcal{V}$ interacting with $\mathcal{P}^*(B)$. The idea is that this prevents a malicious prover from doing trivial attacks like duplicating elements in its set B to inflate the cardinality returned to the verifier. Of course, a malicious prover can always run the protocol on some subset of B, which would with high probability under-report the cardinality. This is unavoidable and is why cardinality soundness is only concerned with over-reporting the cardinality. As it turns out, this property will be the reason why the HW construction in Section 4 is *not* an Honest-Verifier PIC protocol. Section 6 will discuss this further.

Since a verifier is allowed to potentially learn $|A \cap B|$ in both the PDT and PIC protocols, the zero knowledge definitions presented in this paper are the same. This relaxation appears in FNP as well, but not KM.

The Malicious-Prover Zero Knowledge (MPZK) property means that no probabilistic polynomial-time potentially malicious prover $\mathcal{P}^*$ can learn anything about a set A from an interaction with $\mathcal{V}$ that it could not simulate on its own. In other words, the verifier's set, for example a database of passwords, remains hidden from even malicious provers. Here the distributions are computationally indistinguishable. Any action that $\mathcal{V}$ takes as a result of a successful protocol invocation, such as allowing $\mathcal{P}^*$ to anonymously login, is considered outside the protocol definition.

Finally, the Honest-Verifier Perfect Zero Knowledge (HVPZK) property implies that a probabilistic polynomial-time semi-honest verifier $\mathcal{V}$ does not learn anything about B beyond the size of the set intersection. There is a subtle point here in the PDT protocol: the verifier is only *guaranteed* to learn the bit $D(A, B)$, but we allow an honest-but-curious verifier to *potentially* learn the size of the intersection. The flexibility suits the applications mentioned in the introduction. In fact, in the semi-honest setting, the distribution an adversary can simulate on its own is perfectly indistinguishable from a real transcript distribution.

Above we do not explicitly consider auxiliary inputs in the zero-knowledge definitions. To do so, we would need to quantify over all polynomial-size advice strings and provide this string to both the party in question and the simulator.

4   HW Private Disjointness Testing

In this section, we present a construction that efficiently implements a PDT protocol. In the full version of this paper, we prove that this construction securely meets the requirements of Definition 3. Overall, this construction is very similar to those of Freedman, Nissim, and Pinkas (FNP) [11] and Kiayias and Mitrofanova (KM) [14].

FNP and KM respectively rely on Paillier's homomorphic encryption system [18, 19] and a Pedersen commitment variant [20] as underlying primitives. This paper offers a new *testable and homomorphic commitment* (THC) primitive that will be used in a FNP-style oblivious polynomial evaluation scheme. The THC construction presented is reminiscent of both Paillier's and Pedersen's schemes. It is very similar to the encryption scheme for small messages due to Boneh, Goh, and Nissim (BGN) [3], but is used for the full range of messages.

The advantage of the HW construction is that it offers a stronger security guarantee than the basic FNP and KM protocols, with equivalent computation and communication costs. Although variants of both FNP and KM can be modified to offer stronger security, they require either the use of random oracles or significantly more computation.

4.1   Verifier System Setup

The verifier's system setup algorithm is as follows:

1. Run $S(1^k)$ to obtain $(\mathbb{G}, p, q)$.
2. Choose two random generators g and u from $\mathbb{G}$.
3. Compute $n = pq$ and $h = u^q$.
4. Publish $(\mathbb{G}, n)$ and keep (p, q, g, h) private.

Note that h is a random generator of the subgroup of order p. The verifier only needs to publish $\mathbb{G}$ and n. The prover will not know p, q, h or even g. Learning h, p, or q would allow a malicious prover to spuriously convince the verifier that an intersection exists.

4.2   Testable and Homomorphic Commitments

The public order n and private values g and h may be used for a *testable and homomorphic commitment* (THC) scheme. This primitive will be the basis of the HW construction. Informally, a THC scheme supports the following operations:

- Commit: $\mathsf{Com}(m, r)$ a message m with randomness r,
- Addition: For all m, r, m', r', $\mathsf{Com}(m, r) \cdot \mathsf{Com}(m', r') = \mathsf{Com}(m + m', r + r')$,
- Constant Multiplication: For all m, r, c, $\mathsf{Com}(m, r)^c = \mathsf{Com}(cm, cr)$
- Equality Test: $\mathsf{Test}(\mathsf{Com}(m, r), x)$, returns 1 if $m = x$.

Definition 5 (Testable and Homomorphic Commitment Hiding Property). *Let n be an integer, and let a_0, a_1, r be values in $\mathbb{Z}_n^*$. Then, we say that* *a testable and homomorphic commitment* Com *set in a group* $\mathbb{G}$ *of order* n *is* computationally hiding *over the distribution of* r *if*

$$\forall a_0, a_1 \in \mathbb{Z}_n^*, \{\mathbb{G}, n, a_0, a_1, \mathsf{Com}(a_0, r)\} \overset{c}{\approx} \{\mathbb{G}, n, a_0, a_1, \mathsf{Com}(a_1, r)\}$$

The encryption scheme for small messages due to BGN is very similar to the HW construction, except for two differences. First, we provide the adversary with even less information about the commitment; that is, the values g and h remain private. Secondly, BGN allow and support bilinear map operations, whereas we do not consider them. Similarly to their scheme, the HW testable and homomorphic commitment primitive operates as shown in Figure 2.

TESTABLE AND HOMOMORPHIC COMMITMENTS OPERATIONS:

1. **Setup:** Let $S(1^k)$ be an algorithm that outputs $(\mathbb{G}, p, q)$ where $\mathbb{G}$ is a group of composite order $n = pq$, and $p < q$ are k-bit primes. Let g, u be random generators of $\mathbb{G}$ and let $h = u^q$. Publish n; keep all else private.
2. **Commit:** Given m and $r \in \mathbb{Z}_n^*$, compute: $\mathsf{Com}(m, r) = g^m h^r$
3. **Addition:** $\mathsf{Com}(m, r) \cdot \mathsf{Com}(m', r') = g^{m+m'} h^{r+r'} = \mathsf{Com}(m + m', r + r')$
4. **Constant Multiplication:** $\mathsf{Com}(m, r)^c = g^{cm} h^{cr} = \mathsf{Com}(cm, cr)$
5. **Equality Test:** If $\mathsf{Test}(\mathsf{Com}(m, r)) = (g^m h^r / g^x)^p = (g^p)^{m-x} = 1$, output 1; else, output 0.

Fig. 2. Testable and homomorphic commitment construction

Lemma 1. *The testable and homomorphic commitment scheme described in Figure 2 is computationally hiding, i.e., it satisfies definition 5.*

This lemma follows, more or less, from the semantic security of the encryption scheme of Boneh, Goh, and Nissim. For completeness, however, we prove in the full version of this paper that this construction is computationally hiding.

4.3 Oblivious Polynomial Evaluation

Suppose a party knowing h has some polynomial $f(x) = \sum \alpha_i x^i \in \mathbb{Z}_q[x]$. This party can publish commitments to f's coefficients as $\mathsf{Com}(\alpha_i, \gamma_i) = g^{\alpha_i} h^{\gamma_i}$, where γ_i values are random. Let $s = \lceil \sqrt{n} \rceil$. Assuming p and q are not twin primes, we have that $p < s < q$. Let the group $\mathbb{Z}_s^*$ be the domain of set values. Due to the homomorphic properties of Com, anyone can obliviously evaluate a commitment to $f(z)$ for any $z \in \mathbb{Z}_s^*$.

The HW construction uses this ability by having a verifier $\mathcal{V}$ compute a polynomial f with A as its set of roots. $\mathcal{P}$ can then obliviously evaluate f and return the result to $\mathcal{V}$. Note, this is not a contribution due to HW. Similar constructions were proposed by Naor and Pinkus [17] and FNP [11]. It is also the basis of the KM scheme [14]. $\mathcal{V}$'s polynomial is constructed as shown in Figure 3.

OBLIVIOUS POLYNOMIAL EVALUATION:

1. $\mathcal{V}$ chooses a random constant or irreducible polynomial $G(x)$.
2. $\mathcal{V}$ computes $f(x) = G(x) \cdot (\prod_{a_i \in A}(x - a_i)) = \sum_{i=0}^{|A|} \alpha_i x^i \in \mathbb{Z}_q[x]$.
3. If any $\alpha_i = 0$, restart the protocol.
4. $\mathcal{V}$ chooses a random polynomial $r(x) = \sum_{i=0}^{|A|} \gamma_i x^i \in \mathbb{Z}_p[x]$.
5. $\mathcal{V}$ publishes commitments $\mathsf{Com}(\alpha_i, \gamma_i) = g^{\alpha_i} h^{\gamma_i}$, for $i = 0$ to $|A|$.

Fig. 3. HW oblivious polynomial evaluation

Given these commitments to the α_i coefficients, $\mathcal{P}$ may use the homomorphic operations to compute a commitment to $f(z)$ for an arbitrary point $z \in \mathbb{Z}_s^*$: $\prod_i \mathsf{Com}(\alpha_i, \gamma_i)^{z^i} = g^{\sum_i \alpha_i z^i} h^{\sum_i \gamma_i z^i} = g^{f(z)} h^{r(z)} = \mathsf{Com}(f(z), r(z))$. Because $\mathcal{P}$ does not want to accidentally reveal information about values $z \notin A$ to $\mathcal{V}$, he can select a random $R \in \mathbb{Z}_n^*$ and compute the value $\mathsf{Com}(Rf(z), Rr(z)) = g^{Rf(z)} h^{Rr(z)} = \mathsf{Com}(f(z), r(z))^R$. If $f(z) \neq 0 \bmod q$, then $Rf(z)$ will be some random value in $\mathbb{Z}_n$, and $\mathsf{Com}(f(z), r(z))^R$ will be a random value in $\mathbb{G}$.

However, if $f(z) = 0 \bmod q$, then $g^{Rf(z)}$ will have order p (or 1). Since h has order p, this means that $\mathsf{Com}(f(z), r(z))^R$ will have order p, which can be tested by $\mathcal{V}$ by checking if the Test operation returns a 1 value. Thus, if $\mathcal{P}$ returns some value with order p, $\mathcal{V}$ concludes that $\mathcal{P}$ obliviously evaluated the polynomial at a root.

Recall that $\mathcal{P}$ does not know p, q, or even g or h. To erroneously convince $\mathcal{V}$ that he knows a root, a malicious $\mathcal{P}^*$ must produce some value of order p. Finding such a value is at least as hard as the Subgroup Computation Problem described in Definition 2.

5   HW Private Disjointness Testing

Given the oblivious polynomial evaluation protocol from the previous section, the HW construction to implement Private Disjointness Testing with a testable and homomorphic commitment primitive is quite simple. As mentioned, the overall protocol paradigm originally proposed by FNP [11]. Figure 4 illustrates the HW private disjointness testing protocol that is specified in Figure 5.

Theorem 1. *The HW construction is correct and secure, i.e., it satisfies Definition 3, under the Subgroup Decision and the Subgroup Computation assumptions.*

Theorem 1 is proven in four steps: completeness, soundness, malicious-prover zero knowledge, and honest-verifier zero knowledge. These proofs appear in the full version of this paper due to space considerations.

Remark: Note that when talking to an honest prover, a verifier will actually learn $|A \cap B|$ in this protocol by counting the number of elements returned with order p. We could somewhat obfuscate this value by having the prover return a

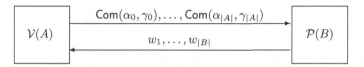

Fig. 4. An illustration of HW private disjointness testing

HW PRIVATE DISJOINTNESS TESTING:

1. $\mathcal{V}$ runs $S(1^k)$ to obtain $(\mathbb{G}, p, q)$, selects random generators g, u in $\mathbb{G}$, and computes $n = pq$ and $h = u^q$.
2. $\mathcal{V}$ publishes $(\mathbb{G}, n)$.
3. $\mathcal{V}$ and $\mathcal{P}$ announce $|A|$ and $|B|$ for respective input sets A and B, which are poly(k)-sized subsets of $\mathbb{Z}_s^*$.
4. $\mathcal{V}$ publishes commitments to polynomial coefficients $\mathsf{Com}(\alpha_i, \gamma_i) = g^{\alpha_i} h^{\gamma_i} \in \mathbb{G}$ for $i = 0$ to $|A|$.
5. For each $b_j \in B$ selected in random order:
   (a) $\mathcal{P}$ obliviously evaluates $f(b_j)$ as $v_j = g^{f(b_j)} h^{r(b_j)}$.
   (b) $\mathcal{P}$ selects a random exponent $R_j \in \mathbb{Z}_n^*$.
   (c) $\mathcal{P}$ sends $\mathcal{V}$ the value $w_j = v_j^{R_j}$.
6. $\mathcal{V}$ halts if any $w_j = 1$.
7. $\mathcal{V}$ tests each w_j by computing w_j^p.
8. If any $w_j^p = 1$, then $\mathcal{V}$ concludes that $A \cap B \neq \emptyset$.
9. Otherwise, $\mathcal{V}$ concludes $A \cap B = \emptyset$.

Fig. 5. HW private disjointness testing

random number of copies of each element in his set. This would not be true zero-knowledge, but it would be good enough for many practical applications. This protocol can be modified to hide $|A \cap B|$ at a cost of increased communication as discussed in Section 7.

6   Semi-honest Private Intersection Cardinality

The construction in Section 4 is *not* an Honest-Verifier Private Intersection Cardinality protocol. Unfortunately, there are trivial ways a malicious-prover can manipulate the actual cardinality value obtained by the verifier. The simplest attack would be to obliviously evaluate each element in B twice. The verifier will think the cardinality is $2 \cdot |A \cap B|$. By the HVPZK property, an honest verifier cannot detect this attack, otherwise it could distinguish different evaluations by the prover.

For this reason, the HW construction violates the Cardinality Soundness property from definition 4. However, we may consider a weaker PIC setting by assuming that both the prover and verifier are honest-but-curious (semi-honest).

Recall that a honest-but-curious party will follow a protocol as specified, but may further examine any received values [12].

Definition 6 (Semi-Honest Private Intersection Cardinality). *An* Semi-Honest Intersection Cardinality *protocol has the same setup as in Definition 3, except for the following difference:*

Completeness: *For semi-honest parties, the protocol works and the verifier learns the cardinality predicate; that is,*

$$\forall A \in U, \; \forall B \in U, \; \Pr\left[\mathcal{P}(B)\mathcal{V}(A) = |A \cap B|\right] \geq (1 - \mathrm{negl}(k))$$

where probability is taken over the randomness of $\mathcal{P}$ and $\mathcal{V}$.

Corollary 1. *The HW construction from Section 4 implements a Semi-honest Private Intersection Cardinality Protocol, under the Subgroup Decision and the Subgroup Computation assumptions.*

Corollary 1 follows directly from the proof of Theorem 1.

7 Discussion

Malicious Verifiers. The HW construction is only secure against honest-but-curious verifiers. A malicious verifier $\mathcal{V}^*$ can choose arbitrary setup parameters $(\mathbb{G}, n)$, such as $\mathbb{G} = \mathbb{Z}_{p'}$ where $p' = 2n + 1$, and send $\mathcal{P}$ an arbitrary set of values $g^{c_i} \in \mathbb{G}$, where the c_i values define some polynomial $f(x) = \sum c_i x^i$. In response, a legitimate $\mathcal{P}$ will send values $w = g^{Rf(b)}$ for each $b \in B$, where R is chosen randomly from $\mathbb{Z}_n^*$.

If $g^{f(b)}$ has order n, then w will be a random element of order n. However, a malicious $\mathcal{V}^*$ can design the polynomial $f(\cdot)$ to have different orders for different inputs. So, if $p' = 2pq + 1$, $\mathcal{V}^*$ might have two sets S, T such that $\forall s \in S, f(s) = 0 \bmod p$ and $\forall t \in T, f(t) = 0 \bmod q$. Thus, $\mathcal{V}^*$ would be able to distinguish how many elements of B were in either S or T. In fact, $\mathcal{V}^*$ could choose n to have many factors. This would allow her to test how many elements of B belonged to several different sets.

To make the HW construction secure against malicious verifiers, $\mathcal{V}$ could provide a zero knowledge proof that n was the product of two large primes p and q. $\mathcal{V}$ could then include a proof that each of her commitments was the product of at least one value with order p. Camenisch and Michels describe efficient proofs which can be used in this setting [4]. Of course, the costs of creating and verifying these proofs may be equivalent to the costs of the existing malicious verifier-secure protocols of FNP and KM.

Computation and Communication Costs. The computation and communication costs of the HW construction are equivalent to the costs of FNP's malicious-prover secure scheme, except the HW construction offers security against malicious provers without random oracles. The costs of HW are as follows:

$\mathcal{V}$ **Computation Costs:** Computing α_i coefficients requires $O(|A|^2)$ modular additions and multiplications. Committing requires $O(|A|)$ modular exponentiations and multiplications. Testing whether responses have order p requires $O(|B|)$ modular exponentiations.

$\mathcal{P}$ **Computation Costs:** Using Horner's method, $\mathcal{P}$ can obliviously evaluate a d-degree polynomial with $O(d)$ modular exponentiations and multiplications. Normally, $\mathcal{P}$ will perform $O(|A||B|)$ operations; that is, one polynomial evaluation at a cost of $O(|A|)$ operations for each of the $|B|$ elements in $\mathcal{P}$'s set. However, as described in FNP, if the balanced hash-bucket scheme of Azar et al. [1] is employed $\mathcal{P}$ can perform only $O(|B|\ln\ln|A|)$ modular operations.

Communication Costs: The total exchange between $\mathcal{P}$ and $\mathcal{V}$ is $O(k(|A| + |B|))$ bits or alternatively $O(k(|A|\ln\ln|A| + |B|))$ if a hash-bucket optimization is used, where 1^k is the security parameter.

Hiding Set Sizes. In the HW construction, the size of the prover and verifier's sets is public information. In practice, however, the prover $\mathcal{P}$ with set B or the verifier $\mathcal{V}$ with set A might wish to mask the true size of their sets using well-known techniques. To do this, the verifier $\mathcal{V}$ can compute a random polynomial $f(\cdot)$ with roots in set A as normal, then multiply it by some irreducible polynomial of arbitrary degree d. Then, $\mathcal{P}$ (or anyone else) will only learn that $\mathcal{V}$'s set is of some size less or equal to $|A| + d$. Similarly, $\mathcal{P}$ can evaluate f on each value in B an arbitrary number of times. Each copy will be randomized by the regular protocol. This will maintain correctness of Private Disjointness Testing, but would obviously change the results of an honest-but-curious private intersection cardinality protocol, as described in Section 6.

Small Set Domains. The HW construction requires that sets A and B are small with respect to the domain of set values. Obviously, in the HW PDT protocol, if $|B| = \Theta(\sqrt{n})$, then a malicious adversary can factor n in time polynomial to the size of its input. This would allow an adversary to generate values of order p and violate the Soundness property.

Private Information Retrieval. Recalling Private Information Retrieval (PIR), one party will have a database of $m + 1$ bits $x_0, \ldots, x_m$, while a second party wishes to privately query a particular bit x_i without revealing i. Putting this in the context of the HW construction, A would be the set of indices where x is 1 and $B = \{i\}$. Unfortunately, it may be the case that $|A|$ is large with respect to the domain $\mathbb{Z}_m^*$.

As a result, the requirement of small set domains mentioned in Section 7 precludes directly using the HW construction for PIR in general. Yamamura and Saito offer a simple PIR solution based on the SDA [21]. However, their PIR solution approach is very inefficient and requires $O(km)$ bits of communication to privately retrieve a single bit from a m-bit database, where k is a security parameter.

Multiparty Extensions. Another interesting variant to the 2-party PDT protocol is considering a multi-verifier, single-prover PDT scenario. For example, suppose that law enforcement agencies from different countries, in the role of verifiers, wish to be assured by an airline, in the role of the prover, that no one on *any* of their watch-lists is getting on the next flight. The law enforcement agencies neither trust each other nor the airline with their individual databases, yet may want to corroborate their watch lists (so as to possibly work together).

Suppose there are two verifiers. The HW construction may be extended as follows. First, each verifier computes his own values $n_i = p_i q_i$ and a group of known order $\prod_i n_i$ is published. Next, both verifiers publish commitments to their own polynomials using a random generator g from the group of order $n_1 n_2$ and, respectively, h_1 of order $(n_1 n_2)/p_1 = q_1 n_2$ and h_2 order $(n_1 n_2)/p_2 = n_1 q_2$. That is, values of the form $g^{\alpha_i} h_1^{r_i}$ and $g^{\beta_j} h_2^{r_j}$, where $f(x) = \sum \alpha_i x^i$ and $z(x) = \sum \beta_j x^j$. A third party can obliviously evaluate commitments to the sum of these polynomials. If the third party's set contains an element c_i such that $f(c_i) = z(c_i) = 0$, then this party can output elements $h_1^r h_2^{r'}$, which have order $q_1 q_2$.

No single party can compute elements of order $q_1 q_2$ by themselves; such an element is produced only after an evaluation on an element in *both* of the law enforcement agencies' sets. Each agency, knowing q_1 and q_2 respectively, could collaborate to detect this fact and take further action. The benefit here is that the contents of the sets of the law enforcement agencies and the airline all remain private, up to knowledge of any three-way intersections. This digression illustrates that unknown order subgroups might be applied in other interesting applications.

Finding Intersection Values with HW. As previously mentioned, basic FNP is actually a Private Intersection or Private Matching protocol. The verifier party learns which specific values are in the set intersection. Essentially, the prover will send homomorphic encryptions of the form $E_{pk}(r \cdot f(b) + b)$ for values $b \in B$. If $b \in A$, then $f(b) = 0$ and the verifier will receive an encryption of b. Otherwise, the verifier receives a random value. Of course, this is still susceptible to malicious prover attacks. A malicious prover can encrypt any value he likes or can encrypt values like $E_{pk}(r_1 \cdot f(b_1) + r_2 \cdot f(b_2) + b_1)$, which can be interpreted as "If $(b_1 \in A)$ and $(b_2 \in A)$, then tell the verifier that $(b_1 \in A)$". FNP's fixes the problem by using the random oracle model to force a prover to use the encrypted coefficient values prepared by the verifier.

This begs the question of whether the HW testable and homomorphic commitment primitive could be used in a private intersection protocol. Initially, one may consider using the exact FNP construction and having the prover obliviously evaluate $g^{Rf(b)+b} h^r$. If $f(b) = 0$, raising this to the power q will result in the value $(g^q)^b$. The verifier can then check whether for any of its own values a, that $(g^q)^a = (g^q)^b$.

Unfortunately, like FNP, a malicious prover could also send conditional evaluations, like "if x is in A, then reveal that y is in B". This would violate the soundness of a private intersection protocol. Thus, a HW-style private intersection protocol offers no advantage over FNP. They have equivalent computation costs and the same level of security.

8 Open Questions

In the full version of this paper, we discuss several open problems related to HW. Briefly, some of them are: (1) Are there natural constructions of more general private set operations like union or intersection? (2) What is the relation between the SCA and SDA assumptions? (3) How does either assumption relate to Diffie-Hellman or factoring?

References

[1] AZAR, Y., BRODER, A. Z., KARLIN, A. R., AND UPFAL, E. Balanced allocations. *SIAM Journal on Computing 29*, 1 (1999), 180–200.

[2] BELLARE, M., AND ROGAWAY, P. Random oracles are practical: A paradigm for designing efficient protocols. In *CCS* (1993), ACM Press, pp. 62–73.

[3] BONEH, D., GOH, E.-J., AND NISSIM, K. Evaluating 2-DNF formulas on cipher-texts. In *TCC* (2005), J. Kilian, Ed., vol. 3378 of *LNCS*, pp. 325–341.

[4] CAMENISCH, J., AND MICHELS, M. Proving in zero-knowledge that a number is the product of two safe primes. In *EUROCRYPT'99* (1999), J. Stern, Ed., vol. 1592 of *LNCS*, pp. 107–122.

[5] CAMENISCH, J., AND SHOUP, V. Practical verifiable encryption and decryption of discrete logarithms. In *CRYPTO '03* (2003), vol. 2729 of *LNCS*, pp. 126–144.

[6] CANETTI, R., AND FISCHLIN, M. Universally composable commitments. In *CRYPTO '01* (2001), J. Kilian, Ed., vol. 2139 of *LNCS*, pp. 19–40.

[7] CANETTI, R., GOLDREICH, O., AND HALEVI, S. The random oracle methodology, revisited. *Journal of the ACM 51*, 4 (July 2004), 557–594.

[8] CANETTI, R., LINDELL, Y., OSTROVSKY, R., AND SAHAI, A. Universally composable two-party and multi-party secure computation. In *STOC* (2002), J. H. Reif, Ed., ACM Press, pp. 495–503.

[9] CRAMER, R., GENNARO, R., AND SCHOENMAKERS, B. A secure and optimally efficient multi- authority election scheme. In *EUROCRYPT '97* (1997), W. Fumy, Ed., vol. 1233 of *LNCS*, pp. 103–118.

[10] DAMGÅRD, I., AND NIELSEN, J. B. Perfect hiding and perfect binding universally composable commitment schemes with constant expansion factor. In *CRYPTO '02* (2002), M. Yung, Ed., vol. 2442 of *LNCS*, pp. 581–596.

[11] FREEDMAN, M. J., NISSIM, K., AND PINKAS, B. Efficient private matching and set intersection. In *EUROCRYPT '04* (2004), vol. 3027 of *LNCS*, pp. 1–19.

[12] GOLDREICH, O., MICALI, S., AND WIGDERSON, A. How to play any mental game. In *STOC* (January 1987), ACM Press, pp. 218–229.

[13] GROTH, J., OSTROVSKY, R., AND SAHAI, A. Perfect non-interactive zero knowledge for NP. In *EUROCRYPT '06* (2006), vol. 4004, pp. 339–358.

[14] KIAYIAS, A., AND MITROFANOVA, A. Testing disjointness of private datasets. In *Financial Cryptography* (2005), vol. 3570 of *LNCS*, pp. 109–124.

[15] KISSNER, L., AND SONG, D. Privacy-preserving set operations. In *CRYPTO '05* (2005), V. Shoup, Ed., vol. 3621 of *LNCS*, pp. 241–257.

[16] MICALI, S., RABIN, M., AND KILIAN, J. Zero-knowledge sets. In *Foundations of Computer Science – FOCS* (2003), M. Sudan, Ed., IEEE Press, pp. 80–91.

[17] NAOR, M., AND PINKAS, B. Oblivious transfer and polynomial evaluation. In *STOC* (May 1999), T. Leighton, Ed., ACM Press, pp. 245–254.

[18] PAILLIER, P. Public-key cryptosystems based on composite degree residuosity classes. In *EUROCRYPT '99* (1999), vol. 1592 of *LNCS*, pp. 223–238.

[19] PAILLIER, P. Trapdooring discrete logarithms on elliptic curves over rings. In *ASIACRYPT '00* (2000), T. Okamoto, Ed., vol. 1976 of *LNCS*, pp. 573–584.

[20] PEDERSEN, T. P. Non-interactive and information-theoretic secure verifiable secret sharing. In *CRYPTO '91* (1991), vol. 576 of *LNCS*, pp. 129–140.

[21] YAMAMURA, A., AND SAITO, T. Private information retrieval based on the private information retrieval based on subgroup membership problem. In *Australasian Conf. on Info. Security and Privacy* (2001), vol. 2119 of *LNCS*, pp. 206–220.

[22] YAO, A. C. How to generate and exchange secrets. In *Foundations of Computer Science – FOCS* (1986), IEEE Press, pp. 162–167.

A Flexible Framework for Secret Handshakes
(Multi-party Anonymous and Un-observable Authentication)

Gene Tsudik[1] and Shouhuai Xu[2]

[1] Department of Computer Science, University of California, Irvine
`gts@ics.uci.edu`
[2] Department of Computer Science, University of Texas, San Antonio
`shxu@cs.utsa.edu`

Abstract. In the society increasingly concerned with the erosion of privacy, privacy-preserving techniques are becoming very important. This motivates research in cryptographic techniques offering built-in privacy. A secret handshake is a protocol whereby participants establish a secure, anonymous and unobservable communication channel only if they are members of the same group. This type of "private" authentication is a valuable tool in the arsenal of privacy-preserving cryptographic techniques. Prior research focused on 2-party secret handshakes with one-time credentials.

This paper breaks new ground on two accounts: (1) it shows how to obtain secure and efficient secret handshakes with reusable credentials, and (2) it represents the first treatment of group (or *multi-party*) secret handshakes, thus providing a natural extension to the secret handshake technology. An interesting new issue encountered in multi-party secret handshakes is the need to ensure that all parties are indeed distinct. (This is a real challenge since the parties cannot expose their identities.) We tackle this and other challenging issues in constructing **GCD** – a flexible framework for secret handshakes. The proposed **GCD** framework lends itself to many practical instantiations and offers several novel and appealing features such as self-distinction and strong anonymity with *reusable* credentials. In addition to describing the motivation and step-by-step construction of the framework, this paper provides a thorough security analysis and illustrates two concrete framework instantiations.

Keywords: secret handshakes, privacy-preservation, anonymity, credential systems, unobservability, key management.

1 Introduction

Much of today's communication is conducted over public networks which naturally prompts a number of concerns about security and privacy. Communication security has been studied extensively and a number of effective and efficient security tools and techniques are available.

Unfortunately, privacy concerns have not been addressed to the same extent. Yet, it is quite obvious to anyone who keeps up with the news that our society is very concerned with privacy. At the same time, privacy is being eroded

G. Danezis and P. Golle (Eds.): PET 2006, LNCS 4258, pp. 295–315, 2006.

by (often legitimate) concerns about crime, terrorism and other malfeasances. Furthermore, the proliferation of wireless communication (among laptops, cell phones, PDAs, sensors and RFIDs) drastically lowers the bar for eavesdropping and tracking of both people and their devices.

Popular techniques to provide communication privacy include email MIX-es, anonymizing routers and proxy web servers as well as purely cryptographic tools, such as private information retrieval. Despite important advances, the privacy continuum has not been fully explored. One particular issue that has not been widely recognized is the need for unobservable, untraceable and anonymous authentication, i.e., **privacy-preserving authentication**. Such a notion might seem counter-intuitive at first, since authentication traditionally goes hand-in-hand with identification. However, in the context of groups or roles, authentication identifies not a distinct entity but a collection thereof. To this end, some advanced cryptographic techniques have been developed, such as group signatures [1] and privacy-preserving trust negotiation [9,25].

We focus on *interactive privacy-preserving mutual authentication*; more specifically, on *secret handshakes*. A secret handshake scheme (SHS) allows two or more group members to authenticate each other in an anonymous, unlinkable and unobservable manner such that one's membership is not revealed unless every other party's membership is also ensured.[1]

In more detail, a secure handshake allows members of the same group to identify each other *secretly*, such that each party reveals its affiliation to others if and only if the latter are also group members. For example, in a 2-party setting, an FBI agent (Alice) wants to authenticate to Bob only if Bob is also an FBI agent. Moreover, if Bob is *not* an FBI agent, he should be unable to determine whether Alice is one (and vice versa). This property can be further extended to ensure that group members' affiliations are revealed only to members who hold specific *roles* in the group. For example, Alice might want to authenticate herself as an agent with a certain clearance level *only if* Bob is also an agent with at least the same clearance level.

In a more general sense, secret handshakes offer a means for privacy-preserving mutual authentication with many possible applications, especially, in hostile environments.

Goals: We set out to develop techniques for supporting efficient **multi-party** secret handshakes while avoiding certain drawbacks present in some or all of the previous **2-party** secret handshake solutions. These drawbacks include: (1) use of one-time credentials or pseudonyms, (2) ability of the group authority to cheat users, (3) requirement to maintain information about many irrelevant groups (groups that one is not a member of), and (4) lack of support for handshakes of three or more parties. Some of these drawbacks are self-explanatory, while others are clarified later in the paper.

---

[1] This informal definition broadens the prior version [3] which limited secret handshakes to two parties.

1.1   Overview and Summary of Contributions

We are interested in multi-party secret handshakes, whereby $m \geq 2$ parties establish a secure, anonymous and unobservable communication channel provided that they are members of the same group. We achieve this by constructing a secret handshake framework called **GCD**. This framework is essentially a *compiler* that transforms three main ingredients – a **G**roup signature scheme, a **C**entralized group key distribution scheme, and a **D**istributed group key agreement scheme – into a secure secret handshake scheme. We formally specify this framework based on desired functionality and security properties.

From the functionality perspective, existing solutions are only able to support 2-party secret handshakes [3,14,36]. Our framework represents the first result that supports truly *multi-party* secret handshakes. Moreover, our work is first to solve the problem of *partially-successful* secret handshakes.[2]

From the security perspective, our framework has two novel features. First, it can be resolved into concrete schemes that provide the novel and important `self-distinction` property which ensures the uniqueness of each handshake participant. In other words, it guarantees that the protocol is a multi-party computation with the exact number of players that claim to be participating. Without `self-distinction`, a malicious insider can easily impersonate any number of group members by simultaneously playing multiple roles in a handshake protocol.[3] Thus, an honest participant may be fooled into making a wrong decision when the number of participating parties is a factor in the decision-making policy. We also note that self-distinction is trivial for 2-party secret handshakes. However, it becomes more challenging for handshakes of three or more, since the parties cannot simply expose their identities; otherwise, anonymity would be lost.

Second, in contrast with prior work [3,14] which relies on one-time credentials to achieve `unlinkability` – this ensures that multiple handshake sessions involving the same participant(s) cannot be linked by an adversary – our approach provides `unlinkability` with multi-show (or reusable) credentials. This greatly enhances its usability. Moreover, our approach does not require users to be aware of other groups, in contrast with [36].

In addition, our framework has some interesting *flexibility* features. In particular, it is model-agnostic: if the building blocks operate in the asynchronous communication model (with guaranteed delivery), so does the resulting secret handshake scheme. Also, it supports a set of selectable properties that can be

---

[2] A partially successful handshake occurs whenever not all parties engaged in a handshake protocol are members of the same group. For example, if 5 parties take part in a secret handshake and 2 of them are members of group A, while the rest are members of group B, the desired outcome is for both the former and the latter to complete the secret handshake protocol and determine that their respective handshakes were performed with 2 and 3 members, respectively. Our scheme achieves this desired goal.

[3] This is reminiscent of the well-known Sybil attack [19], which is nevertheless different and not addressed in the present paper.

tailored to application needs and semantics (e.g., the two specific instantiations have two different sets of properties). Finally, it lends itself to many practical instantiations: we present two concrete examples where a handshake participant computes only $O(m)$ modular exponentiations and sends/receives $O(m)$ messages, where m is the number of handshake participants.

Organization: Section 2 presents our system model and definitions of secret handshake schemes. Then we proceed to discuss the design space and lay the foundation for the framework in Section 3. The models and definitions for the three building blocks are discussed in Sections 4, 5, and 6. Next, Section 7 presents the actual **GCD** framework and the analysis of its properties, followed by two concrete instantiations in Section 8. Some practical issues are considered in Section 9 and related work is overviewed in Section 10. The paper concludes with the summary and future research directions. Due to space limitation, we placed some technical material into the full version of the present paper [32].

2   Secret Handshakes: Model and Definition

Let κ be a security parameter and $\mathcal{U}$ be a set of all users: $\mathcal{U} = \{U_i \mid 0 < i < n\}$ where n is bounded by $poly(\kappa)$. Let **G** be a set of groups, where each group[4] $G \in \mathbf{G}$ is a set of members managed by a *group authority* $\mathcal{GA}$, which is responsible for admitting members, revoking their membership and updating system state information. For simplicity's sake we assume that each user is a member of exactly one group. (Of course, all results can be easily generalized to the case that users are allowed to join multiple groups.) An adversary $\mathcal{A}$ is allowed to corrupt various participants. All participants (including $\mathcal{A}$) are modeled as probabilistic polynomial-time algorithms.

We assume the existence of *anonymous* channels between all the legitimates participants, where the term "anonymous" means that an outside attacker cannot determine identities of the $\mathcal{GA}$, group members, as well as the dynamics and size of a group, and that a malicious insider cannot determine the identities of other honest group members as well as the the dynamics and size of the group. This assumption is necessary in most privacy-preserving authentication schemes; otherwise, anonymity could be trivially compromised. However, we note that the fact that secret handshake protocols themselves rely on anonymous channels does *not* necessarily present a problem. This is because a typical secret handshake application would be in a wireless setting where all communication is done via *broadcast* which offers receiver anonymity as a "built-in" feature.[5] (See Section 9 for further discussion of practical issues.)

---

[4] We use "group" to refer to a set of users, unless explicitly stated otherwise.

[5] This does not contradict our claim in Section 1 that wirelessness heightens privacy concerns. Although eavesdropping is easier in wireless networks, receiver anonymity is, at the same time, also easier to achieve in wireless (rather than in wired) networks.

Definition 1. *A secret handshake scheme (*SHS*) consists of the following algorithms and protocols:*

SHS.CreateGroup: *executed by $\mathcal{GA}$ to establish a group G. It takes as input appropriate security parameters, and outputs a cryptographic context specific to this group. The context may include a certificate/membership revocation list, $\mathcal{CRL}$, which is originally empty. The cryptographic context is made public, while the $\mathcal{CRL}$ is made known only to current group members.*

SHS.AdmitMember: *executed by $\mathcal{GA}$ to admit a user to the group under its jurisdiction. We assume that $\mathcal{GA}$ admits members according to a certain admission policy. Specification and enforcement of such policy is out the scope of this paper. After executing the algorithm, group state information has been appropriately updated, the new member holds some secret(s) as well as a membership certificate(s), and existing members obtain updated system information from $\mathcal{GA}$ via the aforementioned authenticated anonymous channel.*

SHS.RemoveUser: *executed by $\mathcal{GA}$. It takes as input the current $\mathcal{CRL}$ and a user identity U_i such that $U_i \in \mathcal{U}$ and $U_i \in G$. The output includes an updated $\mathcal{CRL}$ which includes the newly revoked certificate for U_i. The state update information is sent to the existing group members through the authenticated anonymous channel.*

SHS.Update: *executed by each current group member upon receiving, via the authenticated anonymous channel, system state update information from $\mathcal{GA}$. It is used to update each member's system state information.*

SHS.Handshake(Δ): *executed by a set Δ of m users purporting to be members of a group G, where $\Delta = \{U_1, \ldots, U_m\}$ and $m \geq 2$. The input to this protocol includes the secrets of all users in Δ, and possibly some public information regarding the current state of the systems. At the end of a protocol execution, it is ensured that each $U_i \in \Delta$ determines that $\Delta \setminus \{U_i\} \subseteq G$ if and only if each $U_j \in \Delta$ ($j \neq i$) discovers $\Delta \setminus \{U_j\} \subseteq G$.*

SHS.TraceUser: *executed by $\mathcal{GA}$. On input of a transcript of a successful secret handshake protocol SHS.Handshake(Δ), $\mathcal{GA}$ outputs the identities of all m participants involved in the handshake, i.e., $U_1, \ldots, U_m$.*

We note that the definition says nothing about the participants establishing a common key following (or during) a successful handshake. It is indeed straightforward to establish such a key if a secret handshake succeeds. However, allowing further communication based on a newly established key would require concealing the outcome of the handshake. (See also Section 9.) The definition also does not ensure any form of "agreement" in the sense of [20], since the adversary is assumed to have complete control over all communication, and can corrupt parties. This also explains why we only achieve a somewhat *weak* form of traceability.

Definition 2. *Desired security properties are informally specified below (the formal treatment is deferred to [32]).*

* **Correctness**: *If all handshake participants $\{U_1, \ldots, U_m\}$ belong to the same group, the protocol returns "1"; otherwise, the protocol returns "0".*
* **Resistance to impersonation**: *an adversary $\mathcal{A} \notin G$ who does not corrupt any members of G has only a negligible probability in convincing an honest user $U \in G$ that $\mathcal{A} \in G$. This remains to be true even if $\mathcal{A}$ plays the roles of multiple participants.*
* **Resistance to detection**: *no adversary $\mathcal{A} \notin G$ can distinguish between an interaction with an honest user $U \in G$ and an interaction with a simulator. This remains to be true even if $\mathcal{A}$ plays the roles of multiple participants.*
* **Full-unlinkability**: *no adversary $\mathcal{A}$ is able to associate two handshakes involving a same honest user $U \in G$, even if $\mathcal{A} \in G$ and $\mathcal{A}$ participated in both executions, and U has been corrupt. This remains to be true even if $\mathcal{A}$ plays the roles of multiple participants.*
* **Unlinkability**: *no adversary $\mathcal{A}$ is able to associate two handshakes involving a same honest user $U \in G$, even if $\mathcal{A} \in G$ and $\mathcal{A}$ participated in both executions. This remains to be true even if $\mathcal{A}$ plays the roles of multiple participants.*
* **Indistinguishability to eavesdroppers**: *no adversary $\mathcal{A}$ who does not participate in a handshake protocol can distinguish between a successful handshake between $\{U_1, \ldots, U_m\} \subseteq G$ and an unsuccessful one, even if $\mathcal{A} \in G$.*
* **Traceability**: *$\mathcal{GA}$ can trace all users involved in the handshake session of a given transcript.*
* **No-misattribution**: *no coalition of malicious parties (including any number of group members and the $\mathcal{GA}$) is able to frame an honest member as being involved in a secret handshake.*
* **Self-distinction**: *each participant is ensured that all the participants are distinct.*

Remark 1. If needed, our definitions of **resistance to impersonation** and **resistance to detection** can be naturally extended to capture the case when $\mathcal{A}$ corrupts some group members but does not use their secrets in the subsequent handshake protocols.

We notice that for certain applications **full-unlinkability** may be desirable, while for certain other applications **unlinkability** and **self-distinction** may be desirable. In other words, the framework specifies the important properties, while leaving the decision on which subset of the properties to satisfy to the specific applications.

The flavor of **traceability** achieved in the framework is relatively weak since the protocol participant who is last to send out the values (to facilitate traceability) can always neglect to do so. However, we observe that this holds in other schemes, even in those based on one-time credentials [3,14]. The subtle issue is that the last sender could always use a "fake" token before other (honest) participants can verify its validity. This is inevitable because of the basic impossibility result in [20]. While there are some purely theoretical ways to mitigate this problem, we are interested in efficient (i.e., practical) solutions. Consequently, we are prepared to tolerate some unfairness, which, nevertheless, only exists between *legitimate* users. As a result, the achieved traceability is still valuable for investigating activities of group members before they become corrupt.

3   Design Space

As mentioned earlier, the **GCD** framework is essentially a compiler that outputs a multi-party secret handshake scheme satisfying all desired propertied specified in Section 2. Its input includes:

- A group signature scheme (GSIG): a scheme that allows any group member to produce signatures on behalf of the group in an anonymous and unlinkable manner; only a special entity (called a group manager) is able to revoke anonymity and "open" a group signature thereby revealing the signer's identity. (See Section 4.)
- A centralized group key distribution (broadcast encryption) scheme (CGKD): a key management scheme for large one-to-many groups that handles key changes due to dynamic group membership and facilitates secure broadcast encryption. (See Section 5.)
- A distributed group key agreement scheme (DGKA): a scheme that allows a group of peer entities to dynamically (on-the-fly) agree on a common secret key to be used for subsequent secure communication within that group. (See Section 6.)

We now discuss the choices made in designing **GCD**. As a first try, one might be tempted to construct a secret handshake scheme directly upon a CGKD that enables secure multicast. It is easy to see that $m \geq 2$ members can conduct efficient secret handshakes based on a group key k. However, this approach would have some significant drawbacks:

(1) No indistinguishability-to-eavesdroppers. A *passive* malicious (or even honest-but-curious) group member can detect, by simply eavesdropping, whenever other members are conducting a secret handshake.
(2) No traceability. A dishonest member who takes part in a handshake (or is otherwise malicious) can not be traced and held accountable.
(3) No self-distinction. For handshakes of more than two parties, self-distinction is not attained since a rogue member can play multiple roles in a handshake.

Alternatively, one could employ a GSIG scheme as a basis for a secret handshake scheme. This would avoid the above drawback (2), however, drawback (1) remains. Also, resistance to detection attacks would be sacrificed, since (as noted in [3]), group signatures are verifiable by anyone in possession of the group public key.

A natural next step is to combine a CGKD with a GSIG. This way, the GSIG group public key is kept secret among all current group members (along with the CGKD group-wide secret key k), and – during the handshake – group signatures would be encrypted under the group-wide key k. Although traceability would be re-gained, unfortunately, drawbacks (1) and (3) would remain.

In order to avoid (1), we need the third component, an interactive distributed key agreement protocol. With it, any member who wants to determine if other parties are members (or are conducting a secret handshake) is forced to participate in a secret handshake protocol. As a result, the group signatures are encrypted with a key derived from both: (a) the group-wide key and (b) the freshly established key. Moreover, we can thus ensure that, as long as a group signature is presented by a corrupt member, the traceability feature enables the group authority to hold that member accountable.

As pertains to drawback (3) above (no self-distinction), we defer the discussion to later in the paper. Suffice it to say that group signature schemes do not provide self-distinction by design, since doing so undermines their version of the unlinkability property. (Unlinkability in group signatures is different from that in group secret handshakes; see Section 8.2.) To remedy the situation, we need some additional tools, as described in Section 8 below.

Since our approach involves combining a group signature scheme with a centralized group key distribution scheme, it is natural to examine potentially redundant components. In particular, both GSIG and CGKD schemes include a revocation mechanism. Furthermore, revocation in the former is quite expensive, usually based on dynamic accumulators [12]. Thus, it might seem worthwhile to drop the revocation of component of GSIG altogether in favor of the more efficient revocation in CGKD. This way, a revoked member would simply not receive the new group-wide key in CGKD but would remain un-revoked as far as the underlying GSIG is concerned. To illustrate the problem with this optimization, consider an attack whereby a malicious but unrevoked member reveals the CGKD group-wide key to a revoked member. The latter can then take part in secret handshakes and successfully fool legitimate members. Whereas, if both revocation components are in place, the attack fails since the revoked member's group signature (exchanged as part of the handshake) would not be accepted as valid.

4   Building Block I: Group Signature Schemes

Let $\mathcal{U}$ be the universe of user identities. In a group signature scheme, there is an authority called a group manager ($\mathcal{GM}$) responsible for admitting users and identifying the actual signer of a given group signature[6]. There is also a set of users who can sign on behalf of the group. In addition, there is a set of entities called verifiers. All participants are modeled as probabilistic polynomial-time algorithms.

A group signature scheme, denoted by GSIG, consists of the following algorithms.

Setup: a probabilistic polynomial-time algorithm that, on input of a security parameter κ, outputs the specification of a cryptographic context including the group manager's public key $pk_{\mathcal{GM}}$ and secret key $sk_{\mathcal{GM}}$. This procedure may be denoted by $(pk_{\mathcal{GM}}, sk_{\mathcal{GM}}) \leftarrow \text{Setup}(1^{\kappa})$.

---

[6] Sometimes, the two functionalities are assigned to two separate entities.

Join: a protocol between $\mathcal{GM}$ and a user (conducted over a private and authenticated channel) that results in the user becoming a group member U. Their common output includes the user's unique membership public key pk_U, and perhaps some updated information that indicates the current state of the system. The user's output includes a membership secret key sk_U. This procedure may be denoted by $(pk_U, sk_U, certificate_U; pk_U, certificate_U) \leftarrow \text{Join}[U \leftrightarrow \mathcal{GM}]$, where $\text{Join}[U \leftrightarrow \mathcal{GM}]$ denotes an interactive protocol between U and $\mathcal{GM}$, $pk_U, sk_U, certificate_U$ is the output of U, and $pk_U, certificate_U$ is the output of $\mathcal{GM}$. Besides, there may be some system state information that is made public to all participants.

Revoke: an algorithm that, on input of a group member's identity (and perhaps her public key pk_U), outputs updated information that indicates the current state of the system after revoking the membership of a given group member.

Update: a deterministic algorithm that may be triggered by any Join or Revoke operation. It is run by each group member after obtaining system state information from the group manager.

Sign: a probabilistic algorithm that, on input of: key $pk_{\mathcal{GM}}$, (sk_U, pk_U) and a message M, outputs a group signature σ of M. This procedure may be denoted by $\sigma \leftarrow \text{Sign}(pk_{\mathcal{GM}}, pk_U, sk_U, M)$.

Verify: an algorithm that, on input of: $pk_{\mathcal{GM}}$, an alleged group signature σ and a message M, outputs a binary value TRUE/FALSE indicating whether σ is a valid group signature (under $pk_{\mathcal{GM}}$) of M. This procedure may be denoted by TRUE/FALSE $\leftarrow \text{Verify}(pk_{\mathcal{GM}}, M, \sigma)$.

Open: an algorithm executed by the group manager $\mathcal{GM}$. It takes as input of a message M, a group signature σ, $pk_{\mathcal{GM}}$ and $sk_{\mathcal{GM}}$. It first executes Verify on the first three inputs and, if the output of Verify is TRUE, outputs some incontestable evidence (e.g., a membership public key pk_U and a proof) that allows anyone to identify the actual signer. This procedure may be denoted, without loss of generality, by $U \leftarrow \text{Open}(pk_{\mathcal{GM}}, sk_{\mathcal{GM}}, M, \sigma)$ if TRUE $\leftarrow \text{Verify}(pk_{\mathcal{GM}}, M, \sigma)$.

Informally, we require a group signature scheme to be **correct**, i.e., any signature produced by an honest group member using Sign is always accepted by Verify.

Following notable prior work [4,7,23], we say a group signature scheme is **secure** if it satisfies the following three properties (see[32] for a formal definition): (1) **full-traceability** – any valid group signature can be traced back to its actual signer, (2) **full-anonymity** – no adversary can identify the actual signer of a group signature, even if the actual signer's secret has been compromised, and (3) **no-misattribution** – no malicious group manager can misattribute a group signature to an honest group member.

In order to achieve secret handshakes of **self-distinction**, we may also adopt group signature schemes achieving a somewhat weaker privacy notion. Specifically, we can substitute the following weaker notion of **anonymity** for the above **full-anonymity**: (2') **anonymity** – no adversary can identify the actual signer of a group signature, as long as the actual signer's secret has *not* been compromised. As we will see, our specific handshake scheme achieving `self-distinction` is based on the variant group signature scheme of [22], which fulfills the above `anonymity` rather than `full-anonymity`.

5   Building Block II: Centralized Group Key Distribution Scheme

Let κ be a security parameter, and $\mathbb{ID}$ be the set of possible group members (i.e., users, receivers, or principals) such that $|\mathbb{ID}|$ is polynomially-bounded in κ. There is a special entity called a *Group Controller* (i.e., key server, center, server, or sender), denoted by $\mathcal{GC}$, such that $\mathcal{GC} \notin \mathbb{ID}$.

Since a (stateful) group communication scheme is driven by "rekeying" events (because of joining or leaving operations below), it is convenient to treat the events occur at "virtual time" $t = 0, 1, 2, \ldots$, because the group controller is able to maintain such an execution history. At time t, let $\Delta^{(t)}$ denote the set of legitimate group members, $k^{(t)} = k_{\mathcal{GC}}^{(t)} = k_{U_1}^{(t)} = \ldots$ the group (or session) key, $K_{\mathcal{GC}}^{(t)}$ the set of keys held by $\mathcal{GC}$, $K_U^{(t)}$ the set of keys held by $U \in \Delta^{(t)}$, $\mathsf{acc}_U^{(t)}$ the state indicating whether $U \in \Delta^{(t)}$ has successfully received the rekeying message. Initially, $\forall\, U \in \mathbb{ID}, t \in \mathbb{N}$, set $\mathsf{acc}_U^{(t)} \leftarrow$ FALSE. We assume that $\mathcal{GC}$ treat joining and leaving operation separately (e.g., first fulfilling the leaving operation and then immediately the joining one), even if the requests are made simultaneously. This strategy has indeed been adopted in the group communication literature.

To simplify the presentation, we assume that during system initialization (i.e., Setup described below) $\mathcal{GC}$ can communicate with each legitimate member U through an *authenticated private* channel. In practice, this assumption can be implemented with a two-party authenticated key-exchange protocol. Further, we assume that $\mathcal{GC}$ can establish a common secret, if needed, with a joining user, and that after the system initialization $\mathcal{GC}$ can communicate with any $U \in \mathbb{ID}$ through an *authenticated* channel.

A centralized group key distribution scheme (CGKD) is specified below. It is adopted from [35].

Setup: The group controller $\mathcal{GC}$ generates a set of keys $K_{\mathcal{GC}}^{(0)}$, and distributes them to the current group members (that may be determined by the adversary), $\Delta^{(0)} \subseteq \mathbb{ID}$, through the authenticated private channels. (If some users were corrupted before this setup procedure, we may let the adversary select the keys held by the corrupt users.) Each member $U_i \in \Delta^{(0)}$ holds a set of keys denoted by $K_{U_i}^{(0)} \subset K_{\mathcal{GC}}^{(0)}$, and there is a key, $k^{(0)}$ that is common to all the current members, namely $k^{(0)} \in K_{\mathcal{GC}}^{(0)} \cap K_{U_1}^{(0)} \cap \ldots \cap K_{U_{|\Delta^{(0)}|}}^{(0)}$.

Join: This algorithm is executed by the group controller $\mathcal{GC}$ at certain time t following a join request by a prospective member. (We abstract away the out-of-band authentication and establishment of an individual key for each new member). It takes as input: (1) a set of identities of current group members

– $\Delta^{(t-1)}$, (2) identities of newly admitted group member, $\Delta' \subseteq \mathbb{ID} \setminus \Delta^{(t-1)}$, (3) keys held by the group controller, $K_{\mathcal{GC}}^{(t-1)}$, and (4) keys held by group members, $\{K_{U_i}^{(t-1)}\}_{U_i \in \Delta^{(t-1)}} = \{K_{U_i}^{(t-1)} : U_i \in \Delta^{(t-1)}\}$.

It outputs updated system state information, including: (1) identities of new group members, $\Delta^{(t)} \leftarrow \Delta^{(t-1)} \cup \Delta'$, (2) new keys for $\mathcal{GC}$ itself, $K_{\mathcal{GC}}^{(t)}$, (3) new keys for new group members, $\{K_{U_i}^{(t)}\}_{U_i \in \Delta^{(t)}}$, which are *somehow* sent to the legitimate users through the authenticated channels (depending on concrete schemes), (4) new group key $k^{(t)} \in K_{\mathcal{GC}}^{(t)} \cap K_{U_1}^{(t)} \cap \ldots \cap K_{U_{|\Delta^{(t)}|}}^{(t)}$. Denote it by $(\Delta^{(t)}, K_{\mathcal{GC}}^{(t)}, \{K_{U_i}^{(t)}\}_{U_i \in \Delta^{(t)}}) \leftarrow \mathsf{Join}(\Delta^{(t-1)}, \Delta', K_{\mathcal{GC}}^{(t-1)}, \{K_{U_i}^{(t-1)}\}_{U_i \in \Delta^{(t-1)}})$.

Leave: This algorithm is executed by the group controller $\mathcal{GC}$ at time, say, t due to leave or revocation operation(s). It takes as input: (1) identities of previous group members, $\Delta^{(t-1)}$, (2) identities of leaving group members, $\Delta' \subseteq \Delta^{(t-1)}$, (3) keys held by the controller, $K_{\mathcal{GC}}^{(t-1)}$, and (4) keys held by group members, $\{K_{U_i}\}_{U_i \in \Delta^{(t-1)}}^{(t-1)}$.

It outputs updated system state information, including: (1) identities of new group members, $\Delta^{(t)} \leftarrow \Delta^{(t-1)} \setminus \Delta'$, (2) new keys for $\mathcal{GC}$, $K_{\mathcal{GC}}^{(t)}$, (3) new keys for new group members, $\{K_{U_i}^{(t)}\}_{U_i \in \Delta^{(t)}}$, which are *somehow* sent to the legitimate users through the authenticated channels (depending on concrete schemes), (4) new group key $k^{(t)} \in K_{\mathcal{GC}}^{(t)} \cap K_{U_1}^{(t)} \cap \ldots \cap K_{U_{|\Delta^{(t)}|}}^{(t)}$. Denote it by $(\Delta^{(t)}, K_{\mathcal{GC}}^{(t)}, \{K_{U_i}^{(t)}\}_{U_i \in \Delta^{(t)}}) \leftarrow \mathsf{Leave}(\Delta^{(t-1)}, \Delta', K_{\mathcal{GC}}^{(t-1)}, \{K_{U_i}^{(t-1)}\}_{U_i \in \Delta^{(t-1)}})$.

Rekey: This algorithm is executed by the legitimate group members at some time t, namely all $U_i \in \Delta^{(t)}$ where $\Delta^{(t)}$ is derived from a Join or Leave event. In other words, $U_i \in \Delta^{(t)}$ runs this algorithm upon receiving the message from $\mathcal{GC}$ over the authenticated channel. The algorithm takes as input the received message and U_i's secrets, and is supposed to output the updated keys for the group member. If the execution of the algorithm is successful, U_i sets: (1) $\mathsf{acc}_{U_i}^{(t)} \leftarrow$ TRUE, (2) $K_{U_i}^{(t)}$, where $k_{U_i}^{(t)} \in K_{U_i}^{(t)}$ is supposed to be the new group key.

If the rekeying event is incurred by a Join event, every $U_i \in \Delta^{(t)}$ erases $K_{U_i}^{(t-1)}$ and any temporary storage after obtaining $K_{U_i}^{(t)}$. If the rekeying event is incurred by a Leave event, every $U_i \in \Delta^{(t)}$ erases $K_{U_i}^{(t-1)}$ and any temporary storage after obtaining $K_{U_i}^{(t)}$, and every *honest* leaving group member $U_j \in \Delta'$ erases $K_{U_j}^{(t-1)}$ (although a *corrupt* one does not have to follow this protocol).

We require for a CGKD scheme to be **correct**, meaning that after each rekey process, all the group members share a common key with the group controller, and **secure**, meaning that no adversary learns any information about a group key at time t_1, even if there are corrupt users at time $t_2 > t_1$. This is the strongest notion, called *strong-security in the active outsider attack model* in [35] (somewhat surprisingly, existing popular group communication schemes do not achieve this property, but many of them can be made secure in this sense without incurring any significant extra complexity [35]). We defer formal definition and discussions to [32].

6   Building Block III: Distributed Group Key Agreement

Let κ be a security parameter. We assume a polynomial-size set $\mathbb{ID}$ of potential players. Any subset of $\mathbb{ID}$ may decide at any point to invoke distributed group key agreement. A distributed group key agreement scheme, DGKA, is specified below; it follows the results in [5] and [21].

Environment: Since each principal can take part it many runs of the GroupKeyA-greement protocol (described below), we denote an instance i of $U \in \mathbb{ID}$ as Π_U^i. Each instance Π_U^i is associated with variables $\mathsf{acc}_U^i, \mathsf{sid}_U^i, \mathsf{pid}_U^i, \mathsf{sk}_U^i$. Initially, $\forall\, U \in \mathbb{ID}$ and $i \in \mathbb{N}$, $\mathsf{acc}_U^i \leftarrow \text{FALSE}$ and $\mathsf{sid}_U^i, \mathsf{pid}_U^i, \mathsf{sk}_U^i \leftarrow \text{UNDEFINED}$.

GroupKeyAgreement: a protocol that performs distributed unauthenticated (or "raw") group agreement between any set of $m \geq 2$ parties. After executing the protocol, each party outputs an indication of the protocol outcome (success or failure), and some secret information, in case of success. In more detail, the protocol is executed by m instances: $\Pi_{U_1}^{i_1}, \ldots, \Pi_{U_m}^{i_m}$, where $\{U_1, \ldots, U_m\} \subseteq \mathbb{ID}$. If the execution of $\Pi_{U_j}^{i_j}$ is successful, it sets:

1. $\mathsf{acc}_{U_j}^{i_j} \leftarrow \text{TRUE}$,

2. $\mathsf{sid}_{U_j}^{i_j}$ as the session id of instance $\Pi_{U_j}^{i_j}$, namely a protocol-specific function of all communication sent and received by $\Pi_{U_j}^{i_j}$ (e.g., we can simply set $\mathsf{sid}_{U_j}^{i_j}$ as the concatenation of all messages sent and received by $\Pi_{U_j}^{i_j}$ in the course of its execution),

3. $\mathsf{pid}_{U_j}^{i_j}$ as the session id of instance $\Pi_{U_j}^{i_j}$, namely the identities of the principals in the group with whom $\Pi_{U_j}^{i_j}$ intends to establish a session key (including U_j itself), and (4) $\mathsf{sk}_{U_j}^{i_j}$ as the newly established session key.

Remark: We stress that this definition does not offer any *authentication*, i.e., it does not capture *authenticated group key agreement*. For example, the above definition can be satisfied (instantiated) with a straight-forward extension to any of the several group Diffie-Hellman protocols, such as BD or GDH [11,30]. Of course, we are aware that unauthenticated key agreement protocols are susceptible to man-in-the-middle (MITM) attacks; this is addressed later, through the use of our second building block – CGKD.

Informally speaking (see [32] for a formal definition), we require for a scheme to have **correctness** and **security**. **Correctness** means that all participants must obtain the same new session secret (key), and **security** means that a passive adversary – who does not compromise any principal during protocol execution – does not learn any information about the new group session key.

7   GCD Secret Handshake Framework

The **GCD** framework has the following components:

GCD.CreateGroup: The group authority ($\mathcal{GA}$) plays the roles of both group manager in GSIG and group controller in CGKD.
  - $\mathcal{GA}$ executes GSIG.Setup. This initializes a group signature scheme.
  - $\mathcal{GA}$ executes CGKD.Setup. This initializes a centralized group key distribution (broadcast encryption) scheme.
  - $\mathcal{GA}$ generates a pair of public/private keys (pk_T, sk_T) with respect to an IND-CCA2 secure public key cryptosystem. This pair of keys enables $\mathcal{GA}$ to identify handshake participants in any handshake transcript.
  - Note that no real group-specific setup is required for initializing the distributed group key agreement component – DGKA. We assume that there is a set of system-wide (not group-specific) cryptographic parameters for the DGKA scheme, e.g., all groups use the same group key agreement protocol with the same global parameters. (More on this below.)

GCD.AdmitMember: $\mathcal{GA}$ executes CGKD.Join and GSIG.Join.
  CGKD.Join results in a new group key and GSIG.Join causes an update to GSIG state information. The updated GSIG state information is encrypted under the new CGKD group key and distributed to all group members through an authenticated anonymous channel, e.g., posted on a public bulletin board.

GCD.RemoveUser: $\mathcal{GA}$ executes CGKD.Leave and GSIG.Revoke, except: (1) the updated system state information corresponding to GSIG is encrypted under CGKD's new group session key, and distributed as part of CGKD's state information updating message, and (2) the update messages are distributed via an authenticated anonymous channel.

GCD.Update: All non-revoked members execute GSIG.Update and CGKD.Rekey, except: (1) the updated system state information is obtained from an authenticated anonymous channel, and (2) if CGKD.Rekey succeeds, the update information corresponding to GSIG is decrypted using CGKD's new group key.

GCD.Handshake: Suppose m (≥ 2) users want to determine if they belong to the same group. We denote their group keys with respect to CGKD as: $k_1, \ldots, k_m$, respectively. Note that, if they belong to the same group, then $k_1 = \ldots = k_m$.

  Phase I: Preparation: All m parties jointly execute DGKA.GroupKeyAgreement. We denote the resulting keys as: $k_1^*, \ldots, k_m^*$, respectively. If the execution is successful, then $k_1^* = \ldots = k_m^*$, and each party computes $k_i' = k_i^* \oplus k_i$.

  Phase II: Preliminary Handshake: Each party publishes a tag $\mathrm{MAC}(k_i', s, i)$ corresponding to a message authentication code MAC (e.g., HMAC-SHA1), where s is a string unique to party i, e.g., the message(s) it sent in the DGKA.GroupKeyAgreement execution.[7]

  Phase III: Full Handshake: There are two cases:

---

[7] If a broadcast channel is available, the tag is sent on it; else, it is sent point-to-point.

CASE 1: If all message authentication tags are valid (i.e., they belong to the same group), each party executes the following:

1. Encrypt k_i' to obtain ciphertext δ_i under the group authority's tracing public key pk_T; $\delta_i \leftarrow \mathsf{ENC}(pk_T, k_i')$.
2. Generate a group signature σ_i on δ_i via GSIG.Sign.
3. Encrypt σ_i using a symmetric key encryption algorithm and key k_i' to obtain a ciphertext θ_i; $\theta_i \leftarrow \mathsf{SENC}(k_i', \sigma_i)$.
4. Publish (θ_i, δ_i).
5. Upon receiving (θ_i, δ_i), execute the following:
   - Obtain the group signature by performing symmetric key decryption algorithm using k_i'; $\sigma_i \leftarrow \mathsf{SDEC}(k_i', \theta_i)$.
   - Run GSIG.Verify to check if σ_i is a valid group signature. If all group signatures are deemed valid, the party concludes that the corresponding parties all belong to the same group and stores the transcript including $\{(\theta_i, \delta_i)\}_{1 \leq i \leq m}$.

CASE 2: If at least one message authentication tag is invalid, each of party picks and publishes a pair (θ_i, δ_i) randomly selected from the ciphertext spaces corresponding to the symmetric key and public key cryptosystems, respectively.

GCD.TraceUser: Given a transcript of a secret handshake instance: $\{(\theta_i, \delta_i)\}_{1 \leq i \leq m}$, the group authority $\mathcal{GA}$ decrypts all δ_i's to obtain the corresponding session keys: $k_1', \ldots, k_m'$. In the worst case, the authority needs to try to search the right session key and decrypt all θ_i's to obtain the cleartext group signatures. Then, it executes GSIG.Open to identify the handshake parties.

Remark 2. In order to enable modular construction, we specify the handshake protocol as a three-phase protocol. Thus, the resulting framework is flexible, i.e., tailorable to application semantics. For example, if traceability is not required, a handshake may only involve Phase I and Phase II.

The following theorems are proved in [32].

Theorem 1. *Assume* GSIG *possesses the properties specified in Section 4, namely* correctness, full-traceability, full-anonymity, *and* no-misattribution. *Assume also that* DGKA *and* CGKD *are secure with respect to their corresponding definitions in Sections 5-6. Then, the* **GCD** *framework possesses the properties specified in Section 2, namely* correctness, resistance to impersonation, resistance to detection, full-unlinkability, indistinguishability to eavesdroppers, traceability, *and* no-misattribution.

Theorem 2. *Assume* GSIG *possesses the properties specified in Section 4, namely* correctness, full-traceability, anonymity, *and* no-misattribution. *Assume* DGKA *and* CGKD *are secure with respect to their corresponding definitions in Sections 5-6. Then, the* **GCD** *framework possesses the properties specified in Section 2, namely* correctness, resistance to impersonation, resistance to detection, unlinkability, indistinguishability to eavesdroppers, traceability, *and* no-misattribution.

Extension: A natural extension of the above framework can fulfill the afore-mentioned *partially-successful* secret handshakes, namely that all such $\Delta \subset \{1,\ldots,m\}$ that consists of $|\Delta| > 1$ members of a same group can always succeed in their handshakes without incurring any extra complexity. Each participant i can immediately tell the Δ such that $i \in \Delta$ as i knows which message authentication tags are valid.

8   Two Concrete Instantiations

We now present two concrete secret handshake schemes. The first scheme employs "raw" (unauthenticated) contributory group key agreement, and the second scheme ensures that all handshake participants are distinct.

8.1   Example Scheme 1

This is a straight-forward instantiation of the **GCD** framework. We simply plug in unauthenticated group key agreement (DGKA) derived from any of [11,30,21], CGKD based on [34,26], and GSIG based on [1,12]. Theorem 1 immediately implies that this instantiation satisfies all properties specified in Section 2, excluding self-distinction.

Computational complexity for each party is the sum of the respective complexities incurred in each of the three building blocks. Note that, in an m-party handshake, each party only needs to compute $O(m)$ modular exponentiations in total. Moreover, the communication complexity is $O(m)$ per-user in number of messages.

8.2   Example Scheme 2

As mentioned above, the first instantiation does not offer self-distinction, i.e., some of the m parties in a handshake protocol could in fact be "played" by the same party. We now discuss the basic idea for attaining the self-distinction property. Naturally, neither group key agreement nor centralized key distribution (i.e., the CGKD and DGKA components) can provide self-distinction. Thus, we turn to group signatures to obtain it. However, group signature schemes do not natively offer self-distinction since it runs against one of their basic tenets, informally summarized as:

> *Given any two group signatures it should be impossible to determine with any certainty whether the same signer (or two distinct signers) generated both signatures*

Nonetheless, the need for self-distinction in group signatures (not in secret handshakes) has been recognized prior to this paper. In particular, the work in [2] introduces the concept of *subgroup signatures* motivated by certain applications, such as anonymous petitions. (In an anonymous petition, t group members want to sign a document in a way that any verifier can determine with certainty that all t signers are distinct.) The example technique for constructing sub-group signatures in [2] involves slight modifications to the underlying group signature scheme. This is very similar to what we need to achieve self-distinction in the proposed framework.

Unfortunately, we cannot use the example in [2] since it is based on a group signature scheme [13] which is inefficient and not provably secure. However, we can modify a more recent (as well as much more efficient and provably secure) group signature scheme by Kiayas and Yung [22]. In this scheme each group signature is accompanied by a pair: $\langle T_6 = g^{\beta\alpha}, T_7 = g^\alpha \rangle$, where β is the signer's secret, and α is the signer's randomness for this specific signature. This structure has a nice feature that T_7 serves only as an "anonymity shield" in the sense that the signer does not even need to prove the knowledge of α. Instead, it is crucial that $T_6 = T_7^\beta$. Intuitively, this allows us to obtain `self-distinction` if we let each handshake participant use the same T_7, since they should all provide distinct T_6's. This can be achieved by simply utilizing an idealized hash function [6] $\mathcal{H} : \{0,1\}^* \to \mathbf{R}$ to the input of, for instance, the concatenation of all messages sent by the handshake participants.[8] This ensures that, as long as there is at least one honest participant, the resulting T_7 is uniformly distributed over $\mathbf{R}$, and the security proof in [22] remain sufficient for our purposes.

We now present a scheme based on the modified version of [22]. In what follows we only illustrate the handshake protocol since it is the only distinctive feature of this scheme.

GCD.Handshake: Assume m (≥ 2) users are taking part in the protocol. We denote their group keys with respect to the CGKD by $k_1, \ldots, k_m$, respectively. As before, if they belong to the same group, $k_1 = \ldots = k_m$.

Phase I: Preparation: m parties jointly execute DGKA.GroupKeyAgreement. Let the resulting keys be denoted as: $k_1^*, \ldots, k_m^*$, respectively. (After a successful run $k_1^* = \ldots = k_m^*$.) Then, each party computes $k_i' = k_i^* \oplus k_i$

Phase II: Preliminary Handshake: Each party publishes a pair MAC(k_i', s, i), where s is a string unique to i.

Phase III: Full Handshake: We consider two cases:

Case 1: If all message authentication tags are valid (i.e., they belong to the same group), each party executes as follows:

1. Encrypt k_i' under the public key pk_T to obtain ciphertext δ_i.
2. Generate a variant group signature σ_i on δ_i on s via GSIG.Sign, which is the same as in [22] except that T_7 is chosen using an ideal hash function as discussed above, and the *same* T_7 is common to all handshake participants. (We stress that `self-distinction` is obtained from requiring all participants to use the same T_7 which forces them to compute distinct T_6 values.)
3. Encrypt σ_i using a symmetric key encryption algorithm and key k_i' to obtain ciphertext $\theta_i \leftarrow$ SENC(k_i', σ_i).

---

[8] While it would suffice for $\mathbf{R}$ to be $QR(n)$, what is needed in [22] is in fact that $g \in QR(n)$ and α is chosen from an appropriate interval, i.e., $\mathbf{R} \subset QR(n)$.

4. Publish (θ_i, δ_i).
5. Upon receiving (θ_i, δ_i), execute as follows:
   (a) Obtain $\sigma_i \leftarrow \mathsf{SDEC}(k_i', \theta_i)$
   (b) Run GSIG.Verify to check if each σ_i is a valid group signature (if all group signatures are valid, it concludes that they all belong to the same group and records the transcript).

Case 2: If at least one message authentication tag is invalid, each party simulates the above execution of the Pederson protocol and then picks a pair of (θ_i, δ_i) randomly selected from the ciphertext spaces corresponding to the symmetric key and public key cryptosystems, respectively.

A proof sketch of the following theorem can be found in [32].

Theorem 3. *Assume that* GSIG *possesses the properties specified in Section 4, namely* correctness, full-traceability, anonymity, *and* no-misattribution. *Assume also that* DGKA *and* CGKD *are secure with respect to their corresponding definitions in Sections 5-6. Then, the above instantiation possesses the properties of* correctness, resistance to impersonation, resistance to detection, unlinkability, indistinguishability to eavesdroppers, no-misattribution, traceability, *and* self-distinction *specified in Section 2.*

Computational complexity in number of modular exponentiations (per-user) remains $O(m)$ and communication complexity (also per-user) in number of messages also $O(m)$, where m is the number of participants.

9   Discussion

There are several practical issues that need to be addressed. First, if there is only a single group that uses a secret handshake scheme, an adversary can simply figure out that the handshake peers belong to that group. In fact, if a secret handshake scheme is implemented as a TLS or IKE cipher suite, then the parties will exchange a cipher suite designator that clearly shows that they wish to engage in a secret handshake. Second, in any secret handshake scheme, utilizing one-time or reusable credentials alike, it is assumed that there is no easy way to identify the party who sent or received a certain message; otherwise, it is easy for an adversary to discover who is interacting with whom. This assumption is also true in privacy-preserving authentication mechanisms [24,8,16,17,28,27]. Third, if an adversary observes that handshake participants continue communicating after finishing the handshake protocol, it can deduce that they belong to the same group. (This applies to any secret handshake scheme utilizing one-time or reusable credentials.)

The above issues can be mitigated by various means. First, it is reasonable to assume that there are many groups, as long as it is not illegal to conduct secret handshakes. Second, there may be settings where the identity (for the purpose of authentication) of a party is not directly derivable from the address that must appear in the clear in protocol messages. A common example is the case of mobile devices wishing to prevent an attacker from correlating their (changing) locations with the device's logical identity [24]. Furthermore, some form of anonymous communication could make it hard to decide exactly who is engaging in a secret handshake. Third, protection against traffic analysis (e.g., an adversary simply observing continued communication after a handshake) can be achieved by utilizing mechanisms such as steganographic techniques, or anonymous communication channels.

In summary, if all assumptions are satisfied, then our secret handshake schemes (as well as [3,24,8]) can provide provable privacy-preserving authentication, whereby two (or in our case, more) participants authenticate each other's membership *simultaneously*. Otherwise, all schemes attain heuristic or *best-effort* anonymity.

10   Related Work

The first secret handshake scheme [3] is based on the protocol of Sakai et al. [29], which targets the key exchange problem. Indeed, a secret handshake can be appropriately turned into an authenticated key exchange, but an authenticated key exchange does not necessarily imply a secret handshake, e.g., the two-party Diffie-Hellman key agreement scheme [18] does not lend itself to solving the secret handshake problem; see [3]. The scheme in [3] is based on bilinear maps in the setting of elliptic curves and its security is based on the associated assumptions. This scheme uses one-time pseudonyms to achieve unlinkability and does not offer the *No-misattribution* property.

A more recent result is due to Castelluccia, et al. [14]. This work constructs several handshake schemes in more standard cryptographic settings (avoiding bilinear maps) and provides some extensions for satisfying *No-misattribution*. However, it still relies on one-time pseudonyms to satisfy unlinkability. Another recent result by [36] requires each player to be aware of the information of other groups and offers weaker anonymity (referred to as k-anonymity).

11   Conclusions and Future Work

To summarize, we present **GCD**– a flexible secret handshake framework. **GCD** is a compiler that can transform a group signature scheme, a centralized group key distribution scheme, and a distributed group key agreement scheme into a secure secret handshake scheme. As illustrated by three concrete examples, **GCD** lends itself to actual practical instantiations and offers several interesting new features. **GCD** avoids the use of one-time pseudonyms and, unlike prior techniques, supports handshakes among an arbitrary number of parties. Furthermore, **GCD** can be instantiated to support the important new property of self-distinction important in handshakes of more than two participants.

We believe that the work described in this paper is a *first* step towards achieving practical anonymous interactive multi-party authentication protocols. Much remains to be done. First, the **GCD** framework needs to be implemented and experimented with. Second, we have made no attempt to optimize the efficiency of the framework. Further investigation is clearly called for. Third, efficient constructions are needed for those settings where the **GCD** framework does not apply (because, e.g., the lack of a centralized group key distribution scheme).

References

1. G. Ateniese, J. Camenisch, M. Joye, and G. Tsudik. A practical and provably secure coalition-resistant group signature scheme. In *Proc. CRYPTO 2000*, pages 255–270. Springer, 2000. Lecture Notes in Computer Science No. 1880.
2. G. Ateniese and G. Tsudik. Some Open Issues and New Directions in Group Signatures. In *Financial Cryptography'99*. Lecture Notes in Computer Science No. 1880.
3. D. Balfanz, G. Durfee, N. Shankar, D. Smetters, J. Staddon, and H. Wong. Secret handshakes from pairing-based key agreements. In *24th IEEE Symposium on Security and Privacy*, May 2003.
4. M. Bellare, D. Micciancio, and B. Warinschi. Foundations of group signatures: Formal definitions, simplified requirements, and a construction based on general assumptions. In E. Biham, editor, *Advances in Cryptology - EUROCRYPT 2003*, volume 2656 of *Lecture Notes in Computer Science*, pages 614–629. Springer, 2003.
5. M. Bellare, D. Pointcheval, and P. Rogaway. Authenticated key exchange secure against dictionary attacks. In *Proc. EUROCRYPT 2000*, pages 139–155. Springer, 2000. Lecture Notes in Computer Science No. 1807.
6. M. Bellare and P. Rogaway. Random oracles are practical: A paradigm for designing efficient protocols. In *First ACM Conference on Computer and Communications Security*, pages 62–73, Fairfax, 1993. ACM.
7. M. Bellare, H. Shi, and C. Zhang. Foundations of group signatures: The case of dynamic groups. Cryptology ePrint Archive, Report 2004/077, 2004. http://eprint.iacr.org/.
8. C. Boyd, W. Mao, and K. Paterson. Deniable authenticated key establishment for internet protocols.
9. R. Bradshaw, J. Holt, and K. Seamons. Concealing complex policies with hidden credentials. In *Proceedings of the 11th ACM conference on Computer and communications security (CCS'04)*, pages 146–157. ACM Press, 2004.
10. E. Bresson, O. Chevassut, and D. Pointcheval. Dynamic group Diffie-Hellman key exchange under standard assumptions. In L. R. Knudsen, editor, *Proc. of Eurocrypt 02*, volume 2332 of *LNCS*, page 321–336.
11. M. Burmester and Y. Desmedt. A secure and efficient conference key distribution system. In A. D. Santis, editor, *Proc. EUROCRYPT 94*, pages 275–286. Springer, 1994. Lecture Notes in Computer Science No. 950.
12. J. Camenisch and A. Lysyanskaya. Dynamic accumulators and application to efficient revocation of anonymous credentials. In M. Yung, editor, *Proc. CRYPTO 2002*, volume 2442 of *Lecture Notes in Computer Science*, pages 61–76.
13. J. Camenisch and M. Stadler. Efficient group signature schemes for large groups. In B.S. Kaliski Jr., editor, *Proc. CRYPTO 1997*, volume 1294 of *Lecture Notes in Computer Science*, pages 410–424. Springer-Verlag, 1997.

14. C. Castelluccia, S. Jarecki, and G. Tsudik. Secret handshakes from ca-oblivious encryption. In *Advances in Cryptology - ASIACRYPT 2004*, volume 3329 of *Lecture Notes in Computer Science*, pages 293–307. Springer, 2004.
15. D. Chaum. Untraceable electronic mail, return addresses, and digital pseudonyms. *Communications of the ACM*, 24:84–88, Feb. 1981.
16. D. Chaum. Blind signatures for untraceable payments. In R. L. Rivest, A. Sherman, and D. Chaum, editors, *Proc. CRYPTO 82*, pages 199–203.
17. D. Chaum and E. V. Heyst. Group signatures. In D. W. Davies, editor, *Advances in Cryptology — Eurocrypt '91*, pages 257–265, Berlin, 1991. Springer-Verlag. Lecture Notes in Computer Science No. 547.
18. W. Diffie and M. E. Hellman. New directions in cryptography. *IEEE Trans. Inform. Theory*, IT-22:644–654, Nov. 1976.
19. J. Douceur. The sybil attack. In *Proceedings of the First International Workshop on Peer-to-Peer Systems (IPTPS'01)*, pages 251–260, 2002. Springer-Verlag.
20. M. Fischer, N. Lynch, and M. Patterson. Impossibility of distributed consensus with one faulty process. *Journal of the ACM*, 32(2):374–382, 1985.
21. J. Katz and M. Yung. Scalable protocols for authenticated group key exchange. In D. Boneh, editor, *Proc. CRYPTO 2003*, volume 2729 of *Lecture Notes in Computer Science*, pages 110–125. Springer-Verlag, 2002.
22. A. Kiayias, Y. Tsiounis, and M. Yung. Traceable signatures. In C. Cachin and J. Camenisch, editors, *Advances in Cryptology - EUROCRYPT 2004*, volume 3027 of *Lecture Notes in Computer Science*, pages 571–589. Springer, 2004.
23. A. Kiayias and M. Yung. Group signatures: Provable security, efficient constructions and anonymity from trapdoor-holders. Cryptology ePrint Archive, Report 2004/076, 2004. http://eprint.iacr.org/.
24. H. Krawczyk. Sigma: The 'sign-and-mac' approach to authenticated diffie-hellman and its use in the ike-protocols. In D. Boneh, editor, *Proc. CRYPTO 2003*, volume 2729 of *Lecture Notes in Computer Science*, pages 400–425. Springer-Verlag, 2002.
25. N. Li, W. Du, and D. Boneh. Oblivious signature-based envelope. In *Proceedings of 22nd ACM Symposium on Principles of Distributed Computing (PODC)*, pages 182–189. ACM, 2003.
26. D. Naor, M. Naor, and J. Lotspiech. Revocation and tracing schemes for stateless receivers. In J. Kilian, editor, *Proc. CRYPTO 2001*, volume 2139 of *Lecture Notes in Computer Science*, pages 41–62. Springer-Verlag, 2001.
27. M. Naor. Deniable ring authentication. In M. Yung, editor, *Proc. CRYPTO 2002*, volume 2442 of *Lecture Notes in Computer Science*, pages 481–498. 2002.
28. R. Rivest, A. Shamir, and Y. Tauman. How to leak a secret. In *Advances in Cryptology–ASIACRYPT '2001*, pages 552–565.
29. R. Sakai, K. Ohgishi, and M. Kasahara. Cryptosystems based on pairing. In *Proceedings of the Symposium on Cryptography and Information Security (SCIS)*, 2002.
30. M. Steiner, G. Tsudik, and M. Waidner. Key agreement in dynamic peer groups. *IEEE Trans. on Parallel and Distributed Systems*, 11(8):769–780, 2000.
31. Y. Sun and K. Liu. Securing dynamic membership information in multicast communications. In *IEEE Infocom'04*.
32. G. Tsudik and S. Xu. A Flexible Framework for Secret Handshakes. Full version of the present paper (available from the authors).
33. D. Wallner, E. Harder, and R. Agee. Key management for multicast: Issues and architectures. Internet Draft, Sept. 1998.

34. C. Wong, M. Gouda, and S. Lam. Secure group communication using key graphs. *IEEE/ACM Transactions on Networking* (Preliminary version in SIGCOMM'98), 8, 2000.

35. S. Xu. On the security of group communication schemes based on symmetric key cryptosystems. In *Proceedings of the Third ACM Workshop on Security of Ad Hoc and Sensor Networks (SASN'05)*, 2005.

36. S. Xu and M. Yung. k-anonymous secret handshakes with reusable credentials. In *Proceedings of the 11th ACM conference on Computer and communications security (CCS'04)*, pages 158–167. ACM Press, 2004.

On the Security of the
Tor Authentication Protocol

Ian Goldberg

David R. Cheriton School of Computer Science, University of Waterloo,
200 University Ave W, Waterloo, ON N2L 3G1
iang@cs.uwaterloo.ca

Abstract. Tor is a popular anonymous Internet communication system, used by an estimated 250,000 users to anonymously exchange over five terabytes of data per day. The security of Tor depends on properly authenticating nodes to clients, but Tor uses a custom protocol, rather than an established one, to perform this authentication. In this paper, we provide a formal proof of security of this protocol, in the random oracle model, under reasonable cryptographic assumptions.

1   Introduction

The Tor anonymous communication system [11] is used by an estimated 250,000 users worldwide [15] to protect the privacy of their Internet communications. Users can maintain their anonymity with Tor while taking advantage of many Internet services, including web browsing and publishing, instant messaging, and ssh.

In order to protect users' privacy, Tor utilizes of a number of *nodes* (also known as "onion routers" or "ORs") situated around the Internet. A *client* (an Internet user, whom we will call Alice, who does not necessarily run a node herself) builds a *circuit* through the network as follows:

- Alice picks a Tor node, n_1, and establishes an encrypted communication channel with it.
- Alice picks a second Tor node, n_2, and, over the previously established channel, instructs n_1 to connect to n_2. Alice then establishes an encrypted communication channel with n_2, tunneled within the existing channel to n_1.
- Alice picks a third Tor node, n_3, and, over the previously established channel, instructs n_2 to connect to n_3. Alice then establishes an encrypted communication channel with n_3, tunneled within the existing channel to n_2.
- and so on, for as many steps as she likes.

The security of the Tor system derives in part from the fact that the various nodes in the circuit are operated in different administrative domains; if one party had access to the internal state of all of the nodes in Alice's circuit, he could easily compromise Alice's anonymity.

G. Danezis and P. Golle (Eds.): PET 2006, LNCS 4258, pp. 316–331, 2006.

For this reason, it is important that Alice be assured that her communications with the various nodes be *authenticated*: if Mallory (a malicious man-in-the-middle) operated (or compromised) any single node n_i, then, without authentication, he could simulate all subsequent nodes $n_{i+1}, n_{i+2}, \ldots$ in Alice's circuit. If Alice were unlucky enough to pick Mallory's node as her n_1, he would be able to control her entire circuit.

Therefore, at each step, Alice (a) establishes a shared secret with a node, and (b) verifies that node's identity, so that it cannot be impersonated. Note that *Alice's* identity is never authenticated; she operates anonymously.

Tor uses a new protocol to achieve this, which we call the Tor Authentication Protocol (TAP) [10]. TAP is not an established authentication protocol, however, and its first deployment had at least one serious weakness [9]. In this paper, we analyze the (updated) TAP, and give a formal proof of security in the random oracle model [3]. This formal proof provides confidence that there are no similar weaknesses remaining in the protocol.

2 The Tor Authentication Protocol

We will first describe TAP in abstract terms. TAP is built from the following pieces:

- There is a trusted PKI that allows Alice to determine each node's public encryption key. Let $\mathcal{E}_\mathcal{B}$ be public-key encryption using $\mathcal{B}$'s public key, and let $\mathcal{D}_\mathcal{B}$ be the corresponding decryption using $\mathcal{B}$'s private key.
- p is a prime such that $q = \frac{p-1}{2}$ is also prime, and g is a generator of the subgroup of $\mathbb{Z}_p^*$ of order q. l_x is an exponent length; when a "random exponent" is required, select an l_x-bit value uniformly from the interval $[1, \min(q, 2^{l_x}) - 1]$.
- f is a hash function, which we will model by a random oracle, taking as input elements of $\mathbb{Z}_p$, and outputting bit strings of length l_f.

The abstract protocol is as follows:

1. Alice selects a node to add to her circuit. Let us suppose she selects Bob ($\mathcal{B}$).
2. Alice picks a random exponent x, and computes g^x (all exponentiations will be assumed to be mod p, and the least nonnegative representative will always be used).
3. Alice sends $c = \mathcal{E}_\mathcal{B}(g^x)$ to Bob.
4. Bob computes $m = \mathcal{D}_\mathcal{B}(c)$, checks that $1 < m < p - 1$, picks a random exponent y, and computes $a = g^y$ and $b = f(m^y)$.
5. Bob sends (a, b) to Alice.
6. Alice checks that $1 < a < p - 1$ and that $b = f(a^x)$.[1]
7. If the checks are successful, Alice accepts Bob's authentication, and they use $a^x = m^y$ as a shared secret in order to communicate privately.

---

[1] The error corrected in [9] was that Alice neglected to check that $1 < a < p - 1$. This allowed Mallory to ignore Alice's first message, reply with $(1, f(1))$, and use the "shared secret" of 1 to read Alice's subsequent messages, pretending to be Bob.

Note that in step 4, it is possible that $m \leq 1$ or $m \geq p - 1$ or even that $\mathcal{D}_{\mathcal{B}}(c) = \perp$; i.e. c is not a valid ciphertext. In these cases, Bob aborts the protocol.

Remember that all of the communication in TAP, other than that between Alice and the first node, is visible to, and modifiable by, the previous node in the circuit. We will assume this node is malicious, and denote it by Mallory ($\mathcal{M}$).

3   Formalization

In this section, we formally define what we mean by the *security* of TAP.

We begin by formally defining, in the usual way, a public-key encryption system (in the random oracle model) Π as a triple $(\mathcal{K}, \mathcal{E}^H, \mathcal{D}^H)$ of algorithms:

- $\mathcal{K}$ is the *key generation algorithm*. It takes as input a security parameter, k, in unary notation, and outputs a pair (pk, sk). pk is the public key, and sk is the private key. $\mathcal{K}$ is a polynomial-time randomized algorithm. If additionally, there is a polynomial-time algorithm κ that inputs pk, and outputs the value of k used to generate it, we say that Π is k-*aware*.[2]
- $\mathcal{E}^H$ is the *encryption algorithm*. It has access to a random oracle H, takes as input a public key output by $\mathcal{K}$ and a plaintext message m, and outputs a ciphertext c. $\mathcal{E}^H$ is also a polynomial-time randomized algorithm, so there are many possible outputs c for the same inputs pk and m.
- $\mathcal{D}^H$ is the *decryption algorithm*. It has access to the same random oracle H, takes as input a private key output by $\mathcal{K}$ and a ciphertext c, and outputs either a plaintext message m, or else a special symbol $\perp$, indicating an invalid input. $\mathcal{D}^H$ is also polynomial-time, but is deterministic.

We of course require that, for any (pk, sk) output by $\mathcal{K}(1^k)$, any plaintext message m in the domain of $\mathcal{E}^H_{\text{pk}}$ (which may depend on pk), and any c output by $\mathcal{E}^H_{\text{pk}}(m)$, it must be the case that $\mathcal{D}^H_{\text{sk}}(c) = m$. Note that we indicate the keys as subscripts to $\mathcal{E}^H$ and $\mathcal{D}^H$.

Next we define a *group parameter generator*. This is a function $\mathcal{G}$, which is possibly, but not necessarily, randomized. $\mathcal{G}$ takes as input a security parameter k, again in unary notation, and outputs a pair (p, g) such that:

- p is prime
- $q = \frac{p-1}{2}$ is also prime
- g is a generator of the subgroup of $\mathbb{Z}_p^*$ of order q
- the length of p, in bits, is $\Omega(k)$, and polynomial in k

Finally, we recall that a function $\epsilon(k)$ is *negligible* with respect to k if for every constant $c \geq 0$, there exists an integer k_c such that $\epsilon(k) \leq k^{-c}$ for all $k \geq k_c$. Throughout this paper, the term "negligible" by itself will mean "negligible with respect to the security parameter k".

---

[2] Almost every reasonable public-key encryption system is k-aware. k-awareness is an easy-to-verify technical condition that will prevent the use of certain pathological systems in section 6.

Definition 1. *For a given public-key encryption system Π, and a given group parameter generator $\mathcal{G}$, we say TAP is $(\Pi, \mathcal{G})$-**insecure** if there exists a polynomial-time randomized algorithm $\mathcal{M}^{f,H,\mathcal{N}}$ such that, for a random output $(\mathrm{pk}, \mathrm{sk})$ of $\mathcal{K}(1^k)$, a (possibly random) output (p, g) of $\mathcal{G}(1^k)$, and a random exponent x, with non-negligible probability, $\mathcal{M}^{f,H,\mathcal{N}}(\mathrm{pk}, p, g, \mathcal{E}_{\mathrm{pk}}^H(g^x)) = (a, a^x)$, for some $1 < a < p - 1$.*

*If no such algorithm exists, we say TAP is $(\Pi, \mathcal{G})$-**secure**.*

As the notation would suggest, $\mathcal{M}^{f,H,\mathcal{N}}$ has access to three oracles: the random oracles f and H, and a *node oracle* $\mathcal{N}$. The node oracle is one which emulates the behaviour of the above Tor node Bob: given an input c, it outputs a pair $\left(g^y, f\left(\mathcal{D}_{\mathrm{sk}}^H(c)^y\right)\right)$ for an exponent y chosen freshly at random on each invocation.[3]

It is easy to see how, if such an algorithm exists, Mallory could compromise the security of Tor: when Alice asks Mallory to extend her circuit to Bob, Alice will choose an x and give him $\mathcal{E}_B(g^x)$. Mallory will run $\mathcal{M}^{f,H,\mathcal{N}}$ on that value, Bob's public key, and the group parameters, replacing every call to $\mathcal{N}$ by contacting Bob, sending c, and receiving Bob's output $(g^y, f(\mathcal{D}_B(c)^y))$ for an exponent y chosen freshly at random each time. Mallory takes the output (a, a^x), with $1 < a < p - 1$, and returns $(a, f(a^x))$ to Alice. Now Alice will send messages protected with the shared secret a^x, thinking that only Bob can read them. But Mallory knows this value, and Tor's security is compromised.

Broadly, there are two main strategies Mallory could use to construct such an algorithm. First, he could perform an attack on $\mathcal{E}_B(g^x)$ to try to recover g^x; in this case, he can pick a random r and output $(g^r, (g^x)^r)$. Second, Mallory could try to construct a "master" (a, a^x) pair that works despite his not knowing g^x. It was this latter strategy that was exploited in the previous version of the Tor protocol, where the restriction $1 < a < p - 1$ was absent. The purpose of this paper is to show that Mallory has no way to succeed using either of these strategies, or indeed any other strategy.

4   IND-CPA

We next recall the definition of IND-CPA (indistinguishability in a chosen plaintext attack) [1]:

Definition 2. *Let $\Pi = (\mathcal{K}, \mathcal{E}, \mathcal{D})$ be a public-key encryption scheme. For a pair of randomized algorithms $A = (A_1, A_2)$, define the **advantage** of A to be*

$$\mathsf{Adv}_{A,\Pi}^{\mathrm{ind-cpa}}(k) = |2 \cdot \Pr\ [\ (\mathrm{pk}, \mathrm{sk}) \leftarrow \mathcal{K}\left(1^k\right); (m_0, m_1, \sigma) \leftarrow A_1\left(\mathrm{pk}\right); b \leftarrow \{0,1\};$$
$$y \leftarrow \mathcal{E}_{\mathrm{pk}}\left(m_b\right) : A_2\left(m_0, m_1, \sigma, y\right) = b] - 1| \ .$$

We additionally require that the outputs m_0 and m_1 of A_1 be of the same length.

Definition 3. *If, for a given public-key encryption scheme Π, any pair of polynomial-time randomized algorithms A has advantage $\mathsf{Adv}_{A,\Pi}^{\mathrm{ind-cpa}}(k)$ negligible in k, we say Π is **IND-CPA**.*

---

[3] So long as $\mathcal{D}_{\mathrm{sk}}^H(c) \neq \perp$ and $1 < \mathcal{D}_{\mathrm{sk}}(c) < p - 1$. Otherwise $\mathcal{N}$ returns $\perp$.

Informally, we say Π is IND-CPA if there is no way for a polynomial-time adversary to win the following game (against a *tester*) non-negligibly more often than half the time:[4]

- (Key generation:) The tester generates a public/private key pair.
- (Message generation:) The adversary is told the public key, and picks two messages m_0 and m_1 of the same length.
- (Challenge:) The tester picks a bit b at random, and produces y, an encryption of m_b using the public key.
- (Response:) The adversary is given y, and tries figure out the value of b.

The adversary can keep state (symbolized by σ in the formalization) between the message generation and the response phases.

5   Reaction Resistance

In this section, we introduce the concept of *reaction resistance*, which is similar to plaintext awareness [1], but weaker. Therefore, we first review the latter. Informally, a public-key encryption system is said to be *plaintext aware* if there is no way to produce a valid ciphertext (one which does not decrypt to $\bot$) without knowing the corresponding plaintext. Even if you observe some valid ciphertexts (say, by intercepting messages), you should be unable to modify them to produce a new ciphertext whose decryption you do not know.

We formalize this by saying that an IND-CPA public-key encryption system is plaintext aware if there is an algorithm K, known as a *knowledge extractor*. K is given the public key pk, a list C of *observed ciphertexts* (for which the plaintext is not necessarily known), a *challenge ciphertext* $y \notin C$, generated by some adversary, and the list η of all of the random oracle queries and responses used by the adversary to construct y. K must then output the correct decryption of y, except with negligible probability.

Plaintext awareness is a very strong property for a public-key encryption system to have; for example, any system which is plaintext aware is also resistant to adaptive chosen ciphertext attacks. We define the weaker property of reaction resistance, which allows the adversary to construct certain valid ciphertexts for which it doesn't know the corresponding plaintext. To do this, we remove the requirements that the system be IND-CPA and that $y \notin C$, and also allow the knowledge extractor to do any of the following:

- output (plain, v) where v is the decryption of y, as in the plaintext awareness case (v is allowed to be $\bot$)
- output (match, i), claiming that the decryption of y is the same as that of C_i (this can be used when $y \in C$, for example)
- output (guess), indicating that the only way for an adversary to know the decryption of y is to guess it (note that the extractor is given the transcript of the adversary's calls to the random oracle, so it would know how y was generated)

---

[4] The adversary can trivially win half the time by simply picking an answer at random.

Formally:

Let $\Pi = (\mathcal{K}, \mathcal{E}^H, \mathcal{D}^H)$ be a public-key encryption system where the encryption and decryption algorithms have access to a random oracle H.

Let B^H be an adversary that is given a public key pk output by $\mathcal{K}$ and a list of ciphertexts C, and outputs a tuple (η, y, m), where:

- η is the list of queries and results that B^H made to the random oracle H
- y is a *challenge ciphertext*
- m is a *guessed plaintext*

Definition 4. Π *is* **reaction resistant (RR)** *if there exists a knowledge extractor* K, *which, for any such adversary* B^H, *has the property that*

$$K(\eta, C, y, \text{pk}) = \begin{cases} (\text{plain}, v) \Rightarrow \mathcal{D}^H_{\text{sk}}(y) = v \\ (\text{match}, i) \Rightarrow \mathcal{D}^H_{\text{sk}}(y) = \mathcal{D}^H_{\text{sk}}(C_i) \\ (\text{guess}) \;\;\Rightarrow \mathcal{D}^H_{\text{sk}}(y) \neq m \wedge \forall i : \mathcal{D}^H_{\text{sk}}(y) \neq \mathcal{D}^H_{\text{sk}}(C_i) \end{cases}$$

for any (pk, sk) *output by* $\mathcal{K}$, *any list of ciphertexts* C *(created by using* $\mathcal{E}^H_{\text{pk}}$ *to encrypt plaintexts selected from some distribution), and any* (η, y, m) *output by* $B^H(\text{pk}, C)$, *except with negligible probability.*

We note that this definition of RR is in the random oracle model, and follows the definition of plaintext awareness from [1]. The methods used in [2] could be used to produce a definition of RR in the standard model, but this is not necessary for our purposes.

Reaction resistance is so named because it is the property a cryptosystem needs in order to prevent reaction attacks [13], such as those against Atjai-Dwork [13], NTRU [14], and PKCS#1-v1.5 [5]. In these attacks, the adversary sends chosen ciphertexts (typically modified versions of intercepted ciphertexts) to one of the participants in the protocol, and watches her reaction in order to determine whether the ciphertext decrypted to something sensible. This information can be enough for the adversary to determine the original plaintext, or sometimes the secret key.

Finally, we define the weaker notion of RR1 (reaction resistance with a single observed ciphertext):

Definition 5. Π *is* **RR1** *if there exists a knowledge extractor* K *that satisfies the conditions of Definition 4, but which may also assume that its second parameter,* C, *is a list consisting of exactly one ciphertext.*

6   Security Reduction

In this section, we provide a reduction from the security of TAP to the security of the underlying public-key encryption system. We start by defining an x-power pair, and the $\mathcal{G}$-restriction of a public-key encryption system. The latter is just a slight modification to the original system that additionally checks that decrypted values are integers from some particular interval.

Definition 6. *For a fixed exponent* x, *an* x-**power pair** *is a pair* (α, α^x) *such that* $1 < \alpha < p - 1$.

Note: It will be important in section 6.2 that an algorithm that knows no information about x, save that is a random exponent, be able to create an x-power pair only with negligible probability. Since $1 < \alpha < p - 1$, and each member of this interval has order either $\frac{p-1}{2}$ or $p - 1$, this is trivially true. However, if the restriction on α were not present, an attacker could choose an element of low order for α, and easily create an x-power pair, so the proof of Theorem 1 would not go through. This was the problem in the earlier version of the protocol.

Definition 7. *If Π is a public-key encryption system, and $\mathcal{G}$ is a group parameter generator, then the $\mathcal{G}$-restriction of Π, denoted $\Pi^\mathcal{G}$, is a public-key encryption system $(\mathcal{K}^*, \mathcal{E}^*, \mathcal{D}^*)$, where*

- $\mathcal{K}^*(1^k) = ((\mathrm{pk}, p, g), (\mathrm{sk}, p, g))$, *where* $(\mathrm{pk}, \mathrm{sk}) \leftarrow \mathcal{K}(1^k)$ *and* $(p, g) \leftarrow \mathcal{G}(1^k)$.
- $\mathcal{E}^*_{(\mathrm{pk}, p, g)}(m) = \mathcal{E}_{\mathrm{pk}}(m)$.
- $\mathcal{D}^*_{(\mathrm{sk}, p, g)}(c) = \begin{cases} \mathcal{D}_{\mathrm{sk}}(c) & \text{if } \mathcal{D}_{\mathrm{sk}}(c) \neq \bot \text{ and } 1 < \mathcal{D}_{\mathrm{sk}}(c) < p - 1 \\ \bot & \text{otherwise} \end{cases}$.

Theorem 1. *Let $\mathcal{G}$ be a group parameter generator, and Π be a k-aware public-key encryption system. If Π is IND-CPA and $\Pi^\mathcal{G}$ is RR1, then TAP is $(\Pi, \mathcal{G})$-secure.*

We will prove the following logically equivalent statement: if $\Pi^\mathcal{G}$ is RR1, and TAP is $(\Pi, \mathcal{G})$-insecure, then Π is not IND-CPA.

Therefore, we now assume that we have in hand a knowledge extractor K for $\Pi^\mathcal{G}$ satisfying the properties of section 5, and an algorithm $\mathcal{M}^{f,H,\mathcal{N}}$ satisfying the properties of section 3, and will try to produce a pair of algorithms (A_1, A_2) that can win the guessing game of section 4. We will do this in two steps: (1) remove the node oracle; (2) win the guessing game.

6.1 Remove the Node Oracle

In this step, we take our algorithm $\mathcal{M}^{f,H,\mathcal{N}}$, which has access to the random oracles f and H and the node oracle $\mathcal{N}$, and produce an algorithm $\mathcal{M}_1^{f,H}$, which just has access to the random oracles.

$\mathcal{M}_1^{f,H}(\mathrm{pk}, p, g, c_0)$, then, is calculated as follows:

- Initialize Γ, Φ, and η to be empty lists.
- Set $out \leftarrow \mathcal{M}^{f',H',\mathcal{N}'}(\mathrm{pk}, p, g, c_0)$. Note that we have replaced each call to $f(m)$ by a call to the following subroutine $f'(m)$:

> append m to the list Φ
> return $f(m)$

each call to $H(m)$ by a call to the following subroutine $H'(m)$:

> set $h \leftarrow H(m)$
> append (m, h) to η
> return h

and each call to $\mathcal{N}(c)$ by a call to the following subroutine $\mathcal{N}'(c)$:

> set $k \leftarrow K(\eta, \{c_0\}, c, \mathrm{pk})$
> if $k = (\mathsf{plain}, \bot)$:
> > return $\bot$
>
> else if $k = (\mathsf{plain}, v)$:
> > pick a random exponent y
> > set $s \leftarrow f(v^y)$
> > return (g^y, s)
>
> else:
> > pick a random exponent y
> > pick a random string s of length l_f
> > append g^y to the list Γ
> > return (g^y, s)

- Pick a random bit β.
- If $\beta = 0$, return *out*.
- If $\beta = 1$, and either Γ or Φ is empty, return $\bot$
- Otherwise, pick a random element γ of Γ and a random element ϕ of Φ, and return (γ, ϕ).

Lemma 1. *If $\mathcal{M}^{f,H,\mathcal{N}}(\mathrm{pk}, p, g, \mathcal{E}_{\mathrm{pk}}^{H}(g^x))$ outputs an x-power pair with non-negligible probability, then $\mathcal{M}_1^{f,H}(\mathrm{pk}, p, g, \mathcal{E}_{\mathrm{pk}}^{H}(g^x))$ outputs an x-power pair with non-negligible probability.*

Proof. The intuition behind the proof is that the input/output behaviours of f and f' are the same, as are those of H and H', so we only have to consider the difference between $\mathcal{N}$ and $\mathcal{N}'$. We can use K, the knowledge extractor for $\Pi^{\mathcal{G}}$, to give us a partial decryption oracle: if K reports that it knows the plaintext corresponding to the given ciphertext, $\mathcal{N}'$ can just use that value to perform the same operations as $\mathcal{N}$ would. On the other hand, if K reports that there's no way to know the plaintext, then $\mathcal{N}'$ can output a value which, by the properties of the random oracle, will be indistinguishable from those of $\mathcal{N}$, except in certain cases we consider separately.

We first note that $\mathcal{N}'$, and thus K, is called only polynomially often. Since each call to K only has a negligible probability of returning an erroneous result, we can conclude that, except with negligible probability, all of the calls to K return a correct result.

We assume, then, that indeed all of the calls to K return a correct result. Since K is a knowledge extractor for $\Pi^{\mathcal{G}}$, if K returns (plain, v), it must be the case that either $v = \bot$ or else $1 < v < p - 1$. In either case, $\mathcal{N}'$ performs the same operations as $\mathcal{N}$.

If K returns (guess), then $\mathcal{M}_1^{f,H}$ (in the role of K's adversary) cannot learn $\mathcal{D}_{\mathrm{sk}}^{H}(c)$ (and in particular $\mathcal{D}_{\mathrm{sk}}^{H}(c)$ cannot be $\bot$), except with negligible probability. In this case, $\mathcal{N}$ will return $(g^y, f(\mathcal{D}_{\mathrm{sk}}^{H}(c)^y))$, while $\mathcal{N}'$ will return (g^y, s), for a randomly chosen exponent y and a randomly chosen string s of length l_f. But $\mathcal{M}_1^{f,H}$ will not be able to compute $\mathcal{D}_{\mathrm{sk}}^{H}(c)^y$, so it will not be able to distinguish the two results. We also note that the probability that two different calls to $\mathcal{N}$ produce the same input to f is negligible: $\mathcal{N}$ only calls f on random powers of numbers d with $1 < d < p-1$. All such numbers have order either q or $2q = p-1$, and note that p was selected to be $\Omega(k)$ bits long. There are only polynomially many of these calls that $\mathcal{N}$ makes to f (since $\mathcal{M}^{f,H,\mathcal{N}}$ runs in polynomial time), so the probability that two of these calls have matching inputs is negligible.

Finally, if K returns (match, i), then i must be 1, since $\{\mathcal{E}_{\mathrm{pk}}^H(g^x)\}$ is a list of length 1, and so $\mathcal{D}_{\mathrm{sk}}^H(c) = g^x$. Again, $\mathcal{N}$ will return $(g^y, f(g^{xy}))$, and $\mathcal{N}'$ will return (g^y, s), for a randomly chosen exponent y and a randomly chosen string s of length l_f. What if $\mathcal{M}^{f,H,\mathcal{N}}$ makes a call to f that happens to match one of these inputs that $\mathcal{N}$ uses in a call to f? Suppose the probability of this event (which we will label C for "Collision") is Δ. Let θ_C be the conditional probability of $\mathcal{M}^{f,H,\mathcal{N}}$ succeeding (i.e. outputting an x-power pair), given that C has occurred. Similarly, let $\theta_{\overline{C}}$ be the conditional probability of $\mathcal{M}^{f,H,\mathcal{N}}$ succeeding, given that C has not occurred. Then the overall probability of $\mathcal{M}^{f,H,\mathcal{N}}$ succeeding is $\Delta \cdot \theta_C + (1-\Delta) \cdot \theta_{\overline{C}}$, which by assumption is non-negligible, so either $\Delta \cdot \theta_C$ or $(1-\Delta) \cdot \theta_{\overline{C}}$ (or both) must be non-negligible.

Note that, if C does not occur, then $\mathcal{M}_1^{f,H}$ will not be able to distinguish outputs of $\mathcal{N}'$ from outputs of $\mathcal{N}$, and so the probability of $\mathcal{M}^{f',H',\mathcal{N}'}$ outputting an x-power pair, given that C does not occur, is at least $\theta_{\overline{C}} - \epsilon$, for some negligible ϵ (which takes into account the negligible probabilities of error mentioned above).

On the other hand, if C does occur, then $\mathcal{M}_1^{f,H}$ will have made a call to f', passing an input g^{xy} (thus entering g^{xy} into the list Φ), where g^y is some value entered into the list Γ. Therefore, this (g^y, g^{xy}) pair is an x-power pair that appears in the set $\Gamma \times \Phi$.

So what is the overall probability of $\mathcal{M}_1^{f,H}$ succeeding? If C does not occur, and $\beta = 0$ (the combined probability of which is $\frac{1-\Delta}{2}$), then $\mathcal{M}_1^{f,H}$ will output out, which will be an x-power pair with probability at least $\theta_{\overline{C}} - \epsilon$. If C does occur, and $\beta = 1$ (the combined probability of which is $\frac{\Delta}{2}$), then $\mathcal{M}_1^{f,H}$ will output a random element of $\Gamma \times \Phi$, a set of polynomial size, of which at least one element is an x-power pair.

Therefore, the overall probability is at least $z = \frac{\Delta}{2} \cdot \frac{1}{|\Gamma \times \Phi|} + \frac{1-\Delta}{2} \cdot (\theta_{\overline{C}} - \epsilon)$. Now recall that either $\Delta \cdot \theta_C$ or $(1-\Delta) \cdot \theta_{\overline{C}}$ (or both) must be non-negligible. If $\Delta \cdot \theta_C$ is non-negligible, then $z \geq \frac{\Delta}{2} \cdot \frac{1}{|\Gamma \times \Phi|} = \frac{1}{2 \cdot |\Gamma \times \Phi|} \cdot \Delta \geq \frac{1}{2 \cdot |\Gamma \times \Phi|} \cdot (\Delta \cdot \theta_C)$, which is non-negligible. If $(1-\Delta) \cdot \theta_{\overline{C}}$ is non-negligible, then $z + \epsilon \geq z + \frac{1-\Delta}{2} \cdot \epsilon \geq \frac{1-\Delta}{2} \cdot (\theta_{\overline{C}} - \epsilon) + \frac{1-\Delta}{2} \cdot \epsilon = \frac{1}{2} \cdot (1-\Delta) \cdot \theta_{\overline{C}}$, which is non-negligible. In either case, z is non-negligible, as required. $\qquad\square$

6.2   Win the Guessing Game

With $\mathcal{M}_1^{f,H}$ in hand, it is now straightforward to win the guessing game of section 4 against Π. Remember that Π is k-aware, so there is an polynomial-time algorithm κ that can extract the security parameter k from a public key pk generated by $\mathcal{K}(1^k)$.

Algorithm $A_1(\text{pk})$:
    set $k \leftarrow \kappa(\text{pk})$
    set $(p, g) \leftarrow \mathcal{G}(1^k)$
    pick two (distinct) random exponents x_0, x_1
    return $(m_0, m_1, \sigma) \leftarrow (g^{x_0}, g^{x_1}, (\text{pk}, p, g, x_0, x_1))$

Algorithm $A_2(m_0, m_1, \sigma, y)$:
    set $(\text{pk}, p, g, x_0, x_1) \leftarrow \sigma$
    set $out \leftarrow \mathcal{M}_1^{f,H}(\text{pk}, p, g, y)$
    if $out = (\alpha, \alpha^{x_0})$ for some $1 < \alpha < p - 1$:
        return 0
    else if $out = (\alpha, \alpha^{x_1})$ for some $1 < \alpha < p - 1$:
        return 1
    else:
        return a random element of $\{0, 1\}$

Why does this work? The tester (in the nomenclature of section 4) will pick a random bit b, and pass $\mathcal{E}_{\text{pk}}^H(m_b) = \mathcal{E}_{\text{pk}}^H(g^{x_b})$ to A_2 as y. A_2 will then calculate $out = \mathcal{M}_1^{f,H}(\text{pk}, p, g, \mathcal{E}_{\text{pk}}^H(g^{x_b}))$, which, by the above, will be a x_b-power pair with non-negligible probability δ. Also, since x_0 and x_1 were picked randomly, and $\mathcal{M}_1^{f,H}$ never learns any value that depends on x_{1-b}, the probability that out is an x_{1-b}-power pair must be some negligible value ϵ. So the probability of A_2 outputting b is then $\delta + \frac{1-\delta-\epsilon}{2} = \frac{1}{2} + \frac{\delta-\epsilon}{2}$, and $\mathsf{Adv}_{(A_1,A_2),\Pi}^{\text{ind-cpa}} = \delta - \epsilon$, which is non-negligible, so Π is *not* IND-CPA.

Therefore, we have that if $\Pi^{\mathcal{G}}$ is RR1, and TAP is $(\Pi, \mathcal{G})$-insecure, then Π is not IND-CPA, which completes the proof of Theorem 1.   □

7   The Concrete Protocol

In this final section, we examine the actual encryption mechanism used by Tor, and show that it indeed satisfies the preconditions of Theorem 1, under reasonable assumptions.

First, we need to work around a slight technicality: so far, all of our analyses have been parameterized by the security parameter k. Unfortunately, the Tor specification [10] is not so parameterized: it specifies a single Diffie-Hellman group, for example. The algorithms we outline here, therefore, are generalizations of the actual Tor algorithms, and reduce to the actual algorithms for a specific value of k.

Let $T_{RSA}(l_N)$ be a lower bound on the expected amount of work an adversary must do to break RSA with an l_N-bit modulus. We of course assume this bound is superpolynomial in l_N.[5] Then select values for parameters $(l_N, l_p, l_x, l_f, l_H, l_s)$, based on a security parameter k, as follows:

---

[5] For concreteness, we use $T_{RSA}(l_N) = \exp\left(\xi\,(\ln 2^{l_N})^{1/3}(\ln\ln 2^{l_N})^{2/3}\right)$, where $\xi = \frac{1}{3}\left(92 + 26\sqrt{13}\right)^{1/3} \approx 1.902$. This is the asymptotic expected running time for factoring an l_N-bit integer using the generalized number field sieve [6].

- l_N will be the bitlength of an RSA modulus. Select a value divisible by 8, such that $\lfloor \log_2 T_{RSA}(l_N) \rfloor = k$.
- l_p will be the bitlength of a Diffie-Hellman modulus. Select $l_p = l_N$.
- l_x will be the bitlength of random exponents. Select a value divisible by 8, such that l_x is $\Omega(k)$.
- l_f and l_H will be the bitlengths of the outputs of random oracles. Select values divisible by 8, such that l_f and l_H are each $\Theta(k)$.
- l_s will be the bitlength of a symmetric key. Select a value divisible by 8, such that l_s is $\Theta(k)$.

It must be the case that $l_N - 2l_H - 16 - l_s$ is positive, and $\Omega(k)$. Define r to be $\frac{1}{8}(l_N - 2l_H - 16 - l_s)$.

In the specified protocol, $k = 85$ and $(l_N, l_p, l_x, l_f, l_H, l_s) = (1024, 1024, 320, 160, 160, 128)$. The random oracles f and H are instantiated by appropriately chosen hash functions with output lengths l_f and l_H bits, respectively. Let S^* be a family of pseudorandom functions (such as a block cipher) with keylength l_s. The specified protocol uses hash functions based on SHA-1 [16], and uses AES-128 [17] as the symmetric encryption function.[6]

For $m \in \mathbb{N}$, define the pair (m^L, m^R) as follows:

- Express the integer m as a sequence mo of octets, most significant first. This sequence should be of minimum length; i.e. no leading 0x00s.
- Let m^L be the first r octets of mo, and let m^R be the remainder of mo.

The public-key encryption system used in Tor is then the following $\Pi_{\mathsf{TAP}} = (\mathcal{K}, \mathcal{E}^H, \mathcal{D}^H)$:

$\mathcal{K}(1^k)$ outputs a randomly generated RSA keypair $(\mathrm{pk}, \mathrm{sk}) = ((N, e), (N, d))$ where the bitlength of N is l_N (which depends on k, as above), and $e = 65537$.
$\mathcal{E}^H_{\mathrm{pk}}(m)$ is as follows:

- Pick a random key s for S^*, of length l_s.
- Let C_1 be the RSA-OAEP encryption (using the hash function H internally, and the key pk) of the concatenation of s and m^L.
- Let C_2 be the encryption (using the cryptosystem S^* in CTR mode with key s and initial counter 0) of m^R.
- Output (C_1, C_2).

$\mathcal{D}^H_{\mathrm{sk}}((C_1, C_2))$ is as follows:

- Decrypt C_1 using RSA-OAEP (with the hash function H and the key sk). Let s be the first l_s bits of the result, and mo_1 be the remainder of the result.
- Decrypt C_2 using the cryptosystem S^* in CTR mode with key s and initial counter 0, yielding mo_2.
- Concatenate mo_1 and mo_2, and turn the result into an MSB-first integer m.
- If any step failed, return $\perp$. Otherwise, return m.

---

[6] AES-128 is indeed an appropriate choice for S^*, as long as an attacker cannot distinguish AES-128 from a family of random functions.

The group parameter generator $\mathcal{G}_{\mathsf{TAP}}$ for Tor returns a deterministic (p, g) for any input 1^k, with p of bitlength l_p, and such that $1 - p \cdot 2^{-l_p}$ is a negligible function of k. This last condition means that a random integer of the same length as p has only a negligible probability of being greater than p.

Now that we have specified TAP for generic k, we must simply check that Π_{TAP} and $\mathcal{G}_{\mathsf{TAP}}$ satisfy the preconditions of Theorem 1, namely:

1. Π_{TAP} is k-aware.
2. Π_{TAP} is IND-CPA.
3. $\Pi_{\mathsf{TAP}}^{\mathcal{G}_{\mathsf{TAP}}}$ is RR1.

7.1 Π_{TAP} Is k-Aware

We need to produce an algorithm κ which outputs k when given a public key output by $\mathcal{K}(1^k)$.

This is easy: given a public key (N, e) output by $\mathcal{K}(1^k)$, let l_N be the bitlength of N. Then output $\lfloor \log_2 T_{RSA}(l_N) \rfloor$, which will equal k, by the choice of l_N.

7.2 Π_{TAP} Is IND-CPA

We first note that, for any one-way trapdoor permutation g, g-OAEP is IND-CPA [4], and that for any pseudorandom function F, F-CTR is IND-CPA[7] [8].

We prove, more generally, that the hybrid construction of Π_{TAP} is IND-CPA, for any choice of underlying public-key encryption system (R) and symmetric-key encryption system (S), so long as they are each IND-CPA themselves.[8]

Let (A_1, A_2) be any polynomial-time adversary in the IND-CPA game of section 4 against Π_{TAP}. Let $[s, \rho]$ denote the concatenation of the l_s-bit value s and the r-octet value ρ. Then define an adversary $A' = (A_1', A_2')$ against S and a pair of adversaries $A_\beta'' = (A_{1,\beta}'', A_{2,\beta}'')$ (for $\beta \in \{0, 1\}$) against R as follows:

Algorithm $A_1'(1^k)$:
    $(\mathrm{pk}, \mathrm{sk}) \leftarrow \mathcal{K}(1^k)$
    $(m_0, m_1, \sigma) \leftarrow A_1(\mathrm{pk})$
    return $(m_0^R, m_1^R, (\mathrm{pk}, m_0, m_1, \sigma))$

Algorithm $A_2'(m_0^R, m_1^R, (\mathrm{pk}, m_0, m_1, \sigma), y)$:
    pick a random l_s-bit key s and a random r-octet string ρ
    return $A_2(m_0, m_1, \sigma, (R_{\mathrm{pk}}([s, \rho]), y))$

---

[7] We have not formally defined the notion of IND-CPA for symmetric encryption, but the definition is analogous to that in section 4; the only changes are that $\mathcal{K}$ returns a single key instead of a keypair, and 1^k (and not pk) is the input to A_1.

[8] Our proof is similar to that of Theorem 5 of [7], though that result pertained to IND-CCA systems, and did not need to deal with part of the plaintext messages being encrypted under the underlying public-key system.

Algorithm $A''_{1,\beta}(\text{pk})$:
 $(m_0, m_1, \sigma) \leftarrow A_1(\text{pk})$
 pick two random l_s-bit keys s_0, s_1 and a random r-octet string ρ
 return $([s_0, m_\beta^L], [s_1, \rho], (m_0, m_1, \sigma))$

Algorithm $A''_{2,\beta}([s_0, m_\beta^L], [s_1, \rho], (m_0, m_1, \sigma), y)$:
 return $A_2(m_0, m_1, \sigma, (y, S_{s_0}(m_\beta^R)))$

For $\beta \in \{0, 1\}$, define μ_β to be the conditional probability that $A_2(m_0, m_1, \sigma, y) = 0$, given that (m_0, m_1, σ) is an output of $A_1(\text{pk})$, and that $y = (R_{\text{pk}}([s, m_\beta^L]), S_s(m_\beta^R))$ for a randomly chosen l_s-bit key s. That is, μ_β is the probability that A_2 outputs 0 as its guess for the tester's value b, when the correct answer was β.

Also for $\beta \in \{0, 1\}$, define ν_β to be the conditional probability that $A_2(m_0, m_1, \sigma, y) = 0$, given that (m_0, m_1, σ) is an output of $A_1(\text{pk})$, and that $y = (R_{\text{pk}}([s_1, \rho]), S_{s_0}(m_\beta^R))$ for randomly chosen l_s-bit keys s_0 and s_1 and a randomly chosen r-octet string ρ. That is, $|\nu_\beta - \mu_\beta|$ is the probability that A_2 can distinguish between a correctly formed value of y, encrypting m_β (namely, $(R_{\text{pk}}([s, m_\beta^L]), S_s(m_\beta^R))$), and one in which the wrong symmetric key (and the wrong m_β^L) is encrypted with the public-key system (namely, $(R_{\text{pk}}([s_1, \rho]), S_{s_0}(m_\beta^R))$).

We now note that $\text{Adv}^{\text{ind-cpa}}_{A, \Pi_{\text{TAP}}} = \left|2\left(\frac{1}{2}\mu_0 + \frac{1}{2}(1 - \mu_1)\right) - 1\right| = |\mu_0 - \mu_1|$. Similarly, $\text{Adv}^{\text{ind-cpa}}_{A', S} = |\nu_0 - \nu_1|$, and $\text{Adv}^{\text{ind-cpa}}_{A''_\beta, R} = |\mu_\beta - \nu_\beta|$.

Therefore, $\text{Adv}^{\text{ind-cpa}}_{A, \Pi_{\text{TAP}}} \leq \text{Adv}^{\text{ind-cpa}}_{A''_0, R} + \text{Adv}^{\text{ind-cpa}}_{A', S} + \text{Adv}^{\text{ind-cpa}}_{A''_1, R}$. So if Π_{TAP} is not IND-CPA, then for some adversary A, $\text{Adv}^{\text{ind-cpa}}_{A, \Pi_{\text{TAP}}}$ is non-negligible, which means at least one of $\text{Adv}^{\text{ind-cpa}}_{A', S}$, $\text{Adv}^{\text{ind-cpa}}_{A''_0, R}$, and $\text{Adv}^{\text{ind-cpa}}_{A''_1, R}$ must be non-negligible, which means at least one of R and S is not IND-CPA, as required.

So under the usual assumption that RSA is a one-way trapdoor permutation, Π_{TAP} is also IND-CPA.

7.3 $\Pi^{\mathcal{G}_{\text{TAP}}}_{\text{TAP}}$ Is RR1

We must produce a knowledge extractor K for $\Pi^{\mathcal{G}_{\text{TAP}}}_{\text{TAP}}$ with the properties of section 5.

From [12], we know that, under the RSA assumption, there is a decryption simulator DS for RSA-OAEP (but *not* f-OAEP in general!) such that $DS(\eta, c^*, c, \text{pk}) = \mathcal{D}^H_{\text{sk}}(c)$, for any (pk, sk) output by $\mathcal{K}(1^k)$, any distinct ciphertexts c, c^*, and the list of oracle queries and responses η used to generate c (but *not* c^*), except with negligible probability.

Given this, the construction of K is straightforward:

$K(\eta, \{(C_1^*, C_2^*)\}, (C_1, C_2), (\text{pk}, p, g))$:
 determine l_p, l_s, and r based on $k \leftarrow \kappa(\text{pk})$
 let r_2 be the length (in octets) of C_2
 if $C_1 = C_1^*$:

(1)   if $8(r + r_2) - l_s > l_p$: return (plain, $\bot$)
(2)   else if $C_2 = C_2^*$: return (match, 1)
(3)   else: return (guess)
      else:
              let $m_1 \leftarrow DS(\eta, C_1^*, C_1, \mathrm{pk})$
              if $m_1 = \bot$: return (plain, $\bot$)
              let s be the first l_s bits of m_1, and let mo_1 be the remainder of m_1
              decrypt C_2 using S^*-CTR$_s$ and initial counter 0, yielding mo_2
              if $mo_2 = \bot$: return (plain, $\bot$)
              concatenate mo_1 and mo_2, yielding mo
              turn mo into an MSB-first integer m
              if $1 < m < p - 1$: return (plain, m)
              else: return (plain, $\bot$)

Remember that (C_1^*, C_2^*) can be assumed to be a valid encryption of the plaintext message g^x for some random exponent x, so if $C_1 = C_1^*$, then (C_1, C_2) will decrypt (under Π_{TAP}) to a value v whose first $8r - l_s$ bits will be the same as those of g^x. Also, still assuming $C_1 = C_1^*$:

- If the length of v is larger than the length of p, then certainly $v > p$, and $\Pi_{\mathsf{TAP}}^{\mathcal{G}_{\mathsf{TAP}}}$ would return $\bot$, so we return (plain, $\bot$) in line (1).
- If $C_2 = C_2^*$, then of course $\mathcal{D}_{\mathrm{sk}}^H((C_1, C_2)) = \mathcal{D}_{\mathrm{sk}}^H((C_1^*, C_2^*))$, so we return (match, 1) in line (2).
- Otherwise, the length of v is at least $8r - l_s$, and at most the length of p, so $1 < v < p - 1$ except with negligible probability, by our choice of p, so $v = \mathcal{D}_{\mathrm{sk}}^H((C_1, C_2))$. Further, $v \neq \mathcal{D}_{\mathrm{sk}}^H((C_1^*, C_2^*))$, since S^*-CTR with an initial counter of 0 is a deterministic encryption function. Finally, no algorithm can predict v, since its first $8r - l_s$ bits are the same as those of the randomly chosen g^x, so we return (guess) in line (3).

If C_1 does not equal C_1^*, then we can use the decryption simulator for RSA-OAEP to decrypt it successfully, except with negligible probability, and then we just perform the same actions as the real $\Pi_{\mathsf{TAP}}^{\mathcal{G}_{\mathsf{TAP}}}$ would.

Therefore, this K satisfies the properties of Definition 5 for $\Pi_{\mathsf{TAP}}^{\mathcal{G}_{\mathsf{TAP}}}$, so $\Pi_{\mathsf{TAP}}^{\mathcal{G}_{\mathsf{TAP}}}$ is RR1, as required.

8   Conclusion

Under the assumptions that RSA is one way, and that an appropriately strong block cipher is used, we have shown that the Tor Authentication Protocol is secure in the random oracle model; that is, without exploiting particular structure of the hash functions, a man-in-the-middle has only a negligible chance of being able to read messages that Alice thinks she's sending to Bob.

It should be noted, however, that the proof is sensitive to specific properties of TAP, and any modifications to the protocol should take care not to destroy these properties. For example, if Bob were to check that the order of the received message m were equal to exactly q, as opposed to merely checking that $1 < m < p - 1$, $\Pi_{\mathsf{TAP}}^{\mathcal{G}_{\mathsf{TAP}}}$ would *not* be RR1. On the other hand, replacing Π_{TAP} with a stronger system, such as one that is plaintext aware, would make TAP more robust to other modifications.

Acknowledgements. We would like to thank Stefan Brands for originally suggesting the problem, Jan Camenisch for his helpful initial discussion, Nikita Borisov and Dennis Kügler for clarifying the presentation of the paper, and the anonymous referees.

References

1. Mihir Bellare, Anand Desai, David Pointcheval, and Phillip Rogaway. Relations Among Notions of Security for Public-Key Encryption Schemes. In *Advances in Cryptology—CRYPTO '98, Lecture Notes in Computer Science 1462*, pages 26–45. Springer-Verlag, August 1998.
2. Mihir Bellare and Adriana Palacio. Towards Plaintext-Aware Public-Key Encryption without Random Oracles. In *Advances in Cryptology—Asiacrypt 2004, Lecture Notes in Computer Science 3329*, pages 48–62. Springer-Verlag, 2004.
3. Mihir Bellare and Phillip Rogaway. Random Oracles are Practical: A Paradigm for Designing Efficient Protocols. In *ACM Conference on Computer and Communications Security*, pages 62–73, 1993.
4. Mihir Bellare and Phillip Rogaway. Optimal Asymmetric Encryption—How to Encrypt with RSA. In *Advances in Cryptology—Eurocrypt '94, Lecture Notes in Computer Science 950*. Springer-Verlag, 1994.
5. Daniel Bleichenbacher. Chosen Ciphertext Attacks Against Protocols Based on the RSA Encryption Standard PKCS#1. In *Advances in Cryptology—CRYPTO '98, Lecture Notes in Computer Science 1462*, pages 1–12. Springer-Verlag, August 1998.
6. Don Coppersmith. Modifications to the Number Field Sieve. *Journal of Cryptology*, 6(3):169–180, 1993.
7. Ronald Cramer and Victor Shoup. Design and Analysis of Practical Public-Key Encryption Schemes Secure against Adaptive Chosen Ciphertext Attack. *SIAM Journal on Computing*, 33(1):167–226, 2003.
8. Anand Desai and Sara Miner. Concrete Security Characterizations of PRFs and PRPs: Reductions and Applications. In *Advances in Cryptology—Asiacrypt 2000, Lecture Notes in Computer Science 1976*, pages 503–516. Springer-Verlag, 2000.
9. Roger Dingledine. Tor security advisory: DH handshake flaw. http://archives.seul.org/or/announce/Aug-2005/msg00002.html, August 2005.
10. Roger Dingledine and Nick Mathewson. Tor Protocol Specification, version 1.112. http://tor.eff.org/cvs/tor/doc/tor-spec.txt, January 2006.
11. Roger Dingledine, Nick Mathewson, and Paul Syverson. Tor: The Second-Generation Onion Router. In *Proceedings of the 13th USENIX Security Symposium*, August 2004.
12. Eiichiro Fujisaki, Tatsuaki Okamoto, David Pointcheval, and Jacques Stern. RSA-OAEP is Secure under the RSA Assumption. In *Advances in Cryptology—CRYPTO 2001, Lecture Notes in Computer Science 2139*, pages 260–274. Springer-Verlag, August 2001.

13. Chris Hall, Ian Goldberg, and Bruce Schneier. Reaction Attacks Against Several Public-Key Cryptosystems. In *International Conference on Information and Communication Security 1999*, November 1999.
14. Jeffrey Hoffstein and Joseph H. Silverman. Reaction Attacks Against the NTRU Public Key Cryptosystem. NTRU Cryptosystems Technical Report #015, Version 2, http://www.ntru.com/cryptolab/pdf/NTRUTech015.pdf, June 2000.
15. Paul Syverson. Personal communication.
16. U.S. Department of Commerce, N.I.S.T. Secure Hash Algorithm. FIPS 180-1, 1995.
17. U.S. Department of Commerce, N.I.S.T. Advanced Encryption Standard (AES). FIPS 197, 2001.

Optimal Key-Trees for Tree-Based Private Authentication

Levente Buttyán, Tamás Holczer, and István Vajda

Laboratory of Cryptography and System Security (CrySyS)
Department of Telecommunications
Budapest University of Technology and Economics, Hungary
{buttyan, holczer, vajda}@crysys.hu

Abstract. Key-tree based private authentication has been proposed by
Molnar and Wagner as a neat way to efficiently solve the problem of privacy preserving authentication based on symmetric key cryptography.
However, in the key-tree based approach, the level of privacy provided
by the system to its members may decrease considerably if some members are compromised. In this paper, we analyze this problem, and show
that careful design of the tree can help to minimize this loss of privacy.
First, we introduce a benchmark metric for measuring the resistance of
the system to a single compromised member. This metric is based on the
well-known concept of anonymity sets. Then, we show how the parameters of the key-tree should be chosen in order to maximize the system's
resistance to single member compromise under some constraints on the
authentication delay. In the general case, when any member can be compromised, we give a lower bound on the level of privacy provided by
the system. We also present some simulation results that show that this
lower bound is quite sharp. The results of this paper can be directly used
by system designers to construct optimal key-trees in practice; indeed,
we consider this as the main contribution of our work.

1 Introduction

Entity authentication is the process whereby a party (the prover) corroborates
its identity to another party (the verifier). Entity authentication is often based
on authentication protocols in which the parties pass messages to each other.
These protocols are engineered in such a way that they resist various types
of impersonation and replay attacks [2]. However, less attention is paid to the
requirement of preserving the privacy of the parties (typically that of the prover)
with respect to an eavesdropping third party. Indeed, in many of the well-known
and widely used authentication protocols (e.g., [8,10]) the identity of the prover
is sent in cleartext, and hence, it is revealed to an eavesdropper.

One approach to solve this problem is based on public key cryptography, and
it consists of encrypting the identity information of the prover with the public
key of the verifier so that no one but the verifier can learn the prover's identity. Another approach, also based on public key techniques, is that the parties

G. Danezis and P. Golle (Eds.): PET 2006, LNCS 4258, pp. 332–350, 2006.
© Springer-Verlag Berlin Heidelberg 2006

first run an anonymous Diffie-Hellman key exchange and establish a confidential channel, through which the prover can send its identity and authentication information to the verifier in a second step. An example for this second approach is the main mode of the Internet Key Exchange (IKE) protocol [7]. While it is possible to hide the identity of the prover by using the above mentioned approaches, they provide appropriate solution to the problem only if the parties can afford public key cryptography. In many applications, such as low cost RFID tags and contactless smart card based automated fare collection systems in mass transportation, this is not the case, while at the same time, the provision of privacy (especially location privacy) in those systems is strongly desirable.

The problem of using symmetric key encryption to hide the identity of the prover is that the verifier does not know which symmetric key it should use to decrypt the encrypted identity, because the appropriate key cannot be retrieved without the identity. The verifier may try all possible keys in its key database until one of them properly decrypts the encrypted identity[1], but this would increase the authentication delay if the number of potential provers is large. Long authentication delays are usually not desirable, moreover, in some cases, they may not even be acceptable. As an example, let us consider again contactless smart card based electronic tickets in public transportation: the number of smart cards in the system (i.e., the number of potential provers) may be very large in big cities, while the time needed to authenticate a card should be short in order to ensure a high throughput of passengers and avoid long queues at entry points.

Recently, Molnar and Wagner proposed an elegant approach to privacy protecting authentication [11] that is based on symmetric key cryptography while still ensuring short authentication delays. More precisely, the complexity of the authentication procedure in the Molnar-Wagner scheme is logarithmic in the number of potential provers, in contrast with the linear complexity of the naïve key search approach. The main idea of Molnar and Wagner is to use key-trees (see Figure 1 for illustration). A key-tree is a tree where a unique key is assigned to each edge. The leaves of the tree represent the potential provers, which we will call members in the sequel. Each member possesses the keys assigned to the edges of the path starting from the root and ending in the leaf that corresponds to the given member. The verifier knows all keys in the tree. In order to authenticate itself, a member uses all of its keys, one after the other, starting from the first level of the tree and proceeding towards lower levels. The verifier first determines which first level key has been used. For this, it needs to search through the first level keys only. Once the first key is identified, the verifier continues by determining which second level key has been used. However, for this, it needs to search through those second level keys only that reside below the already identified first level key in the tree. This process is continued until all keys are identified, which at the end, identify the authenticating member. The key point is that the verifier can reduce the search space considerably each time

---

[1] This of course requires redundancy in the encrypted message so that the verifier can determine if the decryption was successful.

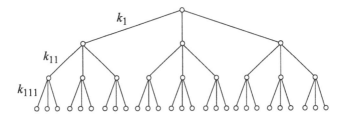

Fig. 1. Illustration of a key-tree. There is a unique key assigned to each edge. Each leaf represents a member of the system that possesses the keys assigned to the edges of the path starting from the root and ending in the given leaf. For instance, the member that belongs to the leftmost leaf in the figure possesses the keys k_1, k_{11}, and k_{111}.

a key is identified, because it should consider only the subtree below the recently identified key.

The problem of the above described tree-based approach is that upper level keys in the tree are used by many members, and therefore, if a member is compromised and its keys become known to the adversary, then the adversary gains partial knowledge of the key of other members too [1]. This obviously reduces the privacy provided by the system to its members, since by observing the authentication of an uncompromised member, the adversary can recognize the usage of some compromised keys, and therefore its uncertainty regarding the identity of the authenticating member is reduced (it may be able to determine which subtree the member belongs to).

One interesting observation is that the naïve, linear key search approach can be viewed as a special case of the key-tree based approach, where the key-tree has a single level and each member has a single key. Regarding the above described problem of compromised members, the naïve approach is in fact optimal, because compromising a member does not reveal any key information of other members. At the same time, as we saw above, the authentication delay is the worst in this case. On the other hand, in case of a binary key-tree, we can observe that the compromise of a single member *strongly*² affects the privacy of the other members, while at the same time, the binary tree is very advantageous in terms of authentication delay. Thus, there seems to be a trade-off between the level of privacy provided by the system and the authentication delay, which depends on the parameters of the key-tree, but it is far from obvious to see how the optimal key-tree should look like. In this paper, we address this problem, and we show how to find optimal key-trees. More precisely, our main contributions are the following:

- We propose a benchmark metric for measuring the resistance of the system to a single compromised member based on the concept of anonymity sets. To the best of our knowledge, anonymity sets have not been used in the context of key-tree based private authentication yet.

---

² The precise quantification of this effect is the topic of this paper and will be presented later.

- We introduce the idea of using different branching factors at different levels of the key-tree; the advantage is that the system's resistance to single member compromise can be increased while still keeping the authentication delay short. To the best of our knowledge, key-trees with variable branching factors have not been proposed yet for private authentication.
- We present an algorithm for determining the optimal parameters of the key-tree, where optimal means that resistance to single member compromise is maximized, while the authentication delay is kept below a predefined threshold.
- In the general case, when any member can be compromised, we give a lower bound on the level of privacy provided by the system, and present some simulation results that show that this lower bound is quite sharp. This allows us to compare different systems based on their lower bounds.
- In summary, we propose *practically usable techniques* for designers of key-tree based authentication systems.

The outline of the paper is the following: In Section 2, we introduce our benchmark metric to measure the level of privacy provided by key-tree based authentication systems, and we illustrate, through an example, how this metric can be used to compare systems with different parameters. By the same token, we also show that key-trees with variable branching factors can be better than key-trees with a constant branching factor at every level. In Section 3, we formulate the problem of finding the best key-tree with respect to our benchmark metric as an optimization problem, and we present an algorithm that solves that optimization problem. In Section 4, we consider the general case, when any number of members can be compromised, and we derive a useful lower bound on the level of privacy provided by the system. Finally, in Section 5, we report on some related work, and in Section 6, we conclude the paper.

2   Resistance to Single Member Compromise

There are different ways to measure the level of anonymity provided by a system [5,14]. Here we will use the concept of anonymity sets [4]. The anonymity set of a member v is the set of members that are indistinguishable from v from the adversary's point of view. The size of the anonymity set is a good measure of the level of privacy provided for v, because it is related to the level of uncertainty of the adversary. Clearly, the larger the anonymity set is, the higher the level of privacy is. The minimum size of the anonymity set is 1, and its maximum size is equal to the number of all members in the system. In order to make the privacy measure independent of the number of members, one can divide the anonymity set size by the total number of members, and obtain a normalized privacy measure between 0 and 1. Such normalization makes the comparison of different systems easier.

Now, let us consider a key-tree with ℓ levels and branching factors $b_1, b_2, \ldots, b_\ell$ at the levels, and let us assume that exactly one member is compromised (see

Figure 2 for illustration). Knowledge of the compromised keys allows the adversary to partition the members into partitions $P_0, P_1, P_2, \ldots$, where

- P_0 contains the compromised member only,
- P_1 contains the members the parent of which is the same as that of the compromised member, and that are not in P_0,
- P_2 contains the members the grandparent of which is the same as that of the compromised member, and that are not in $P_0 \cup P_1$,
- etc.

Members of a given partition are indistinguishable for the adversary, while it can distinguish between members that belong to different partitions. Hence, each partition is the anonymity set of its members.

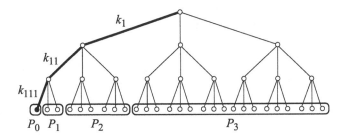

Fig. 2. Illustration of what happens when a single member is compromised. Without loss of generality, we assume that the member corresponding to the leftmost leaf in the figure is compromised. This means that the keys k_1, k_{11}, and k_{111} become known to the adversary. This knowledge of the adversary partitions the set of members into anonymity sets P_0, P_1, ... of different sizes. Members that belong to the same partition are indistinguishable to the adversary, while it can distinguish between members that belong to different partitions. For instance, the adversary can recognize a member in partition P_1 by observing the usage of k_1 and k_{11} but not that of k_{111}, where each of these keys are known to the adversary. Members in P_3 are recognized by not being able to observe the usage of any of the keys known to the adversary.

The level of privacy provided by the system can be characterized by the level of privacy provided to a randomly selected member, or in other words, by the expected size of the anonymity set of a randomly selected member. By definition, the expected anonymity set size is:

$$\bar{S} = \sum_{i=0}^{\ell} \frac{|P_i|}{N} |P_i| = \sum_{i=0}^{\ell} \frac{|P_i|^2}{N} \tag{1}$$

where N is the total number of members, and $|P_i|/N$ is the probability of selecting a member from partition P_i. We define the *resistance to single member compromise*, denoted by R, as the normalized expected anonymity set size, which can be computed as follows:

$$R = \frac{\bar{S}}{N} = \sum_{i=0}^{\ell} \frac{|P_i|^2}{N^2}$$

$$= \frac{1}{N^2} \left(1 + (b_\ell - 1)^2 + ((b_{\ell-1} - 1)b_\ell)^2 + \ldots + ((b_1 - 1)b_2 b_3 \ldots b_\ell)^2\right)$$

$$= \frac{1}{N^2} \left(1 + (b_\ell - 1)^2 + \sum_{i=1}^{\ell-1} (b_i - 1)^2 \prod_{j=i+1}^{\ell} b_j^2\right) \tag{2}$$

where we used that

$$|P_0| = 1$$
$$|P_1| = b_\ell - 1$$
$$|P_2| = (b_{\ell-1} - 1)b_\ell$$
$$|P_3| = (b_{\ell-2} - 1)b_{\ell-1}b_\ell$$
$$\ldots \quad \ldots$$
$$|P_\ell| = (b_1 - 1)b_2 b_3 \ldots b_\ell$$

As its name indicates, R characterizes the loss of privacy due to the compromise of a single member of the system. If R is close to 1, then the expected anonymity set size is close to the total number of members, and hence, the loss of privacy is small. On the other hand, if R is close to 0, then the loss of privacy is high, as the expected anonymity set size is small. We use R as a benchmark metric based on which different systems can be compared.

Obviously, a system with greater R is better, and therefore, we would like to maximize R. However, there are some constraints. We define the *maximum authentication delay*, denoted by D, as the number of basic operations needed to authenticate any member in the worst case. The maximum authentication delay in case of key-tree based authentication can be computed as $D = \sum_{i=1}^{\ell} b_i$. In most practical cases, there is an upper bound D_{max} on the maximum authentication delay allowed in the system. For instance, in the specification for electronic ticketing systems for public transport applications in Hungary [6], it is required that a ticket validation transaction should be completed in 250 ms. Taking into account the details of the ticket validation protocol, one can derive D_{max} for electronic tickets from such specifications. Therefore, in practice, the designer's task is to maximize R under the constraint that $D \leq D_{max}$. We will address this problem in Section 3.

In the remainder of this section, we illustrate how the benchmark metric R can be used to compare different systems. This exercise will also lead to an important revelation: key-trees with varying branching factors at different levels could provide higher level of privacy than key-trees with a constant branching factor, while having the same or even a shorter authentication delay.

Example: Let us assume that the total number N of members is 27000 and the upper bound D_{max} on the maximum authentication delay is 90. Let us consider a key-tree with a constant branching factor vector $B = (30, 30, 30)$, and another key-tree with branching factor vector $B' = (60, 10, 9, 5)$. Both key-trees can serve the given population of members, since $30^3 = 60 \cdot 10 \cdot 9 \cdot 5 = 27000$. In addition, both key-trees ensure that the maximum authentication delay is not longer than D_{max}: for the first key-tree, we have $D = 3 \cdot 30 = 90$, whereas for the second one, we get $D = 60+10+9+5 = 84$. Using (2), we can compute the resistance to single member compromise for both key-trees. For the first tree, we get $R \approx 0.9355$, while for the second tree we obtain $R \approx 0.9672$. Thus, we arrive to the conclusion that the second key-tree with variable branching factors is better, as it provides a higher level of privacy, while ensuring a smaller authentication delay.

At this point, several questions arise naturally: Is there an even better branching factor vector than B' for $N = 27000$ and $D_{max} = 90$? What is the best branching factor vector for this case? How can we find the best branching factor vector in general? We give the answers to these questions in the next section.

3   Optimal Trees in Case of Single Member Compromise

The problem of finding the best branching factor vector can be described as an optimization problem as follows: *Given the total number N of members and the upper bound D_{max} on the maximum authentication delay, find a branching factor vector $B = (b_1, b_2, \ldots b_\ell)$ such that $R(B)$ is maximal subject to the following constraints:*

$$\prod_{i=1}^{\ell} b_i = N \tag{3}$$

$$\sum_{i=1}^{\ell} b_i \leq D_{max} \tag{4}$$

We analyze this optimization problem through a series of lemmas that will lead to an algorithm that solves the problem. Our first lemma states that we can always improve a branching factor vector by ordering its elements in decreasing order, and hence, in the sequel we will consider only ordered vectors:

Lemma 1. *Let N and D_{max} be the total number of members and the upper bound on the maximum authentication delay, respectively. Moreover, let B be a branching factor vector and let B^* be the vector that consists of the sorted permutation of the elements of B in decreasing order. If B satisfies the constraints of the optimization problem defined above, then B^* also satisfies them, and $R(B^*) \geq R(B)$.*

Proof. The proof can be found in the Appendix.

The following lemma provides a lower bound and an upper bound for the resistance to single member compromise:

Lemma 2. *Let $B = (b_1, b_2, \ldots b_\ell)$ be a sorted branching factor vector (i.e., $b_1 \geq b_2 \geq \ldots \geq b_\ell$). We can give the following lower and upper bounds on $R(B)$:*

$$\left(1 - \frac{1}{b_1}\right)^2 \leq R(B) \leq \left(1 - \frac{1}{b_1}\right)^2 + \frac{4}{3b_1^2} \tag{5}$$

Proof. The proof can be found in the Appendix.

Let us consider the bounds in Lemma 2. Note that the branching factor vector is ordered, therefore, b_1 is not smaller than any other b_i. We can observe that if we increase b_1, then the difference between the upper and the lower bounds decreases, and $R(B)$ gets closer to 1. Intuitively, this implies that in order to find the solution to the optimization problem, b_1 should be maximized. The following lemma underpins this intuition formally:

Lemma 3. *Let N and D_{max} be the total number of members and the upper bound on the maximum authentication delay, respectively. Moreover, let $B = (b_1, b_2, \ldots, b_\ell)$ and $B' = (b'_1, b'_2, \ldots, b'_{\ell'})$ be two sorted branching factor vectors that satisfy the constraints of the optimization problem defined above. Then, $b_1 > b'_1$ implies $R(B) \geq R(B')$.*

Proof. The proof can be found in the Appendix.

Lemma 3 states that given two branching factor vectors, the one with the larger first element is always at least as good as the other. The next lemma generalizes this result by stating that given two branching factor vectors the first j elements of which are equal, the vector with the larger $(j+1)$-st element is always at least as good as the other.

Lemma 4. *Let N and D_{max} be the total number of members and the upper bound on the maximum authentication delay, respectively. Moreover, let $B = (b_1, b_2, \ldots, b_\ell)$ and $B' = (b'_1, b'_2, \ldots, b'_{\ell'})$ be two sorted branching factor vectors such that $b_i = b'_i$ for all $1 \leq i \leq j$ for some $j < \min(\ell, \ell')$, and both B and B' satisfy the constraints of the optimization problem defined above. Then, $b_{j+1} > b'_{j+1}$ implies $R(B) \geq R(B')$.*

Proof. The proof can be found in the Appendix.

We will now present an algorithm that finds the solution to the optimization problem. However, before doing that, we need to introduce some further notations. Let $B = (b_1, b_2, \ldots, b_\ell)$ and $B' = (b'_1, b'_2, \ldots, b'_{\ell'})$. Then

- $\prod(B)$ denotes $\prod_{i=1}^{\ell} b_i$;
- $\sum(B)$ denotes $\sum_{i=1}^{\ell} b_i$;
- $\{B\}$ denotes the set $\{b_1, b_2, \ldots, b_\ell\}$ of the elements of B;
- $B' \subseteq B$ means that $\{B'\} \subseteq \{B\}$;
- if $B' \subseteq B$, then $B \setminus B'$ denotes the vector that consists of the elements of $\{B\} \setminus \{B'\}$ in decreasing order;
- if b is a positive integer, then $b|B$ denotes the vector $(b, b_1, b_2, \ldots, b_\ell)$.

We define our algorithm as a recursive function f, which takes two input parameters, a vector B of positive integers, and another positive integer d, and returns a vector of positive integers. In order to compute the optimal branching factor vector for a given N and D_{max}, f should be called with the vector that contains the prime factors of N, and D_{max}. For instance, if $N = 27000$ and $D_{max} = 90$ (we use the same parameters as in the example in Sec 2, to compare the naïve and algorithmical results), then f should be called with $B = (5, 5, 5, 3, 3, 3, 2, 2, 2)$ and $d = 90$. Function f will then return the optimal branching factor vector.

Function f is defined as follows:

$f(B, d)$
1   if $\sum(B) > d$ then exit (no solution exists)
2   else find $B' \subseteq B$ such that
          $\prod(B') + \sum(B \setminus B') \leq d$ and
          $\prod(B')$ is maximal
3   if $B' = B$ then return ($\prod(B')$)
4   else return $\prod(B')|f(B \setminus B', d - \prod(B'))$

The operation of the algorithm can be described as follows: The algorithm starts with a branching factor vector consisting of the prime factors of N. This vector satisfies the first constraint of the optimization problem by definition. If it does not satisfy the second constraint (i.e., it does not respect the upper bound on the maximum authentication delay), then no solution exists. Otherwise, the algorithm successively improves the branching factor vector by maximizing its elements, starting with the first element, and then proceeding to the next elements, one after the other. Maximization of an element is done by joining as yet unused prime factors until the resulting divisor of N cannot be further increased without violating the constraints of the optimization problem.

Theorem 1. *Let N and D_{max} be the total number of members and the upper bound on the maximum authentication delay, respectively. Moreover, let B be a vector that contains the prime factors of N. Then, $f(B, D_{max})$ is an optimal branching factor vector for N and D_{max}.*

Proof. We will give a sketch of the proof. Let $B^* = f(B, D_{max})$, and let us assume that there is another branching factor vector $B' \neq B^*$ that also satisfies the constraints of the optimization problem and $R(B') > R(B^*)$. We will show that this leads to a contradiction, hence B^* should be optimal.

Let $B^* = (b_1^*, b_2^*, \ldots, b_{\ell^*}^*)$ and $B' = (b_1', b_2', \ldots, b_{\ell'}')$. Recall that B^* is obtained by first maximizing the first element in the vector, therefore, $b_1^* \geq b_1'$ must hold. If $b_1^* > b_1'$, then $R(B^*) \geq R(B')$ by Lemma 3, and thus, B' cannot be a better vector than B^*. This means that $b_1^* = b_1'$ must hold.

We know that once b_1^* is determined, our algorithm continues by maximizing the next element of B^*. Hence, $b_2^* \geq b_2'$ must hold. If $b_2^* > b_2'$, then $R(B^*) \geq R(B')$ by Lemma 4, and thus, B' cannot be a better vector than B^*. This means that $b_2^* = b_2'$ must hold too.

By repeating this argument, finally, we arrive to the conclusion that $B^* = B'$ must hold, which is a contradiction. ◇

Table 1 illustrates the operation of the algorithm for $B = (5, 5, 5, 3, 3, 3, 2, 2, 2)$ and $d = 90$. The rows of the table correspond to the levels of the recursion during

Table 1. Illustration of the operation of the recursive function f when called with $B = (5, 5, 5, 3, 3, 3, 2, 2, 2)$ and $d = 90$. The rows of the table correspond to the levels of the recursion during the execution.

recursion level	B	d	B'	$\prod(B')$
1	$(5, 5, 5, 3, 3, 3, 2, 2, 2)$	90	$(3, 3, 2, 2, 2)$	72
2	$(5, 5, 5, 3)$	18	(5)	5
3	$(5, 5, 3)$	13	(5)	5
4	$(5, 3)$	8	(5)	5
5	(3)	3	(3)	3

the execution. The column labelled with B' contains the prime factors that are joined at a given recursion level. The optimal branching factor vector can be read out from the last column of the table (each row contains one element of the vector). From this example, we can see that the optimal branching factor vector for $N = 27000$ and $D_{max} = 90$ is $B^* = (72, 5, 5, 5, 3)$. For the key-tree defined by this vector, we get $R \approx 0.9725$, and $D = 90$.

4   Analysis of the General Case

So far, we have studied the case of a single compromised member. This already proved to be useful, because it allowed us to compare different key-trees and to derive a key-tree construction method. However, one may still be interested in what level of privacy is provided by a system in the general case when any number of members could be compromised. In this section, we address this problem.

In what follows, we will need to refer to the non-leaf vertices of the key-tree, and for this reason, we introduce the labelling scheme that is illustrated in Figure 3. In addition, we need to introduce some further notations. We call a leaf compromised if it belongs to a compromised member, and we call a non-leaf vertex compromised if it lies on a path that leads to a compromised leaf in the tree. If vertex v is compromised, then

- K_v denotes the set of the compromised children of v, and $k_v = |K_v|$;
- $\mathcal{P}_v$ denotes the set of partitions (anonymity sets) that belong to the subtree rooted at v (see Figure 3 for illustration); and
- $\bar{S}_v$ denotes the average size of the partitions in $\mathcal{P}_v$.

We are interested in computing $\bar{S}_{\langle - \rangle}$. We can do that as follows:

$$\bar{S}_{\langle - \rangle} = \sum_{P \in \mathcal{P}_{\langle - \rangle}} \frac{|P|^2}{b_1 b_2 \dots b_\ell}$$

$$= \frac{((b_1 - k_{\langle - \rangle}) b_2 \dots b_\ell)^2}{b_1 b_2 \dots b_\ell} + \sum_{v \in K_{\langle - \rangle}} \sum_{P \in \mathcal{P}_v} \frac{|P|^2}{b_1 b_2 \dots b_\ell}$$

$$= \frac{((b_1 - k_{\langle - \rangle}) b_2 \dots b_\ell)^2}{b_1 b_2 \dots b_\ell} + \frac{1}{b_1} \sum_{v \in K_{\langle - \rangle}} \bar{S}_v \tag{6}$$

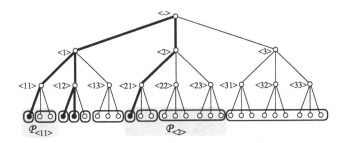

Fig. 3. Illustration of what happens when several members are compromised. Just as in the case of a single compromised member, the members are partitioned into anonymity sets, but now the resulting partitions depend on the number of the compromised members, as well as on their positions in the tree. Nevertheless, the expected size of the anonymity set of a randomly selected member is still a good metric for the level of privacy provided by the system, although, in this general case, it is more difficult to compute.

In general, for any vertex $\langle i_1, \ldots, i_j \rangle$ such that $1 \le j < \ell - 1$:

$$\bar{S}_{\langle i_1, \ldots, i_j \rangle} = \frac{((b_{j+1} - k_{\langle i_1, \ldots, i_j \rangle})b_{j+2} \ldots b_\ell)^2}{b_{j+1} \ldots b_\ell} + \frac{1}{b_{j+1}} \sum_{v \in K_{\langle i_1, \ldots, i_j \rangle}} \bar{S}_v \quad (7)$$

Finally, for vertices $\langle i_1, \ldots, i_{\ell-1} \rangle$ just above the leaves, we get:

$$\bar{S}_{\langle i_1, \ldots, i_{\ell-1} \rangle} = \frac{(b_\ell - k_{\langle i_1, \ldots, i_{\ell-1} \rangle})^2}{b_\ell} + \frac{k_{\langle i_1, \ldots, i_{\ell-1} \rangle}}{b_\ell} \quad (8)$$

Expressions (6 – 8) can be used to compute the expected anonymity set size in the system iteratively, in case of any number of compromised members. However, note that the computation depends not only on the number c of the compromised members, but also their positions in the tree. This makes the comparison of different systems difficult, because for a comprehensive analysis, all possible allocations of the compromised members over the leaves of the key-tree should be considered. Therefore, we would prefer a formula that depends solely on c, but characterizes the effect of compromised members on the level of privacy sufficiently well, so that it can serve as a basis for comparison of different systems. In the following, we derive such a formula based on the assumption that the compromised members are distributed uniformly at random over the leaves of the key-tree. In some sense, this is a pessimistic assumption as the uniform distribution represents the worst case, which leads to the largest amount of privacy loss due to the compromised members. Thus, the approximation that we derive can be viewed as a lower bound on the expected anonymity set size in the system when c members are compromised.

Let the branching factor of the key-tree be $B = (b_1, b_2, \ldots, b_\ell)$, and let c be the number of compromised leaves in the tree. We can estimate $k_{\langle - \rangle}$ for the root as follows:

$$k_{\langle - \rangle} \approx \min(c, b_1) = k_0 \tag{9}$$

If a vertex $\langle i \rangle$ at the first level of the tree is compromised, then the number of compromised leaves in the subtree rooted at $\langle i \rangle$ is approximately $c/k_0 = c_1$. Then, we can estimate $k_{\langle i \rangle}$ as follows:

$$k_{\langle i \rangle} \approx \min(c_1, b_2) = k_1 \tag{10}$$

In general, if vertex $\langle i_1, \ldots, i_j \rangle$ at the j-th level of the tree is compromised, then the number of compromised leaves in the subtree rooted at $\langle i_1, \ldots, i_j \rangle$ is approximately $c_{j-1}/k_{j-1} = c_j$, and we can use this to approximate $k_{\langle i_1, \ldots, i_j \rangle}$ as follows:

$$k_{\langle i_1, \ldots, i_j \rangle} \approx \min(c_j, b_{j+1}) = k_j \tag{11}$$

Using these approximations in expressions (6 – 8), we can derive an approximation for $\bar{S}_{\langle - \rangle}$, which we denote by $\bar{S}_0$, in the following way:

$$\bar{S}_{\ell-1} = \frac{(b_\ell - k_{\ell-1})^2}{b_\ell} + \frac{k_{\ell-1}}{b_\ell} \tag{12}$$

$$\cdots \quad \cdots$$

$$\bar{S}_j = \frac{((b_{j+1} - k_j)b_{j+2} \ldots b_\ell)^2}{b_{j+1} \ldots b_\ell} + \frac{k_j}{b_{j+1}} \bar{S}_{j+1} \tag{13}$$

$$\cdots \quad \cdots$$

$$\bar{S}_0 = \frac{((b_1 - k_0)b_2 \ldots b_\ell)^2}{b_1 \ldots b_\ell} + \frac{k_0}{b_1} \bar{S}_1 \tag{14}$$

Note that expressions (14 – 12) do not depend on the positions of the compromised leaves in the tree, but they depend only on the value of c.

In order to see how well $\bar{S}_0$ estimates $\bar{S}_{\langle - \rangle}$, we run some simulations. The simulation parameters were the following:

- total number of members $N = 27000$;
- upper bound on the maximum authentication delay $D_{max} = 90$;
- we considered two branching factor vectors: $(30, 30, 30)$ and $(72, 5, 5, 5, 3)$;
- we varied the number c of compromised members between 1 and 270 with a step size of one.

For each value of c, we run 100 simulations[3]. In each simulation run, the c compromised members were chosen uniformly at random from the set of all members. We computed the exact value of the normalized expected anonymity set size $\bar{S}_{\langle - \rangle}/N$ using the expressions (6 – 8). Finally, we averaged the obtained values over all simulation runs. Moreover, for every c, we also computed the estimated value $\bar{S}_0/N$ using the expressions (14 – 12).

The simulation results are shown in Figure 4. The figure does not show the confidence interwalls, because they are very small (in the range of 10^{-4} for all simulations) and thus they could be hardly visible. As we can see, $\bar{S}_0/N$ approximates $\bar{S}_{\langle - \rangle}/N$ quite well, and in general it provides a lower bound on the normalized expected anonymity set size.

---

[3] All computations have been done in Matlab, and for the purpose of repeatability, the source code is available on-line at http://www.crysys.hu/~holczer/PET2006

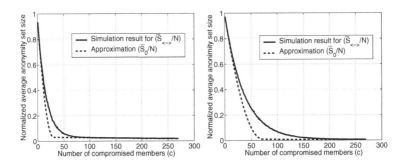

Fig. 4. Simulation results for branching factor vectors $(30, 30, 30)$ (left hand side) and $(72, 5, 5, 5, 3)$ (right hand side). As we can see, $\bar{S}_0/N$ approximates $\bar{S}_{\langle-\rangle}/N$ quite well, and in general it provides a lower bound on it.

In Figure 5, we plotted the value of $\bar{S}_0/N$ as a function of c for different branching factor vectors. This figure illustrates, how different systems can be compared using our approximation $\bar{S}_0/N$ of the normalized expected anonymity set size. On the left hand side of the figure, we can see that the value of $\bar{S}_0/N$ is greater for the vector $B^* = (72, 5, 5, 5, 3)$ than for the vector $B = (30, 30, 30)$ not only for $c = 1$ (as we saw before), but for larger values of c too. In fact, B^* seems to lose its superiority only when the value of c approaches 60, but at this range, the systems nearly provide no privacy in any case. Thus, we can conclude that B^* is a better branching factor vector yielding more privacy than B in general.

We can make another interesting observation on the left hand side of Figure 5: $\bar{S}_0/N$ starts decreasing sharply as c starts increasing, however, when c gets close

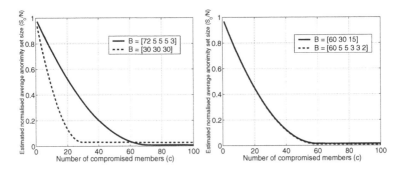

Fig. 5. The value of $\bar{S}_0/N$ as a function of c for different branching factor vectors. The figure illustrates, how different systems can be compared based on the approximation $\bar{S}_0/N$. On the left hand side, we can see that the value of $\bar{S}_0/N$ is greater for the vector $(72, 5, 5, 5, 3)$ than for the vector $(30, 30, 30)$ not only for $c = 1$ (as we saw earlier), but for larger values of c too. On the right hand side, we can see that $\bar{S}_0/N$ is almost the same for the vector $(60, 5, 5, 3, 3, 2)$ as for the vector $(60, 30, 15)$. We can conclude that $\bar{S}_0/N$ is essentially determined by the value of the first element of the branching factor vector.

to the value of the first element of the branching factor vector, the decrease of $\bar{S}_0/N$ slows down. Moreover, almost exactly when c reaches the value of the first element (30 in case of B, and 72 in case of B^*), $\bar{S}_0/N$ seems to turn into constant, but at a very low value. We can conclude that, just as in the case of a single compromised member, in the general case too, the level of privacy provided by the system essentially depends on the value of the first element of the branching factor vector. The plot on the right hand side of the figure reinforces this observation: it shows $\bar{S}_0/N$ for two branching factor vectors that have the same first element but that differ in the other elements. As we can see, the curves are almost perfectly overlapping.

Thus, a practical design principle for key-tree based private authentication systems is to maximize the branching factor at the first level of the key-tree. Further optimization by adjusting the branching factors of the lower levels may still be possible, but the gain is not significant; what really counts is the branching factor at the first level.

5   Related Work

The problem of private authentication has been extensively studied in the literature recently, but most of the proposed solutions are based on public key cryptography. One example is Idemix, which is a practical anonymous credential system proposed by Camenisch and Lysyanskaya in [3]. Idemix allows for unlinkable demonstration of the possession of various credentials, and it can be used in many applications. However, it is not applicable in resource constraint scenarios, such as low-cost RFID systems. For such applications, solutions based on symmetric key cryptography seem to be the only viable options.

The key-tree based approach for symmetric key private authentication has been proposed by Molnar and Wagner in [11]. However, they use a simple b-ary tree, which means that the tree has the same branching factor at every level. Moreover, they do not analyze the effects of compromised members on the level of privacy provided. They only mention that compromise of a member has a wider effect than in the case of public key cryptography based solutions.

An entropy based analyzis of key trees can be found in [12]. Nohara *et al.* prove that their K-steps ID matching scheme (whitch is very similar to [11]) is secure against one compromised tag, if the number of nodes are large enough. They consider only b-ary trees, no variable branching factors. The entropy based analysis leads to a slightly different optimization problem. We leave the detailed comparison of the entropy based and the anonimity set based approach for future work.

Finally, Avoine *et al.* analyze the effects of compromised members on privacy in the key-tree based approach [1]. They study the case of a single compromised member, as well as the general case of any compromised members. However, their analysis is not based on the notion of anonymity sets. In their model, the adversary is first allowed to compromise some members, then it chooses a target member that it wants to trace, and it is allowed to interact with the chosen member. Later, the adversary is given two members such that one of them is the target member chosen by the adversary. The adversary can interact with the given members, and it must decide which one is its target. The level of privacy provided by the system is quantified by the success probability of the adversary. This model is similar to ours in case of a single compromised member, but it is slightly different in the general case. Moreover, Avoine *et al.* do not consider the problem of how to optimize the key-tree, instead, they suggest a time-memory trade-off to reduce the authentication delay.

6   Conclusion

Key-trees provide an efficient solution for private authentication in the symmetric key setting. However, the level of privacy provided by key-tree based systems decreases considerably if some members are compromised. The main message of this paper is that this loss of privacy can be minimized by the careful design of the tree. Based on our results presented in this paper, we can conclude that a good practical design principle is to maximize the branching factor at the first level of the tree such that the resulting tree still respects the constraint on the maximum authentication delay in the system. Once the branching factor at the first level is maximized, the tree can be further optimized by maximizing the branching factors at the successive levels, but the improvement achieved in this way is not really significant; what really counts is the branching factor at the first level.

Acknowledgements

This work has partially been supported by the Hungarian Scientific Research Fund (T046664), the Mobile Innovation Center, Hungary, and the SeVeCom Project (IST-027795). The first author has been further supported by the Hungarian Ministry of Education (BÖ2003/70).

References

1. G. Avoine, E. Dysli, and P. Oechslin. Reducing time complexity in RFID systems. In *Proceedings of the 12th Annual Workshop on Selected Areas in Cryptography (SAC'05)*, 2005.
2. C. Boyd, A. Mathuria. Protocols for Authentication and Key Establishment. Springer-Verlag, 2003
3. J. Camenisch, A. Lysyanskaya. A Efficient Non-transferable Anonymous Multishow Credential System with Optional Anonymity Revocation. In *Advances in Cryptography – EUROCRYPT 2001*. Springer, 2001.
4. D. Chaum. The Dining Cryptographers Problem: Unconditional sender and recipient untraceability. *Journal of Cryptology*, 1(1):65–75, 1988.
5. C. Díaz, S. Seys, J. Claessens, and B. Preneel. Towards measuring anonymity. In Dingledine and Syverson (Eds.), *Designing Privacy Enhancing Technologies*, Springer LNCS 2482, pp. 54–68, 2002.

6. Elektra Hungaria (In Hungarian)
   http://www.gkm.gov.hu/data/357863/kovetelmeny1215.pdf
7. IKE, The Internet Key Exchange, RFC 2409, http://www.ietf.org/rfc/rfc2409.txt
8. ISO 9798-2. Mechanisms using symmetric encipherment algorithms
   http://www.iso.org
9. A. Juels. RFID security and privacy: a research survey. Manuscript, condensed
   version will appear in the *IEEE Journal on Selected Areas in Communication*,
   September 2005.
10. Kerberos. RFC 1510, http://www.ietf.org/rfc/rfc1510.txt
11. D. Molnar and D. Wagner. Privacy and security in library RFID: issues, prac-
    tices, and architectures. In *Proceedings of the ACM Conference on Computer and
    Communications Security*, 2004.
12. Y. Nohara, S. Inoue, K. Baba, H. Yasuura. Quantitative Evaluation of Unlinkable
    ID Matching Schemes. In Workshop on Privacy in the Electronic Society, WPES,
    2005.
13. A. Pfitzmann and M. Khntopp. Anonymity, unobservability and pseudonymity –
    a proposal for terminology. In *Proceedings of the Privacy Enhancing Technologies
    (PET) Workshop*, Springer LNCS 2009, pp. 1–9, 2001.
14. A. Serjantov and G. Danezis. Towards an information theoretic metric for
    anonymity. In *Proceedings of the Privacy Enhancing Technologies (PET) Work-
    shop*, Springer LNCS, 2002.

A   Proof of Lemma 1

B^* has the same elements as B has, therefore, the sum and the product of the
elements of B^* are the same as that of B, and so if B satisfies the constraints
of the optimization problem, then B^* does so too.

Now, let us assume that B^* is obtained from B with the bubble sort algorithm.
The basic step of this algorithm is to change two neighboring elements if they
are not in the right order. Let us suppose that $b_i < b_{i+1}$, and thus, the algorithm
changes the order of b_i and b_{i+1}. Then, using (2), we can express $\Delta R = R(B^*) - R(B)$ as follows:

$$
\Delta R = \frac{1}{N^2} \left((b_{i+1} - 1)^2 b_i^2 \prod_{j=i+2}^{\ell} b_j^2 + (b_i - 1)^2 \prod_{j=i+2}^{\ell} b_j^2 \right) -
$$

$$
\frac{1}{N^2} \left((b_i - 1)^2 b_{i+1}^2 \prod_{j=i+2}^{\ell} b_j^2 + (b_{i+1} - 1)^2 \prod_{j=i+2}^{\ell} b_j^2 \right)
$$

$$
= \frac{\prod_{j=i+2}^{\ell} b_j^2}{N^2} \left((b_{i+1} - 1)^2 b_i^2 + (b_i - 1)^2 - (b_i - 1)^2 b_{i+1}^2 - (b_{i+1} - 1)^2 \right)
$$

$$
= \frac{\prod_{j=i+2}^{\ell} b_j^2}{N^2} \left((b_{i+1} - 1)^2 (b_i^2 - 1) - (b_i - 1)^2 (b_{i+1}^2 - 1) \right)
$$

$$
= \frac{(b_i - 1)(b_{i+1} - 1) \prod_{j=i+2}^{\ell} b_j^2}{N^2} \left((b_{i+1} - 1)(b_i + 1) - (b_i - 1)(b_{i+1} + 1) \right)
$$

Since $b_i \geq 2$ for all i, ΔR is non-negative if

$$\frac{b_i + 1}{b_i - 1} \geq \frac{b_{i+1} + 1}{b_{i+1} - 1} \qquad (15)$$

But (15) must hold, since the function $f(x) = \frac{x+1}{x-1}$ is a monotone decreasing function, and by assumption, $b_i < b_{i+1}$. This means, that when sorting the elements of B, we improve $R(B)$ in every step, and thus, $R(B^*) \geq R(B)$ must hold. ⋄

B   Proof of Lemma 2

By definition

$$R = \frac{1}{N^2} \left(1 + (b_\ell - 1)^2 + \sum_{i=1}^{\ell-1} (b_i - 1)^2 \prod_{j=i+1}^{\ell} b_j^2 \right)$$

$$= \left(\frac{b_1 - 1}{b_1} \right)^2 + \frac{1}{N^2} \left(1 + (b_\ell - 1)^2 + \sum_{i=2}^{\ell-1} (b_i - 1)^2 \prod_{j=i+1}^{\ell} b_j^2 \right) \qquad (16)$$

where we used that $N = b_1 b_2 \ldots b_\ell$. The lower bound in the lemma[4] follows directly from (16). In order to obtain the upper bound, we write b_i instead of $(b_i - 1)$ in the sum in (16):

$$R < \left(\frac{b_1 - 1}{b_1} \right)^2 + \frac{1}{N^2} \left(1 + \sum_{i=2}^{\ell} \prod_{j=i}^{\ell} b_j^2 \right)$$

$$= \left(\frac{b_1 - 1}{b_1} \right)^2 + \frac{1}{b_1^2} \left(1 + \sum_{i=2}^{\ell} \prod_{j=2}^{i} \frac{1}{b_j^2} \right)$$

Since $b_i \geq 2$ for all i, we can write 2 in place of b_i in the sum, and we obtain:

$$R < \left(\frac{b_1 - 1}{b_1} \right)^2 + \frac{1}{b_1^2} \left(1 + \sum_{i=2}^{\ell} \prod_{j=2}^{i} \frac{1}{4} \right)$$

$$= \left(\frac{b_1 - 1}{b_1} \right)^2 + \frac{1}{b_1^2} \left(1 + \sum_{i=2}^{\ell} \left(\frac{1}{4} \right)^{i-1} \right)$$

$$< \left(\frac{b_1 - 1}{b_1} \right)^2 + \frac{1}{b_1^2} \left(1 + \sum_{i=2}^{\infty} \left(\frac{1}{4} \right)^{i-1} \right)$$

$$= \left(\frac{b_1 - 1}{b_1} \right)^2 + \frac{1}{b_1^2} \frac{1}{1 - \frac{1}{4}}$$

and this is the upper bound in the lemma. ⋄

---

[4] Note that we could also derive the slightly better lower bound of $\left(\frac{b_1 - 1}{b_1} \right)^2 + \frac{1}{N^2}$ from (16), however, we do not need that in this paper.

C   Proof of Lemma 3

First, we prove that the statement of the lemma is true if $b_1' \geq 5$. We know from Lemma 2 that

$$R(B') < \left(1 - \frac{1}{b_1'}\right)^2 + \frac{4}{3b_1'^2}$$

and

$$R(B) > \left(1 - \frac{1}{b_1}\right)^2 \geq \left(1 - \frac{1}{b_1' + 1}\right)^2$$

where we used that $b_1 > b_1'$ by assumption. If we can prove that

$$\left(1 - \frac{1}{b_1'}\right)^2 + \frac{4}{3b_1'^2} \leq \left(1 - \frac{1}{b_1' + 1}\right)^2 \tag{17}$$

then we also proved that $R(B') \leq R(B)$. Indeed, a straightforward calculation yields that (17) is true if $b_1' \geq 2 + \sqrt{\frac{15}{2}}$, and since b_1' is an integer, we are done.

Next, we make the observation that a branching factor vector $A = (a_1, \ldots, a_k, 2, 2)$ that has at least two 2s at the end can be improved by joining two 2s into a 4 and obtaining $A' = (a_1, \ldots, a_k, 4)$. It is clear that neither the sum nor the product of the elements changes with this transformation. In addition, we can use the definition of R to get

$$N^2 \cdot R(A) = ((a_1 - 1) \cdot a_2 \cdot \ldots \cdot a_k \cdot 2 \cdot 2)^2 + \ldots + ((a_k - 1) \cdot 2 \cdot 2)^2 + ((2 - 1) \cdot 2)^2 + (2 - 1)^2 + 1$$

and

$$N^2 \cdot R(A') = ((a_1 - 1) \cdot a_2 \cdot \ldots \cdot a_k \cdot 4)^2 + \ldots + ((a_k - 1) \cdot 4)^2 + (4 - 1)^2 + 1$$

Thus, $R(A') - R(A) = \frac{1}{N^2}(9 - 4 - 1) > 0$, which means that A' is better than A. Now, we prove that the lemma is also true for $b_1' \in \{2, 3, 4\}$:

- $b_1' = 2$: Since B' is an ordered vector where b_1' is the largest element, it follows that every element of B' is 2, and thus, N is a power of 2. From Lemma 2, $R(B') < (1 - \frac{1}{2})^2 + \frac{4}{3 \cdot 2^2} = \frac{7}{12}$ and $R(B) > (1 - \frac{1}{b_1})^2$. It is easy to see that $(1 - \frac{1}{b_1})^2 \geq \frac{7}{12}$ if $b_1 \geq \frac{1}{1 - \sqrt{\frac{7}{12}}} = 4.23$. Since $b_1 > b_1'$, the remaining cases are $b_1 = 3$ and $b_1 = 4$. However, $b_1 = 3$ cannot be the case, because N is a power of 2. If $b_1 = 4$, then B can be obtained from B' by joining pairs of 2s into 4s and then ordering the elements. However, according to our observation above and Lemma 1, both operations improve the vector. It follows that $R(B) \geq R(B')$ must hold.
- $b_1' = 3$: From Lemma 2, $R(B') < (1 - \frac{1}{3})^2 + \frac{4}{3 \cdot 3^2} = \frac{16}{27}$ and $R(B) > (1 - \frac{1}{b_1})^2$. It is easy to see that $(1 - \frac{1}{b_1})^2 \geq \frac{16}{27}$ if $b_1 \geq \frac{9}{9 - 4 \cdot \sqrt{3}} = 4.34$. Since $b_1 > b_1'$, the

only remaining case is $b_1 = 4$. In this case, the vectors are as follows:

$$B = (\overbrace{2^2,\ldots,2^2}^{i}, \overbrace{3,\ldots,3}^{j}, \overbrace{2,\ldots,2}^{k})$$

$$B' = (\overbrace{3,\ldots,3}^{j}, \overbrace{2,\ldots,2}^{2i+k})$$

where $i, j \geq 1$ and $k \geq 0$. This means that B can be obtained from B' by joining i pairs of 2s into 4s and then ordering the elements. However, as we saw earlier, both joining 2s into 4s and ordering the elements improve the vector, and thus, $R(B) \geq R(B')$ must hold.

- $b'_1 = 4$: Since B' is an ordered vector where b'_1 is the largest element, it follows that N is not divisible by 5. From Lemma 2, $R(B') < (1-\frac{1}{4})^2 + \frac{4}{3\cdot 4^2} = \frac{31}{48}$ and $R(B) > (1-\frac{1}{b_1})^2$. It is easy to see that $(1-\frac{1}{b_1})^2 \geq \frac{31}{48}$ if $b_1 \geq \frac{1}{1-\sqrt{\frac{31}{48}}} = 5.09$. Since $b_1 > b'_1$, the remaining case is $b_1 = 5$. However, $b_1 = 5$ cannot be the case, because N is not divisible by 5. $\diamond$

D   Proof of Lemma 4

By definition

$$R(B) = \frac{1}{N^2}\left(1 + (b_\ell - 1)^2 + \sum_{i=1}^{\ell-1}(b_i - 1)^2 \prod_{j=i+1}^{\ell} b_j^2\right)$$

$$= \left(\frac{b_1 - 1}{b_1}\right)^2 + \frac{1}{b_1^2}\left(\frac{1}{(N/b_1)^2}\left(1 + (b_\ell - 1)^2 + \sum_{i=2}^{\ell-1}(b_i - 1)^2 \prod_{j=i+1}^{\ell} b_j^2\right)\right)$$

$$= \left(\frac{b_1 - 1}{b_1}\right)^2 + \frac{1}{b_1^2}\cdot R(B_1)$$

where $B_1 = (b_2, b_3, \ldots, b_\ell)$. Similarly,

$$R(B') = \left(\frac{b'_1 - 1}{b'_1}\right)^2 + \frac{1}{b'^2_1}\cdot R(B'_1)$$

where $B'_1 = (b'_2, b'_3, \ldots, b'_{\ell'})$. Since $b_1 = b'_1$, $R(B) \geq R(B')$ if and only if $R(B_1) \geq R(B'_1)$. By repeating the same argument for B_1 and B'_1, we get that $R(B) \geq R(B')$ if and only if $R(B_2) \geq R(B'_2)$, where $B_2 = (b_3, \ldots, b_\ell)$ and $B'_2 = (b'_3, \ldots, b'_{\ell'})$. And so on, until we get that $R(B) \geq R(B')$ if and only if $R(B_j) \geq R(B'_j)$, where $B_j = (b_{j+1}, \ldots, b_\ell)$ and $B'_j = (b'_{j+1}, \ldots, b'_{\ell'})$. But from Lemma 3, we know that $R(B_j) \geq R(B'_j)$ if $b_{j+1} > b'_{j+1}$, and we are done. $\diamond$

Simple and Flexible Revocation Checking with Privacy

John Solis and Gene Tsudik

Computer Science Department
University of California, Irvine
{jsolis,gts}@ics.uci.edu

Abstract. Digital certificates signed by trusted certification authorities (CAs) are used for multiple purposes, most commonly for secure binding of public keys to names and other attributes of their owners. Although a certificate usually includes an expiration time, it is not uncommon that a certificate needs to be revoked prematurely. For this reason, whenever a client (user or program) needs to assert the validity of another party's certificate, it performs revocation checking. There are many revocation techniques varying in both the operational model and underlying data structures. One common feature is that a client typically contacts an on-line third party (trusted, untrusted or semi-trusted), identifies the certificate of interest and obtains some form of a proof of either revocation or validity (non-revocation) for the certificate in question.

While useful, revocation checking can leak potentially sensitive information. In particular, third parties of dubious trustworthiness discover two things: (1) the identity of the party posing the query, as well as (2) the target of the query. The former can be easily remedied with techniques such as onion routing or anonymous web browsing. Whereas, hiding the target of the query is not as obvious. Arguably, a more important **loss of privacy** results from the third party's ability to tie the source of the revocation check with the query's target. (Since, most likely, the two are about to communicate.) This paper is concerned with the problem of privacy in revocation checking and its contribution is two-fold: it identifies and explores the loss of privacy inherent in current revocation checking, and, it constructs a simple, efficient and flexible privacy-preserving component for one well-known revocation method.

1 Introduction and Motivation

As is well-known, public key cryptography allows users to communicate privately without having pre-established shared secrets. While parties can be assured that communication is private, there is no guarantee of authenticity. Authenticity is obtained by binding a public key to some identity or name which is later verified via digital signatures in conjunction with public key certificates. A public key certificate, signed by a recognized certification authority (CA), can be used to verify the validity, authenticity and ownership of a public key. As long as the issuing CA is trusted, anyone can verify the CA's certificate signature and bind

G. Danezis and P. Golle (Eds.): PET 2006, LNCS 4258, pp. 351–367, 2006.

the included name/identity to the public key. Digital certificates work best in large interconnected open systems, where it is generally infeasible to directly authenticate the owners of all public keys. X.509 [24] is one well-known certificate format widely used in several Internet-related contexts. The peer-based PGP/GPG [2,8] format represents another popular approach.

Since a certificate is essentially a capability, one of the biggest problems associated with large-scale use of certificates is revocation. There are many reasons that can lead to a certificate being revoked prematurely. They include [24]: private key loss or compromise, change of affiliation or job function, algorithm compromise, or change in security policy. To cope with revocation, it must be possible to check the status of any certificate at any time.

Revocation techniques can be roughly partitioned into implicit and explicit classes. In the former, each certificate owner possesses a timely proof of non-revocation which it supplies on demand to anyone. Lack of such a proof implicitly signifies revocation. An example of implicit revocation is Micali's Certificate Revocation System (CRS) [20]. Most revocation methods are explicit, i.e., they involve generation, maintenance and distribution of various secure data structures that contain revocation information for a given CA or a given range of certificates.

Well-known explicit revocation methods (data structures) include Certification Revocation Lists (CRLs) and variations such as Δ-CRLs, CRL Distribution Points (CRL-DPs), Certificate Revocation Trees (CRTs) [15] and Skip-Lists [9]. Another prominent technique is the On-line Certificate Status Protocol (OCSP) [21] which involves a multitude of "somewhat-trusted" validation agents (VAs) which respond to client queries with on-demand signed replies indicating current status of a target certificate.

Regardless of their particulars, all current explicit revocation methods have an unpleasant side-effect: they divulge too much information. Specifically, a third party (agent, server, responder or distribution point) of dubious trustworthiness knows: (1) the entity checking revocation status (source), and (2) the entity whose status is being checked (target). An even more important **loss of privacy** results from the third party tying the source of the revocation checking query to that query's target. This is significant, because the revocation status check typically serves as a prelude to actual communication between the two parties.[1]

In the society preoccupied with gradual erosion of (electronic) privacy, loss of privacy in current revocation checking is an important issue worth considering. Consider, for example, certain countries with less-than-stellar human rights records where mere intent to communicate (indicated by revocation checking) with a "unsanctioned" web-site may be grounds for arrest or worse. In the same vein, sharp increase in popularity (deduced from being a frequent target of revocation checking) of a web-site may lead authorities to conclude that something "subversive" is going on. The problem can also manifest itself in less sinister

---

[1] We assume that communication between clients and on-line revocation agents (third parties) is private, i.e., conducted over secure channels protected by tools such as IPSec [12] or SSL/TLS [10].

settings. Many internet service providers keep detailed statistics and build elaborate profiles based on their clients' communication patterns. Current revocation checking methods – by divulging both sources and targets or revocation queries – represent yet another source of personal information that can be exploited by potentially unscrupulous providers.

The primary motivation for this paper is current lack of privacy in certificate revocation checking. The intended contribution of this paper is two-fold: first, it explores the loss of privacy inherent in current certificate revocation checking, and, second, it constructs a simple, efficient and flexible privacy-preserving add-on component for one well-known revocation method. We believe that the simplicity of our approach has a good chance of enabling its eventual adoption by the Internet *masses* most of whom at present (unfortunately) ignore revocation checking.

1.1 Focus

The first problem mentioned above (hiding the source of a revocation query) can be easily remedied with modern anonymization techniques, such as onion routing, anonymous web browsing or remailers. While this might protect the source of a revocation query, the target of the query remains known to the third party. Furthermore, although anonymization techniques are well-known in the research community, their penetration remains, overall, fairly low. Also, in order to take advantage of an existing anonymization infrastructure, one either needs to place some trust in unfamiliar existing entities (e.g., remailers, re-webbers or onion routers) or make the effort to create/configure some of these entities.

In this paper we focus on the second problem – hiding the targets of revocation queries. We start by examining current revocation techniques and settle on the one that is most amenable to supporting efficient privacy-preserving querying.

Note that the privacy problem of the type described above is not unique to revocation checking. A very similar problem arises in the context of a name service, e.g., the Internet Domain Name System (DNS) [14]. In DNS, at least one (and potentially many) name servers become privy to both the source and target of a name-to-address resolution query. For the same reasons as revocation checking, information culled from DNS queries can be used for sinister, or at least unintended, purposes. In fact, the privacy problem in DNS is much more rampant and thus more important than that in revocation checking. This is because revocation checking is still a niche' activity among Internet users, in contrast to DNS which is used by nearly all.

1.2 Related Work

There is very little in terms of closely related work. However, this paper is not the first to consider privacy in revocation checking. The honor belongs to the recent work of Kikuchi [13]. This work identified the problem and proposed a fairly heavy-weight (inefficient) cryptographic technique specific to CRLs. The solution relies on so-called cryptographic accumulators which are, unfortunately, quite expensive.

A related research topic is Private Information Retrieval (PIR) [4,16]. PIR refers to a set of cryptographic techniques and protocols that – in a client-server setting – aim to obscure the actual target(s) of database queries from potentially malicious servers. Although PIR techniques could be applicable in our context, they tend to be relatively inefficient owing to either (or both) many communication rounds/messages or expensive cryptographic operations. As will be seen in subsequent sections, PIR techniques would amount to overkill in the context of privacy-preserving revocation checking.

2   Certificate Revocation Techniques

In this section, we briefly overview certificate revocation techniques and associated data structures. In the following, we refer to the entity validating certificates (answering certificate status queries) as a Validation Authority (VA). A distinct entity – Revocation Authority (RA) – is assumed responsible for actually revoking certificates, i.e., generating secure data structures such as CRLs. Unlike a CA, which is always off-line, an RA may be partially on-line to facilitate fast distribution of revocation information.

CRLs and Δ-CRLs: These are the most common ways to handle certificate revocation. The Validation Authority (VA) periodically posts a signed list (or a similar structure) containing all revoked certificates. Such lists are placed on designated servers, called CRL Distribution Points. Since a list can get quite long, a VA may post a signed Δ-CRL which only contains the list of certificates revoked since the last CRL was issued. In the context of encrypted email, at the time email is sent, the sender checks if the receiver's certificate is included in the latest CRL. To verify a signature on a signed email message, the verifier first checks if (at present time) the signer's certificate is included in the latest CRL.

OCSP: The Online Certificate Status Protocol (OCSP) [21] avoids the generation and distribution of long CRLs and provides more timely revocation information. To validate a certificate in OCSP, a client sends a certificate status request to a VA. The latter sends back a signed response indicating the status (revoked, valid, unknown) of the specified certificate.

Certificate Revocation Trees: In 1998, Kocher suggested an improvement for OCSP [15]. Since the VA is a global service, it must be sufficiently replicated in order to handle the load of all the validation queries. This means the VA's signature key must be replicated across many servers which is either insecure or expensive. (VA servers typically use tamper-resistance to protect the VA's signing key). Kocher's idea is a single highly secure VA which periodically posts a signed CRL-like data structure to many insecure VA servers. Users then query these insecure VA servers. The data structure proposed by Kocher is a hash tree[2] where the leaves represent currently revoked certificates sorted by serial number (lowest serial number is the left-most leaf and

---

[2] More, accurately, a Merkle Hash Tree (MHT) [19].

the highest serial number is the right-most leaf). The root of the hash tree is signed by the VA. This data structure is called a Certificate Revocation Tree (CRT). When a client wishes to validate a certificate CERT, she issues a query to the nearest VA server. Any insecure VA can produce a proof that CERT is (or is not) on the CRT. If n certificates are revoked, the length of the proof is $O(\log n)$. In contrast, the length of the validity proof in plain OCSP is $O(1)$.

Skip-lists and 2-3 trees: One problem with CRTs is that, each time a certificate is revoked, the whole tree must be recomputed and distributed in its entirety to all VA servers. A data structure allowing for dynamic updates would solve the problem since a secure VA would only need to send small updates to the data structure along with a signature on the new root of the structure. Both 2-3 trees proposed by Naor and Nissim [22] and skip-lists proposed by Goodrich, et al. [9] are natural and efficient for this purpose. Additional data structures were proposed in [1]. When a total of n certificates are already revoked and k new certificates must be revoked during the current time period, the size of the update message to the VA servers is $O(k \log n)$ (as opposed to $O(n)$ with CRT's). The proof of certificate's validity is of size $O(\log n)$, same as with a CRT.

3   Zooming In

Looking at the approaches reviewed above, it seems that retrofitting privacy into CRLs or Δ-CRLs is not easy. This observation is supported by the recent attempt by Kikuchi in [13]. As mentioned in Section 1.2, the cryptographic accumulator approach is inefficient in terms of both bandwidth and computation. There is, of course, a trivial solution that would entail, for each revocation check, requesting the entire CRL (or Δ-CRL). Although effective – the target of the revocation check remains unknown – this approach is grossly inefficient in terms of bandwidth and client storage.

Similarly, making plain OCSP privacy-preserving is difficult because the type of a revocation/non-revocation *proof* it employs is basically an on-demand public key signature by the VA. It does not rely, at least as far as clients are concerned, on any specific data structure for representing revoked certificates.

This leaves us with CRTs and related structures, such as 2-3 trees and skip-lists. We start with CRTs (skip-lists are discussed in the Appendix) since they turn out to be quite amenable to supporting privacy and inherently guarantee *completeness* of query replies. (*Completeness* means that a lazy or malicious server can not omit leaf nodes in response to a query without causing verification of the root hash to fail.) Admittedly, our approach is simple (even trivial) and relies on two basic tools:

- **Range Queries:** Because the number of revoked certificates typically constitutes only a small fraction of issued certificates, we suggest, instead of posing revocation queries by a specific target, to query a range or certificates. The size of the range is determined by the combination of two basic

parameters: (1) the degree of privacy desired by the querier, and (2) the density/number of revoked certificates. The latter directly influences bandwidth and client storage overhead.
- **and**
- **Permuted Ordering:** As designed, CRT involves ordering of revoked certificates by (typically) certificate serial numbers. Since most CAs assign consecutive serial numbers to consecutively issued certificates (which makes perfect sense) groups of related certificates, e.g., issued to the same company, would have consecutive serial numbers. Thus, we need to avoid situations where querying for a range of certificates betrays some information about somehow related consecutive blocks of serial numbers contained in the range.

In the rest of this paper we describe CRTs in more detail (Section 42), present our modifications to support privacy (Section 5, describe our prototype implementation (Section 6) and conclude with examples (Section 7) and future directions (Section 8). Our approach in the context of skip-lists is presented in the Appendix.

4   CRT Details

We now describe the CRT/OCSP scheme in more detail and, in the process, introduce the notation used in the rest of this paper.

Consider a CRT corresponding to a specific CA and/or a block of certificates. Let lo and hi be the lowest- and highest-numbered certificates, respectively and $n = (hi - lo + 1)$ be the total number of certificates. A certificate with the serial number i is denoted C_i. To simplify the description, we assume that the total number of revoked certificates $2 < m \leq n$ (leaf nodes) is a power of 2. [3] Let $L_1, ..., L_m$ represent the leaf nodes of the CRT. Each leaf contains the serial number of the corresponding revoked certificate and possibly other information, such as the certificate hash, data/time of, and reason for, revocation. Finally, the notation $N(L_p)$ means the serial number of the certificate referred to by L_p for $1 \leq p \leq m$, and, for all L_p, $C(L_p) = i$ where $lo \leq i \leq hi$. Conversely, $L(C_i)$ is the leaf index of a revoked certificate, i.e., for each revoked C_i, there exists a unique p, such that: $1 \leq p \leq m$ and $L(C_i) = p$.

Consider two revoked certificates C_j and C_k such that $j < k$ and, for each i, $j < i < k$, C_i is **not** revoked. (In other words, all certificates with serial numbers between j and k are valid.) Then, it is easy to see that there exists p such that $C(L_p) = j$ and $C(L_{p+1}) = k$. In most cases (with over 75% probability) any two adjacent leaf nodes are either siblings or cousins.

Another requirement for building a CRT is a cryptographically suitable (efficient, one-way and second pre-image collision-resistant) hash function $H()$ such as SHA-256 [23]. As in any Merkle Hash Tree [19], each non-leaf node is recursively computed bottom-up by hashing the concatenation of its left and right

---

[3] In practice, a CRT does not need to be perfectly balanced.

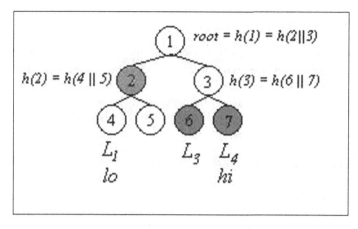

Fig. 1. An example CRT query for node L_3

children. Once the root node is computed, its hash, along with additional information such as issuance and expiration date, is signed by the CA. Finally, the signed CRT is distributed to all VAs (responders or distribution centers).

For any node in the tree, we use the term *co-path* to mean a sequence of nodes representing siblings of all direct ancestors of that node.

To check revocation status, a client sends a request containing the certificate serial number, say i, to its closest VA. If C_i is not revoked, the response consists of:

1. Two adjacent leaf nodes L_p, L_{p+1} such that $N(L_p) < i < N(L_{p+1})$
2. Three co-paths: one from L_p and one from L_{p+1}, to their LCA, and a third co-path from the LCA to the root.
3. The signed root node.

If C_i is revoked, the response includes:

1. Two adjacent sibling leaf nodes L_p, L_{p+1} such that either $N(L_p) = i$ or $N(L_{p+1}) = i$.
2. A co-path to the root starting with the sibling of their parent.
3. The signed root node.

In each case, using the data in the response, the client recomputes the root of the CRT and compares it to the signed root. It then (in case it has not done so yet for some previous query) verifies the CA's signature on the root. This forms a proof of the target certificate's status.

The CRT/OCSP scheme is computation-efficient since it obviates the need to sign each reply. Moreover, it removes most of the trust from VAs which are no longer required to maintain on-line keys, as in plain OCSP. Also, the bandwidth overhead is modest, logarithmic in terms of m – the number of revoked certificates. However, bandwidth overhead is higher than in plain OCSP which has constant-sized query replies. Figure 1 illustrates an example CRT with a query to node L_3. The co-path returned to the client is denoted by the green nodes.

5   Range Queries

The basic idea behind range queries is very simple, even trivial. Instead of querying by a specific certificate serial number i, the client queries a range of serial numbers (j, k) with $j \le i \le k$. This allows us to effectively hide the certificate of interest. The only information divulged to the VA (third party) is that the target certificate lies in the interval $[j, k]$ which translates into the probability of correctly guessing i: $P_i = \frac{1}{k-j+1}$. Each number in the range is equally likely to be the serial number of interest and the third party has no means, other than guessing, of determining the target certificate.

Furthermore, the third party has no way of telling whether the target is a revoked or a non-revoked certificate. Assuming uniform distribution of revoked certificate serial numbers over the entire serial number range, $\frac{m}{n}$ is the fraction of revoked certificates. The very same fraction of certificates would then be revoked in any (j, k) range and hence $(k-j+1)*\frac{m}{n}$ adjacent leaf nodes would be contained in the query reply.

We stress that using range queries in conjunction with CRTs does not involve any modifications to the basic CRT data structure.

5.1   Range Size

As with many simple solutions, the challenge lies in the details. Clearly, there is no perfect privacy attainable with range queries. The highest possible privacy is $\frac{1}{n}$ which corresponds to querying the full certificate serial number range, i.e., $[j = lo, k = hi]$, and entails receiving the entire set of CRT leaf nodes.[4] The lowest privacy level corresponds to querying – as currently done – by a specific serial number, i.e., setting $j = k = i$.

The optimal query range is determined by the source of the query, i.e., the client. Several factors must be taken into account: (1) desired level of privacy, e.g., the probability of guessing equal to 0.001 which, equivalently, the desired level of privacy equal to $k - j + 1 = 1000$, (2) additional bandwidth and storage overhead stemming from a set of adjacent leaf nodes in the reply. It is important to note that additional bandwidth overhead does not depend on the height of the CRT. This is because, in the plain CRT scheme, any query reply always includes a co-path. The same holds for our modification. The only "new" overhead is incurred due to the number of adjacent leaf nodes returned. As described in Section 4, at most two leaf nodes are returned if a certificate-specific query $(j = k = i)$ is posed. In contrast, a range query of size r entails returning $\lceil \frac{r*m}{n} \rceil$ contiguous leaf nodes.

Once the range size (r) is decided, the client proceeds to set the actual range boundaries: j and k. To do so, it first generates a b-bit random number X where $b = log(r)$ or the bit-length of r. X determines the position, within the range, of the actual target certificate serial number. This step is necessary to randomize/vary the placement of the target. Next, the boundaries are set as:

---

[4] This is equivalent to obtaining an entire CRL.

$j = i - X$ and $k = j + r - 1$. (Special care must be taken if $i < X$ or $i - X < lo$. More on this below.)

Incidentally, we observe that, if a client poses **repeated queries** against the same target certificate, varying the query range and boundaries is not advisable. This is because, otherwise, the adversary can gradually narrow down the set of possible targets by repeatedly computing the intersection of multiple query ranges. To avoid this situation, our prototype implementation – described in Section 6 – keeps a cache of previously queried certificates along with corresponding ranges.

A related privacy-enhancing measure is to reuse previously queried ranges. If a certificate of interest is contained within a previously queried range, then re-using an old query range that contains the (new) certificate of interest leaks no additional information.

5.2 Range Size Analysis

The intuition behind our claim that a range query provides privacy is fairly straightforward. It is impossible for the distribution center, and indeed anyone intercepting traffic, to determine with any significant advantage the targeted certificate in the returned range. Put another way, we claim that:

> *Given a client query range (j, k) and corresponding results from the server, no adversary can distinguish with probability neglibly over 50% among two certificates $a, b \in (j, k)$ where a is the certificate of interest and b is not.*

The only information learned by an adversary about the potential target of the query is the range. Since we require the range to be randomly determined (as long as the certificate of interest is within the range) and a client performing repeated queries against the same certificate uses the same range (j, k), the attacker gains no additional information about the actual certificate of interest. Each certificate in the range is equally likely to be the certificate of interest with probability $\frac{1}{k-j}$. However, we concede that, if revocation status of a particular certificate is being queried by *many* clients – and each client picks its own random range – the target certificate will be contained within the intersection of all such queires' ranges.

5.3 Revocation Density

In order to achieve a tailored trade off between privacy and (mostly bandwidth) overhead, the client has to be aware of the revocation density, i.e., the ratio of revoked-to-unrevoked certificates, denoted by $\frac{m}{n}$. We suggest two simple ways of obtaining this value.

The simpler method requires no modifications whatsoever to the CRT data structure. A client merely poses a dummy revocation query with a randomly generated certificate serial number (no range query). The purpose is to elicit a reply in the form of the proof containing a CRT co-path. Verifying the reply securely convinces the client of the CRT's height. Given the height, the number of leaf nodes is easily computed, assuming again that the the tree is balanced. The revocation density immediately follows. (Note that the dummy query is needed only once per CRT, supposing that the CRT update interval is globally known.)

If dummy queries are undesirable or keeping the CRT balanced is not practical, a minor modification solves the problem. Recall that the root of the CRT is always signed by the issuing CA or its trusted off-line agent. One obvious modification is to include the number of leaf nodes (or the actual ratio) in the computation of the root node's signature. A client initially obtains the signed root and obtains the associated tree revocation density as a consequence of successfully verifying the root signature.

5.4   Query Response

Upon receipt of a range query (j, k), the VA first determines the contiguous sequence of leaf nodes corresponding to all revoked certificates within the range. It then adds to this sequence two sentinel leaf nodes: one just beyond k and one immediately preceding j (unless either j or k correspond to the leftmost of rightmost leaves in the CRT, respectively). This is needed to prove completeness of the query reply. Completeness in this context refers to expectation that a client will receive *all* nodes within the range, i.e., a server can not omit leaf nodes without causing root hash verification to fail.

All of these leaf nodes have the lowest common ancestor denoted by LCA. The reply must includes the sequence of leaf nodes and a co-path from the LCA up to the root. In addition, the reply needs to include two partial co-paths to enable the client to recompute the LCA. This differs from the plain CRT scheme where a single co-path to the root is sufficient. Of course, the additional (over plain CRT) overhead is mainly due to returning *multiple* leaf nodes as part of the verification object. As long as the revocation density – which is used to determine the query range – is uniform, on the average $\lceil r * (\frac{m}{n}) \rceil$ leaf nodes are returned. Also, of the two co-paths leading up to the LCA, one represents additional overhead imposed by our method.

The respective bandwidth costs (ignoring constants) of plain CRT and the range query extension can be compared as follows:

- Plain CRT: $log(m)$ – two leaf nodes and a co-path from their parent (or grandparent) to the root.
- Range Query: $log(m) + log(\frac{r*m}{n}) + \lceil \frac{r*m}{n} \rceil$ – a set of $\lceil \frac{r*m}{n} \rceil$ contiguous leaf nodes, a co-path from their LCA to the root and two co-paths from sentinel leafs to the LCA.

Figure 2 illustrates an example with two co-paths necessary to compute the root hash. The first co-path includes all nodes on the left side of the subtree and the second includes all nodes on the right. These nodes, along with the leaf nodes in the (j, k) range, are used to compute the root of the CRT. The figure also illustrates how computing the LCA for nodes returned in the (j, k) range results in shorter co-paths, i.e., by computing the LCA, the co-path can begin from the sibling node of the LCA instead of the leaf nodes.

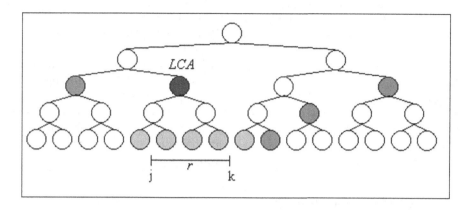

Fig. 2. The LCA and co-path nodes for a given (j, k) range

5.5   Forcing Uniform Distribution

In a worst-case scenario, all certificates in the desired range are revoked and corresponding r leaf nodes must be returned to the client. The simplest solution to this is to force all revoked certificate serial numbers to be uniformly distributed over the entire serial number range. However, this is unrealistic, since, in practice, certificate issuers assign serial numbers to certificates consecutively over well-defined subranges. [5] Each subrange can be used to indicate a different product or class of products, e.g., VeriSign supports the following classes: Standard, Commerce and Premium [5]. Requiring uniform non-sequential certificate distribution would create a maintenance nightmare for both issuers and certificate-holders. Furthermore, gathering and analysis of statistical data would become problematic.

We propose a simple extension to the range query technique that addresses the problem while guaranteeing uniformity among the CRT leaf nodes. Instead of sorting according to serial numbers, we sort leaf nodes along *permuted* serial numbers. One obvious choice of suitable permutation that ensures uniformity is a block cipher, e.g., DES, with a known and fixed key. Note that the brute-force resistance of the block cipher is not important here. The only issue of concern is the block cipher's quality – for a fixed key – as a pseudo-random permutation (PRP). Ideally, the space of all possible serial numbers would match the set of all possible block cipher outputs. For example, DES-ECB mode outputs 64-bit blocks which matches the size of certificate serial numbers for many X.509v3 CAs. However, the underlying permutation can be resolved with any good block cipher, such as Blowfish or AES. We further observe that a cryptographic hash function is not a good choice for the kind of a PRP we require. Unlike a PRP, a

---

[5] This is true even in light of certain new attacks [18]. Such attacks allow an adversary to construct a pair of valid X.509 certificates when the template for the certificate is known or easily guessed, i.e., with high probability two sequential certificates will have near identical header templates.

hash function "reduces" its input and collisions are expected, however difficult they might be to compute. Whereas, a PRP resolved with a block cipher such as DES-ECB with a fixed key, guarantees no collisions.

The primary advantage of this extension is that certificate issuers can continue issuing sequentially-numbered certificates over well-defined subranges. As long as an appropriate PRP is used, we can assure uniform distribution of the CRT leaf nodes. An unfortunate drawback of this technique is that revoking a whole block of consecutive certificate serial numbers becomes inefficient. This is because permuted serial numbers are scattered throughout the total range of serial numbers, which complicates the corresponding CRT.

6   Prototype Implementation

The range query approach described above has been implemented as a stand-alone proof-of-concept prototype available for both Linux and Win32 platforms. The tools and the source code are available for download at `http://sconce.ics.uci.edu/ppr`. The toy prototype consists of the client and server components and utilizes the popular OpenSSL crypto library [10]. There is also a separate CA component which issues certificates and CRTs.

The prototype components are configured with the following parameters:

- Pseudo-Random Permutation Function: $PRP(\cdot)$
- CA Public/Private Key-Pair: (PK, SK)
- The CRT Root Hash and its RSA signature

In this implementation, the permutation function can be one of the following block ciphers supported by OpenSSL: Blowfish, DES, RC4.

The server component takes as input the path to an ASCII configuration file, or loads from a default file if one is not supplied. Currently, there is no interactive way of configuring the server. The configuration file allows for selecting a (PRP) block cipher (or none, if so desired), the keys to be used, as well as the information about each revoked certificate in the CRT. The information required for each revoked certificate includes: certificate certificate number, reason for revocation, and path to a (file) copy of the revoked certificate. The certificates are assumed to be in the X.509v3 format, generated by the OpenSSL CA tool, in the default .pem output. A more complete description of the configuration file is included in the *default.conf* file distributed with the tool.

Once all settings are loaded from the configuration file, the server generates the corresponding CRT based on the permuted (via $PRP(\cdot)$) serial numbers and waits for clients to initiate a connection. When a client initially connects, the server responds with the global parameters for the system and waits for an actual query. When a query is received, the server returns all appropriate leaf nodes in the range requested by the client as well as the interior nodes corresponding to the co-paths, as described in Section 5.4 above.

The client component takes as input the server's IP address, the desired privacy level $p = \frac{1}{r}$ (where r is the query range size) and the serial number (C_i) of the target certificate. It then computes $PRP(K, C_i)$, and performs two queries on the server. The first query refers to a specific but random certificate. As described in Section 5.3, this is needed to establish revocation density. The client verifies the first reply, and, using, the length of the returned co-path in the reply, computes the number of leaf nodes. Then, it generates the random range boundaries necessary for the desired privacy level. The formulation of the second query, its processing by the server and reply verification by the client follow the protocol as described above.

The current prototype is a mere proof-of-concept of little practical use. Work is currently underway to construct a privacy-preserving CRT plug-in for the Mozilla Thunderbird and Eudora e-mail clients. These plug-ins will have the functionality roughly equivalent to the stand-alone prototype and will allow user-transparent certificate status checking for the intended email destination (in case of sending) and for the email source (as part of processing received email).

7 Real World Scenarios

Public Key Infrastructures (PKIs) are already well-established in commercial, educational and government venues. For example, VeriSign, one of the leading certificate issuers has more than $450,000$ public key certificates in many different countries throughout the world [6]. The majority of e-commerce sites utilize VeriSign certificates. Additionally, the United States Army has instituted a program that issues public keys (contained on a personal smartcard) to all military personnel, selected reservists, civilian employees, and on-site contractors in the Department of the Army [17]. This initiative is quite remarkable because of its huge scale. The Department of the Army is expecting to issue a total of around 1.4 million smartcards. Researchers have already started pointing out potential problems with the planned implementation of the PKI infrastructure [11,3].

Both VeriSign and the Department of the Army use CRLs as the primary means of distributing information about invalid certificates. VeriSign hosts a public website with all CRLs [7]. Each CRLs issued includes the certificate serial numbers along with a hash of the certificate. The CRLs combined together represent over $115,000$ revoked certificates and take up 3.6 MBytes of space. The situation is worse for the Department of the Army. In a study by the National Institute of Standards and Technology (NIST), Berkovits, et al. [3] predict certificate revocation frequency as high as 10%. This is based on the relatively fast re-issue rate (every three years) and the high fluidity of the user base. Supporting CRLs with upwards of $140,000$ certificates translates into a bandwidth nightmare requiring each of the 1.4 million smart card owners to periodically download the CRLs.

With such high bandwidth requirements for traditional CRLs, alternate solutions providing low bandwidth costs need to be explored. Our approach offers client-selectable bandwidth/privacy trade-off.

8   Future Directions

The proposed range query approach takes advantage of the CRT structure to offer low bandwidth overhead and obtain client-specified level of privacy. The CRT structure has the additional benefit of providing efficient (in terms of computation) cryptographic proofs for target certificates. However, our approach represents only the initial simple step in this line of research and much more remains to be done.

One outstanding issue is the analysis of privacy loss in the presence of repeated queries. If we assume that multiple clients, at about the same time, are all interested in a particular target certificate (e.g., because of a breaking news article) and the adversary (third party or VA) is aware of the potential target, co-relating multiple range queries does not seem difficult since all the range queries in question would have at least one certificate in common. A similar situation occurs if a single client, over time, repeatedly queries the status of the same target certificate – in this case, narrowing the overlap of all queries' ranges gradually erodes privacy and might eventually yield a single target certificate.

Finally, the usability factor remains largely unexplored. Many wonderful security- and privacy-enhancing techniques have been proposed and lauded by the research community only to quietly fade into obscurity due to usability issues. As mentioned earlier in the paper, revocation checking is unfortunately all but ignored by the majority of Internet users. For this reason, finding simple and unobtrusive ways of making average users aware of both the need for revocation checking and the need to protect their privacy (as part of revocation checking) is a major challenge.

9   Conclusions

The work described in this paper represents a very simple yet novel approach for addressing privacy concerns in revocation checking. Each client, depending on the desired level of privacy, can determine a query range that best suits its needs. This results in a fundamental trade-off between privacy and bandwidth overhead. In the worst case, the overhead can be significant if the desired privacy level is high and as is the number of revoked certificates. However, if only a small fraction of all certificates are revoked, our approach results is reasonably efficient. Furthermore, experience from real-world environments (based on revocation statistics from government, commercial, and military sources) suggests that the proposed solution would work well since revoked certificates represent a tiny fraction of the total numbers of issued certificates.

Acknowledgments

We thank Einar Mykletun, Maithili Narasimha and Marina Blanton for their comments on the draft of this paper.

References

1. W. Aiello, S. Lodha, and R. Ostrovsky. Fast digital identity revocation. In Hugo Krawczyk, editor, *Proceedings of Crypto'98*, number 1462 in LNCS. IACR, Springer Verlag, 1998.
2. The OpenPGP Alliance. Openpgp: Open pretty good privacy, http://www.openpgp.org/.
3. S. Berkovits, S. Chokhani, J. Furlong, J.Geiter, and J. Guild. Public key infrastructure study: Final report, April 1994. Produced by the MITRE Corporation for NIST.
4. C. Cachin, S. Micali, and M. Stadler. Computationally private information retrieval with polylog communication. In *Proceedings of Eurocrypt'99*, LNCS. IACR, Springer Verlag, 1999.
5. Verisign Corporation. Compare all ssl certificates from verisign, inc. http://www.verisign.com/products-services/security-services/ssl/buy-ssl-certificates/compare/index.html.
6. Verisign Corporation. Corporate overview: Fact sheet from verisign, inc. http://www.verisign.com/verisign-inc/corporate-overview/fact-sheet/index.html.
7. Verisign Corporation. Public online crl repository. http://crl.verisign.com/.
8. Inc. Free Software Foundation. Gnu privacy guard, http://www.gnupg.org/.
9. M. Goodrich, R. Tamassia, and A. Schwerin. Implementation of an authenticated dictionary with skip lists and commutative hashing. In *Proceedings of DARPA DISCEX II*, 2001.
10. OpenSSL User Group. The openssl project web page, http://www.openssl.org.
11. J. Hackerson. Rethinking department of defense public key infrastructure. In *Proceedings of 23rd National Information Systems Security Conference*, October 2000.
12. S. Kent and R. Atkinson. Security architecture for the internet protocol. Internet Request for Comments: RFC 2401, November 1998. Network Working Group.
13. H. Kikuchi. Privacy-preserving revocation check in pki. In *2nd US-Japan Workshop on Critical Information Infrastructure Protection*, pages 480–494, July 2005.
14. J. Klensin. Role of the domain name system (dns). Internet Request for Comments: RFC 3467, February 2003. Network Working Group.
15. P. Kocher. On certificate revocation and validation. In *Proceedings of Financial Cryptography 1998*, pages 172–177, 1998.
16. E. Kushilevitz and R. Ostrovsky. Computationally private information retrieval with polylog communication. In *Proceedings of IEEE Symposium on Foundation of Computer Science*, pages 364–373, 1997.
17. US Army Research Laboratory. Using the cac with pki - faqs. http://www.usaarl.army.mil/CBT/EndUser/chapter_06b/chapter06b.html.
18. Arjen Lenstra, Xiaoyun Wang, and Benne de Weger. Colliding x.509 certificates. Cryptology ePrint Archive, Report 2005/067, 2005. http://eprint.iacr.org/.
19. R. Merkle. *Secrecy, Authentication, and Public-Key Systems*. PhD thesis, Stanford University, 1979. PH.D Dissertation, Department of Electrical Engineering.
20. S. Micali. Certificate revocation system. United States Patent 5666416, September 1997.
21. M. Myers, R. Ankney, A. Malpani, S. Galperin, and C. Adams. Internet public key infrastructure online certificate status protocol - OCSP. Internet Request for Comments: RFC 2560, 1999. Network Working Group.

22. M. Naor and K. Nissim. Certificate revocation and certificate update. *IEEE Journal on Selected Areas in Communications (JSAC)*, 18(4):561–570, April 2000.

23. National Institute of Standards and Technology. Federal information processing standards (fips), publication 180-2, secure hash standard (shs), February 2004.

24. International Telecommunication Union. Recommendation x.509 (1997 e): Information technology open systems interconnection - the directory: Authentication framework, 6-1997, 1997. Also published as ISO/IEC International Standard 9594-8.

Appendix A: Range Queries in Skip-Lists

The ranqed query technique can also be applied to other revocation structures mentioned in Section 2. We now discuss providing privacy in the context of skip-lists which were proposed for revocation purposes by Goodrich, et al. [9] The authenticated dictionary approach based on skip-lists and commutative hashing [9] can be used as a certificate revocation structure. The resultining data structure is a traditional skip-list amended with commutative hashing. A hash function is said to be commutative if $h(x,y) = h(y,x)$ for all x and y. A candidate construction for such a hash function is:

$$h(x,y) = f(min\{x,y\}, max\{x,y\})$$

Here, $h()$ is a hash function that takes two integer arguments, x and y of equal bit-size and maps them to a k-bit integer $h(x,y)$. Additionally, sequences of integers $(x_1, x_2, ..., x_n)$ can be hashed together by using the resultant hash as the input for the next iteration of the hash function: $h(x_1, h(x_2, ...h(x_{n-2}, h(x_{n-1}, h_n))\cdots))$

This notion of commutative hashing allows for the creation of authenticated dictionary based on skip-lists. Each node in the skip-list contains the hash of its neighbor to the right causing a hash chain up to the root. The root node represents the combined hash of all nodes in the skip-list. Further details of the hashing process (for both tower and plateau nodes) can be found in [9].

When used as certificate revocation structure, a skip-list with commutative hashing can also provide a short proof. When a query for a target node is posed, the nodes along the search path are returned to the client who, by repeated commutative hashing, can verify the hash of the root. If the hash value matches the signed root then

Figure 3 shows the query path for value 75 in the skip-list. The colored nodes represent the search path taken to locate the node. These colored nodes become the hash values returned to the user to verify the root the hash. We can now easily extend this data structure to preserve privacy. The technique is similiar to the original CRT solution. Instead of querying for a single node, we query for a single node and for a range of nodes to return. The result from the server is the search path for the smallest node in the query and all nodes in the query range.

Since each node contains the hash value of the node immediately to its right, the client takes each returned node and computes the hash for the smallest node.

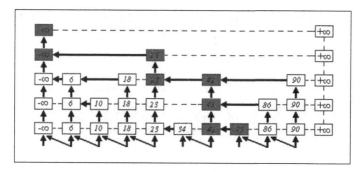

Fig. 3. Query for 75 on a skip-list with commutative hashing. Colored nodes represent search path and arrows represent direction of hash flow to root.

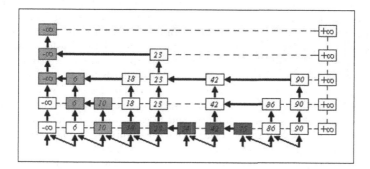

Fig. 4. Range query (10,60) using skip-lists and commutative hashing

If the computed value correctly matches the value returned by the server the client can be assured that no nodes have been omitted from the search results, and that the results are *complete*.

The second step of the verification process involves using the search path to the smallest node and the smallest node itself to compute the hash value of the root node. If the computed value matches the signed root hash value then the client can be assured that all nodes returned are revoked and that none have been omitted. An example of this process can be seen in Figure 4. In this example, a client makes a query on node 10 with a range of 60, making the complete search range from 10 to 70. Node 75 must be included in the results to prove to the client that no nodes have been omitted from the search results.

The green nodes represent the search path to node 10, while the red nodes represent all nodes in the range returned to the client. A client can then verify the validity of the results using the process described above. In this example, nodes are hashed from 73 down to 10 and then verified that this value is the hash value returned by the server. If this verifies then the root hash is computed by using the search path (green) nodes.

Breaking the Collusion Detection Mechanism of MorphMix

Parisa Tabriz and Nikita Borisov

University of Illinois at Urbana-Champaign
{tabriz, nikita}@uiuc.edu

Abstract. MorphMix is a peer-to-peer circuit-based mix network designed to provide low-latency anonymous communication. MorphMix nodes incrementally construct anonymous communication tunnels based on recommendations from other nodes in the system; this P2P approach allows it to scale to millions of users. However, by allowing unknown peers to aid in tunnel construction, MorphMix is vulnerable to colluding attackers that only offer other attacking nodes in their recommendations. To avoid building corrupt tunnels, MorphMix employs a collusion detection mechanism to identify this type of misbehavior. In this paper, we challenge the assumptions of the collusion detection mechanism and demonstrate that colluding adversaries can compromise a significant fraction of all anonymous tunnels, and in some cases, a majority of all tunnels built. Our results suggest that mechanisms based solely on a node's local knowledge of the network are not sufficient to solve the difficult problem of detecting colluding adversarial behavior in a P2P system and that more sophisticated schemes may be needed.

1   Introduction

Over 20 years ago, David Chaum introduced the *mix* as a communication proxy to hide the correspondence between messages coming into and going out of a system [4]. Since then, this design has been extensively used to build anonymous systems ranging from remailers [6] to low-latency communication systems for anonymous Internet access [2,8,10,20].

Most mix network designs use a relatively small and fixed set of mix servers for forwarding all traffic, usually on the order of several dozen. The current deployment of the Tor [8] network has been pushing this limit somewhat, with several hundred servers in operation, but the network cannot grow much larger without major changes to its design and implementation. This imposes a limit on how much traffic these networks can handle and therefore the size of the user population; already, the Tor network carries close to half the amount of traffic of its stated capacity. Furthermore, some recent traffic analysis techniques take advantage of the relatively small number of nodes to enumerate them all in the search for the forwarders of a particular stream [13].

MorphMix [20] represents an alternative, peer-to-peer design for anonymous networks. Each MorphMix user runs a node that both generates anonymous

G. Danezis and P. Golle (Eds.): PET 2006, LNCS 4258, pp. 368–383, 2006.

traffic of its own and acts as a mix server, forwarding anonymous traffic for others. This allows the capacity of the network to grow in proportion to the number of users. Even as the number of users reaches millions, the requirements on any single node are small; in particular, each node knows only a limited number of other nodes, and uses recursive queries of neighbors and neighbors' neighbors in order to find other nodes. For these reasons, MorphMix, or a similar design, holds the most promise for providing a global, widely-used anonymous communications infrastructure.

The limited knowledge at each node, however, can create a problem for Morph-Mix security. As each node relies on its neighbors to learn about other nodes in the system when building anonymous tunnels, a set of colluding malicious nodes could easily direct many tunnels to the colluding set and therefore compromise anonymity. To defend against such attacks, MorphMix introduced a new collusion detection mechanism (CDM). The original analysis of this mechanism considered several attack strategies and determined that in all cases, the number of tunnels that could be compromised by all colluding nodes is small [20].

In this paper, we present a new attack on the MorphMix collusion detection mechanism that is far more effective than those considered in the original analysis. Our key observation is that because the CDM relies solely on local knowledge and observations, attackers can effectively model the state of the CDM at each node and tailor their strategy accordingly. The attackers can therefore avoid detection for much longer and compromise a significant percentage of all tunnels constructed in MorphMix; in some cases, attackers can compromise the majority of all tunnels built. Our results show that the CDM introduced by MorphMix is not an effective means of defending against collusion attacks and that further research is needed to solve this important problem in decentralized peer-to-peer anonymous networks.

This paper is organized as follows. In Section 2, we review MorphMix and its collusion detection mechanism. In Section 3, we describe our attack. We present simulation results in Section 4 and in Section 5, we present both immediate countermeasures and permanent changes necessary to prevent this attack.

2 MorphMix

2.1 MorphMix and Anonymous Tunnels

MorphMix is a circuit-based mix network consisting of many MorphMix clients, or *nodes*, that act as both connection initiators and routers for the network. Each MorphMix node maintains a limited number of *virtual links* via TCP connections to *neighbor* nodes within the system. One unique feature of MorphMix is that the route a node uses for its connection, an *anonymous tunnel*, is constructed iteratively by other participating nodes in the system. We briefly describe Morph-Mix's anonymous tunnel construction, and refer the reader to [18] for a more detailed look at the MorphMix system and tunnel construction protocol.

An anonymous tunnel consists of the node establishing the connection, the *initiator*, zero or more *intermediate* nodes, and the *final* node of the anonymous tunnel. Similar to other onion routing mix networks like Tor, MorphMix uses fixed size messages and layered encryption across each link of the anonymous tunnel to prevent against traffic analysis attacks and protect message content, respectively.

When an initiator node, a, wants to create an anonymous connection, it first establishes a shared key with one of its neighboring nodes, say b, which will be used to encrypt messages sent across that link of the tunnel. If a decides to extend the tunnel, it asks node b to recommend a *selection* of nodes from b's neighbors to use as a next hop in the anonymous tunnel. Node a then chooses from the offered selection a node, say c, to append to b in the tunnel. Node a establishes a symmetric key with c via b that it will use for encryption across the next link in the tunnel. To prevent against b performing a man-in-the-middle attack between a and c, a selects a *witness* node from the nodes it already knows[1] to establish the symmetric key between a and c. There are other attacks that can be considered if the witness is in collusion with b, but to simplify our presentation, we ignore this case and assume the witness is always an honest node. Once a tunnel to c is established, a can ask c for a selection of nodes to extend the tunnel further; this process continues until a has finished appending nodes to the tunnel.

By having the last node select the next hop to append during tunnel construction, MorphMix nodes only need to maintain state information about their local neighbors. This allows MorphMix to scale independently of the number of nodes in the system. However, an immediate threat is introduced when a malicious node is appended because it helps determine the next hop in the tunnel. To prevent a malicious node from offering selections biased with other malicious nodes, MorphMix employs a *collusion detection mechanism* (CDM) to identify this behavior and prohibit this form of attack. MorphMix assumes that a tunnel is compromised, or *malicious*, if the first intermediate and final node are both controlled by an attacker. Otherwise, it considers the tunnel *fair*.

2.2   Collusion Detection Mechanism

Similar to other anonymous systems, we assume the primary goal of an attacker in MorphMix is to link communications between initiators and recipients of a connection. While low-latency systems are generally more susceptible to traffic analysis, MorphMix is vulnerable to a more immediate attack when colluding nodes try to append other colluding nodes during tunnel construction. MorphMix detects this behavior by performing collusion detection on each offered selection.

If attackers own a whole range of IP addresses, it would be easy for them to operate many MorphMix nodes. To limit this threat, MorphMix distinguishes individual nodes from each other by their 16-bit IP address prefix. We refer to this prefix as the node's /16 subnet. It is much more costly and difficult for attackers to own nodes in many unique /16 subnets than it is for them to own many nodes in one or fewer /16 subnets. The CDM is built on the following two assumptions: honest selections will be comprised of nodes selected randomly from

---

[1] MorphMix uses a peer discovery mechanism to learn about other nodes in the network to use for witness and neighbor selections.

many different /16 subnets and malicious selections will be comprised of mostly or all colluding nodes coming from a limited portion of /16 subnets in MorphMix.

Each MorphMix node maintains a fixed size *extended selection list*, L_{ES}, of entries consisting of the concatenation of the selection and the 16-bit IP prefix of the node that sent that selection; we refer to this entry as an *extended selection* and each 16-bit IP prefix in the entry as the node's subnet. When a tunnel initiator receives a new selection, it compares it to each entry in its L_{ES} and calculates the proportion of node subnets that have been seen multiple times to those that have been seen only once. The computed correlation is expected to be larger for a colluding selection than it is for an honest selection because colluding nodes will limit their selections to only other nodes in their colluding set and honest nodes will offer selections consisting of neighbors that have been chosen more or less randomly from all nodes in the system. The algorithm, described in [20], is repeated below:

Correlation Algorithm
1. Build a set ES_N consisting of the 16-bit IP address prefixes of the nodes in the new extended selection.
2. Define a result set ES_R which is empty at first.
3. Compare each extended selection ES_L in the extended selections list L_{ES} with ES_N. If ES_N and ES_L have at least one element in common, add the elements of ES_L to ES_R.
4. Count each occurrence of elements that appear more than once in ES_R and store the result in m.
5. Count the number of elements that appear only once in ES_R and store the result in u.
6. Compute the correlation c which is defined as $c = \frac{m}{u}$ if $u > 0$, or ∞ otherwise.

Each MorphMix node remembers the correlations it has computed over recent extended selections and represents these in a *correlation distribution*. Every time a node receives a new extended selection, it computes a correlation and updates this distribution according to an exponential weighted moving average. The results in [18] show that these distributions can often be characterized as having two peaks, one formed by the aggregate contribution of honest nodes and one formed by the aggregate contribution of malicious nodes (see Figure 2a). From this distribution, MorphMix determines a threshold point between the two peaks, the *correlation limit*, which has the property that correlations greater than this limit are malicious with high probability and correlations less than this limit are honest with high probability.

During tunnel construction, the initiator calculates the correlation of every extended selection it receives and compares this to its correlation limit. If any extended selection during the setup is detected as malicious, the tunnel is torn down and not used. Otherwise, the tunnel is considered fair and used for anonymous connections.

There are two important assumptions to highlight from the collusion detection mechanism that form the intuition behind our attack:

1. An extended selection from a colluding node will overlap with many other colluding entries stored in the L_{ES}, resulting in a large c.
2. The c of a malicious extended selection will, in general, be higher than the correlation limit determined for that node.

By limiting the number of selections that overlap in a victim's L_{ES}, a colluding adversary can keep c low such that it frequently falls beneath the correlation limit and is not detected during tunnel construction.

3   Attacking the Collusion Detection Mechanism

In this section, we define the adversary necessary to perform this attack, describe the attacker's goal, and present a general description of the attack.

3.1   Attacker Model

Anyone with access to the Internet and a MorphMix client can actively partici-pate in MorphMix. Because attackers can so easily join, contribute, and exit the system, we assume an active, internal adversary. Specifically, we assume that there is some subset, n_c, of all MorphMix nodes, n, that is comprised of collud-ing nodes from unique subnets that are participating in MorphMix. In reality, the number of colluding nodes may be larger than n_c, but because the CDM does not differentiate between two nodes from the same subnet, we only con-sider the number of colluding nodes that can be represented by unique subnets. We assume the colluding set will conspire to choose how they offer selections to a victim node, but otherwise, behave honestly.

We specify that n_c will be comprised of nodes representing a percentage, C, of the unique subnets in MorphMix, where C can realistically range from 0% to 40%. This range represents different attackers present in the system, from a small group of attackers to an organization of moderate resources to an even larger network of compromised zombie machines. This range similarly follows the assumptions made by the MorphMix authors. Consequently, we analyze the success of our attack using a colluding set ranging in size from 5% to 40% of the unique subnets in MorphMix.

3.2   Attacker Goal

We assume that the goal of attackers is to link a connection initiator with some outgoing stream. Attackers can achieve this goal by owning the first intermediate and final node in an anonymous tunnel. This will happen with probability C^2 during normal MorphMix behavior. Our attackers, however, accomplish linkabil-ity by owning every node in the tunnel. We aim to show that by using intelligent selections, colluding attackers can expect to compromise every node in C anony-mous tunnels built by some victim node.

3.3   Attack Description

Our attack is based on this simple intuition: Because each node's CDM is based on only the local knowledge stored in its L_{ES}, attackers can model and manipulate the L_{ES} to avoid being detected. To accomplish this, colluding nodes should only offer other colluding nodes in their selections, and they should organize and offer selections to a victim in such a way that they have the least overlap with other malicious selections in the victim's L_{ES}. The analysis in [18] simulates attackers offering selections that are comprised of nodes *randomly* chosen from the set of all colluding nodes. By being more intelligent with their selections, colluding attackers can limit the number of nodes in extended selections that contribute to m in the correlation algorithm. The attack works as follows:

Intelligent Selection Attack
1. For every victim, v, construct a list of selections, S_v, comprised of only colluding nodes such that there is no overlap in node subnets between any selection entry in S_v.
2. Maintain a global pointer, p_g, that keeps reference to a selection in S_v to be offered in the next attack attempt.
3. When v contacts any colluding node to be a first intermediate node and any subsequent node in a new anonymous tunnel, we offer to v the selection pointed to by p_g and increment p_g. If p_g pointed to the last element in S_v, we set p_g to be the first element of S_v and iterate once again through all elements in the list.

The above attack assumes that a colluding node can determine if it is the first intermediate node *during* tunnel construction. MorphMix makes this difficult by using the same witness mechanism for every step of tunnel construction, including the first. Therefore, a node cannot determine whether it is the first node or a later node from only the messages exchanged in the append protocol. Measuring message delays can help determine the position in the list, but in our attack, a node must decide if it is in the first position before returning the selection, with not enough messages exchanged to measure timings.

We therefore modify our attack to return selections from S_v for all tunnels arriving at a colluding node from v, including ones that may have originated from nodes other than v. After the fact, once the tunnel is fully constructed, it is easy to determine whether it originated from v by counting the number of links after v, since all nodes past v will be colluding. (The effects of variable tunnel lengths will be discussed in Section 5.)

Intelligent Selection Attack (Revised)
1. Whenever v requests a selection from a colluding node, we begin the attack by assigning a local pointer, p_l to the selection referenced by p_g and offer that selection to v. We cannot verify if v is the initiator of the tunnel or a node appended to a tunnel started by some other node, v'.
2. For every successive selection request, we increment p_l in S_v and offer the new selection that p_l points to.
3. After the tunnel is created, we determine if the tunnel initiator was v or some v' by measuring the tunnel length.

4. If the tunnel was initiated by v, we update p_g to hold the value referenced by p_l. Otherwise, some v' was the initiator of this tunnel. Since our attack selections are stored in the L_{ES} of v', they can still be used against v. In this case, p_g maintains its original value.

Next we will use simulations to determine how effective this attack is at avoiding the collusion detection mechanism.

4   Simulation

4.1   MorphMix Settings

Because MorphMix does not have a substantial user base, we are unable to execute this attack on a live system. Instead, we simulate many tunnel constructions using the CDM from the MorphMix client prototype [19] and investigate the effects of the attack on one node, the victim node. We evaluate how successful the attack is based on how many tunnels we can compromise, what proportion of all tunnels constructed can be compromised, and how long the attack can run successfully.

The analysis in [18] simulates construction of 5000 anonymous tunnels from a network of 10,000 MorphMix nodes with every node coming from a unique /16 subnet. We believe this is not indicative of a realistic user distribution for an unstructured, decentralized network such as MorphMix. The real Internet is composed of a high concentration of users from certain subnets and we choose to represent this imbalance. Additionally, each node's correlation limit in Morph-Mix is based on the correlations of all recent selections it has seen, both honest and malicious. Because of this, it is important to simulate as realistic a network distribution as possible, namely, one that consists of users coming from both common and unique subnets. We look to a popular P2P system of similar structure, the Overnet/eDonkey file-sharing system, to provide more realistic statistics [1].

Resulting from traffic probes taken during 2003, Overnet consisted of the subnet to node distribution displayed in Table 1 [3]. We simulated 5000 tunnel constructions consisting of only honest selections from both the original node distribution in [18] and our own node distribution based on the Overnet traces. The average correlation limit in the original distribution was .145 ($\sigma = .005$) and the average correlation limit using the Overnet trace was .172 ($\sigma = .005$), a significant difference given identical network parameters between the two simulations aside from the underlying node distribution. From Figure 2a, we can see that the distance between the peak formed by honest selections and the peak formed by malicious selections is already very small. Increasing the correlation limit by even a small amount will make this distance even closer and the correlation limit harder to define. While the Overnet spread may not exactly represent a deployed MorphMix system, we believe it is more indicative of P2P use than the one used in the original MorphMix simulation. For this reason, we follow this distribution during our experimentation.

Table 1. Node distribution according to Overnet traffic traces. For example, 72% of Overnet is composed of users coming from unique subnets, 14% of Overnet is composed of users coming from subnets with two active users, etc.

Users per Subnet	Percentage of Overnet
1	72%
2	14%
3	7%
4	4%
5	2%
6	1%

Aside from this change, we use the same fixed tunnel size of 5 nodes and compute the size of the L_{ES} and the size of node selections identical to [18].[2] Every node in MorphMix maintains virtual links to neighbors that are chosen as the first intermediate node during tunnel construction. Virtual links with other nodes are established more or less randomly from all of the nodes known to a user. We consider that C tunnels will actually begin with a colluding node and $(1 - C)$ will begin with an honest node and be impossible to compromise.

In [17], the authors of MorphMix do an additional analysis of the CDM, taking into account node tunnel acceptance rates and uptime probabilities. We have chosen to ignore these additional constraints in our simulation for simplicity, but believe they would only strengthen the success of the attack: while honest nodes may occasionally refuse to accept new tunnels and leave the network due to limited capabilities, malicious nodes are likely to devote more resources to their attacks and have higher acceptance probabilities and network uptimes. Therefore, we can expect even fewer than $(1 - C)$ tunnels would have a first intermediate honest node.

4.2 Attacker Settings

Attackers will blindly assume that any initial selection request from v (and all subsequent selection requests) are contributing to a tunnel initiated by v. If v was not the tunnel initiator though, the attack selections destined for v actually arrived at some other node, v', and are stored in that node's L_{ES}.

If our attack is being executed against many victim nodes in MorphMix, attacker selections destined for one victim may accidentally be misdirected to a different victim. To minimize the effect these misdirected selections have on the collusion detection mechanism, the attackers should use a different random permutation of n_c when constructing S_v for each different victim v. When v' receives a selection destined for v, it will appear as a random sample of nodes from $S_{v'}$,

---

[2] In MorphMix, tunnel size is fixed for the duration of the session and has a default value of 5 nodes. While this value can be changed upon restart, we assume most users would keep the default configuration. We address the effects of violating this assumption in Section 5.

Table 2. Tunnel construction for range of attackers

(a) Uninterrupted attack execution.

C	Honest Tunnels	Malicious Tunnels	Percentage Compromised
5%	3337.9	6.8	0.2% ($\sigma = 0.1\%$)
10%	2951.4	33.8	1.1% ($\sigma = 0.2\%$)
15%	2283.2	470.1	17.1% ($\sigma = 1.5\%$)
20%	1930.0	860.4	30.8% ($\sigma = 1.1\%$)
30%	1171.5	1384.0	54.2% ($\sigma = 2.4\%$)
40%	450.9	1847.5	80.4% ($\sigma = 2.3\%$)

(b) Optimized attack execution.

C	Honest Tunnels	Malicious Tunnels	Percentage Compromised
5%	4251.9	51.8	1.2% ($\sigma = .2\%$)
10%	4161.2	146.9	3.4% ($\sigma = .2\%$)

and that is in fact how we model misdirected selections in our simulations. More specifically, whenever a node tries to extend a tunnel that starts with an honest node, with probability C a malicious next node is chosen, who will then return a misdirected selection. The misdirected selection is represented as a random set of nodes from n_c. If the tunnel is then extended further, we assume the malicious node will carry out the attack and provide more misdirected selections, once again represented by a random sample from n_c.

We simulate the modified attack as described in Section 3.3 by first creating a random permutation of attacking nodes and storing this ordering into S_v. We select the first k nodes, where k is the selection size, and continue to cycle through S_v to create unique selections.

We briefly explored more sophisticated ways of creating S_v such that more selections can be made with minimal overlap, however, our initial results showed that even a basic organization of how colluding selections are offered is enough to result in significant attacker success.

4.3   Attack Execution

We execute the attack during 5000 tunnel construction attempts by a single victim node and calculate how many successful tunnels are constructed. In Morph-Mix, a node creates, on average, a new anonymous tunnel every 2 minutes. Therefore, creating 5000 tunnels is roughly equivalent to one week of constant MorphMix usage. In Table 2a, we can see that the attack results in a significant portion of anonymous tunnels being compromised using intelligent selections. If colluding adversaries control nodes in more than 15% of the represented subnets in MorphMix, they are able to compromise at least that percentage of tunnels constructed by victims. Attacking levels above 30% result in the majority of all constructed tunnels being compromised by an attacker. While adversaries that control nodes in less unique subnets cannot claim quite as high statistics, by

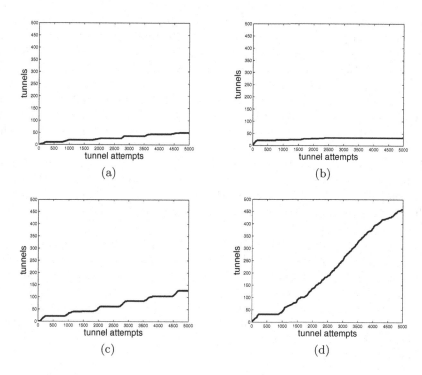

Fig. 1. Successfully constructed tunnels from colluding adversaries with (a) $C = 5\%$ executing an optimized attack, (b) $C = 10\%$ executing an uninterrupted attack and (c) an optimized attack, and (d) $C = 15\%$ executing an uninterrupted attack

slightly adjusting the attack, they can still successfully compromise more than C^2 anonymous tunnels.

4.4 Optimized Execution for Smaller Adversaries

The main problem that attackers have when they own few nodes in unique subnets is that they are more limited in the number of unique selections they can create. If they continue the attack uninterrupted, these selections will begin to overlap in a victim's L_{ES}, causing the correlation and chance of detection to raise. If attackers owning nodes in less than 15% of the unique subnets in MorphMix attack uninterrupted, they will eventually saturate the victim's L_{ES} and be detected with high probability once they starts repeating selections. In this case, they can optimize their attack by using intelligent selections to build tunnels until they runs out of unique selections and then behave normally until the victim's L_{ES} has cleared. Because nodes evict the oldest entries from their L_{ES}, attackers can estimate how long it will take for the victim's L_{ES} to be cleared based on how often and at what rate the victim creates tunnels. Both of these parameters have initial values in each MorphMix client, and even if they are changed, they are limited by a small range of realistic values.

We test this strategy during 5000 tunnel attempts using identical simulation parameters and present the results in Table 2b. In Figure 1, we compare the results of the uninterrupted and optimized attack for C ranging from 5% to 15%. We note that attackers with $C = 10\%$ executing an uninterrupted attack can only compromise around 30 tunnels before they have saturated the L_{ES} and cannot compromise any more tunnels. However, if they attack until they run out of unique selections and then wait until the node's L_{ES} has cleared, they can compromise almost five times as many tunnels and can continue to attack the victim in this manner indefinitely.

This interrupted strategy is only necessary for colluding attackers with limited resources. Specifically, it is only necessary for those with nodes in less than 15% of the uniquely represented subnets in MorphMix. As seen in Figure 1d, attackers with $C = 15\%$ can continue to compromise tunnels indefinitely without waiting for a victim's L_{ES} to clear.

In theory, there is an improved strategy that a limited attacker can use when behaving honestly. Attackers should provide selections that consist of very few malicious nodes and many other unique honest nodes during this honest behavior period. This way, the victim's L_{ES} becomes filled with selections that will overlap with future attacking selections, yet make a large contribution to u in the correlation algorithm. This will, in turn, lower the correlation and decrease the chance of future detection.

5   Attack Countermeasures

In Section 2.2, we reviewed the CDM and how the correlation limit is determined in practice. As shown in [18], when colluding adversaries provide selections of nodes that are *randomly* selected from only participating attackers, the contribution of these selections to the correlation distribution forms a distinguishable second peak to the right of the contribution of honest selections. We reproduce this effect by simulating an attacker that controls nodes in 20% of the unique subnets in MorphMix and attacks with selections of only randomly chosen malicious nodes. The resulting correlation distribution and correlation limit are displayed in Figure 2a. Next, we simulate the same adversary using *intelligent* selections. The results in Figure 2b show that using this method destroys the dual-peak characteristic of the correlation distribution. This, in turn, creates a less meaningful correlation limit, crippling the detection mechanism.

An immediate countermeasure to this attack might be to increase the number of nodes in the tunnel and increase the number of entries in the L_{ES}. Increasing the number of nodes in the tunnel would force the attackers to use more selections for each tunnel. This would cause their attacking selections to overlap much sooner in the L_{ES}, driving up the correlation before as many tunnels can be compromised. Increasing the number of entries in the L_{ES} has a similar consequence because it allows each node to store more attacker selections at one time. An immediate drawback to this approach is that it has a two-fold impact on system performance. Increasing the size of the tunnel will increase

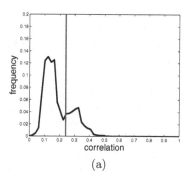
(a)

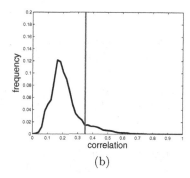
(b)

Fig. 2. Correlation distribution and correlation limit of (a.) random colluding selections and (b.) intelligent colluding selections

connection latency as messages will need to be routed through more nodes. Increasing the size of the L_{ES} will require greater storage and more computation for each execution of the CDM during tunnel construction.

Alternatively, one might introduce variable length tunnels into MorphMix. If an attacker doesn't initially know the true length of the tunnel, it is more difficult to determine if he owns the first and last nodes; however, tunnel length is limited by a small range of realistic values. The analysis in [18] noted that while longer tunnels (eg. 10 nodes) offer greater protection than shorter tunnels (eg. 3 nodes), they also incur a higher connection latency and result in higher bandwidth usage by the MorphMix network. They also will increase the chances of tunnel failure if a node leaves the network or purposefully breaks a connection. Taking this into account, an attacker can estimate the distribution of tunnel lengths in MorphMix and the probability that it has compromised the entire tunnel.

We briefly evaluate a scenario where initiators create anonymous tunnels with lengths between 5 and 7, chosen at random. Because of the variable tunnel lengths, an attacker cannot be positive about whether to roll back selections when the number of appended nodes is either 5 or 6. We use a simple strategy of rolling back whenever the appended tunnel length is less than 6; this results in some number of incorrect rollbacks, which re-send the same selections to the same victim node, and some missed rollbacks, where some selections are skipped and never sent to the victim. However, these problems are relatively infrequent, and our simulations of an adversary who has compromised 20% of the MorphMix nodes can still compromise 18% of all MorphMix tunnels. Thus, the use of variable tunnel lengths slows down, but does not eliminate our attack. The scenario we considered produces a marginal increase in security, but introduces higher latency for constructed tunnels. Introducing even greater variability will result in still higher costs and thus reduced adoption by users.

New users to MorphMix are especially vulnerable to the intelligent selection attack. Since new users enter the system with an empty L_{ES}, attackers are guaranteed to successfully compromise a significant portion of a new user's initial tunnels, regardless of the L_{ES} size. This type of initial behavior in MorphMix will presumably limit its adoption. Most importantly, neither of these methods prevents the attack, and instead, only delays its success. As described in Section 4.2, attackers can optimize their attack strategy so that they can still build a significant number of anonymous tunnels given fewer unique attack selections.

The general limitation of the CDM is that it only considers a node's local knowledge when detecting collusive behavior. Specifically, it distinguishes between honest and colluding selections based only on the selections the individual node has previously seen, not taking into account the behavior of the rest of the network when calculating its own correlation limit. Also, because nodes evict the oldest entries from their L_{ES}, attackers can estimate when a victim's L_{ES} will be cleared of attacking selections and then once again begin the attack. These two factors make it easy for attackers to not only model and manipulate what a node has stored in its L_{ES}, but improve their attack strategy based on this information. Although the CDM may be adjusted to capture some possible attack strategies, attackers can stay one step ahead by modeling the state and algorithms of the CDM at each node and crafting the best possible response, consisting of both honest and colluding selections.

An effective collusion detection mechanism for MorphMix requires a more global perspective of the network. One instance of this might be to enforce a double check on any offered selection during tunnel construction. Every time a tunnel initiator wants to append a node to its tunnel, he contacts a unique witness to help establish the symmetric key between the initiator and the new end node. Additionally, it is the witness that chooses which node from the offered selection to use for the next hop. Requiring that a selection correlation fall beneath the correlation limit of the initiator and witness when appending a node may double the chances of it being detected; however, it may also adversely affect the false positive rate when evaluating honest selections. Nevertheless, while this may improve the mechanism's detection rate, it still doesn't provide a thorough view of network behavior and more sophisticated schemes are likely needed.

6   Related Work

6.1   P2P Anonymous Systems

In response to some of the weaknesses of single point proxy systems and centralized mix networks, attention turned toward distributed solutions to anonymous networking. Crowds [16] aims to provide anonymity to people using the Internet by blending and forwarding web requests among other users in their "crowd". Because no user can distinguish between receiving a web request from an initiator or just another forwarding user, sender anonymity is preserved. Hordes [12] is a variant of Crowds that uses multicast services to anonymously route replies back to the initiator. From a high level, both Crowds and Hordes provide anonymity through plausible deniability because each user issues requests on behalf of other unidentifiable users in the crowd. Both systems are examples of condensed P2P systems and use a central directory to keep track of users currently in the crowd. Whenever a user enters of leaves the system, each node in the crowd must be updated with this change in status. A major disadvantage to this approach is it severely restricts the number of users a crowd can support; thus, these systems are only appropriate for small sized networks.

Mix networks, on the other hand, enforce anonymity by providing sender and receiver unlinkability. Tarzan [10] is a P2P overlay for anonymous networking. Like MorphMix, each Tarzan client is a mix. Users achieve anonymity by using layered encryption and multi-hop routes relayed through other Tarzan nodes. Distinctive to Tarzan, each user selects its own route through a restricted set of nodes and cooperates in system cover traffic to prevent initiator identification from traffic analysis. To learn about other nodes in the system for anonymous routes, Tarzan users continually contact their peers and download current neighbor lists which provide each Tarzan node with a shared global view of the network. This approach, however, severely limits the scalability of the system. Tarzan peer selection is similar to MorphMix in that peers are chosen among distinct IP prefixes instead of their whole IP address; however, no additional collusion detection mechanism is present in the system.

6.2   Collusion Detection

The problem of detecting colluding adversaries in distributed systems is not unique to MorphMix. Without a trusted central authority, it was shown in [9] that large P2P systems are vulnerable to "Sybil attacks" in which a small number of entities can present multiple identities and compromise a disproportionate share of the system. Techniques for avoiding Sybil attacks in ad-hoc wireless and sensor networks have been studied extensively [14]. In Internet overlays such as MorphMix, a common defense against Sybil attacks is to allow one node per IP address to limit the number of identities an attacker can present.

Collusion detection, however, still remains a problem even when Sybil attacks are impossible. Daswani *et al* studied collusion attacks to poison pong caches in unstructured P2P networks; they suggest using a most-recently-used (MRU) cache replacement policy to slow down the rate of such attacks [7]. However, they admit that, just as in MorphMix, their collusion detection scheme is susceptible to a sophisticated coordinated attack that takes into account the detection state at each node. Collusion has also been examined in the realm of reputation based systems, such as information retrieval on the web [15] and P2P file sharing networks. In [22], they study the effects of collusive behavior to improve Google page rank of indexed web pages and propose modifications to the page rank algorithm to prevent this type of gaming. The Eigentrust algorithm [11] for P2P file sharing networks provides a way to compute a global trust value of peers based on their peer interactions in the system. One limitation of this approach is the requirement of universally trusted root nodes, a feature often lacking in most P2P systems. The authors in [5] propose a reputation management protocol, P2PRep, for peers participating in P2P file sharing networks. Their protocol consists of weighted voting according to peer credibility that determines the reputation of other peers in the network. As opposed to peer reputation,

Credence [21] attempts to deter pollution in file sharing systems by computing reputations on the actual shared information as opposed to the peers.

While the success of these P2P approaches is promising, many seem specifically suited for file sharing networks where the ultimate goal is detecting malicious content in the system. Also, there is often clear evidence of misbehavior in file sharing networks, however, this is rarely the case in anonymous networking systems. It is still uncertain if reputation management schemes can be applied to anonymous systems like MorphMix without disrupting node anonymity and user unlinkability within the system.

7   Conclusion

We have presented an attack to MorphMix that breaks the collusion detection mechanism during anonymous tunnel construction, thus devastating the anonymity guarantees initially proposed by the system. We assume an internal adversary of different resource levels and demonstrate that this attack can successfully compromise many tunnels in both a strong and weak setting. This attack highlights an inherent weakness in the MorphMix CDM. Namely, the mechanism only considers a node's local view of the network when detecting collusive behavior. This allows attackers to model a victim's local knowledge and manipulate its content to prevent detection of compromised anonymous tunnels.

Our results show that MorphMix does not effectively address the problem of detecting colluding nodes in peer-to-peer anonymous networks and this problem is worthy of future research. Peer-to-peer approaches such as MorphMix are currently the only solution that can scale to very large numbers of users and offer a promise of a truly global and widely used anonymous communication infrastructure. Therefore, solving the problem of collusion is an important step towards widespread adoption of anonymity technologies.

Acknowledgements

We would like to thank Marc Rennhard for providing access to the MorphMix prototype and for his valuable comments concerning this attack. We would also like to thank Ian Goldberg, Andrei Serjantov, and the anonymous reviewers for their useful suggestions.

References

1. eDonkey File Sharing System, 2003.
2. Oliver Berthold, Hannes Federrath, and Stefan Köpsell. Web MIXes: A System for Anonymous and Unobservable Internet Access. In *Workshop on Design Issues in Anonymity and Unobservability*, pages 115–129, 2000.
3. R. Bhagwan, S.Savage, and G. Voelker. Understanding Availability. In *2nd International Workshop on Peer-to-Peer Systems*, 2003.

4. David Chaum. Untraceable Electronic Mail, Return Addresses, and Digital Pseudonyms. *Communications of the ACM*, 24(2):84–88, 1981.
5. Fabrizio Cornelli, Ernesto Damiani, Sabrina De Capitani di Vimercati, Stefano Paraboschi, and Pierangela Samarati. Choosing Reputable Servents in a P2P Network. In *WWW*, pages 376–386, 2002.
6. George Danezis, Roger Dingledine, and Nick Mathewson. Mixminion: Design of a Type III Anonymous Remailer Protocol. In *Proceedings of the 2003 Symposium on Security and Privacy*, pages 2–15. IEEE Computer Society, May 11–14 2003.
7. N. Daswani and H. Garcia-Molina. Pong-cache poisoning in GUESS. In *11th ACM Conference on Computer and Communications Security*, 2004.
8. Roger Dingledine, Nick Mathewson, and Paul F. Syverson. Tor: The Second-Generation Onion Router. In *USENIX Security Symposium*, pages 303–320, 2004.
9. Douceur. The Sybil Attack. In *International Workshop on Peer-to-Peer Systems (IPTPS), LNCS*, volume 1, 2002.
10. Freedman and Morris. Tarzan: A Peer-to-Peer Anonymizing Network Layer. In *SIGSAC: 9th ACM Conference on Computer and Communications Security*. ACM SIGSAC, 2002.
11. Sepandar D. Kamvar, Mario T. Schlosser, and Hector Garcia-Molina. The Eigentrust Algorithm for Reputation Management in P2P Networks. In *WWW*, pages 640–651, 2003.
12. Brian Neil Levine and Clay Shields. Hordes: a Multicast-Based Protocol for Anonymity. *Journal of Computer Security*, 10(3):213–240, 2002.
13. Steven J. Murdoch and George Danezis. Low-Cost Traffic Analysis of Tor. In *IEEE Symposium on Security and Privacy*, pages 183–195, 2005.
14. James Newsome, Elaine Shi, Dawn Song, and Adrian Perrig. The Sybil Attack in Sensor Networks: Analysis & Defenses. In *Proceedings of the Third International Symposium on Information Processing in Sensor Networks (IPSN-04)*, pages 259–268, New York, April 26–27 2004. ACM Press.
15. Lawrence Page, Sergey Brin, Rajeev Motwani, and Terry Winograd. The PageRank Citation Ranking: Bringing Order to the Web. Technical Report SIDL-WP-1999-0120, Stanford University, November 1999.
16. Reiter and Rubin. Crowds: Anonymity for Web Transactions. *ACMTISS: ACM Transactions on Information and System Security*, 1, 1998.
17. Rennhard and Plattner. Practical Anonymity for the Masses with MorphMix. In *FC: International Conference on Financial Cryptography*. LNCS, Springer-Verlag, 2004.
18. Marc Rennhard. PhD thesis, Swiss Federal Institute of Technology Zurich.
19. Marc Rennhard. MorphMix prototype v0.1, 2004.
20. Marc Rennhard and Bernhard Plattner. Introducing MorphMix: Peer-to-Peer Based Anonymous Internet Usage with Collusion Detection. In *WPES*, pages 91–102, 2002.
21. Kevin Walsh and Emin Gun Sirer. Fighting Peer-to-Peer SPAM and Decoys with Object Reputation. In *Proceedings of the Third Workshop on the Economics of Peer-to-Peer Systems (P2PECON)*, 2005.
22. Zhang, Goel, Govindan, Mason, and Van Roy. Making Eigenvector-Based Reputation Systems Robust to Collusion. In *International Workshop on Algorithms and Models for the Web-Graph (WAW), LNCS*, volume 3, 2004.

Linking Anonymous Transactions: The Consistent View Attack

Andreas Pashalidis[*] and Bernd Meyer

Siemens AG, Corporate Technology,
Otto-Hahn-Ring 6, 81739 Munich, Germany
{andreas.pashalidis, bernd.meyer}@siemens.com

Abstract. In this paper we study a particular attack that may be launched by cooperating organisations in order to link the transactions and the pseudonyms of the users of an anonymous credential system. The results of our analysis are both positive and negative. The good (resp. bad) news, from a privacy protection (resp. evidence gathering) viewpoint, is that the attack may be computationally intensive. In particular, it requires solving a problem that is polynomial time equivalent to ALLSAT. The bad (resp. good) news is that a typical instance of this problem may be efficiently solvable.

1 Introduction

Anonymous credential or 'pseudonym' systems enable a user to interact with organisations using distinct pseudonyms that hide their relation to each other and to the user's identity. In particular, the user can obtain a credential (a statement of a designated type that attests to one or more of his attributes) using one of his pseudonyms from one organisation and then 'show' it to another organisation using a different pseudonym, such that transactions of issuing and showing credentials do not reveal the identity of the user. Pseudonym systems must prevent users from showing credentials that have not been issued (i. e. they must guarantee 'credential unforgeability'), and prevent users from pooling their credentials (for example, to collectively obtain a new credential that each user individually would not be able to). This latter property is usually referred to as 'credential non-transferability' (see, for example, [2,11]). Note that a number of pseudonym systems have been proposed in the literature (e. g. [2,3,4,5,6,9,12,15]).

As a result of the property of credential non-transferability, it is possible for cooperating organisations to link user transactions based on the type of the credential. If, for example, only one credential is ever issued with a particular set of attributes, i. e. type, then clearly all credential showings containing this set of attributes can be linked to each other because they must have been initiated by a single user.

---

[*] This author is also affiliated with the Information Security Group at Royal Holloway, University of London.

G. Danezis and P. Golle (Eds.): PET 2006, LNCS 4258, pp. 384–392, 2006.

In this paper, we extend the above simplistic observation to the setting with arbitrarily many users, pseudonyms, and credential types. We show that linking transactions and pseudonyms in this setting requires solving an NP-complete problem. Moreover, we show that linking pseudonyms and transactions in *all* permissible ways is polynomial time equivalent to ALLSAT, i. e. the problem of enumerating all boolean assignments that satisfy a given boolean formula [7]. We stress that linking transactions and pseudonyms in this way does not require breaking any cryptographic properties of the underlying system.

The rest of the paper is organised as follows. The next section briefly overviews related work. Section 3 describes our attack and Section 4 provides an analysis of its complexity. Finally, Section 5 concludes.

2 Related Work

In [8], Kesdogan, Agrawal, and Penz present the 'disclosure' attack which may be launched against a MIX network, and which bears certain similarities to our 'consistent view' attack. In particular, in both attacks, the adversary collects information during the normal operation of the system and then, based on this information, tries to defeat a certain user privacy property that the system is meant to protect. However, the MIX network model that is used in [8] cannot be directly applied to the setting of anonymous credential systems due to the inherent differences of the two types of system. A few notable differences between the disclosure attack and the consistent view attack that arise as a result of this incompatibility are the following.

- The disclosure attack is a traffic analysis attack where senders and recipients are typically identified by the use of network layer identifiers (e. g. IP addresses). In the consistent view attack, by contrast, users are identified based on application layer identifiers, i. e. pseudonyms.
- The disclosure attack is on the anonymity of users, while the consistent view attack is on the unlinkability of the pseudonyms and transactions of users (see, for example, [14] for a treatment of these two types of attack).
- The adversary of the disclosure attack is an external player. In the consistent view attack it is an internal player, i. e. a set of cooperating organisations.
- In the disclosure attack, the adversary is required to read all the messages that enter and leave the MIX network. The consistent view attack, by contrast, is based on data that is typically found in the audit records of the system, i. e. it does not require the adversary to acquire data from the network.

3 The Attack

Our attack is based on the following assumptions. We assume that the system's lifetime is limited, i. e. that only a finite number of events occur. We also assume that no two users have the same pseudonym, and that the pseudonym system has the 'credential non-transferability' property (or, equivalently, that the system has the 'credential unforgeability' property and that users do not share their credentials).

In order to describe the attack, we require some notation. We denote by P and T the finite sets of pseudonyms and credential types, respectively, that are used in the system. Due to our assumption that no two users have the same pseudonym, there exists a partition $Q_1, \ldots, Q_k \subseteq P$ that divides the set of pseudonyms P into as many equivalence classes (i.e. disjoint subsets) as there are users in the system, such that, for all $1 \leq j \leq k$, the class Q_j contains only the pseudonyms of the user j. We write $p \equiv q$ if $p, q \in P$ belong to the same class with respect to a partition of P.

The adversary $\mathcal{A}$ in our setting is a subset of cooperating organisations and proceeds in two consecutive phases, namely the 'learning phase' and the 'linking phase'. We now describe these phases.

Learning phase: As users obtain and show credentials during the lifetime of the system, $\mathcal{A}$ creates and maintains records, as follows. For each issuing and showing event that occurs, $\mathcal{A}$ records the pseudonym that was used, the type of the credential, and the type of the event (i.e. issuing or showing). We call the resulting collection of records, the 'history file' $\mathcal{H}$. Formally, $\mathcal{H}$ is a finite list. The entries of $\mathcal{H}$ are of the form $(p, t, event) \in P \times T \times \{issue, show\}$. Note that, as a result of the 'credential unforgeability' property of the underlying pseudonym system, for every $(p, t, show)$-entry in $\mathcal{H}$ there exists at least one preceding $(q, t, issue)$-entry. Also note that $\mathcal{A}$ does not get to know the identities of the users; $\mathcal{A}$ only sees their pseudonyms[1].

Linking phase: $\mathcal{A}$ examines the recorded history file $\mathcal{H}$ and divides the pseudonyms into equivalence classes. The result of this phase is a set of partitions of P that all satisfy the constraints implied by the events of issuing and showing in the history file $\mathcal{H}$. In the optimal case, $\mathcal{A}$ is able to uniquely link the pseudonyms and the transactions that occur in $\mathcal{H}$.

We require some more notation, as follows. A partition of P is called $\mathcal{H}$-*consistent* if and only if, for each $(p, t, show) \in \mathcal{H}$, there exists a preceding $(q, t, issue) \in \mathcal{H}$ such that $p \equiv q$ with respect to this partition. In this case, $\mathcal{H}$ is also said to *admit* the partition. The $\mathcal{H}$-consistent partitions represent all the information, in an information-theoretical sense, that $\mathcal{A}$ can extract from the history file $\mathcal{H}$.

The partition of P that contains a single element equal to P is always $\mathcal{H}$-consistent and is called the *trivial* partition. Note that, since we assume that the pseudonym system has the 'credential non-transferability' property, there exists an $\mathcal{H}$-consistent partition that divides P into exactly those equivalence classes that correspond to the users in the attacked system.

We now define the LINKING problem, which $\mathcal{A}$ must solve in the linking phase.

---

[1] In the sequel we assume that all pseudonyms in P appear in $\mathcal{H}$, i.e. we ignore the case where pseudonyms have been established in the system but have not been used to obtain or show a credential.

Definition 1. (LINKING) *On input $\mathcal{H}$, obtained from the learning phase, output descriptions of all non-trivial $\mathcal{H}$-consistent partitions of P.*

If an adversary that solves LINKING outputs only a single partition, then it has unambiguously linked all pseudonyms and transactions in the system. If an adversary that solves LINKING does not output any partitions, then the only $\mathcal{H}$-consistent partition is the trivial one. This represents the scenario where all pseudonyms belong to a single user.

Remark 1: In practical terms, the learning phase is a timing attack where the cooperating organisations maintain clocks that are sufficiently synchronised to enable them to unambiguously establish the order of events that occur in the system and keep records. Then they proceed to the linking phase. Although, as we show below, this may be a resource intensive task, cooperating organisations are in an advantageous position as they can, by definition, pool their resources.

Remark 2: Using the attack, organisations can link different pseudonyms of a single user. In theory, the identity of this user remains unknown. In practice, however, the anonymity of this user may be affected since, if one pseudonym p can be associated with the user's real identity, then all pseudonyms that are linked to p can be associated with that identity, too.

Remark 3: While some pseudonym systems permit users to show a credential an arbitrary number of times (e.g. [2]), others impose an upper limit on the number of times that a credential may be shown. In [5], for example, a credential may be shown only once without loss of unlinkability. Moreover, certain anonymous credential systems enable users to 'selectively disclose' a subset of the attributes that are encoded into a credential (e.g. [1]). It follows from the construction of our reduction that our attack applies to all above types of anonymous credential system.

4   The Complexity of the Linking Phase

In this section we show that LINKING is polynomial time equivalent to ALLSAT, i. e. the problem of enumerating all satisfying truth assignments of a given boolean formula. First, we prove that the problem of deciding whether or not a given history file admits a non-trivial partition, is NP-complete. We call this problem the 'decision version' of LINKING.

Definition 2. (DV − LINKING) *Given a history file $\mathcal{H}$, obtained from the learning phase, decide whether or not a non-trivial $\mathcal{H}$-consistent partition exists.*

Theorem 1. DV − LINKING *is* NP-*complete.*

In order to prove this theorem, we provide a polynomial time reduction of CIRCUIT SATISFIABILITY, as defined in [13, p. 328], to DV − LINKING. We assume that the input and the output of the reduction is encoded in a 'reasonable' way, i. e. that the length of the encoding of a boolean circuit is polynomially bounded in the number of its inputs, gates, and interconnecting wires, and that the length of the encoding of the history file is polynomially bounded in the number of pseudonyms, credential types, and events in the list. Furthermore, we assume that boolean circuits are acyclic and consist only of gates of type NAND where each gate has two inputs. The above assumptions are made without loss of generality (see, for example, [10,13]).

Given a description of a boolean circuit, our reduction generates a history file where each $(p, t, show)$-entry is preceded by a $(q, t, issue)$-entry. In particular, given the description of a circuit C with n inputs, a single output, and m interconnecting wires (excluding the inputs and the output), the reduction generates a history file $\mathcal{H}_C$ in which the set of pseudonyms that appear is

$$P = \{in_1, \ldots, in_n, w_1, \ldots, w_m, out, true, false\}, \tag{1}$$

where $in_1, \ldots, in_n$ correspond to the inputs of C, $w_1, \ldots, w_m$ to its interconnecting wires, and out to its output. The pseudonyms $true$ and $false$ are auxiliary pseudonyms that are used for the representation of boolean values.

The history file $\mathcal{H}_C$ is constructed in a way that guarantees that, if it admits a non-trivial $\mathcal{H}_C$-consistent partition, this partition will have exactly two elements $Q_1, Q_2 \subset P$ where $true \in Q_1$, $false \in Q_2$, and that, therefore, for all $p \in P$, either $p \equiv true$ or $p \equiv false$. Furthermore, for all such partitions, setting the inputs of C that correspond to pseudonyms in Q_1 to 'true' and the remaining inputs (i.e. those that correspond to pseudonyms in Q_2) to 'false' yields a satisfying truth assignment for C.

The history file $\mathcal{H}_C$ consists of two parts, namely the 'setup' part and the 'main' part. The setup part is constructed using the setup algorithm which is shown in Figure 1. Note that this algorithm generates $3(n+m)+2$ entries in $\mathcal{H}_C$, and that the amount of different types appearing in these entries is $n + m + 1$.

Lemma 1. *The entries in the setup part of $\mathcal{H}_C$ ensure that any non-trivial $\mathcal{H}_C$-consistent partition has exactly two elements $Q_1, Q_2 \subset P$ with $true, out \in Q_1$ and $false \in Q_2$.*

Proof. It follows from the entries that are added to $\mathcal{H}_C$ in Step 4 of the setup algorithm that, for all $p \in P - \{out\}$, either $p \equiv true$ or $p \equiv false$. Consider an $\mathcal{H}_C$-consistent partition $Q_1, \ldots, Q_k \subseteq P$. If the partition is such that $true \equiv false$, then $p \equiv true \equiv false$ for all $p \in P$. Thus, the partition is the trivial partition $Q_1 = P$. If the partition contains two sets $Q_1, Q_2 \subset P$ with $true \in Q_1$ and $false \in Q_2$, then, since either $p \equiv true$ or $p \equiv false$ for all $p \in P - \{out\}$, it follows that $Q_1 \cup Q_2 = P$. Moreover, the entries added to $\mathcal{H}_C$ in Step 6 imply that $out \equiv true$. The result follows.   □

The main part of $\mathcal{H}_C$ encodes the gates in C. We first describe an algorithm that encodes a single NAND-gate G into $\mathcal{H}_C$, and leave the encoding of the entire circuit for later.

As determined by the setup algorithm, each gate G is associated with three pseudonyms. Let $a, b \in P$ be the pseudonyms that correspond to the two inputs of G and $c \in P$ be the pseudonym that corresponds to its output. The NAND-gate algorithm, shown in Figure 2, adds entries for the encoding of G to the main

Setup algorithm (input: a description of a boolean circuit C):

1. Generate the set of pseudonyms P according to Equation 1 and uniquely assign each pseudonym (except *true* and *false*) to either an input, an interconnecting wire, or the output of C, as described above.
2. Generate the set of types $T = \{t_1, \ldots, t_{4m+n+4}\}$.
3. Start with an empty list $\mathcal{H}_C$ and set the global counter $i \leftarrow 0$.
4. For each $p \in P - \{true, false, out\}$ do the following.
   (a) Increase i by one.
   (b) Append the three entries $(true, t_i, issue)$, $(false, t_i, issue)$, and $(p, t_i, show)$ in this order to $\mathcal{H}_C$.
5. Increase i by one.
6. Append the entries $(out, t_i, issue)$ and $(true, t_i, show)$ in this order to $\mathcal{H}_C$.

Fig. 1. Generation of the setup part of $\mathcal{H}_C$

NAND-gate algorithm (input: pseudonyms a, b, c that are associated with a gate G, a history file $\mathcal{H}_C$, a counter value i):

1. Increase i by one.
2. Append the three entries $(a, t_i, issue)$, $(c, t_i, issue)$, $(true, t_i, show)$ in this order to $\mathcal{H}_C$.
3. Increase i by one.
4. Append the three entries $(b, t_i, issue)$, $(c, t_i, issue)$, $(true, t_i, show)$ in this order to $\mathcal{H}_C$.
5. Increase i by one.
6. Append the four entries $(a, t_i, issue)$, $(b, t_i, issue)$, $(c, t_i, issue)$ $(false, t_i, show)$ in this order to $\mathcal{H}_C$.

Fig. 2. Generation of the encoding of a NAND-gate

part of $\mathcal{H}_C$. It is assumed that the algorithm runs after the setup algorithm has completed.

Note that the NAND-gate algorithm generates 10 entries in which three different types appear.

Lemma 2. *The entries generated by the NAND-gate algorithm, together with the entries generated by the setup algorithm, encode gate G into $\mathcal{H}_C$, i. e. they ensure that, for all non-trivial $\mathcal{H}_C$-consistent partitions, it holds that $c \equiv false$ if and only if $a \equiv b \equiv true$.*

Proof. By Lemma 1 it follows that, for any given non-trivial $\mathcal{H}_C$-consistent partition of P and for all $p \in \{a, b, c\}$, either $p \equiv true$ or $p \equiv false$. Furthermore, the entries that are generated by the NAND-gate algorithm enforce that each of the sets $\{a, c\}$ and $\{b, c\}$ contains at least one element that is equivalent to *true*, and that at least one element in $\{a, b, c\}$ is equivalent to *false*.

We now show that all non-trivial $\mathcal{H}_C$-consistent partitions of P are such that the pseudonyms a, b and c are equivalent with either *true* or *false* in a way that is consistent with the boolean behaviour of G. Consider any such partition. If $a \equiv b \equiv$ *true*, then the last four entries imply that $c \equiv$ *false*. Also, no contradiction arises from the first six entries. Since $c \equiv$ *false*, the behaviour of G is correctly encoded in this case. In all other cases (i.e. if $a \equiv b \equiv$ *false* or if $a \not\equiv b$), the first six entries imply that $c \equiv$ *true*. Also, no contradiction arises from the last four entries. Since $c \equiv$ *true*, the behaviour of G is correctly encoded in these cases as well.   □

The encoding of the entire circuit C into $\mathcal{H}_C$ amounts to calling the NAND-gate algorithm for each gate G in C in turn, and setting the pseudonyms a, b and c to those that correspond to G, as this correspondence was determined by the setup algorithm. Note the total number of gates in the circuit is $m + 1$: one for each interconnecting wire, plus one output gate. This results in $10(m+1)$ entries in the main part of $\mathcal{H}_C$, where $3(m + 1)$ different types appear. Thus, the total amount of entries in $\mathcal{H}_C$ is $13m + 3n + 12$, and the total amount of different types that appear is $4m + n + 4$.

We can now prove Theorem 1.

Proof. There exists an obvious polynomial time algorithm that, given a partition of P and a history file $\mathcal{H}$, checks whether or not the partition is consistent with all events in $\mathcal{H}$. Thus, DV − LINKING ∈ NP.

By Lemma 1, the setup part of $\mathcal{H}_C$ makes sure that all non-trivial $\mathcal{H}_C$-consistent partitions of P are such that all pseudonyms that are associated with the inputs and the interconnecting wires of C are either equivalent to *true* or *false*. Furthermore, the pseudonym that corresponds to the output of C is equivalent to *true*. By Lemma 2, it can be proven using induction on the number of gates in C that the main part of $\mathcal{H}_C$ guarantees that all non-trivial $\mathcal{H}_C$-consistent partitions are such that the pseudonyms are either equivalent to *true* or *false* in a way that is consistent with the boolean behaviour of the circuit. Thus, DV − LINKING is NP-complete.   □

It follows from the construction of our reduction that the partition of the pseudonyms $in_1, \ldots, in_n$, which correspond to the inputs of the circuit, uniquely determines the partition of all other pseudonyms in the system, in accordance with the boolean behaviour of the circuit. Therefore, there exists a one-to-one correspondence between the non-trivial $\mathcal{H}_C$-compliant partitions and the satisfying truth assignments for the circuit.

By a standard complexity-theoretical argument, the algorithm for the verification of the non-trivial $\mathcal{H}$-consistency of a given partition can be efficiently transformed into a family of boolean circuits of polynomial size. We thus arrive at the following corollary.

Corollary 1. LINKING *is polynomial time equivalent to* ALLSAT.

5   Conclusion

In this paper we studied the 'consistent view' attack that may be launched by cooperating organisations in order to link the transactions and the pseudonyms of the users of an anonymous credential system. The attack is based on the information in a 'history file' that describes the events that take place during the lifetime of the system. We showed that extracting all the information from such a history file is polynomial time equivalent to solving ALLSAT, by providing a polynomial time reduction. This, however, is a statement about the *worst-case* complexity of the attack. Our reduction produces history files that are unlikely to be similar in structure to the history files of real-world pseudonym systems; in a typical real-world scenario, extracting all the information from the history file is therefore likely to be significantly more efficient than polynomial equivalence to ALLSAT might suggest. Moreover, since LINKING can be formulated as an instance of ALLSAT, the adversary can use state-of-the-art SAT solvers [7,16].

Unfortunately, making more precise statements about the complexity and the efficiency of our attack in a real-world scenario requires making assumptions about the behaviour of the users in the system. It is conceivable that there may exist certain user strategies that lead to history files that, with at least non-negligible probability, make the 'consistent view' attack computationally expensive. However, this is rather unlikely, as the existence of a generic strategy could be used as the basis to prove that $P \neq NP$.

Studying the efficiency of the attack under a reasonable user behaviour model is a subject for further research.

Acknowledgements

The authors would like to thank Michael Braun, Erwin Heß, Anton Kargl, Chris J. Mitchell, Torsten Schütze, and Susanne Wetzel for their help and encouragement. The authors would also like to thank the anonymous reviewers for their stimulating comments.

References

1. S. Brands. *Rethinking Public Key Infrastructures and Digital Certificates — Building in Privacy*. The MIT Press, Cambridge, Massachusetts, 2000.
2. J. Camenisch and A. Lysyanskaya. An efficient system for non-transferable anonymous credentials with optional anonymity revocation. In B. Pfitzmann, editor, *Advances in Cryptology — EUROCRYPT 2001, International Conference on the Theory and Application of Cryptographic Techniques, Innsbruck, Austria, May 6-10, 2001, Proceedings*, volume 2045 of *Lecture Notes in Computer Science*, pages 93–118. Springer Verlag, Berlin, 2001.
3. J. Camenisch and A. Lysyanskaya. Signature schemes and anonymous credentials from bilinear maps. In M. Franklin, editor, *Proceedings of the 24th Annual International Cryptology Conference, Santa Barbara, California, USA, August 15-19 — CRYPTO 2004*, volume 3152 of *Lecture Notes in Computer Science*, pages 56–72. Springer Verlag, Berlin, 2004.

4. D. Chaum. Showing credentials without identification: Transferring signatures between unconditionally unlinkable pseudonyms. In J. Seberry and J. Pieprzyk, editors, *Advances in Cryptology – AUSCRYPT 90*, volume 453 of *Lecture Notes in Computer Science*, pages 246–264. Springer Verlag, Berlin, 1990.

5. L. Chen. Access with pseudonyms. In E. Dawson and J. D. Golic, editors, *Cryptography: Policy and Algorithms, International Conference, Brisbane, Queensland, Australia, July 3-5, 1995, Proceedings*, number 1029 in Lecture Notes in in Computer Science, pages 232–243. Springer Verlag, Berlin, 1995.

6. I. Damgård. Payment systems and credential mechanisms with provable security against abuse by individuals. In S. Goldwasser, editor, *Advances in Cryptology — CRYPTO '88: Proceedings*, number 403 in Lecture Notes in Computer Science, pages 328–335. Springer Verlag, Berlin, 1990.

7. H. Jin and F. Somenzi. Prime clauses for fast enumeration of satisfying assignments to boolean circuits. In *DAC '05: Proceedings of the 42nd Annual Conference on Design Automation*, pages 750–753, New York, NY, USA, 2005. ACM Press.

8. D. Kesdogan, D. Agrawal, and S. Penz. Limits of anonymity in open environments. In F. Petitcolas, editor, *Proceedings of the 5th International Information Hiding Workshop, IH 2002*, volume 2578 of *Lecture Notes in Computer Science*, pages 53–69. Springer Verlag, Berlin, 2003.

9. A. Lysyanskaya, R. L. Rivest, A. Sahai, and S. Wolf. Pseudonym systems. In H. M. Heys and C. M. Adams, editors, *Selected Areas in Cryptography, 6th Annual International Workshop, SAC'99, Kingston, Ontario, Canada, August 9-10, 1999, Proceedings*, volume 1758 of *Lecture Notes in Computer Science*, pages 184–199. Springer Verlag, Berlin, 2000.

10. M. Mano. *Digital Design*. Prentice Hall, third edition, 2001.

11. A. Pashalidis and C. Mitchell. A security model for anonymous credential systems. In S. J. Y. Deswarte, F. Cuppens and L. Wang, editors, *Information Security Management, Education and Privacy, Proceedings of the 3rd Working Conference on Privacy and Anonymity in Networked and Distributed Systems (I-NetSec'04)*, pages 183–199. Kluwer Academic Publishers, August 2004.

12. G. Persiano and I. Visconti. An efficient and usable multi-show non-transferable anonymous credential system. In A. Juels, editor, *Proceedings of the Eighth International Financial Cryptography Conference (FC '04)*, volume 3110 of *Lecture Notes in Computer Science*, pages 196–211. Springer Verlag, Berlin, 2004.

13. M. Sipser. *Introduction to the Theory of Computation*. PWS Publishing Company, 1997.

14. S. Steinbrecher and S. Köpsell. Modelling unlinkability. In R. Dingledine, editor, *Privacy Enhancing Technologies, Third International Workshop, PET 2003, Dresden, Germany, March 26-28, 2003, Revised Papers*, volume 2760 of *Lecture Notes in Computer Science*, pages 32–47. Springer Verlag, Berlin, 2003.

15. E. R. Verheul. Self-blindable credential certificates from the Weil pairing. In C. Boyd, editor, *ASIACRYPT '01: Proceedings of the 7th International Conference on the Theory and Application of Cryptology and Information Security*, volume 2248 of *Lecture Notes in Computer Science*, pages 533–551. Springer Verlag, Berlin, 2001.

16. L. Zhang and S. Malik. The quest for efficient boolean satisfiability solvers. In A. Voronkov, editor, *Automated Deduction - CADE-18, 18th International Conference on Automated Deduction, Copenhagen, Denmark, July 27-30, 2002, Proceedings*, volume 2392 of *Lecture Notes in Computer Science*, pages 295–313. Springer Verlag, Berlin, 2002.

Preserving User Location Privacy in Mobile Data Management Infrastructures

Reynold Cheng[1], Yu Zhang[2], Elisa Bertino[2], and Sunil Prabhakar[2]

[1] The Hong Kong Polytechnic University, Hung Hom, Kowloon, Hong Kong
csckcheng@comp.polyu.edu.hk
[2] Purdue University, West Lafayette, IN 47907-1398, USA
{zhangyu,bertino,sunil}@cs.purdue.edu

Abstract. Location-based services, such as finding the nearest gas station, require users to supply their location information. However, a user's location can be tracked without her consent or knowledge. Lowering the spatial and temporal resolution of location data sent to the server has been proposed as a solution. Although this technique is effective in protecting privacy, it may be overkill and the quality of desired services can be severely affected. In this paper, we suggest a framework where uncertainty can be controlled to provide high quality and privacy-preserving services, and investigate how such a framework can be realized in the GPS and cellular network systems. Based on this framework, we suggest a data model to augment uncertainty to location data, and propose imprecise queries that hide the location of the query issuer and yields probabilistic results. We investigate the evaluation and quality aspects for a range query. We also provide novel methods to protect our solutions against trajectory-tracing. Experiments are conducted to examine the effectiveness of our approaches.

1 Introduction

Positioning technologies like the Global Positioning Systems (GPS), GSM, RF-ID and the Wireless LAN have undergone rapid developments in recent years [1,2]. These new technologies allow locations of users to be determined accurately, and enable a new class of applications known as Location-Based Services (LBS). An important LBS is the E-911 application mandated by the U.S. (correspondingly E-112 in Europe), which requires cell phone companies to provide an accurate location (i.e., within a few hundred feet) of a cell phone user who calls for emergency help [2]. In another application, a user may want to know the waiting time for a table in a restaurant close to her. A user may also wish to be notified when her friend is located within her walking distance. All these applications require an extensive use of location data [3].

Although LBS applications hold the promise of safety, convenience, and new business opportunities, the ability to locate users and items accurately also raises a new concern – intrusion of *location privacy*. According to [4], location privacy is "the ability to prevent other parties from learning one's current or past location".

G. Danezis and P. Golle (Eds.): PET 2006, LNCS 4258, pp. 393–412, 2006.

Using locationing technologies, a service provider can track the whereabouts of a user and discover her personal habits. These pieces of sensitive information can be sold to third parties without the user's consent or knowledge. It is often feared that government agencies can monitor the behavior of individuals, or know the places they have visited. Preventing location privacy from being invaded is thus of utmost importance.

Recently several solutions for location privacy protection have been proposed. Some researchers suggest the use of "policies", in which the service provider is required to state explicitly how user's location information can be used [5,6,7]. In another proposal, a user "cloaks" her information before sending it to the LBS, by providing her location at a lower resolution in terms of time and space [2,4]. In other words, rather than giving a precise location and time instant, a larger region covered in a time frame is reported. This solution, known as *location cloaking*, provides the user with more flexibility in controlling her information.

By reducing the granularity of spatial and temporal information, location cloaking allows a user's privacy to be better protected. Unfortunately, this scheme can also reduce the quality of service provided by the LBS. This is simply because the LBS does not have the most accurate information to provide the best service. Consider a remote cab service that allows a subscriber to call for a cab nearby. If the subscriber reports her precise location, the service provider can find her the closest cab, and can tell the cab driver how to reach the customer. However, if only a vague location is given, it may take more time for a cab to reach the customer. Thus, by adjusting the accuracy of the location information sent to the service provider, a tradeoff can be achieved between: (1) privacy of the user, and (2) quality of a service requested. To the best of our knowledge, the interaction of these factors has only been briefly mentioned in [8,9]. In this paper, we propose a framework to study this problem more extensively. We also describe how this framework can be realized in commonly-used systems like the GPS and cellular network systems.

We then focus on data modeling and query evaluation issues in this system. We propose an intuitive model for representing cloaked location data, and present a metric for measuring the privacy of location cloaking. Moreover, we study the evaluation of a particular query called the *Location-based Range Query* (LRQ), where a user issuing an LRQ is notified of any object of interest within a fixed distance from her current location. This kind of query is commonly used in location-based applications [10]. We propose an "imprecise" version of the Location-based Range Query, namely ILRQ, which processes cloaked location data. Since the location of the query issuer is also inexact, the query result is "imprecise". That is to say, there is no single, definite answer to the query. To capture the answer imprecision, ILRQ provides probabilistic guarantees to the query answers that indicates the degree of confidence about these answers. For example, an answer for the ILRQ is $\{(S_1, 0.4), (S_2, 0.8)\}$, which means that users S_1 and S_2 have probabilities of 0.4 and 0.8 respectively of satisfying the query. We will present algorithms for computing probabilistic answers for ILRQ, based on computational geometry techniques.

Another important use of "probabilistic answers" is to quantify the ambiguity of a query answer due to the inexactness of cloaked location data. We define metrics for evaluating the quality of a service, allowing a user to decide whether she should adjust the granularity of her cloaked location information in order to obtain a better service.

We also address the issues of inference attacks, where future locations can be inferred based on tracing the movement in the past. We present two approaches, namely *patching* and *delaying*, in order to prevent the user's location from being deduced, thereby reducing the impact of this kind of threats.

The rest of this paper is organized as follows. We first describe related works in Section 2. We propose a framework to capture data uncertainty, privacy and quality of service in Section 3. In Section 4, we formally present the data cloaking model. Section 5 presents an algorithm for evaluating an ILRQ, and Section 6 describes service quality metrics for this query. Experimental results are presented in Section 7. We conclude the paper in Section 8. Appendix A discusses how our framework can be used in real systems, and Appendix B investigates a type of inference attacks to our system and their corresponding solutions.

2   Related Works

Data privacy has been a subject of active research in recent years. Pfitzmann et al.[11] explain various terms related to privacy, such as "linkability" and "anonymity". The notion of k-anonymity, first proposed in [12], has been widely studied. The main idea of k-anonymity is to make a data attribute indistinguishable with $k - 1$ other values. Recent work in k-anonymity include [13], which presents efficient query algorithms for a k-anonymity model; and [14], which uses k-anonymity for privacy and copyright protection.

The notion of k-anonymity has also been used in a number of works that study location privacy [2,4,15]. How k-anonymity is defined depends on the particular type of LBS application. According to [4], LBS applications can be non-anonymous, pseudonymous and anonymous. A non-anonymous LBS needs a user's location information and her true identity; a pseudonymous LBS needs a user's pseudonym but not her real identity; an anonymous LBS does not require a user's true identity.

For an anonymous LBS, Gruteser et al. define k-anonymity in the context of location cloaking [2], which is the method that we will study in this paper. In location cloaking, a middleware is proposed to transform each tuple (x, y, t) (i.e., location (x, y) at time t) to $([x_1, x_2], [y_1, y_2], [t_1, t_2])$ where $([x_1, x_2], [y_1, y_2])$ is the rectangular area within which (x, y) is found, between the time interval $[t_1, t_2]$. The middleware then sends the transformed tuple to the system. Here the k-anonymity requirement is that the time interval $[t_1, t_2]$ there must be at least k users in the same spatial vicinity $([x_1, x_2], [y_1, y_2])$. Notice that this location cloaking technique is not limited to anonymous applications [2]; it can also be applied to location data in order to enhance the privacy of non-anonymous and pseudonymous LBS applications. In [16], a personalized version of k-anonymity is proposed.

Although k-anonymity is a simple metric and can be applied to different LBS applications, it has several problems. First, the scheme may not be used if there are fewer than k users in the system. Secondly, even if there are more than k users, they may span in a large area over an extended time period, in which case the cloaked location can be very large and cause a severe degradation of service quality, due to the large amount of ambiguity in the cloaked location. In this paper, we suggest the size of a cloaked location to be controlled by the user's policy, which can be independent of the number of users inside the uncertainty region. This can also avoid the cloaked location from being too large, which can adversely affect the service quality.

In [9], Atallah et al. studied the idea of perturbing the location of a query issuer for protecting location privacy, and its effect on the accuracy of nearest-neighbor queries. Here we investigate the provision of probabilistic guarantees for range queries.

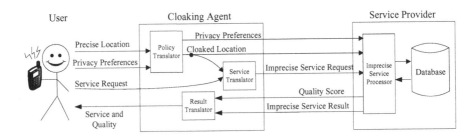

Fig. 1. Managing Privacy and Service Quality with the Cloaking Agent

3   A Framework for Capturing Location Privacy and Service Quality

In this section, we will describe a system model that connects privacy, cloaked information and service quality. This model forms the basis for subsequent discussions. Figure 1 illustrates this system model. Its main idea is to allow the user to specify her location, service request and privacy requirements to the **cloaking agent**, which then produces the cloaked location (i.e., a larger region that contains the user's true location) and an "imprecise" service request. On receiving these pieces of information, the service provider processes the request and sends back the service and feedback to the user. The cloaking agent can either be implemented in the user's device, or provided by a third-party system.

In Figure 1 we see that a user can first specify her privacy preferences through a privacy language. This language, that we are planning to develop, allows a subject to specify her privacy preferences with respect to:

- Locations – a user may specify that when being near to a given object, cloaking is required, and the accuracy requirements. Locations can be logical or physical; logical position may identify a specific spatial entity (like the "Purdue Hospital") or a set of spatial entities (like "Any Hospital").

– Other users and service providers – a user may also specify that her presence be made known (or hidden) to specific users and service providers. For example, a physician while being in the hospital may require that her position be notified only to the head nurse and only to emergency services.

The user's privacy preferences are then passed to the **policy translator** inside the cloaking agent. The policy translator produces a cloaked location based on the precise location of the user as well as her privacy requirements. For instance, if the user's requirement is "generate a cloaked location that covers five buildings when I am in Area X", the policy translator produces the corresponding cloaked location when it detects the user is in Area X. The policy translator also forwards to the service provider the user's privacy preference concerning other users and service providers if needs.

Based on the cloaked location and the service request, the service translator produces an "imprecise" service request that processes cloaked data. For example, the LRQ is a service request from the user, and the service translator transforms the LRQ to ILRQ, an imprecise service request that processes cloaked location data. Both the cloaked location and the imprecise service request are then shipped to the **imprecise service processor**, which stores the cloaked location in a spatial-temporal database and processes the service request. Since location values are imprecise, the service processor produces a "probabilistic service result" i.e., answers are augmented with probability to indicate the confidence of their presence [17]. For example, the result of ILRQ contains user names together with their probabilities. In addition, a score indicating the quality of the service is generated. We will revisit the query and quality evaluation details in Sections 5 and 6.

Both the probabilistic service result and the quality score can be transferred directly to the user, or optionally to the **result translator** inside the cloaking agent. The main purpose of the result translator is to hide the technical details of the probabilistic service result (e.g., probability, quality scores), and converts the answers to a higher-level form that casual users can understand. For an ILRQ, the translator can choose to return only the names for which there is a high confidence (e.g., $p_j > 0.8$) and not return any probability value. It can also describe to the user the quality as LOW, MEDIUM and HIGH for quality score ranges between $(0, 0.2], (0.2, 0.8], (0.8, 1]$ respectively, instead of requiring the user to interpret the numerical values. Based on the recommendation from the cloaking agent, the user can then decide if the degree of privacy should be reduced.

In Appendix A we will describe how this framework may be deployed in practical systems like the GPS and cellular network systems. Let us now focus on data modeling, query evaluation, quality and privacy protection issues for this system.

4   Cloaking and Privacy

In this section, we present a formal model of location cloaking, based on which location privacy is defined.

4.1   Location Cloaking Model

As mentioned before, a cloaked location data is essentially a region that contains the user's true location [2,4]. To define this notion formally, assume that the system has n users with names $S_1, S_2, \ldots, S_n$. Suppose that the location of each user S_i at time t is $L_i(t)$, then location cloaking can be defined as follows.

Definition 1. Location Cloaking: *At time t, a user S_i reports to the service provider a closed region called uncertainty region, denoted $U_i(t)$, such that $L_i(t)$ has an even chance of being located inside $U_i(t)$.*

In other words, the probability density function (pdf) of the user's location within the uncertainty region is $\frac{1}{\text{Area}(U_i(t))}$. If the user moves outside the uncertainty region given earlier, she has to report to the service provider a new uncertainty region. A user may also send an uncertainty region if she wants to issue a query that requires her current location information (e.g., a location-based range query).

Our solution does not limit the geometric shape of the uncertainty region. The only requirement is that the uncertainty region is closed. The rationale is that the evaluation of probabilities and quality scores needs integration over the uncertainty regions, as illustrated in subsequent sections. The user can define the geometric shape required through the privacy language discussed in Section 3. For example, if the uncertainty region is a circle of radius r, the cloaking agent can select the center of the circle randomly with distance less than r from the user's actual location.

We remark that the user assumes the service provider only knows her position accurate to the size of the uncertainty region she has provided. This may not be necessarily true, since the service provider can use various methods to reduce the uncertainty about the cloaked location. We investigate this issue in Appendix B. Furthermore, the service provider may be able to infer a higher pdf to some areas in the cloaked region if it has some information about it, instead of assuming a uniform distribution within $U_i(t)$. For now, we assume the service provider holds the same view of the cloaked location data as that of the user.

4.2   Measuring Privacy of Cloaking

By "injecting" different amount of spatial uncertainty to her location, cloaking provides a simple way for a user to control the release of her private information to untrusted parties. The degree of privacy can be measured in two ways: (i) size of uncertainty region and (ii) coverage of sensitive area.

1. Size of uncertainty region. By providing a larger uncertainty region, the spatial resolution of a location is reduced, making the user's location more difficult to be guessed. The size of the uncertainty region can thus be used to reflect the degree of privacy: the larger the region size, the more the privacy.

2. Coverage of sensitive region. The second means of quantifying privacy depends on the location of the user. To see this, assume the size of the uncertainty region is fixed. Suppose the user is inside a hospital (which she does not want people to know about this), and her uncertainty region has a fraction of 90% overlap with the hospital. One can easily guess she is in the hospital. On the other hand, if the user is shopping in a mall, she may not be very concerned even if her location is known.

From this example, we can see that whether the user's located in a "sensitive region" (e.g., hospital, nightclub) affects the degree of privacy. Based on this observation, we define the "coverage" of sensitive region for user S_i as follows:

$$\text{Coverage} = \frac{\text{Area}(\text{sensitive regions of } S_i \cap U_i(t))}{\text{Area}(U_i(t))} \tag{1}$$

In general, the higher the coverage, the lower the privacy. In the previous example, the coverage is 90%, and thus the user can be easily guessed that she is in the hospital. Thus the uncertainty region should be enlarged in order to assure that the user's location cannot be easily associated with a sensitive region.

It is also worth mention that the definition of sensitive region is user-specific. For example, while for a physician a hospital may not be a sensitive region, the same cannot be said about a patient. The system described in Section 3 should allow the users to specify what places are sensitive to them.

Although cloaking lessens the threat to location privacy, it can affect the *quality* of service provided. In particular, since the service provider does not receive accurate location information, it may not be able to generate a precise answer, leading to a lower service quality. In the next section, we develop algorithms to quantify the "imprecision" of query answers through the use of probability values. Section 6 further illustrates how the query answer quality can be evaluated based on the probabilistic answers.

5   Evaluation of Imprecise Queries

We now study query evaluation over cloaked location data. We focus on the *location-based range query* (LRQ), which is a range query with the range depending on the position of the query issuer. We propose an "imprecise" form of this query for evaluating cloaked data, and techniques for evaluating it.

5.1   Precise and Imprecise Queries

Suppose the current time instant is t_c. A user of the system, S_i (where $i \in [1, n]$), issues a snapshot query on the uncertainty regions $U_j(t_c)$ of objects S_j (with $j \neq i$ and $j \in [1, n]$). For ease of presentation, let us use S to refer to S_i. We denote her location $L(t_c)$ and uncertainty region $U(t_c)$ as L and U respectively. Moreover, $U_j(t_c)$ is represented as U_j unless stated otherwise. Given a circle C with L and r as its center and radius respectively, we can define a location-based range query as follows.

Definition 2. *A* **Location-based Range Query (LRQ)** *returns* $\{S_j | j \neq i \wedge j \in [1, n]\}$, *where user S_j is located within C, at the current time instant.*

Essentially, LRQ asks the question: "who is within r units from me?". As an example, Figure 2(a) shows that S issued an LRQ (a range query with L as the center and r as the radius), and obtains S_4 as the only answer. Notice that the query range of the LRQ is defined to be a circle for the purpose of easier explanation; our methods can be generalized to deal with range queries with any geometric shape. Moreover, the system needs to know the current location of S_i, and it also knows the positions of the objects being queried. Location privacy of the database is not protected.

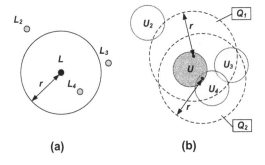

(a)	**(b)**

Fig. 2. Location-based Range Query: (a) exact locations, and (b) cloaked locations

Location cloaking can alleviate the threat to location privacy. Instead of supplying exact locations, users only supply their cloaked locations in order to achieve higher anonymity, or lower entropy [18]. How should a query be defined and executed over this kind of data? To address this question, we term the version of LRQ that employs cloaked location data as the **Imprecise Location-based Range Query**. The word "imprecise" comes from the fact that both the locations of the query issuer and those of objects being queried are ambiguous.[1] This query is formally defined as follows:

Definition 3. *An* **Imprecise Location-based Range Query (ILRQ)** *returns a set of tuples* $\{(S_j, p_j) | j \neq i \wedge j \in [1, n]\}$, *where $p_j > 0$ is the non-zero probability that user S_j is located within C at the current time instant.*

---

[1] Although we assume objects being queried are moving objects, static objects like buildings can also be queried. These objects have no ambiguity in locations. However, our queries can still be applied by modeling the uncertainty regions of these objects as points.

Figure 2(b) shows a scenario where an ILRQ is computed over cloaked locations, with two range queries, namely Q_1 and Q_2, issued at two different locations in U. For Q_1, the answer is $\{(S_2, 0.2), (S_3, 0.6), (S_4, 0.7)\}$, while for Q_2, the answer is $\{(S_3, 0.9), (S_4, 1)\}$. After considering the probabilities of objects satisfying the queries issued at all possible points in U_1, the answer is:

$$\{(S_2, 0.1), (S_3, 0.7), (S_4, 0.9)\}$$

The probabilities allow the user to place confidence in the answers, which is the consequence of evaluating cloaked (or imprecise) location values. Depending upon the requirements of the application, one may choose to report only the object with the k highest probability value, or only those objects whose probability values exceed a minimum threshold. Our work will be able to work with any of these models. Next, let us examine how an ILRQ can be evaluated.

5.2   Evaluation of ILRQ

The ILRQ is evaluated in three phases:

1. Pruning Phase, which removes all the objects that do not have any chance of satisfying the ILRQ.
2. Transformation Phase, which converts an ILRQ into subqueries, and
3. Evaluation Phase, which computes probabilistic answers for the ILRQ.

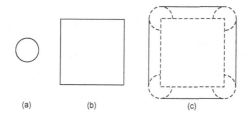

Fig. 3. Illustrating the Minkowski Sum

1. Pruning Phase. In the first step, we retrieve objects from the database that are candidates for the query answer. It prunes away objects that have no chance of satisfying the query, and hence allows us to manipulate a smaller set of objects for further processing (e.g., calculating their probabilities).

There are a number of ways to achieve the pruning effect. First of all, the service provider can exploit the privacy preferences of the users as suggested in Section 3. For example, user S_j may specify that she does not want user S to know that they are close to each other. Moreover, S may have defined the list of the people of interest to her, and she only requires the subset of the names of these people to appear her query answer. By using these policies, the service provider can filter away objects before further processing.

The second pruning technique is specific to ILRQ. Notice that the objects that do not need to be considered for an ILRQ are those that have zero chance of being located inside the query range C. To prune away these objects, we must take into account all the possible locations of the query issuer S. Here we employ the concept of the *Minkowski Sum*, which is commonly studied in computational graphics and motion planning. Given two point sets or polygons, A and B, the Minkowski Sum is defined as follows [19]:

$$A \oplus B = \{x + y | x \in A, y \in B\}$$

Figure 3 illustrates an example, where the Minkowski Sum of the circle in (a) and the square in (b) is shown in (c). Conceptually, the Minkowski Sum is the union of all translations of A by a point y located in B.

We can view the Minkowski Sum of the query range C and the uncertainty region U, that is, $U \oplus C$, as the union of all range queries, by considering all the possible positions of S who resides somewhere in U. If the uncertainty region of any object being queried does not overlap $U \oplus R$, we can be assured that this object does not have any chance of satisfying any range query issued at any position in U. Thus we can use $U \oplus R$ as a query range to obtain objects that have non-zero probability of satisfying the query (i.e., their uncertainty regions overlap with the query range). The objects retrieved from this range query will be the ones that are processed in the subsequent phases.

Standard algorithms for computing the Minkowski Sum are discussed in [19], and here we do not present the details due to space limitation. The worst-case complexity of these algorithms, given a circle and a polygon with e sides, can have a complexity of $O(e^2 \log e)$ (if the polygon is non-convex).To reduce the complexity of these algorithms, notice that the Minkowski Sum is used solely to improve the efficiency of our methods. It is not necessary that we obtain the exact shape, although that may result in getting false hits that do not contribute to the query answers. If U is a non-convex polygon, we can first approximate it with a convex polygon that circumscribe it (e.g., compute its convex hulls, which needs $O(e \log e)$ times for a e-sided polygon) [19]. We can also circumscribe the circular query range, C, with a m-sided polygon (e.g., a square). The resulting Minkowski sum then produces a convex polygon with at most $m + e$ edges, and requires only $O(m + e)$ time to compute. A range query using this approximate version of Minkowski Sum can then be issued to produce a set of objects (denoted by K) for the next phase.

2. Transformation Phase. In LRQ, the query range of the user S is a circle C with radius r and center L. If the user transmits her cloaked location, the query range is no longer C, since the service provider has no idea of where L exactly is. The service provider does know that L is within U, so it transforms the query into sub-queries over all possible locations of S. In other words, at each point $(u, v) \in U$, a query is issued to find out which user(s) from the set K is(are) within the region $C'(u, v)$, where $C'(u, v)$ is the circle with radius r centered at (u, v). The result of ILRQ is essentially the union of the results of the range queries issued at each point in U.

3. Evaluation Phase. This phase computes the actual probability that each object in K satisfies the ILRQ. Notice that the probability $p_j(u,v)$ of user S_j satisfying S's request at point $(u,v) \in U$ is given by

$$p_j(u,v) = \frac{\text{Area}(U_j \cap C'(u,v))}{\text{Area}(U_j)} \tag{2}$$

where $U_j \cap C'(u,v)$ is the common region between U_j and $C'(u,v)$. Essentially, $p_j(u,v)$ is the fraction of U_j that overlaps $C'(u,v)$.

The total probability of S_j satisfying the ILRQ issued by S is given by the integration of the product of the pdf of user S's location at (u,v) (i.e., $\frac{1}{\text{Area}(U)}$) and $p_j(u,v)$ over all $(u,v) \in U$. Therefore,

$$p_j = \int_U \frac{1}{\text{Area}(U)} p_j(u,v) du dv \tag{3}$$

$$= \frac{\int_U \text{Area}(U_j \cap C'(u,v)) du dv}{\text{Area}(U)\text{Area}(U_j)} \tag{4}$$

by substituting $p_j(u,v)$ with Equation 2. The probability so computed serves indicates the confidence placed on the answer. For example, in Figure 2(b), p_2 is only 0.1, showing that S_2 is unlikely to be the answer, while S_3 and S_4 have a much higher chance (0.5 and 0.9 respectively) of being the answers.

In practice, p_j can be evaluated with numerical integration techniques. The basic idea is to collect a set of sampling points (u,v) for U. Then $p_j(u,v)$ is computed for each sampling point. The sum of these $p_j(u,v)$ values divided by Area(U) yields the approximate value of p_j. Here an important issue is to use suitable number of sampling points to achieve an accurate answer. We have implemented numerical integration in our experiments (Section 7), and have also determined the number of sampling points experimentally. In our technical report, we have also shown how the evaluation can be expressed as a SQL query in a spatial database [20].

6   Quality of Imprecise Queries

Due to the inherent imprecision in location data and the query itself, an imprecise query returns probabilistic answers, which can be ambiguous. Here we investigate the notion of quality for imprecise queries that quantifies query ambiguity. It also serves as an indicator to the query issuer to see whether she should adjust the degree of her location uncertainty. For ease of exposition, we again use the simplified notions as described in Section 5.1.

The quality of an imprecise query is affected by the uncertainty of the query issuer's location. In an ILRQ, for example, the position of the query issuer S, which is part of the query, is only known to be accurate within the uncertainty region U. As a result, there can be numerous possible answers, where only one of them is correct. However, the final answer returned to the user is the union of all possible answers, and this reduces the overall answer quality.

To illustrate, consider Figure 4 which shows the uncertainty region U of S, and also the uncertainty regions of two objects being queried, S_2 and S_3. Some sub-queries of the ILRQ issued by S (in dotted line) are also shown. When the same query C is issued at different points in U, the query results can also vary. For example, the range query issued in the region A_1 yields S_2 as the result, while for the query issued in the region A_3, the answer is S_3. In reality, S is only positioned in one point in U, so the true answer is only one of the possible answers. However, the final answer returned to S contains both S_2 and S_3. Thus, the inconsistency of results can affect the overall quality of a query answer.

Our goal is to provide a quality metric to quantify the quality of the query result due to the ambiguity of the query issuer. The metric should take into account (1) how many different answers are produced and (2) how different these answers are. Intuitively, the quality should be the best when the uncertainty region U is reduced to a single point, since in that case there is only one single answer. In Figure 4, for instance, if the uncertainty region is simply the point in A_2, then the set $\{S_2, S_3\}$ is the only answer.

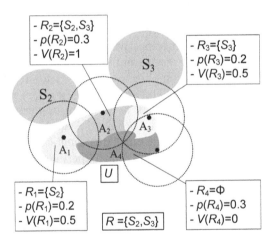

Fig. 4. Illustrating the query score of ILRQ

Let R be the set of answers that are actually returned to the user. In Figure 4, R equals to $\{S_2, S_3\}$. Our approach is to partition U into subregions according to their answer sets. For example, in Figure 4, U is partitioned into four subregions, namely A_1, A_2, A_3 and A_4. Moreover, if a query is issued at any one point in A_1, the answer set R_1, i.e., $\{S_2\}$, is produced. Notice that for all values of $i, j \in [1, 4]$ (with $i \neq j$), some objects in R_i and R_j can be the same, but $R_i - R_j \neq \emptyset$. The final answer R is the union of all the answer sets $R_1, \ldots, R_4$.

Now we can measure the similarity between the answer returned R, and each sub-result R_k. Specifically, we define the *precision* of R with respect to R_k as

$$V(R_k) = \frac{|R_k|}{|R|} \tag{5}$$

where $V(R_k)$ indicates the amount of "impurities" injected to R_k in order to become R. As $V(R_k)$ increases from 0 to 1, R_k is closer to R. Thus $V(R_k)$ serves as a score for measuring the closeness of R to R_k, if S is located in A_k. In Figure 4, if S is located in A_1, the score obtained for this query answer, i.e., $V(R_1)$, is $\frac{1}{2}$.

However, S has only a certain probability of being located in A_1. Let this value be $p(R_1)$, which is also the probability that S_1 yields R_1 as the answer. The product $p(R_1) \cdot V(R_1)$ can then be viewed as the precision weighted by the probability of S_1 having R_1 as the true answer.

In general, given that U is partitioned into B subregions according to the difference in their answers, the *query score* of ILRQ can be measured by the sum of the weighted precision values at all the subregions of U,

$$\text{Query score} = \sum_{k=1}^{B} p(R_k)V(R_k) \tag{6}$$

which varies between 0 (lowest quality) and 1 (highest quality). For example, the query score shown in Figure 4 is $0.2 \cdot 0.5 + 0.3 \cdot 1 + 0.2 \cdot 0.5 + 0.3 \cdot 0 = 0.32$.

An important question is how to compute $p(R_k)$, i.e., the probability that S gets the answer R_k. Let us assume that each sub-query of ILRQ issued at point (u, v) returns a set of answers $Q'(u, v)$. Then,

$$p(R_k) = \int_{(u,v) \in U \wedge R_k = Q'(u,v)} \frac{1}{Area(U)} \, du\, dv \tag{7}$$

that is, the integration of the uniform pdf over all points in U that evaluate the same result R_k.

The answer quality metric allow a user to trade-off privacy for a potentially better answer quality. In particular, the query score depends on the size of the uncertainty region – a larger uncertainty region potentially yields more distinct answers and lower query scores. Therefore, a low query score indicates that the user may reduce the size of her uncertainty region and resubmit the query.

7   Experimental Results

We have performed an extensive simulation study on the behavior of location cloaking. Our experiments are based upon data generated by the City Simulator 2.0 [21] developed at IBM. The City Simulator simulates the realistic motion of 10,000 people moving in a city. The input to the simulator is a map of a city. We used the sample map provided with the simulator that models a city of size

840 × 1260 square units, with 71 buildings, 48 roads, six road intersections and one park. The simulator models the movement of objects within the buildings, as well as their relatively faster movement on the roads and highways.

Each object reports its location to the server at an average rate of 0.5sec^{-1}. An ILRQ is generated by randomly choosing a user as the query issuer. The ILRQ has a range of radius r of 150 units. Each user has an uncertainty region with a radius of $U_i(t).r$, equal to 30 units. The radius is denoted as "privacy" in the graphs shown. In our experiments, since both the query range and the query issuer (S_i)'s uncertainty region are circles, their Minkowski Sum is simply a circle centered at the query issuer's location, with a radius of $(r + U_i(t).r)$. Each data point is the average value over 200 location update cycles. We use the radius of uncertainty region as a measure of the location privacy of user – a larger radius implies a higher degree of privacy.

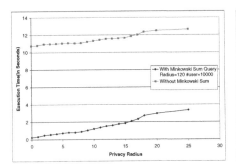
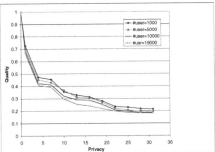

Fig. 5. Execution time vs. Privacy   **Fig. 6.** Quality vs. Privacy

7.1 Effectiveness of Location Cloaking

Quality and Performance. In Figure 5 we see that an increase in privacy value lengthens the execution time of ILRQ. With a higher privacy (or uncertainty region of the query issuer), the ranges of sub-queries cover a larger area. Thus more objects are involved in computation, resulting in a higher execution time. We can also see from the same figure that when the Minkowski Sum is used as an initial filtering phase, the performance improves by at least a factor of three. Thus, the use of the Minkowski Sum in the first step is effective in improving the query evaluation performance.

Quality and Privacy. We investigate the effect of location privacy on query score of the ILRQ. Figure 6 shows the result for different number of users. The quality is 1 (highest) when there is no privacy at all. As privacy (i.e., uncertainty region area) increases, the query score drops. This is because the larger uncertainty region increases the number of distinct query answers, thereby lowering the query score. We also observe the difference in quality when the number of users varies. In general, for the same privacy value, a larger population produces a lower score, since more distinct answer sets are produced.

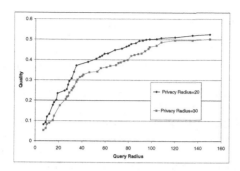

Fig. 7. Quality vs. Query Radius

Quality and Query Size. Next, we study the effect of query size on answer quality. Figure 7 illustrates that answer quality increases with query size. With a fixed privacy value (uncertainty radius), an increase in the query size creates less distinct answer sets. For example, when the query range has a very large radius (140) compared with the radius of the uncertainty region (which is equal to 20), the query ranges created will render many similar answers, since the difference in the answers to the queries at different points in the uncertainty region is small. As shown in the same graph, at a larger uncertainty region radius (30), the relative difference between the uncertainty size and privacy is smaller than when the radius is 20, and thus the quality is lower too.

8   Conclusions

In this paper we suggested a framework to connect privacy, information cloaking and service quality. We proposed imprecise queries, which hide the identity of the query issuer and enable evaluation of cloaked information. We studied an evaluation algorithm and quality metrics of moving range queries. We also performed an extensive simulation to investigate the behavior of our proposed methods.

References

1. Warrior, J., McHenry, E., McGee, K.: They know where you are. IEEE Spectrum **40**(7) (2003) 20– 25
2. Gruteser, M., Grunwald, D.:   Anonymous Usage of Location-Based Services Through Spatial and Temporal Cloaking. In: Proc. 1st Intl. Conf. on Mobile Systems, Applications, and Services. (2003)
3. Varshney, U.: Location management for mobile commerce applications in wireless internet environment. ACM Transactions on Internet Technology **3**(3) (2003)
4. Beresford, A.R., Stajano, F.: Location Privacy in Pervasive Computing. IEEE Pervasive Computing **2**(1) (2003) 46–55
5. Snekkenes, E.: Concepts for personal location privacy policies. In: Proceedings of the 3rd ACM conference on Electronic Commerce, ACM Press (2001) 48–57

6. Hengartner, U., Steenkiste, P.: Protecting Access to People Location Information. In: Proc. 1st Intl. Conf. on Security in Pervasive Computing. (2003)
7. Hengartner, U., Steenkiste, P.: Access control to information in pervasive computing environments. In: Proc. 9th USENIX Workshop on HotOS. (2003)
8. Cheng, R., Prabhakar, S.: Using uncertainty to provide privacy-preserving and high-quality location-based services. In: Workshop on Location Systems Privacy and Control, MobileHCI 04. (2004)
9. Atallah, M., Frikken, K.: Privacy-preserving location-dependent query processing. In: Proc. ACS/IEEE Intl. Conf. on Pervasive Services (ICPS). (2004)
10. Mokbel, M., Xiong, X., Aref, W.: SINA: Scalable incremental processing of continuous queries in spatio-temporal databases. In: Proc. ACM SIGMOD. (2004)
11. Pfitzmann, A., Hansen, M.: Anonymity, unobservability, psuedonymity, and identity management - a proposal for terminology. (2004)
12. Sweeney, L.: k-anonymity: a model for protecting privacy. Intl. Journal on Uncertainty, Fuzziness and Knowledge-based Systems **10**(5) (2002)
13. LeFevre, K., DeWitt, D., Ramakrishnan, R.: Incognito: efficient full-domain k-anonymity. In: Proc. ACM SIGMOD Intl. Conf. (2005)
14. Bertino, E., Ooi, B., Yang, Y., Deng, R.: Privacy and ownership preserving of outsourced medical data. In: Proc. IEEE ICDE. (2005)
15. Gruteser, M., Liu, X.: Protecting privacy in continuous location-tracking applications. IEEE Security and Privacy **2**(2) (2004)
16. Gedik, B., Liu, L.: A customizable k-anonymity model for protecting location privacy. In: ICDCS. (2005)
17. Cheng, R., Kalashnikov, D., Prabhakar, S.: Evaluating probabilistic queries over imprecise data. In: Proc. ACM SIGMOD. (2003)
18. Serjantov, A., Danezis, G.: Towards an information metric for anonymity. In: Privacy Enhancing Technologies: 2nd Intl. Workshop, PET 2002. (2002)
19. Berg, M., Kreveld, M., Overmars, M., Schwarzkopf, O.: Computational Geometry – Algorithms and Applications, 2nd ed. Springer Verlag (2000)
20. Cheng, R., Zhang, Y., Bertino, E., Prabhakar, S.: Querying private data in moving-object environments. Technical Report CERIAS TR #2005-45, Purdue U (2005)
21. Kaufman, J., Myllymaki, J., Jackson, J.: IBM City Simulator Spatial Data Generator 2.0 (2001)
22. Stallings, W.: Wireless Communications and Networks. Prentice Hall (2005)
23. Wong, V., Leung, V.: Location management for next-generation personal communications network. IEEE Network (2000)

A   Applicability to Real-World Systems

Can the framework proposed in Section 3 be deployed in systems like the GPS and cellular network systems? Here we describe how this is possible for two major classes of systems:

– **Systems that do not track a user's location regularly.** Typical examples are the GPS and RF-ID systems. In particular, the GPS receiver that resides in the user's device obtains location information from 24 satellites and gets a location precision ranging from a few to several hundred meters [3]. Our framework is readily used here, where the user's device can generate location data spontaneously.

– **Systems that track a user's location regularly.** The cellular network system (such as GSM and PCS) are representative examples, where the cellular network system has to identify the user's location (in terms of a hexagonal cell with radius ranging from 0.1 to 1 km [22]) in order to deliver phone calls. If the system is trusted, the user can contact it directly before sending her location to the service provider [15].

Here we describe how a user can place less trust on the cellular network system compared to [15]. In this solution, the user only lets the cellular network know a rough position of her, by specifying a cloaked location that is represented by a set of neighboring cells. The cloaking agent should map the cloaked location into cells before sending them to the system. This may result in an increase in connection cost, due to the additional effort in finding out the user in a particular cell for making a connection. Without going into further details, we would like to point out that such a scheme (that allows a user to notify the cellular network her approximate positions) has already been implemented in cellular networks [23]. Thus it is possible to deploy our framework in these systems.

B   Threat Analysis and Solutions

In this paper, we have assumed the service provider holds the same amount of location uncertainty as reported by the user. In this section, we investigate how the service provider can improve its knowledge about the user's location. Specifically, we describe a technique called "trajectory tracing" that can reduce the effectiveness of cloaking in Section B.1. We then describe solutions to reduce this threat in Section B.2, and present experimental results in Section B.3.

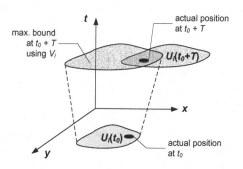

Fig. 8. Illustrating trajectory tracing

B.1   Trajectory Tracing

Suppose the service provider saves all the cloaked locations it has received from a user. The service provider may also capture the maximum velocity information of the user through her movement record, her vehicle, etc. We now show that it is possible for the service provider to reduce the size of uncertainty region reported by the user.

Specifically, let the maximum velocity of a user S_i be V_i. Assume S_i sent her last cloaked location at time t_0, i.e., $U_i(t_0)$, and then again after T time units, i.e., $U_i(t_0 + T)$. Using the values of V_i and $U_i(t_0)$, the service provider can know the possible location of S_i. As shown in Figure 8, the service provider derives the bound enclosing S_i's location at time $t_0 + T$ (called *maximum bound*) Thus, even if S_i says she is located somewhere in $U_i(t_0 + T)$, her possible location is actually limited within the overlapping region between $U_i(t_0 + T)$ and the maximum bound, which is smaller than $U_i(t_0 + T)$. Notice that this is an accumulative effect, since the service provider can derive an even smaller bound based on the overlapping region.

If the service provider is able to reduce the location uncertainty of the user, the location privacy may be threatened. In non-anonymous applications, for example, the user's identity is also transmitted to the service provider, and hence the service provider can associate with the user's identity with a smaller uncertainty region. Even in anonymous applications, the service provider can use a map to help identifying the owner of the location. For instance, if the uncertainty region has significant overlap with a residential area, the owner of the location may be discovered and her movement can then be tracked. We propose two techniques, namely **patching** and **delaying**, in order to alleviate this problem.

B.2   Patching and Delaying

The first solution is to combine the cloaked locations released in the past with the current cloaked location before it is sent. We call this technique *patching*. Figure 9(a) illustrates this concept. At time $t_0 + T$, in place of $U_i(t_0 + T)$, the user S_i sent the region $U_i'(t_0 + T) = U_i(t_0) \cup U_i(t_0 + T)$. As a result, the "loss" of uncertainty in $U_i(t_0 + T)$ due to trajectory tracing is "compensated" by the inclusion of $U_i(t_0)$, which is assured to be within the maximum bound. Essentially, the spatial accuracy of the location is further relaxed. Notice that this may cause a degradation in query quality due to the increase in uncertainty, as shown in our experimental results.

Another solution is based on relaxing the timing requirement, which we termed "*delaying*". The idea is to suspend the request until the cloaked location fits into the maximum bound. As shown in Figure 9(b), $U_i(t_0 + T)$ is not sent until after δ_t more time units, when $U_i(t_0 + T)$ is guaranteed to be within the maximum bound. The value of δ_t can be estimated based on distance between the edges of the adjacent uncertainty regions, and the value of the maximum velocity. The advantage of this scheme over patching is that the extent of the cloaked location remains unchanged and so the quality is not affected. However, the response time of the query can be increased due to the delay introduced, which can be an important Quality-of-Service parameter in time-critical applications.

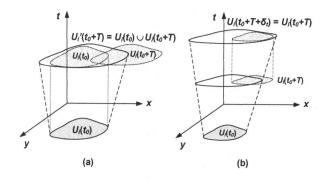

Fig. 9. (a) Patching and (b) Delaying

B.3   Effectiveness of Patching and Delaying

We examine experimentally the behaviors of the patching and delaying policies. We compare these two policies with the case when these two policies are not used (denote this case as *normal*). We first investigate the impact of the knowledge about the maximum velocity of the query issuer on the amount of uncertainty reduced. Figure 10 shows that regardless of whether patching or delaying is used, the area of uncertainty region reduced is lower with increase in the maximum velocity. As illustrated in Figure 8, a faster velocity increases the amount of overlap of the maximum bound with the next reported uncertainty region, and thus the portion of uncertainty reduced also decreases. While both patching and delaying have lower amount of uncertainty reduced than *normal*, patching performs the best due to the enlargement of the uncertainty region sent.

Next, we examine the effect of privacy of the query issuer on query quality. Figure 11 shows that as privacy increases, the three policies suffer from different degrees of quality degradation. While both *normal* and delaying perform similarly, patching performs the worst. This is because patching augments the previously reported uncertainty region, which is enlarged with a larger privacy

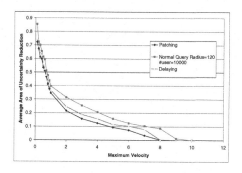

Fig. 10. Uncertainty vs. Velocity

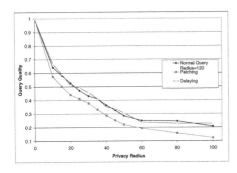

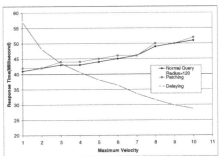

Fig. 11. Quality vs. Privacy   **Fig. 12.** Time vs. Velocity

radius. This results in a more ambiguous query issuer location and a poorer query quality. This is the price paid for a lower reduction of uncertainty area, as we have described previously.

Finally, Figure 12 illustrates the response time (i.e., the duration between the time that the user submits a query and the time that the query is finished). Delaying outperforms both *normal* and patching at a maximum velocity higher than 3. This is because the maximum bound can cover the newly reported uncertainty region faster (c.f. Figure 9). However, delaying does not work well when the maximum velocity is small, since the cloaking agent has to wait for a longer time until the uncertainty region can be covered by the maximum bound. In these cases, it may be necessary to limit the waiting time, and the uncertainty region is sent even though it may not be fully covered by the maximum bound.

The Effects of Location Access Behavior on Re-identification Risk in a Distributed Environment

Bradley Malin* and Edoardo Airoldi**

* Department of Biomedical Informatics, Vanderbilt University, Nashville, TN 37232 USA
** School of Computer Science, Carnegie Mellon University, Pittsburgh, PA 15213 USA
b.malin@vanderbilt.edu, eairlodi@cs.cmu.edu

Abstract. In this paper, we investigate how location access patterns influence the re-identification of seemingly anonymous data. In the real world, individuals visit different locations that gather similar information. For instance, multiple hospitals collect health information on the same patient. To protect anonymity for research purposes, hospitals share sensitive data, such as DNA sequences, stripped of explicit identifiers. Separately, for administrative functions, identified data, stripped of DNA, is made available. On a hospital by hospital basis, each pair of DNA and identified databases appears unlinkable, however, links can be established when multiple locations' database are studied. This problem, known as trail re-identification, is a generalized phenomenon and occurs because an individual's location access pattern can be matched across the shared databases.

Data holders can not exchange data to find and suppress trails that would be re-identified. Thus, it is important to assess the re-identification risk in a system in order to develop techniques to mitigate it. In this research, we evaluate several real world datasets and observe trail re-identification is related to the number of people to places. To study this phenomenon in more detail, we develop a generative model for location access patterns that simulates observed behavior. We evaluate trail re-identification risk in a range of simulated patterns and our findings suggest that the skew of the distribution of people to places is one of the main factors that drives trail re-identification.

1 Introduction

DNA sequences are becoming an integral part of electronic patient medical records [1, 2]. Collections of detailed genomic data that are tied to clinical information are poised to yield significant healthcare breakthroughs [3], ranging from personalized medicine to drug discovery. However to share person-specific genomic data collections for research, data holders must adhere to legal regulations, such the Privacy Rule of the Health Insurance Portability and Accountability Act [4]. Though an individual's genome is unique, a database of DNA records, with no accompanying explicit demographic information or identifiers included, appears anonymous. But patients leave information behind at multiple institutions and the collections are autonomously controlled. As a result, the location-access patterns, or trails, of an individuals DNA can be extracted from shared databases. DNA trails are not necessarily re-identifiable, but

G. Danezis and P. Golle (Eds.): PET 2006, LNCS 4258, pp. 413–429, 2006.

publicly available information, such as hospital discharge databases, are available and reveal identified individuals' trails. Uniqueness of an individuals discharge and DNA trails leads to re-identification.

Healthcare is one realm in which trail re-identification poses a privacy threat [5], but trails arise in many other environments [6,7]. Though domains change the goal remains constant: share data such that the identity of sensitive information, can not be linked to the individual from which it was derived. Privacy protection methods have been proposed and adopted, such as [8] and [9], which advocate the removal or encryption of explicit identifiers associated with sensitive data. However, such methods do not prevent trail re-identification since the identities of the individuals are available in other shared or public databases.

Trail re-identification is a real concern. Inability to address the problem will prevent organizations, such as biomedical data holders, from sharing data [3, 10]. As an alternative to ad hoc protection methods, we propose formally evaluating the re-identification risk of a set of database entries prior to release.[1] The actual number of re-identifications can be measured as the number of shared database entries that are re-identifiable. Yet, when data can not be shared prior to re-identification evaluation, we must approximate the number of re-identifications that can be made. To do so we need to isolate the processes that influence re-identification, such as 1) the data generating process (e.g. How do people visit places?) and 2) the re-identification process (e.g. How are trails linked?) [12]. Then, for a given method of re-identification, substitute characteristics of location access patterns, as opposed to the actual patterns, to estimate of re-identification risk.

In this paper, we model the underlying processes governing trail re-identification to evaluate risk in a distributed environment. We have two goals. First, we tie together results from our previous case studies to conjecture how the number of people and locations in a system relates to the number of re-identifications that can be made. Second, we step back from specific cases and develop a statistical model to examine why different populations have varying degrees of re-identification in a distributed environment. Using this model, we then simulate several fundamental location visit strategies employed by individuals in the real world and assess the re-identification risk they entail.

The remainder of this paper is organized as follows. In the following section we review the formal basis and methods for trail re-identification. The methods are amenable to combinatoric proof, which suggests that the number of re-identifications scales with the number of subjects and locations. However, with real world populations, we demonstrate that such scaling does not exist. In addition, we show the power law feature of online environments, as well as how highskew populations are generated. Next, we simulate and perform linkage analysis on several types of simulated datasets corresponding to a range of distributions. Then, we investigate the relationship of trail re-identification risk to information theoretic principles. Finally, this work addresses limitations and extensions for future research.

---

[1] Provable solutions to guarantee trails can not be re-identified exist [11], but they require the use of third parties, which are not always practical due to trust or regulatory constraints.

2   Background

In this section we survey related research and provide an overview of several basic concepts for the trail re-identification problem.

2.1   Related Work

In the past, it was generally believed that person-specific data collections could be shared somewhat freely, provided none of the features of the data included explicit identifiers, such as name, address, or Social Security number. However, an increasing number of data detective-like investigations have revealed that collections of "de-identified" data, derived from ad hoc protection models, can often be linked to other collections that do include explicit identifiers to uniquely, and correctly, re-identify disclosed information by personal name [13, 14, 15, 16, 17]. Fields appearing in both de-identified and identified tables can link the two, thereby relating names to the subjects of the de-identified data. For example, Sweeney's analysis of the fields {*date of birth, gender, 5-digit zip code*}, which, until recently, commonly appeared in both de-identified databases and publicly available identified data, such as voter registration lists, uniquely represented approximately 87% of the U.S. population [16].

Trail re-identification [5, 7] extends traditional re-identification and illustrates how the pattern of locations people visit, or trails, can be used for linkage. First, we provide an informal view of trail re-identification, which will be followed by a more formal presentation of the problem. The main premise of trail re-identification is based upon the observation that people visit different sets of locations where they can, and do, leave behind similar pieces of de-identified information. The de-identified data can consist of only one or very few fields. Each location visited collects and, subsequently, shares de-identified data on people who visited their location. In addition, locations also collect and share, in separate releases devoid of de-identified data, explicitly identified data (i.e. name, residential address, etc.), thereby naming some people. Individually, a single locations releases appear unrelatable, and thus identity and sensitive information appear unlinkable. However, when multiple locations share their respective data, this allows for trails, a characterization of the locations that an individual visited, to be constructed. Similar patterns in the trails of de-identified and identified data can then be used for linkage purposes.

The trail re-identification attack is related to other attack that have been studied in anonymous communications, such as the interaction attack [18, 19].

2.2   Elements of a Formal Re-identification Model

We now describe the problem in a more formal manner. Let L be a set of locations collecting data. At each location, data is organized as a database, which we model as a table of rows and columns. Each column corresponds to an attribute, which is a semantic category of information that refers to people, machines, or other entities. Each row contains attribute values specific to a person, machine, or other entity. A database is represented by $\tau(A_1, A_2, \ldots, A_p)$, where the set of attributes is $A^\tau = \{A_1, A_2, \ldots, A_p\}$ and each attribute is associated with its own domain of specific values. Each row in the database is a p-tuple, which we represent in vector form $[a_1, \ldots, a_p]$, such that each value a_i is in the domain of attribute A_i. We define the size of the database as the number of tuples and use cardinality, denoted with $|\tau|$.

A database τ is said to be *identified* if A^τ includes explicit identifying attributes, such as name or residential address, or attributes known to be directly linkable to explicit identifiers. If τ is not identified, then it said to be *de-identified*. Data holding locations attempt to protect the anonymity of sensitive data by stripping explicitly identifying attributes from sensitive data. In doing so, locations partition identified and de-identified data and make separate database disclosures. As such, in our model, each data holder releases a two-table vertical partition of its internal data by splitting τ into two tables $\psi(A_1, \ldots, A_i)$ and $\delta(A_{i+1}, \ldots, A_j)$, with attributes $A^\psi \subset A^\tau$ and $A^\delta \subset A^\tau$. For illustration, several tables are depicted in Figure 1.

2.3   The Trail Re-identification Problem

Given the tables of a particular type (e.g. the sensitive data tables), we can construct a matrix X that is referred to as a trail matrix. The trail matrix X is the join of all locations' tables over a set of related attributes, such as when we trace an individuals DNA sequence from one location to another.[2] This matrix has a row for each distinct data element and $|L|$ columns, one for each location. Values in the matrix are drawn from $\{1, 0, *\}$. A "1" a cell denotes the data element for the row definitely visited the location corresponding to the column, while a "0" denotes a definite non-visit. A "*" is an ambiguous value and indicates that we are unsure if the data element was collected at the location. We use $X[x, :]$ to denote the trail of data element x in trail matrix X.

The basis behind trail re-identification is that there exist two different types of data collected at the set of locations in the environment. Thus two trail matrices, X and Y, can be constructed, and it assumed that both trail matrices are drawn from the same population of entities. An example of trail matrices are depicted in Figure 2(a).

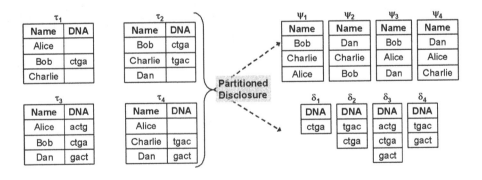

Fig. 1. Sample disclosures for four locations

---

[2] This join can be constructed from traditional record linkage algorithms for tables with common attributes [20, 21].

The main distinguishing feature of trail re-identification algorithms is their characterization of data completeness. Trail matrices are said to be *unreserved*, if an entity's data is always collected and disclosed from a location. In some situations, a location can collect data of both types, but it undercollects (or underreports) data of one type (i.e. the data is not in the location's table). In this case, trail matrix X is said to be *reserved* to Y if the trail of each entity in matrix X, $X[x, :]$ can be transformed into the entity's corresponding $Y[y, :]$ in matrix Y by replacing only *'s with 0's and 1's. When this transformation can be performed, $X[x, :]$ is said to be a subtrail (represented with the $\preceq$ symbol) of $Y[y, :]$. Similarly, y_Y is said to be the supertrail of $X[x, :]$, or $Y[y, :] \succeq X[x, :]$. Figure 2(a) provides an example of trail matrices where X is reserved to matrix Y. Notice $Y[actg, :] \preceq X[Alice, :]$ and $Y[actg, :] \preceq X[Charlie, :]$.

Trail Matrix X				
Name	l_1	l_2	l_3	l_4
Dan	0	1	1	1
Bob	1	1	1	0
Charlie	1	1	0	1
Alice	1	0	1	1

Trail Matrix Y				
Name	l_1	l_2	l_3	l_4
actg	1	*	1	*
gact	*	*	1	1
tgac	*	1	*	1
ctga	1	1	1	*

	Dan	Bob	Charlie	Alice
actg	0	1	0	1
gact	1	0	0	1
tgac	1	0	1	0
ctga	0	1	0	0

(a) Trail Matrix Y is reserved to X (b) Trail Re-identification

Fig. 2. (a) Trail matrices built from Fig. 1. (b) *Bob* is re-identified to *ctga* in the first iteration

Recall, the goal of trail re-identification is to match the rows of two trail matrices to re-identify sensitive data to identity. In related research, [5, 7] introduced an algorithm called REIDIT (RE-Identification of Data In Trails) to perform such a task, such that every match is guaranteed to be a correct re-identification. Informally, REIDIT works as follows. First, we construct a $|Y| \times |M|$ matrix, called M, such that cell $M[i, j] = 1$ if $i_Y \preceq j_X$, and 0 otherwise. When we find a row or column that has only one cell $M[i, j] = 1$, we re-identify the corresponding data elements in the cell. We iterate this process until no more matches can be made. Figure 2(b) illustrates the initial matrix for Figure 2(a) and the first trail re-identification of *ctga* to *Bob* is made. In the next iteration *actg* will be re-identified to *Alice*, and so on.

3   Empirical Evidence: Lesson Learned

We assessed the feasibility of trail re-identification in several different domains. The first population we studied consisted of individuals visiting physical hospitals for treatment. The second population consisted of individuals visiting sites on the World Wide Web (i.e. a virtual world) for performing various functions, such as purchasing goods.

Healthcare Case Study. We analyzed the trails of DNA database records in a distributed healthcare environment. The observations were hospital discharge data for the state of Illinois from 1990 to 1997 [22]. Trails were derived for eight different patient populations, each with a distinctive DNA-based disorder. In these populations, the entities were hospital patients and the locations were hospitals. The size of the populations ranged from 4 to 8,000 patients over 8 to 200 hospitals and the distribution of individuals to hospitals varies from uniform to approximately Gaussian, which are relatively low skew.

Internet Case Study. We studied the trails of IP addresses in a distributed online environment. The dataset used in this study was compiled by the Homenet project at Carnegie Mellon University, who provide families in the Pittsburgh area with Internet services in exchange for the monitoring and recording of the families' online services and transactions [23]. We studied URL access data collected over a two-month period that included 86 households and 144 individuals. Each individual was provided with a unique login and password for fine-grained monitoring. Overall, approximately 5,000 distinct website domains and 66,000 distinct pages were accessed. We analyzed the traffic at each domain with respect to the number of distinct visitors and discovered a generalized Zipf distribution, which represents high skew.

In both case studies, we found that re-identification rates correlate with the average number of people visiting a location. When we investigated this relationship in more detail, we found particular types of locations influence trail re-identification. For example, we ranked the popularity of each location by the number of distinct subjects visiting the location. When we measured trail re-identification from the least popular location to a location with a specific popularity, we found the re-identification rate correlated the average number of people per location. The result is shown in Figure 3, where we depict re-identification rates for three different populations. In Figure 3, the term "discovered" corresponds to the number of individauls' data that are observed given the set of locations that trails are constructed from. As we increase the number of locations considered, we increase the number of individuals that have their data discovered, but not necessarily re-identified.

The first two populations are derived from the healthcare case study. The first corresponds to a population afflicted with cystic fibrosis (CF) and the second to a population afflicted with phenylketonuria (PK). These two cases establish a comparison between the feasibility of trail re-identification on a population in which the number of subjects per location is relatively large (CF - approximately 6.60), with a population in which the average is closer to a single subject per location (PK - approximately 1.35). The third population corresponds to the online Homenet dataset, where the ratio of subjects per location is relatively small (approximately 0.017).

We observe that as the ratio of subjects per location grows large, such as in the CF dataset shown in Figure 3(a), we find evidence of an exponential relation between the number of locations considered (the X axis), and the number of people that are trail re-identifiable (the Y axis). As the ratio becomes negligible, as observed in the Homenet dataset in Figure 3(c), we find evidence of a logarithmic relation between the number of locations considered and the number of trail re-identifications. Furthermore, the PK dataset in Figure 3(b) supports this trend; in this case the ratio of people to locations is approximately 1, and we find evidence of a linear relation between the number of locations considered and the number of trail re-identifications.

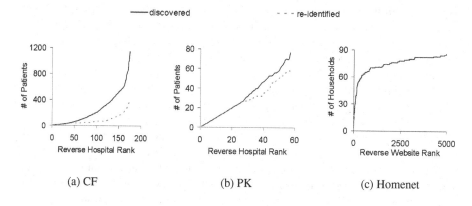

Fig. 3. Trail re-identification in unreserved systems for case studies. Number of locations increase from least-visited to most-visited.

The evidence from the case studies suggests that different types of location access patterns have an effect on trail re-identification. In the following section we study the degree to which specific types of access distributions influence re-identification.

4   Simulation Experiments and Results

There are many aspects of location-based information which influence trail re-identification. The main contributing components include the number of subjects, the number of locations, the distribution of subjects to locations, as well as the parameters controlling said distributions. In this research, we concentrate on the number of locations and the distributions guiding subject access to these locations. For our analysis, we fix the number of subjects to 1000. We simulate uniform and high skew distributions of subjects per location. We simulate both unreserved systems, i.e. neither trail matrix has *'s, and reserved systems, where one trail matrix has *'s. From an operational point of view, in the simulation of unreserved systems, we generate two equivalent trail matrices. In the simulation of reserved systems, instead, we generate trail matrices for an unreserved environment, and then we change all 0's in a matrix to *'s. For each distribution type and parameterization, these populations are allocations to sets of locations over the range of 3 to 40 locations.

Uniform Simulation. In this setting, subjects visit locations with uniform probability. We control the average number of subjects per locations, by specifying the probability that a subject visits each location, $p \in [0.1]$. This sampling mechanism is from a location perspective. From a subject perspective, however, given that subjects act independently and there is no difference among locations, each subject's trail is a string of 0s and 1s, where the probability of observing a 1 at each location is also given by $p \in [0, 1]$. We perform different simulations by fixing p on a grid in.[3]

---

[3] In theory, any number of points on the $[0, 1]$ interval will suffice.

Zipf Simulation. In this setting, subjects visit locations according to Zipf distributions, which lead to the desired high skew in the location access patterns. The set of available locations is denoted by L, and the population of subjects visiting those locations is denoted by S. The expected number of subjects who visit location $l_i \in L$ is equal to the mean of the corresponding distribution, e.g., equals $|S| \cdot r_i^{-\alpha}$, where r_i is the rank of l_i's popularity, and α is a real number greater than zero. When α equals 1, then the distribution is a true Zipf and when $\alpha < 1$ the Zipf distribution is said to be in a generalized form. Given the high skew of the distribution, the log-log plot of "number of visitors" to "location rank" is linear, while the α coefficient serves as a dampening factor on the slope of the fitted curve. As with the uniform distribution, the Zipf is studied by varying the parameter α over the same interval $[0, 1]$, and sample points, as the p parameter of the uniform distribution. Note that the exponent of a Zipf distribution is allowed to vary in the larger interval, $\alpha \in (0, \infty)$, with $\alpha = 0$ corresponding to the case of a Zipf distribution that degenerates into a Uniform distribution, and $\alpha = 1$ corresponding to the case of moderate skew. Thus, our choice of studying the exponent in the smaller interval $[0, 1]$ allows us to explore how the re-identification risk changes as location access patterns smoothly change from uniform to skewed. An exponent larger than one would not add much to our study, beside adding coverage of different degrees of skewness, hence it is reasonable to truncate the range of α at 1. For example, the empirical evidence we presented in Section 3 supports (estimated) Zipf exponents as large as $\alpha = 0.6$. For each tested data point, such as $\langle |L| = 10, p = 0.3 \rangle$, we generate 100 populations. Populations that are guided by the Zipf distribution are generated using the formula described above.

4.1   Distribution Effect on Re-identification

The resulting 10-point plots for unreserved and reserved systems are depicted in Figures 4 and 5. In these plots the mean percentage and plus/minus one standard deviation[4] for the 100 simulated populations are depicted. The x-axis corresponds to the parameter of the distribution in question and the y-axis corresponds to values of the mean percent of the population that is trail re-identified.

From the re-identification plots, though there is no direct way to compare the parameterizations of the uniform and Zipf distribution, there are several interesting observations that can be made. First with respect to both the unreserved and reserved systems, it is apparent that the uniform distribution consistently yields a larger number of re-identifications than the Zipf distribution. This can be seen by comparing the re-identification maximum, or peaks, in the left and right panels. Consider Figure 4, for example, in a situation with 10 locations, we re-identify a maximum of approximately 40% of the subjects distributed uniformly (which occurs when $p = 0.5$), as opposed to around 16% of the subjects that are distributed in Zipf high skew (which occurs when $\alpha = 0.4$). This finding is consistent across all systems as the number of the locations in consideration is increased.

Second, we consider a less readily observable feature that directly relates to the general success of re-identification, given a specific distribution for location access patterns.

---

[4] In Figure 4, the error bars are too small to be visible.

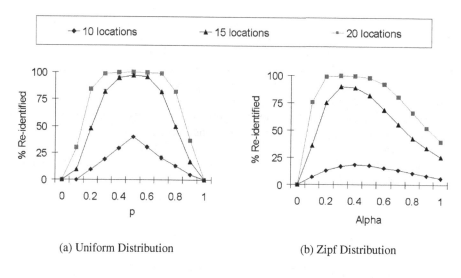

(a) Uniform Distribution   (b) Zipf Distribution

Fig. 4. Re-identification of simulated unreserved location access distributions

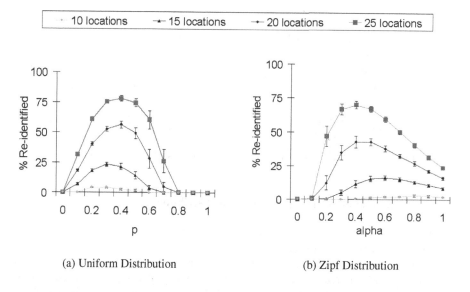

(a) Uniform Distribution   (b) Zipf Distribution

Fig. 5. Re-identification of simulated reserved location access distributions

To compare distribution archetypes, such as uniform vs. Zipf, we measure the area under the re-identification curve. This is calculated as the total area under the 10-point mean re-identification curve (average number of re-identifications in 100 simulated populations). The results of this calculation with respect to distributions and algorithm results are presented in Figures 6(a) and 6(b). Though the uniform distribution always yields the larger maximum number of re-identifications, the Zipf distribution is almost always the more linkable when considering all parameterizations. This is obviously so in the case of the reserved system, where Figure 6(b) shows that the Zipf always dominates. Similarly, in an unreserved system, Zipf is both the initial and inevitable dominant. However, this analysis reveals an unanticipated and intriguing finding. In certain ranges, the uniform distribution is dominant to the Zipf! In Figure 6(a), this finding is observed between approximately 8 and 18 locations.

The flip in distribution linkage capability dominance occurs for two reasons. First, Zipf dominates when there are not many locations in consideration because it is more difficult to realize complete vectors of all 1's. Second, Zipf dominates as the number of locations increase because it is easier for lesser accessed locations, which is what the newly considered locations are, to convert an unlikely trail into an extremely unlikely trail.

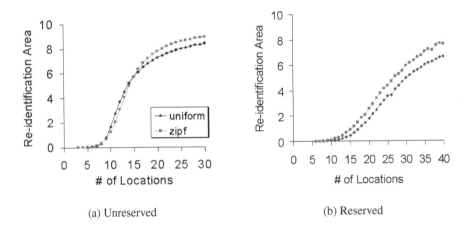

(a) Unreserved   (b) Reserved

Fig. 6. Area under the mean re-identification curves for simulated populations

4.2   Information and Re-identifiability of a Distributed System

In this section we relate the re-identifiability of trails in a distributed system to the Shannon entropy of the set of trails. [24, 25]

Each trail is a Boolean vector of 0's and 1's, and, as such, we can compute its entropy as measure of information. If we consider all the possible trails with a given information score, we note that the more entropic a trail is, i.e., the more random looking an individual's location access pattern is, the larger is the set of trails that relate to it. Therefore, entropy is a measure that inversely relates to a notion of distinguishability of one trails from others. To what extent does this notion of distinguishability relate to the notion of distinguishability (via uniqueness and re-identifiability) we studied in the previous section? In other words, there are many random looking location access patterns with high entropy, and fewer random looking location access patterns with low entropy, and we are interested in assessing to what extent we can relate the indistinguishability of trails according to their entropy score with the indistinguishability of trails from the standpoint of existing re-identification algorithms. If so, this would suggest that a low entropy systems leads to a low risk of re-identification.

For our purposes, let us assume we have the trail matrix that maps a population of subjects S to a set of locations L. Also, let f_l be the proportion of subjects in S that visit location l. Then, the entropy for location l, $H(l)$, equals

$$H(l) = -f_l \cdot \log \left(f_l \right) - (1 - f_l) \cdot \log \left(1 - f_l \right).$$

Under the assumption that individuals decide whether to visit each location independently of other locations, the entropy of the set of location access patterns of the population S to the set of available locations L is given by $H(L) = \sum_{l=1}^{|L|} H(l)$.

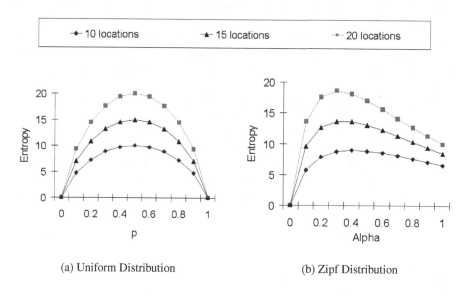

(a) Uniform Distribution   (b) Zipf Distribution

Fig. 7. Entropy plots corresponding to parameter values in the left and right panels of Figure 4

In order to assess whether entropy and re-identifiability are capturing the same notion of distinguishability we need to compute a measure of correlation among the corresponding scores, as the number of locations changes. In an additional set of experiments, we observed that the entropy curves display a behavior that is similar to that of the percentage of people re-identified, displayed in Figures 4 and 5. In Figure 7 we report the results for the unreserved case.

Here we perform a formal correlation study of these two sets of behaviors by introducing a distance metric, σ, between two curves, which measures the absolute difference of their areas modulo a scaling factor. The scaling factor is proportional to the ratio between the peaks of the two curves. Let us denote the entropy curve by $E(i)$, and the actual linkage curve by $R(i)$, where i is a point in the grid, G, for the interval $[0, 1]$ we used to generate the re-identification curves in Figures 4 and 5. Let $\max(R) = R(i^*)$ where $i^* = \arg\max\{R(i), i \in G\}$, and let $\max(E) = E(j^*)$ where

$j^* = \arg\max\{R(j), j \in G\}$. The scaling factor is then $\frac{\max(R)}{\max(E)}$, and the distance metric, σ, is defined as follows,

$$\sigma(E, R) = \sum_{i=1}^{10} \sigma_i(E, R) = \sum_{i=1}^{10} \left| E(i)\frac{\max(R)}{\max(E)} - R(i) \right|.$$

Note that whenever $i^* = j^*$, i.e., whenever the entropy and re-identification curves peak at the same point $i^* = j^*$ on the grid G, it follows that $\sigma_i(E, R) = 0$. That is,

$$\sigma_i(E, R) = \left| E(i)\frac{\max(R)}{\max(E)} - R(i) \right| = \left| E(i^*)\frac{R(i^*)}{E(i^*)} - R(i^*) \right| = 0.$$

The resulting information from the shape metric is summarized in Figure 8. As values for shape tends toward 0, the curves converge. As expected, the curves tend toward convergence as the number of locations increase. Yet after convergence begins to come into the line of sight, a counter-intuitive phenomenon occurs. Specifically, after a certain number of locations are considered for a particular distribution, the E and R curves begin to diverge from each other. This is an artifact of the limits of re-identifiability. Notice that in Figure 4, when a lesser number of locations are considered the linkage curve has a well defined peak. This peak corresponds to the parameter at which the distribution is most amenable to linkage. But this peak is only discernible when less than all of the trails are linked. Thus, when the system is fully linked at multiple parameterizations of the distribution, the linkage curve plateaus at 100% at its peak, while the entropy continues to be well defined. This limit to linkage causes the observed linkage curve to be improperly matched to the entropy of the system. There is no divergence observed, but rather a limit to independent use of the entropy metric.

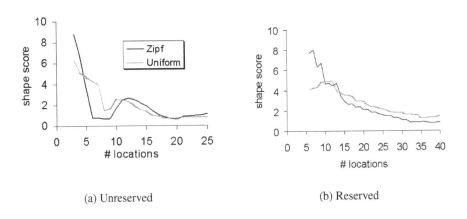

(a) Unreserved   (b) Reserved

Fig. 8. Shape metric for similarity in simulated distributions and entropy

The shape metric allows for the discovery of another notable feature that captures how the distribution type influence different trail linkage algorithms. Note that in the unreserved system, the uniform distribution converges earlier than the Zipf distribution.

In contrast, when subject to the reserved system, the uniform distribution converges after the Zipf distribution. Ah, a paradox! At first consideration, one would expect that one distribution type, either uniform or Zipf, would converge earlier in both algorithms. However, this paradox results from how trails are generated under the two distributions as well as how the re-identification method leverages trails. First, consider the linkage algorithms. In an unreserved system, the re-identification method looks for a unique bit pattern because there are no *'s. So both 1's and 0's are contributing evenly to the re-identification process. This is why the re-identification curve for the uniform distribution is balanced and has no shift around the midpoint of p. In other words, the percent re-identified is approximately equivalent for +/-x around the parameterization of $p = 0.5$. With respect to an reserved environment though, a * value in a trail functions as fuzzy bit, since it can be used as either a 0 or a 1. Thus, as p tends toward 1, trails with a lesser number of unambiguous values become more difficult to re-identify. As a consequence, the re-identification curve shifts away from high values of p which allow for trails with large amounts of 1's. The Zipf distribution should be hindered by this problem as well, but because it allows for locations to have different entropy values, the Zipf reveals more re-identifications. Thus, the total quantity of re-identifications the Zipf is capable of tends to be greater than the uniform. If one wanted to validate this claim, it is simple to observe that the average number of re-identifications, but not the maximum, for the Zipf is greater than the uniform.

5   Discussion

The above analysis provide a wealth of insight into the effects of location access patterns on the degree to which trail re-identification can be achieved in a distributed system. It also provides intuition into the relation between re-identifiability of a set of trails and the information they carry, as measured by the corresponding Shannon entropy. In this section we briefly address some findings of particular interest. After discussing revelations from our investigations, we consider some of the limitations and possible extensions of our framework. We conclude by presenting a conjecture that emerges from consideration of the empirical evidence we presented in Section 3.

5.1   Location Access Patterns and Re-identification

One of the more interesting findings of our experiments is that high-skew location access patterns yield higher *overall* re-identification when compared with low-skew location access patterns. This result holds despite the fact that low-skew distributions lead to a larger number of *peak* re-identifications, with respect to the parameter underlying the distribution of location access patterns, as well as for any given number of locations in the distributed environment. Further, this result holds in both situations where there is certainty about the information collected and released at the various locations, i.e. the unreserved case, and in situations where there is uncertainty about the information collected and released at the various locations. This finding has immediate implications for the design of solutions to limit trail re-identification in disclosed databases. For example, one solution we could employ is to entrust an independent third party to identify the set of locations that contribute the most to the skewness of location access patterns, and prevent them from releasing some, or all, of their de-identified data. By doing so, we do not need to provide the third party with data per se, as is the case in prior solutions [11], but rather essential components of the distribution of people to places. Nonetheless, risk analysis is not a substitute for formal privacy protection to prevent trail re-identification, which can be subject to rigorous proof. Re-identification risk provides a proxy by which we can develop provable protection models.

Further, we find there is a strong correlation between the entropy of the system and re-identification. In particular, the lower the entropy in a the set of trails, the more individual trails can be re-identified. This correlation is stronger for distributed systems with more locations, but hold for smaller systems as well. With respect to minimizing risk, our experiments suggest that in order to predict the number of trail re-identifications that can be made, the distribution of location access patterns, or the entropy, should be modelled. In pursuing these strategies, it becomes crucial that the information which released is reliable. In fact, reliability of the information bears relevance to the expected quality of the estimates of both the parameters underlying the distribution of location access patterns, and the entropy of the set of trails of the population of interest.

5.2 Limitations and Extensions

An aspect of our analysis that requires further attention is the correlation between the entropy of a set of trails and the number of re-identifications that can be made. However intriguing, the fact that low entropy systems correlate with high re-identifiability, our experiments offer little intuition into what mechanism may link the two phenomena in a causal manner. We cannot explain "in what sense" low entropy location access patterns explain re-identifiability.

Though this research provides a theoretical investigation into how particular distributions of location access patterns influence trail re-identification, there are certain caveats of the simulation design which limit the extension of these results. First, the entropy computations are carried out under the assumption that individuals decide whether to visit each location independently. As a consequence, our simulations do not completely replicate the behavior of real world populations. This is because in the real world most entities are not random agents visiting locations independently. Rather they can play an active role in choosing which locations to visit. This manifests in the form of correlations between locations in the patterns of access. As a consequence of this dependence, the resulting location access patterns can be different than those obtained under the independent locations assumption. For example, individuals may tend to visit multiple locations in co-location patterns. As a result of such location access behavior, the re-identification capability of the synthetic populations used in this research may be inflated.

Second, the distributions used in this study consist of homogenous populations, such that location access to all locations adheres to a single distribution. However, we should ask, "What is the effect of mixture models of populations on trail re-identification?" For instance, to what extent is re-identification facilitated when half the population is uniformly distributed while the other half is Zipf distributed? It is possible to speculate on the results, but it is a complex problem that is difficult to reason. As a result, another feasible direction for research into the fundamentals of trail re-identification is to study the effect of mixture models of distributions on re-identification.

5.3   A Conjecture: Re-identification Risk Through Subject-Location Ratio

The empirical evidence presented in Section 3 suggested we explore how different distributions of individuals' location access patterns influences the number of re-identifications in a distributed environment. However, in the case studies it is the ratio of subjects per location that correlates strongly with the number of re-identifications. In particular we observed that: (i) as the ratio of subjects per location grows large, we find evidence of an exponential relation between the number of locations considered and the number of people that are trail re-identifiable, in the CF dataset; (ii) as the ratio becomes negligible, we find evidence of a logarithmic relation between the number of locations considered and the number of trail re-identifications, in the Homenet dataset; and (iii) when the ratio of subjects per location is approximately 1, we find evidence of a linear relation between the number of locations considered and the number of trail re-identifications, in the PK dataset.

The evidence from the case studies also suggests that the number of re-identifications can be explained by a simpler relation centered around the ratio of subjects per location. This may be due to statistical limiting phenomena that occur in the re-identification of individuals in a distributed environment. This will require further investigation. Specifically, if we denote the ratio of subjects per location with $\frac{|S|}{|L|}$, we conjecture that the number of re-identifications, R, can be expressed as $R \propto f(S, L)^{\frac{|S|}{|L|}}$. Therefore, if the exponent is greater than, equal to, or less than 1, the function may replicate the observed shape of the relations shown in Figure 3.

6   Conclusions

In this paper we proposed a model to estimate re-identification risk when an individual's data is distributed across a set of locations. Specifically, we introduced methods and metrics for studying the effect of different location access behaviors on trail re-identification. We provided experimental evidence that implies the skew of the distributions of location access patterns is one of the main factors that influences re-identification. Though our models are based on simulation, this work provides a foundation for both basic and applied trail linkage research. One possible extension to this work is to study distributions with location dependencies, as well as mixture models of location access distributions.

Acknowledgements

The authors thank Kathleen Carley, Latanya Sweeney, and Stephen Fienberg for insightful discussions. This work was partially supported by the Data Privacy Laboratory at Carnegie Mellon University, NSF IGERT grant 9972762 in CASOS, NSF grant DMS-0240019, NIH Grant 1 R01 AG023141-01, ONR grant N00014-02-1-0973, and DOD grant MKIDS IIS0218466. The views and conclusions contained in this document are those of the authors and should not be interpreted as representing the official policies of the U.S. government.

References

1. Altman, R.: Bioinformatics in support of molecular medicine. In: Proceedings of the American Medical Informatics Association Annual Symposium, Miami Beach, FL (1998) 53–61
2. Sax, U., Schmidt, S.: Integration of genomic data in electronic health records: opportunities and dilemmas. Methods of Information in Medicine **44** (2005) 546–550
3. Altman, R., Klein, T.: Challenges for biomedical informatics and pharmacogenomics. Annual Review of Pharmacology and Toxicology **42** (2002) 113–133
4. Department of Health and Human Services: 45 cfr (code of federal regulations), parts 160 - 164. standards for privacy of individually identifiable health information, final rule. Federal Register **67** (2002) 53182–53273
5. Malin, B., Sweeney, L.: How (not) to protect genomic data privacy in a distributed network: using trail re-identification to evaluate and design anonymity protection systems. Journal of Biomedical Informatics **37** (2004) 179–192
6. Karat, C., Brodie, C., Karat, J.: Usable privacy and security for personal information management. Communications of the ACM **49** (2006) 51–55
7. Malin, B.: Betrayed by my shadow: learning data identity via trail matching. Journal of Privacy Technology (2005) 20050609001
8. de Moor, G., Claerhout, B., de Meyer, F.: Privacy enhancing technologies: the key to secure communication and management of clinical and genomic data. Methods of Information in Medicine **42** (2003) 148–153
9. Gulcher, J., Kristjansson, K., Gudbjartsson, H., Stefansson, K.: Protection of privacy by third-party encryption in genetic research. European Journal of Human Genetics **8** (2000) 739–742
10. Lin, Z., Owen, A., Altman, R.: Genomic research and human subject privacy. Science **305** (2004)
11. Malin, B., Sweeney, L.: Composition and disclosure of unlinkable distributed databases. In: Proceedings of the 22nd IEEE International Conference on Data Engineering, Atlanta, GA (2006)
12. Airoldi, E.M.: A statistical theory of record linkage with applications to privacy. Technical Report CMU-ISRI-05-112, School of Computer Science, Carnegie Mellon University (2004) Revision, December 2005.
13. Bender, S., Brand, R., Bacher, J.: Re-identifying register data by survey data: an empirical study. Statistical Journal of the United Nations ECE **18** (2001) 373–381
14. Griffith, V., Jakobsson, M.: Messin' with texas: deriving mother's maiden name using public records. In: Proceedings of the Applied Cryptography and Network Security Conference, New York, NY (2005)
15. Malin, B., Sweeney, L.: Determining the identifiability of dna database entries. In: Proceedings of the American Medical Informatics Association Annual Symposium, Los Angeles, CA (2000) 537–541
16. Sweeney, L.: Uniqueness of simple demographics in the us population. Technical Report LIDAP-WP04, Data Privacy Laboratory, Carnegie Mellon University, Pittsburgh, PA (2000)
17. Willenborg, L., de Waal, T.: Statistical Disclosure Control in Practice. Springer, New York, NY (1996)

18. Danezis, G., Serjantov, A.: Statistical disclosure or intersection attacks on anonymity systems. In: LNCS 2119: Proceedings of the 6th International Workshop on Information Hiding. (2004)

19. Kesdogan, D., Agrawal, D., Penz, S.: Limits of anonymity in open environments. In: LNCS 2119: Proceedings of the 5th International Workshop on Information Hiding. (2002)

20. Winkler, W.E.: Matching and record linkage. In Cox et al., B., ed.: Business Survey Methods. J. Wiley, New York, NY (1995) 355–384

21. Winkler, W.: Data cleaning methods. In: Proceedings of the ACM SIGKDD Workshop on Data Cleaning, Record Linkage, and Object Consolidation, Washington, DC (2003)

22. State of Illinois Health Care Cost Containment Council: Data release overview. State of Illinois Health Care Cost Containment Council, Springfield, IL (March 1998)

23. Kraut, R., Mukhopadhyay, T., Szczypula, J., Kiesler, S., Scherlis, B.: Information and communication: alternative uses of the internet in households. Information Systems Research **10** (2000) 287–303

24. Shannon, C.E.: A mathematical theory of communication. Bell System Technical Journal **27** (1948) 379–423

25. Shannon, C.E.: A mathematical theory of communication. Bell System Technical Journal **27** (1948) 623–656

Author Index

Lecture Notes in Computer Science

For information about Vols. 1–4248

please contact your bookseller or Springer

Vol. 4287: C. Mao, T. Yokomori (Eds.), DNA Computing. XII, 440 pages. 2006.

Vol. 4286: P. Spirakis, M. Mavronicolas, S. Kontogiannis (Eds.), Internet and Network Economics. XI, 401 pages. 2006.

Vol. 4285: Y. Matsumoto, R. Sproat, K.-F. Wong, M. Zhang (Eds.), Computer Processing of Oriental Languages. XVII, 544 pages. 2006. (Sublibrary LNAI).

Vol. 4284: X. Lai, K. Chen (Eds.), Advances in Cryptology – ASIACRYPT 2006. XIV, 468 pages. 2006.

Vol. 4283: Y.Q. Shi, B. Jeon (Eds.), Digital Watermarking. XII, 474 pages. 2006.

Vol. 4282: Z. Pan, A.D. Cheok, M. Haller, R.W.H. Lau, H. Saito, R. Liang (Eds.), Advances in Artificial Reality and Tele-Existence. XXIII, 1347 pages. 2006.

Vol. 4281: K. Barkaoui, A. Cavalcanti, A. Cerone (Eds.), Theoretical Aspects of Computing - ICTAC 2006. XV, 371 pages. 2006.

Vol. 4280: A.K. Datta, M. Gradinariu (Eds.), Stabilization, Safety, and Security of Distributed Systems. XVII, 590 pages. 2006.

Vol. 4279: N. Kobayashi (Ed.), Programming Languages and Systems. XI, 423 pages. 2006.

Vol. 4278: R. Meersman, Z. Tari, P. Herrero (Eds.), On the Move to Meaningful Internet Systems 2006: OTM 2006 Workshops, Part II. XLV, 1004 pages. 2006.

Vol. 4277: R. Meersman, Z. Tari, P. Herrero (Eds.), On the Move to Meaningful Internet Systems 2006: OTM 2006 Workshops, Part I. XLV, 1009 pages. 2006.

Vol. 4276: R. Meersman, Z. Tari (Eds.), On the Move to Meaningful Internet Systems 2006: CoopIS, DOA, GADA, and ODBASE, Part II. XXXII, 752 pages. 2006.

Vol. 4275: R. Meersman, Z. Tari (Eds.), On the Move to Meaningful Internet Systems 2006: CoopIS, DOA, GADA, and ODBASE, Part I. XXXI, 1115 pages. 2006.

Vol. 4274: Q. Huo, B. Ma, E.-S. Chng, H. Li (Eds.), Chinese Spoken Language Processing. XXIV, 805 pages. 2006. (Sublibrary LNAI).

Vol. 4273: I. Cruz, S. Decker, D. Allemang, C. Preist, D. Schwabe, P. Mika, M. Uschold, L. Aroyo (Eds.), The Semantic Web - ISWC 2006. XXIV, 1001 pages. 2006.

Vol. 4272: P. Havinga, M. Lijding, N. Meratnia, M. Wegdam (Eds.), Smart Sensing and Context. XI, 267 pages. 2006.

Vol. 4271: F.V. Fomin (Ed.), Graph-Theoretic Concepts in Computer Science. XIII, 358 pages. 2006.

Vol. 4270: H. Zha, Z. Pan, H. Thwaites, A.C. Addison, M. Forte (Eds.), Interactive Technologies and Sociotechnical Systems. XVI, 547 pages. 2006.

Vol. 4269: R. State, S. van der Meer, D. O'Sullivan, T. Pfeifer (Eds.), Large Scale Management of Distributed Systems. XIII, 282 pages. 2006.

Vol. 4268: G. Parr, D. Malone, M. Ó Foghlú (Eds.), Autonomic Principles of IP Operations and Management. XIII, 237 pages. 2006.

Vol. 4267: A. Helmy, B. Jennings, L. Murphy, T. Pfeifer (Eds.), Autonomic Management of Mobile Multimedia Services. XIII, 257 pages. 2006.

Vol. 4266: H. Yoshiura, K. Sakurai, K. Rannenberg, Y. Murayama, S. Kawamura (Eds.), Advances in Information and Computer Security. XIII, 438 pages. 2006.

Vol. 4265: L. Todorovski, N. Lavrač, K.P. Jantke (Eds.), Discovery Science. XIV, 384 pages. 2006. (Sublibrary LNAI).

Vol. 4264: J.L. Balcázar, P.M. Long, F. Stephan (Eds.), Algorithmic Learning Theory. XIII, 393 pages. 2006. (Sublibrary LNAI).

Vol. 4263: A. Levi, E. Savaş, H. Yenigün, S. Balcısoy, Y. Saygın (Eds.), Computer and Information Sciences – ISCIS 2006. XXIII, 1084 pages. 2006.

Vol. 4262: K. Havelund, M. Núñez, G. Roşu, B. Wolff (Eds.), Formal Approaches to Software Testing and Runtime Verification. VIII, 255 pages. 2006.

Vol. 4261: Y. Zhuang, S. Yang, Y. Rui, Q. He (Eds.), Advances in Multimedia Information Processing - PCM 2006. XXII, 1040 pages. 2006.

Vol. 4260: Z. Liu, J. He (Eds.), Formal Methods and Software Engineering. XII, 778 pages. 2006.

Vol. 4259: S. Greco, Y. Hata, S. Hirano, M. Inuiguchi, S. Miyamoto, H.S. Nguyen, R. Słowiński (Eds.), Rough Sets and Current Trends in Computing. XXII, 951 pages. 2006. (Sublibrary LNAI).

Vol. 4258: G. Danezis, P. Golle (Eds.), Privacy Enhancing Technologies. VIII, 431 pages. 2006.

Vol. 4257: I. Richardson, P. Runeson, R. Messnarz (Eds.), Software Process Improvement. XI, 219 pages. 2006.

Vol. 4256: L. Feng, G. Wang, C. Zeng, R. Huang (Eds.), Web Information Systems – WISE 2006 Workshops. XIV, 320 pages. 2006.

Vol. 4255: K. Aberer, Z. Peng, E.A. Rundensteiner, Y. Zhang, X. Li (Eds.), Web Information Systems – WISE 2006. XIV, 563 pages. 2006.

Vol. 4254: T. Grust, H. Höpfner, A. Illarramendi, S. Jablonski, M. Mesiti, S. Müller, P.-L. Patranjan, K.-U. Sattler, M. Spiliopoulou, J. Wijsen (Eds.), Current Trends in Database Technology – EDBT 2006. XXXI, 932 pages. 2006.

Vol. 4253: B. Gabrys, R.J. Howlett, L.C. Jain (Eds.), Knowledge-Based Intelligent Information and Engineering Systems, Part III. XXXII, 1301 pages. 2006. (Sublibrary LNAI).

Vol. 4252: B. Gabrys, R.J. Howlett, L.C. Jain (Eds.), Knowledge-Based Intelligent Information and Engineering Systems, Part II. XXXIII, 1335 pages. 2006. (Sublibrary LNAI).

Vol. 4251: B. Gabrys, R.J. Howlett, L.C. Jain (Eds.), Knowledge-Based Intelligent Information and Engineering Systems, Part I. LXVI, 1297 pages. 2006. (Sublibrary LNAI).

Vol. 4250: H.J. van den Herik, S.-C. Hsu, T.-s. Hsu, H.H.L.M. Donkers (Eds.), Advances in Computer Games. XIV, 273 pages. 2006.

Vol. 4249: L. Goubin, M. Matsui (Eds.), Cryptographic Hardware and Embedded Systems - CHES 2006. XII, 462 pages. 2006.